Poetry
for Students

Poetry for Students

Presenting Analysis, Context, and Criticism on Commonly Studied Poetry

Volume 14

Anne Marie Hacht, Editor

Foreword by David Kelly

GALE GROUP

™

THOMSON LEARNING

Detroit • New York • San Diego • San Francisco
Boston • New Haven, Conn. • Waterville, Maine
London • Munich

Poetry for Students

Staff

Editor: Anne Marie Hacht.

Contributing Editors: Michael L. LaBlanc, Ira Mark Milne, Jennifer Smith, Daniel Toronto, Carol Ullmann.

Managing Editor, Content: Dwayne D. Hayes.

Managing Editor, Product: David Galens.

Publisher, Literature Product: Mark Scott.

Literature Content Capture: Joyce Nakamura, *Managing Editor.* Madeline Harris, *Associate Editor.*

Research: Victoria B. Cariappa, *Research Manager.* Sarah Genik, Ron Morelli, Tamara Nott, Tracie A. Richardson, *Research Associates.* Nicodemus Ford, *Research Assistant.*

Permissions: Maria Franklin, *Permissions Manager.* Shalice Shah-Caldwell, *Permissions Associate.*

Manufacturing: Mary Beth Trimper, *Manager, Composition and Electronic Prepress.* Evi Seoud, *Assistant Manager, Composition Purchasing and Electronic Prepress.* Stacy Melson, *Buyer.*

Imaging and Multimedia Content Team: Barbara Yarrow, *Manager.* Randy Bassett, *Imaging Supervisor.* Robert Duncan, Dan Newell, Luke Rademacher, *Imaging Specialists.* Pamela A. Reed, *Imaging Coordinator.* Leitha Etheridge-Sims, Mary Grimes, David G. Oblender, *Image Catalogers.* Robyn V. Young, *Project Manager.* Dean Dauphinais, *Senior Image Editor.* Kelly A. Quin, *Image Editor.*

Product Design Team: Pamela A. E. Galbreath, *Senior Art Director.* Michael Logusz, *Graphic Artist.*

Copyright Notice

ISBN 0-7876-4692-X
ISSN 1094-7019
Printed in the United States of America.

10 9 8 7 6 5 4 3 2 1

National Advisory Board

Table of Contents

Just a Few Lines on a Page

I have often thought that poets have the easiest job in the world. A poem, after all, is just a few lines on a page, usually not even extending margin to margin—how long would that take to write, about five minutes? Maybe ten at the most, if you wanted it to rhyme or have a repeating meter. Why, I could start in the morning and produce a book of poetry by dinnertime. But we all know that it isn't that easy. Anyone can come up with enough words, but the poet's job is about writing the *right* ones. The right words will change lives, making people see the world somewhat differently than they saw it just a few minutes earlier. The right words can make a reader who relies on the dictionary for meanings take a greater responsibility for his or her own personal understanding. A poem that is put on the page correctly can bear any amount of analysis, probing, defining, explaining, and interrogating, and something about it will still feel new the next time you read it.

It would be fine with me if I could talk about poetry without using the word "magical," because that word is overused these days to imply "a really good time," often with a certain sweetness about it, and a lot of poetry is neither of these. But if you stop and think about magic—whether it brings to mind sorcery, witchcraft, or bunnies pulled from top hats—it always seems to involve stretching reality to produce a result greater than the sum of its parts and pulling unexpected results out of thin air. This book provides ample cases where a few simple words conjure up whole worlds. We do not actually travel to different times and different cultures, but the poems get into our minds, they find what little we know about the places they are talking about, and then they make that little bit blossom into a bouquet of someone else's life. Poets make us think we are following simple, specific events, but then they leave ideas in our heads that cannot be found on the printed page. Abracadabra.

Sometimes when you finish a poem it doesn't feel as if it has left any supernatural effect on you, like it did not have any more to say beyond the actual words that it used. This happens to everybody, but most often to inexperienced readers: regardless of what is often said about young people's infinite capacity to be amazed, you have to understand what usually does happen, and what could have happened instead, if you are going to be moved by what someone has accomplished. In those cases in which you finish a poem with a "So what?" attitude, the information provided in *Poetry for Students* comes in handy. Readers can feel assured that the poems included here actually are potent magic, not just because a few (or a hundred or ten thousand) professors of literature say they are: they're significant because they can withstand close inspection and still amaze the very same people who have just finished taking them apart and seeing how they work. Turn them inside out, and they will still be able to come alive, again and again. *Poetry for Students* gives readers of any age good practice in feeling the ways poems relate to both the reality of the time and place the poet lived in and the reality of our emotions. Practice is just another word for being a student. The information given here helps you understand the way to read poetry; what to look for, what to expect.

With all of this in mind, I really don't think I would actually like to have a poet's job at all. There are too many skills involved, including precision, honesty, taste, courage, linguistics, passion, compassion, and the ability to keep all sorts of people entertained at once. And that is just what they do with one hand, while the other hand pulls some sort of trick that most of us will never fully understand. I can't even pack all that I need for a weekend into one suitcase, so what would be my chances of stuffing so much life into a few lines? With all that *Poetry for Students* tells us about each poem, I am impressed that any poet can finish three or four poems a year. Read the inside stories of these poems, and you won't be able to approach any poem in the same way you did before.

David J. Kelly
College of Lake County

Introduction

Purpose of the Book

The purpose of *Poetry for Students* (*PfS*) is to provide readers with a guide to understanding, enjoying, and studying poems by giving them easy access to information about the work. Part of Gale's "For Students" Literature line, *PfS* is specifically designed to meet the curricular needs of high school and undergraduate college students and their teachers, as well as the interests of general readers and researchers considering specific poems. While each volume contains entries on "classic" poems frequently studied in classrooms, there are also entries containing hard-to-find information on contemporary poems, including works by multicultural, international, and women poets.

The information covered in each entry includes an introduction to the poem and the poem's author; the actual poem text; a poem summary, to help readers unravel and understand the meaning of the poem; analysis of important themes in the poem; and an explanation of important literary techniques and movements as they are demonstrated in the poem.

In addition to this material, which helps the readers analyze the poem itself, students are also provided with important information on the literary and historical background informing each work. This includes a historical context essay, a box comparing the time or place the poem was written to modern Western culture, a critical overview essay, and excerpts from critical essays on the poem. A unique feature of *PfS* is a specially commissioned critical essay on each poem, targeted toward the student reader.

To further aid the student in studying and enjoying each poem, information on media adaptations is provided (if available), as well as reading suggestions for works of fiction and nonfiction on similar themes and topics. Classroom aids include ideas for research papers and lists of critical sources that provide additional material on the poem.

Selection Criteria

The titles for each volume of *PfS* were selected by surveying numerous sources on teaching literature and analyzing course curricula for various school districts. Some of the sources surveyed included: literature anthologies; *Reading Lists for College-Bound Students: The Books Most Recommended by America's Top Colleges*; textbooks on teaching the poem; a College Board survey of poems commonly studied in high schools; and a National Council of Teachers of English (NCTE) survey of poems commonly studied in high schools.

Input was also solicited from our advisory board, as well as educators from various areas. From these discussions, it was determined that each volume should have a mix of "classic" poems (those works commonly taught in literature classes) and contemporary poems for which information is often hard to find. Because of the interest in expanding the canon of literature, an emphasis was also placed on including works by international, multicultural, and women poets. Our advisory board members—educational professionals—helped pare down the list for each volume. If a work was not selected for the present volume, it was often noted as a possibility for a future volume. As always, the editor welcomes suggestions for titles to be included in future volumes.

How Each Entry Is Organized

Each entry, or chapter, in *PfS* focuses on one poem. Each entry heading lists the full name of the poem, the author's name, and the date of the poem's publication. The following elements are contained in each entry:

Introduction: a brief overview of the poem which provides information about its first appearance, its literary standing, any controversies surrounding the work, and major conflicts or themes within the work.

Author Biography: this section includes basic facts about the poet's life, and focuses on events and times in the author's life that inspired the poem in question.

Poem Text: when permission has been granted, the poem is reprinted, allowing for quick reference when reading the explication of the following section.

Poem Summary: a description of the major events in the poem, with interpretation of how these events help articulate the poem's themes. Summaries are broken down with subheads that indicate the lines being discussed.

Themes: a thorough overview of how the major topics, themes, and issues are addressed within the poem. Each theme discussed appears in a separate subhead and is easily accessed through the boldface entries in the Subject/Theme Index.

Style: this section addresses important style elements of the poem, such as form, meter, and rhyme scheme; important literary devices used, such as imagery, foreshadowing, and symbolism; and, if applicable, genres to which the work might have belonged, such as Gothicism or Romanticism. Literary terms are explained within the entry, but can also be found in the Glossary.

Historical Context: this section outlines the social, political, and cultural climate *in which the author lived and the poem was created*. This section may include descriptions of related historical events, pertinent aspects of daily life in the culture, and the artistic and literary sensibilities of the time in which the work was written. If the poem is a historical work, information regarding the time in which the poem is set is also included. Each section is broken down with helpful subheads.

Critical Overview: this section provides background on the critical reputation of the poem, including bannings or any other public controversies surrounding the work. For older works, this section includes a history of how the poem was first received and how perceptions of it may have changed over the years; for more recent poems, direct quotes from early reviews may also be included.

Criticism: an essay commissioned by *PfS* which specifically deals with the poem and is written specifically for the student audience, as well as excerpts from previously published criticism on the work (if available).

Sources: an alphabetical list of critical material used in compiling the entry, with full bibliographical information.

Further Reading: an alphabetical list of other critical sources which may prove useful for the student. It includes full bibliographical information and a brief annotation.

In addition, each entry contains the following highlighted sections, set apart from the main text as sidebars:

Media Adaptations: if available, a list of audio recordings as well as any film or television adaptations of the poem, including source information.

Topics for Further Study: a list of potential study questions or research topics dealing with the poem. This section includes questions related to other disciplines the student may be studying, such as American history, world history, science, math, government, business, geography, economics, psychology, etc.

Compare and Contrast: an "at-a-glance" comparison of the cultural and historical differences between the author's time and culture and late twentieth century or early twenty-first century Western culture. This box includes pertinent parallels between the major scientific, political, and cultural movements of the time or place the poem was written, the time or place the poem was set (if a historical work), and modern Western culture. Works written after the mid-1970s may not have this box.

What Do I Read Next?: a list of works that might complement the featured poem or serve as a contrast to it. This includes works by the same author and others, works of fiction and nonfiction, and works from various genres, cultures, and eras.

Other Features

PfS includes "Just a Few Lines on a Page," a foreword by David J. Kelly, a professor of English, College of Lake County, Illinois. This essay provides a straightforward, unpretentious explanation of why poetry should be marveled at and how *Poetry for Students* can help teachers show students how to enrich their own reading experiences.

A Cumulative Author/Title Index lists the authors and titles covered in each volume of the *PfS* series.

A Cumulative Nationality/Ethnicity Index breaks down the authors and titles covered in each volume of the *PfS* series by nationality and ethnicity.

A Subject/Theme Index, specific to each volume, provides easy reference for users who may be studying a particular subject or theme rather than a single work. Significant subjects from events to broad themes are included, and the entries pointing to the specific theme discussions in each entry are indicated in **boldface**.

A Cumulative Index of First Lines (beginning in Vol. 10) provides easy reference for users who may be familiar with the first line of a poem but may not remember the actual title.

A Cumulative Index of Last Lines (beginning in Vol. 10) provides easy reference for users who may be familiar with the last line of a poem but may not remember the actual title.

Each entry may include illustrations, including a photo of the author and other graphics related to the poem.

Citing Poetry for Students

When writing papers, students who quote directly from any volume of *Poetry for Students* may use the following general forms. These examples are based on MLA style; teachers may request that students adhere to a different style, so the following examples may be adapted as needed.

When citing text from *PfS* that is not attributed to a particular author (i.e., the Themes, Style, Historical Context sections, etc.), the following format should be used in the bibliography section:

Angle of Geese. *Poetry for Students.* Eds. Marie Napierkowski and Mary Ruby. Vol. 2. Detroit: Gale, 1997. 5–7.

When quoting the specially commissioned essay from *PfS* (usually the first piece under the "Criticism" subhead), the following format should be used:

Velie, Alan. Essay on "Angle of Geese."*Poetry for Students.* Eds. Marie Napierkowski and Mary Ruby. Vol. 2. Detroit: Gale, 1997. 8–9.

When quoting a journal or newspaper essay that is reprinted in a volume of *PfS*, the following form may be used:

Luscher, Robert M. "An Emersonian Context of Dickinson's 'The Soul Selects Her Own Society.'" *ESQ: A Journal of American Renaissance* Vol. 30, No. 2 (Second Quarter, 1984), 111–16; excerpted and reprinted in *Poetry for Students*, Vol. 1, eds. Marie Napierkowski and Mary Ruby (Detroit: Gale, 1997), pp. 266–69.

When quoting material reprinted from a book that appears in a volume of *PfS,* the following form may be used:

Mootry, Maria K. "'Tell It Slant': Disguise and Discovery as Revisionist Poetic Discourse in 'The Bean Eaters,'" in *A Life Distilled: Gwendolyn Brooks, Her Poetry and Fiction.* Edited by Maria K. Mootry and Gary Smith. University of Illinois Press, 1987. 177–80, 191; excerpted and reprinted in *Poetry for Students*, Vol. 2, eds. Marie Napierkowski and Mary Ruby (Detroit: Gale, 1997), pp. 22–24.

We Welcome Your Suggestions

The editor of *Poetry for Students* welcomes your comments and ideas. Readers who wish to suggest poems to appear in future volumes, or who have other suggestions, are cordially invited to contact the editor. You may contact the editor via E-mail at: *ForStudentsEditors@galegroup.com.* Or write to the editor at:

Editor, *Poetry for Students*
The Gale Group
27500 Drake Rd.
Farmington Hills, MI 48331–3535

Literary Chronology

1340: Geoffrey Chaucer is born.

1400: Geoffrey Chaucer dies on October 25.

1400: Geoffrey Chaucer's *The Canterbury Tales* is published.

1554: Walter Raleigh is born in Hayes Barton, Devonshire.

1600: Walter Raleigh's "The Nymph's Reply to the Shepherd" is published.

1618: Walter Raleigh is beheaded outside the Palace of Westminster on October 29.

1788: Lord Byron is born in London, England.

1815: Lord Byron's "She Walks in Beauty" is published.

1824: Lord Byron dies ten days after April 9 when he was soaked in the rain and contracted a fever.

1830: Christina Rossetti is born in December in London, England.

1842: Sidney Lanier is born in Macon, Georgia.

1862: Christina Rossetti's "Remember" is published.

1877: Sidney Lanier's "Song of the Chatta-hoochee" is published.

1881: Sidney Lanier dies in North Carolina.

1884: Sara Teasdale is born in August in St. Louis, Missouri.

1887: Marianne Moore is born in Kirkwood, Missouri.

1894: Christina Rossetti dies in December in London.

1916: Peter Viereck is born in August in New York City.

1920: Sara Teasdale's "There Will Come Soft Rains" is published.

1920: Howard Nemerov is born in March in New York City.

1921: Marianne Moore's "The Fish" is published.

1923: Louis Simpson is born in Kingston, Jamaica, in the West Indies.

1925: Donald Justice is born in Miami, Florida.

1928: Anne Sexton (born Anne Gray Harvey) is born in Weston, Massachusetts.

1933: Sara Teasdale commits suicide in January in New York City.

1936: Lucille Clifton is born in Depew, New York.

1948: Peter Viereck's "Kilroy" is published.

1949: Peter Viereck wins the Pulitzer Prize for poetry for *Terror and Decorum*.

1951: Marianne Moore wins the Pulitzer Prize for *Collected Poems*. This work wins the National Book Award in 1952 and the Bollingen Prize in 1953.

1951: Andrew Hudgins is born on April 22 in Killeen, Texas.

1954: Louise Erdrich is born in Little Falls, Minnesota.

1955: Howard Nemerov's "Deep Woods" is published.

1963: Louis Simpson's "In the Suburbs" is published.

1964: Louis Simpson wins the Pulitzer Prize for poetry for *At the End of the Open Road*.

1967: Anne Sexton wins the Pulitzer Prize for Poetry for *Live or Die*.

1967: Donald Justice's "An Incident in a Rose Garden" is published.

1968: Joel Brouwer is born in Grand Rapids, Michigan.

1972: Marianne Moore dies on February 5 in New York City.

1974: Anne Sexton commits suicide on October 4.

1975: Anne Sexton's "Courage" is published.

1978: Howard Nemerov wins the Pulitzer Prize for poetry for *Collected Poems* in 1978.

1979: Lucille Clifton is made the Poet Laureate of the State of Maryland from 1979 to 1982.

1980: Donald Justice wins the Pulitzer Prize for poetry for *Selected Poems*.

1989: Louise Erdrich's "Bidwell Ghost" is published.

1991: Donald Justice wins the Bollingen Prize for poetry.

1991: Andrew Hudgins's "Elegy for My Father, Who Is Not Dead" is published.

1991: Howard Nemerov dies of cancer at his home in Missouri in July.

1993: Lucille Clifton's "Climbing" is published.

1999: Joel Brouwer's "Last Request" is published.

2000: Lucille Clifton wins the National Book Award for poetry.

Acknowledgments

The editors wish to thank the copyright holders of the excerpted criticism included in this volume and the permissions managers of many book and magazine publishing companies for assisting us in securing reproduction rights. We are also grateful to the staffs of the Detroit Public Library, the Library of Congress, the University of Detroit Mercy Library, Wayne State University Purdy/Kresge Library Complex, and the University of Michigan Libraries for making their resources available to us. Following is a list of the copyright holders who have granted us permission to reproduce material in this volume of *Poetry for Students (PfS)*. Every effort has been made to trace copyright, but if omissions have been made, please let us know.

COPYRIGHTED MATERIALS IN *PfS*, VOLUME 14, WERE REPRODUCED FROM THE FOLLOWING PERIODICALS:

Bulletin of John Rylands Library of Manchester, v. 74, Spring, 1992. © The John Rylands University Library of Manchester 1992. Reproduced by courtesy of the Director and University Librarian, the John Rylands University Library of Manchester.—*Chaucer Review*, v. 5, Fall, 1970; v. 15, Fall, 1981; v. 18, 1983. Copyright © 1970, 1981, 1983 The Pennsylvania State University, University Park, PA. All reproduced by permission.—*College English*, v. 27, November, 1965, for "Criticism and the Old Man in Chaucer's 'Pardoner's Tale,'" by Alfred David. Copyright © 1965 by the National Council of Teachers of English.

Reproduced by permission of the publisher and the author.—*Comparative Studies in Society and History*, v. 12, January, 1970 for "Chaucer's General Prologue as History and Literature," by R. T. Lenaghan. Reproduced by permission of the publisher and the author.—*Critical Quarterly*, v. 1, 1959. Reproduced by permission.—*Essays in Literature*, v. 15, Fall, 1988. Copyright 1988 by Western Illinois University. Reproduced by permission.—*The Literary Review*, v. 23, Summer, 1980 for "'The Struggle between Noble Designs and Chaos': The Literary Tradition of Chaucer's 'Knight's Tale,'" by Robert W. Hanning. Reproduced by permisison of the author.—*Modern Language Quarterly*, v. 33, September, 1972. Copyright © 1972 by Duke University Press, Durham, NC. Reproduced by permission.—*Prairie Schooner*, Fall, 1989 for "Bidwell Ghost" by Louise Erdrich. © 1989 by University of Nebraska Press. Reproduced from Prairie Schooner by permission of the University of Nebraska Press.

COPYRIGHTED MATERIALS IN *PfS*, VOLUME 14, WERE REPRODUCED FROM THE FOLLOWING BOOKS:

Clifton, Lucille. From *The Garden Thrives: Twentieth-Century African-American Poetry*. HarperPerennial, 1996. Copyright © 1996 by Clarence Major. All rights reserved.—Conley, Susan. From *The Culture of Christina Rossetti*. Edited by Mary Arseneau, Anthony H. Harrison, and Lorraine Janzen Kooistra. Ohio University Press, 1999. © by Mary Arseneau, Anthony H. Harrison, and Lorraine Janzen Kooistra. Reproduced by permission.—De Bellis, Jack. From *Sidney Lanier*. Twayne Publishers, Inc., 1972. Copyright © 1972 by Twayne Publishers, Inc. The Gale Group.—Donaldson, E.T. From *Chaucer's Poetry*. The Ronald Press Company, 1958. Copyright © 1958, 1975 by The Ronald Press Company. Reproduced by permission.—Lenhart, Charmenz S. From *Musical Influence on American Poetry*. The University of Georgia Press, 1956. © Copyright 1956, The University of Georgia Press. Renewed 1984 by Charmenz S. Lenhart. Reproduced by permission.—Mann, Jill. From *Medieval Literature: Chaucer and the Alliterative Tradition*. Edited by Boris Ford. Penguin Books Ltd., 1982. Copyright © Boris Ford, 1982. Reproduced by permission of Penguin Books, Ltd.—Martin, Taffy. From *Marianne Moore: Subversive Modernist*. University of Texas Press, 1986. Copyright © 1986 by the University of Texas Press. Reproduced by permission.—Moore, Marianne. From *Collected Poems*. The Macmillan Company, 1952. Copyright 1935, 1951 by Marianne Moore, renewed 1963 by Marianne Moore and T.S. Eliot. Reproduced by permission of Simon & Schuster Macmillan and Faber & Faber Limited.—Phillips, Elizabeth. From *Marianne Moore*. Frederick Ungar Publishing Co., Inc., 1982. Copyright © 1982 by Frederick Ungar Publishing Co., Inc. Reproduced by permission of The Continuum International Publishing Company.—Sexton, Anne. From *The Complete Poems*. Houghton Mifflin Company, 1981. Copyright © 1981 by Linda Gray Sexton and Loring Conant, Jr., executors of the will of Anne Sexton. Reproduced by permission.—Simpson, Louis. From *At the End of the Open Road*. Wesleyan University Press, 1963. Copyright © 1960, 1961, 1962, 1963 by Louis Simpson. Reproduced by permission.—Teasdale, Sara. From *Flame and Shadow*. The Macmillan Company, 1935. Copyright, 1920 by The Macmillan Company. All rights reserved. Reproduced by permission of Simon & Schuster Macmillan and the Lit. Est of Sara Teasdale.—Williams, David. From *The Canterbury Tales: A Literary Pilgrimage*. Twayne Publishers, 1987. Copyright © 1987 by G.K. Hall & Co. The Gale Group.

PHOTOGRAPHS AND ILLUSTRATIONS APPEARING IN *PfS*, VOLUME 14, WERE RECEIVED FROM THE FOLLOWING SOURCES:

Byron, George Gordon (short curly hair), engraving. The Library of Congress.—Brouwer, Joel, photograph. Reproduced by permission.—Chaucer, Geoffrey, illustration.—Erdrich, Louise, photograph by Jerry Bauer. Reproduced by permission.—German soldiers advancing through French lines, photograph. Bettmann/Corbis. Reproduced by permission.—Hudgins, Jr., Andrew L, photograph by Joanna Eldredge Morrissey. Reproduced by the permission of Andrew Hudgins Jr.—Justice, Donald R., photograph. © Miriam Berkley. Reproduced by permission.—Lanier, Sidney, photograph. The Library of Congress.—Lucille Clifton, photograph by Chris Felver. Reproduced by permission.—Moore, Marianne, photograph. The Library of Congress.—Nemerov, Howard, photograph. Oscar White/Corbis-Bettmann. Reproduced by permission.—Rising sun shining on the Chattahoochee River, photograph by Galen Rowell. Corbis. Reproduced by permission.—Rossetti, Christina, portrait by James Collinson, photograph.—Sexton, Anne, 1962, photograph. AP/ Wide World Photos. Reproduced by permission.—Simpson, Louis, photograph. The Library of Congress.—"Sir Walter Raleigh and His Son, Wat," painting, photograph. The Library of Congress.—Teasdale, Sarah, photograph. Archive Photos, Inc. Reproduced by permission.—Viereck, Peter, photograph by Clemens Kalischer. Mount Holyoke College. Reproduced by permission of Clemens Kalischer.

Contributors

Emily Archer: Archer holds a Ph.D. in English from Georgia State University, has taught literature and poetry at several colleges, and has published essays, reviews, interviews, and poetry in numerous literary journals. Entry on *Elegy for My Father, Who Is Not Dead.*

Bryan Aubrey: Aubrey holds a Ph.D. in English Literature from the University of Durham, England. He has worked as editor for Lynn C. Franklin Associates and as a freelance writer and editor. Original essay on *Elegy for My Father, Who Is Not Dead.*

Adrian Blevins: Blevins is a poet and essayist who has taught at Hollins University, Sweet Briar College, and in the Virginia Community College system. She has published poems, stories, and essays in many magazines, journals, and anthologies. Original essays on *Courage, Elegy for My Father, Who Is Not Dead,* and *In the Suburbs.*

Erik France: France is a librarian and teaches history and interdisciplinary studies at University Liggett School in Grosse Pointe Woods, Michigan. Original essay on *Elegy for My Father, Who Is Not Dead.*

Joyce Hart: Hart is a freelance writer of literary themes. Original essays on *Climbing* and *Incident in a Rose Garden.*

Pamela Steed Hill: Hill is the author of a poetry collection, has published widely in poetry journals, and is an associate editor for a university publications department. Entries on *Deep Woods, Kilroy, Last Request, Remember,* and *There Will Come Soft Rains.* Original essays on *Deep Woods, Kilroy, Last Request, Remember,* and *There Will Come Soft Rains.*

David Kelly: Kelly is a writer and a teacher at two colleges in Illinois. Entries on *Bidwell Ghost, The Canterbury Tales, The Nymph's Reply to the Shepherd, She Walks in Beauty,* and *Song of the Chattahoochee.* Original essays on *Bidwell Ghost, The Canterbury Tales, The Nymph's Reply to the Shepherd, She Walks in Beauty,* and *Song of the Chattahoochee.*

Judi Ketteler: Ketteler has taught literature and English composition and is currently a freelance writer based in Cincinnati, Ohio. Original essays on *Bidwell Ghost* and *Climbing.*

Laura Kryhoski: Kryhoski is currently working as a freelance writer. Original essay on *Bidwell Ghost.*

Uma Kukathas: Kukathas is a freelance writer and editor. Original essay on *She Walks in Beauty.*

Daniel Moran: Moran is a secondary school teacher of English and American literature. Original essays on *The Nymph's Reply to the Shepherd* and *She Walks in Beauty.*

Carl Mowery: Mowery has a Ph.D. in literature and composition and has written extensively for the Gale Group. Original essays on *Deep Woods* and *Courage.*

Doreen Piano: Piano is a Ph.D. candidate in English at Bowling Green State University. Original essay on *There Will Come Soft Rains.*

Chris Semansky: Semansky publishes widely in the field of twentieth-century poetry and culture. He holds a Ph.D. in English from Stony Brook University and teaches writing and literature at Portland Community College in Portland, Oregon. His collection of poems *Death, But at a Good Price* received the Nicholas Roerich Poetry Prize for 1991 and was published by Story Line Press and the Nicholas Roerich Museum. Semansky's most recent collection, *Blindsided*, has been published by 26 Books of Portland, Oregon. Entries on *Climbing, Courage, The Fish, Incident in a Rose Garden,* and *In the Suburbs.* Original essays on *Climbing, Courage, The Fish, Incident in a Rose Garden,* and *In the Suburbs.*

Erika Taibl: Taibl has a master's degree in English writing and has published widely in poetic studies. Original essay on *The Nymph's Reply to the Shepherd.*

Bidwell Ghost

Louise Erdrich
1989

"Bidwell Ghost" is an example of Erdrich's use of myth or legend in her poetry, a practice which is a firmly rooted tradition in her Chippewa heritage. It's difficult to tell what "Bidwell Ghost" is a reference to—possibly a family name or the name of a small town in Minnesota, the state where Erdrich was raised. Included in the collection *Baptism of Desire* in 1989, this poem recounts the myth of an orchard haunted by a young girl's ghost. Presumably killed in a house fire twenty years earlier, she still waits at the edge of the road for passing cars; if you stop she'll climb in but "not say where she is going." By using vivid images throughout, Erdrich describes the burned trees waiting for someone to pick their fruit, as well as the girl's ghost waiting for anyone to pass by, in turn blurring the lines between the human and the natural, and the natural and the supernatural. The poem ends with a question, perhaps asking the reader to ponder the cycle of death and new life.

Author Biography

Erdrich was born Karen Louise Erdrich in Little Falls, Minnesota, in 1954, the eldest of seven children of German-born Ralph Erdrich and Rita Gourneau Erdrich, a Chippewa. Both parents worked for the Bureau of Indian Affairs. Erdrich grew up in Wahpeton, North Dakota, near the Turtle Mountain Chippewa reservation, where her maternal grandparents lived. The story-telling tra-

Louise Erdich

ditions of her heritage stimulated her to write her own pieces, an activity encouraged by her parents. In 1972, Erdrich enrolled in Dartmouth College. There she met her future husband and literary collaborator, anthropologist Michael Dorris, who was the chair of the Native American Studies department. While in college, she worked at a wide variety of jobs, including beet weeder, psychiatric aide, lifeguard, waitress, poetry teacher at prisons, and construction flag-signaler. She also became an editor for the *Circle*, a Boston Indian Council newspaper. She enrolled in a graduate program at Johns Hopkins University in 1978, earning a master's degree the following year and then returning to Dartmouth as a writer-in-residence. During this period, Erdrich began collaborating with Dorris, and one of their stories,"The World's Greatest Fisherman," was awarded first prize in *Chicago* magazine's Nelson Algren Fiction Competition in 1982. Erdrich subsequently expanded this work into a novel, *Love Medicine*, which was published in 1984. That same year, she published *Jacklight*, her first collection of poems. In 1985, Erdrich received the National Book Critics Circle Award and numerous other prizes for *Love Medicine*. She has continued to write novels, short stories, and poems, publishing a second volume of verse, *Baptism of Desire*, in 1989.

Poem Text

Each night she waits by the road
in a thin white dress
embroidered with fire.

It has been twenty years
since her house surged and burst in the dark trees.   5
Still nobody goes there.

The heat charred the branches
of the apple trees,
but nothing can kill that wood.

She will climb into your car   10
but not say where she is going
and you shouldn't ask.

Nor should you try to comb the blackened nest of
    hair
or press the agates of tears
back into her eyes.   15

First the orchard bowed low and complained
of the unpicked fruit,
then the branches cracked apart and fell.

The windfalls sweetened to wine
beneath the ruined arms and snow.   20
Each spring now, in the grass, buds form on the
    tattered wood.

The child, the child, why is she so persistent
in her need? Is it so terrible
to be alone when the cold white blossoms
come to life and burn?   25

Poem Summary

Lines 1–3

Here the poet introduces the ghost, a girl, caught in a pattern of waiting, standing by the road "each night" in the same white dress. Using figurative language to describe the dress as "embroidered with fire," the poet suggests this is probably the same outfit the girl died in years ago.

Lines 4–6

These lines establish how long ago the fatal fire occurred, destroying the house in the orchard along with the girl, though there is no mention of her family. These lines also inform us that even after this long, the place is still abandoned; no one ever visits.

Lines 7–9

Here the poet describes the effects of the fire's heat on the surrounding orchard. The branches were burned, though the trees didn't die. Notice the similarity between the tree and the girl thus far in the poem: both show evidence of the fire, yet both still "survive," the trees still standing in the orchard, the ghost still haunting the road.

Lines 10–12

Note how the tone of the speaker's voice shifts here from third person description to second person direct address. But who is the "you" being spoken to? Since there's only one person—the girl—introduced in the poem, we might conclude that we, the readers, are being directly spoken to, are being given instructions. This personal and immediate connection with the reader might help create a spookier feeling, as if we let the ghost right into our own car. Once she's in the car with us, the ghost won't tell us where to drive, and the poet suggests we "shouldn't ask," perhaps for fear of what the answer might be.

Lines 13–15

In these lines, the poet continues offering instructions in the event we meet this ghost. Using a disturbing and vivid image, Erdrich suggests the girl's hair was burned in the fire, now resembling a "black nest." Note how this comparison reminds us again of the trees in the orchard, where a real bird's nest might be found. In line 14, the image implies the girl ghost is still crying after all these years, her tears like "agates," which are colorful layered stones found abundantly in Minnesota, where the poet grew up.

Lines 16–18

Here the poet returns us again to the orchard after the fire. In these lines, she personifies the orchard, giving it human qualities, suggesting the trees were unhappy because no one showed up anymore to pick the fruit from their branches. Then, as if because of the lack of attention, the burned branches "cracked apart and fell." Note, again, the similarities of emotion between the girl and the orchard, both lonely and waiting for someone to come back.

Lines 19–21

"Windfalls" are unpicked apples which fall to the ground near the end of the season, sometimes even at the slightest wind. At the literal level, these apples then begin to break down and ferment, much in the same way fermented grapes are used to make wine. The verb "sweetened" here might suggest something becoming better. Note here how the burned branches are now called "ruined arms," once again blending the line between the natural and human realms. On a figurative level, the im-

Media Adaptations

- Caedmon Audio has a three-hour audiocassette of Erdrich's book *Tracks*, which features Louise Erdrich and her husband, Michael Dorris, describing the daily life of Native Americans of North Dakota during the nineteenth century and the clash of their native legends and beliefs with white culture. It was recorded in 1989, the year "Bidwell Ghost" was published.

- An abridged version of Erdrich's most famous novel, *Love Medicine*, is read by Erdrich and Dorris on a two-cassette recording from Harper and Row, released in 1990.

- Erdrich's short story "The Bingo Van" is read by Joe Spano on Volume Ten in the series of cassettes produced by Symphony Space called *Selected Shorts*. This volume was recorded in 1986.

- Erdrich is one of several authors examined on the videocassette *Voices on the Water*, which is a documentary of the International Festival of Writers, originally released in 1988 under the title *Authors of the World* and re-released in 1993 by Chip Taylor Productions.

- A videocassette entitled "Louise Erdrich and Michael Dorris" features Erdrich and Dorris being interviewed by Paul Bailey in 1989. It is available from the Anthony Roland Collection of Films on Art of Northbrook, Illinois.

- Erdrich and Dorris were interviewed by Bill Moyers for the Public Broadcasting System's series *A World of Ideas*. This interview is available on videocassette under the title "Louise Erdrich and Michael Dorris: Searching for a Native American Identity" from Films for the Humanities and Sciences, 1988.

ages in this stanza—forgotten apples becoming wine, the snow giving way to spring, new buds growing from "tattered wood"—perhaps all point to a sense of renewal, a larger cycle of nature, life emerging from what has passed away.

Lines 22–25

In this last four-line stanza, after such a close description of the orchard, the speaker suddenly reminds us of the girl ghost again, asking us questions perhaps she has been unable to answer for herself. With the repetition of the phrase "the child, the child," the tone becomes suddenly insistent, echoing the persistence of the girl, who "in her need" waits every night for a car to jump into. It's in these questions that the emotion of the poem, the extreme sense of loneliness, seems to focus itself most explicitly, the poet wondering if it is "so terrible" for the ghost to still be alone season after season, even when the flowers bloom. In this final image, Erdrich describes the "cold white blossoms" of the apple trees in the spring, as they "come to life and burn," perhaps suggesting the bright flowers resemble tiny fires. Note, too, how this image ties together one of the poem's central themes: fire and rebirth, "life and burn." These last lines are phrased as questions, suggesting that the poet wonders if perhaps the ghost finds comfort in the new blossoms every season and the larger cycle of death and rebirth they represent. By ending the poem with these unanswered questions, the poet forces us to leave the poem without a set conclusion, instead asking each of us to think of our own answer.

Themes

Horror

Louise Erdrich's poem "Bidwell Ghost" is about a child who died in a fire twenty years earlier and who continues to show up as a ghost at the abandoned land where her home was. The poem uses many familiar elements that readers will associate with horror stories. The presence of the ghost is, of course, frequently used in horror stories, making use of the fact that no one knows what the afterlife might hold. In "Bidwell Ghost," Erdrich uses the idea of a ghost haunting its former earthly home in order to capture the longing that a ghost must feel to return to a place after death. Stories like this often concern a tragedy that occurred at some significant time in the past: in Erdrich's poem, the tragedy happened more than twenty years ago. Ghost stories often take place one, ten, or even a hundred years after the event they memorialize. Horror stories also frequently rely on the existence of a particular haunted location, such as the apple grove in "Bidwell Ghost," which marks the place of the girl's death. Erdrich reveals the symbolic significance of this haunted location by showing its parallel to the girl's tragic life, its fruit abandoned by society just as her spirit has been.

Erdrich even incorporates a particular familiar horror story into this poem. The tale of the girl who can be found out hitchhiking alone at night is one that is common throughout many communities and one that is well documented in books about contemporary myth and legend. Often the girl is said to be wearing a nightgown, as the Bidwell Ghost does, but she is also described as wearing a prom dress in versions of the story in which her death occurred on the day of the school dance. By using elements of familiar horror stories and basing her work on a particular myth, Erdrich makes readers feel that they have heard this story before. This allows her to expand beyond the familiar situation, which is often told just for shock value, and to explore the dead girl's feelings in depth.

Nature

The ghost is supernatural, meaning that she occurs outside of the laws of nature as people generally understand them, but she is described using imagery that is drawn from nature. Her nightgown is compared to fire in the first stanza, and her hair is compared to a bird's nest and her tears to beautiful stones in stanza 5. Overall, the poem centers on the unfulfilled, abandoned feeling that links the spirit of the dead girl with the abandoned apple orchard, where sweet fruit, like her youth, is left to rot. In particular, the phrase "nothing can kill that wood" in line 9 draws a direct connection between the trees and the ghost, which also cannot die.

The relationship between the natural and the supernatural is a timeless one in literature. Writers used it most often during the romantic period of the early-nineteenth century. Writers such as Washington Irving ("The Legend of Sleepy Hollow"), Mary Wollstonecraft Shelley (*Frankenstein*), and Edgar Allan Poe wrote about issues of life and death, knowledge and mystery, using natural symbolism to represent the things that were beyond human understanding. This trend has diminished some as the world has been paved over with human-made objects, from buildings and trees to reservoirs and engineered genes; still, there is an element to nature that makes it an obvious doorway for writers writing about the supernatural. Horror movies such as *The Blair Witch Project* often take place in the woods, where the rules of society do not apply, and the same can be said of this charred and abandoned apple orchard, where people do not go.

Loneliness and Isolation

The poem, like many ghost stories, holds back on giving the reason for the ghost's behavior until it has shown in detail just how she does behave, so that readers find their curiosity raised with every line until the explanation comes at the end. The last stanza reveals what is driving the ghost to stay on earth at the same time that it questions her for haunting the land as she does. Being alone is given as the ghost's motive, making her "so persistent in her need." It certainly makes sense that, in order to avoid loneliness, she would wait by the road and climb into cars and that she would cry for twenty years. Having died as a child, she would not have formed enough of a self-identity to feel comfortable without anyone else around. Since ghosts are considered to be unsettled spirits who lack fulfillment, it makes sense that, in the case of a dead child, she or he would desperately miss the presence of another person's company.

At the same time, though, the poem asks, "Is it so terrible to be alone?" From the speaker's adult perspective, the apple orchard seems a satisfying place to spend eternity, with the seasons changing, the flowers blossoming into life year after year in the spring. There is a hint here that the speaker of the poem actually envies the situation that the ghost finds so intolerable. The speaker sees tranquility where the ghost, a perpetual child, sees only loneliness.

Style

"Bidwell Ghost" is written in eight short free verse stanzas, each usually three lines long. Unlike traditional verse, where each line is determined by a set number of accents or metric feet, the line lengths in this poem vary widely, ranging anywhere from four to sixteen words each. In free verse, the form of the poem grows from the poem's changing moods and subject matter—in this case, the poet chooses short, individual stanzas to organize her images. Stanza, in Italian, literally means *room*, so it might be useful to think of reading this poem as walking through eight small rooms and seeing, smelling, hearing, and touching the images placed in each. Erdrich closes every stanza with a period, not letting any images flow into the next. These lines ending on a period are called end-stopped lines, unlike enjambed lines, which have no punctuation at the end and "run over" to the next line or stanza.

Topics for Further Study

- Discuss the nature images—apple trees, nests, agates, snow, etc.—that are associated with the ghost. What relationship between natural and supernatural does this poem imply?

- Choose a story that you have been told as "true" and research it on one of the Internet sites devoted to urban legends. Then write a poem about it.

- Research some of the scientific processes described in this poem. How long, for instance, would it take apple trees that have been charred in a fire to grow enough to start bearing fruit again? What chemicals will apples decomposing on the ground turn into? What are the chances that new trees will grow and blossom from charred wood?

- Write an explanation for why this poem changes at the end with four lines in the last stanza whereas all of the other stanzas had three.

- Examine some ghost stories from Native American tribes of the American Midwest and identify particular elements that seem to be related to this poem.

Historical Context

Louise Erdrich grew up in a small town in North Dakota, where her parents taught at a school run by the Bureau of Indian Affairs. "Bidwell Ghost" reflects both her Native American heritage, with its rich history of oral storytelling, and the contemporary American culture that surrounded her. Oral storytelling has always been an integral part of the culture of the North American tribes, in which stories have a spiritual and ceremonial function that they lack in Western literature. They are used to relate history, social lessons, religion, and a general understanding of the world from one generation to the next. The traditional stories often combine elements of nature with the behaviors of humans: for instance, many Native American

Compare & Contrast

- **1989:** The world economy is in recession with several countries suffering from huge, hyper-inflation rates in the triple digits.

  Today: The United States, as well as much of the world, has enjoyed a prolonged period of economic stability, mostly due to new technologies developed for and requiring computers.

- **1989:** Many of the countries in eastern Europe and western Asia belong to the Union of Soviet Socialists Republic, or U.S.S.R., which was formed after the Russian Revolution of 1917.

Today: After the Soviet Union disbanded in 1991, some of its former member countries joined the Commonwealth of Independent States, but this group is not nearly the world-class superpower that the U.S.S.R. was.

- **1989:** Ghost stories, such as this one, traveled by word of mouth from one person to another.

  Today: Stories travel the world within minutes via the Internet. There are also Web sites devoted to distinguishing urban legends from true, bizarre events.

---

myths incorporate some form of a "trickster" figure to show humans that the world is not always as simple as it might seem to the naked eye. The form the trickster takes varies from one Indian nation to the next. The trickster is a raven among Indians of the Northwest coast, a coyote in the Southwest region, a spider in the Plains states, and a rabbit in the Southeast. In the trickster stories, children are taught to see and understand the limitations of the physical world, as the trickster often relies on some unexpected element to ward off evil and save humanity or to take advantage of humanity's ignorance. For example, a trickster figure might cheat some humans out of their food in one story, but the same trickster might, in another story, save humanity from a natural disaster that is being initiated by a more powerful supernatural figure.

Trickster stories are by no means the only kind of stories among the indigenous peoples of this continent, but they offer a good example of the way that information has traditionally been conveyed through telling stories. Like the myths of other cultures, Native American myths do include gods that appear to humans in the forms of animals, but there are also stories about historical events, including personal family histories, that are passed along in spoken rather than written form.

For this poem, Erdrich has drawn on a familiar urban folk tale, one that has been in circulation in American society for at least a hundred years.

Jan Harold Brunvand, a renowned sociologist, included several versions of the story that Erdrich tells in his 1981 study of urban legends called *The Vanishing Hitchhiker*. Brunvand notes that stories like this are modernized versions of the returning-ghost tale that was popular at the end of the nineteenth century. The subsequent popularity of automobiles, he explains, added the element of the ghost getting into a car and riding along for a while and then disappearing from the car when the driver is distracted; usually, the driver finds out later that the place where the ghost disappeared was the place of its death. Brunvand's book, one of the first studies of contemporary urban legends to make it beyond the academic presses and onto best-seller lists, points out how such stories, distributed throughout the culture in the same way that the Native American traditional stories are, exist in different forms in different parts of the country. Different localities at different parts of the country are likely to have some form of the story that is at the heart of "Bidwell Ghost."

With the spread of the Internet in the 1990s, urban legends have a new way to travel. Stories are spread around in a matter of hours, not years. E-mail messages ask receivers to spread to everyone on their address list the warnings about such fanciful stories as gang initiations that have potential members driving with their lights off, then killing motorists who flash their own headlights as a reminder; HIV-infected needles hidden in strategic places to pierce and infect unsuspecting victims; or valuable corporate secrets worth millions that are released by irate employees. In each case, the teller of the tale will insist it is true, usually adding that it happened to someone they know. Studying such stories, as with poetry and the oral tales of the Indians and the urban legends that came after them, helps sociologists understand the cultures from which they derive.

In modern Indian culture, this oral tradition has become mixed with the methods of communication that are made available by technology. Stories are transcribed and then printed, or they are posted on the Internet; they are recorded by native tellers and translated into other languages; they are interpreted into paintings, dance, and other forms. Contemporary American authors with Native American roots recognize the importance of "told" stories, and they use stylistic devices of the storytelling tradition in their works. In describing her view of writing, Erdrich said in an interview with *Writers Digest* that storytelling is of prime importance to her, that she is "hooked on narrative." She sees the importance of it in all cultures, not just the Native Americans. "Why is it that, as humans, we have to have narrative?" she mused in an interview with Michael Schumacher. "I don't know, but we do. I suppose it goes back to before the Bible; that storytelling cycle is in the traditions of *all* cultures."

Critical Overview

Several critics point out Erdrich's use of specific locations in her poetry as a means to discover a subject fully. Carolyne Wright, in her essay published in the *Northwest Review*, points out that Erdrich's "work is so clearly rooted in its setting and milieu as to enable her to achieve access to the invisible: the realm of myth, which must always be grounded in the actual and tangible." Literally a "ghost story," this specific description of location and movement toward the invisible realm of myth is evident in "Bidwell Ghost." Also apparent, according to other critics, is a sense of blending between the human and natural worlds. In a book review published in *Poetry*, Vernon Shetley terms this effect Erdrich's "landscape of human loneliness." Wright agrees, concluding that "Erdrich's poetry responds to this aim by finding in the patterns of the visible world of nature and the received legacy of family and tribal history a vast fund of material."

Criticism

David Kelly

Kelly is a writer and a teacher at two colleges in Illinois. In this essay, he examines the harsh attitude taken by the speaker of Erdrich's poem and how its fractured time sequence helps readers understand this attitude.

Louise Erdrich's "Bidwell Ghost" is a strange and difficult poem that presents a sympathetic situation in the voice of a speaker who is not sympathetic. Readers are faced with two possible ways to read the poem, and the two conflict with one another. Everything about the poem's subject and structure evokes a sense of pity for the unhappy, powerless ghost, but in the end the poem questions whether that pity is really appropriate.

The poem is based on a story that almost everyone is bound to have heard at some time, about a girl who died long ago under tragic circumstances and who walks the earth, seeking the company of the living. At different times throughout history, she has been called by different names, localizing her, affixing her sad story to the location where it is being told at the time. The details may be different—in some versions, she died in a car crash, in some she was murdered, and in some she took her own life—but the story always has her making contact with unsuspecting participants, in the way that the Bidwell Ghost, as Erdrich tells it, "will climb into your car."

If the poem were only about this strange event that is rumored to occur now and then, it would be just another ghost story, amusing enough to be told around Halloween time or to make a campfire even more unnerving. The fact of the ghost's existence, told with intricate details, is enough to justify this as a worthwhile piece to read. But the last stanza adds a new element to it: the personality of the poem's speaker. It forces readers to go back and reevaluate all that they have learned about the Bidwell Ghost in the three-line stanzas that come before.

The girl's fate is tied to that of the orchard, which has died twice, by fire first and then by neglect. Years after the fire, it is so healthy that the trees' branches, full of ripe fruit, break off and fall to the ground, wasted by people too superstitious to harvest this bounty. The ghost-child suffers the same way. First, there is her actual death, twenty years ago. More recently, she suffers the same neglect as the apple trees, with her existence ignored. People are advised not to speak to her or touch her

> *Her loneliness is fed by human superstition, which warns people not to touch her or speak to her, but then, the trees have been just as forsaken by society, and they have come out fine.*"

(if they even need such advice). Readers who have heard ghost stories since childhood, as most in American culture have, know that the spirits of the dead are assumed to walk the earth because they have some unfinished business here. They might seek revenge, they might seek mercy, they might seek forgiveness for the sins of their lives, but they are always looking for some sort of fulfillment that will give them peace and let them go off to the spirit world the way most dead people do. It is quite clear that the Bidwell Ghost is unable to find peace because she suffers from loneliness.

The poem leads readers to understand just how awful it would be to be a perpetual child, forced to wander the earth alone, avoided by frightened people. Just as the ghost's obsession with companionship with the living becomes clear, however, the poem's speaker draws away from the ghost, implying that she worries too much about loneliness. The question raised in the last three lines, "Is it so terrible?," is surprisingly harsh for several reasons. The question introduces a mocking tone that has not appeared anywhere else previously. Being alone is established as the ghost's fear, and the poem seems to respect this fear throughout the first seven stanzas, but the word "so" in "Is it so terrible?" implies that the speaker does not feel it is very terrible at all. This sarcastic use of "so" is typically used to show that the other person's concern is exaggerated, blown out of proportion. Furthermore, the circumstance that the poem's speaker questions actually *is* terrible. In the last two lines, there are unsettling images presented by the words "alone," "cold," and "burn." The confusing thing about this poem is that the same speaker who provides these obviously negative images is the person who is asking whether they are so bad after all.

The only way to pass over the feeling of misery that the loneliness causes this neglected child is to emphasize the splendor of the blossoms' new life. Fire, in this last stanza, has a mixed meaning: it is the source of the Bidwell Ghost's misery. But, the poem goes on to suggest that the scorched apple trees are getting beyond both their destruction by fire and their neglect by humans by growing a whole new orchard from the seeds of the fruit left to decay. Erdrich balances the horror of the past with some hope for the future, implying that the child could, like the orchard, grow into something much greater and stronger. If this is the point of taking the child's "need" so lightly in the final stanza, it is not as heartless as the words used to express it make it sound.

The missing element, which connects the speaker's somewhat cruel dismissal of the ghost's concerns and the sympathy that the poem itself grants her, is hidden somewhere within the poem's distorted presentation of time. It starts with the words "Each night," and as a result readers often are likely to focus their attention on the present tense and on the ongoing situation. In fact, there are four different time frames presented in the poem, which is actually quite a wide span to be compacted into a twenty-five-line piece. Arranging them in chronological order, starting with the farthest past, offers some insight into why this poem is able to capture complex emotions within its limited scope.

The first step in the Bidwell Ghost's development was the fire that killed her. The apple trees in the orchard were hardened and blackened, "charred," and "her house surged and burst." There is the implication that this was a violent night, even though the word "burst" does not seem intended to say that the house literally exploded. More likely, this graphic visual description might be seen as an overstatement, in order to link the house to the blossoms described in the final line as coming to life and "burning." There is no mention of how the fire started, or of others who may have lived there with the girl: these glaring omissions add to the poem's aura of mystery, as if twenty years ago was before records, before memory, in a time that is only knowable through legend.

The second area of time concerns the following twenty years. Instead of focusing on the ghost, part of her development is explained indirectly, in terms of how the apple orchard has evolved. The charred branches were replaced with new, live ones, which grew so heavy with fruit that they were torn right off of the trees by their own fecundated weight. Fertilized by charred and fallen wood, new apple seeds have taken root and started a whole new, clean generation of blossoms. The poem does not describe how the Bidwell Ghost developed over the course of twenty years. The ghost has, in fact, not developed at all. Nature follows its course in the apple orchard, but the ghost's situation has not been affected by time, and as a result (or possibly, as a cause), humanity has feared the situation and has stayed away.

The third time frame is the present. It describes what the ghost does every night, wandering her familiar road, waiting for something that will fulfill her.

The fourth, only slightly different than the present tense, is the near future. She *will* get into your car, the poem explains, and it then goes on to tell readers what they should not do in response to her presence; they should not comb her hair or touch her tears, the way one might be tempted to do for a distraught child. Perhaps most importantly, and certainly most mysteriously, readers are told to not ask the Bidwell Ghost where she is going. This rule, like the others, is presented as absolute law but not explained. It may be that conversations with ghosts are forbidden, although there is no clue of who might make or enforce such a rule. What is more important than the fact that "you" are told to not talk to the ghost is the question itself: if the ghost were forced to think about where she is going, she might not carry out the same ghostly behavior night after night.

Arranging the facts of the case in chronological order puts the ghost's situation in a clearer, more direct light. Instead of seeing her as a victim of fate, she appears to be stuck in a rut, unwilling to grow and change in the same way that the trees in the devastated orchard, which suffered along with her, were able to go on. Her loneliness is fed by human superstition, which warns people not to touch her or speak to her, but then, the trees have been just as forsaken by society, and they have come out fine.

If the story this poem tells had been presented more directly, in clear chronological order, the speaker's tough attitude at the end would not seem so much a harsh insult to the ghost-child as it would seem a way of urging her to get on with her existence, to take it to another phase, to learn, as the trees have, how to thrive on loneliness. Such clarity might make the poem easier for readers, but it would not force them to experience the complexity of the issues involved. Louise Erdrich uses the

frame of a familiar ghost story, but the true source material at the heart of this story is that of any little child who has fallen victim to tragedy. Almost anyone is inclined to feel sorry for such a helpless, suffering figure, and it is to this poem's credit that it uses this emotional situation, stretching it, looking at implications that go beyond human kindness to consider other ways to react to a child who cannot find peace.

Source: David Kelly, Critical Essay on "Bidwell Ghost," in *Poetry for Students*, The Gale Group, 2002.

Laura Kryhoski

Kryhoski is currently working as a freelance writer. In this essay, she considers Erdrich's work in relation to the author's Chippewa heritage.

Erdrich's "Bidwell Ghost" is a work shaped primarily by mythic folklore and spiritual beliefs, the rhythms of nature and the author's Chippewa ancestry. A consideration of the poem uncovers themes in keeping with universal folklore and Native American philosophy and tradition. The significance of the work is primarily rooted, however, within the belief system of the native people to whom the author herself is related. A sense of Chippewa spirituality creates a cadence or balanced, rhythmic flow within the narrative.

As the title "Bidwell Ghost" suggests, the poem is a ghost story with a rhythm and feel of a tale that will continue to be passed along orally. The reader is immediately captivated by a ghostly figure in the first stanza, a woman who "Each night . . . waits by the road in a thin white dress." In the next stanza, the legendary encounter with the supernatural, anticipated by the reader, is forewarned: "she will climb into your car / but not say where she is going." The poet also warns, "you shouldn't ask" of her destination. The mythic quality of this encounter creates an impression of a personal account related, thereby giving the poem an almost historical flavor.

In various interviews, Erdrich claims her creative inspirations stem from her native heritage. She often mentions that several members of her family are storytellers. She claims that her heavy and repeated exposure to a family tradition of storytelling shapes her ability as a writer. It is not surprising, then, that the mythic quality of this "ghost story" is in keeping with Erdrich's background and native heritage.

The creation imagery appearing within the text on several different levels supports the unifying thematic force of the poem. D'Arcy Rheault, Na-

> *To the Chippewa, the Circle of Life, or Sacred Circle, is a cultural code that binds the people together because all have a place in creation and all are dictated by the cycles driving it."*

tive American scholar, explains in his work "Anishinaabe Philosophy: An Introduction" the concept of creation in the Anishinaabe (Chippewa) culture as one of dependency for native peoples. Central to the concept of creation is the Earth Mother, to whom the Chippewa are physically and spiritually bound: "Without Mother Earth there would be no life and no reason to live," writes Rehault. Essentially, the quality of the Earth Mother dominating Chippewa philosophy is the Circle of Life. Rheault adds, "We are witnesses to the circularity of the seasons, of life and death and life again, to the cycles that drive our very existence." To the Chippewa, the Circle of Life, or Sacred Circle, is a cultural code that binds the people together because all have a place in creation and all are dictated by the cycles driving it.

"Bidwell Ghost" is filled with images of spring, renewal, and reproduction. These images, in turn, serve as a device to create a movement within the piece, a movement through seasonal cycles and transitions from one stage of womanhood to the next. A closer look at the work uncovers the interrelationship between the elements of the poem itself and the mysterious woman moving through its cycles. The images of fertility, the topical seasonal changes, parallel the "seasons" or cycles of a woman's life.

One of the first, the most powerful, sensual, and perhaps violent images of the poem appears in the guise of the apple tree. Dr. Clarissa Estes, in her discussion of myth and tradition in *Women Who Run With the Wolves* expounds on the image of the psychic tree: "it grows, it lives, it is used up, it leaves its seeds for new, it loves us." In folklore, the tree is symbolic of the feminine nature.

Erdrich's work relies heavily on the image of the psychic tree to create movement in the poem, movement set in motion by milestones in a woman's experience during a reproductive lifetime. In the second stanza of the poem, a house has "surged" and "burst" into flame, "charring" the branches of the surrounding apple trees. "Surged" can also be represented as a flow, pour, gush, stream, or flood, whereas "burst" is more aptly likened to eruption, rupture, or explosion. It is "her house" that has undergone such violent change, a change occurring "in the dark trees." If the house in this instance is her womb, then the imagery accompanying it takes on a much deeper significance. The surging and bursting of "her house" represent the onset of the female menstrual cycle. Looking ahead, similar imagery within the poem supports this notion of the transition from virginity to womanhood as the "cold white blossoms come to life and burn," with fruitfulness, as the "unpicked fruit" becomes burdensome, or barrenness in the tree's "charred branches."

Color imagery present within the poem also contributes to this cyclical movement—white, red, and black dominate the poem, be it the cold white blossoms blazing red fire or the darkness of agates. These color choices, appearing throughout the work, are identified with specific stages of womanhood, those of the virgin (white) maiden, motherhood (red), and the image of the crone, the elderly woman approaching death (black).

The spirit in white, or the white maiden appearing in the beginning of the poem, resembles this guide or helper of the mother/crone who appears later within the work. Folklore surrounding the spirit guide, according to Estes, characterizes her as a piece of old and precious shattered God, still invested in each human. In folklore, she is identified as the helper of the mother crone, or the Life/Death/Life Goddess. Her image, presented at the beginning of the poem, is one of youth, of freshness, as mirrored by the white dress and the ring of fire that passionately encircles it. But the figure present in the car paints a much different picture, that of a woman with an unkempt "blackened nest of hair." She fits the portrait of Mother/Crone. A mythological figure, she is a fertile image, she is the mother, a rich, moist, dark and inviting giver of life. The "blackened nest" of her hair, as it is described in the poem, could be likened to closely intertwined roots blackened with soil.

What is missing from this portrait of life is the image of womanhood. A succinct lack of harmony is also evident within the movement of the cycles—

the ghostly figure in the poem experiences no summer, no state of motherhood, and this disjointedness has an unsettling effect on the mood of the overall work and creates a mood of hopelessness, of lost opportunity. Seasonally, the poem does not progress logically in accordance with natural law. Spring, fall, and winter cycle helplessly out of sync without the appearance of summer, as are the seasons of a woman's life, heightening a mood of despair implicit within the text.

The description of the haunted figure of the woman is also fleshed out symbolically in natural terms: her emotions like "charred wood," her appearance, characterized by her "blackened nest of hair" or "agates of tears," ground the figure firmly on Earth. In addition to the creative imagery propelling the female spirit through the lifecycle, the author employs duality in her use of images to further assert a strong relationship between the main character of the poem and the natural world swirling about her. Dual images include, but are not limited to, those of maiden and crone, of white blossoms and darkened wood, of virgin frailty and passionate anger. The dual images set up a natural harmony or balance within the overall work for the reader. This duality is a reflection of native world values, according to D'Arcy Rheault in "Anishinaabe Philosophy: An Introduction." Rheault claims the Anishinaabe (or Chippewa) view of creation to be "a movement in unity rather than a unity towards movement. Creation is harmony seen in duality."

Louise Erdrich's "Bidwell Ghost" captures all of the beauty and harmonious movement of a woman's reproductive journey. In this "Creation sequence," the author relies on the beliefs of her Chippewa ancestry to flesh out and give great spiritual depth to the poem and to the tragedy of lost opportunity that inspires it. As the poem progresses, the reader is left to contemplate a haunting female image and the mystery behind her silence, and perhaps also with a yearning to wriggle her toes in the warm, moist soil.

Source: Laura Kryhoski, Critical Essay on "Bidwell Ghost," in *Poetry for Students*, The Gale Group, 2002.

Judi Ketteler

Ketteler has taught literature and composition. In this essay, she discusses the way the poem "Bidwell Ghost" is shaped and informed by Native American spirituality.

"Bidwell Ghost" by Louise Erdrich is, on one level, a ghost story. The poem tells the story of a

> *Sharing is the backbone of native societies. To achieve a 'resurrection,' one must honor the memory. "Bidwell Ghost" is a poem about memory and about loneliness."*

young girl, killed twenty years ago in a house fire. Since her death, the girl haunts the road by the house, inviting herself into the cars and thoughts of passers-by. But the ghost-child is much more than an eerie presence on a lonely stretch of road.

Erdrich is a gifted storyteller, and both her novels and her poetry reflect her gift for language. She also has Native American heritage, which shapes and informs her writing in many ways. Knowing that Erdrich is Native American and writes about Native Americans can sharpen and enrich our reading of "Bidwell Ghost"—though it certainly does not box Erdrich into only one identity or meaning. We might, however, expect to find certain elements literary critics have highlighted in Native American poetry in Erdrich's poetry as well.

In the Native American tradition, storytelling is about community. Telling stories is a way of organizing culture. Richard Erdoes and Alphonso Ortiz, Native American scholars and authors of *American Indian Myths and Legends*, explain that stories and legends "are magic lenses through which we can glimpse social orders and daily life: how families were organized, how political structures operated, how men caught fish, how religious ceremonies felt to the people who took part, how power was divided between men and women." Erdrich is drawing upon this tradition of storytelling to communicate to her readers. The form she chooses—poetry—has many advantages. One might say that what separates a written poem from a story or novel is a certain economy of words and a heightened sense of language: in other words, every word counts and is used to create a certain mood or feeling. Norma C. Wilson, author of *The Nature of Native American Poetry*, comments: "Poetry allows a rhythmic and emotional expression closer than any other written genre to the songs and chants that are integral to oral tradition and ceremony."

In "Bidwell Ghost," the mood is eerie and wistful. Like any good ghost story, the poem has a communal feeling about it. The reader might imagine a group of friends seated around a campfire, retelling the story. And this is exactly the atmosphere Erdrich wants to create. Ghost stories are an integral part of many Native American cultures. Erdoes and Ortiz explain: "Ghost stories and tales of the dead are essential parts of almost every people's folklore and American Indians are no exception. The ghosts, here, however, are not necessarily always evil or threatening." It's important not to assume the ghost in this poem represents evil—ghosts can be symbolic of many things. As beings belonging to the supernatural world, ghosts have special powers, and their presence can often suggest a healing power, as will be discussed later in this essay.

The opening lines of the poem create a very forlorn mood; the place where the girl waits by the road is deserted and has been for some time: "It has been twenty years / since her house surged and burst in the dark trees / Still nobody goes there." Her waiting is habitual; she returns night after night, as suggested by the first line: "Each night she waits by the road." The reader learns that the cause of the girl's death was a housefire. Erdrich uses vivid language to describe the event. The house "surge and burst"; "the heat charred the branches." There is a sense of violence and destruction, and while Erdrich does not describe the death of the young girl, the reader uses his/her imagination to fill in the unpleasant details. Her "thin white dress" is "embroidered with fire"—the girl is forever marked by the violence of the fire.

The next set of images describes the violence the natural world around the house suffered. "The heat charred the branches / of the apple tree"; "the Orchard bowed low and complained / of unpicked fruit, / then the branches cracked apart and fell." The tree branches have become "ruined arms." Erdrich personifies—or gives human characteristics to—the natural world. The orchard bows and complains and the limbs of the trees are described as "arms." Many poets use the technique of personification to achieve different effects. For Erdrich, it is about connecting to the natural world. "An understanding of the interrelatedness of humans and the rest of the natural world is pervasive both in traditional songs and chants and in contemporary Native poetry of the United States," explains Norma Wilson.

It is a seemingly barren world the ghost inhabits, yet she continues to appear every night, and the cycles of nature keep moving forward. Line 21 underscores this point: "Each spring now, in the grass, buds form on the tattered wood." Wood is referred to at another place in the poem as well; in line 9, the speaker states, "but nothing can kill that wood." As a natural element, wood is stronger than the eerie sense of destruction and desolation. It stands the test of time. Despite the tragedy of the event, time cannot be stopped. The natural world around the tragedy is trying to heal itself. Just as the "windfalls sweetened to wine / beneath the ruined arms and snow," the cycle of life continues.

One way to read the ghost, then, is as a healing force. She represents past tragedies and memories. The nature of a ghost is somewhat like the nature of memory—fleeting, haunting, seemingly from another dimension which a person generally has no control over. Memories grab us and take us along for a ride, similar to the way the ghost forces itself into the car of drivers passing by: "She will climb into your car / but not say where she is going / and you shouldn't ask." The message is that our memories will take us where we need to be, heal us in the way we need healing. Robin Riley Fast, literary critic and author of *The Heart as a Drum: Continuance and Resistance in American Indian Poetry*, speaks to the importance of memory: "All across Native America, dream, vision and myth are essential to spirituality, along with memories, which keeps them alive; they are thus essential to the ways of healing these poets offer."

But what healing is Erdrich addressing? The answer lies in many things, but mostly it is the healing of a culture and of a bloody history. Like the young girl whose life was tragically ended before it reached fulfillment, throughout the eighteenth and nineteenth centuries hundreds of Native American cultures were systematically destroyed through brutal fighting and scheming tactics on the part of the United States government. The sadness and shame of this history is ever present, like the tears of the ghost. "Nor should you try to comb the blackened nest of hair / or press the agates of tears / back into her eyes." In other words, as a culture and a country, we cannot forget what happened or try to conceal it or make it go away. The history will live with us, but it does not determine the future. The natural world has suffered, like the branches that "cracked and fell apart," but it is not destroyed.

What Do I Read Next?

- Louise Erdrich is one of the writers featured in the anthology *Growing Up Native American*, a collection of works from noted Indian authors of the past two centuries writing about their childhoods. Some other authors included are Leslie Marmon Silko, Black Elk, Michael Dorris, and Linda Hogan. This anthology, edited by Patricia Reilly, was published in 1995.

- Erdrich's short story "A Place of the True Cross" is included in the anthology *Ghost Writing: Haunted Tales by Contemporary Writers*, published in 2000 by Invisible Cities Press.

- Louise Erdrich is not included in the short story collection *Ghosts of the Heartland: Haunting, Spine-Chilling Stories from the American Midwest*, but these stories come from the same geographic region where her works always take place. This 1990 anthology from Rutledge Hill Press was edited by Frank D. McSherry Jr., Charles G. Waugh, and Martin H. Greenberg.

- One of the basic texts for studying contemporary American folklore is Jan Harold Brunvand's 1981 *The Vanishing Hitchhiker: American Urban Legends and their Meaning*. The title refers to a series of ghost stories similar to the one told in "Bidwell Ghost."

- Karl Shapiro's poem "Auto Wreck" captures much of the same sense of numb wonder over the immutable forces of life and death, using a similar, detached tone. It can be found in Shapiro's *The Wild Card: Selected Poems, Early and Late* (1998) from University of Illinois Press.

- Starting as a poet, Louise Erdrich later concentrated on writing fiction, for which she has received international recognition. Her five novels, interconnected by characters that appear in various books, take place on the Ojibwe reservation in North Dakota. They include *Tracks* (1988), *The Last Report on the Miracles at Little No Horse* (2001), *Love Medicine* (1984), *The Beet Queen* (1986), and *The Bingo Palace* (1994).

- Much is made of Erdrich's background as an Ojibwe and its influence on her as a storyteller. The Minnesota Historical Society has recently published a collection called *Living Our Language: Ojibwe Tales and Oral Histories* (2001), translated by Anton Treuer.

- One of the most serious and respected investigators of ghosts in the past half-century is Hans Holzer. Several of his writings were compiled into one volume in 1997 under the title *Ghosts: True Encounters with the World Beyond*.

- Edgar Allan Poe wrote some of the greatest poetry ever written about ghosts. His poem "Lenore" and "To Helen," in particular, capture the eerie mood of Erdrich's poem. They are all collected in *Edgar Allan Poe: Complete Poems*, reprinted in 2001 by Grammarcy Press.

- Erdrich is often mentioned along with N. Scott Momaday because they are among the preeminent Native American authors writing today. In fact, they do share similar sensibilities, which can be observed by reading Momaday's 1969 novel, *House Made of Dawn*, about life on the Jimez Reservation in New Mexico.

Erdrich ends "Bidwell Ghost" by asking a question: "The child, the child, why is she so persistent / in her need?" The repetition of "the child" suggests a sort of pleading or cooing tone. The speaker continues her questioning: "Is it so terrible / to be alone when the cold white blossoms / come to life and burn?" Here Erdrich is juxtaposing the sense of loneliness with the idea of resurrection. The "cold white blossoms" of the last stanza hearken back to the "thin white dress" mentioned in the first stanza. White is the color of purity, of hope, and of resurrection. Erdrich makes an allusion to the myth of the phoenix—the bird that rises from the ashes of its own destruction. Similarly, the blossoms seem to come to life as they burn.

The "need" addressed in the beginning of the stanza refers to the ghost's need for companionship. She waits for drivers to pass by so she can climb into their car. Her loneliness stems not so much from the fact that she is a ghost—after all, the mythic world is full of such supernatural presences—but from the fact that she needs to tell her story. She needs to be mourned for, and to mourn with someone—someone still alive, someone who can still appreciate life. Her story will be dead, just like her physical body, if there is no one to pass it on. The speaker is asking a rhetorical question in the last stanza, asking if it is so terrible to be alone in our memories.

The answer depends upon one's cultural perspective. For a culture built upon collectivity, upon storytelling and collaborative thinking and effort, it is a terrible thing to not be able to share memories and history. Sharing is the backbone of native societies. To achieve a "resurrection," one must honor the memory. "Bidwell Ghost" is a poem about memory and about loneliness. It is a sad story of a terrible tragedy—on many levels. But the story doesn't end with the tragedy; instead it begins there, retelling the event, passing it on to future generations so that the memory may be preserved.

Source: Judi Ketteler, Critical Essay on "Bidwell Ghost," in *Poetry for Students*, The Gale Group, 2002.

Sources

Brunvand, Jan Harold, *The Vanishing Hitchhiker: American Urban Legends and Their Meanings*, W. W. Norton & Company, 1981.

Erdoes, Richard, and Alfonso Ortiz, *American Indian Myths and Legends*, Pantheon, 1984.

Estes, Clarissa Pinkola, *Women Who Run with the Wolves*, Ballantine, 1995, pp. 399–425.

Fast, Robin Riley, *The Heart as a Drum: Continuance and Resistance in American Indian Poetry*, University of Michigan Press, 1999.

Rehault, D'Arcy, "Anishinaabe Philosophy: An Introduction," http://www.sky-lynx.com/Articles/Anishinaabephil.htm (June 4, 2001).

Schumacher, Michael, "Louise Erdrich and Michael Dorris: A Marriage of Minds," in *Conversations with Louise Erdrich and Michael Dorris*, University of Mississippi Press, 1994, pp. 173–83.

Shetley, Vernon, Review of *Jacklight*, in *Poetry*, Vol. CXLVI, No. 1, April 1985, pp. 40–41.

Wilson, Norma C., *The Nature of Native American Poetry*, University of New Mexico, 2001.

Wright, Carolyne, "Women Poets: Seven New Voices" in *Northwest Review*, Vol. 23, No. 1, 1985, pp. 118–33.

Further Reading

Beidler, Peter, and Gay Barton, *A Reader's Guide to The Novels of Louise Erdrich*, University of Missouri Press, 1999.
    Fans of Erdrich's writing will find this comprehensive guide useful in untangling the rich complexity of the plots of her novels.

Bloom, Harold, ed., *Native American Woman Writers*, Chelsea House Publishers, 1998.
    A section of this book contains a brief biography of Erdrich, followed by excerpts from critical essays about her works.

Smith, Jeanne Rosier, *Writing Tricksters: Mythic Gambols in American Ethnic Literature*, University of California Press, 1997.
    There are other books that study the magical image of the trickster in Native American writing, but Smith uses a large section of her book to apply this concept to Erdrich's writing in particular.

Stookey, Lorena L., *Louise Erdrich: A Critical Companion*, Greenwood Press, 1999.
    This book focuses on Erdrich's fiction, but the introductory material about her life and writing style illustrates her poetic style.

Van Dyke, Annette, "Of Vision Quests and Spirit Guardians: Female Power in the Novels of Louise Erdrich," in *The Chippewa Landscape of Louise Erdrich*, edited by Allan Chavkin, University of Alabama Press, 1999, pp. 130–43.
    Though focused on Erdrich's novels, this essay can help readers gain insight into the significance of the ghost in "Bidwell Ghost" being a young girl; it examines attitudes prevalent throughout Erdrich's works.

The Canterbury Tales

Geoffrey Chaucer
1400

Geoffrey Chaucer began writing *The Canterbury Tales* sometime around 1387 A.D.; the uncompleted manuscript was published in 1400, the year he died. Having recently passed the six hundredth anniversary of its publication, the book is still of interest to modern students for several reasons. For one thing, *The Canterbury Tales* is recognized as the first book of poetry written in the English language. Before Chaucer's time, even poets who lived in England wrote in Italian or Latin, which meant that poetry was only understandable to people of the wealthy, educated class. English was considered low class and vulgar. To a great degree, *The Canterbury Tales* helped make it a legitimate language to work in. Because of this work, all of the great writers who followed, from Shakespeare to Dryden to Keats to Eliot, owe him a debt of gratitude. It is because Chaucer wrote in English that there is a written record of the roots from which the modern language grew. Contemporary readers might find his words nearly as difficult to follow as a foreign language, but scholars are thankful for the chance to compare Middle English to the language as it is spoken now, to examine its growth.

In the same way that *The Canterbury Tales* gives modern readers a sense of the language at the time, the book also gives a rich, intricate tapestry of medieval social life, combining elements of all classes, from nobles to workers, from priests and nuns to drunkards and thieves. The General Prologue alone provides a panoramic view of society that is not like any found elsewhere in all of liter-

Geoffrey Chaucer

ature. Students who are not particularly interested in medieval England can appreciate the author's technique in capturing the variations of human temperament and behavior. Collections of stories were common in Chaucer's time, and some still exist today, but the genius of *The Canterbury Tales* is that the individual stories are presented in a continuing narrative, showing how all of the various pieces of life connect to one another. This entry does not cover all the tales, only some of the most studied.

Author Biography

Geoffrey Chaucer came from a financially secure family that owned ample wine vineyards but held no title, and so from birth he was limited in his capacity for social growth. His date of birth is uncertain but is assumed to be around 1340–1345. While he was still a child in London, it became clear that Chaucer was a brilliant scholar, and he was sent to the prestigious St. Paul's Almonry for his education. In 1357, he rose in society by taking a position in the royal court of Elizabeth, Countess of Ulster. His duties as a squire in court would have included those that are usually associated with domestic help: making beds, carrying candles, helping the gentleman of the house dress. Chaucer was given an education in his association with the

household, and he met some of England's exalted royalty.

He left in 1359 to join the army to fight the French in the Hundred Years' War (1337–1453). Captured near Rheims, he was ransomed the following year and returned to being a squire. Being intelligent and witty, he became increasingly valuable at court for the entertainment of his poetry. By 1367, he was the valet for the King himself, and that same year, he married a woman whose rank added to his social standing: Philippa de Roet, the sister to Catherine of Swynford, the third wife of John of Gaunt. John of Gaunt, the Duke of Lancaster, was later to take over the responsibility for ruling England when his father, Edward III, became too senile to rule before a successor was crowned.

As a valued and trusted member of the court, Chaucer was sent on several diplomatic missions, giving him a rare opportunity to see Italy and France. The influences of these languages can be traced in his poetry, and the worldliness of travel affected his storytelling ability. His political influence grew with a series of appointments: to Comptroller of taxes on wools, skins, and hides at the Port of London in 1374; Comptroller of petty customs in 1382; Justice of the Peace for the County of Kent in 1385; and Knight of the Shire in 1386.

In December of 1386, he was deprived of all of this political influence when his patron, John of Gaunt, left the country on a military expedition for Spain and the Duke of Gloucester replaced him. It is assumed that it was during this period of unemployment that Chaucer planned out and started writing *The Canterbury Tales*. When John of Gaunt returned to England in 1389, he was given a new government post, and Chaucer lived a prosperous life from then on.

There is no record of his progress on *The Canterbury Tales*. The plan that he laid out in the Prologue was left unfinished when he died on October 25, 1400. He was buried in Westminster Abbey and was the first of the writers to be entombed there in the area known as the Poets' Corner.

Poem Summary

The Prologue

In the Prologue to *The Canterbury Tales*, Geoffrey Chaucer introduces the speaker of the poem as a man named Chaucer, who is traveling from London with a group of strangers to visit Canterbury, a borough to the southeast of London. This group of people is thrown together when they travel together on a trip to the shrine of Saint Thomas à Becket, who was murdered in Canterbury in 1170. The Prologue gives a brief description of the setting as they assemble at the Tibard Inn in Southwark to prepare for their trip. It describes each of the pilgrims, including ones who were meant to be discussed in sections of the book that were never written before Chaucer died. After the introductions, the Host, who owns the inn that they gather at and who is leading the group, suggests that they should each tell two stories while walking, one on the way to Canterbury and one on the way back, to pass the time more quickly. He offers the person telling the best story a free supper at the tavern when they return.

The Knight's Tale

The first pilgrim to talk, the Knight, tells a long, involved tale of love from ancient Greece about two knights, Arcite and Palamon. They were captured in a war between Thebes and Athens and thrown into an Athenian prison to spend the rest of their lives there. From the tower they were locked in, they could see a fair maiden, Emily, in the window of her chamber every morning, and they each fell in love with her. An old friend of Arcite arranged for his release, and the ruler of Athens, Duke Theseus, agreed with just one condition: that Arcite had to leave Athens forever or be killed if he ever returned. In exile, all he could do was think about Emily, while Palamon, who was in prison, could at least look at her every day.

For two years Arcite wandered, suffering so much from lovesickness that he became worn and pale. When the god Mercury came and told him to return to Athens, he realized that he did not even look like the man he had once been. Upon returning, he secured a job in Emily's court and became one of her servants. Meanwhile, Palamon, after seven years in prison, escaped. The two former companions soon ran into each other in the forest and fought. While they were fighting, Theseus stumbled upon them and, finding out who they were, was ready to have them both killed. His wife, however, was moved by their love for Emily and convinced them to settle their argument by leading the best soldiers in the land against each other, with the winner marrying Emily.

The Knight's Tale goes on for hundreds of lines detailing the historic noble personages who participated in the battle and the preparations they made, including sacrifices to gods. In the battle,

Palamon was injured, but no sooner was Arcite declared the winner than his horse reared up and dropped him on his head. He died that night and was given a hero's funeral, and Palamon married Emily. They lived happily ever after: "Thus endeth Palamon and Emelye," the Knight's Tale ends, "And God save al this faire companye! Amen."

The Miller's Tale

The Miller is the next speaker; he is drunk and picks an argument with the Reeve before beginning a story about a carpenter at Oxford, who was rich and miserly. To make extra money, the carpenter rented a room to a poor student, Nicholas, who lived with the carpenter and his young, beautiful wife. Eventually, Nicholas and the young wife, Alison, started scheming about how they could have an affair without the carpenter finding out. They made use of the fact that the parish clerk, Absalon, had a crush on the wife, and would sing songs outside of her window at night. Once, Nicholas stayed up in his room, and didn't come down for days, having prepared by hoarding enough food for a long period. When the carpenter sent a servant to get him, he found Nicholas lying as if he had suffered a seizure. The fit was caused, Nicholas explained, by a startling discovery he had made while studying astrology: that a terrible flood was coming. He convinced the carpenter to hang three tubs from the roof, so that both men and Alison would be safe from the rising waters. On the appointed day, they climbed into their separate tubs, but once the carpenter was asleep Alison and Nicholas sneaked down to the bedroom together. While they were in bed, Absalon came to the window, and, thinking Alison was alone, demanded a kiss; she put her naked backside out the window, and he kissed it in the dark. When he climbed the ladder again to object, Nicholas put his own behind out and passed gas in Absalon's face. When John, the carpenter, came out of his basket, the young lovers told everyone in town that he was insane and had made up the crazy story about the flood, ruining his reputation forever.

The Wife of Bath's Tale

The Wife of Bath's tale starts with a long Prologue, much longer than the tale she eventually tells, in which she describes to her fellow pilgrims the history of her five previous marriages and her views about relations between men and women. She defends at length the moral righteousness of people who marry often, as long as their spouses are dead, quoting the Bible as only stating that sexual abstinence is preferred but not required. In fact, she explains, the sexual organs are made to be used for sex and supports this claim with a quote from the Book of Proverbs, "Man shal yelde to his wyf hire dette" ("Man shall yield to his wife her debt").

After the Pardoner interrupts to say that he has been thinking of being married soon, the Wife of Bath describes marriage to him, using her own marriages as examples. The first three, she says, were to old men who were hardly able to have sex with her. She flattered these men by pretending to be jealous of them, using the excuse of keeping an eye on them as an explanation for why she was always out at night. She also argued with them constantly, bringing up every stereotype about women they had ever uttered and every suspicion that they'd had about her in particular so that she could argue from a defensive position. By arguing, she was able to make them appreciate her more when she did decide to be nice to them. Her fourth husband was younger, but he made her jealous by having a mistress so she made him miserable by making him jealous too: not, as she points out, by having a sexual affair, but simply by having a good time. Her fifth and last husband, Jankin, was physically abusive, but she loved him best nonetheless because he was a good lover. She met him while still married to her fourth husband when he was living next door to her godmother. When her fourth husband died, she married Jankin and signed over to him all that she had inherited from her four previous husbands. She continued her active social life, and her sarcastic talk. One night, as Jankin was reading aloud from a scholarly work about the evils of women, she became exasperated and, reaching over, tore a page out of the book. He hit her, which permanently made her deaf, but when he realized what he had done he apologized, and after that, she explains, they have been happy together.

There is a brief interval, during which angry words are exchanged between the Friar, who mocks the Wife of Bath for her long preface, and the Summoner, who tells him to leave her alone. The wife then begins her tale, which takes place during the time of King Arthur, which was ancient legend even in Chaucer's time. In the tale, a knight came upon a maiden walking beside the river one afternoon and raped her, for which he was condemned to death. The queen interceded, asking the king to spare the knight. When he could not answer her question about what women really desire most, the knight was sent off for a year to try to find the answer. The Wife of Bath relates several of the answers he received, including the one she favors,

which is that women want to be flattered. On the day he was to return from his quest, the knight came across several dozen women in the forest, but when he approached them they disappeared, leaving an old lady in their place. She told him that the answer was that women wanted equality, which is what he told the queen, sparing his life. For giving him the right answer, the knight was obliged to marry the old woman.

On their wedding night, when he would not take her to bed, she talked to him about the difference between being born noble and being truly noble. Gentleness is a virtue, she told him, as are poverty and age. She then gave him a choice: he could have her old and ugly and faithfully devoted, or young and pretty and courted by other men. He left the choice to her, proving her equality with him, and for that she kissed him and turned into a young maiden, faithful to him forever after.

The Franklin's Tale

A Franklin was a person who held property but no title of nobility. In the Prologue to his tale, the Franklin explains that he is going to tell a story that has been passed down in English from troubadours, who traveled from town to town, singing the story with musical accompaniment. He apologizes for lacking the verbal skill to color in the details of the story as clearly as a skilled speaker might be able to do.

His tale takes place in Brittany, a region of France that was settled by English emigrants around the year 500 A.D. A knight loved a beautiful lady named Dorigene, and when she finally consented to marry him, he promised to never do anything that would embarrass her and treat her as a respected equal. When the knight, Arveragus, was called upon to fight in England, Dorigene was left home alone. Friends took her out for walks along the ocean, but all she noticed was the dangerous rocks along the shore that Arveragus' ship might crash onto when he returned.

Her friends took her to a dance on the sixth of May, and there Dorigene was approached by a handsome young squire, Aurelius, who declared his love for her. Aurelius had all masculine attributes possible: he was "Yong, strong, right vertuous, and riche and wys, and wel biloved, and holden in great prys." Dorigene was too in love with her husband to care about Aurelius. To discourage him, she told him that he could have her if he could clear all of the rocks off the shoreline within two years. Aurelius set about to pray to various gods for help, ask-

Media Adaptations

- The 2001 movie *A Knight's Tale*, starring Heath Ledger and Mark Addy, is only loosely based on the Knight in *The Canterbury Tales*: it concerns a young squire who meets Chaucer and enlists his help in becoming a full-fledged knight. It was written and directed by Brian Helgeland and is distributed by Columbia Tristar.

- A compact disc of Trevor Eaton reading selections from *The Canterbury Tales* was released in 2000, marking the six hundredth anniversary of Chaucer's death. It is available from Pearl, of Sussex, England.

- The Penguin Library edition of the *Canterbury Tales*, translated into modern English by Nevill Coghill, is available on six audiocassettes from Penguin. It was released in 1995 and again in 1999.

- *The Canterbury Tales* were adapted to an opera, sung in English, available on two compact discs from Chandos Records of Colchester, England. The performers, recorded in 1996, include Yvonne Kenny, Robert Tear, Stephen Roberts, and the London Symphony Orchestra.

- A 1995 audiocassette of *The Canterbury Tales* is available from Durkin Hayes of Niagara Falls, New York, with Fenella Fielding and Martin Starkie reading.

- Recorded Books has a thirteen-hour recording on nine audiocassettes, edited and hosted by Michael Murphy of Brooklyn College.

- A compact disc of songs that Chaucer mentioned or that were popular in his day was released in 2000. Recorded by Carol Wood, its title is *The Chaucer Songbook: Celtic Music and Early Music for Harp and Voice*.

- Several of the *Canterbury Tales* can be found on a 1961 recording available from Caedmon on a 1988 audiocassette release. Dame Peggy Ashcroft reads "The Wife of Bath's Tale," and Stanley Holloway and Michael MacLiommoir read "The Miller's Tale" and "The Pardoner's Tale."

- A feature film of *The Canterbury Tales* was made in Italy in 1971, starring Hugh Griffith, Franco Citti and Tom Baker, and it is available dubbed into English on both videodisc and videocassette from Image Entertainment of Chatsworth, CA.

- A 1991 videocassette of the Prologue to *The Canterbury Tales* is available from Educational Video Network of Huntsville, Texas.

- A 1944 feature movie, entitled *A Canterbury Tale*, retells the story in an updated version, setting it in the same location during World War II. It stars John Sweet and Eric Portman, and it is available on videocassette from Public Media Incorporated.

---

ing them to raise the ocean. Meanwhile, Arveragus came home and was reunited with his wife.

Aurelius' brother, a scholar, took him to the place where he had studied, and there they consulted with a man who had studied magic. This magician made them hallucinate so that they saw various scenes, including deer in a forest, knights battling, and Dorigene dancing. For a thousand pounds in gold, he agreed to make Dorigene think the rocks had sunk into the ocean.

Aurelius went to Dorigene after the spell was cast on her and reminded her that she had agreed to go to bed with him. Distressed about the prospect of losing her honor by either breaking her word or being unfaithful to her husband, she considered killing herself. Arveragus noticed how upset she was, and she explained the situation. He told her that she would have to sleep with Aurelius rather than break her word.

When she went to offer herself to Aurelius, he asked why she had changed her mind, and she explained that she was there because her husband had insisted that she keep her promise. Aurelius was so impressed with Arveragus and his concern that

Dorigene should stay honest that he freed her from her promise without touching her. Then he realized that he was financially ruined by the thousand gold pieces he had promised to pay the magician.

When he went to ask the magician to work out payment terms, Aurelius ended up telling him the whole story about letting Dorigene out of her promise. The magician was so impressed by his nobility, that he let Aurelius out of his own promise, and let him go without paying.

The Pardoner's Tale

Before telling his tale, the Pardoner expresses his need for a drink; this raises the fear in the other pilgrims that he will tell a crude or dirty joke, but he promises not to. The Prologue to "The Pardoner's Tale" is about his life, detailing how he makes his living by going from town to town with phony relics and documents allegedly signed by the pope and curing such ailments as snake bites and jealousy. He announces his ability to charm simple people with a well-told story, noting that they love stories that they can remember and retell: "lewd (unlearned) peple loven tales of olde; / Swich thinges can they wel reporte and holde." When he has had enough to drink the Pardoner starts telling a tale that he often tells, promising that it will be moral and not dirty.

He starts his tale by mentioning a gang of tough youths in Flanders but soon digresses from them for a detailed discussion of sin, not only the specific sins committed by the rough characters in his story but sin in general. The irony of his lecture is that these are sins, like gambling and drinking and swearing, that the Pardoner himself is guilty of. The tale itself is about three men who were drinking in a tavern one morning when they heard the funeral of an old friend going by. Their friend died that morning, a tavern employee explained, killed by the plague, his life ended by the thief called "Death." They set off to find Death and came across an old man who complained that, as old as he was, he could not die, but he was able to direct them to a park where he had seen Death lingering. Instead of Death, they found a pile of gold coins. One of the three was sent off to get tools to carry the gold with, and while he was gone, the other two plotted to murder him and divide his share of the gold. He had the same basic idea, however, and returned with poisoned drinks for them. They fatally stabbed him, then drank the drinks, which in turn killed them.

When he is done, the Pardoner tries to sell the other pilgrims pardons for their sins, taking advantage of their attention and their feelings of piety after hearing about such wicked men. The Host, annoyed, threatens to cut off his testicles and make relics of them, which makes the Pardoner turn quiet, seething, until the Knight intercedes and has the two men make up.

The Prioress's Tale

A Prioress is the head nun at an abbey, or convent, and is therefore a very religious person. The irony of the tale that this Prioress tells is that she piously invokes the name of the Virgin Mary and then goes on to tell one of the most violent, bloody tales in the whole collection. The Prioress starts her short piece with an introductory poem, praising God for His goodness and praising Mary for Her great humility. From the introduction, readers are led to expect the Prioress to be a meek person who tells a simple, gentle story. Instead, she talks about an unnamed Christian town in Asia that had a Jewish ghetto. The inhabitants of the ghetto, the Prioress explains, were full of hate and anger toward the Christians, but the country's ruler kept the Jews around for their value in money-lending, or usury. As she puts it, they were "sustained by a lord of that contree / For foule usure and lucre of vileynye, / Hateful to Crist and to his compaignye." A seven-year-old boy, the son of a widow, lived in that town. One day, when the boy heard the other children singing the Latin hymn *O Alma Redemptoris*, he was immediately smitten with the beauty of the song, so he set about to learn it, even though he didn't understand the words. One day, he walked through the Jewish ghetto singing the hymn, and the Jews, offended, hired a murderer to kill the boy. He was chased down an alley and had his throat slit and his body thrown into a drainage ditch that collected bodily waste.

The boy's mother went searching for him when he did not come home. She found no sign of him until, passing by the drain, she heard him singing *O Alma Redemptoris*. A lawman was summoned, and he passed a harsh sentence against the Jews, commanding that their bodies be drawn apart by horses and then hung on spikes from a wagon. Then an abbot came and asked the boy how he was still able to sing when his throat seemed to be cut. The boy explained that his throat was indeed cut, to the bone, but that Mary came down to him and commanded that he keep singing. She placed a piece of grain on his tongue, he explains, and told him that he would only stop singing when the grain was removed. The abbot removed the grain, the singing stopped, and the boy was buried. The tale ends with the Prioress calling for guidance for Hugh of Lincoln, a martyr who was also murdered as a child.

The Nun's Priest's Tale

When the Knight declares the story that they have just heard to be too depressing, the Host asks the priest who is travelling with the nun to tell them a story that is more uplifting. His story concerns a widow who, he says, lived long ago on a farm. The widow's two daughters, three pigs, three cows, and a sheep also lived on the farm. A rooster named Chaunticleer and seven hens, who were his wives, lived in the yard. One morning, Chaunticleer told the prettiest of his wives, Pertelote, that he had dreamt about being attacked by a hound-like creature. She responded by calling him a coward for being afraid of a dream, explaining that dreams were a sign of an unsettled digestive system. She offered to make him a laxative that would empty his system out. In response, he cited numerous examples from the Bible and from ancient mythology that illustrated how dreams accurately predicted the future. Having said this, he let the matter drop, and it was forgotten for a little over a month.

On the third of May, a fox sneaked into the farm yard, waiting patiently until Chaunticleer came down out of the barn rafters and onto the ground. Chaunticleer was alarmed, and ready to fly away, until the fox flattered him, telling him that he had a beautiful singing voice, as did his mother and father. At the fox's request, Chaunticleer threw back his shoulder, ready to sing out a song, when the fox reached over and grabbed him by the neck.

When all of the hens he was married to screamed an alarm, the fox tried to escape with the rooster in his mouth, but the widow and her daughters, hearing the alarm, ran out of the house and joined the other barnyard animals in chasing the fox. Coming to his senses, Chaunticleer suggested to the fox that he should taunt the people chasing him, telling them that they could never catch him; when the fox opened his mouth to do this, Chaunticleer flew free. The fox tried once more to convince the rooster that it was all a misunderstanding, that he actually had a secret reason for carrying him away in his mouth, but Chaunticleer, having learned his lesson, refused to go near him. The Nun's Priest ends this tale by reminding his listeners about the dangers of falling for flattery. In the epilogue to this story, the Host expresses his delight with the story that they have just heard, and he congratulates the Priest for being such a strong, brawny man, which is not what one expects from someone in his profession.

Themes

Christianity

When *The Canterbury Tales* were written, Christianity was the dominant social force throughout western Europe, including England. Its influence stretched across the social spectrum from nobles to poor beggars. In 1388, while Chaucer was working on the tales, a change occurred in the way that Christianity was perceived and practiced when John Wycliffe, an English reformer, released a version of the Bible translated into English. For the first time, people from the lower classes, who had not been educated in Latin, could read the Bible themselves instead of having its word interpreted to them by members of the clergy.

The influence of Christianity can be seen in *The Canterbury Tales* by the variety of social types presented. Fourteenth century Christian society had room for different ways of incorporating faith into lifestyle. The Knight, for instance, espouses romantic love and brotherliness, and the Franklin tells a tale that ends with mercy and forgiveness for all. The Prioress, on the other hand, tells a story that propagates hatred toward non-Christians, making them out to be evil and relishing their punishment. The Wife of Bath proves to be very familiar with Biblical Scripture, finding her own sexuality to be acceptable, if not ideal, by Biblical standards. The Pardoner is the most cynical Christian, condemning the very behaviors that he indulges in and trying to sell salvation by way of the counterfeit icons and the signed certificates from the pope he carries with him. It was in fact the sort of fraud perpetuated by people like the Pardoner, as well as actions by angry reformers like Wycliffe to make religion accessible to the common people, that eventually led to the Protestant Reformation in the sixteenth century that weakened the Catholic Church's powerful hold over Western thought.

Deception

Many of the stories in this book deal with deception—the potential to mislead people with words and the consequences that result. In some cases, decent people are compelled to employ deception, such as when Arcite from "The Knight's Tale" disguises himself to enter the court of Emily, whom he loves, or when Aurelius from "The Franklin's Tale" is driven by love to trick Dorigene so that she will leave her husband for him. Other characters are deceptive for purely greedy reasons, such as the fox who charms Chaunticleer twice (once successfully, once not) in "The Nun's Priest's

Topics for Further Study

- Have your own storytelling contest. Make sure that each participant tells two stories, since Chaucer originally intended each traveler to tell one story on the way to Canterbury and one on the way back home.

- Assign people from your class to play the parts of storytellers from *The Canterbury Tales* and have them describe to one another an experience they have had in the twenty-first century. Vote on the stories that were the best and talk about why.

- Find out what kind of food these pilgrims would have eaten when they stopped at inns on their trip, and try making some of it.

- Using words found throughout the text of *The Canterbury Tales*, try to translate a favorite song into Middle English.

- Write an essay explaining how these tales are or are not like the urban folk legends that are constantly circulated on the Internet.

Tale," and the three thieves who plot to kill each other to increase their share of the found gold in "The Pardoner's Tale." Still, other characters in the tales deceive people for the noble cause of teaching them a lesson about how to behave. For instance, the "old woman" in "The Wife of Bath's Tale" only pretends to be old and ugly until the knight in that story proves that he has thought about how women should be treated and that he has learned to respect more than superficial beauty.

Spring

There is excitement in the air as this band of pilgrims travels toward the religious shrine at Canterbury, where they all hope to gain God's grace. Their trip begins in April, and the very first lines of the book emphasize the significance of that time of year: "Whan that Aprill with his shoures sote / The droghte of Marche hath perced to the rote." In other words, the poem begins by evoking the process of rainwater reaching dormant roots, revi-

talizing them. It is the period of revitalization that happens over and over in the earth's cycle each spring. It is a time of renewal, of life, of the glories of nature shaking off the mundane. It is a time of beginnings and a time of hope.

In addition to this beginning of the General Prologue, there are several additional places where the time of year is mentioned, referring back to springtime in several of the tales. In "The Franklin's Tale," the young wife who misses her husband while he is away is approached by a handsome, muscular, wealthy stranger while she is at a dance on the sixth of May, adding even more temptation to that presented by his charms. Spring is the time of fertility for plants, which has evolved over time to it being associated with romantic love. The text is also very specific in stating that it was the third of May when Chaunticleer forgot his foreboding dream and allowed himself to be tricked by the fox who asked him to sing. The implication is that the beauty of the season may have pushed the premonition of death from Chaunticleer's mind, driving his concentration toward more uplifting things (such as the sound of his own singing) and away from life's more frightening prospects.

Reputation

The characters in the tales told by the pilgrims on their way to Canterbury show more concern about their social reputations than the pilgrims themselves show. In part, this is due to the instructive nature of tales in general: many of these tales are told to teach a "moral" to their listeners, and so they often include advice about personal behavior, with an emphasis on observable behaviors. The most obvious example of one of these pilgrims preaching the need for a good reputation is the Pardoner, who claims that he cannot start his story until he has taken a drink and then immediately starts by warning his listeners against drinking with several stories from the Bible to illustrate his point that "The Holy Writ take I to my witness / That luxurie (lechery) is in wyn and drunkenness." The Knight, on the other hand, seems to live by the same code of nobility that the knights in his story live by, while the Nun's Priest, a meek man who almost escapes notice, tells the story of the danger that pride and bragging bring to the rooster Chaunticleer. Perhaps the most powerful story about keeping a good reputation is the Franklin's. In it, Dorigene is so torn by the prospect of having to cheat on her husband to stay true to her promise that she considers suicide as a way of avoiding either prospect, while her husband, who is just as concerned about her reputation, would rather have her sleep with another man than break her word. The story rewards them both by having Aurelius forgive the wife her promise because he is so moved by the honor they both show, and it rewards Aurelius by having the magician forgive his huge debt because he has shown himself noble enough to recognize the nobility of the couple.

Style

Heroic Couplets

The poetic meter, or rhythm, used throughout *The Canterbury Tales* is iambic pentameter. This means that each line is based on pairs of syllables, proceeding from one that would be unstressed in normal speech to one that is stressed. This pattern is called the *iamb*, and a poetic structure based on it is called *iambic*. When the English language is spoken, this pattern occurs naturally, so the rhythm of an iambic poem is hardly noticeable when read aloud. Because the lines generally have five iambs each, for a total of ten syllables per line, the rhythm is described as *iambic pentameter*—"penta" is the Greek word for "five."

Throughout *The Canterbury Tales*, lines are paired off into rhyming *couplets*, which means that each pair of lines has similar-sounding words that rhyme at the end. A poem that is written in iambic pentameter and has rhyming couplets is said to be written using *heroic couplets*. This structure drives the poem along, page after page, giving it a sense of order that it would lack if it were written without any structure but using a natural rhythm that readers do not have to focus on. Because the language of Chaucer's time is not familiar to modern ears, students, stopping frequently to look up pronunciations and spellings, often have trouble recognizing the ease of the rhythm unless the poem is read aloud by a reader experienced with Middle English.

Speech

One of Chaucer's greatest achievements with this poem is his ability to alter his style for the different speakers. The meter (rhythmic scheme) stays consistent throughout, but he is able to give distinctive personalities to each of the speaking characters by giving them different vocabularies and having them express themselves with different images. "The Knight's Tale," for example, is told with a more gentle and mannerly voice than, say, the

Wife of Bath's or the Pardoner's. This can be seen when the Knight notices he has strayed from an important subject, at the start of the third section of his tale, and he chastises himself, saying, with formal diction, "I trowe men wolde deme it neglicence / If I foryete to tellen the dispence / Of Theseus." The Wife of Bath, by contrast, is so self-centered that she becomes caught up in talking about herself and nearly forgets to tell a tale. Her lack of refinement can be seen in her language, from the use of shorter words to the fact that she tells her tale in the present tense. A common example of her language comes from line 1022 of her tale: "When they be comen to court, this knight / seyde he had holde his day, as he hadde hight, / And redy was his answere, as he sayde." Each character speaks in a distinctive style that is appropriate to his or her social situation and, more importantly, to his or her specific personality.

Historical Context

The Black Plague

During Chaucer's lifetime, the Black Plague swept across Europe, causing hundreds of thousands of people to die in a gruesome way and changing the way that common citizens looked at mortality. The plague originated in the north of India during the 1330s and spread quickly, affecting much of Asia by the mid-1340s. Its spread to Europe was no accident. Mongol-Tartar armies, in an attempt to discourage Italian trade caravans from crossing their territory on their way to and from China, catapulted bodies of infected victims over the walls of their fortresses at the Italians, who subsequently brought the disease back to their country. While carrying on their trade, they infected other travelers, who carried the disease to the most crowded cities on the continent. The plague struck Spain and France in 1348 and reached England the following year. By the time that *The Canterbury Tales* was published in 1400, a third of the people of Europe had died of the Black Plague. During the last half of the fourteenth century, though, scientific inquiry about the plague led to the discovery that it was spread by fleas that had picked up the virus from rats. Chaucer's pilgrims may seem lax in their hygienic practices: for instance, the specific point of the Nun being noteworthy for not getting grease into the wine cup when she drank from it and passed it on, or the characters who share beds with strangers. Still, their practices reflect a height-

Compare & Contrast

- **Fourteenth Century:** The Bible is published in English for the first time in 1382 by John Wycliffe, in a protest against the power of the Catholic Church.

  Today: English is the language recognized in most countries and is the unofficial language of international trade.

- **Fourteenth Century:** The world's most powerful nations are ruled by monarchs who inherit their political power as part of their birthright. The king of France takes the throne in 1388, at age nineteen, while the King of England is twenty-two when he takes the throne in 1389.

  Today: Many countries have democratically elected governments. The most populous country in the world, China, is a socialist dictatorship.

- **Fourteenth Century:** London, England's largest city, has a population of 50,000. No other city in England has even half that many citizens.

  Today: London is still England's largest city, with a population of nearly seven million.

- **Fourteenth Century:** The revolution in art and science known as the Renaissance is just beginning. New theories develop about the nature of humanity and artistic means to represent humanity in painting, sculpture, music, and literature.

  Today: Some consider humanity to be at the beginning of a new age, spurred by the fact that the personal computer has given ordinary individuals access to millions of pieces of information and the means to create complex artistic works.

- **Fourteenth Century:** The Roman Catholic Church, though corrupted by a series of popes who rose to power using financial means, is a powerful influence on all of western society.

  Today: Christianity, which split during the Protestant Reformation of the sixteenth century, still has the most members worldwide, but the West is becoming increasingly aware of religions like Hinduism and Islam, which have hundreds of millions of adherents around the world.

---

ened sense of the ways in which lethal diseases can spread, and their physical interactions with each other are more cautious than they would have been a generation earlier. The characters in *The Canterbury Tales*, such as the Pardoner, who mentions a death by plague in his poem, reflect an enlightened and cautious generation that is familiar with sudden illness and death and that hopes for a better life.

The Hundred Years' War

When Chaucer wrote this work, and throughout his entire lifetime, England was at war with France. The two countries had suffered strained relations for a long time before 1328, when war broke out between them following the death of France's king, Charles IV. Charles's daughter was rejected as a ruler, and so Edward II, the king of England, thought that he should be named king of France as well, for Edward's mother was Isabella, the sister of Charles IV. The French people did not want their country subservient to England in any way, and so they chose Philip Valois to rule as Philip VI. Edward, feeling that his claim on the French throne was stronger, led an invasion with 30,000 men. He was spectacularly successful, but the French had strong defenses around and within their major cities, and they were dug in to defend themselves in a series of battles fought during the ensuing century.

Of Edward's sons, one, also named Edward but called the Black Prince, led the British forces to victory in several battles, taking most of the south of France for the throne of England. The Black Prince died in 1376, after turning over his French holdings to John of Gaunt, another of Edward's sons. Geoffrey Chaucer was a squire in the household of John of Gaunt and was married to the sister of his wife. He served with John on several campaigns during the Hundred Years' War. In Edward III's last years, when he was too ill to oversee his government, John ruled England; he gave up his power when Richard II was named as successor in 1377. After that, John worked to bring peace between the English and the French, with Chaucer as a trusted aid.

Despite the military superiority of the English, the French resisted, fighting until 1453 and eventually taking back almost all of their land. The result of the war was to clarify France's identity as a separate social and political entity (one of the heroes of the Hundred Years' War was Joan of Arc, who remains today an important symbol of the French spirit) and to establish international relations between the countries of Europe.

The Renaissance

The word renaissance comes from the Old French word for rebirth and is commonly used to refer to the period of time, starting in 1350 and lasting into the seventeenth century, when a sudden, powerful thirst for knowledge swept through the western world's cultural institutions, signifying the start of modern thought. Renaissance art was derived from the art and ideas of ancient Greece and Rome, which had been ignored since the fall of Rome after the overthrow of Romulus Augustulus in 476 A.D. From 476 to 1350, generally identified as the Middle Ages, there was little scientific inquiry and development of the arts. Renaissance thinkers considered this middle period to be the Dark Ages, during which all prior discoveries had been lost, and they set the enormous task of reinventing human knowledge.

Several cultural elements came together in the fourteenth century to bring about the Renaissance. For several hundred years, Christians from Europe had invaded the Middle East in an attempt to chase the Muslims out of the Holy Land. One result of these Crusades was that much of the presumably lost knowledge of the Roman Empire was found to survive in Constantinople, the seat of the Eastern Roman Empire. With a renewed sense of history, scholars and artists basked in relative financial security, with wealthy nobles giving them financial support while they worked on intellectual pursuits. Such relationships worked to mutual advantage, as the patrons were often glorified in art, architecture, and music. Starting in Northern Italy, concentrated efforts were made to assemble the scattered records of past civilizations, piecing together knowledge and artistic theory from frag-

ments of old Roman and Latin texts found in private libraries and abbeys. Because of this interest in knowledge for its own sake, the Renaissance figure came to be a person who was skilled in many different subjects. Leonardo da Vinci, for example, is known equally for his paintings of the Last Supper and Mona Lisa as for designing flying machines four hundred years before the Wright Brothers. Michelangelo's fame would have survived for his skilled architecture alone, even if he had not also painted the Sistine Chapel or carved his statue of David. Chaucer was a Renaissance Man of this sense, proficient in court politics as well as in writing.

Critical Overview

In an age when authors announce with pride when their book has continuously been in print for twenty years, there cannot be enough said about the significance of *The Canterbury Tales*, which has been with us for six centuries. It is the first poem written in the English language and is therefore given much credit for actually inventing modern English, recording words and phrases that were commonly spoken but had never been put on paper before. As the first English poet, Chaucer is considered the model and inspiration for the grand history of English poetry that followed him. Because it uses the overall narrative structure of the pilgrimage to hold all of the individual tales together, *The Canterbury Tales* is also considered to be the first English novel, with sharply defined characters that remain consistent throughout.

Over time, thousands of essays have been written about Chaucer, but, as Thomas C. Stillinger points out in his introduction to a recent collection of *Critical Essays on Geoffrey Chaucer*, most recent criticism can be broken down into two categories: "he is an ancient writer, his texts silent monuments of a lost world; and, at the same time, he is a living poetic voice." One of the principle reasons that Chaucer is still studied so actively today is that critics can find such a wide range of things to say about him. Lee Patterson, in a brief review of the criticism written in the twentieth century about *The Canterbury Tales*, cited a 1906 essay by Robert Root as saying that "we turn to [Chaucer] . . . for refreshment, that our eyes and ears may be opened anew to the varied interest and beauty of the world around us." Patterson also includes the thoughts of other important critics:

some fifty years after Root's book, one of the greatest of the next generation of Chaucerians, E. Talbot Donaldson, described Chaucer as possessed of "a mind almost godlike in the breadth and humanity of its ironic vision"

Patterson also shares Derek Pearsall's introduction to his excellent Chaucer study by insisting that "*The Canterbury Tales* neither press for [n]or permit a systematic kind of ideological interpretation." In short, critics continue to find issues of both human behavior and historical significance in this complex work.

In some cases, such universal approval can dull critics' understanding of an author, as the British novelist and essayist G. K. Chesterton pointed out in his 1932 essay "The Greatness of Chaucer." Chesterton felt that critics tended not to take Chaucer seriously:

> there has been a perceptible, in greater or less degree, an indescribable disposition to *patronize* Chaucer. Sometimes he is patted on the head like a child because all our other poets are his children. Sometimes he is treated as the Oldest Inhabitant, partially demented and practically dead, because he was alive before anybody else in Europe to certain revolutions of the European mind. Sometimes, he is treated as entirely dead; a bag of dry bones to be dissected by antiquarians, interested only in matters of detail.

Chesterton's observation about the danger of patronizing critics is even more relevant today, in a world that is moving forward so quickly that there is hardly time to give the past its due consideration; still, *The Canterbury Tales*, which was there at the beginning of the English language, is likely to be there until the end.

Criticism

David Kelly

Kelly is an instructor of creative writing and literature at Oakton Community College in Illinois and is currently working on a book about comedy in twentieth century America. In this essay, he compares Chaucer's constant inventiveness to techniques used throughout the centuries by jesters and stand-up comics to hold their audiences' attention.

One of the first things that students learn when they begin to study *The Canterbury Tales* is that Geoffrey Chaucer, its author, is frequently called "the father of English poetry." He was the first significant poet to write in the English language, as opposed to Italian, Latin, or French, which were the languages favored by educated people of his

time, the late fourteenth century. The entire tradition of English literature, therefore, points back to Chaucer. He deserves respect, but, unfortunately, respect too often makes readers feel that they have to be reverential and solemn when considering *The Canterbury Tales*.

Over the centuries, Chaucer scholars have attempted to show that the book is not just a dry textbook and is actually quite a lot of fun, but their attempts consistently fall on deaf ears. English teachers see episodes like the flatulence scene in the "The Miller's Tale" as the same gross-out comedy that Jim Carrey or Tom Green would use for laughs today. Students today are more inclined to view Chaucer's low-brow moments as a senior family member struggling to be hip, like a grandfather wearing a shockingly loud tie to show that he still remembers fun. It is hard to think of the father of English poetry as working for attention because he had to.

But *The Canterbury Tales* is all about the struggle to keep audiences entertained. The central conceit is that a group of pilgrims enter into a storytelling competition to take their minds off the labor and monotony of their journey. They are not competing to see who will tell the most uplifting story or the most intellectually enriching; they are each trying to be the most entertaining (although some do abuse their forum and sneak in moral tales about spiritual correctness). Designed around performers who are fighting for attention, the book has more in common with a court jester doing handsprings and backflips for the king's pleasure than it does with the sort of staid literature that it is often shelved with. Chaucer was a raconteur, a teller of amusing stories, and he did whatever he had to do to keep audiences interested.

Like a jester, Chaucer's audience was the royal court. He was an attendant to royalty throughout his adult years, starting in the house of Elizabeth of Ulster and rising to be the valet to the King himself. In later years, he left domestic service and was given political responsibilities that were better suited for his intelligence. By all accounts, and as evinced by his poetry, Chaucer was a man of incredible intellect. His intellect alone could have accounted for his fortune in government matters, but there are and always have been bland functionaries who understood issues but cannot draw enough attention to let their knowledge be known. Chaucer was lucky enough to be a true Renaissance man, talented in several fields, with each feeding the other. The stories and poems that he wrote and recited assured that the rulers of England knew who Geoffrey Chaucer was.

The court that he served in expanded during Chaucer's stay there. Historically, the English government had been mobile, not only to deal with matters of law in different parts of the kingdom at a time when there was no reliable system of communications, but for the very practical reason that there were few places that could provide for all of the government functionaries for any length of time. In his book *Chaucer in His Time*, Derek Brewer explains that "such large gatherings were difficult to feed at a time when communications were slow and almost every household had to be self-sufficient. The court had to move about the country so as to spread the burden of its maintenance." This practice changed in 1382, when King Richard II married Anne of Bohemia and established a permanent court patterned on the French court in Paris and the Papal court at Avignon. Settled, the ranks of the court grew, with dozens of royals and the hundreds of attendants that each required. In such a crowded environment, it helped Chaucer to be known as a wit and as one whose reputation as a poet had spread to France and Italy. A wit becomes tiresome when he runs out of things to say, but Chaucer was clever enough to never run out of new items or new methods.

We think of jesters as being self-deprecating fools, willing to humiliate themselves if that is what is required to keep the royal family amused. Modern performers are given more respect if they are considered artists, but those who are thought of as mere entertainers are still considered somewhat embarrassing. What they both have in common with Chaucer's "performance" in *The Canterbury Tales* is that they all are continuously in motion, struggling for innovation, line after line, sentence after sentence, valuing attention before respect.

It may be difficult for some contemporary readers to accept that the primary purpose of the tales is to entertain, even when the Host focuses on that as the purpose of each narration. Some of the tales seem just too complex, too tied up in learning to fit in with modern standards, which separate learning from entertainment and see them as being mutually exclusive. Still, if the purpose of entertainment is to keep one interested, then some education is bound to become part of the process. And if the main lever of humor is, as many have claimed, the element of surprise, then the most amusing tales are the ones that establish a sense of familiarity that they can eventually disturb.

> *Chaucer was a raconteur, a teller of amusing stories, and he did whatever he had to do to keep audiences interested."*

The tale that uses the broadest humor is, of course, the Miller's tale, which has no reason for existing other than to see an unpleasant man, a "riche gnof," gotten the best of. It is a pretty straightforward joke, about a man thinking that he is going to survive a flood while his fellow citizens drown, unaware of the fact that his wife and lodger are sleeping together in his own bed. The most noteworthy thing about this tale is that it is so silly as to include the nonsense, already mentioned, about a man breaking wind in another man's face. There really is no place for the flatulence episode in the story that the Miller tells, but its complete inappropriateness is what makes it funny: readers expect the drunken Miller to be tasteless, and he is warned by the Host to watch his manners. That concern is forgotten as the story turns out to be a mild tale of adultery, until a superfluous character appears out of nowhere. Readers are prepared for this level of vulgarity, but are then surprised by it all the same.

"The Pardoner's Tale" works on a similar comic device, of bad people unwittingly participating in their own downfall. The story itself has a surprise, ironic ending, as the man who prepared poisonous drinks is stabbed and the men who did the stabbing unknowingly drink poison. There is a richer layer here, though: while the Miller came across with exactly the sort of crude story that was expected of him, the Pardoner preaches a tale about conventional morality but turns out to be a con man looking to sell religious icons. Chaucer does not make much of this contradiction, but it is clear, and it makes the story more engaging and interesting. A similar level of irony invigorates "The Prioress' Tale": the introduction prepares readers for a shy, gentle soul, but the tale she tells reveals the imagination of a bloodthirsty anti-Semite with true hatred in her heart. In both cases, Chaucer gives a text—the tale—and a context—the personality of the teller—that contrast with one another. Modern comedy might achieve the same results by having an unscrupulous, oily character pose as priest or politician, or by having a meek nervous character suddenly fill up with angry ferocity.

The tales that are hardest to recognize as entertainment are those that do not find humor at the expense of some braggart, poseur, or deluded fool. There are tales, like the Knight's and the Franklin's, that celebrate noble behavior and mourn the tragedy of the death of a good person. Though not funny, these tales fit loosely into the definition of humor as surprise. Not all surprises are humorous, but the basic element of a sort of gallows humor is at least nearby, even in the most serious turns of events presented in these tales. It would not take much to see Arcite's fall from his horse as a deadpan punchline that is meant to contrast the huge buildup preceding it in "The Knight's Tale,'' with pages and pages of battle preparation and combat mocked by stupid, ignoble fate. Similarly, it would not take much to make a comic buffoon out of Arveragus, who is so committed to the abstract concept of keeping one's vow that he is willing to give up his beloved wife. In each case, readers' expectations are set up and then demolished with such an ease of presentation that the readers do not even notice Chaucer's presence, looking instead to the characters who tell the stories.

The main thing that makes contemporary stand-up comedy an appropriate analogy for *The Canterbury Tales* is the desperation required by each. Comedy, often dismissed as mere entertainment, is able to make its audience think, but only when it has their attention. Some comedians are all about drawing attention to themselves, but once they have that attention, they have nothing to say; others have serious points to make, but they forget to entertain. The best will be able to make audiences think, but they also know that on some level they are the heirs of the court jester who would jump, shout, and ring bells just to keep his audience from looking anywhere but at him. This is the tradition of the entertainer that is too often overlooked by people who read Chaucer as if he were some sort of icon. His tales can turn vulgar or sentimental, didactic or warmhearted, but he was not afraid to use any trick at his disposal—and he had quite a few—to make sure that they stayed interesting.

Source: David Kelly, Critical Essay on *The Canterbury Tales*, in *Poetry for Students*, The Gale Group, 2002.

Philip S. Alexander

In the following essay, Alexander examines the treatment of Jews and anti-Semitism in the "Prioress's Tale."

The history of the criticism of Chaucer's "Prioress's Tale" affords proof, if proof be needed, that the attitudes and events of their own days affect how critics read literature, even literature of the distant past. As Florence Ridley notes, the question of anti-semitism in the "Prioress's Tale" has in recent years become an important critical issue, to the extent that most contemporary readings of the text seem to involve, explicitly or implicitly, a response to this problem. The explanation is not far to seek. Critics cannot view the "Tale" after the holocaust in quite the same way as they viewed it before. Since the holocaust anti-semitism has become academically discredited: it is now one of the few generally acknowledged intellectual heresies. So for a critic today to expound the "Tale" and to ignore the question of anti-semitism would strike most educated people as displaying a detachment from life bordering on the irresponsible, if not on the perverse.

Most who have written on the problem of the anti-semitism in the "Prioress's Tale" have been literary critics by calling. Few historians of Judaism, or of anti-semitism, seem to have addressed the question. As a result some of the analysis, though painstaking and well intentioned, has been historically and philosophically confused. The sort of confusion that can arise is illustrated by John Archer's article, "The structure of anti-semitism in the 'Prioress's Tale'." Archer, unlike some, perceives the importance of defining anti-semitism. His stated aim is 'to examine the operation of the imagery in the "Prioress's Tale" against the background of the tradition, and in the process to extrapolate three or four categories of imagery that might be used to analyze anti-semitism in so far as it functions in other literary works.' He stresses the transformation of society that takes place within the "Tale." The opening lines depict the secular authorities as being subservient to the Old Law: they sustain the Jews in their usurious practices, which are 'hateful to Crist.' At the end of the "Tale," however, in the person of the Provost, they break with the Jews and with the old dispensation, and embrace the New Law of Christ. The decisive change is wrought by the clergeon's death, which is 'a sacrifice as well as a murder because it has loosened the hold of the Old Law over the secular positive law'. The clergeon is a Christ-figure and his death recapitulates

Christ's death, which by redeeming man from the curse and bondage of the Old Law transformed society. All this is moderately persuasive till we recall that the purpose of Archer's article is to lay bare the structure of anti-semitism in the "Prioress's Tale." Anti-semitism turns out for Archer to be identical with the central tenets of the Christian faith! Archer shows not a flicker of awareness of the radical implications of this analysis, which at a theological level risks delegitimizing Christianity, and at a literary level, if extrapolated, appears to brand much of European literature as anti-semitic.

Clearly we need a more historically-informed view of the nature of anti-semitism if we are to deal responsibly with the question of anti-semitism in a given piece of literature. Anti-semitism is not a charge to be lightly bandied about: it is more than 'queasy, resentful feelings about Jews.' The definition of the phenomenon is not self-evident. The term 'anti-semitism' itself did not emerge till the late nineteenth century, when it was used by the proponents of a world-view (widely deemed then as acceptable), which embraced three main tenets: first, Jewish culture is inferior to Germanic culture; second, the Jews are plotting to undermine Germanic culture and to foist their own cultural values on society; and, third, in the interests of progress and civilization society has a duty to defend itself against Jewish domination and to purge itself of decadent Jewish culture. Nineteenth-century anti-semitism was often racist in that it espoused the belief that culture and race were interconnected, and so the inferior Jewish culture was seen as the product of inferior Jewish genes. However, racism, in this precise technical sense, was not fundamental to the anti-semitic point of view.

Nineteenth-century anti-semitism presented itself, often aggressively, in secular and scientific terms, and some of its proponents fastidiously distanced themselves from the crude 'Jew bashing' of earlier centuries. It has, consequently, been argued that modern secular anti-semitism should not be confused with the religious anti-Judaism of the middle ages. If this view is correct, then the problem of anti-semitism in the "Prioress's Tale" is solved at a stroke. What we have in Chaucer may be anti-Judaism (and deplorable), but not anti-semitism in any exact sense. The dissimilarities can, however, be overplayed. The fact is that mediaeval christendom espoused a set of beliefs which are strikingly congruent in content and structure with the nineteenth-century anti-semitic creed: Judaism is inferior to Christianity; the Jews, motivated by

> *Most who have written on the problem of the anti-semitism in the 'Prioress's Tale' have been literary critics by calling. Few historians of Judaism, or of anti-semitism, seem to have addressed the question."*

malevolence, and in alliance with the powers of darkness, are seeking to overthrow Christian society; the Church, in the interests of humanity, has a sacred duty to protect society from the baleful influence of the Jews and Judaism. Nineteenth-century anti-semitism was not a bolt from the blue. Rather it represented the modernization of the anti-semitism of the middle ages. At a time when religious language and religious categories were losing their power, nineteenth-century anti-semites found a modern, intellectually more acceptable way of restating the mediaeval position. In much the same way nineteenth century Christian theologians, in the face of the onslaught of Darwinism, found more modern and acceptable ways of restating the biblical doctrine of creation. There is, then, a deep, underlying continuity between the modern and the mediaeval phenomena, and in virtue of this continuity the term anti-semitism can be applied properly to both.

There is a consensus among critics that the "Prioress's Tale" has been carefully constructed not simply in terms of a limited, local incident, but in terms of timeless absolutes. It is intended to represent the conflict between truth and error, between good and evil. The clergeon died as a martyr, because he testified to his faith, not because he disturbed the peace and quiet of the neighbourhood. It was the content of his song that raised the Jews' ire. The Jews *as a whole* are blackened, and it is this which makes the story anti-semitic. They conspire as a group to kill the boy (even though only one of them actually slits his throat), and this is recognized by the Provost who holds them all guilty and has them all killed. The confrontation between the seeking mother and the Jews is handled in a masterly way, so as to put the Jews as a whole in the worst possible light. Unmoved by the mother's pitiful distress, each and every Jew denies that he has seen the boy: 'they seyde "nay."' Not a flicker of conscience, no attempt to soften the answer, or even to be economical with the truth, only barefaced villany! There are racist undertones here. It is often said that mediaeval Christian anti-semitism was not, unlike much modern anti-semitism, racist, in that it always left open a way of escape for the Jew through conversion. This is broadly true, but it should also be borne in mind that there were some Christian authorities in the middle ages who found it very hard to accept the sincerity of *any* Jewish conversion. Hence the whole tragic problem of the Conversos in Spain. Conversion did not always save the Jew from harrassment or even death. It is chilling so early in the Tale to find the line: 'Children an heep, ycomen of Cristen blood.' Why 'blood'? Was Chaucer strapped for a rhyme for 'stood', or is there a more sinister note here? Is Christian blood any different from Jewish blood?

Running like a refrain through the "Tale" is the description of the Jews as 'cursed.' 'Cursed Jews' is not a generalized term of abuse like 'damned Frenchies'. It means very literally that Jews are under a divine curse, a curse which they called down upon their own heads when they goaded Pilate into crucifying Jesus: 'When Pilate saw that he could prevail nothing, but that rather a tumult was made, he took water, and washed his hands before the multitude, saying, I am innocent of the blood of this just person: see ye to it. Then answered all the people, and said, His blood be on us, and on our children' (Matthew 27:24f). Jews were Christ-killers, and they killed Christ with their eyes open, thus taking upon themselves and their descendants the consequences of that dreadful deed. This charge was used throughout the middle ages to deny Jews the due process of law, and to justify lynchings and pogroms. Note in this context line 578: 'The blood out crieth on youre cursed dede'. There is a clear echo here of the story of Cain and Abel. God says to Cain: 'What hast thou done? The voice of thy brother's blood crieth unto me from the ground. And now thou art cursed from the earth, which hath opened her mouth to receive thy brother's blood from thy hand ... a fugitive and a vagabond shalt thou be in the earth. And Cain said unto the Lord, My punishment is greater than I can bear. Behold thou has driven me out this day from the face of the earth; and from thy face shall I be hid; and I shall be a fugitive and a vagabond

in the earth; and it shall come to pass, that everyone that findeth me shall slay me' (Genesis 4:10–14). In Christian exegesis Cain is often seen as typifying the Jew (the wanderer rejected by both God and man); Abel is taken as a type of the just man, or of the Christian, or (most significantly) of Christ, on whom the Jew tries to vent his spite.

The Prioress invites us in all kinds of subtle but not unmistakable ways to see the death of Mary's little devotee as being parallel to the death of Mary's son. To this extent Archer's analysis of the "Tale" is sound. In murdering the clergeon the Jews are giving rein to the same evil nature which led them to kill Christ. The parallelism is very explicit in some forms of the tradition on which Chaucer has drawn: the boy is ritually murdered, crucified in repetition and mockery of the death of Christ. There is no hint of ritual murder in Chaucer. Nevertheless the parallelism between Jesus and the clergeon is clearly implied. It comes out, for example, at 574f: 'O cursed folk of Herodes all newe, / What may youre yvel entente yow availle?' Just as the Jew Herod had tried to kill the infant Christ, but killed the holy innocents instead, so had the Jews killed the innocent clergeon. The reference to the slaughter of the innocents, which picks up allusions to the liturgy for Childermas in the Prioress's Prologue is further strengthened by 625ff: 'His mooder swownynge by his beere lay; / Unnethe myghte the peple that was theere / This newe Rachel brynge fro his beere'. This echoes the application in Matthew 2:18 of Jeremiah 40:1 to the slaughter of the innocents: 'In Rama was there a voice heard, lamentation, and weeping, and great mourning, Rachel weeping for her children, and would not be comforted, because they were not'. Implicit parallelism between Christ and the clergeon may also lie behind 628–34: 'With torment and with shameful deeth echon, / This provost dooth thise Jewes for to sterve / That of this mordre wiste, and that anon. / He nolde no swich cursednesse observe. / "Yvele shal have that yvele wol deserve"; / Therfore with wilde hors he dide hem drawe, / And after that he heng them by the lawe'. Though the Provost may have been acting within his legal powers (a point carefully stressed in 'by the lawe'), the execution is, in effect, summary. Why the haste? Because the Provost was unwilling to abide such 'cursednesse'. The murder of the clergeon was a curse-bringing act, like the murder of Jesus. By taking prompt and decisive action the Provost ensured that the divine curse would fall on the Jews and not on the community at large.

At 558ff the Prioress gives expression to one of the standard charges of mediaeval anti-semitism, namely, that the Jews are in league with the devil: 'Oure first foo, the serpent Sathanas, / That hath in Jues herte his waspes nest, / Up swal, and seide, "O Hebrayk peple, allas! / Is this to yow a thyng that is honest, / That swich a boy shal walken as hym lest / In youre despit, and synge of swich sentence, / Which is agayn youre lawes reverence?"' As early as the New Testament a special relationship is alleged to exist between the Jews and the devil. John 8:44 is the *locus classicus:* 'Ye are of your father the devil, and the lusts of your father ye will do. He was a murderer from the beginning, and abode not in the truth, because there is no truth in him.' The Book of Revelation twice savagely refers to 'the synagogue of Satan.' Such language may have begun as straightforward abuse, but later it took on more sinister, theological connotations: the Jews were sorcerers able to do evil by the power of the devil. Some even regarded them as devils incarnate. The pact between the devil and the Jews is a common theme of the mystery plays. Lines 558ff of the "Prioress's Tale" are strongly reminiscent of the scenes in the mystery plays in which devils are shown inciting the Jews to demand the crucifixion of Jesus.

At the very outset of the "Tale" the Jews are put in a bad light by linking them with usury—the activity which more than any other distorted their relationships with their non-Jewish neighbours and brought down opprobrium on their heads: 'Ther was in Asye, in a great citee, / Among Cristene folk a Jewerye, / Sustened by a lord of that contree / For foul usure and lucre of vileynye, / Hateful to Crist and to his compaignye'. The Prioress could have found no surer way to dispose her audience against the Jews than by raising the charge of usury. The charge is incidental to the main thrust of the story and plays no direct part in the development of the plot, but it is more than local colour. Dramatically it helps to justify the gory punishment meted out to the Jews at the end.

There are, in fact, as Yunck has pointed out, technically two distinct charges here: usury was the lending of money on interest; 'lucre of vileynye' was profiteering. Both were condemned in canon law, and in using such precise legal terms the Prioress is showing herself a well-informed daughter of the Church. Her knowledge also comes out in her claim that usury and profiteering are 'hateful to Crist and to his compaignye'. At first sight this is odd since one would assume that at least the prohibition of usury was based on the Old Testament,

and not on the New. However, canon lawyers often appealed to Luke 6:35 (Vulgate: *mutum date, nihil inde sperantes*), a fact which the Prioress is presumably supposed to know. A New Testament text certainly lies behind 'lucre of vileynye'. As the gloss *turpe lucrum* in the Ellesmere and Hengwrt manuscripts indicates, it is 1 Timothy 3:8: 'Likewise must the deacons be grave, not doubletongued, not given to much wine, not greedy of filthy lucre' (Vulgate: *diaconos similiter pudicos, non bilingues, non multo vino deditos, non turpe lucrum sectantes*).

The charge of usury was well founded: Jews *were* heavily involved in moneylending in the middle ages. There were a number of reasons for this. Other professions and means of livelihood were not readily open to them. Since the various trades and crafts were dominated by guilds which were often anti-Jewish, it was difficult for a Jew to become, for example, a carpenter or a stone-mason. It was also difficult for them to break into the feudal system of land tenure. In fact it was not advisable for them to hold much land, for if they tied up their wealth in real estate they ran the risk of losing everything when, as so often happened, they were forced to flee. The only means of livelihood readily open to them were trading and moneylending, in which they put to some use the surplus of money they acquired through trading.

The civil authorities actively encouraged Jewish moneylending. They used the Jews as a caste of untouchables to do a necessary but 'dirty' job. The financial systems of the mediaeval world were primitive in the extreme. There was only a rudimentary bureaucracy to collect taxes, and few sources of cash existed from which one could get a loan to finance a project or to tide one over a financial crisis. The chronic shortage of money and credit particularly affected kings and princes, who, though potentially rich, were often short of hard cash if the need to wage war or to build a castle made sudden demands on the exchequer. Jews were encouraged to perform the function both of substitute tax-collectors and bankers. Through various privileges the state promoted their wealth, and then creamed off a proportion of that wealth into the state coffers. As Lilian Winstanley succinctly puts it: 'The Jews were permitted to fleece thoroughly the people of the realm on condition that the king fleeced them'. This placed the Jews in an invidious position socially and exacerbated their already fraught relations with the Christian population.

The social basis of Jewish moneylending is not entirely lost on the Prioress: the ghetto is sustained by 'a lord of that contree'. Once again the Prioress reveals that she is *au fait* with Church teaching and politics. The Church often had occasion to rebuke Christian princes for allowing and for benefiting from Jewish usury. The Church had only limited powers of physical coercion. To compel compliance with its wishes it had to rely on the secular authorities, whom it had to persuade to do its will. The negative picture of civil authority at the beginning of the "Tale" is offset, as Archer rightly notes, by the picture of the Provost at the end. Here was a secular authority who, acting in concert with the Church, knew how to defend good Christians against the blaspheming Jews. Article LXVII ('On Jewish Usury') of the decrees of the Fourth Lateran Council of 1215 provides an illuminating commentary on the opening lines of the "Tale:"

> The more the Christian religion refrains from exacting interest [*usura*], the more does the perfidy of the Jews in this practice increase, so that, in a short time, they exhaust the wealth of Christians. Desiring, therefore, to protect the Christians in this matter from being immoderately burdened by the Jews, we ordain by synodal decree that if, on any pretext, Jews extort heavy and excessive interest from Christians, all relationships with Christians shall be withdrawn from them, until they make adequate restitution for their exorbitant exactions. The Christians also shall be compelled, if need be, by ecclesiastical punishment against which no appeal will be heard, to abstain from business dealings with the Jews.
>
> Moreover, we enjoin princes not to be hostile to the Christians on this account, but rather to endeavour to restrain the Jews from so great an oppression.
>
> And under threat of the same penalty we decree that the Jews shall be compelled to make good the tithes and offerings owed to the Churches, which the Churches were accustomed to receive from the houses and other possessions of the Christians, before these came, by whatever entitlement, into the hands of the Jews, in order that the Churches may be preserved against loss.

Though the Prioress is Chaucer's creature, her voice cannot automatically be identified with his. An author, holding up a mirror to life, may express through his characters ideas which he himself would repudiate. However, the author may find himself on morally dubious ground if he insists on being an out-and-out realist, a recorder but not a commentator. He is responsible for his creatures, and he cannot be allowed *carte blanche* to publicize any point of view purely and simply on the grounds that there are people who say such things. Inevitably he has his own perspective and where this clashes with the perspective of his characters he can reasonably be expected to find ways of dis-

tancing himself from them. The more momentous the issues and the deeper the clash, the more imperative does such distancing become. If the author is totally self-effacing he can hardly complain if the reader assumes that his voice and the voice of his character are one and the same. Is it possible to distance Chaucer from the Prioress? An influential body of criticism claims that it is. Two main lines of argument have been followed.

The first involves playing off the General Prologue against the Tale. An ironic, satirical tone pervades Chaucer's treatment of the Prioress in the General Prologue. Her nice manners (139–40: 'And peyned hire to counterfete cheere / Of court') and fashionable dress (151: 'Ful semyly hir wympul pynched was') sit uneasily with her spiritual calling. She is lax in the observance of monastic rules: she eats roast meat, keeps lap-dogs and wears a brooch with the ambiguous inscription *Amor vincit omnia*. The description of her physical charms in terms of the conventions of courtly love poetry, ending with the understatement, 'For, hardily, she was not undergrowe', is comical. Even her linguistic accomplishments (and her finishing school) are made the butt of barbed comment: 'And Frenssh she spak ful faire and fetisly, / After the scole of Stratford atte Bowe, / For Frenssh of Parys was to hire unknowe.' She weeps easily—at the suffering of small animals: 'She was so charitable and so pitous / She wolde wepe, if that she saugh a mous / Kaught in a trappe, if it were deed or bledde.' The bathetic 'mous' is surely mocking. A picture emerges of a rather large, sentimental, vain woman. But against all this must be set the verve and passion of the Prioress's actual words. The brilliance of her narrative, its burning sincerity and its persuasiveness show that Chaucer was prepared to give her a fair hearing, without a shadow of satire or mockery to cloud her actual speech. Critics have rightly remarked in particular on the power of the Prologue to the "Tale." Here is a liturgical composition of the very highest order. Whether or not we feel a tension between the Tale and the "General Prologue," and how we interpret that tension, once felt, will depend in the final analysis on our own innate moral sense. We may see the Prioress's concern for the suffering of small animals, in contrast to her relish at the hanging and drawing of the Jews, as evidence of her stunted moral development. But we may equally choose to see her love of small animals (so modern in its concern for animal welfare!) as all of a piece with her horror at the fate of the little clergeon. Chaucer keps his own counsel, and offers no clear guidance. He has simply given us a slice of life—a well-observed, full-blooded portrait of a certain human type. If he meant to distance himself from the Prioress's views then the means by which he has chosen to do so are inadequate.

A second line of argument used to exculpate Chaucer is to urge that he is simply drawing on traditional material: he is repeating what was in his sources, not inventing anything significantly new. In fact, the "Prioress's Tale" can be seen as representing one of the more moderate forms of the tradition; it could have been worse, a lot more lurid and virulently anti-semitic. At least in Chaucer, as we noted earlier, the clergeon is not crucified, as he is in some other versions; the murder is not a ritual murder, nor is the blood used for nefarious purposes. Moreover, it is urged, since Jews had been expelled from England in 1290, the Jews of the "Prioress's Tale" are not drawn from life, but from literature and folklore. They are not perceived as real people, but almost as mythical beings, like hobgoblins. These arguments, however, can easily be stood on their head. It is the very fact that Chaucer is writing within a well established tradition that demonstrates beyond all doubt the anti-semitic character of the "Tale." The tradition was so well known that the audience would have confidently classified and interpreted it in a certain way. Elements not explicitly mentioned could still have been read in by them. And although the Prioress may not have been to 'Parys', Chaucer himself had travelled widely on the continent. In fact a realistic topographical detail at lines 493–4 suggests that he was directly acquainted with Jewish ghettoes. The implication that because the Jews of the "Tale" may not be perceived as real people, Chaucer or the Prioress are in some sense exonerated, shows insensitivity to the history of anti-semitism. It was precisely such mythologization (a process of dehumanization unchecked, as history shows, by face-to-face contact with Jews in the flesh) which hardened people to committing appalling atrocities against them.

"The Prioress's Tale" belongs to the large and varied mediaeval genre of Miracles of the Virgin. More precisely it can be assigned to a sub-group of that genre consisting of tales which link the Virgin's miracle to the blood-libel. The first recorded mediaeval case of the blood-libel was at Norwich in 1144: the story was written up with considerable flair by Thomas of Monmouth. The veneration of the Blessed William of Norwich provided a useful source of income for centuries for Norwich cathedral, and to this day on rood screens in churches around Norwich representations of the foul murder of William can be found. Within a short time of the Norwich incident blood-libel accusations were springing up all over Europe. Between 1144 and the 1390s, when Chaucer composed the bulk of the Canterbury Tales, at least twenty-three instances in England, France, Germany, Spain and Czechoslovakia are documented. Another famous English example was the case of Hugh of Lincoln, supposedly done to death by the Jews in 1255. Hugh, like the Blessed William of Norwich, was venerated in the local cathedral. Hugh's story is recounted in the Annals of Waverley and by Matthew Paris. Significantly, it is the subject of a ninety-two stanza Anglo-Norman ballad dating probably from the late thirteenth century—a hint, perhaps, of how these stories were spread. Hugh's case is particularly relevant because it is mentioned at the end of the Prioress's Tale: 'O yonge Hugh of Lyncoln, slayn also / With cursed Jewes, as it is notable, / For it is but a litel while ago, / Preye eek for us, we synful folk unstable, / That of his mercy God so merciable / On us his grete mercy multiplie, / For reverence of his mooder Marie. Amen.' Chaucer had close connections with Lincoln cathedral. He clearly knew Hugh's story. Indeed, it is puzzling that he did not simply tell Hugh's story, which is in all essentials parallel to the clergeon's. Why does he go back in time, to a nameless Christian youth in a distant land when he knows a recent case so close to home? Have we here, perhaps, a later edition to the "Tale?" This, then, is the tradition within which Chaucer was working. He knew what he was doing, and his readers knew what he was doing. He set out to create a version of a well-known type of anti-semitic tale, and he succeeded wonderfully well.

Chaucer's "Prioress's Tale" may fairly be described as an anti-semitic tract. Most anti-semitic writing has been poor and shabby, but here is a piece which displays fine intellect and consummate artistry. Artistically it may be the best anti-semitic tract ever written. Chaucer was a child of his time—no better, no worse in his attitudes towards the Jews than many of his contemporaries. But that is hardly a defence. The verdict that he was anti-semitic is not entirely based on hindsight or on the morality of a later age. There were wiser heads throughout the middle ages ready to defend the Jews, at least against grosser charges such as the blood libel. There were even some who argued, on good theological grounds, that the Gospel demanded that the Jews be treated with compassion and respect.

This sorry conclusion leaves us with a reflection and a problem. The reflection is on the amorality of art. Art, being largely a matter of form and proportion, can, it seems, be used to articulate morally bad ideas as well as morally good. One may acknowledge the aesthetic power of a piece of writing without endorsing its sentiments.

The problem is what to do with the "Prioress's Tale" today, now that it has entered the canon of English literature. Lumiansky's exclusion of it from his 1948 prose version of the *Canterbury Tales* does more credit to his heart than his head. Such censorship is dangerous and futile. We should also resist the temptation of apologetically re-reading the text in such a way that it is made to say the opposite of what it appears to say, and to express politically correct opinions. That sort of hermeneutic has been widely used within religions to make classic religious texts acceptable to later ages. It is hardly proper in the academic study of Chaucer. Chaucer, though a classic, does not have the status of Scripture. Applied to Chaucer such an approach is fundamentally dishonest, and the dishonesty will be rapidly perceived. The only course of action left open is to ensure that when the "Prioress's Tale" is expounded, the basic facts of anti-semitism are expounded as well. Some critics may be irked when asked to play the historian or the moral 'nanny', but in this case there is no honourable alternative. Art may be neutral on morality; the criticism and appreciation of art cannot.

Source: Philip S. Alexander, "Madame Eglentyne, Geoffrey Chaucer, and the Problem of Medieval Anti-Semitism," in *Bulletin of John Rylands Library of Manchester*, Vol. 74, No. 1, Spring 1992, pp. 109–20.

David Williams

In the following essay excerpt, Williams explores how the Pardoner poses a threat to the other authors and to Chaucer himself in Canterbury Tales.

There are several similarities between the Wife of Bath and the Pardoner, not the least of which is the intimate relation between the prologue and tale of each author. If it can be said that the basis of this relation between prologue and tale in the Wife's case is that she denies and destroys reality to make her fictional life valid, perhaps it may then be said that the Pardoner in turn destroys fiction in order to complete the process of rendering everything subjective and meaningless. In this sense they are in league with each other, and we see this in several ways. Whereas the Wife may be seen as a figure who distorts reality through a carnal willfulness and weakness of which she is

only partially aware, the Pardoner emerges as a highly astute figure who has developed his depravity into a powerful intellectual theory, which in his prologue and tale he attempts to impose on the pilgrimage in order to destroy it. Unlike other flawed characters in the company who, despite themselves, reveal the intellectual or moral basis of their corruption (which, in many cases, they do not fully understand), the Pardoner intentionally exposes his vice in the prologue in order to raise evil to a theoretical level on which he can confront good. For if, in fact, the various authors of the pilgrimage have shown themselves as imperfect, each would seem to have also shown the origin of this imperfection to be misunderstanding or moral weakness. The great challenge to a figure like the Pardoner is to provide a theoretical basis for his fellow authors' misconstructions and for the audience's misinterpretations, and so trap them intellectually, as well as morally, in error. The Pardoner is, then, a formidable challenge not only to the authors of the Canterbury pilgrimage but also to the author of the *Canterbury Tales,* and to its audiences.

The nature of that challenge is a form of radical nominalism that calls into question the function of language in revealing truth, our ability to know truth, and consequently (in this kind of reductive logic), the objective existence of truth.

On the surface, nominalism would seem to favor the fictive use of language, since its basic claim is that universals and abstract concepts are merely names, or words, which do not correspond to or represent any objective reality. In the medieval context, however, this did not lead to a greater prestige of the imaginative use of language, but rather, just the opposite; under nominalism, the interest in language became increasingly speculative and severely logical, and literary analysis of texts lost importance. The force of imaginative creation, in the medieval view, existed precisely in the correspondences that could be perceived to what lay outside the text, and part of the delight of the beautiful was generated through the multiple analogies that could be perceived between the fiction of the created artifact and the realities beyond it. Naturally, when beyond the text there is nothing other than more words, these analogies are not possible, or, at least, not delightful. In other words, the basis of fiction is reality, and when that is removed all communication becomes expository. Harry Bailly realizes this keenly, although not at a theoretical level, and continually tries to keep the "fun" in fiction; his good instinct for literature, limited though it may be, is what accounts for his eventual rage against the Pardoner.

The Pardoner is an enemy not only of orthodox medieval philosophy, but of poetry as well. His challenge to a certain theory of universals and of language is felt directly as a threat to the activity of the Canterbury authors and to the act of pilgrimage itself. By constructing the figure of the Pardoner in this way, Chaucer succeeds both in raising the theory of poetry to the level of the theme of his work, and in forcing the audience to reflect on the process of understanding and interpretation in which they are engaged.

The Pardoner's attack on the audience is launched at the outset of his introduction. The Host instructs the Pardoner to "Telle us som myrthe or japes", but having perhaps perceived by his appearance and earlier behavior the Pardoner's inclination to depravity, some of the other pilgrims countermand the Host: "Nay, lat hym telle us of no ribaudye [ribaldry]!" The Pardoner realizes that the pilgrims would be safer with a ribald tale than that which he has in store for them, and his ironic use of the contraries of honesty and drunkenness in agreeing to their demand expresses the disdain with which he regards their self-righteousness: "'I graunte, ywis,' quod he, 'but I moot thynke / Upon som honest thyng while that I drynke.'"

He begins by telling the audience how he uses rhetoric and for what purpose, revealing that in his tale-telling his theme is always the same: "*Radix malorum est Cupiditas* [Cupidity is the root of all evil]." The irony that he intends is in the double sense that he preaches against the sin of cupidity while having cupidity itself as his personal motive for such preaching. For the several members of his audience who are slow in catching irony, he spells it out. With papal documents, the seals of church powers, and his own ecclesiastical title, he establishes his authority and attempts to win the respect and confidence of his audience. He then reveals his glass boxes full of old rags and bones, which the audience believes, based on the authority of the speaker, are relics. And their belief, the Pardoner tells us, is all that matters: "Relikes [relics] been they, as wenen [imagine, suppose] they echoon [each one of them]." This is an important statement, for it reveals the basis of the epistemology of the Pardoner as author, and, of course, it foreshadows his final proposition to his fellow pilgrim-authors at the end of his tale.

It is unlikely that this revelation is merely more of the Pardoner's considerable cynicism toward his

> *The great challenge to a figure like the Pardoner is to provide a theoretical basis for his fellow authors' misconstructions and for the audience's misinterpretations, and so trap them intellectually, as well as morally, in error."*

audience and his fellow man. Rather, it is a statement of principle. For the Pardoner, all signs are systems of discourse, language and relics alike, and what is significant in them is their manner of communication, not the validity of what they communicate. The Pardoner himself is an expert in the analysis of communications, as he amply demonstrates, and this expertise is built on the idea that no objective truth can be communicated by any system because there is none to communicate. Therefore, whatever the audience believes, or can be made to believe, through a particular discourse is, indeed, correct. That is to say, since words and other signs do not correspond to any reality other than their own process of signifying, whatever meaning they are understood to have is as good as any other; therefore, what the audience is led to believe is the best understanding that can occur. These are the pragmatics born of extreme nominalism, which make of the lie, misrepresentation, and propaganda intellectual virtues, and identify nominalism as a descendant of sophistry.

The self-revelations of his prologue present us with the paradox of the dishonest man being honest about his dishonesty. That is not to say that the Pardoner is above seduction; for, indeed, he seems to gear his words initially to the individual pilgrims seemingly most vulnerable to his rhetoric. His sheep's shoulder bone, he says, cures not only animal illnesses, but, he adds with an eye to the Wife of Bath no doubt, it cures the jealousy of husbands, even those who are quite correct in their suspicions of their wives' adultery. He has a mitten, too, that multiplies the grain it handles. The Miller is likely to have an interest in it. But his ultimate ploy is one that few in his audience are likely to be strong enough to refuse. "Anyone," he seems to say, "who is guilty of truly horrible sin, particularly women who have committed adultery, must not come forward to venerate my relics." With this trick, as he boldly tells the pilgrims, he makes a very good living.

The Pardoner is not now playing his tricks, but describing them. Since he is a pardoner, he is more than personally concerned with sin, for penance and contrition are his professions, and he soon reveals his theory on this subject, as well. The rest of his prologue is devoted largely to the broad topic of intention and effect:

> Thus kan I preche [preach] agayn [against] that
>   same vice
> Which that I use, and that is avarice.
> But though myself be gilty in that synne,
> Yet kan I maken oother folk to twynne [separate
>   from],
> From avarice, and soore to repente.
> But that is nat my principal entente [intention].

The Pardoner here engages a topical subject of the Middle Ages—whether an evil man can know, and thus teach, the truth. On the one hand was the position generally associated with Augustine and the Neoplatonists that true knowledge presupposed a union between knower and known, which knowledge was love. Therefore, he who did not love the truth could not be described as having real knowledge of it. On the other hand was the equally orthodox position of the Scholastics that knowledge was a function of intellect and love a function of the will. Theoretically, these faculties were separate although related, and the possibility of the co-existence of a correct intellect and a corrupt will existed. Therefore, a thoroughly evil man might know and accurately express the truth.

The Pardoner obviously allies himself with the Scholastic position, for he sees the many advantages to himself that lie therein. The fully articulated theory is sufficiently complex for there to be plenty of room for distortion. By extension, it also applies to tale-telling and thus becomes a pertinent consideration for poetry. Must a poet be a good man in order to practice his art? Or, to restate it, what is the relationship of the practice of fiction and the moral probity of the practitioner? What, in addition, is the role of authorial intention in the construction of meaning in a tale? The Pardoner provides implicit answers to these questions in his prologue and tale, and Chaucer suggests alternative responses within the larger structure of the *Canterbury Tales*.

The Pardoner ends his introductory words with a statement of principle concerning virtue, knowledge, and truth, and from this theory flows his tale. A vicious (in the original sense: full of vice) man can tell a virtuous tale, he claims, and it is clear that this implies the ability of the vicious man to know that the content of the tale is, indeed, virtuous. This is possible on the basis of the theory mentioned above that intellect and will can function independently. Thus a separation of the two faculties is introduced. This disjunction, in the Pardoner's presentation, reminds us of the Wife of Bath, who separates and divides, but never unifies, and like her, he is engaged in his storytelling in a plan to separate word from meaning, language from reality, in such a way that signs will mean anything he wants them to.

That a vicious man can tell a moral tale indicates that there really exists a moral truth that can be known. But the separation between universals and particulars is posited on the idea that if there is universal truth, it cannot be known because only particulars can be known. The further separation between signs (words, things, and concepts) and what they signify (represent, symbolize, make known) makes impossible both real knowledge of the truth and accurate expression of it. Thus, analogies between these separations can be, and in the case of the Pardoner certainly are, misleading. In Scholastic theory the truth spoken by a vicious man remains the truth, totally independent of his love or knowledge of it. Indeed, it is precisely because of its independent existence that the truth can be attained by the correct intellect despite the subject's moral condition. In nominalist theory, on the other hand, the intellect, regardless of its condition, cannot know anything beyond what the particulars of experience yield. The Pardoner, whose intellect is governed by the principle that truth cannot be known because reality is essentially a linguistic construct, can only preach the most relative kind of morality and will only create fiction of the most self-referential kind.

The Pardoner, then, because he believes that truth can never be known, lies through mental reservation in his claim about the easy accommodation of immoral author with moral fiction, just as he lies in his claim concerning the efficacy of false relics for the repenting of sin. Whereas a genuine desire to turn away from error remains genuine regardless of the authenticity of any sign which may have inspired it, the Pardoner is saying, as if in response to the Wife's earlier lament about sin and love, that "there is no sin." In this view, the repentance related to sin is illusory, and the words, objects, and ideas employed to produce this illusion are of little consequence, as long as they are believed. Reality has become an enormous pile of old rags and bones.

As with other figures of the pilgrimage, Chaucer (as author) establishes the significance of the Pardoner by his appearance and by the authoritative texts he gives him to cite. In the *"General Prologue,"* several details of the Pardoner's description suggest effeminacy and even eunuchry. The Narrator clearly sees and states the physical dimension of the Pardoner's condition through equine analogies: "I trowe [believe] he were a geldyng or a mare." His sexual orientation is alluded to in the description of his relationship with the apparently leprous Summoner: "Ful loude he soong [sang] 'Com hider, love, to me!'." The Summoner, it is said, bore him a "stif" accompaniment. The Pardoner's lack of virility, his sexual impotency and sexual orientation, are not the result of genetic chance, a dominant mother, or the unfortunate consequence of disease, as our modern sciences might try to explain such characteristics. Instead, according to the medieval science of physiognomy, the Pardoner's physical endowments and health are direct reflections of his intellectual and moral condition, and the same holds true for all the pilgrims. Just as his intellect is divorced from reality, self-referential, and incapable of fruitful relation with the world, so his sexuality is narcissistic, divorced from nature, sterile, and nonlife-giving. In this way Chaucer incarnates in the very physical condition of the Pardoner the philosophy and morality that the pilgrim will attempt to promote.

The Pardoner's perverse use of Scripture also harmonizes with his other characteristics. Like the Wife, the Pardoner refers only to that part of the text that serves his immediate purpose, usually distorting it, and Chaucer relies on the audience's familiarity with the true sense of the text to introduce a meaning ironically contrary to that which the Pardoner intends. Such is the case with the Pardoner's motto, *"Radix malorum est Cupiditas,"* which he takes from Saint Paul's letter to Timothy (one of Paul's most prominent disciples), in which Paul gives instructions on the creation and maintenance of the Christian community. Much of the letter is concerned with false teaching and empty speech, and these are connected with cupidity by Paul: "Now the end of the commandment is charity out of a pure heart, and of a good conscience, and of

faith unfeigned: From which some having swerved have turned aside unto vain jangling." Chaucer encourages and expects his audience to go beyond the lines of the text quoted by his pilgrim and to consider it in its wider context, which ironically reflects on the storytelling author-pilgrim.

There is much in the Pauline text from which the Pardoner extracts his dictum that reflects directly on the Pardoner himself, but perhaps nothing quite so pertinent as the following: "He is proud, knowing nothing, but doting about questions and strifes of words, whereof cometh envy, strife, railings, evil surmisings, Perverse disputings of men of corrupt minds, and destitute of the truth, supposing that gain is godliness." The irony of the Pardoner's citing of Saint Paul is not only that the Pauline text exposes the vice of the very one who cites it, but also that it provides an alternative position on the function of language to that held by the Pardoner. Paul's view, stated here and elsewhere, is that true language and true doctrine come directly from God so that man may know the truth, which is divine in origin and eternal: "Whereunto I am ordained a preacher, and an apostle, (I speak the truth in Christ, and lie not;) a teacher of the Gentiles in faith and verity." Thus, before the pilgrim-author has succeeded in establishing his intended meaning, the text is invested by a higher authorship with an alternative meaning capable of changing the nature of the whole text. The audience need only be capable of finding it.

Apparently originating in the East in Buddhist literature, versions of the *"Pardoner's Tale"* are found throughout the world in all times up to our own (John Huston's film *The Treasure of the Sierra Madre* is such a version). Its timeless appeal certainly has something to do with its enigmatic quality and the multiple layers of meaning and of irony it contains. Chaucer's original contribution is in the development of the figure of the old man who points the way to the final denouement. Chaucer's rendering of the tale, however, is one that maintains the commentary of the Pilgrim-Author throughout in the form of the sermon, which also characterized his prologue. Having established the three protagonists of the tale as figures of capital sins, many of which he has accused himself of earlier, the author interrupts the narrative of the tale to comment on its moral significance.

Gluttony, avarice, and idolatry are the chief sins of the Pardoner's characters, and as he enumerates and describes them he also shows them to be related to each other. Appealing to a series of ancient sources, including both wise pagans and

Scripture, the Pardoner creates a powerful condemnation of these sins:

> Allas! a foul thyng is it, by my feith,
> To seye this word, and fouler is the dede,
> Whan man so drynketh of the white and rede
> That of his throte he maketh his pryvee [privy / toilet],
> Thurgh thilke cursed superfluitee.

In this formulation, the Pardoner alludes to the relationship between the word and that which it signifies, declaring the reality (gluttony or fornication) the signifier, to be more than the "word", or signifier, but, also, the word to be appropriate to what it expresses; both are "foul." However, were the author sincere in this belief, he would personally repudiate the thing he so describes. Rather, in the case of the Pardoner, who has openly established himself as the personification of these vices, we are treated to a display of rhetorical skill, for he is engaged in creating a fiction about three characters guilty of these vices. By interspersing the fictional narrative with a discourse on the nature of those sins, he deliberately blurs the boundaries between the fictional universe of the tale and the real world to which it should correspond. In other words, by reweaving into the fiction the lesson, or meaning, that may be derived from it, the Pardoner attempts to neutralize that meaning by making it fictive.

Like the Pardoner himself, the three rioters of his tale take signs of all kinds for reality. Hearing that Death has slain one of their companions, they set out to find and to slay Death, swearing by "God's bones" to accomplish the deed before nightfall. This additional reference to bones recalls the author's earlier description of his false relics, and associates the rioters' quest to control the reality of death with the Pardoner's theory of reality as illusion. This brotherhood, whose members have sworn to live and die for each other, encounter in their quest an old man whose quest is not to slay Death but to join it, to remedy a life overextended and empty of vigor. His instructions to the youths are correct:

> To fynde Deeth, turne up this croked wey,
> For in that grove I lafte hym, by my fey,
> Under a tree, and there he wole abyde;
> Noght for youre boost he wole him no thyng hyde.
> Se ye that ook? Right there ye shal hym fynde.

The old man not only pursues Death, but knows where, for all but himself, it is to be found, as his advice to the youths demonstrates. Yet he, himself, is unable to possess Death, condemned, as he tells us, forever to wander in search of what he knows but cannot become one with. Like the Par-

doner, according to his own boast, the old man can lead others to what they seek, but is forever separate from it. The three rioters conceive of reality in a material and literalist way, thinking that death is a tangible, and thus controllable, phenomenon. Their dedication to food and drink is another dimension of their materialism, and so for them, signs, words, and concepts, such as the death bell they hear, the oaths they swear, and Death whom they pursue, contain no greater reality than their experiential existence. The old man, on the other hand, has lost this naive enthusiasm for the world of particulars, having long lived the bitter experience of a radically nominalist world disconnected from the real. He has become the empty sign: "Lo how I vanysshe, flessh, and blood, and skyn! / Allas! whan shul my bones been at reste?" Still another reference to bones! He is the very sign of Death by his appearance and words, but he cannot connect with the reality that he signifies and remains a particular in search of a universal. He is the living death, the oxymoron, the contradiction that so permeates the Pardoner's prologue and tale.

All the characters of the tale, then, constitute the pilgrim-author and reveal him. The Pardoner's gluttony and swearing is echoed in the rioters who further establish his materialist-relativist philosophy in the narrative, while his eunuchry and spiritual oldness are reflected in the old man's physical lifelessness; that figure further establishes his author's nominalist philosophy in the tale through his isolation from what he knows. The tale is brought to a wonderfully ironic end through the Pardoner's brilliant use of a Eucharistic metaphor when, having found gold instead of Death under the tree, one of the trio is sent for bread and wine to celebrate their fortune. After murdering their brother, who has brought back the food, so as to divide the gold between them, the two survivors drink the wine, which the younger victim has poisoned in the hope of having the treasure all for himself. For the first and only time in the tale, the sign (gold: cupidity) and what it signifies (death) are brought together to the confounding of character and author alike.

At various levels of the tale, the Pardoner's authorial intentions are fulfilled. As a moral sermon the tale conditions the audience to repent of the various sins that they have seen so dramatically depicted and punished, and as an intellectual proposition it sufficiently confuses the nature and efficacy of signs so as to gain possible acceptance for his nominalist literary theory. But most important, from the author's point of view, the tale has set the stage for his ultimate extension of both theory and practice, the use of morality to destroy morality and the use of literature to destroy literature. The Pardoner hurries at the end of his tale toward that goal, immediately offering to his audience his false relics as means of redemption.

The Pardoner has good reason to hurry, realizing, perhaps, that within his tale, for all his careful rhetoric, lurks another possible significance antithetical to the meaning and application he intends. The longer the audience explores the text's allegorical relations to the world and to other texts, the more this meaning emerges from it. The bread and wine that bring death expand in significance as they are inevitably associated with the bread and wine that truly slay death; the oak under which the rioters find gold and death similarly unfolds into symbol when associated with the tree of life and the text "the wages of sin is death"; the numerous partial citations from Scripture and other authoritative texts reach out to their full contexts to create a larger and inevitably contradictory meaning to that intended by the author. But nothing so menaces the Pardoner's success as the figure of the old man who, as the personification of the author, reveals the Pardoner's way as living death. With the memory of the skeletal old man who points the way to death so fresh in their minds, how terrifying to the pilgrims must seem the old bones which the Pardoner now offers to them as relics.

In order to ensure the self-referentiality of the tale (so important to the success of his enterprise), the Pardoner attempts to extend its terms into the world of the Canterbury pilgrimage itself by urging his fellow travelers to accept his false relics and thereby give assent to the ideology of empty signs, meaningless experience, and positivist art:

> But, sires, o [one] word forgat I in my tale:
> I have relikes and pardoun in my male [pouch],
> As faire as any man in Engelond,
> Whiche were me yeven [given] by the popes hond.
> If any of yow wole, of devocion,
> Offren, and han myn absolucion,
> Com forth anon, and kneleth heere adoun,
> And mekely receyveth my pardoun.

While we cannot know which, if any, of the pilgrims reached for coins in order to buy into the Pardoner's proposition, we see the destruction of his scheme when he appropriately singles out Harry Bailly as his main target. As Harry has, in fact, invented the idea of a tale-telling pilgrimage and acts as the official literary critic, his assent to the Pardoner's theory is most crucial. For, just as the pilgrimage itself is a physical journey toward an objective reality in time and space, that is, the

shrine of Canterbury and its relics, which is a sign of a spiritual journey toward salvation, so too the tales told during the pilgrimage are an intellectual use of sign implying such a spiritual reality and the purposeful mental journey toward it. Harry's assent to the Pardoner's epistemological principles would have destroyed the meaning of both the physical and mental journeys and would have provided the Pardoner with the vengeance and the leadership he seems to desire.

The Host's ferocious rejection of the Pardoner's philosophy arises out of both his abilities and his limitations. Although he has shown himself throughout to be unable to interpret the tales beyond their level of entertainment, he nevertheless has a strong and correct instinct for what makes fiction work: Harry knows what constitutes tedium and what constitutes delight, and as far as his judgments go, they are correct. This common man's intuition about art's need for reality, for mimesis, coupled with his natural, virile heartiness, define Bailly as the Pardoner's contrary and his natural antagonist. When these opposites clash, the violence is considerable:

> "Nay, nay!" quod he, "thanne have I Cristes curs [curse]!
> Lat be," quod he, "it shal nat be, so theech [as I hope to prosper]!
> Thou woldest make me kisse thyne olde breech [breeches],
> And swere it were a relyk of a seint,
> Though it were with thy fundement depeint [stained by your buttocks]!
> But, by the croys [cross] which that Seint Eleyne fond,
> I woulde I hadde thy coillons [testicles] in myn hond
> In stide of relikes or of seintuarie [holy objects].
> Lat kutte [cut] hem of, I wol thee helpe hem carie;
> They shul be shryned [enshrined] in an hogges toord [turd]!"

This very personal attack on the Pardoner addresses his intellectual position as well as his corporeal condition and is both appropriate and extremely telling, rendering the Pardoner speechless in defeat. The Host has at once cruelly unmasked his adversary's physical deficiency and the sterility of his philosophy. "Your relics and your theories," Harry storms, "are as worthless as your testicles," thus knitting up and exposing all the elements of this author's motives and methods.

That the Pardoner's downfall comes through his misuse of relics is significant. By his forceful rhetoric he has succeeded in purging verbal signs of their significance, but his war on meaning is total. Like words, relics were also conceived of as signs, but as signs with a simpler and more direct relationship to what they signified. As the etymology of the word suggests, a relic was considered the "remains" of a person or object especially sanctified. Often they were parts of a saint's body or something that had touched the body and had thus taken into themselves a degree of the power of the sacred object. Like icons, relics do much more than represent what they signify; they cause the reality to be present: "The icon is not consubstantial with its prototype and yet, while employing symbolism, is not itself a symbol. It causes to emerge, not without a certain artistic rigidity, a personal presence; and it is symbolism which reveals this presence, as well as the entire cosmic context that surrounds it."

Differing from the usual function of words, relics incarnate what they stand for and are a conduit for a power no longer present. Their authenticity, then, is more obviously crucial to their function, although, like the false words of the Pardoner, a false relic may inspire real faith and devotion. Relics and icons are, therefore, more powerful than words and yet far less supple. Language, even false language, does, in fact, participate in the making of meaning, whereas a false relic, like an impotent man, can engender nothing, as Harry Bailly so bluntly puts it. According to medieval theory, a false relic will under no circumstances have the effect it is supposed to have, although the subjective belief that it inspires may have merit as piety. The relic, then, depends completely for its power on the objective, independent existence of that of which it is the remains and the sign.

The Canterbury pilgrimage is one directed toward a relic, the remains of Saint Thomas à Becket. The Pardoner realizes that it is not only the stories told on the journey that must be the object of his attack, but also the goal of the journey itself, if he is to impose his view of reality upon the pilgrims. But at the same time that he voids words of their signifying power and relics of their incarnating power, he also assults a third category of sign, one preeminent and unique in medieval Christian thought, the Eucharist. The Pardoner's central allusion to this "sign of signs" comes in his insincere denunciation of gluttony: "Thise cookes, how they stampe, and streyne, and grynde, / And turnen substaunce into accident."

The theory of the Eucharist is that through the repetition of Christ's words at the Last Supper, bread and wine become the Body and Blood of Christ while retaining their natural form and appearance. Through this transubstantiation the *accidents,* or visible and tangible aspects of the bread and wine, remain while the *substance,* or essence, is changed to that of the Divinity. Just as the Pardoner uses the image of bread and wine at the end of the tale to denote death, so here he uses the theory of transubstantiation to describe gluttony and luxury, and for good reason. For in the Eucharist is discovered the highest order of the real, in that it is both sign and signified simultaneously. For it is not a true sign of something else, nor only a representation, nor even an icon that calls forth the divine presence in the Eucharist, but it is a complete union of symbol and reality, which, as it is eaten by the faithful, denotes the complete union of knower and known, creator and created, universal and particular.

For the radical nominalist, the possibility that every day, in every church, the particulars of bread and wine not only communicated a universal, but became the universal of universals (Plato's *nous,* Christianity's superessential Being), posed a serious problem, and in Chaucer's time more than in any other the question of transubstantiation was hotly argued. Robert E. Nichols, Jr., in his study of the Eucharistic symbolism in the *"Pardoner's Tale,"* describes one side of the controversy: "Wyclif, who declared that hypocritical clergy by their actions 'ben made wafreris,' protested the fiction that any priest can 'make' the body of Christ daily by saying mass, arguing that he simply 'makes' in the host a sign of the Lord."

We see how far-reaching is the Pardoner's attack on cognition when we realize that the three cornerstones of knowledge—language, icon, and Eucharist—which he attempts to undermine, constitute the epistemological structure of the Middle Ages. Just as he empties signs of their signification through his manipulation of language, and just as he demotes the function of the relic to that of the empty sign, so, too, he attempts to devalue the mystery of the Eucharist to the status of a human sign. Attempting to project his own spiritual decay onto the world through the use of fiction in his tale, this author threatens the basis of fiction itself. But in Chaucerian poetics there is within language, and thus within fiction, the power to reassert the essential connection with reality, as is revealed in this case through the unlikely agency of the Host, "moost envoluped in synne."

Source: David Williams, "Language Redeemed: 'The Pardoner's Tale,'" in *"The Canterbury Tales": A Literary Pilgrimage,* Twayne Publishers, 1987, pp. 53–100.

David Williams

In the following essay excerpt, Williams examines how the Wife of Bath wields her own version of experience and authority in telling her tale.

Whatever may be the interpretation she places on the "Miller's Tale," the Wife of Bath must have enjoyed it thoroughly. Her own prologue and tale are similar exercises in turning everything upside down, but with the Wife of Bath, Chaucer seems to be exploring similar questions under a different theme, a theme that the Wife herself identifies as experience and authority as alternative means of understanding the truth. In his important study *Chaucerian Fiction,* Robert Burlin has shown the central importance of this theme in all of Chaucer's work, but nowhere is it as explicitly addressed as in the "Wife of Bath's Tale": "She was preserved illiterate, allowed only the puny weapon of her own 'experience' to contend with an armory of masculine 'auctoritee'. No wonder, then, that the Wife uses any strategy that comes to hand to establish and defend her identity. No wonder, either, that she finds herself uncomfortably contrary, consistently obliged to assume the very position she is opposing." Philosophically she is off to a bad start, however, since in the Middle Ages this somewhat complicated concept of authority and experience as the basis of human cognition normally regarded both elements as necessary for correct understanding. But the Wife is a dualist in all she undertakes; she divides, differentiates, and emphasizes conflict wherever possible.

Ideally, human knowledge of truth is achieved through both experience and authority, although each, and the sources of each, are different. In this tradition, all texts represent authority; all interpretation is experience. The ultimate textual authority is Scripture, of course, because God is its Author. The ideal of experience, it follows, is to be found in the life of Christ, who is seen as the definitive interpreter of Scripture, the paradigmatic exegete. It is here in the authoritative Word of God as revealed in Scripture and in the historical life of Christ, the *Verbum Dei,* that the junction of experience and authority is to be found. Beyond these models lie numerous other examples of authority and experience: truth is authority, language is experience; meaning is authority, signification is experience; the knowable is authority, reason is experience; universals are authority, particulars are experience. Usually authority is superior to experience, but this is not always the case. Particularly when the authority is human—for instance, a man-

> **"** *Through the fiction of her tale the author has fulfilled her desires and resolved the oppositions they engendered in life."*

made text—the right use of reason, which is experience, may be the better guide. In any case, both ideally coincide in the Augustinian "good man skilled in teaching [*vir bonus discendi paritus*]" whose experience guided by authority leads to correct perception and communication of the knowable.

The "Wife of Bath's Prologue" begins for the *Canterbury Tales* a debate on the question of marriage in which several other pilgrims participate. It is the woe in marriage that the Wife announces as her theme, while declaring that were there no authority on which to base her understanding of the subject, her own experience would be sufficient. On at least one level this is quite true, since she herself is the "author" of that woe experienced by her five husbands. Immediately, then, we see that the terms and concepts of authority and experience are to be used in several ways typical of Chaucerian irony. It is clear, for instance, that the Wife's use of "experience" has little to do with Thomas Aquinas's *experimentum,* the intellectual ordering and unifying of present perceptions with previous remembered perceptions.

While the Wife's entire prologue consists of memories of her past, neither her reasoning in the present about them nor her interpretation of other tales that she hears in the present pilgrimage bring order, or understanding, or meaning to her life. To cite Burlin's convenient summary of the medieval sense of experience: "This, then, is the 'experience' that underlies the Middle English definitions. It is more than the apprehension of the senses, or a collection of remembered objects; it is a unifying activity linking actual perception to what has been apprehended in the past." The Wife's sense of experience is hardly a unifying activity, but rather one that separates her from everything she seeks. As opposed to integrating present with past, it leads only to a melancholy desire for what was. As the champion of experience over authority, she fails dismally, since the one thing that eludes her is real experience in the meaningful sense. To the Wife of Bath, experience is understood only in its most literal and banal senses: it means sex and power. Significantly, in her prologue, experience is something that exists only in the past and in the future, and, as the Wife makes clear, she looks forward hopefully to more sex and power as soon as possible. Experience for the Wife has become memory and anticipation without reality in the present.

Ironically, it is to authority that the Wife appeals in her assertion of the superiority of experience, and we are treated to a sustained demonstration of reason applied to text. She begins with scriptural stories of the wedding at Cana and the oft-married Samaritan encountered by Jesus at the well. Her exegesis of these passages is forthright: she has no idea, she declares, what they could possibly mean! She is much more comfortable with the Old Testament, particularly the commandment of Genesis, "Go, wax and multiply!" Wax she will, but she prefers division and subtraction to multiplying and goes on to cite the command that *husbands* must leave fathers and mothers, dividing it from the commandment to wives about their obligations.

Several scriptural figures are used to characterize the Wife. We recall her introduction in the "General Prologue": "A good Wif was ther Of biside BATHE, / But she was somdel deef [somewhat deaf], and that was scathe [a pity]". Her own reference to the Samaritan woman whom Jesus meets by a *well* identifies her, a woman from near *Bath,* with that other, five-time-wedded figure. But the Samaritan understands the words of Christ ("I perceive that thou art a prophet", whereas the Wife is "somdel deef." She prefers to be the vessel of wood or earth (dishonor) rather than one of gold or silver (honor) and is content to be humble barley bread as long as she does not have to be refined white bread, especially when she recalls that it was with "barly-breed [bread]" that "Oure Lord Jhesu refresshed many a man." She is associated with multiplicity and the "old," both physically and spiritually, as she complains of advancing years and as she adopts the literalist, "old-law" interpretation of life.

The Wife's prologue is the longest by far of all the pilgrims', and in its biographical character seems to grow into a tale in its own right, one that is intimately related to the story of the rapist knight she tells later on. The Wife's life, then, becomes her text and sole authority. Since we find no indication that the account she gives is not accurate, the fictitiousness of that text arises, rather, from the basic fiction of its model: that is, her life is shown to be a lie, a flawed text giving no authoritative knowledge of the real.

The Wife has a strong effect on her audience as we see when the Pardoner interrupts her during her prologue to compliment her for being a "noble prechour [preacher]" on the subject of marriage. She has just finished misinterpreting Saint Paul: "The wife hath not power of her body, but the husband: and likewise also the husband hath not power of his own body, but the wife." As she disjoins the unity of authority and experience, so too, here, as in all other authorities she cites, the Wife fragments the text and cites only the part that advances her interpretation: "I have the power durynge al my lyf / Upon his propre body, and noght he." The Pardoner, like the Wife, approves the text he hears for his own reasons, and will adopt her method of interpreting texts when his turn comes. He was about to marry, he says, but has learned the disadvantages of such a course from the Wife's description of wedded life. Throughout the *Canterbury Tales,* the Pardoner is a figure anxious to conceal and to rationalize his lack of virility; his "celibacy" is thus given a rational basis in the Wife's text. But this author encourages her audience to believe that there is more complicated matter in her tale to come and by careful attention the listener, in this case the Pardoner, may better judge the proper application of the fiction they are about to hear to the reality they live.

"Telle forth youre tale . . . / And teche us yonge men of your praktike [practice]" urges the Pardoner, and the Wife goes on to conclude this contract with the audience in the now-familiar formula: "For myn entente is nat but for to pleye." The Pardoner has good reason to welcome the Wife's fiction, for as a perceptive interpreter of tales, he has already gleaned this author's poetics as one grounded in the pleasant relativist theory that isolates fiction from reality in order to assert the one for the other.

Although still only at the beginning of her prologue, the Wife proclaims, "Now, sire, now wol I telle forth my tale," and proceeds with an account of her married life with five spouses. In a way, this point in her prologue really is the beginning of her tale, for as we shall see, her tale proper becomes a metaphoric representation of the life she describes in the prologue, while the meaning she ascribes to her autobiography is firmly grounded in fantasy.

Alisoun boasts of her triumph over her husbands and describes the techniques by which she mastered them. The husbands fall into two categories: three were rich and old but inadequate to her erotic demands; the last two were sexually vigorous but more difficult to control. In the one kind of relationship the Wife achieves half of what she desires—power; in the other, she achieves the rest—sex; but at the end of her prologue we see that she has failed to attain the unity of the two, which she desires. Like her method of reasoning, her experience is fragmented and divided, ever at war with itself, and as she attains satisfaction in one way, she loses it in another. Her situation is not without pathos, for as a sensualist and materialist, she is doomed to a life of fleeting experiences, which never quite attain the real and which are, thus, interpretable only within the limitations of the flux of time and matter. It is this materialism that gives such prominence to memory and anticipation in her moving lament:

> But, Lord Crist! whan that it remembreth me
> Upon my yowthe, and on my jolitee,
> It tikleth me aboute myn herte roote.
> Unto this day it dooth myn herte boote [good]
> That I have had my world as in my tyme.
> But age, allas! that al wole envenyme [poison],
> Hath me biraft [robbed] my beautee and my pith
> [vigor].
> Lat go, farewel! the devel go therwith!
> The flour is goon, ther is namoore to telle;
> The bren [bran], as best I kan, now moste I selle;
> But yet to be right myrie wol I fonde [invent].

With her last husband, Jankyn, the clerk, the Wife is seen anew in the role of audience, for her learned spouse has taken to educating her through readings from several authoritative texts, which include those of Theophrastus, Tertullian, and Saint Jerome. She is a most unwilling audience, and in her fury against these antifeminist readings she demonstrates something of the powerful relation of literature to life. The tales that Jankyn reads are of evil women throughout history and legend, and they largely preach chastity and marital affection, virtues not likely to excite the Wife's sympathies. She is particularly enraged when her husband continues to read these texts instead of coming to bed, so much so that she finally tears pages from the book, strikes him, and knocks him into the fireplace. In the ensuing battle, the Wife's persistence is sufficient to overcome Jankyn's scholarship; the book is burned, and according to one party, at least, they live for a while in a harmony based upon her mastery and his capitulation, described in terms that echo those of the ending of the tale the Wife is about to tell.

The irony of the Wife's feminism as seen in her literary creation—her tale—is that the tale not only subscribes to the antifeminist cliché that all women, in their heart of hearts, desire to be raped, but it reinforces it. We see this first at the very outset, in her lament for the disappearance of incubi and spirits, who, according to the Wife, were capable in former ages of relieving women of reticence in sexual affairs, and perhaps teaching them a thing or two. In her day, alas, there were only inept (or, perhaps, incapable) begging friars lurking behind every bush. We see the pro-rape theme next in the construction of the tale, in which female authority forgives rape, and we see it finally, when the denouement of the tale becomes an occasion for the universalized mutual rape of mind as well as body. As a tale to illustrate her theme, in which female authority deposes male authority, it serves particularly poorly, just as her apologia in her prologue turns her argument upside down. For in the Wife's "faerie-lond" there are no men or women, just morally androgynous personifications of herself, and the dialectic that she attempts to set up between the male and the female shows itself false. The only authentic figures of womanhood and manhood are the aggrieved maiden seeking justice and the abdicating King Arthur possessing just authority, and these two characters are quickly disposed of by the carnal author to make room for the personifications of herself in the queen, the hag, and the knight.

The queen's usurpation of authority and the transformation of justice into a game prefigure the hag's preempting of the knight's will at the end of the tale, turning moral choice into an illusion of shape-shifting and fantasy. But this inversion has already been established for the tale in the knight's aggression against the maid, in which he has allowed the hag of lust to usurp the moral choice of his victim, imposing his will on hers. Thus the fantasy of the Wife's world is that of the shell game, and the con man, where despite the physical shape-shifting of the tale and the conceptual shape-shifting of her interpretation, nothing changes because nothing has any substance to change. Feminism is another form of antifeminism, love another form of lust, and the possibility of rational understanding, a fantasy.

In the conclusion to the "Wife of Bath's Tale" we see the triumph of her theme—tyranny. The author herself is the rapist knight. In her relationship with her five husbands, she has imposed her will and her desires; in her exegesis of Scripture and authoritative texts, she has imposed her interpretation. She abuses both. Authority, represented by the king, would have inflicted the appropriate punishment on the violent knight, but the Wife in her role as fairy queen commutes his sentence in order to rape him back in a kind of eye-for-an-eye ("gat-tooth-for-gat-tooth") justice. The knight will be raped morally when he relinquishes his integrity to the hag and gives up the power of choice in order to live happily ever after in the world of rape, which the Wife as author promotes. But, as we have seen, he has already accomplished this, without any help from the hag, in his encounter with the maiden, by abdicating to carnal impulse. He has, as it were, raped himself, just as the tale's author, the Wife of Bath, who has created him and the theme of rape, is a perpetual self-rapist.

The Wife's tale is set in the past, for which she expresses a nostalgic preference. It is a past so remote as to constitute for Chaucer's time an epoch of myth and fantasy, and it is this fantastic dimension that makes "th'olde dayes of the Kyng Arthour" so much more attractive than the present to the aging Wife. As in her personal past history there were youth, vigor, and unlimited sensuality (or so she now believes), so she posits in the days of Camelot a world of magic and lawlessness. Nowadays, she laments, a woman may go where she pleases with no fear of rape, for all the fantastic elements have been chased from the world by religion and law. In the world that the Wife constructs for her tale, all desires, no matter how contradictory, no matter how base, come true. The author's prologue has revealed an experience of life in opposition to reality and the sorrow it entails: "Allas! allas! that evere love was synne!" In her tale the opposition is resolved by doing away with reality altogether. It is only in unified reality, a reality that the Wife's dualistic experience has concealed from her, that love is never sin. She therefore seeks this unification in fiction, both in the necessarily incomplete fiction of her life and in the more complete fiction of her tale.

What law is found in fairyland is soon overturned when Arthur, like the Wife's husbands, capitulates to the queen and her ladies. Feminine justice seems more merciful, since unlike established law, which prescribed death for rape, the queen merely assigns a riddle: "What thyng is it that wommen moost desiren"; only in failing to obtain the right answer will the knight die. The false solutions to the riddle offered to him by those he questions constitute a justification of the author's theoretical position, for they are, by and large, the same as the accusations against women that her last husband asserted: desire for wealth, flattery, lust, and license. The true answer comes by magic when in the place where he has been watching a fairy dance, he discovers a "wyf"—old and foul—who teaches the young knight, just as the Pardoner had urged the author to do, the right response. The knight thus wins his life and the old hag a young husband by the formula that what women most want is power over men. But the knight finds that he is immediately faced with still another riddle, which, like the first, is deeply rooted in dualism: how can a woman be both beautiful and faithful?

Through the fiction of her tale the author has fulfilled her desires and resolved the oppositions they engendered in life. In the allegory of her tale, the narrative relates only to the biography of her own desired future life, not to a higher level of meaning in reality external to the text. Merging with her characters, she is the raped maiden, but delighting in the lawless and violent sexuality she complains has disappeared from the contemporary world; she is the queen wresting from her husband the administration of the law; and she is, of course, the hag, suffering the rejection of the youthful knight because of her age. But in fairyland and in fiction this, too, is easily overcome: the author and the knight merge into one, in a dialogue between young husband and old wife that constitutes a monologue in which the author communicates only with herself.

Source: David Williams, "Language Redeemed: 'The Wife of Bath's Tale,'" in *"The Canterbury Tales": A Literary Pilgrimage*, Twayne Publishers, 1987, pp. 53–100.

Patrick J. Gallacher

In the following essay, Gallacher applies Maurice Merleau-Ponty's ideas on perception to "the much-discussed portrait of Alison and to the perceptual responses of John, Absolon, and Nicholas" in "The Miller's Tale."

The "Miller's Tale," if not the fabliau as a genre, presents us with a pattern of mistakes in perception, a sharp, dramatic contrast between the real and the imaginary, which confirms basic assumptions about our world at the same time that it raises important questions. Although our sense of the real begins with what is both actual and possible in perception, it is easy to confuse the two, or to underestimate one or the other. The relevant truism, of course, is that we usually think we know what's there, but we often don't. In fact, the main comic incidents in the "Miller's Tale"—kiss, laying on of hot ploughshare, falling off the roof—belong to that type of slapstick comedy based on such confusion. Our response to the confusion derives from assumptions concerning perception, or, according to Maurice Merleau-Ponty, from the fact that the perceived world is an ensemble of routes taken by the body. The characters portrayed by the brilliant practitioners of this kind of comedy—Charlie Chaplin, Peter Sellers, or Jacques Tati—cannot discover these routes. Given a metaphysical ungainliness in such clowns, the ordinary routes of the body are like mysterious passages sought by legendary navigators. Inspector Clouzot cannot walk into a room without being ambushed by lamps and chairs, or becoming locked in mortal combat with a telephone.

In what follows, I shall give a much abbreviated summary of Merleau-Ponty's ideas on perception, the most important of which are immanence and transcendence, or presence and absence, which, in turn, are basically different aspects of the more inclusive antithesis of the actual and the possible. I shall then apply these ideas to the much-discussed portrait of Alison and to the perceptual responses of John, Absolon, and Nicholas.

Merleau-Ponty attempts to explain the sense of the real that begins in perception through a program of perceptual calisthenics that both trims our assumptions and tones up our expectations. Perception, he points out, is always both more and less than we think, potential and actual in surprising ways, both unlimited and limited, transcendent and immanent. We always see, hear, and touch from the point of view of a limited perspective; but within that limited point of view there are clues, reflections, implied textures of "an immense latent content of the past, the future, and the elsewhere." We are always confronted by the unchallengeable presence and the perpetual absence of things, and nothing reveals itself without thereby hiding most of itself. Perception then is paradoxically both immanent and transcendent: immanent because I cannot conceive a perceptible place in which I myself am not present. Even if I try to imagine some place in the world which has never been seen, the very fact that I imagine it makes me present at that place. By transcendence in perception is meant that the things which I see are things for me only under the condition that they always recede beyond their immediately given aspects. I never see a house in its entirety, or the house as seen from everywhere. The house is given as an infinite sum of perspectives, a series of partial views in each of which it is given, but in none of which is it given exhaustively. An observation of Paul Claudel's brilliantly dramatizes

> *John and Absolon most obviously and habitually have situated themselves in relation to static worlds, one defined by narcissism, the other defined by anti-intellectual credulity; whereas Nicholas has situated himself beyond these structures.*"

the paradox: "a certain blue of the sea is so blue that only blood would be more red." Itself paradoxical, this poetically schematic insight captures that sense of expansiveness and singularity which describes perception, the synecdoche or metonymy within the basic act itself.

In general, then, our perceptual existence is fully accounted for by what we actually and potentially see, hear, smell, touch, and taste. This actuality and possibility are inextricably bound together in the same act of perception, with an emphasis, however, on what can be, on the fact that a thing continues to be defined by that which is beyond our immediate sense experience. The contrast between the real and the imaginary, an essential feature of the climactic incidents in the "Miller's Tale," invokes a special manifestation of this transcendence. When an illusion dissipates, when an appearance suddenly breaks up, it is always for the profit of a new appearance which takes up again for its own account the ontological function of the first. The dis-illusion is the loss of one evidence only because it is the acquisition of another evidence. A convincing substitution of the real for the imaginary reveals the "prepossession of a totality which is there before one knows how or why, whose realizations are never what we would have imagined them to be, and which nonetheless fulfills a secret expectation within us, since we believe in it tirelessly." The least particle of the perceived incorporates it from the first into this paradoxical totality and the most credible phantasm glances off at the surface of the world, because the whole world is present in one reflection and is irremediably absent in the richest and most systematic deliriums. The act of judgment, by distinguishing the real from the imaginary, by saying that one thing is not and that something else is, invokes the mysterious totality of what is, of being, which is all there is, because outside of this, there is nothing.

The portrait of Alison provides not only an emblem of totality by the encyclopedic variety of its imagery, but introduces us also to the insistent presence and absence in perception itself. Images of things that are early, young, new, or fresh give us a sense of unchallengeable presence akin to seeing something for the first time. She is more joyous to look at than the "newe pere-jonette tree." Other images, such as the primrose, cuckoo flower, and the latten pearls on her leather purse, suggest a filling out of vegetative and mineral categories; and, indeed, the *effictio* as a device is intended to give satisfaction precisely by its completeness. Again, it is the actuality of presence and immanence that we primarily experience in Alison's resemblance to young animals in her sudden, playful bursts of vitality; and yet the skittish, elusive quality of these images suggests the unforeseen, the unpredictable—Alison's enticing possibilities, which in turn reflect a seductiveness in reality itself. With this elusiveness, a kind of absence comes into her portrait that has further sensuous developments: "Hir mouth was sweete as bragot or the meeth, / Or hoord of apples leyd in hey or heeth." The apple simile, with its circular rhythms, directs perception sensuously to Alison, who, though not seen in her entirety, is nevertheless amply comprehended. The rotund depth of the store of apples intimates the unseen, unfelt, secret life of what is perceived. What is inviting to taste and sight here is potential, not actually tactile or visible and hence part of the perceptually transcendent. The most compelling union of presence and absence, however, of the actual and the possible, is the image of the doll—*popelote*, which, by evoking the urge to grasp and fondle, elicits such a lively possibility that its realization seems already present. The response intended by the portrait is perhaps summed up in Absolon's reaction: "if she hadde been a mous, / And he a cat, he wolde hire hente anon." In a word, there is a *pounceability* about Alison that sets in motion the exploration of physical and moral space. Just as the courtly heroine often has a philosophical dimension, Alison, her rural counterpart, brings us uniquely into contact with what is real. In reacting to Alison, her two suitors and husband display ludicrous, but unmistakable metaphysical

gestures. Nicholas is precipitous in seizing upon the newly perceived and manifests a raunchy grabbiness. Absolon courts the real by dandyism. The apprehensive husband, John, only wants to imprison the real, which is unpredictable in its hiddenness, and to keep Alison "narwe in cage."

John's view of the world rejects what is transcendent in the real, a rejection that begins in his habits of perception and becomes especially clear in his boastfully ignorant attitude towards "Goddes pryvetee." Two uses of this phrase, which richly suggests the mysterious totality of the real, occur in a sequence that begins when Nicholas sequesters himself in his room: for John, this hiddenness refers to things that men should not know; for Nicholas, it is an effectively persuasive reason for not informing Robin and Gill of the flood. At John's anxious insistence, his "knave" goes up to the room "ful sturdily," in that manner of confidently and precisely taking hold of things that characterizes the tricksters in the story, recalling the directness of Nicholas's first approach to Alison. Receiving no response to his knock, he opens another route to his perception. His gaze enters through a hole in the door and encounters a gaze of Nicholas in the act of seeming to pry open the universe:

> An hole he foond, ful lowe upon a bord,
> Ther as the cat was wont in for to crepe,
> And at that hole he looked in ful depe,
> And at the laste he hadde of hym a sight.
> This Nicholas sat evere capyng upright,
> As he had kiked on the newe moone.

The manner in which the "knave" looks in has those aspects of limited perspective—its immanent particularity—that foreshadow much of the action. In contrast, the bodily posture of Nicholas reveals someone exhausted by looking, someone who has tried to see things as they are in themselves, that is, from all perspectives. Nicholas's pretended overgaping at the stars shows a perceptual hubris, a cocky omniscience that will be chastened by the hot coulter, whereas Robin's peeping through the hole is a more accurate example of limited, serial human perception. John's first reaction to his servant's report—"Men sholde nat knowe of Goddes pryvetee"—anticipates his credulity and determines his subsequent remarks about perception. With an uneasy mixture of fear and scorn, he focuses warily on transcendence, on what can happen—"A man woot litel what hym shal bityde"—on the planes and routes within our perception that escape us:

> So ferde another clerk with astromye;
> He walked in the feeldes, for to prye

Upon the sterres, what ther sholde bifalle,
Til he was in a marle-pit yfalle;
He saugh nat that.

For John, to employ anachronism, clerks belong with men in top hats and monocles who slip on banana peels, who forget the routes taken by the body. The anecdote typifies the comic confusion of immanence and transcendence in perception, of thinking we know what's there. John prides himself on his grasp of the obvious, but nothing, of course, can be so elusive. He is betrayed by the transcendence of what is in front of him. Having boasted of pious ignorance, he will be reproved for his superstition. His manner of entering Nicholas's room—prying under the door with a staff while Robin knocks it off its hasp—shows his artless, downright style of being; and his exhortation to Nicholas reveals attitudes towards the transcendent that undo him:

Awak, and thenk on Cristes passioun!
I crouche thee from elves and fro wightes.
Therwith the nyght-spel seyde he anon-rightes
On foure halves of the hous aboute,
And on the thresshfold of the dore withoute:
"Jhesu Crist and seinte Benedight,
Blesse this hous from every wikked wight,
For nyghtes verye, the white *pater-noster*!
Where wentestow, seinte Petres soster?"

Superstition characterizes John's sense of the unseen. He cannot grasp the fact that mystery begins in perception itself: that "Goddes pryvetee" is the theological resolution of a more prosaic transcendence that begins in the senses. For him, elves and "creatures" people horizons that he fears to acknowledge. He has changed the reflections and clues of an elsewhere into beings that can threaten the security of his immediate perception. Closing off his thresholds, he uses religion to avoid risks and construct defenses against reality. His secret preparations for the flood, designed to escape the notice of Robin, Gill, and others, remove him from that social contact that adds to our own perspectives and ironically distances him from the open totality suggested by the phrase, "Goddes pryvetee." A ludicrous obsession with the wrong perceptual clues, especially a "listening in depth," chronicles his final experience of gravity and solidity. Appropriately situating himself in darkness, which is the absence of figure and ground, he gives himself to prayer, and "stille he sit, / Awaitynge on the reyn, if he it heere." Sleeping soundly through the romp below him, he is awakened by Nicholas's loud, wild pleas for water, and once more gives into fantasy, thinking

"Allas, now comth Nowelis flood!"
He sit hym up withouten wordes mo,
And with his ax he smoot the corde atwo,
And doun gooth al; he foond neither to selle,
Ne breed ne ale, til he cam to the celle
Upon the floor, and ther aswowne he lay.

Having desired to keep Alison "narwe in cage," praying to be secure from the elves and wights of feared perceptual horizons, he plunges with due justice into what is not actually perceived, the perceptually transcendent, the real possibilities of "Goddes pryvetee." That a real perception dissipates an illusion could not be more emphatically dramatized; and with authentic perception comes the presence of the whole world, a definitive experience of the real, whose accomplishment, however, is still deferred. For the sobering future that awaits John begins with the neighbors who run to "gauren on this man"; his broken arm; oaths proclaiming his madness; the failure of his own explanation; and the general laughter. Although the victim of yet another fiction, he, of course, is not deceived; and, although isolated once again, he is situated within a more reliable and enlarged perceptual field, whose pungent reality is incontestable, for "stonde he moste unto his owene harm . . . ".

The prelude to Absolon's perceptual experience is the immanent, self-regarding way in which he defines the space of his world, an attitude manifested especially in two passages. First, the virtuosity of his dancing is presented as an unsituated physical dexterity. Exceeding the properly gratuitous movements of dance, Absolon seems to indulge a kind of unattached flurry that anticipates his failures to locate himself in real perceptual fields:

In twenty manere koude he trippe and daunce
After the scole of Oxenforde tho,
And with his legges casten to and fro . . .

This prodigality of movement affects mastery of the body's routes belied by later developments. The second characterizing passage occurs when, taking his gitern to the carpenter's house and dextrously poising himself by the shuttered window, he makes musical advances to a wife actually in bed with her husband. The insouciance of the exchange between John and Alison reverses Absolon's own opinion of his adroitness and proficiency:

This carpenter awook, and herde him synge,
And spak unto his wyf, and seyde anon,
"What! Alison! herestow nat Absolon,
That chaunteth thus under oure boures wal?"

And she answerde hir housbonde therwithal,
"Yis, God woot, John, I heere it every deel."

Attaching so little importance to the husband's presence shows a carelessness of figure and ground in perception that makes him especially vulnerable to the punitive effects of an unwary imagination. When, therefore, John ceases to be in evidence because of his hidden preparations for the flood, such total perceptual absence guarantees misadventure.

Immediately for Absolon, as previously for John, fantasy begins to outrun perception, the imaginary to usurp the real, which will, however, soon return with an earthy tenacity. His sense of taste becomes the focus of the tension between perceptual immanence and transcendence: "My mouth hath icched al this longe day; / That is a signe of kissyng atte leeste" (3682–83). The initial clue of a future elsewhere—an itching mouth—builds lavishly to the dream of a feast, and, as he rises and prepares himself to visit Alison, becomes a sensual concern with oral messages:

But first he cheweth greyn and lycorys,
To smellen sweete, er he hadde kembd his heer.
Under his tonge a trewe-love he beer,
For therby wende he to ben gracious.

There may be something even in his manner of walking—"He *rometh* to the carpenteres hous" (my italics)—that suggests inattention to the body's proper routes. Worsted in his first exchange with Alison, he is promised a kiss. Most deliciously, a false transcendent anticipation bids him open his taste buds to the fullest. His imagination is already actually enjoying the kiss before the message of the real perception enters his consciousness:

This Absolon gan wype his mouth ful drie.
Derk was the nyght as pich, or as the cole,
And at the wyndow out she putte hir hole,
And Absolon, hym fil no bet ne wers,
But with his mouth he kiste hir naked ers
Ful savourly, er he were war of this.

Having wiped his mouth with expectant certainty, he prolongs this assurance into the manner of the act itself—"Ful savourly"—a phrase which itself suggests lingering exploration. The reversal of this virtually absolute assumption that we know what's there becomes only slowly instructive for Absolon. His answer to the real sense experience is once more fantasy, this time, to the delight of Nicholas, a beard, "a thyng al rough and long yherd." Biting his heretofore pampered lip, Absolon contemplates revenge, while taking temporary comfort in the different textures of sand, straw, cloth and chips, which parody the opulent, sensual transcendence that he sought in the kiss. The chaste plainness of these purifying textures—granular, fibrous, smooth, incisive—corrects his wayward labial expectations and recommends a more plausible world. Narcissism has humiliatingly distorted his capacity for accurate perceptual transcendence. Therefore, just as John, pushed across the threshold guarded by the elves and wights of his superstition, will fall into the real world, so with Absolon. Unsentimental, functional anatomy presses through his fantasies to reach his actual senses. An unforeseen possible has become actual. Having selectively defined the world by dandyism, he has been exquisitely apprised of a more inclusive view.

Finally, the nemesis of the arrogantly successful lover provides for the tale's perceptual experiences a generalization that is spatial and concrete, but philosophical as well. Nicholas, having successfully manipulated John by the phrase, "Goddes pryvetee," believes himself to be in control of the actual and possible structure of space, but fails, like John and Absolon, to realize the range of perceptual transcendence. Laying the plot for John and watching Alison entice Absolon to the disillusioning kiss, he has contained their perspectives and situated their worlds within his own. In seeking to amend the jape, Nicholas wants to ascend to a new level of trickery, a parody of further transcendence. The motif of secrecy is cumulatively present, as Nicholas once more attempts to manipulate the hiddenness of things: "up the wyndowe dide he hastily, / And out his ers he putteth *pryvely* . . . " (my italics). This final repetition of a secrecy word invokes the whole pattern—the Miller's jibe about not being inquisitive, Nicholas's plot, John's anti-intellectualism, the clandestine preparation of the tubs—but especially the ontological ground of the action, that totality on whose threshold their perceptions take place—"Goddes pryvetee." Furthermore, "pryvely" may suggest that Nicholas's attempt at a new level of trickery parodies Theseus's ascent to a new understanding of mystery in the *"Knight's Tale."* A startlingly different possibility, however, is actualized. When Absolon requests the object of his vengeance to speak, because he doesn't know where she is, we are reminded, for the last time, of the night's darkness which creates a space of almost pure possibility and transcendence, without figure and ground. Mortifyingly situated by the fart that gives a final response to his own squeamishness, Absolon "was redy with his iren hoot, / And Nicholas amydde the ers he smoot." Having fouled the air, burned in his tout, Nicholas cries out for water; John awakens to his fantasy of a flood and falls to the ground. A parodic succession of the elements that bind Theseus's fair chain of love—air, fire, water, earth—attends upon this nearly apocalyptic triumph of the real over the imaginary, and alludes to the principles of material totality in the medieval world. Nicholas, who had pretended to view things from a kind of ubiquity, is reintroduced to the situated world of comic limitation. Having presumptuously exploited the mysterious for the purpose of sexual gratification, he is surprised by that literal, immediate world which he has considered his domain. His mad plea for water testifies to the fecundity of those astonishing possiblities that he has considered so predictable.

Each of Alison's three suitors, on one dramatic occasion, fails to gear himself successfully onto the real world. John and Absolon most obviously and habitually have situated themselves in relation to static worlds, one defined by narcissism, the other defined by anti-intellectual credulity; whereas Nicholas has situated himself beyond these structures. Because of the inflexible nature of these other worlds, Nicholas, as trickster, has been able to exploit the possibilities of real space. His own world, though combining the actual with the possible, is, in turn, limited by the trickster's own narrowly focused conception of this scheme. All these worlds lack a due regard for perceptual transcendence. The fact that Absolon's revenge, which initiates the tale's climax, takes the specific form of the trickster tricked makes a final essential point. If the trickster can be tricked, he can also further trick those who are trying to trick him, a complication which in fact develops in the "Reeve's Tale." This unlimited vulnerability suggests a definition of human experience, at least in the fabliau, as an open process of interactions between actual and possible, a process which points to what in the Middle Ages was the true field of fields. The ubiquity that Nicholas has assumed does not pertain to the real nature of human space, which is, instead, a pact between the virtual body and the actual body, a physical experience of potency and act, terms which for the Middle Ages encompass what is real, or being itself. This pact is a function of the immanence and transcendence of perception, and emphasizes what can happen, that range of very concrete possibilities that is partly the subject matter of human choice, divinely foreknown but no obstacle to human freedom, in a phrase, "Goddes pryvetee." The structure of perception, as described by Maurice Merleau-Ponty and dramatized, as I hope to have shown, in the "Miller's Tale," provides for this metaphysical principle a concrete manifestation. It is, I believe, partly for this reason that in the "Miller's Tale," as Charles Muscatine observed, the "genre is virtually make philosophical" and so completely fulfills its "fabliau entelechy."

Source: Patrick J. Gallacher, "Perception and Reality in the 'Miller's Tale,'" in *Chaucer Review*, Vol. 18, No. 1, 1983, pp. 38–48.

Jill Mann

In the following essay, Mann explains how understanding "The Franklin's Tale" and its theme of patience can lead to a greater understanding of the Canterbury Tales *as a whole.*

The "Franklin's Tale" is not only one of the most popular of Chaucer's tales, it is also one whose emotional and moral concerns lie at the centre of Chaucer's thinking and imaginative activity. It is usually thought of as a tale about 'trouthe'—or perhaps about 'gentillesse'—but it is equally concerned with the ideal of patience and the problems of time and change, which are subjects of fundamental importance not in this tale alone but in the *Canterbury Tales* as a whole. What follows is intended to be not only a close discussion of the "Franklin's Tale," but also an attempt to indicate how a proper reading of it can help with a proper reading of the rest of the *Tales*—and indeed, of Chaucer's work in general.

The "Franklin's Tale" begins by introducing a knight who has, in best storybook fashion, proved his excellence through 'many a labour, many a greet emprise' and thus finally won his lady who, likewise in best storybook fashion, is 'oon the faireste under sonne'. 'And they lived happily ever after' is what we might expect to follow. And so far from trying to dispel the reader's sense of the familiar in this situation, Chaucer takes pains to increase it. He refers to the actors only in general terms ('a knyght', 'a lady'), and attributes to them the qualities and experiences normally associated with tales of romantic courtship (beauty, noble family, 'worthynesse', 'his wo, his peyne and his distresse'). Only after eighty lines are the knight and the lady given the names of Arveragus and Dorigen. This generality cannot be accidental, for Chaucer's apparently casual comments are designed precisely to emphasize that this individual situation takes its place in a plural context:

> But atte laste she, for his worthynesse,
> And namely for his meke obeisaunce,
> Hath such a pitee caught of his penaunce
> That prively she fil of his acord
> To take him for hir husband and hir lorde,
> Of swich lordshipe *as men han over hir wives.*

> " *Only through a perpetual readiness to adapt, to change, in each of the actors in the tale, can the status quo be preserved. Or, in Chaucerian language, 'trouthe' is the product of patience.* "

What is more, they stress this plural context even in describing the feature of the situation which seems to make it an unusual one: the knight's promise to his lady that he

> Ne sholde upon him take no maistrye
> Again hir wil, ne kithe hire jalousye,
> But hire obeye, and folwe hir wil in al,
> *As any lovere to his lady shal.*

And after the lady's delighted promise of her own faithfulness and humility, we have a warm outburst of praise which again consistently sets this mutual understanding in the context of a whole multiplicity of such relationships.

> For o thing, sires, saufly dar I seye,
> That freendes everich oother moot obeye,
> If they wol longe holden compaignye.
> Love wol nat been constreined by maistrye.
> Whan maistrye comth, the God of Love anon
> Beteth his winges, and farewel, he is gon!
> Love is a thing as any spirit free.
> Wommen, of kinde, desiren libertee,
> And nat to been constreined as a thral;
> And so doon men, if I sooth seyen shal.

'Love . . . maistrye . . . freendes . . . wommen . . . men'—the terms are abstract, plural, general. They relate general human experience to this situation, and this situation to general human experience, with no sense of conflict or discontinuity between the two.

I stress the importance of the general here for two reasons. The first is that this interest in the *common* features of human experience is characteristic of Chaucer. The parenthetical comments which transform the singular of the story into the plural of everyday experience are not confined to this passage or this tale alone; on the contrary, they are so ubiquitous in Chaucer that we may take them for

granted and fail to question their significance. The second reason is that the unusualness of the relationship between Arveragus and Dorigen has often been taken as a sign that it is aberrant—that it represents an attempt to break away from the normal pattern of marital relationships which inevitably invites problems to follow. Against this view we should note that however unusual the *degree* of generosity and humility in this relationship, Chaucer very firmly roots it in the normal desires and instincts of men and women.

Nor is there any reason given for supposing that these desires and instincts are merely human weaknesses. Chaucer's own comments, some of which have been quoted, constitute an unhesitating endorsement of the wisdom of this situation and of the participants in it. The relationship between the knight and his lady is called 'an humble wys accord', and the knight himself 'this wise, worthy knight'. It would not affect this point were anyone to argue that the comments are the Franklin's, not Chaucer's. For in either case any reader who wishes to dissociate him- or herself from the warm approval in these lines will face the same difficulty—and that is the difficulty of finding a location in the tale for true wisdom and worthiness, if both characters and narrator offer only false images of these qualities. The only way out of this difficulty would be to claim that the reader already knows what true wisdom and worthiness are, and brings this knowledge to bear on the tale, in criticism of its values. But this idea assumes that it is possible for his or her knowledge to remain detached from the tale in a way that the passage we are considering simply refuses to allow. For if the reader is a woman, to refuse to acknowledge the truth of what is said about her sex is, *ipso facto*, to accept the legitimacy of her own 'thraldom':

> Wommen, of kinde, desiren libertee,
> And nat to been constreined as a thral.

If, on the other hand, the reader is a man, and feels inclined to respond to these lines with a knowing smile at the ungovernable nature of women, then the following line—

> And so doon men, if I sooth seyen shal

—immediately challenges him in turn to measure the reasonableness of the female desire for liberty by matching it against his own. The result is that both men and women readers are made aware of the need for the liberty of the opposite sex through the recognition that it is a need of their own. The use of the plural, the appeal to the general, is indeed an invitation to readers to bring their own experience and feelings to bear, but it invites them to an identification with the narrative, not to a critical dissociation from it.

Chaucer's use of the plural is thus intimately connected with his use of the second person, an equally pervasive and significant feature of his style. His appeals to the reader as judge have often been discussed—'Who hath the worse, Arcite or Palamon?' ("Knight's Tale"); 'Which was the moost fre, as thinketh yow?' ("Franklin's Tale"). But to emphasize these formal appeals alone is to imply, again, that the reader, in the role of judge, remains detached from and superior to the narrative. If, on the other hand, we look at the whole series of addresses to the audience in Chaucer, we shall see that the situation is more complicated. Certainly it is true that the narrative is subordinate to the reader, in the sense that it acknowledges that it relies on a particular experience of the reader for its life and depth; the appeal for judgement on the situations of Arcite and Palamon, for example, is specifically addressed to 'Yow loveres'. The opening of *Troilus and Criseyde* similarly invites 'ye loveres' to read the narrative in the light of their own experience. This call for 'supplementation' of the narrative from one's own experience is often implicitly, as well as explicitly, made. Such an appeal can, for example, be felt in the rhetorical question that concludes the praise of the marriage in the "Franklin's Tale":

> Who koude telle, but he had wedded be,
> The joye, the ese, and the prosperitee
> That is betwixe an housbonde and his wif?

The rhetorical question here makes a space for the reader's own experience to give full meaning to the description, just as it makes space for a very different kind of experience to give a very different kind of meaning to the apparently similar question in the "Merchant's Tale." But if the story needs the reader, it can also make claims on the reader. Precisely because the narrative is based on 'common knowledge', on experiences and feelings shared by the narrator, the readers, and the characters in the story, it is possible for its third-person generalizations to issue into second-person imperatives. Thus, when Troilus falls in love, the generalizations about Love's all-conquering power ('This was, and is, and yet men shal it see') issue naturally into a command:

> Refuseth nat to Love for to ben bonde,
> Syn, as himselven list, he may yow binde.

We can thus see that in the narrator's comments on the marriage of Arveragus and Dorigen,

the apparently casual insertion of 'sires' in the first line is a deliberate preparation for the intensification of the narrative's claims on the reader—claims which make themselves known not only as commands but also as threats.

> Looke who that is moost pacient in love,
> He is at his avantage al above.
> Pacience is an heigh vertu, certeyn,
> For it venquisseth, as thise clerkes seyn,
> Thinges that rigour sholde never atteyne.
> For every word men may nat chide or pleyne.
> Lerneth to suffre, or elles, so moot I goon,
> Ye shul it lerne, wherso ye wole or noon;
> For in this world, certein, ther no wight is
> That he ne dooth or seith somtime amis.

The command 'Lerneth to suffre' does not stand alone; if we disobey it, we face a threat, an 'or elles'. If we search for the authority on which we can be thus threatened, we find it, I think, in the appeal to *common* human experience that I have been describing, in the generalizations from which the imperative issues and into which it returns. And because the experience is common, the speaker himself is not exempt from it; it is perhaps possible to detect in the parenthetical 'so moot I goon' a rueful admission that he has learned the truth of his statement the hard way. At any rate, the phrase stands as an indication that the speaker offers his own individual experience as a guarantee of the truth of the generalizations.

It is because Chaucer wishes to appeal to the general that he so often uses proverbs as the crystallizations of episodes or whole narratives. The proverb which underlies the description of the marriage in the "Franklin's Tale" is perhaps the most important one of all to him; the attempt to understand the paradoxical truth 'Patience conquers' is at the heart of the *Canterbury Tales* and much of Chaucer's other work besides. It animates the stories of Constance and Griselda; it is celebrated in Chaucer's own tale of Melibee. It undergoes, as we shall see, a comic—realistic metamorphosis in the "Wife of Bath's Prologue," and it also stimulates Chaucer's exploration of the qualities that represent a rejection of patience—'ire', 'grucching', 'wilfulnesse'. It is tinged with a melancholy irony in *Troilus and Criseyde*, where Criseyde quotes another version of the proverb—'the suffrant overcomith'—in the course of persuading Troilus of the wisdom of letting her go to the Greeks. This latter instance shows us that an understanding of the truth to be found in such proverbs does not give us clues to the instrumental manipulation of life—quite the reverse, in fact. The parallel truism that Criseyde also quotes—'Whoso wol han lief, he lief moot lete'—does not become the less true because in this case Troilus fails to keep possession of his happiness even though he follows her advice. It is precisely the knowledge that proverbs carry with them the memory of human miseries as well as human triumphs and joys that gives depth and emotional power to the apparently worn phrases.

But of course it is also the story, the new setting which will give fresh meaning, that gives new depth and emotional power to the old words, and we should therefore look to the rest of the "Franklin's Tale" to see how much it can help us to understand the nature of patience and 'suffrance'. The first thing that the story shows us is the link between patience and change. In the first place, it is because human beings are inevitably and constantly subject to change, not just from day to day but from moment to moment, that the quality of patience is needed. In his list of the influences that disturb human stability, Chaucer makes clear that they come both from within and from without the person.

> Ire, siknesse, or constellacioun,
> Win, wo, or chaunginge of complexioun
> Causeth ful oft to doon amis or speken.
> On every wrong a man may nat be wreken.
> After the time moste be temperaunce
> To every wight that kan on governaunce.

All these things disturb the stability of a relationship by altering the mood or feelings or behaviour of an individual. Thus, the only way that the stability and harmony of a relationship can be preserved is through constant adaptation, a responsiveness by one partner to changes in the other. The natural consequence of this is that patience is not merely a response to change; it *embodies* change in itself. And this is at first rather surprising to us, since we tend to think of patience as an essentially static quality, a matter of gritting one's teeth and holding on, a matter of eliminating responses rather than cultivating them. But it is the responsive changeability of patience which is emphasized in Chaucer's final lines of praise for the marriage of Arveragus and Dorigen.

> Heere may men seen a humble, wys accord:
> Thus hath she take hire servant and hir lord—
> Servant in love, and lord in mariage.
> Thanne was he bothe in lordshipe and servage.
> Servage? nay, but in lordshipe above,
> Sith he hath bothe his lady and his love;
> His lady, certes, and his wif also,
> The which that lawe of love acordeth to.

It is often said that this passage illustrates Chaucer's belief in an ideal of equality in marriage. But the patterning of the language does not give us a picture of equality; it gives us a picture of alternation. The constant shifts in the vocabulary suggest constant shifts in the role played by each partner: 'servant . . . lord . . . servant . . . lord . . . lordshipe . . . servage . . . servage . . . lordshipe . . . lady . . . love . . . lady . . . wif'. The marriage is not founded on equality, but on alternation in the exercise of power and the surrender of power. The image it suggests is not that of a couple standing immutably on the same level and side-by-side, or marching in step, but rather of something like the man and woman in a weather-house, one going in as the other comes out. Except of course that this image gives a falsely mechanical idea of what is, as Chaucer describes it, a matter of a living organic responsiveness, and that it is also incapable of expressing an important aspect of the relationship—that the ceaseless workings of change lead to an unchanging harmony, and to the creation of a larger situation in which each partner simultaneously enjoys 'lordshipe' and 'servage', as the passage itself stresses. The result of these constant shifts could be called equality (though I should prefer to call it harmony), but the term equality is too suggestive of stasis to be an accurate description of the workings of the ideal involved here. The ideal of patience better befits the way human beings are, because the simplest and most fundamental truth about people, for Chaucer, is that they change. 'Newefangelnesse', the love of novelty, is part of their very nature ('propre kinde'; "Squire's Tale").

Human beings are not only subject to change in themselves; they also live in a changing world. The opening of the "Franklin's Tale" might seem at first to belie this, since it reads more like an ending than a beginning, so that the story seems, with the long pause for the eulogy of the marriage, to have reached a full stop before it has begun. What prevents a sense of total stagnation is that the unusualness of the situation—of Arveragus' surrender of absolute control—creates a powerful expectation that something is going to happen. This is not just a stratagem for holding our interest; on the contrary, Chaucer uses narrative expectation as a way of indicating the persistence of change even when events have apparently reached a standstill, of making us feel the potentiality for change within the most apparently calm and closed of situations. Thus, as Chaucer allows himself his leisured commentary on the 'humble, wys accord', we find ourselves asking not 'Is this a good thing?', but 'How will this turn out?' We await the completion which the development of events will bring to our understanding and evaluation, and we are thus taught to expect development, the breaking of stasis, as natural.

The stasis is first broken in a very simple way: Arveragus departs for England, and Dorigen's contentment changes into a passionate grief. This grief is described in a long passage which takes us from her first agonies, through her friends' attempts at comfort, to her final subsidence into a kind of resignation which creates a new, if provisional, stasis. Two features of this passage are important: the first is that Dorigen's experience is, once again, placed in a general context.

> For his absence wepeth she and siketh
> *As doon thise noble wives whan hem liketh.*

Secondly, her experience is not only generalized, it is also abbreviated:

> She moorneth, waketh, waileth, fasteth, pleyneth.

Dorigen experiences her grief intensely and at length, but it is described summarily and—*ipso facto*—with a sort of detachment. This does not mean, however, that we need to qualify what was said earlier about the identification established between character, writer and reader; the detachment here is not due to lack of sympathy or to criticism, but to a difference of position in time. Dorigen moves slowly through a 'process' which is for her personally felt and unique; the image of the slow process of engraving on a stone emphasizes its gradualness, its almost imperceptible development. The teller of the story (and the reader of it), on the other hand, can from the outset see Dorigen's experience in a general context of human suffering, and from a knowledge of the general human experience which is embodied in the formulae of traditional wisdom—'Time heals', 'It will pass'—can appreciate not only what is pitiable about Dorigen's misery but also the inevitability of its alleviation, and thus, what is slightly comic about it. The amusement denotes no lack of sympathy, no sense that Dorigen's grief is melodramatic or insincere; it is the kind of amusement which might well be felt by Dorigen herself, looking back on her former agonies six months after her husband's safe return. As time goes on, and Dorigen succumbs to the natural 'proces' of adjustment, she herself comes nearer to this view, so that the passage ends with a rapprochement between her position and that of the storyteller and the reader, and the calmer wisdom of 'wel she saugh that it was for the beste' is shared by all three.

The celebrated Chaucerian 'ambiguity of tone', of which this passage might well be taken as an example, is often regarded as an equivocation between praise and blame, a confusion in our impulse to approve or disapprove. Complex the tone may be, but it does not lead to confusion if we read it aright. The complexity is often due, as it is in this case, to Chaucer's habit of fusing with the narrative account of an event or situation the differing emotional responses it would provoke—and with complete propriety—at different points in time. Different contexts of place and time allow and even demand quite different emotional and intellectual responses. In common experience we take this for granted; we find it entirely proper and natural that a widow should be consumed with grief at her husband's death and equally proper and natural that several years later she should have found equanimity. Time thus affects not only decorum, but also morality; were the widow to show at the time of her husband's death the reactions of a widow several years later, we should find her behaviour unfeeling and wrong. Chaucer's complexity arises from the fact that he encourages us to bring to bear our knowledge of both points in the process at the same time. He is helped in this by the fact that a story always abbreviates experience; the protracted time-scale of experience is condensed in the time-scale of the narrative, so that we can more easily and more swiftly achieve those shifts of perspective which are in life so laboriously accomplished. This is, of course, even more true in short narrative, because in such a narrative the disparity between the time-span of the occurrences and the time-span of the relation of them is most striking. Chaucer's interest in short narrative, the beginnings of which can be seen in the *Legend of Good Women*, and which finally achieved success in the *Canterbury Tales*, seems to me, therefore, to be a natural consequence of what he sees as interesting in human experience. The short narrative is a powerful way of provoking reflection on the process of change and of vitalizing our sense of the moral and emotional complications created by change, by our existence in the 'proces' of time. And a multiplicity of short narratives can suggest the multiple individual forms in which a common experience manifests itself, and the constitution of common experience out of a multiplicity of variant instances.

The processes of time and change are not all, however, a matter of the development of inner feeling; change, as we have already observed, can equally originate in the outer world—in its most dramatic form, in the kind of sudden chance or accident for which Chaucer uses the Middle English word 'aventure'. This is a word that can be used with deceptive casualness to refer to the most mundane and minimal sort of occurrence, but also, more emphatically, to refer to the strange and marvellous. The other words which Chaucer uses to mark the operations of chance are 'hap', 'cas' and 'grace', the last of these being usually reserved for *good* luck unless accompanied by an adjective like 'evil' or 'sory'. Chaucer's concern with the problems of chance, with human helplessness before it, and with the difficulties it opposes to any belief in the workings of a co-ordinating providence, is something that can be observed throughout his literary work. The operations of 'aventure' are often examined, (as they are in the "Franklin's Tale") in the sphere of love, and for good reason. The disruptive, involuntary, unforeseeable and unavoidable force of love is perhaps the most powerful reminder of the power of chance over human lives. What is more, it increases human vulnerability to other chances, as Dorigen, in her persistent fears for her husband's possible shipwreck on the 'grisly rokkes blakke', is only too well aware. What she at first fails to perceive is her possible vulnerability to an 'aventure' which is closer at hand: the 'aventure' of Aurelius' love for her.

> This lusty squier, servant to Venus,
> Which that ycleped was Aurelius,
> Hadde loved hire best of any creature
> Two yeer and moore, as was his aventure.

Chaucer's description of the wearing away of Dorigen's grief means that we can dimly see several possible patterns into which the coalescence of inner 'proces' and outer 'aventure' might fall. Were Arveragus' ship in fact, to be wrecked, we could visualize not only Dorigen's passionate grief but also its susceptibility to slow assuagement, so that when healing processes of time have done their work, Aurelius *might* hope at last to win his lady (as Palamon does). Or Arveragus might simply be forced to stay away so long that by the same process of imperceptible adaptation, Dorigen finds Aurelius a more vivid and powerful presence to her thoughts and feelings than her husband, and changes her initial rejection into acceptance—in which case the story would come closer to the pattern of *Troilus and Criseyde*. The openness of Chaucer's stories to other possible developments makes us aware that they are not fixed into inevitable patterns; like life itself, they are full of unrealized possibilities. In this case, the menace symbolized in the black rocks is not realized, and the other possibilities thus evaporate. 'Aventure' does not take the form of shipwreck and Arveragus returns. But that there is no other

kind of disaster is due also to the power of patience, of the ability to 'suffer' the shocks of 'aventure'.

In order to understand this conception of 'suffering' more fully, I should like to make some comparisons with another example of the genre to which the "Franklin's Tale" belongs, the Breton lay, a comparison which will have the incidental advantage of suggesting why Chaucer assigns the tale to this genre, even though his source was probably a tale of Boccaccio. The "Franklin's Prologue" suggests that the Breton lays are centrally concerned with 'aventures':

> Thise olde gentil Britouns in hir dayes
> Of diverse aventures maden layes . . .

The notion that this is the proper subject of the lays can be traced back to one of their earliest composers, the late twelfth-century writer Marie de France, who says that each lay was written to commemorate some 'aventure'. There is no direct evidence that Chaucer knew Marie's work, but a brief comparison with some aspects of the lay of *Guigemar* will help to illustrate the literary tradition which lies behind Chaucer's thinking on 'aventure', and also to understand the imaginative core of the "Franklin's Tale," the underlying pattern of experience which it shares with a lay like *Guigemar*. Like the "Franklin's Tale," *Guigemar* deals with 'aventure' in relation to love; it is interested both in the way that love is challenged by 'aventure', by the shocks of chance, and equally in the way that love itself *is* an 'aventure', a force which is sudden and overwhelming in its demands, and to which the only fitting response is surrender or commitment of the self. What we also find in Marie's lays is the idea that such a surrender acts as a release of power. It is this pattern—surrender to 'aventure' followed by release of power—which can be linked with the 'Patience conquers' of the "Franklin's Tale."

The hero of the lay, Guigemar, is a young man endowed with every good quality, but strangely resistant to love. One day while out hunting he shoots a white deer; the arrow rebounds and wounds him in the thigh, and the dying deer speaks to him, telling him that he will only be cured of this wound by a woman who will suffer for love of him greater pain and grief than any woman ever suffered, and that he will suffer equally for love of her. Guigemar's actions indicate an immediate and unquestioning acceptance of the doom laid on him by the deer. He invents an excuse for dismissing his squire, and rides off alone through the wood, not following any predetermined direction, but led by the path. That is, he follows not the dictates of his own wishes, but the dictates of chance. Eventually he comes to the sea, and finds a very rich and beautiful ship, entirely empty of people. Having boarded the ship, Guigemar finds in the middle of it a bed, sumptuously and luxuriously arrayed. The bed is an emblem of an invitation to rest, to relax, to surrender control—or rather to surrender it still further, since he in fact lost control at the moment when he shot the white deer. He climbs into the bed and falls asleep; the boat moves off of its own accord, taking him to the lady who is to be his love, and who is kept imprisoned by her jealous husband in a castle surrounded by a high walled garden, open only to the sea. The castle and the sea, and their relation to each other, are images that the tale endows with symbolic meaning. The sea (as often in medieval literature) is an image of flux or chance, of something vast and unpredictable which can carry one with the force of a tide or a current to strange harbours. The image of the imprisoning castle which is nonetheless open to the sea suggests the openness of even the most restrictive marriage relationship to the threat of 'aventure'. The jealous husband cannot shut out the power of chance; his marriage—and equally the generous marriage of the "Franklin's Tale"—must remain vulnerable to the assaults of chance.

Guigemar, in contrast, surrenders to the dictates of chance. When he wakes from his sleep on the boat, he finds himself in mid-ocean. Marie's comment on this situation brings a new extension to our notion of 'suffering'; she says

> Suffrir li estut l'aventure.

Both the infinitive 'suffrir' and the noun 'aventure' seem to call for a double translation here. 'Aventure' simply means, in the first place, 'What was happening'; but the word also emphasizes the strangeness and arbitrariness of the event, its lack of background in a chain of causes. 'Suffrir' seems to ask to be translated not only as 'suffer, endure', but also as 'allow', a usage now familiar to us only in archaic biblical quotations such as 'Suffer the little children to come unto me'. So that the line cannot be confined to a single interpretation: 'He had to endure / allow / what was happening / chance'. Guigemar prays to God for protection, and goes back to sleep, another acknowledgement that control is not in his hands. So it is in the surrender or abandon of sleep that he arrives at the lady's castle, is found by her, and becomes the object of her love.

Guigemar's 'suffering' can help with the understanding of the 'suffering' urged in the "Franklin's Tale:"

> Lerneth to suffre, or elles, so moot I goon,
> Ye shul it lerne, wherso ye wole or noon

This sort of 'suffering' is not simply a matter of enduring pain or vexation; it is a matter of 'allowing', of standing back to make room for, the operations of 'aventure', and thus of contributing to the creation of something new by allowing the natural process of change to work. It is the generous in spirit who do this, in both Marie's work and Chaucer's, and it is the mean-spirited, such as the lady's jealous husband, who vainly try to close off possibilities for change, to wall up what they have and to preserve it in a state of fixity.

It is a later moment in the lay, however, that provides the most powerful image of a surrender of the self which miraculously releases power. After Guigemar and the lady have enjoyed each other's love for some time, his presence is discovered by the lady's husband, and he is put back on to the magic ship (which has miraculously reappeared) and sent back to his own country. After his departure, the lady suffers intensely, and finally she cries out with passion that if only she can get out of the tower in which she is imprisoned, she will drown herself at the spot where Guigemar was put out to sea. As if in a trance, she rises, and goes to the door, where, amazingly, she finds neither key nor bolt, so that she can exit freely. The phrase that Marie uses is another that seems to call for a double translation:

> Fors s'en eissi par aventure.

'Par aventure' is a casual, everyday phrase, meaning simply 'by chance, as it happened'; thus on one level, all this line means is 'By chance she got out'. But the miraculous nature of the event, and the way that the phrase recalls the other miraculous 'aventure' of the ship, suggest something like 'By the power of "aventure", she got out'. The intensity of the lady's surrender to her grief, which is imaged in her wish to drown herself, to 'immerse' herself in her love and sorrow, magically transforms external reality. 'Aventure', which had earlier been a force that impinged on people and acted on them, here becomes something which is itself acted on by emotion, which miraculously responds to its pressure. When the lady goes down to the harbour she finds that the magic ship is once again there, so that instead of drowning herself, she boards it, and is carried away to an eventual reunion with Guigemar. Her readiness to 'suffer', the depth of her surrender, magically transforms her external situation and releases the power for a new departure. A surrender paradoxically creates power.

The surrender that leads to the release of power is also at the heart of the narrative in the "Franklin's Tale." It can be seen, first of all, in Arveragus' surrender of 'maistrye', which wins in return Dorigen's promise of truth and humility. Neither of them knows what their promises are committing them to, and it is precisely such ignorance that makes the commitments generous ones. But the underlying principle can operate in far less noble and generous situations, as Chaucer shows us by repeating such a pattern of reciprocal surrender in varying forms, through the rest of the *Canterbury Tales*. The most comic and 'realistic' version is to be found at the end of the "Wife of Bath's Prologue," in the quarrel provoked by the Wife's fifth husband, who insists on reading to her his 'book of wikked wives'. The Wife, in fury, tears three leaves from his book, and he knocks her down. With instinctive shrewdness, the Wife exploits the moral advantage that this gives her, and adopts a tone of suffering meekness.

> 'O! hastow slain me, false theef?' I seyde,
> 'And for my land thus hastow mordred me?
> Er I be deed, yet wol I kisse thee'.

Such a display of submissiveness elicits a matching submissiveness from the aghast Jankin, and he asks for forgiveness. The quarrel ends with the establishment of a relationship that follows, in its own more robust way, the pattern of that between Arveragus and Dorigen: the husband's surrender of 'governance' is met by unfailing truth and kindness on the part of his wife. The description of this reconciliation stays within the sphere of comic realism, however, not least because every gesture of surrender carries with it an accompanying gesture—albeit softened and muted—of self-assertiveness: the 'false theef' of the Wife's first speech; Jankin's excusing of himself for striking the blow by insisting that she provoked him; the Wife's final tap on his cheek to settle the score and make their kind of equality. The generosity here is a matter of letting these last little pieces of self-assertiveness pass, of 'allowing' them to be submerged in the larger movements of self-abasement which are being enacted. Such a comic-realistic version of the notion that surrendering power gives one back power enables us to see that although its operations may be 'magical' in the sense that they are not easy to rationalize, the roots of this principle lie in the everyday world of instinctive inter-

action between human beings. The fairyland world where wishes come true is not an alternative to this everyday experience, but a powerful image of its more mysterious aspects.

Such an image is offered us, of course, by the end of the Wife's tale, in the account of the working out of the relationship between the knight and the ugly old lady he has been forced to marry. After lecturing the knight on the value of age, ugliness and poverty, the old lady offers him a surprising choice: whether he will have her 'foul and old', but a 'trewe, humble wif', or whether he will have her 'yong and fair', and take the chance ('take the aventure') that others will compete to win her favours away from him. The knight's response is to make the choice over to her, to put himself in her 'wise governaunce', and the miraculous result of this is that the ugly old lady is transformed into a beautiful young one, who promises to be faithful in addition. As in the lay of *Guigemar*, a mental surrender has magical effects on physical reality. But the magical transformation in physical reality is the manifestation of an equally magical inward transformation which accompanies and causes it: the knight who began the tale with a particularly brutal assertion of masculine 'maistrye', the rape of a young girl, is transformed into a husband who humbly relinquishes control to his wife. What is more, he must accept that possession can never be complete in the sphere of human relations; to accept happiness is to accept the possibility of its loss, and to take a beautiful wife is to incur the risk of unhappiness at losing her ('Whoso wol han lief, he lief moot lete', as Criseyde puts it).

In the "Franklin's Tale," the magic has rather a different role to play. The magic does not bring about the dénouement of the tale: on the contrary, it creates the problem. The clerk from Orléans uses it to remove all the rocks from the coast of Brittany so that Aurelius may fulfil the apparently impossible condition for winning Dorigen's love. As Dorigen herself says of their removal: 'It is agains the proces of nature'. The magic is used to create an 'aventure'—a sudden, disruptive happening that interrupts the gradual rhythms of natural change. It is as an 'aventure' that the situation created by the removal of the rocks presents itself to Arveragus; he says to Dorigen, 'To no wight telle thou of this aventure.' But he has also told her, 'It may be wel, paraventure, yet today.' There is the same kind of 'hidden pun' in the qualifying 'paraventure' here as there is in Marie de France's use of the phrase. On the face of it, it simply means 'perhaps'. But it also suggests a deeper appeal to the power of chance—the power of 'aventure' which has created the problem and which has, therefore, also the power to resolve it *if* it is allowed to operate. Arveragus allows it; he stands back, as it were, to make room for it, subduing his own claims and wishes. The test of his relinquishment of 'maistrye' is that he must submit himself to his wife's independently-made promise so far that he is forced to order her to keep it; the test of Dorigen's promise to be a 'humble trewe wyf' is that she must obey her husband's command that she fulfil her independent promise to be unfaithful. The structure of their relationship at this point, therefore, is a poignant illustration of the simultaneity of 'lordshipe' and 'servage' which had earlier been described; each of the marriage-partners is following the will of the other and yet also acting out an assertion of self. And just as this moment in the tale provides an illustration of the fusion of 'lordshipe' and 'servage', so it provides an illustration of what is meant by the command 'Lerneth to suffre'. Arveragus 'suffers' in the double sense of enduring pain and 'allowing'; in bidding his wife to keep her promise, he provides a compelling example of patience in Chaucer's sense of the word, of adaptation to 'aventure', of allowing events to take their course. And he shows us very clearly that such an adaptation is not, as we might idly suppose, a matter of lethargy or inertia, of simply letting things drift. The easy course here would be to forbid Dorigen to go; Chaucer makes clear the agonizing effort that is required to achieve this adaptation.

> 'Trouthe is the hyeste thing that man may kepe.'
> But with that word he brast anon to wepe.

In this tale, as in *Guigemar*, a surrender to 'aventure' is met by a response of 'aventure'. In this case, it takes the form of the meeting between Dorigen and Aurelius, as she sets out to keep her promise. Chaucer emphasizes the chance nature of this meeting: Aurelius 'Of aventure happed hire to meete', he says, and a few lines later, 'thus they mette, of aventure or grace'. Yet nothing is more natural, since we are told that Aurelius was watching and waiting for Dorigen's departure. These comments point, therefore, not so much to the fact that this meeting is an amazing coincidence, as to the operation of 'aventure' within it. The intensity of Dorigen's surrender to the situation in which she has been trapped, perceptible in her anguished cry 'half as she were mad',

> 'Unto the gardin, as min housbonde bad,
> My trouthe for to holde, allas! allas!'

has a dramatic effect on Aurelius; it mediates to him Arveragus's surrender to 'aventure' and stimulates him to match that surrender with his own. He releases Dorigen from her promise and sends her back to her husband. He accepts the chance by which he has come too late, by which his love for Dorigen post-dates her marriage—one of the arbitrary cruelties of time—and having perceived the inner reality of the marriage, the firmness with which each is linked in obedience to the other in the very act of consenting to Dorigen's 'infidelity', Aurelius 'allows' that relationship its own being, undisturbed; he too exercises patience and 'suffers' it.

But what if he had not? What if he had insisted on the fulfilment of the promise? For if Chaucer is pointing to the power of chance in human lives, he is bound to acknowledge that chance might well have had it so. One critic who correctly observes the perilous ease with which either development could realize itself at this point has written a conclusion to the episode in which Aurelius does just that. The freedom and openness of events in the Chaucerian world means that romance is always open to turn into fabliau—or into tragedy. But I think that in this tale the nature of such a tragedy would be qualified by our sense that Aurelius would have 'enjoyed' Dorigen in only a very limited sense; his possession of her would have been as much a matter of 'illusion' and 'apparence' as the removal of the rocks that made it possible. The magic, in this tale, suggests the illusory, forced quality of Aurelius's power over Dorigen (in contrast to the natural power won by Arveragus, spontaneously springing into life at the end of the long process of his courtship). That is why the magic removal of the rocks is presented as a laborious, technologically complex operation, rather than the wave of a sorcerer's wand. The real magic in this tale is Aurelius's change of heart, which is as miraculous as that of the knight in the "Wife of Bath's Tale." The magic removal of the rocks is merely a means by which we can measure the immensity of this 'human magic'; we can gauge as it were, the size of the problem it is able to solve. And this 'human magic' is nothing other than the human power to change. What the development of the tale brings to our notion of the human tendency to change is that it is not just an everyday, humdrum matter of our moods fluctuating with the passage of time, but that it is a source of power; its role can be creative.

As I have already suggested, Chaucer is well aware of the tragic aspects of the human propensity to change, as his constant preoccupation with the theme of betrayal shows. He is also aware of the saving power of human resilience, a sort of comic version of patience, which can nullify the tragic aspects of 'aventure'; thus beside the serious transformation of the rapist knight in the "Wife of Bath's Tale" we can set the figure of Pluto in the "Merchant's Tale," the ravisher who has clearly been worn down by feminine rhetoric so that he presents the ludicrous picture of a henpecked rapist. Romances such as the tales of the Knight and Franklin, however, offer us a serious celebration of patience, of the creative power of change. 'Pitee' may be the quality that leads Criseyde's emotions away from Troilus to Diomede, or it may be ironically appealed to as the cause of May's amazing readiness to respond to Damian's advances ("Merchant's Tale"), but it is also the quality that enables Theseus to adapt himself to each new claim that chance events impose on him ("Knight's Tale"), or that leads Dorigen to accept Arveragus' suit, and it is 'routhe' (another word for pity) that leads Aurelius to release Dorigen. Moreover, as the passage on patience makes clear, the responsiveness implied in the ideals of patience and 'pitee' must be exercised continually; the balance and poise achieved at the end of the "Franklin's Tale" is reached by a 'proces', a chain of ceaseless adjustment in which the magician-clerk, as well as the other three figures, must play his part. Ceaseless adjustment is, as we saw, something that characterizes the marriage, with its endless alternation of 'lordshipe' and 'servage', and it is for that reason that it can survive 'aventure'; it is founded on it. Only through ceaseless change can there be stability. Only through a perpetual readiness to adapt, to change, in each of the actors in the tale, can the status quo be preserved. Or, in Chaucerian language, 'trouthe' is the product of patience.

Chaucer's strength is that he gives us a creative sense of order; he makes us aware that static formulae, of whatever nature—the husband's sovereignty, equality in marriage—are inappropriate to human beings, since they are subject to change from within and chance from without. What is needed instead is an ideal such as the ideal of patience, which is founded on change, on the perpetual readiness to meet, to accept and to transform the endless and fluctuating succession of 'aventures' that life offers.

Source: Jill Mann, "Chaucerian Themes and Style in the 'Franklin's Tale,'" in *Medieval Literature: Chaucer and the Alliterative Tradition*, edited by Boris Ford, Penguin Books, 1982, pp. 133–53.

Carolyn P. Collette

In the following essay, Collette contends that the Prioress exhibits a "sensibility that dwells on the small, the particular . . . as a means of arousing deep emotional response."

Chaucer's Prioress has been the subject of lively literary debate for the better part of the twentieth century. Not content to let her go, in the words of Cummings's poem, "into the now of forever," modern critics have insisted that Madame Eglentyne face the now of the twentieth century and answer for her faults. Critics have reproved her vanity, chastized her worldliness, shaken their heads over her exaggerated sensibility, and even explored the hidden anal-sadistic focus of her tale. Where, we might ask, in all of this is Chaucer's Prioress? The answer may lie in the fact that Chaucer's fashionable Prioress and her *litel* tale were more fashionable than most modern critics realize. Her concern with emotion, tenderness, and the diminutive are part of the late fourteenth-century shift in sensibility, which, following the so-called triumph of nominalism, produced the flowering of English mysticism, a highly particularized, emotional style in the arts, and the ascendancy of the heart over the reason in religious matters. In both her portrait and her tale the Prioress reflects these developments as she focuses on the physical, tangible, often diminutive—mice, dogs, and little children—as objects of her "tendre herte" and symbols of her understanding of Christian doctrine; the same attitudes and assumptions about the centrality of the heart and of the emotions dominate her use of the rhyme royal stanza in one of the most sensitively orchestrated narrations of the tales, wedding form and content absolutely. Because the Prioress's sensibility is the product of Chaucer's craft and of late medieval attitudes about religion, God, and man's relationship to God, it might be useful to review what is already common knowledge about late medieval culture before looking closely at her tale.

In literary criticism, art history, or historical analysis of the mid-to late-fourteenth century one hears sounded again and again the note of ritual and the ascendancy of the emotional over the rational. Obviously a simplification of a complex process not restricted to that century, this shift in emphasis produces the impression that the late Middle Ages valued emotion—intense, devout, almost sensual, religious emotion—as man's surest path to the knowledge of God. The reasons for such a stress remain obscure, too complicated to explore in a paper devoted to a reading of a single tale. Suffice it to repeat what is already well known, that the "triumph of nominalism," as David Knowles calls the Ockhamite revolution in medieval thought, denied the possibility of rational demonstrations of the truths of natural religion, while at the same time it declared God's revelations to be arbitrary, to be accepted without comment or explanation: " . . . Nominalism under the guise of a devout humility, left the door open for agnosticism or incredulity as well as for a fideistic acceptance of religious teaching." Charles Musçatine characterizes the thought of the age in a similar fashion: "The cleavage between reason and faith, characteristic of post-Ockhamite thought, not only generated an unsettling scepticism, but also drove faith itself further and further into the realm of the irrational."

One senses such a reaction in the mystics' intense concentration on Christ's passion and the love it manifests. Richard Rolle, writing in the earlier part of the century, stresses the power of love in his poem "Love is Life," communicating the mystery of divine love through a rhetoric of emotion and human love: "Luf rauysches Cryst intyl owr hert . . . "; "Lere to luf, if þou wyl lyfe when þou sall hethen fare"; "Luf es Goddes derlyng; luf byndes blode and bane." Julian of Norwich, writing in the last third of the century, sounds the same theme in her *Revelations of Divine Love*, as she uses the now famous image of the hazelnut to symbolize the tender, all-encompassing nature of God's love which marks even the smallest and humblest of creation as miraculous. "What is this?" she asks, answering, "It is all that is made . . . In short, everything owes its existence to the love of God." She underscores the universal significance of the hazelnut, perceiving and wishing us to perceive the miracle of God's universe, the miracle of the macrocosm, in that small, particular form. She writes, "In this 'little thing' I saw three truths. The first is that God made it; the second is that God loves it; the third is that God sustains it."

One finds a similar emphasis on the apprehension of divine mysteries through concentration on the small, particular elements of our world, and through the power of love, in countless late fourteenth-century lyrics. In hymns to the Virgin and songs of the Virgin, the physical element manifests itself in increased tenderness and in the depiction of Mary's relation to Christ in the intensely human terms of a mother's love for an infant child. A song of the Virgin in Harley MS. 7322 typifies the late fourteenth-century conception of the physical bases

> *The child's martyrdom and explanation are emblems of the sort of faith the Prioress espouses—ritualistic, rooted in phenomena perceptible in this world, intensely emotional.*

of the relationship. The Virgin addresses her infant son not as the savior of the world, the Godhead incarnate, but as a child, vulnerable to earthly suffering:

> Iesu, swete, beo noth wroþ,
> þou ich nabbe clout ne cloþ
> þe on for to folde,
> þe on to folde ne to wrappe . . .

The poem ends with an image both surprising and effective, for it drives home the physical basis of their relationship while it stresses human love and vulnerability over omnipotence and divinity: "Bote ley þou þi fet to my pappe, / And wite þe from þe colde."

We see equivalent processes in art of the period. Ockham's *Via Moderna* emphasized that all men could know surely was the experiential, the particular, that which one could comprehend through the senses. Emile Mâle traces the development of stylistic tendencies in art at the end of the Middle Ages, tying these new styles to this change in sensibility and outlook which social historians of the period regard as one of its hallmarks:

> From the end of the thirteenth century on, the artists seem no longer able to grasp the great conceptions of earlier times. Before, the Virgin enthroned held her Son with the sacerdotal gravity of the priest holding the chalice. She was the seat of the All-Powerful, 'the throne of Solomon,' in the language of the doctors. She seemed neither woman nor mother, because she was exalted above the sufferings and joys of life. She was the one whom God had chosen at the beginning of time to clothe His word with flesh. She was the pure thought of God. As for the Child, grave, majestic, hand raised, He was already the Master Who commands and Who teaches.

This conception, however, disappears. What replaces it is intense human tenderness captured in gestures between the Virgin and Christ. The forms no longer symbolize intellectual conceptions but exist in and for themselves. In contemplating the tenderness between the Virgin and Child we comprehend the nature of love. The art is no longer metaphor, or vehicle, but the image, the focus; it no longer symbolizes, it is. Fourteenth-century art, more particularized, often more highly detailed than twelfth- and thirteenth-century art, focuses on scenes, on moments that speak to the heart.

In both the form and content of her narrative the Prioress, by concentrating on the diminutive, on the detail, not so much for its symbolic significance, but for its emotional value, gives literary expression to the attitudes and assumptions we have traced in religion and art. Her portrait has been treated too often and too thoroughly to be reviewed here, except to note that its major elements—her concern with manners and outward form, the court cheer she "peyned her" to copy, her tender conscience, and the rosary beads with the dependent motto, *Amor vincit omnia*—are all typical of and consonant with the patterns we have been tracing. In her concern with the small, with the particular, with the emotional, the Prioress is unquestionably a woman of "fashion."

It is often said that the *"General Prologue"* tells us very little of the Prioress's inner spiritual state, very little of her comprehension of the mysteries involved in her sacred vocation. We wonder about a woman whose conscience and charity work through a concern for mice and dogs, and whose apparent interest in sacred liturgy is the song, not the substance. The sensible world, and an immediate response to it, rather than any abstract philosophy, seems to form the basis of her faith. Apparently for the Prioress the wide, deep spirit of forgiveness of the Gospels and the charity implicit in the doxology become real in the physical expression of love and conscience between herself and the small creatures that surround her. Mâle speaks of the influence of St. Francis on religious thought in the later Middle Ages; the Prioress's "conscience and tendre herte" follow in that tradition.

In any case, in all that she appears to be and does as a nun, the outward, physical sign is foremost, the substance of her religion either misunderstood or, more likely, reduced in scale and dimension to the humanly comprehensible, the emotionally appealing. Her tale reflects the same tendency. As a result, in both the *"Prologue"* and the *"Tale"* itself the mysteries of Christianity appear to us refracted through a lens of motherhood. Mary the mother of Christ is the subject of the *"Prologue."* The Prioress, who seems to worship a God who is to be identified above all as the Son of Mary, refers to herself as like "a child of twelf month oold, or lesse, / That kan unnethes any word expresse." The *"Tale,"* set against a chronological background of the three seasons of the Christian year devoted to the nativity—Advent, Christmas, and Epiphany—turns on the learning of an anthem to the Virgin, an anthem especially appropriate to these seasons, an anthem devoted to the mother of the Redeemer. The Prioress refers repeatedly to the martyr as the "litel child" and to the Virgin as "Christes mooder," in effect recalling our attention to the Nativity, to the humanity of Christ as the means of approaching the greater mysteries of the incarnation and salvation. Mary in her motherhood helps man to understand the love of the Father and of the Son. She is the bridge. At the end of the tale her experience of earthly, maternal love is reflected in the words she speaks to the child, words generations of mothers have spoken: "Be nat agast, I wol thee nat forsake." In these words we can hear Christ's own promise, "Lo, I am with you always."

Set in the proverbial long ago and far away of "a greet citee" in Asia, the tale is introduced almost as a fable, a romance. There is no effort to create a realistic setting, no attention to the possibilities and inevitabilities of life in such a place. The Jews in the Jewry are shadowy, not real. With the myopia characteristic of her approach to life and religion, the Prioress focuses on the center of the tale, that which for her does have reality, the "wydwes sone" who will be the martyred child-hero and in so dying will become an example for us of true love and devotion. We are told that this child is a student in a school as vaguely presented as the Jewry and the city, indeed as vague as the whole continent of Asia is for the Prioress; what is accomplished in the school we do not know, what is learned we are not told, except that the scholars

> . . . lerned in that scole yeer by yere
> Swich manere doctrine as men used there,
> This is to seyn, to syngen and to rede,
> As smale children doon in hire childhede.

Even the widowed mother is in the background at this point. What we remember of this child, this "litel clergeon," is his smallness; he is young, *sely*. His youth is emphasized by the repeated stress on the word *child:* "As smale children doon in hire childhede." There is an active, particular imagination here that responds to and can visualize the minute.

The child's youthful curiosity and his natural reverence for the Virgin, a reverence fostered by his own devoted mother, lead him to inquire about a song he hears his elder classmate sing, *Alma Redemptoris Mater*. In that exquisitely pictured and phrased stanza where the Prioress describes the child listening to the song we see a visual, metaphorical representation of the approach to God typical of the late fourteenth century—the heart is touched while the reason is bypassed; the soul seeks that which nourishes it:

> And as he dorste, he drough hym ner and ner,
> And herkned ay the wordes and the noote,
> Til he the firste vers koude al by rote.

Time here is virtually suspended as we see him, childlike, creeping closer and closer to that which for him has a magnetic attraction, the song in praise of the Virgin. For the Prioress what is real here is the child and his natural affinity for religious beauty; she responds to and asks us to respond to the same elements. When the little child asks about the meaning of the song, his *felawe* tells him it is of the Virgin, but that he cannot say more of its significance: "I lerne song, I kan but smal grammeere." That line and the child's determination to learn the song, come what may, by rote, are the heart of the tale and the key to both it and the Prioress. One cannot escape the fundamental parallel between her religious practices and the children's attitude toward the song. To *lerne* the song, the outward, by rote, not to gain a full understanding, but in order to manifest praise and love, is for her, if not for us, an emblem of true, innocent faith. She seems to take literally Christ's words, "Except ye be converted and become as little children, ye shall not enter into the kingdom of heaven."

The child, in his innocence, which is stressed throughout, sings the song on his way home through the Jewry, where Satan inspires certain Jews to plot to destroy him. It is in these stanzas, through the contrast they present between what precedes and what follows them, that we see how effectively the Prioress manipulates the stanzaic form of her tale to stress emotion. Up to this point, each stanza has been a separate unit devoted to presenting and exploring an idea. For example, the stanza about the child's creeping closer to hear the song achieves its effect largely because its periodicity encloses a discursive, detailed account of a simple action:

> This litel child, his litel book lernynge,
> As he sat in the scole at his prymer,
> He *Alma redemptoris* herde synge,
> As children lerned hire antiphoner;

> And as he dorste, he drough hym ner and ner,
> And herkned ay the wordes and the noote,
> Til he the firste vers koude al by rote.

The stanza images for us the sweet faith of the child, opening our hearts to his youth and his innocent devotion.

Those stanzas devoted to the Jews' motivation, action, and punishment are handled differently; each line is a unit, each line a new thought. In effect each stanza contains seven times as much "action" as the stanzas devoted to the child:

> Fro thennes forth the Jues han conspired
> This innocent out of this world to chace.
> An homycide therto han they hyred,
> That in an aleye hadde a privee place;
> And as the child gan forby for to pace,
> This cursed Jew hym hente, and heeld hym faste,
> And kitte his throte, and in a pit hym caste.

> I seye that in a wardrobe they hym threwe
> Where as thise Jewes purgen hire entraille.
> O cursed folk of Herodes al newe,
> What may youre yvel entente yow availle?
> Mordre wol out, certeyn, it wol nat faille,
> And namely ther th'onour of God shal sprede;
> The blood out crieth on youre cursed dede.

The Prioress's narrative technique dwells on devices directed at our emotions. In the next stanza the focus shifts to the child-martyr. Sonorous "o's" slow the movement, calling our attention to the mystery of his martyrdom:

> O martir, sowded to virginitee,
> Now maystow syngen, folwynge evere in oon
> The white Lamb celestial—quod she—
> Of which the grete evaungelist, Seint John,
> In Pathmos wroot, which seith that they that goon
> Biforn this Lamb, and synge a song al newe,
> That nevere, flesshly, wommen they ne knewe.

The next truly visual part of the tale, the next scene to bear the stamp of the Prioress's true interest, is the exquisite passage devoted to the mother's search for her son. Obviously the mother-child relationship parallels the Virgin-Christ relationship. It calls to mind the most human aspect of the most ineffable, mystical relation the world has known, the love of a virgin-mother for a God-child. No hint of that mystery appears here; what does appear is the closest human equivalent—deep emotion. In a tale so short, apparently so formal, the Prioress leads herself and her audience to a double pitch of emotion, both at the end of the tale, as we should expect, and also just beyond mid point:

> This poure wydwe awaiteth al that nyght
> After hir litel child, but he cam noght;
> For which, as soone as it was dayes lyght,
> With face pale of drede and bisy thoght,
> She hath at scole and elleswhere hym soght,

Til finally she gan so fer espie
That he last seyn was in the Juerie.

With moodres pitee in hir brest enclosed,
She gooth, as she were half out of hir mynde,
To every place where she hath supposed
By liklihede hir litel child to fynde;
And evere on Cristes mooder meeke and kynde
She cride, and atte laste thus she wroghte:
Among the cursed Jues she hym soghte.

It is as if she meant us to experience the religious significance of her tale through the same intense, emotional reaction she obviously has to the action of her own story. In this effect the rhyme royal stanza, intensely expressive in its inherent periodicity, works as part of the story, not just as form, but as form become content. The sound echoes the sense as emotion builds through each line of the stanza. In the beginning the two adjectives, *poure* and *litel*, used to describe the widow and her son, catch our attention. Our sympathies are aroused as they would be if we, too, saw the defenseless and helpless suffering. The Prioress's narrative style plays on these sympathies—through the grammatical structure which saves till the end of the first clause the fact "but he cam noght," and hurries in the third line, in a verbal foreshadowing of the distress and anxiety tearing at the mother's heart. Finally, near desperation, she discovers that he was last seen in the Jewry. She does not act on that knowledge, though. It is as if she wanted to ignore the dreadful news and its implicit horror. Psychologically valid, the continuing search also allows the Prioress simultaneously to develop our emotional response and to direct it toward a religious subject. The second stanza begins by focusing our attention on what is central, the emotional state of the mother; she becomes through the first line an emblem of all suffering mothers, of Rachel crying after her lost children, but especially of the Virgin mourning her crucified son. While the scene culminates both with the end of the search and the cry of help to the Virgin, *meek* and *kynde*, it seems clear that the Prioress sees the Virgin here less as queenly intercessor than as a mother; that, for this moment at least, Mary comes to mind because she, too, suffered the pain of losing a child. In short, the Prioress's primary focus here is on emotion, only secondarily on Christian doctrine.

The miracle, much like the miracle of Christ's resurrection, occurs in the Jewry. The Prioress's account instructs us both about the God who creates the miracle and about her conception of that God:

O grete God, that parfournest thy laude
By mouth of innocentz, lo, heere thy myght!
This gemme of chastite, this emeraude,

And eek of martirdom the ruby bright,
Ther he with throte ykorven lay upright;
He *Alma Redemptoris* gan to synge
So loude that al the place gan to rynge.

The God of Abraham and Joseph, the God of mercy and justice, becomes the God of innocents who reveals his might through the lowly. One might well infer here the lesson that Christianity teaches, that this God, being all-powerful, is so loving that He humbles himself. One might well infer, as critics have done, that the Prioress's humility stems from this divine example. Yet, typically, the focus of this miracle is not on God's divine power or His infinite humility. The focus is on the little boy himself. The child is imaged in those brilliant hues one so often associates with manuscript illumination; the gems here signify the refraction of the pure white light of God. In the midst of the miracle what emerges as central is not God but the child's perfect, albeit uncomprehending, faith. The grandeur of this miracle lies not in God's awful power but in the little boy's touching song. The effect, not the cause, is central; our attention is once more directed to the physical, the emotional, rather than to the grand conception behind the action of the tale.

By the same token the treatment of the Jews in the tale is also subordinated to the central point, the child. The Prioress, whose vision focuses always on the small, the physical, whose heart is touched by the tenderness of the story of the child-martyr, whose idea of God, Christ, and the Virgin is shaded in terms of sentiment and pity, simply does not regard the Jews in any thinking fashion. The Jews are not real in any living sense, certainly not as the child and his mother are real, invested with emotions and personalities. The Jews are part of the plot, the necessary background of her story; they are but pale shadows beside the overwhelming reality of the little child. Like the setting in Asia they are a convenient backdrop, a catalyst necessary for the central action, the child's demonstration of innocent faith and the Virgin's maternal devotion to those who turn to her. Compare the treatment of the child with the treatment of the Jews:

This child with pitous lamentacioun
Up taken was, syngynge his song alway,
And with honour of greet processioun
They carien hym unto the nexte abbay.
His mooder swownynge by the beere lay;
Unnethe myghte the peple that was theere
This newe Rachel brynge fro his beere.

The descriptive, metaphorical quality here stands in sharp contrast to the almost aphoristic, matter-of-fact tone used to describe the fate of the Jews:

> With torment and with shameful deeth echon
> This provost dooth thise Jewes for to sterve
> That of this mordre wiste, and that anon.
> He nolde no swich cursednesse observe.
> "Yvele shal have that yvele wol deserve";
> Therfore with wilde hors he dide hem drawe,
> And after that he heng hem by the lawe.

The natural periodicity of the stanza form here builds not to a climax but falls flat. The description of the Jews' punishment creates the impression of reason, deliberateness, and inevitability. "He nolde," "therfore," "and after that" are the three phrases which encapsulate the sequential nature of the summary justice they receive. Of course the Prioress may mean deliberately to denigrate the Jews by using such a flat style to describe their ends, but Chaucer, behind both tale and teller, may mean to tell us something about the speaker. Indeed the simplicity of the Prioress's world view, implicit in her apparently unthinking adoption of the motto *Amor vincit omnia*, surfaces here in her phraseology. The provost "with torment and with shameful deeth" put the Jews who knew of the murder to death. Love may conquer all, but it is love of a particular sort, not the light of charity, but a narrow beam directed at the child. The rest of the world may suffer as it must.

In the bier scene the Prioress reveals the effect of the child's holiness. When the Abbot asks him how he can continue to sing, "Sith that thy throte is kut to my semynge", the emphasis both in his question and in our understanding of the story is on the physical phenomenon. The little martyr responds with an explanation that, in its dwelling on detail, echoes the question, calling our attention to the sad end of his physical body:

> "My throte is kut unto my nekke boon,"
> Seyde this child, "and, as by wey of kynde,
> I sholde have dyed, ye, longe tyme agon.
> But Jesu Crist, as ye in bookes fynde,
> Wil that his glorie laste and be in mynde,
> And for the worship of his Mooder deere
> Yet may I synge *O Alma* loude and cleere."

The child's martyrdom and explanation are emblems of the sort of faith the Prioress espouses—ritualistic, rooted in phenomena perceptible in this world, intensely emotional. The child's suffering, martyrdom, and death, as well as the faith which originally prompted him to learn the song by rote, lead our souls to God. He is the channel both for us and for the Prioress, whose religion is one of approaching God through the sensible manifestations of His love. Like fourteenth-century statues and illuminations, the child's martyrdom is not a static, intellectual ikon, a symbol to be understood, but a moving, temporal image which we contemplate with emotion and through which we come to understand in our hearts if not our heads the message of Christianity.

As the Abbot removes the grain from the child's tongue, the little boy's soul ascends and the Abbot's tears fall. The child's innocent faith overcomes and instructs even the convent. In two lines which seem almost to relish the prostration of the monk, the Prioress says, "And gruf he fil al plat upon the grounde, / And stille he lay as he had ben ybounde." Before the example of the boy's faith holy men fall down, and, like the convent, weep. The point of the story, then, is the power of emotion, of touching, overwhelming emotion exemplified by the child's faith and by the martyrdom of his "litel body sweete." The Prioress seems almost overcome by her own tale as she concludes "Ther he is now, God leve us for to meete!", yet hurries on to appeal to the *auctoritee* of Hugh of Lincoln as well as to pray for his intercession, finally concluding with the hope that Christ will grant us His mercy for his mother's sake. In her final appeal to Hugh of Lincoln she tries to ground the tale in fact, to remove it from the realm of the emotional, from the distant world where it takes place. It is as if the Prioress were saying, "And this is all true, as you know, because you all know about Hugh of Lincoln." Try as she might to fix the tale in physical, historical reality by such allusions, the story she tells is still a miracle story, preeminently suited to her own outlook and to the religious fashion of the time. Of all the sorts of religious tales the Prioress could tell, surely the miracle story is the one least rational, most suited to the assumptions and attitudes of late fourteenth-century religion in its revelation of a God so arbitrary, so powerful, that He can and does suspend the operation of His own natural laws. What is left to the Prioress and to us is to worship Him as best we can. For the Prioress such worship involves two touchstones—emotion and the Virgin Mary, the hand-maiden of the Trinity.

In retrospect one remembers the Prioress best for her motto, *Amor vincit omnia*. The words seem especially fitted to be her creed once we consider the dynamics of her tale and its relation to the spirit of art and religion we may suppose she came in contact with. What Chaucer meant to suggest in the person of the Prioress we cannot know for sure. To discover that this woman, so careful to do the "right" thing, had also developed a "fashionable" sensibility leaves unanswered the larger question of Chaucer's attitude toward that sensibility. What we can say is that her tale in both its theme and structure reflects late fourteenth-century ideas, that the Prioress's stress on love, emotion, and pity are all consonant with what we might call a fashion in religious taste. If we accept her on these terms, we find that, odd and inconsistent as the tale seems in its excessive pity for the child and its disregard for the Jews, there is yet a consistent sensibility behind it, a sensibility that dwells on the small, the particular, not as a symbol or even as a type but as a means of arousing deep emotional response; this sensibility also seeks wherever possible to understand the divine through the human; moreover, this sensibility is myopic in its tendency to select and focus on only that narrow range of experience which satisfies it. In all these ways, then, the sense of the "Prioress's Tale" lies in the Prioress's sensibility.

Source: Carolyn P. Collette, "Sense and Sensibility in "The Prioress's Tale,'" in *Chaucer Review*, Vol. 15, No. 2, Fall 1981, pp. 138–50.

Robert W. Hanning

In the following essay, Hanning compares "The Knight's Tale" with epics by Boccaccio and Statius to gain a greater understanding of the themes of nobility and order in the poem.

There is perhaps no better illustration of the processes of continuity and change in medieval literature than the relationship between Geoffrey Chaucer's "Knight's Tale" (1386?), first of the *Canterbury Tales*, and its literary antecedents, both proximate—Giovanni Boccaccio's *Teseida delle nozze d'Emilia* (ca. 1340)—and remote—the *Thebaid of Statius* (ca. 92 AD). Moreover, a comparison of Chaucer's poem with Statius's epic and Boccaccio's epic romance offers important clues to the meaning of one of the most problematic tales in the Canterbury collection.

To Boccaccio and Chaucer, and to medieval authors generally, Statius was *the* authority on the fall of Thebes, one of the most traumatic events of classical legend. Charles Muscatine, in the most influential, and perhaps the finest recent assessment of the "Knight's Tale," states, "the history of Thebes had perpetual interest for Chaucer as an example of the struggle between noble designs and chaos," a struggle which Muscatine finds at the heart of the tale. According to Muscatine, "the noble life . . . is itself the subject of the poem and the object of its philosophical questions", and the man-

ifestations of that life, "its dignity and richness, its regard for law and decorum, are all bulwarks against the ever-threatening forces of chaos, and in constant collision with them." In this reading, the significance of the "Knight's Tale" lies in Theseus' "perception of the order beyond chaos," revealed in his final speech urging a distraught Palamon and Emelye to marry, despite their grief at the death of Arcite, and thus to conform to the scheme of the universe's "Firste Moevere." As Muscatine puts it, "when the earthly designs suddenly crumble, true nobility is faith in the ultimate order of all things."

The present essay responds to Muscatine's analysis of the "Knight's Tale" in two ways. First, it examines two main sources of Chaucer's attitude toward Thebes, in order to confirm the contention that the English poet found in Boccaccio and Statius models for "the struggle between noble designs and chaos"—found, that is, a tradition of concern with the tense relationship between the human capacity to control and order life and the forces, internal and external, that resist or negate order. But if Chaucer is profoundly traditional in composing the "Knight's Tale," he is also profoundly original in telling it not *in propria voce*, but as the utterance of "a worthy man" and "a verray par-fit gentil knyght"—an exponent of the "noble life" of chivalry as Chaucer and his age knew it. By putting the Knight between us and the world of Theseus, Palamon, Arcite, and Emelye, Chaucer invites us to see the conflict of order and disorder as a reflection of the Knight's particular perspective on life. The "Knight's Tale" thus becomes simultaneously a comment on the possibilities for order in human life and a comment on the tensions Chaucer perceived within the system of late medieval chivalry. Further, since the Knight makes us painfully aware of his difficulties as an amateur story-teller, Chaucer innovates again in inviting us to equate Theseus' problems in seeking to control the realm of experience with his pilgrim-creator's trials in seeking to control the realm of art. The coincidence of problems faced by Duke, gentil knight, and poet makes the "Knight's Tale" an even more complex and original poem than its most perceptive critics have noticed. Accordingly, an assessment of the tension between the Tale's levels of meaning will constitute my second, more revisionist response to Muscatine's thesis.

I

The *Thebaid* recounts the fratricidal war between Oedipus's sons, Polynices and Eteocles, for the throne of Thebes. Its twelfth and last book contains the germ of Boccaccio's *Teseida*, and thus of the "Knight's Tale." In the twelfth book, after the brothers have destroyed each other in a final, emblematic single combat, Creon, their uncle and now ruler of Thebes, forbids burial rites for Polynices and the Greek warriors who beseiged the city with him. The grief-stricken widows of the unburied, outraged at the sacrilegious edict but powerless to contest it, are advised by a Theban soldier to turn to Theseus, ruler of Athens, for succor. The greater part of Book Twelve comprises a double action attendant upon Creon's prohibition and the widows' response. Spurred on by desperation, Argia, the Greek widow of Polynices, and Antigone, Polynices' sister, attempt to perform funeral rites for the slain prince, defying the edict. They find the body and put it on a pyre with another, half-consumed corpse who turns out to be none other than Eteocles. Implacable foes in death as in life, the brothers resist the joint immolation; the fire divides into warring tongues of flame while the women watch in helpless terror. The posthumous struggle shakes the pyre, and the noise arouses Creon's guards, who apprehend Argia and Antigone and bring them before Creon to be executed—victims, it would seem, of yet another grotesque manifestation of the curse on the house of Cadmus. Meanwhile, the rest of the widows journey to Athens, where, under Juno's tutelage, they win the sympathy of the Athenians and encounter Theseus as he returns in triumph from Scythia, victor over the Amazons and lord of Hippolyta. He learns the cause of the widows' sorrow and, his army swollen by recruits enraged at Creon's behavior, sets out for Thebes. Creon learns of Theseus' arrival as he prepares to punish Argia and Antigone; despite his speech of defiance, his troops are no match for Theseus, who seeks out and dispatches the Theban tyrant. The epic ends on a muted note of grief and resignation as the widows perform the obsequies for their men.

The *Thebaid* offers a dark view of life, shaped as it is by a legend that stresses the inescapable destiny which destroys a family and leads to fratricidal wrath between its protagonists. Yet the last act of the epic incorporates a movement back from the abyss of rage and destruction, and toward a reestablishment of civilized control over the darker impulses that have reigned throughout. Theseus, whose intervention saves Argia and Antigone and allows the fallen warriors to have the funeral rites owed them by heroic society, represents the belated, partial, but real triumph of civilization over passion, both at Thebes and in Scythia. The image of Hippolyta, brought back to Athens in triumph

> *The 'Knight's Tale' thus becomes simultaneously a comment on the possibilities for order in human life and a comment on the tensions Chaucer perceived within the system of late medieval chivalry."*

by Theseus, sums up his achievement and his function in the epic's economy: "Hippolyta too drew all toward her, friendly now in look and patient of the marriage-bond. With hushed whispers and sidelong gaze the Attic dames marvel that she has broken her country's austere laws, that her locks are trim, and all her bosom hidden beneath her robe, that though a barbarian she mingles with mighty Athens, and comes to bear offspring to her foemanlord." Every detail of this striking portrait testifies to the subduing of wildness by its opposite. The Amazon queen, sworn to enmity toward men, accustomed to flaunting her freedom from male (and social) restraint by her flowing hair, her dress with its one exposed breast (an affront to canons of feminine modesty), and her fierce demeanor, has become a neat, proper, smiling wife and mother-to-be. And as Theseus has tamed the savage Amazon, so will he tame the sacrilegious Creon, rescue Argia and Antigone from being punished for wishing to perform the rituals by which civilization imposes order even on death, and permit the comfort of those rituals to all the bereaved.

Of course, Theseus paradoxically quells rage and violence by unleashing his own, righteous wrath. In his speech to his soldiers as they set out for Thebes, he declares that they fight in a just cause, and against the Furies, emblems of primal chaos; then he hurls his spear and dashes forth on the road to the rage-torn city. This is no statesmanship of sweetness and light, but the sanctioned unleashing of irresistible energy to assure the triumph of "terrarum leges et mundi foedera"—the laws of nations and the covenants of the world. A similar ambivalence hovers over Theseus' shield, on which is portrayed the hero binding the Minotaur on Crete, yet another emblem of terrifying force subjugated by a greater and more licit violence. All of these deeds of conquest take place away from home—in Scythia, at Thebes, on Crete; Athens, like the Rome of Virgil and Statius, remains the peaceful center of civilization, where mourning women are instructed by Juno in the proper decorum of grief, and where there is a temple dedicated to Clementia, the spirit of mildness and forgiveness.

Despite Theseus' authority and easy victory over Creon, there is still no erasing the terrible memory of the death and destruction which fate and the gods have rained down on Thebes throughout the epic, nor can any image of rage subdued by civilization—not even the domesticated Hippolyta—match for sheer evocative power the horror of that moment when the charred remains of Polynices and Eteocles continue in death the fratricidal fury that ruined their lives. Statius's vision of the noble life offers as its highest realization the double-tongued flame and trembling pyre, and the hysterical pleas of Argia and Antigone that the rage cease before it compels them to leap into the flames to separate the brothers. It was to such a pessimistic vision that Boccaccio, and later Chaucer, responded in taking up the poetic challenge of the *Thebaid*.

II

Writing over twelve hundred years after Statius, Giovanni Boccaccio undertook in the *Teseida* to compose the first martial epic in Italian. He placed epic formulae of invocation at the beginning of the poem, and equally conventional addresses to his book and to the Muses at its conclusion; he imitated epic structure (the *Teseida*, like the *Aeneid* and the *Thebaid*, has twelve books) and diction, reinforcing the latter by some nearly verbatim translations from Statius. But if, in all these ways, Boccaccio self-consciously donned the epic mantle, he also brought to his encounter with Statius literary sensibilities formed by medieval courtly romance and lyric, and thereby created in the *Teseida* a new, hybrid version of the noble life. Boccaccio's eclecticism declares itself at the poem's beginning; he will tell of "the deeds of Arcita and of Palemone the good, born of royal blood, as it seems, and both Thebans; and although kinsmen, they came into conflict by their excessive love for Emilia, the beautiful Amazon . . ." The fate of a love affair, not a city, provides a suitably elevated subject. (Even the full title of the work is eclectic: *The Thesiad* [epic] of *Emily's Nuptials* [romance].)

The first book of the *Teseida* cleverly splices Boccaccio's story into Statius's epic world by recounting Teseo's war against the Amazons (mentioned but not described by the Roman poet) and his marriage to Ipolita. Early in the second book, Boccaccio links up with the *Thebaid*'s account of the last stages of the Theban war, and moves quickly to Teseo's encounter with the Greek widows at his triumphant homecoming from Scythia. The bulk of Book Two recounts Teseo's triumph over Creon (whom he kills, as in Statius) and the funeral observances for the Greek warriors. Neither Argia, Antigone, nor the pyre with the twin-tongued flame appear; Teseo is at stage center throughout. Then, as a coda to the action at Thebes, the Greeks who are searching the battlefield for their dead and wounded find two young men, badly wounded and calling for death, whose demeanor and dress proclaim them to be of royal blood. The princes are taken to Teseo, who treats them with respect and holds them in comfortable detention in Athens as Book Two ends. Thenceforth Palemone and Arcita, the young Thebans, usurp the plot from Teseo, thanks to their love for Emilia, Ipolita's sister (and a character unknown to Statius), which transforms their friendship into a near-mortal rivalry.

The first two books of the *Teseida* abound with self-conscious references to Boccaccio's appropriation of the epic heritage for his own uses. The most obvious emblem of poetic metamorphosis is the discovery and "resurrection" of the half-dead Palemone and Arcita from the field of corpses that constitutes the end of the Theban war and the end of Statius' epic about it. In *The Thebaid*, Polynices and Eteocles "overcome" death by the sheer force of their mutual hatred, becoming, through the image of the warring flames, a symbol of destructive destiny's extension beyond the limits of any single life. Boccaccio replaces the pyre scene by the discovery scene, substituting a new beginning for epic closure, and his own heroes for Statius'. Moreover, Teseo responds to the new protagonists in a courteous, refined manner that distinguishes him from the spirit of the epic universe. When Palemone and Arcita are brought before him, he hears the *sdegno real* (royal disdain) in their voices, but doesn't respond to such *ira* as it deserves. Instead he is *pio* (compassionate), heals them, and, despite their danger to his rule, refuses to kill them, as that would be a great sin; as Book Two ends, he installs them in his palace, to be served "at their pleasure."

One more emblem of the transformation the Italian poet has wrought on his Roman master's view of the noble life deserves special mention. After Teseo defeats Ipolita in battle, he falls in love with her, and his sudden subjection to Cupid is accompanied by an equally unexpected collective metamorphosis of all Ipolita's Amazon followers: as soon as they put down their arms, they revert to being paragons of beauty and grace; their stern battle cries become pleasant jests and sweet songs, and even their steps, which were great strides when they fought, are dainty once again. Boccaccio was inspired to this felicitous passage by Statius' image of the domesticated Hippolyta, arriving in Athens as Theseus' captive and wife. But here a whole society of wild Scythian women spontaneously suffers a sea-change of beautifying refinement, manifesting precisely the transformation that *courtoisie* as a behavioral ideal imposed on the ruder manners of European feudal society in the centuries just prior to Boccaccio's own, and that the courtly romance and lyric imposed on the martial style of the classical and feudal epic.

In deflecting the *Thebaid* from epic into a new, mixed genre, the *Teseida* comes to grips with the epic theme of order versus chaos in new ways, such as the emphasis on control and refinement implicit in Teseo's courteous treatment of Palemone and Arcita when they are first brought to him as captives, and in the metamorphosis of Ipolita's warriors after their defeat. Control also manifests itself in other elements of the poem. Boccaccio's mastery of epic conventions—those already mentioned, plus personified prayers flying to heaven, catalogues of heroes arriving for battle, descriptions of funeral obsequies and games—is a self-conscious exercise of poetic control, and the summit of literary self-consciousness is the temple Palemone builds to honor Arcita's memory: it is decorated with pictures that recapitulate the entire story of the *Teseida* (except Arcita's mortal fall from his horse!), and the narrator characterizes it as "a perfect work by one who knew how to execute it superbly"—that is, by Boccaccio himself. The fact, however, that the "perfect work" omits the one detail of its protagonist's story—his death—that has called the temple and its pictures into being suggests that perfect control in art (and life?) is an illusion, created by overlooking those situations in which chaos erupts.

A similar cynicism about control underlies the manipulative gamesmanship used from time to time by Boccaccio's characters in dealing with persons and events. Emilia, having realized that Palemone and Arcita are watching her from their prison when she plays in her garden, encourages their ardor by flirtatious behavior—but out of vanity, not love. Arcita, having been released from prison by Peritoo's intercession with Teseo, speaks ambiguously to his benefactors, and lies outright to his kinsman Palemone, the better to hide his passion and his plans to assuage it. Nor is desire the only nurse of deceit; in Book Nine, after Palemone and Arcita, with one hundred followers each, have fought a tournament with Emilia as the prize, Teseo consoles those on the losing side with diplomatic words, blaming the defeat on the will of Providence, and complimenting them as the best warriors he has ever seen. The beneficiaries of Teseo's game of diplomacy are pleased, even though they don't believe all they have heard!

The *Teseida*'s ironic view of strategies for controlling life and art ripens at times into open recognition of how attempts to defeat chaos falter when faced by its irresistible forces. When Arcita, having encountered Palemone in the woods outside Athens, attempts to dissuade him from a fight to the finish over Emilia, he recalls the wrath of the gods against the Theban lineage to which they both belong; he points out that they are victims of Fortune, and says that in any case the winner of such a battle still will not have Emilia—and then, having marshalled all these sound arguments against strife, ends with the thumping non-sequitur that since Palemone wishes the battle, he shall indeed have it. Dominated by love's passion, Arcita can see (and speak) the truth, but cannot act on it. Later, at the climax of the story, the gods whose wrath Arcita has invoked as a reason for not fighting, intervene decisively (but not on epic grounds) when the young kinsmen commit themselves to battle for Emilia under Teseo's aegis. Arcita, who has prayed to Mars for victory, wins the tournament, only to be thrown from his horse and fatally wounded as he rides about the arena in triumph; Venus sends a Fury to startle the horse, so that she can award Emilia to Palemone, her votary. Emilia, denied her desire to remain chaste and marry neither Theban, can only blame Love for her sorry state.

To the extent that the poem's characters can control their fates by manipulation, their strategies of control and deceit make them figures of irony. But when they become prisoners of larger forces, they (and the poem's rhetoric about them) become pathetic and sentimentalized. This polarity of responses between ironic comedy, when characters act artfully, and pathetic melodrama, when they suffer victimization, differs markedly from our responses to the struggle between order and chaos in Book Twelve of the *Thebaid*. There Theseus' championship of civilized values is intended to provoke admiration, not cynical amusement, and the furious excesses of Polynices, Eteocles, and Creon horrified repugnance, not sentimental involvement. Sometimes, in the *Teseida*, sentiment and irony seem to pervade a scene simultaneously, especially a scene conceived in terms of the literary conventions of courtly love. The hot sighs of Palemone and Arcita in prison, as they debate whether Emilia is a goddess or a woman, and then languish and grow pale with love-sickness, conform so completely to those conventions as to invite us to smile at the predictability of it all, even as we sympathize with the helplessness of the imprisoned lovers. Elsewhere, our compassionate response to the affection the young men frequently express for each other must battle with our sense of the absurdity implicit in the repeated spectacle of the two dear friends trying to beat each other's brains out to win Emilia.

Much more than the *Thebaid*, then, the *Teseida* moves toward an interpretive impasse, resulting from the tense equilibrium between activity and passivity, irony and pathos, in its portrayal of the issues at stake in the noble life. Only Teseo's commanding presence seems to offer a way out of this labyrinth. Except for the brief period in Book One where he suffers from lovesickness for the vanquished Ipolita, Teseo is the active principle throughout the poem. He lacks the symbolic integrity of Statius' Theseus, the agent of civilization in a world driven mad with rage; rather, he functions as an emblem of controlled variousness in a world where variety of response and perception continually leads to situations of collision between and within selves. For example, when Teseo addresses the Greek widows who have sought his aid against Creon, he moves within a single stanza from being "wounded in his heart by profound pity" to speaking "in a loud voice kindled by rage." Unlike Palemone or Arcita, Teseo is not hindered by such extremes. He acts with complete martial authority, killing Creon and capturing Thebes, then responds to the wrath of the distraught, newly captured Theban princes when they are brought before him by a show of magnanimity beyond their deserts; or, finding them later fighting in the woods, he not only grants them the amnesty they request for having broken his laws, but rewards them richly. He presides gravely over Arcita's obsequies and then, in a triumphant show of authority, convinces Palemone and Emilia to marry, despite their deeply felt unwillingness so to sully the memory of the departed prince.

Teseo, in short, makes everything look easy, and in so doing, he seems less to reflect a large view of the noble life as the triumph of order over chaos than to represent within the poem the virtuosity of its creator in assimilating and combining epic and courtly romance conventions, and thus the triumph of ingenuity over disparateness. The *Teseida*'s major concerns are finally aesthetic rather than moral or philosophical; its ultimate referent is literature, not experience.

III

When Geoffrey Chaucer undertook to adapt the *Teseida* for his "Knight's Tale," he performed an impressive feat of truncation, shortening Boccaccio's nearly 10,000 lines to 2250 and compressing twelve books into four. Chaucer's omissions, and the way he has the Knight call attention to them, affect the meaning as well as the length of his revision of the *Teseida*. The change most immediately noticeable to a reader of both texts is Chaucer's wholesale jettisoning of Boccaccio's self-consciously literary epic trappings—invocations, glosses, catalogues of warriors—so that the story, as told by the Knight, sounds much less like a virtuoso performance, much more like the effort of an amateur—a soldier, not a poet—who, far from taking pride like Boccaccio in his poetic achievement, wishes primarily to finish his task as quickly as possible. (The one exception to the Knight's attitude of self-abnegation, his description of the tournament lists constructed by Theseus, will be discussed shortly.) The Knight shares his creator's desire to abridge his "auctor," although, unlike other, more learned or artistic Chaucerian narrators, he never alludes to his source either by real name (as in the reference to "Petrark" in the "Clerk's Tale") or pseudonymously (the "Lollius," alias Boccaccio, of *Troilus and Criseyde*). The rhetorical device by which the Knight (and behind him, Chaucer) calls attention to the process of abridgment is *occupatio*, the deliberate refusal to amplify (or describe completely) some aspect of the narrative. The Knight's first use of *occupatio* comes only fifteen lines into his tale:

> And certes, if it nere to long to heere,
> I wolde have toold yow fully the manere
> How wonnen was the regne of Femenye
> By Theseus and by his chivalrye;
> And of the grete bataile for the nones
> Bitwixen Atthenes and Amazones;
> And how asseged was Ypolita,
> The faire, hardy queene of Scithia;
> And of the feste that was at hir weddynge,

And of the tempest at hir hoom-comynge;
But al that thyng I moot as now forbere.

Chaucer here digests the first book and beginning of the second of the *Teseida* by having the Knight, in effect, tell us what he won't tell us. Chaucer included these details of his omission, not because the story as he tells it needs them, but in order to dramatize the fact that story-telling requires the constant exercise of control in selecting material from a potentially much greater reservoir—ultimately, in fact, from all experience and all antecedent literature. *Occupatio* is an emblem of the hard choices and discipline of art: what do I leave out? And the Knight, as an amateur, is particularly troubled by this aspect of his task, given the scope of his chosen story and his lack of skill. As he puts it:

I have, God, woot, a large feeld to ere,
And wayke been the oxen in my plough.
The remenant of the tale is long enough.

Although the Knight's reference to his limited powers is a traditional *captatio benevolentiae*, it strikes a very different note from Boccaccio's self-confident epic invocations. The image of the oxen and plough is homely and unpretentious, and the idea it conjures up of the rest of the tale stretching before its teller like a great, untilled field conveys some of the nervous discomfort felt by the amateur who sets out to tell a story without fully controlling it, knowing that in any case his best hope is to shorten it where he can.

The Knight's difficulties in discharging his unaccustomed artistic responsibilities surface most spectacularly in his description of Arcite's funeral rites. He recounts in some detail the procession of mourners from Athens to the place of immolation (the same grove where Palamon and Arcite first fought for Emelye), and then launches into an *occupatio* forty-seven lines long, in which he describes the rest of the obsequies (including funeral games) while protesting that he will not do so! The distension of a curtailing device to a size that completely defeats its rhetorical intent is a masterful comic stroke on Chaucer's part, but also a strategy designed to drive home the impression of the amateur poet unable to control his material.

Precariousness of control in fact constitutes a main theme of the "Knight's Tale," linking the Knight's ad hoc artistic activities with the political, and finally philosophical, program of Theseus by which the Athenian duke attempts to solve the potentially disruptive problem of Palamon and Arcite. And behind Theseus lies yet a deeper level of unresolved tension: the ambivalence of the Knight about life's meaning, as revealed in his treatment of his characters. At this last, most profound level, Chaucer confronts the paradoxes inherent in chivalry, and thereby transforms Boccaccio's literary tour de force into a troubling anatomy of an archaic but, in his day, still influential ideal of the noble life.

The theme of precarious control finds emblematic embodiment in a detail included by the Knight in his description (absent in Boccaccio) of the preparations for the tournament battle between Palamon and Arcite. Amidst the bustle of knights, squires, blacksmiths, musicians, and expert spectators sizing up the combatants, he directs our attention to "the fomy stedes on the golden brydel / Gnawynge"—a superb image of animal passion at its most elemental, restrained by the civilizing force of the (symbolic, we feel) golden bridle, but clearly anxious to throw off restraint and liberate energy.

The golden bridle is a microcosm of the entire artifice of civilization—the officially sanctioned tournament and the lists in which it is held—with which Theseus seeks to enclose and control the love-inspired martial energy of Palamon and Arcite. The lists deserve attention as a focal point of the "Knight's Tale" that illustrates with special clarity Chaucer's intent in transforming the *Teseida*. Chaucer has Theseus build them especially for this battle (in Boccaccio the *teatro* where the tournament is held pre-exists the rivalry of Palemone and Arcita); they are thus an emblem of his authority and wisdom in dealing with the young Thebans who threaten him politically and who wish to marry his ward. Furthermore, the description of the lists constitutes the sole instance when the Knight, abandoning *occupatio*, waxes eloquent and self-confidently poetic. The lists, therefore, fuse the high point of the Knight's art of language and Theseus's art of government.

Theseus orders the lists to be built after he interrupts Palamon and Arcite fighting viciously, up to their ankles in blood, in the woods outside Athens to decide who will have Emelye. The tournament which the lists will house, and of which Theseus will be the "evene juge . . . and trewe", represents a revision of his first intention, which was to kill the young combatants when he accidentally comes upon them—one a fugitive from his prison, the other under sentence of perpetual exile from Athens—fighting on his territory without his permission: "Ye shal be deed, by myghty Mars the rede!" This second, less furious response of Theseus to the love-inspired violence of his former prisoners is also a second, more legal chance for

What Do I Read Next?

- One of the most famous writers living during Chaucer's lifetime was Giovanni Boccaccio. Boccaccio's most famous work, *The Decameron* (1350), was a collection of one hundred short tales that may have influenced the structure that Chaucer used. In addition, some of the stories Chaucer used in his work were taken from *The Decameron*.

- The "Chaucer Metapage" is a project initiated in 1998 by the Thirty Third International Congress of Medieval Studies, aimed at coordinating all Chaucer sources on the internet. It can be located at http://www.unc.edu/depts/chaucer/index.html (August 6, 2001).

- *The Canterbury Tales* has been translated into Modern English by Nevill Coghill, whose translation was, in turn, adapted to a Broadway musical in 1968. This translation, from Penguin Classics, is considered to be the best of modern translations. Penguin USA published a recent edition in 2000.

- Nevill Coghill also translated *Troilus and Criseyde* (1483), Chaucer's other famous work. It is also available from Penguin Classics.

- Some of Chaucer's minor works have been compiled in a book from Penguin Classics called *Love Visions*. Included in the book are "The Book of the Duchess," "The House of Fame," "The Parliament of Birds," and "The Legend of Good Women." It was translated by Brian Stone and published by Viking Press in 1985.

- Sir Edmund Spenser's epic poem *The Faerie Queen* was published two centuries after Chaucer in 1590, but it was an historic piece, looking back at a time of knights and medieval folklore, which is why it is often linked with *The Canterbury Tales*. Spenser's poem is available as a Penguin Classic from Viking Press, and a reissued edition was published in 1988.

- *Sir Gawain and the Green Knight* is a tale of chivalry that goes back before Chaucer's time, to the thirteenth century. It is available in a modern translation from 1925 by J. R. R. Tolkien, author of *The Hobbit* and *The Lord of the Rings*. It was reissued by Ballantine Books in 1988.

- One of the most influential poetic works ever written, *The Divine Comedy* by Dante Alighieri, concerns the author's journey through hell and purgatory and finally to heaven. It was published in 1321, and Chaucer would certainly have read it, as have millions of poetry lovers in the centuries since then.

Palamon and Arcite to fight over Emelye. Theseus controls himself, and thus controls the lovers' behavior. And since the lists are built on the very spot where Theseus found Palamon and Arcite in battle, the imposition of the constructed edifice on the hitherto wild grove provides yet another image of civilized control, this time over nature.

The significance of the lists grows as we learn that Theseus calls together all the master craftsmen and artists of his realm to perform the work of construction; indeed, in the light of these facts, and of the extended description of the finished product, we are justified in hearing echoes of Genesis (echoes that emphasize Theseus' powers of control) in the Knight's comment ending his account:

"Theseus, / That at his grete cost arrayred thus / The temples and the theatre every deel / Whan it was doon, hym lyked wonder weel." But if Theseus is the deity behind this work of art and government, he must share the honors of godhead with the Knight, who not only uses the same verb, "devyse," to denominate the activities of those who made the lists and his own activity in describing it, but also (with artistic ineptitude but, for Chaucer, thematic significance) destroys the distance between his reality and that of his tale by describing, as if he had seen them, the insides of the temples built at three compass points atop the round enclosure of the lists ("Ther saugh I . . ."). Although the Knight clearly admires Theseus more than any

---

other character throughout his tale, nowhere does he identify himself so directly with his surrogate as here, where both are constructing a universal image of their willed authority over their respective poetic and political worlds.

In the *Teseida*, we hear of the "teatro eminente," where the tournament will be held, at the beginning of Book Seven, but no details of its construction are given until stanzas 108–110, and then a mere twenty-four lines suffice (as opposed to Chaucer's two hundred). In between, various activities and speeches reduce the *teatro* to the periphery of our attention. Chaucer, instead, moves directly from Theseus' decision to build the lists to the elaborate description of them. He also includes in the description (and the structure) the temples to Mars, Venus, and Diana, which in the *Teseida* are not earthly but celestial edifices to which the prayers of Palemone, Arcita, and Emilia ascend. The cumulative effect of Chaucer's compression and redistribution of Boccaccian detail is to make of the lists the poem's dominant image, and a true *theatrum mundi:* an image of the universe, with men below and gods above (the temples are located above the gates or in a turret), and Theseus in the middle, imposing order and public legitimacy on the private passions of Palamon and Arcite.

Seen in this light, the lists are also a concrete, palpable version and foreshadowing of the cosmic order, held together by Jupiter's "cheyne of love", which Theseus invokes in his last act of control, his proposal and arrangement of a marriage between Palamon and Emelye some years after Arcite's death. And, because of the self-consciousness of the Knight about his artistry, the lists also claim a place in the cosmic order for poetry—not Boccaccio's epic-revival art, with its purely literary and aesthetic triumphalism, but a socially useful poetry that reflects and promotes cosmic order in a manner analogous to the deeds of a good governor. The close relationship between the enterprises of Theseus and the Knight is suggested by the direct juxtaposition of the passage expressing the Duke's godlike satisfaction in his creation and this other judgment on the quality of the painting (i.e., of the poetic description) in the temples: "Wel koude he peynten lifly that it wroghte; / With many a floryn he the hewes boghte."

The mention of the costs attendant upon the artist's triumph provides a transition to the larger costs of the ordering activities undertaken by Theseus. First of all, the gods Mars, Venus, and Diana are presented by Chaucer as much more threatening to human happiness than their Boccaccian

equivalents, thanks to the later poet's insertion into the temple ecphrases of an accumulation of details illustrating catastrophic divine intervention in human life. More crucially, Chaucer invents the figure of Saturn, grandfather of Venus and Mars and presiding deity over the greatest human disasters, who undertakes to solve the problem created by his grandchildren's respective partisanship for Palamon and Arcite: Venus has promised to answer Palamon's prayer for Emelye, Mars Arcite's for victory. Theseus, acting as patron of the Theban princes, calls the lists into being, but the last word belongs to Saturn, who undertakes to use Theseus' creation to assert his own patronage over the celestial counterparts of Palamon and Arcite. Hence the question arises: has Theseus's activity, culminating in the building of the lists, really imposed order on potentially disruptive passions of love and prowess, or has it merely provided a compact and intensified "inner circle" within which the passions—and the uncontrollable divine destiny that sponsors them—can operate to intensify human misery?

This is a sobering question, and not, I believe, one that can easily be answered positively or negatively from the data given us by the "Knight's Tale," albeit many critics have tried, over the years, to argue for Chaucer's philosophical optimism (or more rarely, pessimism) on the basis of the "Tale." It seems to me more useful to search out the source of this deep ambivalence about human happiness—about whether the golden bridle and the lists control human violence or merely license and intensify it—and thereby to understand more clearly the poet's intent in creating the "Knight's Tale." And here, in my view, is where the fact that the Tale is told by a professional warrior becomes extremely important.

Chaucer establishes the Knight's professional perspective on the tale he tells—and on life itself—in several passages, too frequently ignored by critics, describing events and feelings directly related to the career of a practitioner of martial chivalry. One such passage I have already mentioned: the powerfully mimetic description of the preparations for the tournament, rich with the closely observed sights and sounds of the stable, the grounds, and even the palace, where would-be experts, like bettors at a race track, choose their favorites in the coming contest:

> Somme helden with hym with the blake berd,
> Somme with the balled, some with the thikke herd;
> Somme seyde, he looked grymme, and he wolde
>   fighte, etc.

In another passage, the Knight describes the various choices of weaponry made by the participants, and ends his catalogue with the purely professional, almost bored comment: "Ther is no newe gyse [of weapon] that it nas old."

The Knight's treatment of the aftermath of the tournament is as professional (almost disturbingly so) in its tone as it is amateurish in its distortion of the narrative line of his tale. When Arcite is thrown from his horse while parading around the lists in apparent triumph, the Knight immediately declares (as Boccaccio's narrator does not) that this is a critical wound; Arcite is borne to bed, "alwey criynge after Emelye." The picture is infinitely pathetic: the tournament's victor pleads, as if to the heavens, for the prize he should now be enjoying, were it not for their intervention to deny it to him just when it seemed in his grasp. At this point, the Knight abruptly forsakes his wounded protagonist (and the story line) to describe in detail how Theseus entertained the rest of the tournament contestants, minimizing Arcite's injury—"he nolde noght disconforten hem alle"—and assuring them that there have been no real losers on this occasion: after all, "fallyng [as Arcite did] nys nat but an aventure," and to be captured (as Palamon was) by twenty men cannot be accounted cowardice or "vileynye." Theseus seeks to head off "alle rancour and envye" that might lead to post-tournament disruptions of the peace, of a kind that Knight would have seen often enough at tournaments in his day: the Duke calms the feelings of the warriors and holds a feast for them, then leads them out of town. The Knight reports Theseus' diplomacy here with the quiet approval of one who has himself been so entertained after numerous melees, and therefore recognizes how the Duke has effectively defused a potentially dangerous situation—yet another instance of his ability to control life. (By contrast, the purely rhetorical performance of Teseo at the analogous point in the *Teseida* is, as we have seen, greeted with some skepticism by its recipients; moreover, Boccaccio's version entirely lacks the verisimilar, "locker room" details of the combatants treating their wounds and talking about the fight after it is over—details that underscore the Knight's familiarity with the scene he is describing.)

The Knight's professional perspective also endows the tournament fighting with a dimension of mimetic power foreign to Boccaccio. The alliterative vigor with which the combat unfolds and the brilliant description of Palamon's capture, despite the fury of his resistance, owing to sheer force of numbers, convince us that a soldier is letting us see

the martial life through his eyes, not (as in the *Teseida*) through the eyes of a poet steeped in epic conventions. But our deepest penetration into the Knight's vocational psyche comes, not in the lists, but when Palamon and Arcite are preparing to fight in the woods for the right to woo Emelye. Arcite, who has gone to Athens for two suits of armor, returns:

> And on his horse, allone as he was born,
> He carieth all the harneys him biforn.
> And in the grove, at tyme and place yset,
> This Arcite and this Palamon ben met.
> Tho chaungen gan the colour in hir face,
> Right as the hunters in the regne of Trace,
> That stondeth at the gappe with a spere,
> Whan hunted is the leon or the bere,
> And hereth hym come russhyng in the greves,
> And breketh both the bowes and the leves,
> And thynketh, 'Heere cometh my mortal enemy!
> Withoute faille, he moot be deed, or I;
> For outher I moot sleen hym at the gappe,
> Or he moot sleen me, if that me myshappe';
> So ferden they in chaungyng of hir hewe...

The Knight evokes a Hemingwayesque moment of truth to describe what it feels like to be about to undertake a "mortal bataille"—an experience the "General Prologue" of the *Canterbury Tales* tells us he has had fifteen times. The loneliness of the moment of truth is stressed at the beginning of this passage, and the role of Fortune ("myshappe") at its conclusion. The chilling insight and particular details of this passage are entirely the Knight's (and Chaucer's), yet it has a Boccaccian point of departure, comparison with which makes Chaucer's skill and his interests even more obvious. In *Teseida* vii, when Palemone and Arcita arrive at the *teatro* on the day of the tournament, each with his hundred followers, Boccaccio sums up the feelings on hearing each other's party and the roar of the crowd by using the simile of the hunter waiting for the lion. But the effect is deflating, not exalting: the hunter is so afraid, he wishes he had not spread his snares; as he waits, he wavers between being more and less terrified. So the young princes, facing their moment of truth, think better of their daring: "within their hearts they suddenly felt their desire become less heated." From this cynical, comic moment, Chaucer fabricates a perception of the teeth-gritting readiness for death that the professional warrior must take with him into battle.

With this moment, we plumb the absolute depths of the Knight's vision of life as a deadly, and arbitrary, business. This sense underlies another wonderfully apt remark he makes just before the escaped Palamon discovers the disguised Arcite in the grove outside Athens:

> No thyng ne knew he that it was Arcite;
> God woot he wolde have trowed it ful lite.
> But sooth is seyd, go sithen many yeres,
> That 'feeld hath eyen and the wode hath eres.'
> It is ful fair a man to bere hym evene,
> For al day meeteth men at unset stevene.

Fortune, that is, will bring together men without an appointment, and the result may well be, as it is this time, that a fight will result. The warrior must live with one hand on the hilt of his sword; he cannot expect ample warning about when to use it.

This fatalistic sense of life, quite amoral in its recognition of the uncontrollable element in human affairs, seems to me to lead the Knight toward two contrary sets of conclusions, reflected in his tale's ambivalence about the possibility of order in the world. First, by stressing the arbitrariness of events, he succeeds in reducing all of his protagonists except Theseus to the level of playthings of large forces they cannot control. Palamon and Arcite are found by *pilours*, pillagers, in a heap of dead bodies on the field outside Thebes. "Out of the taas the pilours han hem torn," and this wrenching, almost Caesarean "birth" of the young heroes into the story, so different in tone from the courteous rescue afforded them by Teseo's men at this point in the *Teseida*, gives way inside three lines of verse to Theseus' decision to send them "to Atthenes, to dwellen in prisoun, / Perpetuelly" in a tower. The import of this brusque movement from *taas* to *tour*, with all Boccaccio's intervening civilities ruthlessly extirpated, is inescapable: life is a prison into which we are born as Fortune's minions. From this point of view, the rest of Palamon's and Arcite's life is a passage in and out of prison, with the differences between captivity and liberation so blurred that at one point Arcite can call his release from the tower through the intervention of Perotheus a sentence "to dwelle / Noght in purgatorie, but in helle", while prison, instead, is "paradys." Furthermore, the subsequent enclosures prepared for them by Theseus seem as imprisoning as the tower; even the lists, in this reading, render the young princes helpless before Saturn's whim, which is as arbitrary as Theseus' initial decision to imprison them, but more deadly. When Arcite is thrown from his horse, he is "korven out of his harneys" and carried off to die—a grim act of release that recalls his being torn out of the *taas*, and supports a dark view of life as a succession of equally brutal operations of imprisonment and release performed upon humanity by an indifferent or hostile universe.

The Knight, when he espouses this dark view, becomes practically as heedless of the feelings of his characters as is Saturn. He makes fun of the young lovers, and turns their heartfelt, Boethian complaints about the meaning of this cruel life into a *dubbio*, or love-problem game, at the end of Part One. He leers at Emelye as she performs her rites of purification before praying to Diana to remain a virgin (a prayer doomed to rejection), and, as we have seen, he leaves the wounded Arcite crying for Emelye while he recapitulates Theseus's diplomatic treatment of the rest of the tournament combatants. We are surely intended by Chaucer to blanch in horror at the grim levity with which the Knight ends his expert description of Arcite's mortal condition:

> Nature hath now no dominacioun,
> And certeinly, ther Nature wol not wirche,
> Fare wel physik! go ber the man to chirche!

It is against this strand of professionally-inspired pessimism and stoicism that the image of Theseus the bringer of order must be placed—as the mouthpiece of a philosophical optimism that expresses the Knight's pulling back from the edge of the abyss to which his sense of death and fortune leads him. Like Statius so many centuries before him, the Knight needs Theseus, and at the ending of his tale allows Theseus' last diplomatic initiative complete success. Invoking the order of the universe to explain to the still grief-stricken Palamon and Emelye why they should no longer mourn for Arcite, Theseus counsels them "to maken vertu of necessitee," and "make of sorwes two / O parfit joye, lastynge everemo" by marrying. The rhetoric here is at least in part Boethian—with, as critics have noted, some odd turns—but the strategy behind it is wholly political. Theseus has been led to propose the marriage by his desire "to have with certeyn countrees alliaunce, / And have fully of Thebans obeisaunce." For him, this is a dynastic alliance, and thus another imposition of political order on human passions (here, grief). Because the Knight has given vent to his darker perceptions elsewhere in his Tale, however, we are allowed, nay, intended to take some of Theseus' philosophic justifications for his political initiative *cum grano salis*. We know by now how precarious and potentially ironic the Duke's structures of control can be, even if the Knight wishes to forget this. Indeed, even here, the phrases from Theseus' speech about virtue and necessity, sorrow and joy, encourage us to detect someone's desperation— whether Theseus' or the Knight's is not clear—to find an alternative to the dark despair that flooded the poem with Arcite's death. The lingering influence of that despair inheres in Theseus' reference to "this foule prisoun of this lyf", a phrase ironically recalling the tower to which he condemned Palamon and Arcite early in the story, thus literally making their life a prison.

The secret of Chaucer's re-creation of the *Teseida* as the "Knight's Tale" lies, then, in his vivid and profound comprehension of the tensions that might well exist within the *Weltanschauung* of a late medieval mercenary warrior. Or perhaps he simply appreciated the contradictions in his society's concept of chivalry. The knight of Chaucer's day carried with him a very mixed baggage of Christian idealism, archaic and escapist codes of conduct, aesthetically attractive routines of pageantry, and a special function as the repository of skills and graces appropriate to the training of young aristocrats. In his famous "General Prologue" portrait, Chaucer's own knight possesses a high moral character of an archaic (if not totally imaginary) kind: "fro the time that he first began / To riden out, he loved chivalrie, / Trouthe and honour, fredom and curteisie". He combines this idealism of outlook and behavior ("he nevere yet no vileynie ne sayde / In al his lyf unto no maner wight") with a thoroughly professional mercenary career that has taken him to most of the places where the noble warrior's virtues and skills could be practiced during Chaucer's day. This synthetic phenomenon, the idealistic killer (he had "foughten for oure feith at Tramyssene / In lystes thries, and ay slayn his foo"), embodies in his person some but not all of the main strands of chivalry. His son, the Squire who accompanies him on the pilgrimage, supplements these by personifying the virtuosic and aesthetic side of late medieval chivalry: he sings, dances, loves hotly, and fights very little. Chaucer's splitting of the chivalric complex into two generationally distinct segments allowed him to isolate what seemed to him the real paradox of chivalry— its imposition of moral idealism on a deadly, and therefore potentially nihilistic, profession—for treatment in the "Knight's Tale," leaving its decorative aspects to be teased in the harmlessly inept story told (but not completed) by the Squire, himself an unfinished creature, when his turn comes on the road to Canterbury.

The "Knight's Tale," reflecting as it does the problematic view of life implicit in a code that seeks to moralize and dignify aggression, looks back across the centuries to enter into dialogue with the last book of Statius' *Thebaid*, as well as with Boccaccio's *Teseida*, on the question of what Charles Muscatine calls "the struggle between noble designs and chaos." Reading Chaucer's chivalric tale with its ancestry in mind heightens our appreciation of both the uniqueness of his art and the continuities of its tradition.

Source: Robert W. Hanning, "'The Struggle between Noble Designs and Chaos': The Literary Tradition of Chaucer's 'Knight's Tale,'" in *Literary Review*, Vol. 23, No. 4, Summer 1980, pp. 519–41.

Britton J. Harwood

In the following essay, Harwood defends his assertion that "Chaucer was creating a human being" when constructing the character of the Wife of Bath.

The sad note some hear in the voice of the Wife of Bath can be interpreted as "die letzte Süsse in den schweren Wein," a hint of sourness showing that, with age, her deep enjoyments have begun to turn. From the viewpoint of those who understand the Wife as a stock character, this sad note, if not attributed to critical ingenuity, is assimilated to the Wife's type as a picturesque, individuating detail or as the bitter recognition, coming amidst our common celebration of the created world, that time holds us "green and dying." Her "allas!," then, would be "the song of the indestructibility of the people," "of the finite with the vulgar interstices and smells, which lies below all categories."

However, to maintain that the "absurdity" of such characters as the Wife "inveigles us into . . . conspiring with them to make them real and lifelike," that she becomes lifelike by representing a class, and that Chaucer manipulates her "with an entire disregard for . . . psychological probability" seems to me to leave many parts of her performance in only the slightest connection with other parts. Assuming for the moment that the sad note is as close to her center as her willful gaiety and her insistence on fleshly enjoyment, I wish to throw in with those who believe that, in writing lines for the Wife, Chaucer was conceiving a human being.

A denial that the Wife's "make-up . . . is subtle or complex" seems to me to encounter difficulty with the third line she speaks:

> Experience, though noon auctoritee
> Were in this world, is right ynogh for me
> To speke of wo that is in mariage.

This unhappiness in marriage is generally equated, *tout court*, with the defeats borne by her subjugated husbands. She does not need second-hand knowledge of this grief, she is taken to mean, because she knows it at first hand, having caused it. "These opening lines of the Wife's Prologue are actually an introduction not to the 'sermon,'" R. A. Pratt has maintained, "but to the account of woe in marriage," not, that is, to lines 9–162, based upon Jerome's *Epistola adversus Jovinianum*, but to the parts of her Prologue which follow the Pardoner's interruption and draw on Deschamps, Theophrastus, and Walter Map as well as Jerome.

In the first place, however, as her first line anticipates, she does in fact proceed to dispute authority—principally the apostle Paul—although not about the misfortunes of milquetoasts. Secondly, it is not true that "the account of woe in marriage" begins only after the Pardoner intrudes. If "wo" and "tribulacion" mean the same thing, the mention of it seems to *cause* the Pardoner's interruption:

> An housbonde I wol have, I wol nat lette,
> Which shal be bothe my dettour and my thral,
> And have his tribulacion withal
> Upon his flessh, whil that I am his wyf.

No more than previously does she dispute Paul in these lines by misunderstanding the plain meaning of his words. With "wo" or "tribulacion" of the "flessh," she echoes 1 Corinthians 7:28 ("Si autem acceperis uxorem, non peccasti, et si nupserit virgo, non peccavit; tribulationem tamen carnis habebunt hujusmodi"), and she means, as Paul did, the painful test posed in marriage by the temptation to lubricity. As Augustine explains, "the Apostle . . . was unwilling to conceal the tribulation of the flesh springing from carnal emotions, from which the marriage of those who lack self-control can never be free. . ." In his comment on the same verse, Rabanus Maurus, having asked why tribulations of the flesh were greater for wedded folk than virgins, responds that these trials arise from the body itself, since these troubles were the satisfaction of the desires of the body. While the Parson will allow "that for thre thynges a man and his wyf flesshly mowen assemble," he knows that "scarsly may ther any of thise be withoute venial synne, for the corrupcion and for the delit." The tribulations, then, are the travail of continence, the efforts with which one controls the emotions that are "rebel to resoun and the body also"; further, they are the temporal punishment for the venial sin of incontinence in marriage. But they are also the appetite and its satisfaction; and by a familiar trick of religious language, the Wife like the Apostle is using "wo" to mean sexual pleasure.

The context in which the Wife mentions the "tribulacion" of the flesh is her defense of sexuality in marriage: because man and wife maintain the other's honor by relinquishing power over the body

> *. . . the Wife has made up a tale in which, without being altogether aware of doing so, perhaps, she submerges the fact of guilt within a dream of innocence."*

to the other, the Wife will have a husband who will "be bothe my dettour and my thral." The context, then, has nothing to do with "tegumenta, . . . uxoris necessitas, mariti dominatio"—"tribulacion" belonging to "another tonne." Similarly with "dette." Before the Pardoner interrupts, the Wife's husbands pay their "dette" by collaborating with her in sexual satisfaction. The sexual organs must have been created "for ese / Of engendrure," she argues: "Why sholde men elles in hir bookes sette / That man shal yelde to his wyf hire dette?" If she were describing herself here as a "whippe," her husband could not possibly love her "weel," as she approvingly quotes Paul as telling him to do. When the husband takes the initiative and wishes to "paye his dette," the Wife says she will use her "instrument . . . frely." Again, the Wife disagrees with Paul about the dangers of carnal pleasure; but she understands "dette" as he did: the spouse's usual obligation, spiritual cost notwithstanding, to give sexual relief and solace. Where she had promised "experience," the Wife's Prologue to this point is highly theoretical—that is, hypothetical. And there is simply no way to predict that "tribulacion" will mean quarreling, and debt and thralldom the plight of the man whose wife will not suffer his advances until he promises to buy her a present.

Before the Pardoner interrupts, then, we have three points which are evidently inconsistent: (1) "wo . . . in mariage" the Wife surely knows to be unpleasant for someone; (2) she insists she may lawfully marry for sexual fruition; and (3) "tribulacion," debt, and thralldom are sexual and participate in that fruition.

This apparent inconsistency is removed if all of the Wife's Prologue up to the Pardoner's intrusion is, as I think, an enormous red herring. This is something quite apart from the invalidity of her arguments, however telling that might be. She no sooner mentions her five marriages to verify her knowledge of married "wo" than she uses the plurality of her marriages as a pivot on which to turn to a diversive defense, first of bigamy and then of carnal pleasure between husband and wife. The very argument for the lawfulness of this pleasure is irrelevant to the Wife, because nearly all of it, she goes on to recall, has been found *outside* her marriages. Even with Jankyn, fun in bed is explicitly part of that first phase of their marriage when he is "daungerous" to her; for after the night they "fille acorded," they "hadden never debaat." On their sexual relationship afterwards, she is significantly silent. There is no question of sexual pleasure with the first three mates. As opposed to the (carnal) love for a woman which the married state pardons and the Wife misleadingly defends, the "love" won by the Wife from her three husbands takes the form of "lond and . . . tresoor"; on the attempts at love-making she derisively exacts from them ("love" in the sense parallel to "tribulacion" in 1 Cor. 7:28), she places no value. In fact, as we shall observe, she may not ultimately use sex for pleasure at all. She holds marriage to be good as a natural context for propagation and pleasure. Yet she herself has had no "delit" in "bacon" and is evidently childless. She insists that she will devote the best of herself to "fruyt of mariage," yet there has been no fruit either in the sense of children or, in her first four marriages at least, sexual *fruitio*. To protest that she is innocent, she exonerates marriage, while the "wo" actually arises with the uses to which she has put marriage.

The Wife's discourse, taking off from the experience of woe into an argumentative evasion full of theological categories and putative pleasure, includes the Pauline (that is, the metaphoric) use of "tribulacion" and "dette." The redundancy of "bothe my dettour and my thral" may be suspiciously vehement, however; and confronted by this aggressive and sturdy matron, the delicately constituted Pardoner penetrates far into her history by archly misinterpreting "tribulacion" in a reductive and literal way: "What sholde I bye it on my flessh so deere?" Since "tribulacion" as the Wife had used it means the temptation to sinful coitus, the Pardoner's question changes the sense of "tribulacion" to agree with his obvious inability to exchange sexual (or at least heterosexual) pleasure. His incapacity may even remind the Wife of her first three husbands'. To this changed sense of "tribulacion," then, she responds with a vengeance, accommodating her own meaning to the Pardoner's: of *this*

"tribulacion in mariage," she says, "myself have been the whippe." And she turns to the notable abuse actually visited upon her mates. The change in meaning is equally clear in her treatment of the marriage "dette": before the Pardoner interrupts, she says that she uses her "instrument . . . frely" whenever her hypothetical husband likes to "paye his dette." After the interruption, she records that, whenever one of her first three husbands was similarly inclined, he found that nothing was free; the "dette" has become quite literal and pecuniary.

The authorities assert that guilt—the arduous resistance to it, the consequences of it—is the "wo" in marriage. While the Wife contends otherwise, her own "experience" is conclusive. Anyone listening for the dominant's persistence in her narrative of married life will soon hear the language of the broker. The Pardoner sets the motif by speaking of buying marriage with his flesh, and the Pauline metaphors of "debt" and "payment" thereafter broaden into a whole vocabulary of commerce. The Wife will trouble to be agreeable only if it is profitable: "What sholde I taken keep hem for to plese, / But it were for my profit and myn ese?" On the other hand, her ability to carp and nag is also lucrative; for to buy relief from it, her husbands hasten to bring her "gaye thynges fro the fayre." Since a husband is a practical necessity, she is careful to buy one against her future needs: she is "purveyed of a make." There is a quid pro quo even in harsh words: she never took criticism without paying her spouse back for it. Because her fourth husband has been particularly difficult, she holds back on the money for his tomb. She and her first three live by the "cheste," and she disposes of the fourth by cheaply burying him in his.

The commerce extends beyond this, for in marriage she approximates the condition of a prostitute. She imputes to the first three mates a statement that may apply to herself: an ugly woman, she makes them say, will covet

> every man that she may se,
> For as a spaynel she wol on hym lepe,
> Tyl that she fynde som man hire to chepe.

Alice is quite clear that she sells her favors: if one of her old husbands ever stinted on the fee, then at night, when she felt his arm come over her side, she would leave the bed "Til he had maad his raunson unto me." Her body is her equity and no husband will expropriate it: "Thou shalt nat bothe, thogh that thou were wood, / Be maister of my body and of my good." He can deal or not, as he likes, but one of them he must "forgo." Although the husband is a rapacious beast, she must trade with him for her profit:

> With empty hand men may none haukes lure.
> For wynnyng wolde I al his lust endure,
> And make me a feyned appetit.

At forty-plus, this Mother Courage has to work harder at her business. One argument for marriage offered sardonically by Jerome is that it is preferable to be a prostitute for one man than for many. While the Wife overlooks it (pointedly, I am tempted to say), some allusion to her being literally a whore is inevitable: you're a lucky man that I'm faithful to you, she tells one or more of her old husbands, "For if I wolde selle my *bele chose*, / I koude walke as fressh as is a rose." She keeps a green memory of her youth, but here is the fruit of her age: "Wynne whoso may, for al is for to selle."

The "sovereignty" and "mastery" that the Wife exercises over her fifth husband (and that the Loathly Lady reveals to be what women most desire) are commonly understood as the Wife's power to obtain such things as fine clothes, her husbands' flattery, and freedom to roam—all the things, in short, we have just heard her buying with her sexual acquiescence. If sovereignty be the sum of these wifely prerogatives, it is curious that they appear in the Tale only to be discarded as wrong answers and that the Loathly Lady takes pains to dissociate herself from them. Before encountering the hag, the rapist knight polls the ladies:

> Somme seyde wommen loven best richesse,
> Somme seyde honour, somme seyde jolynesse,
> Somme riche array, somme seyden lust abedde.

These and others (flattery, gallivanting, and so on) are precisely the profits won by the Wife with her hard bargains. They are also short of the mark, for they are not sovereignty, unless that is only the power to obtain all of them—and this would seem a barren quibble. What appears most striking is that the Loathly Lady, who will enjoy "maistrie" over her own knight even as the Wife has "maistrie . . . [and] soveraynetee" over Jankyn, repudiates exactly the commerce already surveyed in some detail. The knight tries to get her secret with a bribe: "Koude ye me wisse, I wolde wel quite youre hire," he says; but she will have no part of it. Constrained to marry her, the knight echoes exactly the commercial alternatives offered by the Wife: "Taak al my good, and lat my body go." But the Lady refuses to negotiate:

> "Nay, thanne," quod she, "I shrewe us bothe two!
> For thogh that I be foul, and oold, and poore,
> I nolde for al the metal, ne for oore,

> That under erthe is grave, or lith above,
> But if thy wyf I were, and eek thy love."

Nor does the hag forgo wealth for sex, as the Wife tries to do with Jankyn. Neither before nor after her transformation does she exhibit a marked sexual interest in the knight; on the contrary, she knows what *he* likes and troubles to satisfy all his "worldly appetit."

For the moment I wish to put aside the question of the meaning of "sovereignty" in order to consider some of the effects of the Wife's having made her way by trading upon her youth and beauty. The basic consequence, of course, is guilt. "I koude pleyne," says the Wife, "and yit was in the gilt," and later: "be we never so vicious withinne, / We wol been holden wise and clene of synne." Hence her hatred of Jankyn's uncomplaisant book. Because "love" to her, when it is not income, is sexual fruition, it is found outside those marriages in which she must feign an interest in the "bacon." Love is "evere . . . synne" because for her it is either prostitution or adultery. Moreover, she seems to understand that sin, being unlovely, makes her unlovely, and that so far as she is not loved she is perceived as guilty. (In the Tale, conversely, the Loathly Lady takes the position that, if she is innocent, she is therefore lovable.) The revels of her fourth husband assume and reflect the very absence of virtue in her that she herself had to assume, from the age of twelve, in negotiating the price of her innocence. The "greet despit" in "herte" which he makes her feel is perhaps not merely sexual jealousy, but rather the suffering—an unredemptive "croce"—that comes from being perceived as unlovely; and the Wife brings death with her even from Jerusalem. Her own guiltiness being a kind of hell (women's love is "helle," she says at one point), and the fourth husband having shown it to her, he is made to share it: "in erthe I was his purgatorie."

Because the husbands of her youth are old and thick with lust, the Wife overpowers and outwits them easily in driving her bargains. There are no sales, however, without buyers. And having conspired in the commerce, they share her guilt and take their punishment:

> As help me God, I laughe whan I thynke
> How pitously a-nyght I made hem swynke!
> And, by my fey, I tolde of it no stoor.

> I sette hem so a-werke, by my fey,
> That many a nyght they songen "weilawey!"

After dishing out such a drubbing, she might say:

Goode lief, taak keep
How mekely looketh Wilkyn, oure sheep!
Com neer, my spouse, lat me ba thy cheke!
Ye sholde been al pacient and meke...
Suffreth alwey, syn ye so wel kan preche;
And but ye do, certein we shal yow teche
That it is fair to have a wyf in pees...
What eyleth yow to grucche thus and grone?
Is it for ye wolde have my queynte allone?
Wy, taak it al! lo, have it every deel!
Peter! I shrewe yow, but ye love it weel; ...
But I wol kepe it for youre owene tooth.
Ye be to blame, by God! I sey yow sooth.

Despite a possible nuance of tormented motherhood (she offers the "queynte" as she might have offered the teat), the pervasive tone is fiercely and sardonically patronizing. She knows that she is "in the gilt" and yet knows also, I think, that in a sense he *is* "to blame." The Wife invents a dream about her bed's being full of blood—blood that actually symbolizes gold, she says. In the Tale, the knight rapes the maiden and tries to bribe the lady; in the Prologue the twelve-year-old girl is raped by *being* bribed. The "haukes" lured to her hand leave the bed bloody with nobles and shillings. That Alice shares the guilt does not lessen the dishonor. As the wife of Midas had to reveal her husband's "vice," Alice admits that she could not keep it a secret if her husbands ever pissed upon a wall, or did anything like that. They do, and she can't.

For the sexual appetite to be imaged as fire is usual enough: the Wife's "queynte" is a kind of lantern, and a little later she describes "wommenes love" as "wilde fyr; / The moore it brenneth, the moore it hath desir / To consume every thyng that brent wole be." More remarkable is the thirst that goes with it for the water that might quench the flame. Women's love is a waterless land. Midas's wife, "hir herte . . . a-fyre," rushes to the marsh and lays her mouth against the water. With her "likerous mouth" and "tayl," Alice thirsts, paradoxically, for the same sexual experience with which she burns. She wishes she might be "refresshed" just half so often as Solomon. Christ may be the "welle" of perfection, but like this woman from "biside Bathe," the Samaritan with her five husbands is linked with another "welle"—the image of the unsatisfied "queynte."

At bottom, the Wife thirsts for innocence, relief from the fact of guilt. Thanks to her nativity, she says,

I koude noght withdrawe
My chambre of Venus from a good felawe . . .
For God so wys be my savacioun,
I ne loved nevere by no discrecioun,
But evere folwede myn appetit,

Al were he short, or long, or blak, or whit;
I took no kep, so that he liked me,
How poore he was, ne eek of what degree.

"Just as long as he liked *me*." Here is every nymphomaniac, whispering in the dark, "Love me a little." In the first phase of their marriage, Jankyn is such a "good felawe," periodically interrupting his clerical castigation of her to "glose" her into producing her *bele chose*." Leading through infinite adultery, thus exacerbating the guilt ("Allas! allas! that evere love was synne!"), and revealing itself as basic to the Wife's sense of "wo" in marriage, this thirst is self-defeating: the more it burns, "the moore it hath desir / To consume every thyng that brent wole be." She attempts to quench it with the "queynte," which is fire itself. Not only the Pardoner has a deadly barrel thrust to his lips.

This "coltes tooth"—not merely undiminished sexual vigor, but, motivating it, a longing that the buried and dishonored child has never ceased to feel—leads on to her bad bargain with Jankyn of the well-turned legs. He entertains her with his pleasant anthology of authors who take her categorical imperatives of instability, violence, and lechery and give them the maddening amplitude and inevitability of history. What maddens her most may be its incompleteness. She has not, after all, done this to herself all by herself:

By God! if wommen hadde writen stories,
As clerkes han withinne hire oratories,
They wolde han writen of men moore wikkednesse
Than al the mark of Adam may redresse.

Holding the trump of sexual uninterest, Jankyn evens an old score by reciting at his leisure the same charges the Wife had imputed to her earlier husbands: the uxorious spouses doubtless knew that the charges were true, and yet knew as well that they had not made them. Therefore, obliged to confirm and deny at the same time, they were too weakened by desire and too confused to do either, and the Wife had swept the field. But Jankyn reads on implacably, overpowering her first in one way, then in another:

And whan I saugh he wolde nevere fyne
To reden on this cursed book al nyght,
Al sodeynly thre leves have I plyght
Out of his book, right as he radde, and eke
I with my fest so took hym on the cheke
That in oure fyr he fil bakward adoun.
And he up stirte as dooth a wood leoun,
And with his fest he smoot me on the heed,
That in the floor I lay as I were deed.
And whan he saugh how stille that I lay,
He was agast, and wolde han fled his way,
Til atte laste out of my swogh I breyde.

Leaving the Wife for a moment at the point of this utter and ludicrous defeat, we may revert briefly to the matter of sovereignty. In the Middle Ages, marriage was sometimes considered the *iurata fornicatio*, in which sexual pleasure was not something freely given, but encumbered and obligated. The thirsty Wife would invoke the *iurata fornicatio* (the "statut") with her Pauline "dettours." Each mate constrains the other, the only question being who gets to the mill first. The Wife believes that each old husband would lock her in his chest if he could or employ Argus as a "wardecors." Nevertheless, because "love"—that is, wealth—has been exacted from them, even a superfluity of it is valueless for her: "They loved me so wel, by God above, / That I ne tolde no deyntee of hir love!" In the Tale, the knight is "constreyned" to marry the Loathly Lady. The ability to constrain is power. In bartering with her first three husbands, the Wife pits one kind of power against another. The coolness of Jankyn and the blow which, permanently deafening the Wife, leaves her prostrate and stunned epitomize the Wife's married life to that point.

In reaction to the *iurata fornicatio*, there seems to have arisen, at least in twelfth-century France, an ethic of love beginning with generosity. In her beautiful softness, the woman is perceived to be the source of goodness, bestowing her gifts or not according to what she judges to be worthy. Outside the *iurata fornicatio*, power can do nothing but put itself at the service of goodness, and the woman remains free to be good. This giving without constraint is what the Loathly Lady means by "gentillesse." Henri Dupin distinguishes ten qualities signified by "gentillesse" or "courtoisie" as these synonymous terms occur in French poetry, "contes et . . . romans," and moral works of the twelfth and thirteenth centuries; and elsewhere in Chaucer they have much of this complexity. The Loathly Lady's meaning, if vague, seems nevertheless reasonably simple: "gentil dedes" depend upon grace. This means, unless she is a heretic, that these must be deeds of charity, "heigh bountee." She distinguishes the uncanny and spontaneous nature of "gentillesse" from the natural functioning of fire: one can set a fire in an isolated house, vacate the house, and still the fire will do its "office natureel . . . til that it dye." It cannot stop burning of its own accord, and yet folk can cease to be generous. Here the grace to do a generous deed is exactly opposed to that fire which the poem identifies with the unquenchable "queynte."

Because the sense of "sovereignty" which comes all too readily to mind with the Wife fits the circumstances a little uneasily, we might consider the alternative. The name given by the man to the lady whom he serves because she is good is *domina*. Aurelius, for example, uses the convention when he tells Dorigen, "Nat that I chalange any thyng of right / Of yow, my sovereyn lady, but youre grace." A woman may well "desiren to have sovereynetee / As wel over hir housbond *as hir love*," because it is the hegemony of gracious liberality over legalized violence.

As the Wife bestirs herself from her swoon, she says,

> O! hastow slayn me, false theef? . . .
> And for my land thus hastow mordred me?
> Er I be deed, yet wol I kisse thee.

Jankyn kneels down beside her and vows never to hit her again. He puts the bridle in her hand, as she says, and burns his book. Why does Jankyn cease to preach? To answer that the Wife has mastered him would be simply tautologous. It is equally futile to believe, as many readers do, that she tricks Jankyn into coming within range and overwhelms him with a dying slap. For this fails to explain not only why he puts a permanent end to his hitherto successful strategy but also why she then goes on to be kind to him where she had abused the others. If this is only a matter of his so satisfying her sexually that she never had cause to chide, it is odd we do not hear of her reveling in "a bath of blisse"; indeed, she recalled that he was "in oure bed . . . so fressh and gay" at the same point she was remembering him as "the mooste shrewe." By contrast, after she has got "the soveraynetee," she describes their emotional relationship as simply "kynde" and "trewe."

Jankyn burns the book because it no longer mirrors the Wife. Have you murdered me for my money? she asks. "Er I be deed, yet wol I kisse thee." The slap she actually gives him does not disconcert him and seems little more than the vestige of a habit dying hard—of always having "the bettre in ech degree" turned now from "substaunce into accident." She depicts it as a gallant effort and her surrender, therefore ("Now wol I dye, I may no lenger speke"), as pathetic. Nevertheless, rather than by a trick, she "masters" Jankyn by appearing in a new way. "Truth comes in blows." At the moment of ridiculous defeat, grace irrupts into her experience. With the offer of one kiss, for the first time in 800 lines she proffers something for nothing. In place of a kiss he gets the nominal slap. But kisses are cheap, the pay-off to a "good felawe," as no one knows better than she. Instead, where she had vowed she would "noght forbere hym in no cas," she does exactly that. By being good—having honor to keep—she is sovereign: Jankyn defers to her because of the way he perceives her. She has described forbearance in a kiss, and he forbears; then she forbears in substance. In recalling the episode, she uses her habitual words, "maistrie" and "soveraynetee," although their meaning has changed. After the arid restlessness of a youth in which everything was up for sale, she becomes another woman with this "gentil dede." And where, in her guilt, she had heaped excruciating abuse upon those who had conspired with her to suborn herself, she pours kindness and fidelity upon Jankyn while he lives and blessings upon him after he dies.

It will be enough simply to record the parallel with the Loathly Lady and the knight. Where the Wife had the grace to do a "gentil dede," the Loathly Lady knows not only *gentillesse* but what women desire and what men ought to desire. The knight's marriage to her can be constrained, but his love must be given. After her bolster sermon, in the dark, the only universe of which he is conscious is her voice, and the unmoved mover of *that* world is her vision of the good. He at last vents many sighs, but they perhaps arise from the kind of turmoil that might precede an act of faith; for it is to her knowledge of goodness that he finally defers: "Cheseth yourself which may be moost plesance, / And moost honour to yow and me also." He amends the dishonor to the maiden by submitting to the honor of the Lady.

Jankyn comes late in a life saturated with the experience of "wo . . . in mariage," and the Wife may well be less than fully conscious of why she blesses him. Except for the gracious interlude with Jankyn, her Prologue establishes the facts of guilt, of a nostalgia for a lost goodness, of factitious gaiety, and of perseverance, not toward a hint of light, but in the gathering darkness. The diminished categories of her realized thought are fairly indicated by the closing lines of her whole performance, in which she wishes for young husbands who are "fressh abedde" and scorns "olde and angry nygardes of dispence." Where the transformed Lady "obeyed" her husband "in every thyng," five lines later the Wife prays for "grace t'overbyde hem that we wedde." With a more conscious and far more sardonic example of the same kind of self-punishing meiosis, the Pardoner, another guilty soul, will make his obscene pitch to Harry Bailley.

This notwithstanding, the Wife has made up a tale in which, without being altogether aware of doing so, perhaps, she submerges the fact of guilt within a dream of innocence. And we may conclude by having another look at the Tale.

In the Tale, the rapacity which the Wife imputes to friars with her triumphant joke anticipates the dishonor done a solitary girl, presumably of the lower class, by one of Arthur's knights: "By verray force, he rafte hire maydenhed." This rape appears in none of the analogues. As we have already noticed, the knight is doomed to rehabilitation: where force had destroyed the cleanness of virginity, it ends by putting itself at the service of virtue. We have not yet noticed, however, the simple and significant structure of the Tale.

Having been dishonored, the maiden becomes a hag. When honor is vested in her once more, she becomes a maiden again. Logic identifies the post hoc fallacy; poetry thrives on it. In the plot, the rape of the maiden is the way to the Loathly Lady; therefore, the rape of the maiden *causes* the Loathly Lady. Chaucer has not only added the rape to his sources; he has left out the motive for the Lady's ugliness found in the principal analogues. At bottom, the rapist is not simply—or perhaps not at all—a cut of red meat calculated to excite the Wife. His "verray force" reintroduces all the violence done to her own innocence when she dangled it to lure the hawks. The passing years, the Wife declares in her Prologue, poison everything. But the years of the hag are the instant tetter of a poison which frustrates all refreshment, the guilt of married prostitution and the thirst for infinite adultery. Age and poverty, however wisely she will analyze them, are also a metaphor for her lost innocence; and thus the "leeve mooder" reintroduces to all *appearances* the salacious experience of Alice's own "dame." She is foul with all the jolly sins that buried the child.

In this dream, age and ugliness will drop away like rags, the child will stand revealed, because the knight will restore her honor by perceiving it; *you are good,* he will say, *you decide.* But since the Loathly Lady has minted a fortune in the nasty sty, it is she who in the same bed must cause the man to make the perception—to have him say, without the sexual inducement, that he liked her. The Wife dreams a second chance for her, in which she can ask, "What is my gilt?," and wait for an answer; for there in the dark she can talk as if her chastity were still to be kept and there were yet "gentil dedes" to be done.

Tell me, says the Wife to the pilgrims... Tell me, says the hag to the knight, as she recites in the dark her implacable, inviolable praise of impossible virtue... Tell me I was a good girl once.

And there in the dark, he does.

Source: Britton J. Harwood, "The Wife of Bath and the Dream of Innocence," in *Modern Language Quarterly*, Vol. 33, No. 3, September 1972, pp. 257–73.

R. T. Lenaghan

In the following essay, Lenaghan examines the "General Prologue" as a historical document, asserting that it offers "a richer sense of a civil servant's values than the usual documents afford."

The "General Prologue" is often called a picture of its age and, frequently in the next breath, a satire. In English Lit. this usually draws a stern lecture about confusing the distinction between literature and history, but in this essay, unobserved by my sophomores, I propose to talk about the "General Prologue" as a picture of its age and then, tentatively, about some uses such history might be put to by historians and literary students.

The "General Prologue" has an obvious historical interest as a series of discrete bits of information about dress, customs, etc.; but if it is to be considered as a more general historical formulation, there is a question of coherence. Is Chaucer's fictional society sufficiently coherent to warrant taking it seriously as fourteenth-century sociology? The best reason for an affirmative answer is rather vague. It is simply the strong sense most readers have that Chaucer is sampling, that his pilgrims are representatives. There are certainly omissions from his roll, but he does give good coverage to the middle segment of society. The nature he is imitating is social in a sense that is worthy of a sociologist's regard. To put it rather grandly, Chaucer's imitation has the same general ontological status as the sociologist's model; both are representative fictions. This analogy serves my purpose by temporarily converting the literary fiction into a series of hypothetical propositions which may be examined and defined before they are verified. What are the hypothetical patterns of social organization? Then, were they truly descriptive?

The "General Prologue" suggests at least three different ways of pinning down my general sense of coherence to a more specific pattern of social organization. One would be to invoke the widely familiar theory of the three estates. Chaucer's Knight, Parson, and Plowman do seem to exist as governing ideals, but the effort to classify the pil-

> *The basic fact of life in the society of the 'General Prologue' is economic struggle. The pilgrims' occupational labels are obvious keys to their individual struggles or exemption from struggle and thus to their social position.*

grims in one or another of the estates makes it clear that this pattern has the same trouble with the world of the "General Prologue" as it has with the real one. It doesn't account for the complexities of commerce. The second way would be to follow up Chaucer's expressed intention to discuss each pilgrim's degree, but once again Chaucer's society is too complex for clear hierarchical classifications, as he himself suggests. The third, and I think the best, way of establishing a pattern of organization is to infer it from Chaucer's practice and say the obvious: he presents his pilgrims by occupational labels, he is concerned with what men do. In the "General Prologue," as elsewhere, what men do falls largely into the category of economics. There is certainly a generous provision of economic information in the description of the pilgrims, and although there is a good deal of other information as well, the economic information is sufficiently cohesive to justify taking it as the basic matter of my argument. This focus certainly places the discussion within the historian's purview, but it may seem rather less useful for literary study. However, the study of history can illuminate the norms that govern the irony of the "General Prologue," and defining that irony is very much a literary question.

Taking the economic information as basic, then, I shall consider the sources of livelihood for the pilgrims and ask how they lived, according to the information Chaucer gives. These sources fall into three large classes: land, the Church, and trade (understood to include everything not in the other two, manufacture, commerce, and services). My intention is not to treat the pilgrims as representatives of classified occupations but rather to regard them collectively and to infer patterns of life from their descriptions. I am not concerned to place the Miller either in land or in trade or to justify placing the Physician with the others in trade. I want to infer from the various descriptions information about the kind of life provided by land, the Church, and trade. For example, the Man of Law lives by his professional services and so I would classify him in trade, but I am mainly interested in some information his description gives about life based on land.

The descriptions of the Plowman, the Reeve, and the Franklin should provide detailed information about the economics of land, but except for the description of the Reeve the yield is slight. There is much detail about the Franklin but it has very little to do with economics. It shows more about spending than getting, a difference I shall come back to. The Reeve's description, however, tells a good deal more. The first point is obvious enough, his expertise is managerial. It is founded on practical agricultural knowledge in that he can calculate exactly the effect of the weather on yield, and it is founded on a practical knowledge of human nature in that he knows the tricks of all the bailiffs and herdsmen. The two kinds of practical knowledge add up to efficient operation of his lord's establishment, but not necessarily to his lord's profit. The tight control he maintains over his operations stops with him; no one above him checks up on him as he checks up on those below him. As a result, "ful riche was he astored prively." This leads to a second and less obvious point, a role change. He uses his personal gains as a landholder's agent to establish himself as a landholder in his own right. That, I take it, is the meaning context indicates for the word *purchase:* "His wonyng was ful faire upon an heeth; / With grene trees yshadwed was his place. / He koude bettre than his lord purchase." What is interesting about this role change is the change in the Reeve's activities that it brings about. From hard-nosed managing, which causes him to be feared, he switches to giving and lending, which his lord mistakenly, or at least uncomprehendingly, regards as generous. From sharp practice to the image of generosity, the calculating agent has become a comfortably situated landholder.

This division of activities is significant in the world of the "General Prologue." It shows the social implication of the economic pattern for prosperity: the profits from efficient operation go into the purchase of land, that is, into capital expansion; profits are earned by "operators," the landholder is economically passive. This division of activity also brings into focus some pilgrims like the Franklin who are associated with land by their occupational designations but whose descriptions contain very little practical economic information. Pilgrims deriving their livelihood from land fall into two Chaucerian sub-classes: agents, who see to the operation and expansion of agricultural enterprises; and principals, the landholders. The agents are described by the work they do, the principals by less clearly economic or non-economic activities, by their social activities, their life style.

In addition to the Reeve's work there is another level of agency and another kind of agent's work. This is the legal work of control and capital expansion. In the Manciple's temple there are a dozen lawyers so expert that they are "Worthy to be stywardes of rente and lond. / Of any lord that is in Engelond." The agent's expertise is still managerial but now the basic knowledge is legal. Even on the Reeve's level the emphasis can be shifted from words like *bynne, yeldynge,* and *dayerye,* to words like *covenant, rekenynge,* and *arrerage* in order to show the lawyer's concern in stewardship of rent. Legal draughtsmanship is the crucial skill here. The Man of Law "koude endite, and make a thyng, / Ther koude no wight pynche at his writyng." The Man of Law was also expert in the second category of stewardship, land: "So greet a purchasour was nowher noon / Al was fee symple to hym in effect; / His purchasyng myghte nat been infect." Because of the contextual emphasis on legal skill I read *purchasour* as implying agency; the lawyer buys land for his client by removing the legal restrictions to make it as available as if it had been held in fee simple. Chaucer has given more information about farm management than about dirt farming, and as a consequence his agriculture seems rather bureaucratic. Different kinds of agents work at different levels of removal from the land, but socially the important point is that they all work.

The other class of pilgrims deriving their livelihood from land do not work, at least not directly for their own monetary gain. The Franklin's description dwells on the quantity and quality of his table with mention of its sources of supply in his pond and mew. Less noticed, because Chaucer emphasizes them less, are his public offices, which indicate significant service and a somewhat higher social station than he is often credited with. We have a landholder, then, who is defined not by the operation of his holdings but by his hospitality and public offices. The Knight and the Squire divide these tendencies, the Knight being defined by his service and the Squire by his style. The Monk, though not indicated as a landholder, enjoys the position of one. Hunting is expensive sport and he is a great hunter, presumably because he can command some of his monastery's wealth. The Prioress is a ladylike equivalent.

In the "General Prologue" landed wealth supports a variety of social activities. There are sports and entertainment, like the Monk's hunting and the Franklin's table. There are the Franklin's political service and the Knight's military service against the heathen. Somewhere between sport and service come the Squire's activities, ostensibly directed to entertainment but carrying enough suggestion of probationary regimen to indicate a *gentil* imperative. These activities, taken all together, do much to define the life style of gentlemen and ladies. The supporting wealth comes obviously from agricultural operations and less obviously from capital expansion, and it is earned by the agents who work for the landholders. The two groups are defined by different activities; the agents get and the principals spend, the agents work and the principals amuse themselves and render public service. This is the central pattern of Chaucer's social structure.

This distinction between principals and agents disappears in the loosely assembled activities of commerce, manufacturing, and service that I have grouped together in trade. There, despite the wide social range from the Cook to the Merchant, each of these pilgrims shares a common necessity to face the rigors of economic competition on his own. The Merchant buys and sells and dabbles in currency exchange. The Wife of Bath is a cloth maker. The Cook puts his culinary skill to hire. Yet somewhat surprisingly the yield of economic particulars is not great. Although we are not definitely told what the commerce of the merchant is, we are given an informal audit of his position, something none of his fellows could get. In other words, the thing that interests the narrator about the Merchant is his balance sheet. It is not perfectly clear whether or not the "dette" is ordinary commercial credit, "chevyssaunce." It is clear, however, that the Merchant thinks his interest requires secrecy, implying an apprehension of vulnerability, insecurity. On a lower level, the Shipman's pilferage, the Miller's gold thumb and the Manciple's percentage show more directly predatory activities and indicate the rule of precarious individual interest. A more indirect suggestion of such a pattern of life occurs in the description of the guildsmen where the narrator's emphasis falls on their appearance, which is

consonant with ceremonial dignity. Each of them was "a fair burgeys / To sitten in a yeldehall on a deys." That status is a reward is not especially illuminating, but the intensity of the competition for it does suggest sharp need and insecurity.

> Everich, for the wisdom that he kan,
> Was shaply for to been an alderman.
> For catel hadde they ynogh and rente,
> And eek hir wyves wolde it wel assente;
> And elles certeyn were they to blame.
> It is ful fair to been ycleped "madame,"
> And goon to vigilies al bifore,
> And have a mantel roialliche ybore.

Likewise the Wife of Bath:

> In al the parisshe wif ne was ther noon
> That to the offrynge bifore hire sholde goon;
> And if ther dide, certeyn so wrooth was she,
> That she was out of alle charitee.

In various ways, then, the descriptions of the pilgrims in trade betray an apprehensiveness. Their positions may deteriorate, and even those of high degree seem vulnerable to a greater extent than more or less equivalently placed pilgrims in the other categories.

Granting the fact of predatory competition and the implicit insecurity, one might still pause before characterizing Dame Alice as a neurotic status seeker. She may be sensitive about the due formalities of the offertory, but it is also true that "In felaweshipe wel koude she laugh and carpe." Her Rome and Jerusalem probably had quite a bit of Miami about them. Since the Miller is a "jangler and a goliardeys," the social life of at least some of the pilgrims in trade seems vigorous and uninhibited. The best sense of this tavern *gemütlichkeit* is conveyed by the narrator's description of the Friar's social style.

> His typet was ay farsed ful of knyves
> And pynnes, for to yeven faire wyves.
> And certeinly he hadde a murye note;
> Wel koude he synge and pleyen on a rote;
> Of yeddynges he baar outrely the pris.
> His nekke whit was as the flour-de-lys;
> Therto he strong was as a champioun.
> He knew the tavernes wel in every toun
> And everich hostiler and tappestere
> Bet than a lazar or a beggestere;

The Host's primary qualification is that he is "myrie." The Merchant, the guildsmen, the Man of Law, and the Physician may be too far up the social ladder for this kind of fun; at any rate they are more sedate. Among the pilgrims who make their living in trade, at least for those on the lower social levels, the reward of their struggle is a free, sometimes boisterous conviviality.

Such blatantly materialistic self-interest would ideally set the churchmen on the pilgrimage apart from the rest, but it is perfectly clear from their descriptions that they are more of the world than they ought to be. The Parson, of course, is an ideal, and though he does move in the world, his sanctity sets him apart. However, even in the Parson's description two of the negative particulars indicate something of the practical economic operations of less saintly parsons who readily cursed for their tithes and would leave their parishes with curates to become chantry-priests or chaplains in London. There are churchmen who want to make money. In the descriptions of the Friar, the Summoner, and the Pardoner this materialistic drive is given sharp focus because, with allowance for institutional differences, they are all selling a service—the remission of sins. The Pardoner also sells fake relics as a sideline. The Friar had to pay for his begging territory, which, presumably, would also have been his confessional territory. The Summoner is an agent, working for the archdeacon's court. As a practical matter he took bribes, and so his remission of sins was simply escape from the archdeacon's jurisdiction. The Pardoner sold papal pardons, a practical short circuit of the sacrament of penance. Such churchmen seem to live lives like those of the Shipman, the Miller, and the Manciple. That is to say, they live by their wits under economic pressure, and furthermore the descriptions of the Friar and the Summoner indicate that the tavern is the scene of their social pleasures.

The Monk and the Prioress are hardly in this class but neither are they as saintly as the Parson. We learn a great deal about the style of their lives but nothing of the economic bases for such lives. The Monk is a great hunter and the Prioress is a refined and delicate lady, so their style is unmistakably *gentil.* Though the narrator says nothing of their economic arrangements, both are associated with landed establishments and presumably base their style of life on that kind of wealth. The social pattern discernible among the pilgrims with a livelihood from land seems applicable among the churchmen also. Landed wealth exempts the beneficiaries from the economic struggle that governs the lives of the others, lesser, churchmen. The churchmen divide socially into those who live on the income from a landed establishment and those who earn their living directly. Of the latter group, the obvious generalization is that the remission of sins has become a commercial transaction. A less obvious but more interesting one follows: this commerce was highly competitive, the competitors

representing different ecclesiastical institutions. It seems that Chaucer does not separate his churchmen into a special category. In other words, except for the saintly, ideal Parson, clerical occupations are social and economic indicators in the same way as lay occupations.

The basic fact of life in the society of the "General Prologue" is economic struggle. The pilgrims' occupational labels are obvious keys to their individual struggles or exemption from struggle and thus to their social position. But there is little value in learning that the Knight does not have to struggle like the Cook and that his degree is higher. The pilgrims' descriptions, however, do more; they imply a sharper general pattern for life in the world of the *"General Prologue."* This pattern is clearest among the pilgrims whose living comes from land. There the distinction between principals and agents marks a man as above the economic struggle or in the middle of it and consequently sets a *gentil* style of life apart from the others. Among the pilgrims making a living in trade the distinction does not appear because each one must struggle in his own interest. These pilgrims seem less secure and there is no *gentilesse.* Since the churchmen are not landholders, their case would seem to be similar; yet there is *gentilesse* among their number. The social implications of the distinction between principals and agents reappears, and once again access to landed wealth is determinative.

Pilgrims are what they do, and what most of them do primarily is work. They work competitively within the rules like the Man of Law or outside them like the Pardoner. This stress on hustle and competition creates a society quite different from that implicit in the pattern of the three estates with its stress on complementary self-subordination in a system of cooperation. To be sure, some of the pilgrims do transcend the common struggle. The exemplars of the three estates, the Knight, the Parson, and the Plowman, do so by a moral force unique to them; the Monk, the Prioress, and the Franklin do so because of economic advantage; their wealth is secure. If one can judge by the Merchant's position on Chaucer's roster of pilgrims, his degree is fairly high, but he does not transcend the struggle, perhaps because in the world of the "General Prologue" his wealth is not secure. At any rate his style of life is different from those who are above competition because he has to compete, as do most of his fellow pilgrims. This difference between landed wealth and other wealth can be clarified by another comparison. The Reeve's peculation links him with the Manciple and the

Friar, and so my threefold division does not seem helpful here. If we move upward within the several groups, however, things look different in that the Merchant's description sets his position apart from that of the Knight or the Monk, who both have the use of landed wealth. The Reeve's switch in economic role and social style would seem to be possible only in land, because when the Reeve becomes a landholder in his own right he is more secure than the Merchant. Chaucer seems to hold with Fitzgerald against Hemingway; the rich, at least the landed rich, are different from the rest.

Just how different they are can be seen in what we learn of their sexual habits. They transcend sexual as well as economic competition. Though there is much less about sex than money in the "General Prologue," there is a pattern to the relatively little we are told. We know nothing about the sex lives of the Knight and the Franklin, and we have only the slightest and most ambiguous hints about the Monk and the Prioress. In contrast, we do know something of the sexual activities and outlook of the Wife of Bath, the Friar and the Summoner. The Squire is the crucial case; he is a lover and he draws his living from the land. But his love seems more a matter of regimen than of sex. There is only one reference to a girl, and the focus is much more on his chivalry than on any practical consequences of his lady's favor. In the "General Prologue," sex, like money, seems to be lower class.

So far I have been talking about fiction and hypotheses, Chaucer's imitation or model. There are still questions of fact. Historian's questions deserve historian's answers, which I shall not try seriously to provide. But one does not have to be a serious historian to question the general proposition that the landed classes were economically and sexually inactive, that there was a categorical distinction between most men who struggled to live and a smaller group of landholders who were above the struggle. Division of society into hustlers and gentlemen sounds questionable, and the Paston letters, to cite the most convenient text, clearly indicate that gentlemen were often effective hustlers. In short, historians are more likely to hold with Hemingway on the subject of difference from the rich. Granting that the most general rule for life in the world of the "General Prologue" does not hold true outside it, and deferring the question of how a shrewd observer like Chaucer went wrong, the historian might still be interested in some of the less general rules for life. For example, was "agency" an avenue of social mobility? If it was, was it equally accessible at all points? Could the Reeve

make the change from agent to landholder that he did? Could he move upward as easily at his level as the Man of Law at his? Could either one of them move upward as easily as the Pastons, smaller landholders serving as the agents of larger landholders? Another focus of interest might be the status distinctions in "public service." Military and political offices went more or less naturally to the landed families, and in the cities a more limited range of offices also went naturally to the chief citizens, presumably because they represented important and separately identifiable interests. What were the status implications of public office? What were the status relations between men in public office because of an independent social and economic identification and those men who worked as career officials, the civil servants? Professor Thrupp has shown that at least some career civil servants were gentlemen *ex officio*. It does seem clear that the civil service was an avenue of social mobility and that it provided a range of acquaintance, but acquaintanceship with landed families might simply underscore differences in social and economic security and in the practical possibility of providing for the future of a family. These questions should give some idea of the historical uses of the "General Prologue." It is a credible fourteenth-century model of the middle range of English society; it sets questions for historical verification.

The major literary use of this model is to fill out or elaborate a connection between Chaucer the man and Chaucer the pilgrim-narrator. The poetic manifestation of a writer's values is certainly an important literary question. Chaucer has been well served by Professor Donaldson, who has nicely described the narrative sympathies and ironies of the "General Prologue" in such a way as to clarify the fine combination of amiability and criticism that emanates from the narrator. The structure and descriptions of the "General Prologue" define the narrator's position; he is diffident but central. They also define his values. His representatives of the three estates are moral and social exemplars; the Knight, the Parson, and the Plowman all strive but they do it selflessly rather than competitively. Less clearly, the two probationers, the Squire and the Clerk, are also selfless. The Monk, the Prioress, and the Franklin are hardly selfless but neither are they vigorously assertive of an economic or sexual interest. Although they fall short of true *gentilesse*, their manners and their life style are *gentil* in a lesser but still valuable sense because they show none of the antagonism inherent in competition. This pattern of approbation implies precepts of orthodox charity and social conservatism. But there is nothing rigid or insensitive about this espousal of establishment values because it is winningly mollified by the suffused amiability of the narration. The pilgrim's tone is eminently charitable. No matter how antiseptic our critical practice is about separating narrator and author, the art work and life, we do look to an ultimate point of contact. Though Shakespeare's sonnets do not tell us anything conclusive about his sex life, the proliferation of their metaphors does tell us about his mental and emotional life. The practical charity, orthodoxy, and social conservatism evident in Chaucer's poetic narrative can likewise be referred to the poet.

The narrator-pilgrim's amiability and clarity of criticism are the poet's, but this connection is more interestingly elaborated by working in the opposite direction, from writer to narrator, to supply a deficiency in the scheme of the "General Prologue." Chaucer the pilgrim failed to provide for himself what he gave for all the other pilgrims—an occupational designation. If we give the poet's to the pilgrim and call him a civil servant, we have a supplementary and external definition of the narrator's position.

This embellishment is attractive because it sets the values of the "General Prologue" in precise historical relief. It refers them to a historically identifiable perspective. I deferred the puzzling question of how a shrewd observer like Chaucer could have been so wrong about his basic distinction between landholders and the rest of society. Landholders were economically and, presumably, sexually competitive, as anyone with a career like Chaucer's must have known. But to a civil servant their social position may well have looked far more secure than his own and their style far more negligent of practical economics than the evidence indicates. The civil servant's perspective would certainly be affected by the mobility aspirations associated with that social role and by the limits on the possibilities for fulfillment of those aspirations. In short, both the distortion and the accuracy of Chaucer's social description are plausible for a civil servant.

The details of Chaucer's observation vivify his use of the commonplace scheme of the three estates by giving the charity of its exemplars a fuller and more realistic setting. In other words, he has asserted orthodox values, spliced them with mobility aspirations, and adjusted them to reality. The same social perspective can be fixed in the literary work and in the real world of the fourteenth century. Chaucer the pilgrim talks like a civil servant and Chaucer the poet is a civil servant. The historian gains a richer sense of a civil servant's values than the usual documents afford, and the literary student gains a fuller sense of the social grounding of the norms that govern the irony of the "General Prologue."

Source: R. T. Lenaghan, "Chaucer's 'General Prologue' as History and Literature," in *Comparative Studies in Society and History*, Vol. 12, No. 1, January 1970, pp. 73–82.

Beryl B. Rowland

In the following essay, Rowland explores connections to the Mystery plays in "The Miller's Tale."

The last line of the Miller's "Prologue" has been variously interpreted as indicative of Chaucer's aesthetic intentions both in the tale itself and in his works as a whole. In it, the narrator, after warning his readers of the kind of tale to follow and disclaiming responsibility should any of them subsequently "chese amys," adds a final rider: "and eek men shal nat maken ernest of game." The phrase itself is sufficiently commonplace to be classified as proverbial, and variations of it occur four times elsewhere in the Tales: January finally settles on one delectable young girl as his bride "bitwixe ernest and game"; Griselda, bereft of her daughter, never mentions her name either "in ernest nor in game," and Walter, despite the murmurs of his subjects, continues to try his wife "for ernest ne for game"; the Host is relieved that wine can resolve the differences between the Cook and the Manciple and "turnen ernest into game." But in these instances the implied polarities are unequivocal. Only in the Miller's "Prologue" does the phrase seem to contain tantalizing ambiguities and to mean more than a prefunctory tag. Some critics differ on whether the narrator is advising the more squeamish of his readers to skip the tale for the immorality of its action, the vulgarity of its speech, or for both reasons. Others, inasmuch as they consider that Chaucer's "game" always has serious intent, appear to regard the statement as ironic.

The assumption in every case is that "game" has the meaning of gaiety or mirth for which numerous instances are cited in the *Middle English Dictionary*. The possibility arises, however, that Chaucer, in adumbrating a particular kind of tale to warn off those of his audience who preferred "storial thyng that toucheth gentilesse, / And eek moralitee and hoolynesse", was using "game" in a specific sense directly pertinent to the action which follows.

For game in this sense, the *Middle English Dictionary* cites only two examples, and the *New English Dictionary* alludes only to games in antiquity. Nevertheless "game" was a common term for the Mystery Drama, and appears in the *Promptorium Parvulorum* as the equivalent of "play" (*ludus*) as well as *iocus*. The matter has been well documented since Rossell Hope Robbins contended that "game" was an equivalent for dramatic performance to support his claim that a proclamation admonishing an audience to keep quiet and not interrupt the "game" was a fragment of a Mystery Play. As evidence, he cited references to "oure game" and "oure play" contained in another fragment, clearly an epilogue to a Mystery Play, and to the proclamation in the *Ludus Coventriae*—"Of holy wrytte þis game xal bene." He also showed similar usage in the earliest extant morality play, *The Pride of Life*, and in a sermon quoted by Owst. Its use in the two fragments, one ascribed to the thirteenth and the other to the sixteenth century, suggests currency over a long period, and apart from various town records concerning "game gear," "game-book," "game pleyers gownes and coats," the "Lopham game," the "Garblesham game," and the "Kenningale game," further evidence has accrued to show conclusively that "game" and "play" were used interchangeably.

If "game" has this specialized meaning in the Miller's "Prologue," "ernest" has a particular relevance. In its general combination with "game" or "play," "ernest" was simply an antonym meaning serious; used with reference to drama, it was reality in contrast to counterfeit. This distinction was made by the Wycliffite preacher to support the argument that the play marked an abstention from the true concerns of life. The meaning was even more strongly defined by Skelton, who took the view that the polarities were reconcilable and that truth could be presented under the guise of play:

> Take hede of this caytyfe that lyeth here on
>   grounde;
> Beholde, howe Fortune of hym hath frounde!
> For though we shewe you this in game and play,
> Yet it proueth eyrnest, ye may se, euery day.

This kind of usage suggests that Chaucer, in juxtaposing "ernest" and "game," may have been making an antithesis meaningful within the terms of the contemporary Mystery play.

That the "Miller's Tale" contains a number of allusions to the Mystery plays has often been noted, and Harder suggested that the tale might be a parody of a particular cycle. Certain references enable us to be more specific and to find in the tale one of the principal themes of the Mystery plays. The

It is clearly revealed in the typology of the protagonists, and, as in the Mystery plays, the link between one Fall and another is neatly and palpably established."

carpenter about whom the Miller promises a "legende and a lyf" directly points to St. Joseph of the Holy Family. Probably because of the late development in the West of his cult as a saint, he was one of the most extensively and independently treated characters in medieval drama, often in a comic mode. Like "selig" John, he too was aged, married to a young wife, and fearful of being cuckolded. The momentous event with which he is associated becomes the pivot of the burlesque.

To confirm the various elements of the "game" Chaucer uses the structural pattern found in the Mystery plays themselves. The creators of these dramas passed over many Biblical stories which seem equal or even superior to those dramatized. The reason was that the form of the pageants was determined by traditional exegesis. The writers sought to impose order and meaning upon their material by stressing correspondences and prefigurings cited in the Biblical text and further developed by hermeneutical writers from Tertullian onwards. As Kolve has observed:

> The dramatist simply took over certain significant patterns that had been long observed and studied in Biblical narrative, and by simplifying, abridging or neglecting entirely the mass of incident and detail that surrounds them, they produced a cycle sequence charged with theological meaning—strong, simple, and formally coherent.

Hence they included the story of Cain and Abel because it prefigured the death of Christ, and the play of Noah and the Flood because it prefigured Baptism, the Crucifixion and the end of the world. Similarly the story of Abraham and Isaac was important because it prefigured God's sacrifice of his own Son.

It is this kind of prefiguring, fundamental to the shaping and the interpretation of the Mystery Drama, that Chaucer observes in comic fashion. With audacious artistry he points up a comparable series of correspondences which are inherent in the central action. The initial event in his tale is a young man's salutation of a young woman. In appearance Nicholas resembles the somewhat effeminate-looking angel of the Annunciation—"lyk a mayden meke for to see"; he also has the attribute for which Gabriel was especially renowned in the Mystery plays: he sings divinely—"ful often blessed was his myrie throte." But his role is confirmed by *what* he sings: *Angelus ad virginem*, the hymn of the Annunciation, and the *Kynges Noote*, whereby he reveals God's purpose. The young woman, likened to the weasel, an animal traditionally compared to the Virgin because of the unnatural method of its conception, appears to play the complementary role. The travesty was probably not new to Chaucer's audience. Mary was supposed to have been abashed at the Annunciation because a young man had "made hym lyk an angyll" with the Devil's help and seduced maidens on pretext of a similar errand, and Boccaccio, in the second story of the fourth day, tells of a clerk who pretended to be Gabriel in order to seduce a young married woman. Here, the *logos* which is whispered in Alison's ear is an immediate reminder of the contrasting prefiguration to which exegetists of the Annunciation almost invariably referred. Instantly superimposed on the scene of the Annunciation is that of the first Temptation. Eve replaces *Ave*, and the "sleigh and ful privee" young man is the Serpent himself.

The role of the rival lover, Absolon, is also clearly defined in the "game." Although his namesake never appears to have been included in the cycles, the parish priest is too important to the tale not to be drawn into the sphere of the Mystery play, albeit obliquely. Prefiguring his own climactic attempt at cauterization or curettage, he is assigned the part of the bombastic villain whose most spectacular appearance concerned the Slaughter of the Innocents. Like Herod, "wel koude he laten blood and clippe and shave," and there is little difference in their instruments: Herod is usually depicted with his curved falchion; Absolon has his coulter. Both of them finally betake themselves to Satan. In displaying his "maistrye," Absolon is, one suspects, showing not only his skill but his profession, his "mystery," which is to be responsible for the dénouement.

As the plot develops, more correspondences become apparent. Essential to the central action is the story of Noah and the Flood, which dramatists treated as one of the most important prefigurations in the cycle. The aged Noah, a carpenter, singled

out by God to be His servant and fulfill His purpose for humanity, was considered to prefigure Christ. But he was also the type of Joseph, similarily a carpenter, and chosen as the divine instrument. John who, Nicholas implies, is also chosen by God, becomes the appropriate third correspondence. He, too, is an aged carpenter, *mal marié* if self-deceived, and like Noah he is subsequently to be mocked by his companions. Nicholas plays a similarly appropriate role: in some versions of the tale, God sends Gabriel or another angel to reveal His purpose to Noah. Moreover, inasmuch as the Flood was traditionally held to prefigure salvation through baptism, it is particularly apposite that Nicholas should regard the event as effecting his Salvation. Of even greater importance, however, is the role of the *uxor* in the episode. A popular development of the Noah episode in the Mystery cycles was the comic quarrel between Noah and his shrewish wife, which turned upon her reluctance to cooperate with him and enter the ark. Such domestic discord prefigures that of Joseph, often depicted in the plays as another aged *mal marié*. Nicholas is forced to draw John's attention to "the sorwe of Noe with his felaweshipe, / Ere that he myghte gete his wyf to shipe" in order to provide a reason for the separate tubs. But the reference sets off yet another correspondence. In the widely diffused folktale, Noah's wife succumbed to the blandishments of the Devil, and in the Newcastle-on-Tyne "Noah's Ark," the Wife's recalcitrance is due to her collusion with the Evil One. In the "Miller's Tale," Alison behaves towards John as the meek wife of the Noah plays in the *Ludus Coventriae* and the French mystère, the wife who was said to prefigure the Virgin, but her involvement again looks back to that of the First Temptation which traditionally prefigured this episode.

The reception of the tale by the pilgrims shows that many interpretations are possible: "Diverse folk diversely they seyde, But for the moore part they loughe and pleyde." This interpretation emphasizes one strand of the humor: the comic travesty of the St. Joseph legend, with Nicholas as the Evil One and Alison as Eve. The ambiguities inherent in the narrator's warning remain unresolved but among the various components of this complex tale, this aspect of "game" appears to be undeniably present. It is clearly revealed in the typology of the protagonists, and, as in the Mystery plays, the link between one Fall and another is neatly and palpably established.

Source: Beryl B. Rowland, "The Play of the 'Miller's Tale': A Game within a Game," in *Chaucer Review*, Vol. 5, No. 2, Fall 1970, pp. 140–46.

Alfred David

In the following essay, David examines various interpretations of the old man in "The Pardoner's Tale."

Probably the main trend in contemporary Chaucer criticism is to look for a symbolic level of meaning in a poet whom most of us were taught to regard as a supremely realistic recorder of medieval life. Of course, realism and symbolism are not necessarily antithetical modes of expression, and a lot of misunderstanding will be avoided if we recognize that the choice is not one of either-or, a realistic Chaucer or an allegorical one. It is rather that we are beginning to see another dimension in Chaucer, something that should not surprise us in a great poet. It goes without saying that symbolic interpretation is subject to abuse by the ingenious critic who can persuade himself and others to see the Emperor's clothes. Nevertheless, it can hardly be denied that we are in the midst of a reappraisal of Chaucer as an artist that is certain to influence the way in which he will be presented in the classroom.

Instead of talking generally about the reasons for such a new appraisal and its theoretical justification, I would prefer to discuss a particular instance that may illustrate this trend—a case history in practical criticism—the interpretation of a passage that everyone who has ever taught Chaucer has almost certainly dealt with at one time or another. One may then draw one's own conclusions about the uses and abuses of modern critical theory in the teaching of Chaucer.

One of the great moments in Chaucer comes in the "Pardoner's Tale" when the three young rioters, seeking Death, are greeted by a poverty-stricken old man, muffled so that only his face is visible. One of the three rudely asks him why he has lived so long and receives this strange and moving reply:

> "For I ne kan nat fynde
> A man, though that I walked into Ynde,
> Neither in citee ne in no village,
> That wolde chaunge his youthe for myn age;
> And therefore moot I han myn age stille,
> As longe tyme as it is Goddes wille.
> Ne Deeth, allas! ne wol nat han my lyf.
> Thus walke I, lyk a resteless kaityf,
> And on the ground, which is my moodres gate,
> I knokke with my staf, bothe early and late,
> And seye 'Leeve mooder, leet me in!'"

> *We might say that the Pardoner has something in common with both the old and the young men in his tale, and we have been prepared for this by his portrait and prologue."*

It is, of course, a passage that seems to demand a symbolic interpretation. One feels that there is a mystery about this old man, that something is being left unsaid. As I hope to make clear, however, our understanding of the symbol and how it works has changed over the years. Who is the old man? Professor Kittredge gave the answer that is probably the most familiar. "The aged wayfarer," Kittredge declared flatly, "is undoubtedly Death in person."

But why should Death be personified as an old man who himself wishes to die? Other scholars tried to uncover the old man's identity by seeking his antecedents in medieval literary history. According to one theory, Chaucer got his idea for the old man from the legend of the Wandering Jew, which first took shape in the thirteenth century. According to another theory, the old man is a personification of old age as one of the three messengers of death, a popular theme in late medieval poetry and sermons.

This is not the place to argue the individual merits of these theories, and scholarly speculations of this sort certainly have no place in the classroom. They are relevant for our purposes, however, because they suggest that the question of the old man's identity does not admit a simple, unambiguous, and definitive answer such as Death or Death's Messenger. In fact, it is doubtful whether Chaucer himself, if he were available to answer questions, could provide us with a ready answer. He has sketched the old man in a few strokes that, like shadows, suggest rather than define. We are given a muffled figure, a withered face, an impression of poverty and meekness, and the staff with which he taps the earth. Where does he come from and where is he going? Where is the chamber with the chest of possessions that he says he would exchange for a hair cloth? These are questions that it would be futile to try to answer. The power of the old man is the power of the symbol to suggest a range of meanings.

To say that the old man in many details resembles the Wandering Jew is, of course, not to say that he *is* the Wandering Jew. The legend of the Jew who struck Jesus (or, according to another version, drove him from his door) and who is condemned to roam the earth until the Second Coming contains one variant of the archetypal figure of the man cursed to wander forever without being able to die. This eternal traveler is the type we may also recognize in Chaucer's old man as well as in the Ancient Mariner and in the Flying Dutchman. These figures are not identical—each is a development of a general type, but assumes a particular meaning in the context of the work in which he appears.

Perhaps the mistaken notion that we are obliged to choose only one of several symbolic interpretations, none of them entirely satisfactory, led one critic to assert that "the old man is merely an old man" and that "The Pardoner's Tale" is thoroughly realistic. This interpretation implies that allegory and realism are alien and mutually exclusive forms—that the one contains personifications and the other actual people. On this assumption, we would have to insist that Kafka, Melville, and Dante are realists, as indeed in one sense they are. Certainly the old man in the "Pardoner's Tale" is first of all an old man, and the story contains elements of blood-curdling realism. We may read it at that level, but that does not preclude the possibility of other kinds of reading. If modern critical theories have one thing to teach us, it is that we need not read or teach literature in accordance with one narrow critical theory, including a narrow theory of realism.

Let me turn now to a more recent interpretation of the old man that illustrates the modern trend most clearly and that may be said to result from a new critical approach, imaginatively applied. According to this theory, most medieval literature, including Chaucer, is allegorical. A medieval tale is conceived of as a shell or a rind that contains a kernel of meaning, generally a Christian meaning. One way to get at this meaning is to look in the story for allusions to Scripture and to trace these allusions back to their source in the Bible and to explication of these Biblical passages by the Church fathers and medieval commentators. Thus traditional interpretation of Scripture provides us with clues to the interpretation of literary texts. An

excellent example of this approach is Robert P. Miller's interpretation of the old man in his article "Chaucer's Pardoner and the Scriptural Eunuch." Mr. Miller's case is carefully reasoned and depends on a great deal of evidence that it will be impossible to summarize here. In essence, however, it links together the Pardoner's portrait, his prologue, and his tale into a unified whole that expresses a traditional Christian meaning through symbolic description and narrative.

The old man, according to Mr. Miller, corresponds to the old man St. Paul speaks of several times as a symbol of the flesh or that part of human nature that must die before the spirit may be reborn through the agency of the new man (or the young man) who is Christ. For example, in Fourth Ephesians Paul tells us "to put off . . . the old man, which is corrupt according to the deceitful lusts, . . ." and "to put on the new man, which after God is created in righteousness and true holiness." The old man, or the old Adam, to give him his popular name, points the way to death, not just to physical death but to the death of the soul, and this is exactly what the old man in the "Pardoner's Tale" does when he directs the three rioters up the "crooked way." The old man is ancient—he is born with sin and death—and he will roam the fallen world until the end of time.

It is difficult to do justice to such an interpretation in outline. Even so, it should be apparent that it does not cancel out other interpretations but instead synthesizes them within a broader context. As soon as we begin thinking about the "Pardoner's Tale" as a story not only about physical life and death but about spiritual life and death, many details, both about the tale and its teller, become meaningful. The difference between a symbolic interpretation such as this and one like Kittredge's is that the former depends on our understanding not of an isolated symbol, used for the immediate occasion, but on an understanding of the Pardoner's portrait and prologue and, indeed, of the *Canterbury Tales* as a whole; for the most interesting ramification of Mr. Miller's interpretation is that it involves the Pardoner himself, an impotent man who sells sterile pardons and who interacts with the other pilgrims on a journey that is not only realistic but symbolic. There is an implied analogy between the old man and the Pardoner. "He is," Mr. Miller argues, "that Old Man as he lives and exerts his influence in the great pilgrimage of life." Like the old man the Pardoner wanders ceaselessly through city and village, sending men up the "croked wey."

Mr. Miller's method could be viewed as a new and fascinating kind of source study, but the real support for his interpretation does not come from the Epistles and obscure medieval commentaries upon them. Like all source studies, his must stand or fall by the text, and he has given us a new key, not merely to one passage, but to the entire sequence formed by the Pardoner's portrait, prologue, and tale. A meaningful pattern that was only dimly felt before begins to emerge.

Suggestive as such an interpretation is, however, I think it would be going too far to maintain that St. Paul's old man contains the only key to the passage; one might even wonder whether Chaucer had this image in mind when he was composing the "Pardoner's Tale." However, the Scriptural metaphor remains relevant because Paul himself, in coining it, was following a natural symbolism that is as old as literature. Something that should be kept in mind whenever one tries to interpret a Scriptural image or allusion in a medieval literary text is the fact that the Bible itself contains literature and that Scriptural exegesis may involve some literary criticism. The fact that such exegesis may help us to understand a work of the imagination does not necessarily mean that the author consciously drew his meaning from Scriptural commentary alone.

Moreover, if we are to see a connection between the Pardoner and the Old Man in the tale, Mr. Miller's interpretation does not account for significant differences between them. He implies that both the Pardoner and his counterpart, the old man, are inveterately evil, and he concludes: "... the Old Man still goes wandering through the world, glaring with sterile lust out of his hare-like eyes." But the old man of the tale speaks meekly to the rioters and prays that God may save them. He sounds in every way like a humble pious old man and not a bit like the Pardoner—except for one brief but memorable passage at the end of his tale where the Pardoner addresses the pilgrims:

> And lo, sires, thus I preche.
> And Jhesu Crist, that is oure soules leche,
> So graunte yow his pardoun to receyve,
> For that is best; I wol yow nat deceyve.

This is the moment that Kittredge called "a paroxysm of agonized sincerity," and it echoes the old man's words to the three ruffians:

> God save yow, that boghte agayn mankynde,
> And yow amende!

Both instances are prayers of grace for others, and both, I feel, are sincere.

What I am suggesting is that the old man does indeed tell us something about the Pardoner but something more profound than the redundancy that the Pardoner is an evil man. The old man tells us something about the frustration, the suffering, and the self-destructiveness of evil. For evil may be both like a young man who defies death and like an old man whose only wish is to die.

We might say that the Pardoner has something in common with *both* the old and the young men in his tale, and we have been prepared for this by his portrait and prologue. One of Mr. Miller's most perceptive insights is the ironic fact that the Pardoner, who corresponds to the old man, affects an appearance of youth. He dresses somewhat flashily "al of the newe jet," rides bare-headed exposing his stringy yellow locks that hang down over his shoulders, proclaims his desire for wine and wenches, and impudently asks the Wife of Bath, in his interruption of her prologue, to "teche us yonge men of youre praktike." Although we are given no indication that he is an old man, he is certainly past his prime. A guess might make him out to be about the same age as the Wife of Bath herself.

It requires only observation, not scholarship, to see what lies behind the pose of an ageing man who dresses like a young man and who affects an air of gay abandon, especially when we are told that he must have been "a geldyng or a mare." The truth about the Pardoner is already hinted at very broadly in the description of his duet with "his freend and his compeer," the Summoner:

> Ful loude he soong "Com hider, love, to me!"
> This Somonour bar to hym a stif burdoun.

Two recent notes on this passage provide convincing evidence that the word "burdoun," which may mean both a musical bass and a pilgrim's staff, would have been recognized in the fourteenth century as an obscene pun that clearly implies that the friendship between the Pardoner and the Summoner is homosexual.

For Chaucer, however, the Pardoner's physical perversion is not the key to his character as it might be for a novelist today. The Pardoner's isolation from natural human love is rather the outward sign of a deeper alienation from divine love. It is a fact that has symbolic as well as realistic value. His disguises as a young man and as a Pardoner (for his role as Pardoner, too, is a kind of disguise) conceal a fascination with death that is projected powerfully into the macabre tale. The old man's death wish and the deaths of the three young men at each other's hands reveal the Pardoner's own preoccupation with death and violence.

The three villains are among the "yonge folk" who haunt the tavern. Their vices—drunkenness, blasphemy, and avarice—are those that the Pardoner boastfully claims as his own. Their quest to slay Death has an ironic resemblance to the mission the Pardoner abuses, that is to absolve men from the seven deadly sins. Their camaraderie suggests the sort of companionship that we have seen between the Pardoner and the Summoner. A sadistic element dominates the association of these three blood brothers and culminates when one of them is stabbed as he wrestles "in game" with one of the other two. There is a perverse gratification in the violence and the violent deaths of the young men.

But the Pardoner, much as he would like to conceal it by his dress and his forced jollity, is not one of the "yonge folk," nor is the pleasure he professes to find in vice a genuine pleasure. If we listen carefully to his Prologue, I think we may detect the false note of bravado and the sense of strain:

> I wol nat do no labour with myne handes,
> Ne make baskettes, and lyve therby,
> By cause I wol nat beggen ydelly.
> I wol noon of the apostles countrefete;
> I wol have moneie, wolle, chese, and whete,
> Al were it yeven of the povereste page,
> Or of the povereste wydwe in a village,
> Al sholde hir children sterve for famyne.

There is something almost hysterical about the reiteration of "I wol" and "I wol not," like an angry child defying its parents. The Pardoner is, in short, a young-old man, and the confrontation between the three rioters and the old man in the tale brings to the surface a moral and psychological conflict that has been latent all along.

The old man's longing for death, his inability to find anyone who will exchange youth for his age—this expresses the other side of the Pardoner's nature. Perhaps St. Paul conceived of the old man not as Mr. Miller might have it, "glaring with sterile lust," but as weary unto death of his burden and seeking only to lay it down. The compulsive wish for the tavern life sought by the three young men is complemented by the old man's death wish. Through the old man Chaucer reveals the Pardoner's real secret, the joylessness of the life he professes to relish so much. And the old man enables us, in this most pitiless of the *Canterbury Tales*, to feel compassion not only for him but, by association, for the Pardoner, a compassion that is denied to none of the pilgrims.

As a final comment on the symbolism inherent in the old man and the Pardoner—for however one conceives of their relationship I feel they are inseparable— let me draw an analogy to a modern symbolic tale about death. Aboard the steamer carrying Gustave von Aschenbach to Venice, he is observing a boisterous group of young clerks on a holiday excursion:

> One of the party, in a dandified buff suit, a rakish panama with a coloured scarf, and a red cravat, was loudest of the loud: he outcrowed all the rest. Aschenbach's eye dwelt on him, and he was shocked to see that the apparent youth was no youth at all. He was an old man, beyond a doubt, with wrinkles and crow's-feet round eyes and mouth; the dull carmine of the cheeks was rouge, the brown hair a wig... Aschenbach was moved to shudder as he watched the creature and his association with the rest of the group. Could they not see he was old, that he had no right to wear the clothes they wore or pretend to be one of them? But they were used to him, it seemed; they suffered him among them, they paid back his jokes in kind and the playful pokes in the ribs he gave them.

This grotesque figure, as we come to realize, is the first apparition of Death in Venice, a moral death as well as a physical one that will swallow up Aschenbach and transform him at the end into the very image of the young-old man. In this story, too, a plague motivates the action and provides a unifying symbol of corruption.

I do not want to force an analogy between works as different as *Death in Venice* and the "Pardoner's Tale," yet I believe that the resemblance between them is not entirely fortuitous because the characters in both stories arise independently out of a basic, archetypal symbolism that is always available. It is a symbolism that is elusive and cannot be reduced to any single or simple meaning.

The "Pardoner's Tale" is a story that can lend itself to a Freudian as well as to a Christian interpretation, neither of which would be exclusively right or totally wrong.

If a practical conclusion may be drawn from such a case history in criticism, perhaps it is that, as teachers, we should resist the natural tendency of critics and students to oversimplify symbols, to impose on them some definite meaning that will provide the stuff for an essay in a journal or in a bluebook. The different critical opinions I have cited all have something to contribute and do not cancel each other out. Kittredge was probably right after all—the old man is Death—but as I hope this analysis has shown, Death may assume many different guises and meanings.

Source: Alfred David, "Criticism and the Old Man in Chaucer's 'Pardoner's Tale,'" in *College English*, Vol. 27, No. 1, November 1965, pp. 39–44.

Richard Neuse

In the following essay, Neuse explores the characters of the Knight and Theseus, and calls the "Knight's Tale" a "testimony to the insufficiency of human wisdom at the same time that it transcends it."

In recent years there seems to have been general agreement that the "Knight's Tale" is a "philosophical romance" which raises the problem of an apparently unjust and disorderly universe. By this reading the "Tale" emerges as a philosophic theodicy culminating in Theseus' speech on cosmic order. The latter implicitly denies the final reality or rule of an arbitrary Fortune, but at the same time stoically accepts the inscrutable workings "in this wrecched world adoun" of an eternal cause. The "Tale" is thus seen as the Knight's—and Theseus'—somewhat wistful "consolation of philosophy," the affirmation of an ultimate order that actual experience seems, often sadly, to deny.

Quite recently a study has suggested that the "Tale" "depicts its human world in a more critical light" than has hitherto been acknowledged. The author challenges the view that Theseus is the spokesman for the poem's concept of order by pointing to the problematic nature of Theseus' actions and to the inadequacies of his philosophic outlook. Nonetheless he continues to regard the "Tale's" central theme as the assertion of a divine order; but instead of finding this theme directly figured forth by Theseus, he sees it embodied in the symmetrical structure of the "Tale" itself. The poetic form is thought to be the vehicle for a philosophic idea.

At first glance, it seems surprising that either the Knight or Theseus, both successful men of action, should feel in need of philosophic consolation. Indeed, the "Tale" could be considered as Theseus' success story: it begins with his triumphant campaign and ends with his plan to have Palamon marry Emily brought to a successful conclusion. It may be objected that Theseus is not the real focus of attention, and that the problem arises from the unequal fates of Palamon and Arcite. Again, however, the story begins with the rescue of these two from almost certain death—a stroke of singularly good fortune—and both get precisely what they asked for. Arcite has his victory and "finest hour"; Palamon and Emily live happily ever after.

What is left of the dark fatality that has been found lurking in the "Tale?" And what of the philosophical problem? With respect to Palamon and

> *In a variety of ways, the Knight is able to suggest an alternative manner of looking at man and society, not least by the comedy of his 'Tale.'"*

Arcite, it is contended, character-differentiation has been deliberately underplayed so that the question of justice in the world must be confronted: when two equally deserving men strive for the same goal, why should one succeed while the other is killed?

"What is this world? What asketh men to have?" the dying Arcite is led to ask, and his question is indeed tragic in suggesting a fatal gap between human expectation and the apparently arbitrary ways of the world. Theseus' final oration only underscores this gap in terms of a theoretical reason and a practical unreason. As it images a world order governed by the Prime Mover, it holds out to man no more than the certainty of death. The human spirit has no discernible place in this cosmos, and yet it is subjected to the corruption of matter. If man is no longer the fool of fortune, he is the victim of necessity.

But Theseus here not only "fails to see the crux of the human situation" philosophically; he also appears as the spokesman and representative of a world-view which the entire narrative places in an ambiguous light. To show how this is so, I shall propose a different view of the *"Knight's Tale,"* with respect to the kind of poem it is, and its place in the scheme of the *Canterbury Tales,* both as the beginning of its human comedy and as the imaginative act of the Knight-narrator.

Like many of the other tales, the "Knight's Tale" reveals a teller self-consciously engaged in reshaping (and adapting) an "olde storie" for the audience and the occasion. This much is clear. But it does not seem to have been argued hitherto that the Knight's approach is basically comic and ironic. We see him in an unbuttoned, holiday mood. Repeatedly, he places his narrative and his audience in a comic light: interrupting his tale in the manner of the *demande d'amour:*

Yow loveres axe I now this questioun,
Who hath the worse, Arcite or Palamoun? . . .

delivering a witty comment on the situation in the grove when Palamon overhears Arcite, or on the behaviour of lovers:

Into a studie he [Arcite] fil sodeynly,
As doon thise loveres in hir queynte geres,
Now in the crope, now doun in the breres,
Now up, now doun, as boket in a welle . . .

At first glance, indeed, there seems to be an inconsistency between this playful narrator and the imposing figure of the "General Prologue" who is yet "as meeke as is a mayde." But we must not be misled by the method of the "General Prologue": there it is mainly external "identity" that counts. The pilgrims appear as self-sufficient "concrete universals" while their potentialities—the incompleteness of their natures—remain largely hidden until they enter upon the stage of action.

Accordingly, the "Prologue" gives us not so much an abstract chivalric ideal as clues for understanding a character conceived in its human complexity. "He loved chivalrie," we are told about the Knight; and this chivalry is intimately linked with the Christian faith, for all the Knight's campaigns involved the cause of religion. It has been plausibly suggested that "in his lordes werre" refers to his warfare in the service of God.

If it is scarcely surprising that the "Knight's Tale" deals with chivalry, it does seem significant that it deals with a chivalry lacking a Christian basis. Indeed, it is here that the "Tale's" central irony develops: a chivalric romance is placed within the framework of the classical epic. The characters act by the conventions of courtly love and mediaeval chivalry, but over all preside the antique gods.

From the fusion of these two motifs, classical and mediaeval, there results the "Tale's" double view of pagan epic sans legendary heroes (if we discount "duc" Theseus) and mythic exploits; and of the chivalric romance shorn of its metaphysically inspired idealism. What the consequences of this central irony are, the following discussion hopes to make clear. At this point we may state by way of anticipation some of the Knight's concerns as they emerge from the "Tale." What, first, becomes of chivalry (and chivalric action) without its religious rationale? What of courtly love without the same transcendental dimension? What are these codes of conduct in themselves? Finally, what are the implications—humanly, socially, politically— of a whole-hearted commitment to this world, to things as they are?

It is the specifically pagan elements that become the source of much of the poem's comedy. The Knight has his fun imagining Emily's rites in the temple of Diana, a matter he won't go into, "And yet it were a game to heeren al." There is the burlesque scene in which the wood-nymphs and other forest deities are unhoused and sent scurrying about when the trees of the grove are cut down for Arcite's pyre. And a kind of Homeric comedy plays around the epic machinery of the gods, whose role at times borders on farce.

As in the classical epic there is in the "Knight's Tale" a consistent counter-pointing of human and divine, earthly and celestial action. Human agents do and suffer in the consciousness or name of cosmic forces that further or thwart their desires, and the conflict of human passions finds its counterpart in the conflicting wills of the gods. Specifically, there are three deities that mirror the "Tale's" love-triangle and, beyond that, figure forth its fictive macrocosm. These two functions can be seen fully conjoined in the central symbolic *locus* of the poem, the building of the lists and temples for the great tournament. The stadium is the artistic microcosm within which is to be performed the central ritual of chivalry, the tournament "for love and for increes of chivalrye." Surrounding the lists and defining in a precise way the limits of this little world are the temples of the gods.

The two-hundred-odd lines that describe the temples (and constitute a kind of epic catalogue) serve to extend the audience's awareness of the gods' significance in the poem. Encyclopaedic and monumental both in a rhetorical and substantive sense, this passage recreates the world as its inhabitants experience it. The baleful influence of the gods is much in evidence, confirming the pessimism voiced by most of the characters at some point in the story. The temple of Venus contains a good gloss on the love action. There "maystow se"

Wroght on the wal, ful pitous to biholde,
The broken slepes, and the sikes colde, . . .
The firy strokes of the desirynge
That loves servantz in this lyf enduren; . . .
Despense, Bisynesse, and Jalousye . . .

But the goddess's temple presents a mixture of love's pleasures and woes; thus it is not as bleak as that of Mars, which portrays every form of violence and brutality:

The crueel Ire, reed as any gleede; . . .
The smylere with the knyf under the cloke;
The shepne brennyng with the blake smoke . . .

At the same time, the gruesomeness is relieved by considerable comedy, as in the juxtaposition of epic catastrophes and trivial accidents; and in the deliberate anachronisms:

> Depeynted was the slaughtre of Julius,
> Of grete Nero, and of Antonius;
> Al be that thilke tyme they were unborn,
> Yet was hir deth depeynted ther-biforn.

In the temple of Diana there is a similarly jocular tone—as when the Knight carefully spells out the difference between Da(ph)ne and Diana—though here again the disastrous and painful aspects of the goddess's domain are stressed.

In the first place, therefore, the gods stand for things as they are, *moira.* The artists who have adorned the temple walls see no chasm between earthly reality and the divinities that rule over it. Second, the divine presences sum up certain ways of life to which men dedicate themselves. In another sense, they have a *psychological* function: the god a person serves is his ruling passion. The gods are men's wills or appetites writ large.

It is the narrator himself who suggests this identification. "For certeinly," he says,

> oure appetites heer,
> Be it of werre, or pees, or hate, or love,
> Al is this reuled by the sighte above.

And he goes on to speak of Theseus, who

> in his huntyng hath . . . swich delit
> That it is al his joye and appetit
> To been hymself the grete hertes bane,
> For after Mars he serveth now Dyane.

Theseus successfully combines the service of Venus, Mars, and Diana, whereas Palamon, Arcite, and Emily are committed exclusively to one deity embodying their appetite and destiny. "I kepe noght of armes for to yelpe," says Palamon to Venus before the tournament, "Ne I ne axe nat tomorwe to have victorie,"

> But I wolde have fully possessioun
> Of Emelye, and dye in thy servyse.

Arcite, convinced that Emily is indifferent and must be conquered anyway, asks Mars for victory and promises to "ben thy trewe servant whil I lyve." Emily prays in vain. She is a pawn in the chivalric game of love, just as Diana must submit to the wills of her fellow deities.

Between the latter a "theomachia" breaks out, for in granting their votaries' prayers Venus and Mars have created a celestial impossibility. Jupiter, father of the gods, is helpless to settle their strife until grandfather Saturn intervenes, who, because of his age and experience, we are told, is well qualified to solve such conflicts of interest. "As sooth is seyd," the Knight observes with sublime irony,

> elde hath greet avantage;
> In elde is bothe wisdom and usage;
> Men may the olde atrenne, and noght atrede.

For to make peace—"Al be it that it is agayn his kynde"—Saturn delivers an idiotic speech to Venus that catalogues his "olde experience," a series of natural and historic disasters caused by his malign planetary influence. He concludes by reassuring her: "I am thyn aiel, redy at thy *wille;* / Weep now namoore, I wol thy lust fulfille."

The tournament on earth over, the celestial comedy resumes. Venus is disconsolate and weeps "for wantynge of hir *wille,* / Til that hir teeres in the lystes fille." Again Saturn consoles her:

> Doghter, hoold thy pees!
> Mars hath his *wille,* his knyght hath al his boone,
> And, by myn heed, thow shalt been esed soone.

And his "solution" has the lack of subtlety we have come to expect from the "aiel" of the gods.

The divine-human parallelism in the poem may be represented schematically:

> Saturn   Egeus
> Jupiter   Theseus
> Mars—Venus—Diana   Arcite—Palamon—Emily

It underscores the "Tale's" comic structure, which doubles the absurdity of the earthly action with that of the celestial. For the conduct of the two young knights is at bottom as laughable as that of their divine counter-parts. Similarly, Egeus' platitudinous garrulity follows in Saturn's rhetorical footsteps. His age and experience are also stressed, and they have led to no more than the Saturnian wisdom:

> "Right as ther dyed nevere man," quod he,
> "That he ne lyvede in erthe in some degree,
> Right so ther lyvede never man," he seyde,
> "In al this world, that som tyme he ne deyde . . ."
> And over al this yet seyde he muchel moore
> To this effect . . .

Like Jupiter, Theseus is momentarily helpless after Arcite's death, until Egeus' "consolation" brings him relief. After a gesture of mourning, Theseus becomes again the human figure in the Tale that most clearly resembles the Jupiter of his own speech, a mover of the destiny of men and nations. He proceeds to order a burial for Arcite as sumptuous as had been the tournament. Finally, after the Greeks have stopped mourning, he convenes his parliament at Athens, on which occasion are discussed certain matters of Athenian foreign policy: "To have with certein contrees alliaunce / And have fully of Thebans obeisaunce." Theseus knows exactly how to accomplish this submission for the sake of international "order":

For which this noble Theseus anon
Leet senden after gentil Palamon,
Unwist of hym what was the cause and why;
But in his blake clothes sorwefully
He cam at his commandement in hye.
Tho sente Theseus for Emelye.

With his hands firmly on the ropes, he goes on to employ his best oratorical skill:

Whan they were set, and hust was al the place,
And Theseus abiden had a space
Er any word cam fram his wise brest,
His eyen sette he ther as was his lest.
And with a sad visage he siked stille,
And after that right thus he seyde his wille.

Given this setting, should we still expect a statement of deeply considered conclusions? Mr. Underwood has noted that the human level is absent from Theseus' speech, without, however, drawing any conclusions from this for the rest of the speech. What, for instance, becomes of the "cheyne of love"? Divorced from its relevance to human beings, it assumes the scientific neutrality of gravitational force (note the wording). Even the rhetorical question,

What maketh this but Jupiter, the kyng,
That is prince and cause of alle thyng,
Convertynge al unto his propre welle
From which it is dirryved, sooth to telle?

views the first cause purely *sub specie naturae*. It does not lead to a spiritual vision but merely to the tyrant's plea, "To maken vertue of necessitee."

The fact is that Theseus does not need to relate the principle of a First Cause to the human realm simply because in this realm he *is* the "prime mover" responsible for almost all its weal and woe. For the successful prince, problems of responsibility, free will, or Fortune's cruelty never really arise. And his watchword is: politics as usual. Hence his philosophical reflections are enlisted rhetorically in the service of his marriage plans for Palamon and Emily. And he has his will with such promptness that the bereaved Palamon does not even have time to change his suit of mourning! Thus, far from being an account of Theseus' attempts to preserve or impose order in the face of Fortune's chaos, the poem shows us a brilliant political opportunist who at the outset mounts to the pinnacle of success—in love and war—by one clean stroke. "He conquered al the regne of Femenye" literally and metaphorically: right after the conquest there ensues his marriage to Hippolyta.

There is an element of "wit" in such skill, and this is characteristic of the poem. Throughout, there are no half-measures, everything—events, situations, actions—being doubled or even tripled. And this massive coincidence (in every sense) is counterbalanced by rhetorical amplification and reduplication. A sense of friction between economy of action and verbal exuberance heightens the impression of a wilful incongruity between literary "form" and "content." The geometric design of the "Knight's Tale" functions more as a comic "mechanism" than as a means for expressing a concept of order.

At the same time the character of Theseus is consistently made to appear in a very ambiguous light. For example, when he discovers Palamon and Arcite duelling in the grove, his first reaction is to have them killed—until the ladies of the court intercede. But it is clear that his pity is no instinctive matter of the gentle heart. He enjoys feminine supplications; and he must *reason* his pity (in a kind of interior monologue):

. . . although that his ire hir gilt accused,
Yet in his resoun he hem bothe excused,
As thus: he thoghte wel that every man
Wol helpe hymself in love, if that he kan,
And eek delivere hymself out of prisoun.
And eek his herte hadde compassioun
Of wommen, for *they wepen evere in oon;*
And in his gentil herte he thoughte anon,
And softe unto hymself he seyde, "Fy
Upon a lord that wol have no mercy,
But been a leon, bothe in word and dede,

As wel as to a proud despitous man
That wol mayntene that he first bigan.
That lord hath litel of *discrecioun,*
That in swich cas kan no divisioun,
But weyeth pride and humblesse after oon.
(my italics)

The irony here as elsewhere derives from the judicious blend of motives reconciled on the ground of reason—which is as much *raison d'état* (the lord's discretion) as a rather comical understanding of women's and love's irrational ways.

Theseus proceeds to settle the lovers' destiny (in effect) by commanding a tournament for Emily's hand. His later decision to make it a bloodless tournament proves a move well calculated to gain the increased enthusiasm of the populace which has been pushing to see him "at a wyndow set, / Arrayed right as he were a god in throne." And so, throughout the poem, Theseus fairly dazzles the beholder with his skill. Yet as we move back and forth from inner to outer man, the ironic disparity between the two ever obtrudes itself. In his world Theseus is a Jovian prime mover, with many of the characteristics of the Renaissance machiavel, as H.J. Webb's indictment of his conduct in the poem strongly suggests. If it is possible to sum up the mainspring of his actions, I would call it the will to power, the determination to "have his world as in his time."

Outwardly, indeed, it seems as though agents and events in the "Knight's Tale" are under the governance of supra-human forces. It has often been noted that the gods double as planets whose conjunctions form a web of astrological fate controlling the events of the "Tale." But despite appearances, it may be argued that the real causality of events lies in the human will or appetite. As we have seen, the gods ultimately function as metaphors of man's will, which (we conclude), instead of being powerless over against Fate, *is* his fate. Hence derives a major irony of the poem, an irony at once tragic and comic, namely that everyone gets precisely what he desires.

Confirmation of this point comes from the Miller, who tells his tale to "quite the Knyghtes tale," as he drunkenly proclaims. In the triangle of Nicholas, Absolon, and Alisoun, each likewise gets what he desires: Absolon his kiss, Nicholas the enjoyment of Alisoun, and John the carpenter gets at the least the cuckolding he expected. But in the *"Miller's Tale"* the conventions of courtly love that play such an important role in the "Knight's Tale" burst like a bubble as love is reduced to its most basic terms. Rhetoric, for Nicholas, comes after the act, instead of being a prologue or a substitute for it. And physical nearness is all, whereas in the "Knight's Tale" it counts for nothing. Hence "Absolon may blowe the bukkes horn" while Nicholas has his way.

Of course, Nicholas himself constructs a gigantic trick to achieve his desire. But here again the joke is on the "Knight's Tale" with its apparent suggestion that the planet-gods shape the outcome of events. Nicholas, we are told, is an expert in astrology, and he will *use* astrology to bring about the desired end. The carpenter, with the practical man's sense of superiority to "clerks," ridicules "astromye" but becomes himself the simple-witted dupe of Nicholas' fantastic astrological joke. He falls—in every sense—because of his belief in the stars, but by their means hende Nicholas achieves his will.

In this sense, the "Miller's Tale" is certainly a parody of the Knight's. It bluntly manifests desire or will as the source of action, which in the other tale seems to be concealed under the drift of events or happenstance. Just as the lovers of the "Knight's

Tale" "suffer" their love, so they seem to be the passive agents of a superior destiny. Actually, however, the Tale constantly reveals that the Knight, though no reductionist like the Miller, has a perspective very similar to the Miller's.

The terminology of will and appetite in the "Knight's Tale" supports this idea. In Palamon's lament to the gods the will is linked with animal impulse in a way that foreshadows the Miller's use of animal imagery:

> What is mankynde moore unto you holde
> Than is the sheep that rouketh in the folde?
> For slayn is man right as another beest,
> And dwelleth eek in prison and arreest . . .
>
> What governance is in this prescience,
> That giltelees tormenteth innocence?
> And yet encresseth this al my penaunce,
> That man is bounden to his observaunce,
> For Goddes sake, to letten of his wille,
> Ther as a beest may al his lust fulfille.

The tragic element here is reduced by the terms of the lament and by the divorce between will and reason that it implies. Life, seen as a process of restless and blind willing, is felt to be dominated by an irrational fate. The pathos as well as the absurdity of Palamon and Arcite lies in their acceptance of the view that man is ruled by his animal will but at the same time bound to act by certain conventions.

Even love in the Tale is a blind appetite, though its formal expression is in the style of courtly love. The result is an essentially loveless lovestory. In the name of that love, the sworn blood-brotherhood of Palamon and Arcite is soon destroyed, and the theme of broken friendship and a disruptive Cupid runs through the poem. Shortly after the quarrel between the former friends, the audience is reminded of another kind of friendship more ideal and durable, the love between Theseus and Perotheus:

> So wel they lovede, as olde bookes sayn,
> That whan that oon was deed, soothly to telle,
> His felawe wente and soughte hym doun in
>   helle,—
> But of that storie list me nat to write.

This love is also a direct commentary on the following action. While Palamon remains in the hell of his prison tower, Arcite wanders about preoccupied with his own lot. In a later scene Palamon accuses Arcite of treachery for loving his lady, bejaping Theseus, and changing his name! He declares his mortal enmity, and, despite the violence of feeling, they arrange a duel for the next day. At the agreed time they fight like wild beasts, though they are careful to do it according to the book (of chivalry): "Everich of hem heelp for to armen oother / As freendly as he were his owene brother." When Theseus arrives on the scene, Palamon (again) makes an immediate confession and asks for death. Moreover, he does not hesitate to reveal Arcite's identity and goes on to request that Arcite be executed first. There is a certain grim comedy in Palamon's wavering as to who should be killed first.

As has often been asserted, the reader's sympathies remain, at length, evenly divided between the two men. Both are seen to behave equally absurdly, badly, and nobly. The truth is that we are not permitted to care greatly about either, and this allows us to appreciate the comic element in the poetic justice meted out to Arcite. For even the "accident" that leads to his death was no divine or demonic "miracle," but rather his own fault. He wasn't looking where he was going:

> This fiers Arcite hath of his helm ydon,
> And on a courser, for to shewe his face,
> He priketh endelong the large place
> Lokynge upward upon this Emelye;
> And she agayn hym caste a freendlich ye
> (For wommen, as to speken in comune,
> Thei folwen alle the favour of Fortune)
> And was al his chiere, as in his herte.

With the co-operation of Emily and the jubilant applause of an equally fickle plebs ringing in his ears, Arcite's excitement sets the scene for a mishap that scarcely needs the *diabolus ex machina* of "a furie infernal." Despite the undeniable pathos of Arcite's death-bed lament, the Knight, who dislikes tragedy, consistently presents his story in such a way as to make genuine tragedy impossible.

Similarly, Emily's character is hardly the kind to inspire a noble passion. She is lovely, no doubt, but not much more than that. This is not altogether her fault, since she is after all merely the prize for which men fight. But, as the tournament scene shows, she plays the part expected of her, and her passivity fits well with the passive role that the society assigns her.

Love in the "Tale" is an essentially amoral and self-regarding passion. Theseus views it chiefly as folly, though with a tolerant irony:

> The god of love, a, *benedicite*!
> How myghty and how greet a lord is he!
> Ayens his myght ther gayneth none obstacles.
> He may be cleped a god for his miracles;
> For he kan maken, at his owene gyse,
> Of everich herte as that hym list divyse.

He admires Cupid as an image of his own ideal of (complete) lordship. At the same time, Cupid's power illustrates for him the folly of letting passion triumph over reason. How could "love, maugree hir eyen two" lead Palamon and Arcite to risk death and fight over one totally ignorant of their existence?

After the latter have decided to duel to the death, the Knight is similarly prompted to exclaim:

> O Cupide, out of alle charitee!
> O regne, that wolt no felawe have with thee!
> Ful sooth is seyd that love ne lordshipe
> Wol noght, his thankes, have no felaweshipe.

But the difference in outlook here between the Knight and Theseus defines the distance between the teller and his tale. By paralleling love and lordship in this fashion, the Knight hints at the major themes of his unfolding Tale. This love is the disrupter of "felaweshipe" and also the will to sexual "lordshipe" analogous to the will to power or political lordship.

Finally, there is a punning comment on this kind of love in the Knight's exclamation. "Out of alle charitee" is first of all a colloquial tag; as such it is applied to the Wife of Bath in the "General Prologue", also in a mildly punning form. In addition, "charitee" denotes the religious *caritas* that in the Prologue is explicitly exemplified by the Plowman, and in a general way forms the backdrop (so to speak) against which are played the endless metamorphoses of human love that we find in the Canterbury pilgrims.

In the "General Prologue," that is, each pilgrim is ruled by a specific *eros* that defines the centre of his being. These loves vary from the most intense self-love to the most ideal and selfless, but they all (it seems to be suggested) participate, however obscurely, in the transcendent-immanent love of the Creator for his creation. At the least, each love is capable of conversion towards that which is at once the motive power and goal of the human pilgrimage. Hence the latter is not to eradicate the "love of the creature," but to purify it by showing its dependence upon the divine.

Put in another way, the comedy of the *Canterbury Tales* sees no real discontinuity between matter and spirit. The wind that "inspires" the "yonge croppes" also inspires folk to make their pilgrimages. It stirs to life the hidden seeds of perfection everywhere, so that the human desire for regeneration is an extension, as it were, of the miracle of spring, ascending by imperceptible degrees from vegetable to rational nature, from matter to spirit. By a happy etymological providence, "spirit" proceeds from "breath."

Man, though he has the freedom to pervert the natural intention (Boethius) of creation, still finds himself caught in its *élan vital.* Hence we discover in the pilgrims a group representative of the spectrum of human nature; saint-like and depraved, they combine to form a society moving towards a goal which, whether they are aware of it or not, represents the ultimate fulfilment of their earthly destiny. This movement towards transcendence is not always apparent in the poem. Certain pilgrims with their full-blown individuality practically burst the bounds of their fictive-symbolic framework. Nor is it difficult to see in the "General Prologue" lineaments of a larger social order in crisis (as evidenced, for instance, by a thoroughly corrupt clergy), indices of that waning of the middle ages historians have taught us to look for.

Over against the symptoms of disorder, however, there emerges from the *Canterbury Tales* the idea of what I would call a "comic society," whose order is not so much conceptual as it is pragmatic, being rooted (as it were) in the nature of things. In such a society the control or order arises from below, we might say, because nature is a function of (the comic) spirit. Men have the freedom to follow their natural inclinations, because by doing so they imitate the inner drive in all things towards their full being or perfection. But in so far as they deviate drastically from the norms of a publicly defined good, they are exposed to the censorship of laughter.

The society that meets at the inn in Southwark is not so much a perfect counterpart as a prototype of the larger society from which it derives. The pilgrims re-enact the fundamental rite on which all community life is based: the being together of people in "sociability." The perfect setting for such sociability is the tavern, which, with the fellowship engendered there by drinking together (*symposion*), has sometimes been thought to be the true place of origin of human society. Sociability, moreover, manifests itself in the sense of freedom and *play* which is so prominent in the *Canterbury Tales* that we might almost speak of the poem as viewing not only society but the world itself *sub specie ludi* (to adopt a phrase of Huizinga's).

The world of the *Canterbury Tales*, then, is in a constant process of becoming. The portrait "stills" of the "General Prologue" are a momentary illusion: their subjects are poised to leap out of their frames into a fuller existence, and the road to Canterbury is the stage on which the *dramatis personae* act out their natures. The tales themselves are part of the progressive unfolding of the pilgrims' selves, and thus a way to new insights and a means of communication strengthening the bonds of community implicit in the pilgrimage. Finally, the self-knowledge gained is a stage in the journey of self-transcendence, a step towards the perfection of the individual.

It is part of Chaucer's brilliant subtlety that the reader remains legitimately in doubt as to the Knight's full understanding of this basic motion toward a higher fulfilment. But it appears that as narrator the Knight becomes increasingly aware of the kind of world his story presents, so that the ambiguity of "Cupid, out of alle charitee!" serves as a reminder or invitation to judge this world by a standard that lies outside it and within the world of the pilgrims at whose head the Knight appears.

In a variety of ways, the Knight is able to suggest an alternative manner of looking at man and society, not least by the comedy of his "Tale." It is he rather than Theseus who resolves the problem of a seemingly unjust world by reminding his audience that Fortuna with her outrageous coincidences is both comic and subject to

> The destinee, ministre general,
> That executeth in the world over al
> The purveiaunce that God hath seyn biforn,
> So strong it is that, though the world had sworn
> The contrarie of a thyng by ye or nay,
> Yet somtyme it shal fallen on a day
> That falleth nat eft withinne a thousand year.
> For certeinly, oure appetites heer, ...
> Al is this reuled by the sighte above.

This conception differs crucially from Theseus' First Mover, who

> Hath stablissed in this wrecched world adoun
> Certeyne dayes and duracioun
> To al that is engendred in this place,
> Over the whiche day they may nat pace,
> Al mowe they yet tho dayes wel abregge.

And significantly, the Knight ends, not here, but with the wedding of Emily and Palamon, as well as a final ambiguity: "And God, that al this wyde world hath wroght, / Send hym his love that hath it deere aboght."

Palamon and Emily live happily ever after, and as the Knight steps out of their world into his wider world his optimism asserts itself triumphantly to encompass "al this faire compaignye." But it does so only after he has, through his "Tale," confronted some of life's baffling complexities. For the price of this comic outlook is a steady vigilance; in short, it requires the qualities that the Prologue tells us the Knight possesses: "And though that he were worthy, he was wys."

This wisdom involves a prudent circumspectness, keeping one's eyes open and being prepared for eventualities. For life always has more in store for man than he bargained for, so that it is likely to make him look foolish if not worse. And from this point of view the "heathens" and their gods in the "Tale" are after all metaphors for the human condition at large, in so far as we all share in that more than partial blindness of a Palamon and Arcite, and hence in their possibilities for appearing tragic, absurd, wicked, and innocent. That, it would seem, is one crux of the human situation.

The other crux is perhaps that of action and commitment, in short, of being "worthy" as well as "wys." And here the missing transcendental link of the "Knight's Tale" is of crucial importance. This link is man himself in the cosmic "cheyne of love." For it is only by placing his actions and aspirations within that context, that man raises them above the level of mere Will and Self.

Is there an element of *paideia* in all this? We have noted that the "Tale" presents an image of different generations, and we can now add to our earlier scheme:

Saturn Egeus
Knight Jupiter Theseus
Squire Mars, etc. Arcite, etc.

Included in the Knight's audience is his son, the very type of a courtly lover. In the "General Prologue," moreover, their portraits suggest two stages of the chivalric life, the father furnishing the model for the "bachelour" who "carf biforn his fader at the table."

The "Tale," then, deals precisely with those themes that most nearly concern the Knight. Yet it appears that the latter casts an ironic eye at the relationship between the generations. Man in the "Tale" does not learn much by age and experience. What wisdom can the older transmit to the younger generation? The "Knight's Tale" is a testimony to the insufficiency of human wisdom at the same time that it transcends it.

Source: Richard Neuse, "The Knight: The First Mover in Chaucer's Human Comedy," in *University of Toronto Quarterly*, Vol. 31, No. 3, April 1962, pp. 299–315.

Rosemary Woolf

In the following essay, Woolf comments on Chaucer's satire in the "General Prologue."

Many people nowadays acquire an early and excessive familiarity with the "General Prologue" to the *Canterbury Tales*, which later blunts their sharpness of perception. Since the "Prologue" is read at school, necessarily out of its literary-historical context, its methods of satire seem to have an inevitability and rightness which preclude either surprise or analysis. This natural tendency to remain uncritically appreciative of the "Prologue" has been partly confirmed by various works of criticism, which, though admirable in many ways, effusively reiterate that "here is God's plenty": they thus awaken an enthusiastic response to the vitality and variety of the characterisation in the "Prologue," at the cost of making the exact manner and tone of Chaucer's satire quite indistinct. Despite the bulk of Chaucerian criticism, there is still need for a detailed and disciplined examination of Chaucer's style and methods of satire, which would include a careful consideration of Chaucer's work against the background of classical and Medieval satire. Such a study would be of considerable scholarship and length: it is the purpose of this short article only to make a few general points about Chaucer's methods of satire.

It is sometimes taken for granted that the satirist speaks in his own voice, and that any reference to his opinions and feelings are a literal record of his experience. This assumption perhaps requires testing and reconsideration with reference to any satirist, but it is never more dangerous than when it is accepted without limitation about Chaucer. Chaucer was writing at a time when there was no tradition of personal poetry in a later Romantic sense: a poet never made his individual emotions the subject-matter of his poetry. Though the personal pronoun "I" is used frequently in Medieval narrative and lyric poetry, it is usually a dramatic "I," that is the "I" is a character in the poem, bearing no different relation to the poet from that of the other characters, or it expresses moral judgments or proper emotions which belong, or should belong, to everybody. Chaucer's use of an "I" character in his early poems belongs to the tradition of such characters in dream visions, but, with an ingenious variation that the character appears naive, well-meaning, and obtuse, and the joke thus depends on the discrepancy between this figure in the poetry and the poet of wit and intelligence who wrote the whole. Thus this treatment of the "I" character is new in that it pre-supposes the poet in a way that the other characters do not.

It is well-known that this character re-appears strikingly in the links of the *Canterbury Tales*, when he is rebuked for telling a dull story, but his presence in the "Prologue" has not been particularly stressed, yet it is through this character that both the apparently vivid individuality of the pilgrims and the satiric aim are achieved. Though there are various departures from consistency (to be noticed later), it is through the eyes of Chaucer the pilgrim, not Chaucer the poet, that the characters in the "Prologue" are chiefly presented. Obviously the choice of detail shows the sharp selectiveness of the satirist, but the friendly enthusiastic, unsophisticated, unjudging tone is that of Chaucer the pilgrim.

From this invention there result two important advantages. Firstly by his fiction of having been a close companion of his characters, Chaucer suggests their reality and individuality, an individuality which is largely an illusion brought about by poetic skill. Chaucer makes us feel that we know them as individuals, though often, apart from physical description, they are simply representative portraits of various groups in society—friars, monks, summoners, nuns, etc. The same details of their tastes and behaviour can be found in any Medieval moral denunciation of these people. Secondly, in his satiric character-sketches, Chaucer achieves a two-fold irony. He implies that most of the information which he gives us derives, not from a narrative-writer's omniscience, but from the characters' own conversation. In other words Chaucer unobtrusively uses a pointed satirical method, by which the characters are shown to have erred so far from the true moral order, that they are not ashamed to talk naturally and with self-satisfaction about their own inversion of a just and religiously-ordered way of life. At the same time Chaucer makes his response to this that of a man who accepts and repeats with enthusiasm, and without criticism, whatever he is told. It has been observed before how often Chaucer implies or states explicitly that each of his characters is an outstanding person (although a distinction should be made here between the statement when made of a virtuous character, such as the parson, when it comes as the climax of a well-ordered enumeration of his virtues, and when it appears as a random remark in the sketches of the satirised characters). This has been explained as part of Chaucer's genial enthusiastic appreciation of all kinds of people or, in a manner less wildly wrong, as part of a literary convention of magnifying each character. But it is surely Chaucer the easily-impressed pilgrim who so indiscriminately praises the characters, sharing with them through an obtuse innocence the immoral premises from which they speak.

Chaucer the poet, for instance, must have shared the common knowledge and opinion in the late 14th century, that the friars, instead of serving

> *The neat grace of Chaucer's lines often deceptively suggests that he has made a sharp and lucid observation, when in fact it is but a commonplace, and the precision lies, not in its thought, but in the style."*

all classes of men indifferently, though with a special tenderness for the poor who reflected the poverty of Christ, instead chiefly sought out the rich and those from whom they could make profit, and took the opportunity given by the privacy of the personal interview and confession for exploitation and unchastity. All this Chaucer could not have failed to have known to be an abuse, evil and widespread, of what had originally been a holy and noble conception. But Chaucer the character relates these details of his fellow pilgrims as though they were both inoffensive and idiosyncratic, and in this way both the satiric point and the illusion of individuality are achieved. Similarly it was a common accusation that daughters of aristocratic households, who entered a convent, often did not discard their former manners and affectations. Genteel table-manners, careful attention to dress, and a narrowly sentimental affection for pet-animals, might possibly in a noble household appear signs of a refined sensibility, but in a convent their worldliness would be plain. But of the distinction between the lady of the house and a nun Chaucer the pilgrim is ignorant, so he records all the details sweetly, as though there were no matter here for blame.

The clearest example, however, of this method is the account of the monk. Just as in the description of the friar Chaucer shows clearly by a sudden change to colloquial rhythms that he is ostensibly repeating the friar's own arguments for not caring for the poor, "It is nat honest, it may nat avaunce ...," so in the account of the monk Chaucer repeats the monk's arguments, and then even adds a reply, "And I seyde his opinion was good," supporting this by two foolish rhetorical questions and a blustering retort "Lat Austyn have his swynk to hym reserved." That Chaucer the poet would reject the authority of St Augustine is as manifestly untrue as that he had not the skill to tell an entertaining story. His protested sympathy with the monk is of the same kind as Juvenal's stated agreement ("you have just cause for bitterness") with the utterly debased and contemptible Naevolus in the ninth satire. To suppose that Chaucer's attitude here is ambivalent is to be deceived by the sweet blandness of Chaucer's mask, just as to search for historical prototypes of the characters is to be deceived by the brilliant accuracy of Chaucer's sleight of hand, whereby he suggests an individuality which is not there.

Amongst many other examples of the simplicity of Chaucer the pilgrim may be noticed the frequent device of giving a false explanation of a statement—the physician loved gold because it was of use in medicine—and the making of absurd judgments: the remark that the wives of the guildsmen would be to blame if they did not support and approve their husbands in their smug prosperity, or the query of whether it was not "by a full fair grace" that the maunciple was able to cheat and outwit his learned employers. It is in passages such as the latter that the ironic tone of Chaucer the satirist can be most clearly heard behind the blank wall of obtuseness of Chaucer the pilgrim. Illustrations of the naivete of Chaucer the character could be multiplied to the point of tediousness, and so too there could be laboured at length the demonstration that the substance of the description of each character consists solely of common Medieval observation about the group to which he belongs. It should be added, however, that the appearance of individuality is not achieved by the intimate tone of Chaucer the character alone: at least equally important is the style. The neat grace of Chaucer's lines often deceptively suggests that he has made a sharp and lucid observation, when in fact it is but a commonplace, and the precision lies, not in its thought, but in the style. Thus his method of pretending that the generalisation about a group is the idiosyncracy of an individual is given persuasive force by his exact use of words and the shapeliness of his couplets. There is an interesting contrast to this in the undisguisedly generalised attack of Langland, the generality of which is driven home by his swift but sometimes indiscriminate use of forceful words, and his form of the alliterative metre, which has within the line a great strength and impressive rhythm, but no larger pattern, so that there seems to be no metrical reason why one line should not succeed another without end.

The question to what extent we are aware of Chaucer the poet in the "Prologue" is not easy to determine. Sometimes an example of obtrusive poetic skill draws attention to him: it is Chaucer the pilgrim who observes mildly of the unhealthy sore on the cook's leg that it was a pity, but the placing of this one line in the middle of the account of the fine dishes made by the cook exceeds the licence of poetic cleverness which may by convention be allowed to a dull character in poetry. Similarly the image which implies censure or ridicule is self-evidently the satirist's: the monk's bridle jingling like a chapel bell, the squire's coat so embroidered with flowers that it was like a meadow, the snowstorm of food and drink in the franklin's house, the fiery-red cherubym's face of the summoner, all undisguidedly spring from the imagination of a satiric poet. Occasionally Chaucer even speaks outright in his own voice, making a pointed exposure of affection or self-deception, which is in a quite different style of satire, and provides an exception to the general truth that the characters are not the result of actual observation. A well-known example is the comment about the lawyer:

Nowher so bisy a man as he ther nas,
And yet he semed bisier than he was.

This kind of remark shows the same mocking penetration into the ridiculous complexities of human feeling and behaviour, as Chaucer had already displayed in *Troilus and Creseide*, from which one striking example may be quoted: it was a commonplace in Medieval descriptions of a lover that by pining he grew pale and thin; but in Chaucer's more subtle description, Troilus in the humourless self-absorption of his love *imagines* that he has grown so pale and thin that everybody notices and comments upon it. At first sight Chaucer seems to be an exception to the general rule of the classical period and 18th century that the satirist is to be feared. His disguise of Chaucer the pilgrim and elsewhere a sustained friendliness and moderation of tone imply that no man could be less alarming to those who knew him. But, whilst undoubtedly he was the less to be feared in that he did not make individual contemporaries the objects of his satire, as a century later Skelton was to do, yet only people free from all excesses of emotion and affectation could be sure that they would not be the source of some detail shrewdly observed in Chaucer's work.

Chaucer also speaks in his own voice in his occasional denunciation of evil in the descriptions of the Miller and the Pardoner, and, most effectively in his descriptions of the virtuous characters, one drawn from each order of society with the addition of the Clerk. In these Chaucer establishes the true moral standard by which the topsy-turvyness of the rest may be measured. It was a tradition of satire to provide an ideal standard: some earlier Medieval Latin satirists made use of the classical fable of the Golden Age, identifying it uneasily with the Garden of Eden: an example is the famous *de Contemptu Mundi* of Bernard of Cluny; Langland in a more complex and magnificent scheme makes his standard the pure charity of the Redemption of man by Christ. But Chaucer, lacking Langland's sublimity of imagination, but with a shrewd, clear thoughtfulness, gives a positive analysis of representative types of a well-ordered society, religious and secular. The detailed justice of these descriptions prevents the actual satire from seeming too mild or perhaps too pessimistic. Without them Chaucer's satire might seem to have too much detachment, too much ironic acquiescence. In Langland's angry denunciatory satire there is by implication a hope of reform; but in Chaucer's one feels the tone of a man, who, aware of the incongruity between the gravity of the abuse and his own inability to help, is moved to an ironic and superficially good-humoured laughter. The virtuous characters, however, by their very presence imply a censure of the rest, which dispels any impression of over-sophisticated aloofness. The idea that Chaucer loved his satirised characters despite or including their faults is of course false, and springs from an imprecise consideration of Chaucer's methods of satire.

To what extent Chaucer was influenced by classical and Medieval traditions of satire remains the final difficult but fascinating question. There is no incontrovertible evidence about his knowledge of classical satirists: Juvenal he quotes from and mentions by name, but the quotations he could very easily have gained at second hand; Horace he does not mention at all, but since, as other critics have pointed out, he does not mention Boccaccio either, this negative evidence is worthless. Juvenal had attacked with moral horror the widespread vices of his own time under the satiric disguise of describing historical personages of a previous age. This device was not imitated by the Fathers or the Medieval satirists who were influenced by him, and the writers of the Middle Ages with their preoccupation with what was common to all men rather than with what makes one man different from another, were not concerned to give any appearance of particularity to their satire. The result was either the blackened generalised picture of all men as

totally corrupt, found in the *de Contemptu Mundi*, or the combination of allegory with satire, ingeniously used, though not invented, by Langland. But though the aim of Chaucer's satire is, like Langland's, the distinctive vices of people in various orders and occupations throughout society, he does not generalise but, like Juvenal, reduces the generalisation to a description of particular characters. This, however, seems to be Chaucer's only resemblance to Juvenal, since self-evidently there could not be a greater difference of tone than there is between Juvenal's savage vehemence and Chaucer's specious mildness.

The resemblances between Chaucer and Horace are more subtle and more specific. The object of Horace's satire had been different from Juvenal's, in that Horace was chiefly concerned with those who disrupted the social harmony of life, the fool, the bore, the miser, and these he portrayed with a minute and particular observation of habit and conversation, which gives the impression that his description is of an individual, though by definition not unique, personality. His account, for instance, of the host who makes dinner intolerable for his guests by a tedious analysis of the sources and method of cooking of each dish, suggests a recognisable personality, not a moral generalisation about excessive eating and drinking. The tone of Horace's satire is not designed to arouse horror or anger, but amused contempt for something worthless. It is obvious that this satiric manner required a sophistication not usually possessed in the Middle Ages, and a point of view less easily identifiable with the Christian than that of Juvenal. For, though evil was seen as a fit object for laughter in the Middle Ages, it was a strong laughter at the ugly and grotesque—the devils in the mystery plays, for example—rather than the slight ironic smile of the civilised man at those who deviate from reason and intelligence.

Chaucer shares some characteristics with Horace, though there is no certainty whether by influence, or by coincidence and some affinity of temper. He has in common with Horace the easy tone of a man talking to friends who share his assumptions and sympathies, though usually with a deceptive twist: for when Horace meets the characters in his satires, he expects his audience to sympathise with his misery, whereas Chaucer, as we have already seen, pretends that the situation was delightful and the characters to be admired. He shares with Horace too some other characteristics already noticed, such as the use of comic images, and, above all, the quick observation of human affectation, and the suggestion of a recognisable personality as in the lines quoted about the lawyer. Chaucer, however, extends Horatian ridicule to the kind of objects satirised in the Juvenalian tradition, and modifies it by the tone of pretended naivete, not found in Horace's style, but almost certainly learnt, at least in part, from Ovid, whose works Chaucer had undoubtedly read and who might indeed be called Chaucer's master.

The fact that it is relevant to ask the question, was Chaucer influenced by classical satirists, is in itself interesting, and throws light on Chaucer's distinctiveness. Though it cannot be answered definitely, his indebtedness to classical writers in general is indisputable, and is most interestingly noticeable in the fact that he thought of himself as a poet in a way that earlier Medieval writers seem not to have done. He is the first English medieval poet explicitly to accept the permanent value of his work, and hence to care about the unsettled state of the language and its dialectal variety, the first to see himself as of the same kind as the classical poets. The writers of medieval lyrics, romances, plays, etc., almost certainly had a workaday conception of themselves, and did not think of a poet as a man of particular perception and judgment, but as a man who wrote verse in a craftsmanlike way for specific use. But Chaucer sees himself as a poet in the classical tradition, and it is for this reason that, despite the fact that the substance of his satiric portraits are medieval commonplaces, and despite his usual disguise of Chaucer the pilgrim, behind this disguise, and sometimes heard openly, is the truly personal tone of the satirist, which is quite unmedieval.

Source: Rosemary Woolf, "Chaucer as Satirist in the 'General Prologue' to the *Canterbury Tales*," in *Critical Quarterly*, Vol. 1, 1959, pp. 150–57.

E. Talbot Donaldson

In the following essay excerpt, Donaldson examines the role of rhetoric in "The Nun's Priest's Tale."

It is the nature of the beast fable, of which the "Nun's Priest's Tale" is an example, to make fun of human attitudes by assigning them to the lower animals. Perhaps no other form of satire has proved so charming throughout literary history. From Aesop's fables through the medieval French mock-epic *Reynard the Fox* (upon a version of which the "Nun's Priest's Tale" relies for its slight plot), down to La Fontaine and Br'er Rabbit, the beast who acts like a man has enjoyed general popularity. In the

"Nun's Priest's Tale" one of the most charming of poets has given the genre a superbly comic expression. Yet much of the tale's humor lies neither in its plot nor in the equivalence of man and beast, but in the extraordinary dilation of the telling. For while Chaucer was endowing his feathered hero and heroine with many of the qualities of a courtly lover and his lady, he was also embellishing his tale with an ample selection of the rhetorical commonplaces of Western civilization. To analyze the effect these have on the story it is necessary to investigate briefly what rhetoric is.

The art of expressive speech and writing or, more narrowly, of persuasive speech is a fair enough definition of rhetoric. But considered as a set of formulas for expressing a recurrent idea or situation, rhetoric may amount to little more than cliché. It is also possible to think of rhetoric, as one frequently does today, as a kind of cosmetic art—that of adorning bare facts. Yet something is lacking here. The rhetorical mode of expression may be said to consist in using language in such a way as to bring about certain preferred interpretations. Compare, for example, an apparently bare statement, "The sun sets," with the rhetorical statement, "The Sun drove his chariot beyond the waters of the western seas." To the ancient mind the last statement would suggest a particular kind of order and meaning in the universe—in other words, a cosmos. This piece of rhetoric was the ancient man's way of reassuring himself that chaos would not come again with the setting of the sun. Today we probably prefer the simplicity of the first statement. Yet "The sun sets" has its residue of rhetoric: we know that the sun does not set but only seems to. We accept this inaccurate and quite rhetorical statement because we are reluctant, even when we know better, to displace ourselves from our inherited position at the center of creation. Rhetoric still stands between us and the fear of something which, even if it is not chaos, is disconcerting.

It follows that rhetoric in this sense is something more than language of adornment. It is, in fact, a powerful weapon of survival in a vast and alien universe. In our own time, as in the Middle Ages and in the Age of Homer, rhetoric has served to satisfy man's need for security and to provide a sense of the importance of his own existence and of the whole human enterprise. It is true that rhetoric, as it operates for persuasion and self-persuasion, may become merely an instrument of deception, a matter of clichés and of superficial and contradictory thinking. One finds examples in advertising and political slogans and in the mutually inconsistent wisdom of proverbs. The excesses of rhetoric invite satire; regarded satirically, rhetoric may be taken as a kind of inadequate defense that man erects against an inscrutable reality. It is in this way that Chaucer is viewing it in the "Nun's Priest's Tale." Most noticeably, of course, he employs the standard rhetoric of heroic poetry in order to give the utmost mock-significance to each of Chantecleer's actions. Even the best of epic heroes suffers from the handicap of being only one of an untold number of people who have lived on earth, and the fact that Achilles and Hector still have significance (if a fading one) is due to the gigantic rhetorical effort of Homer, who persuades his reader that these were the very best in their kind who ever lived. By a similar technique Chantecleer is made the best rooster that ever lived, so that his death amid the teeth of Dan Russel—if it had occurred—could have provided a tragic episode every bit as significant to mankind as the death of Hector. Or so the Nun's Priest would have us believe, what with his epic manner and his full-dress similes, his references to the fall of Troy, the burning of Rome, the destruction of Carthage, to Sinon, Ganelon, and Judas Iscariot, to the awful problems of free will and foreordination. And, if this were not sufficient to persuade us of the importance of Chantecleer to the scheme of things, the divine powers take the trouble to send the rooster a monitory dream concerning his impending fate. The logic of the comedy is unexceptionable: these are the devices that made Hector and Achilles, and hence all men in their persons, significant; will not the devices do the same for Chantecleer?

While he deals largely in the rhetorical commonplaces appropriate to epic heroes, the Nun's Priest does not ignore commonplaces less exalted. The discussion of the significance of dreams reflects one of man's most enduring attempts to enhance his importance, and the basic disagreement between the cock and the hen regarding dreams is an embarrassing instance of the rhetorical tradition's having produced two entirely antipathetic answers to the same problem: Similarly, the age-old question of woman is answered—in one breath, as it were—by two equally valid if mutually exclusive commonplaces: woman is man's ruination and woman is all man's bliss. Especially prominent is the rhetoric of "authority," by which poets assure themselves that what they are doing is unexceptionable: when the rooster's singing is compared with the singing of mermaids, the expert on mermaids' singing is named—Physiologus, whose authority presumably makes the simile respectable. It

> *It is almost as if the Creator were watching with loving sympathy and humorous appreciation the solemn endeavors of His creatures to understand the situation in which He has placed them."*

is inevitable that the Friday on which Chantecleer's near-tragedy occurs should be castigated in the terms set by that most formidable and dullest of medieval rhetoricians, Geoffrey of Vinsauf, who carried almost to its ultimate point formalization of expression and stultification of thought.

The "Nun's Priest's Tale" is full of what seem to be backward references to the preceding tales, so that it is sometimes taken as a parody-summary of all that has gone before. The reason for this is probably less that Chaucer had the other tales in mind as he wrote (indeed, he could have written the "Nun's Priest's Tale" without having any thought of the others) than that in it he employs comically all the rhetorical devices that were a part of his own poetical inheritance. But with the "Monk's Tale," which immediately precedes, the Nun's Priest's does seem to have a more organic connection. The Monk had pitilessly labored the emasculated notion of tragedy current in the Middle Ages, with all its emphasis on the dominance of Fortune, viewed apart from human responsibility. In taking by turns the attitude toward Chantecleer of the Monk ("Oh destiny that mayst not be eschewed") and the more ethical attitude that the cock was fondly overcome by female charm (he "took his counsel of his wife, with sorrow"), Chaucer is comically exploiting a paradox the two ends of which are played against the poor narrator, caught in the middle and not knowing whether to blame fate or rooster and compromising by doing both by turns. Yet this elusive interaction between man's nature and his destiny is one of the concomitants of a far more profound kind of tragedy than anything the Monk's definition could produce: Macbeth also had his fatal influences and his deliberate wrongdoings. As a work of the intellect, even though it is wholly comic, the "Nun's Priest's Tale" is far more serious and mature than the Monk's. Its author might well have produced a Shakespearean tragedy—provided he could have stopped laughing.

The man who is able to maintain a satiric view toward rhetoric—the sum of the ideas by which people are helped to preserve their self-respect—is not apt to be popular with his victims. Inevitably, they will search him out to discover the pretensions under which he subsists. Aware that in the personality of the satirist will always exist grounds for rebutting the satire, Chaucer carefully gives us nothing to work on in the character of the Nun's Priest: there is no portrait of him in the "General Prologue," and the introduction to his tale reveals only the most inoffensive of men. But in one important respect he is very like his creator: he can survey the world as if he were no part of it, as if he were situated comfortably on the moon looking at a human race whom he knew and loved wholeheartedly but whose ills he was immune from. This is the same godlike detachment that characterizes the incident of the telling of *Sir Thopas* and also, in another way, *Troilus*. It is almost as if the Creator were watching with loving sympathy and humorous appreciation the solemn endeavors of His creatures to understand the situation in which He has placed them.

Source: E. Talbot Donaldson, "Commentary: The 'Nun's Priest's Tale,'" in *Chaucer Poetry*, selected and edited by Talbot Donaldson, Ronald Press Company, 1958, pp. 1104–08.

R. M. Lumiansky

In the following essay, Lumiansky contends that "The Nun's Priest's Tale" reveals the Nun's Priest to be "frail, timid, and humble."

Among the best liked and most widely known sections of *The Canterbury Tales* is the Nun's Priest's story of the regal Chanticleer and the lovely Dame Pertelote. For a long time critics have realized that this tale skilfully reflects facets of its teller's character, but only recently have detailed attempts been made to suggest just what sort of person Chaucer intended his audience to visualize as the Nun's Priest. Since Chaucer did not include in the "General Prologue" a portrait of this Pilgrim, whatever view one takes of the Nun's Priest must be based on the comments to and about him by the Host, on his own short comment to the Host, on the Narrator's brief remark about him, and on the superb tale which he relates to the company. This

is to say that any acceptable portrait of Chaucer's Nun's Priest must of necessity derive primarily from the personal interplay during the Canterbury pilgrimage.

Recent criticism has presented the Nun's Priest to us as a brawny and vigorous man with stature and muscles which justify his serving for the duration of the pilgrimage as one of three bodyguards for the Prioress and the Second Nun. This view is based, first, on an acceptance as direct description of the Host's extreme comments in the Nun's Priest's Epilogue concerning the physical prowess of the priest; and, second, on the existence of documents which show that contemporary travel was particularly dangerous for women, even nuns—the assumption being that the Prioress and the Second Nun would therefore need husky bodyguards for protection. While the documents concerned are of great interest to anyone working with *The Canterbury Tales*, it is true of course that Chaucer was not always controlled in his writing by a desire for historical accuracy. Accordingly, even the presence of more numerous and apt documents of this nature than are available could not dictate a brawny physique for the Nun's Priest. And whatever the extent to which Chaucer may have had in mind the perils of the road when (and if) he wrote "preestes thre," he was sufficiently unmindful of those perils when he wrote the "Nun's Priest's Prologue" to reduce the Prioress and the Second Nun to one male attendant "*the* Nonnes Preest."

Where but one brief explicit statement is available—and that one to the effect that this Pilgrim is "swete" and "goodly"—considerable difference of opinion concerning the Nun's Priest is at least permissible, if it can be supported. Thus, the purpose of this paper will be to maintain through a reexamination of the pertinent passages that the Nun's Priest is most convincingly visualized as an individual who is scrawny, humble, and timid, while at the same time highly intelligent, well educated, shrewd and witty. As an important part of this portrait, the Host's remarks in the "Nun's Priest's Epilogue" will be considered as broadly ironic, and Harry Bailly will assume a larger role in the dramatic interplay surrounding the Nun's Priest's performance than he has hitherto been granted by the commentators. Numerous suggestions made by other critics concerning this dramatic interplay—most notably those by William W. Lawrence—will be used here. However, no one, so far as I can find, has previously called attention to the important and easily acceptable function of the "Nun's Priest's Epilogue" when it is read as broad irony on the part of Harry Bailly. Such an interpretation of that Endlink serves as foundation for the argument presented here; and, as will appear at length below, it furnishes a reasonable explanation for the unanswerable question which arises if the "Nun's Priest's Epilogue" is taken as straightforward description: namely, why would the Host, who has prudently retreated before the Miller's impressive strength and the Shipman's evident hardihood, feel free to speak rudely and contemptuously to a large and muscular Nun's Priest? The supposition of a patronizing attitude on the part of the henpecked Host towards a man who is under the supervision of a woman, the Prioress, is simply not adequate explanation for the extreme rudeness and contempt of Harry's remarks to the Nun's Priest, if the latter is conceived of as possessing strength sufficient to make Harry fearful of physical violence.

The order to be used here for the fragments of *The Canterbury Tales* is that set forth recently and convincingly by R. A. Pratt, whereby Fragment VII comes immediately before Fragment III and after Fragment II. The Nun's Priest occupies the final position in Fragment VII, in many ways as carefully prepared a fragment of the Canterbury collection as is the first. The Host, up until the time that he calls upon the Nun's Priest for a story, has fared rather badly on the pilgrimage. After his success in the "General Prologue" and his pleasure arising from the "Knight's Tale," he was successfully challenged by the Miller, somewhat annoyed by the Reeve's "sermonyng," and shortly thereafter threatened by the Cook. Then his satisfaction with the Man of Law's performance was quickly dampened by the Shipman's revolt against his authority. Though the latter's tale concerning the merchant of Saint Denis restored the Host's good spirits, he seemed not too pleased with the sobriety resulting from the miracle related by the Prioress. Next, his patience was strained beyond its limits by the Pilgrim Chaucer's "Sir Thopas," and he was moved to a lengthy recollection of his domestic woes by the "Melibeus." In the succeeding instance, he was offered no relief by the Monk, whose tragedies he found exceedingly boring. Finally, when the Monk haughtily refused to relate gayer material, Harry impolitely turned upon the Nun's Priest with a demand that this cleric "Telle us swich thyng as may oure hertes glade."

Looked at in this fashion, the sequence and the nature of the performances in Fragments I, II, and VII seem to have been considerably influenced by Chaucer's desire to represent a regular rise and fall in the Host's spirits, with the humorous deflating

> *The high comedy for the reader and for Chaucer the poet lies, of course, in the Host's missing the subtler points of the tale and holding up to ridicule the meek little priest who has superbly defended him."*

of the Host as a steady theme running through the three successive fragments. Though this surmise may be open to debate, the fact should be noted that in the course of the first three fragments, Harry plays an important role in connection with every Pilgrim's recital. The point is that through these three successive fragments the Host's reactions are a vital part of the drama surrounding the various Pilgrims' performances. We therefore may not be far wide of the mark if, in trying to derive an acceptable portrait of the Nun's Priest, we examine that Pilgrim and his tale as they reflect against and fit with the Host's recent behavior; and we should bear steadily in mind that in this section of *The Canterbury Tales* the continuity of very probably nine and certainly four of the preceding recitals is beyond dispute. Particularly important here are the Host's behavior before and reaction after the immediately preceding performance, that of the Monk.

From this line of reasoning—based upon consideration of relationships which Chaucer certainly must have been aware of as he wrote—the following view is deduced as a defensible statement concerning the character of the Nun's Priest and the function of his tale in their dramatic context. The Host is the central figure in the personal interchanges surrounding the Monk's and the Nun's Priest's performances. He addresses the physically impressive Monk with a lengthy sexual joke; the Monk, by means of his dull tragedies, then rebuffs the Host for the latter's disrespectful and vulgar jocularity towards him. The Host therefore gladly seconds the Knight's interruption of the Monk's series of tragedies, but is again left with injured feelings when the Monk refuses to comply with his demand for a merry tale about hunting. As a consequence, the Host quickly turns upon the feeble and timid Nun's Priest as a cleric upon whom he can *safely* vent the displeasure which the Monk has caused him. The Nun's Priest meekly accepts the Host's brusque orders for a merry tale, and then brilliantly carries them out. In the tale he even subtly challenges two of the Host's attackers: he offers direct rebuttal for the theme of the prose narrative told by the Pilgrim Chaucer, and he satirizes both the manner and the matter of the Monk's recital. Though the Host may not realize that he has thus acquired a defender brilliant though physically weak, the gaiety of this tale dissipates most of Harry's displeasure, which arose most recently from his treatment by the Monk. Then, in the "Epilogue" which follows the Nun's Priest's Tale, the Host completely regains his good spirits, for there he is able to use successfully, in a broadly ironic manner, something of the same sexual joke to which the Monk earlier took exception. The high comedy for the reader and for Chaucer the poet lies, of course, in the Host's missing the subtler points of the tale and holding up to ridicule the meek little priest who has superbly defended him.

The analysis to support the statement in the preceding paragraph should begin with the performance by the Pilgrim Chaucer. To dispel the sobriety that has fallen upon the company as a result of the Prioress' story, the Host begins to jest; then he calls upon Chaucer for a merry tale, after having poked fun at him for his large waistline and his quiet manner. Chaucer proceeds by means of the burlesque "Sir Thopas" and the moralistic "Melibeus" to repay the Host in two complementary ways for his mockery. First, the Host's disgust with the entertaining and skilful "Sir Thopas" and his hearty approval of the interminable "Melibeus" make humorously apparent Harry's sad lack of the literary critical ability upon which he prides himself. Second, Harry's approving the "Melibeus," which has as its theme female "maistrye," and his consequent lengthy account of the difficulties he suffers at home under his wife Goodelief's "maistrye," make him a laughing-stock, for he lacks the critical insight to note the very point of that story which his own marital experience puts him in a position to refute.

Following his revelations of the bitter life Goodelief leads him, the Host turns to the Monk: "My lord, the Monk . . . be myrie of cheere, / For ye shul telle a tale trewely." As has not, I think, been noted elsewhere, from the first of these lines one should perhaps understand that the Monk's facial expression and manner indicate considerable

displeasure, for my lord the Monk certainly has no reason to be pleased with the treatment he has received on this pilgrimage. When, after the "Knight's Tale," the Host with due regard for "degre" called upon the Monk for a story, the drunken Miller rudely took over the Note the repetition here of the emphatic affirmative "yis" in place of the usual "yes." Also, though it is true that for the Host to request a merry tale, or for another Pilgrim to promise one, is a frequent occurrence in *The Canterbury Tales*, a noteworthy part of the unction here may rest in the Nun's Priest's echoing the Host's earlier unsuccessful command to the Monk to be merry. The Nun's Priest thus may be saying, in effect, "Even though the Monk would not do as you told him, *I will*." If such a reading is defensible, then already we can see that the lowly Nun's Priest is unsympathetic towards his high-ranking fellow churchman. As will appear shortly, there is considerable evidence in the "Nun's Priest's Tale" of his lack of sympathy for the Monk. In any event, in his answer here, the Nun's Priest is running no risk of incurring the Host's wrath; and the Narrator's calling him "swete" and "goodly" serves to emphasize the accommodating haste with which he has just accepted Harry's orders.

But, though the Nun's Priest may be weak in body and fawning in manner, there is nothing wrong with his intellect and education. In complying with the Host's request, he relates what is in many ways the outstanding story in the whole collection. And in so doing he manages to include two clear implications which reveal his own point of view and which can also be taken as defenses of the Host. In the first place, the story presents a husband who is right and a wife who is wrong in the interpretation of Chanticleer's dream. Further, though the ostensible moral of the story is that one should not be so careless as to trust in flattery, the Nun's Priest slyly places greater emphasis upon another point:

> Wommennes conseils been ful ofte colde;
> Wommannes conseil broghte us first to wo,
> And made Adam fro Paradys to go,
> Ther as he was ful myrie and wel at ese.
> But for I noot to whom it myght displese,
> If I conseil of wommen wolde blame,
> Passe over, for I seyde it in my game.
> Rede auctours, where they trete of swich mateere,
> And what they seyn of wommen ye may heere.
> Thise been the cokkes wordes, and nat myne;
> I kan noon harm of no woman divyne.

These antifeminist aspects of the tale represent the Nun's Priest's ways of hinting his dissatisfaction at being under the "petticoat rule" of the

Prioress. But they also serve another important function: they are the Nun's Priest's efforts to comfort the Host, who at home must cope with the dictatorial Goodelief. Further, they furnish a direct answer to the theme of the prose tale told earlier by the Pilgrim Chaucer, wherein Melibeus was greatly aided by his wife's counsel. Though Harry Bailly—favorably impressed by the fact that Prudence advised Melibeus to avoid strife, while his own wife urges him to do violence upon both his serving boys and his neighbors—may have failed to notice any incongruity between his praise on the one hand of a story which preaches that a husband should accept his wife's advice, and on the other his unpleasant situation at home, the Nun's Priest quickly saw the point. Therefore, by means of his story, the brilliant gaiety of which contrasts sharply and perhaps purposefully with the lengthy and dull "Melibeus," he makes clear that a husband is not always wise in following his wife's counsel. As J. B. Severs has shown, Chaucer's originality in the tale consists largely in his changes to emphasize just this point. Also, we should note that in the last lines of the passage quoted above, the Nun's Priest does not really withdraw his derogatory comments about women's counsel; rather, he furnishes authority for such views, for in suggesting that his listeners read the authors who treat such matters, he has in mind the same antifeminist writings from which Jankyn read to the Wife of Bath, writings which most certainly do not present a sympathetic view of women's counsel.

The second implication present in the tale is directed against the Monk, who, as we saw, completely discomfitted the Host. The Monk's confidence and general affluence are in as striking contrast with the Nun's Priest's timidity and poverty as is his fine palfrey with the latter's lean and foul nag; thus, it is not unnatural for the Nun's Priest to feel certain twinges of antagonistic jealousy toward his wealthy fellow churchman, and in his tale to hold up the Monk to subtle ridicule. The story of Croesus was one of the dull tragedies related by the Monk, and when Chanticleer refers to this story we are tempted to see a parallel between the strutting manner of both the outrider and the cock. Later, the Nun's Priest says:

> For evere the latter ende of joye is wo.
> God woot that worldly joye is soone ago;
> And if a rethor koude faire endite,
> He in a cronycle saufly myghte it write
> As for a sovereyn notabilitee.

In connection with this passage we observe that this same commonplace idea of mutability was

the central theme of the Monk's performance; and the Nun's Priest's calling such a routine concept a "sovereyn notabilitee" is almost certainly a thrust at the Monk's sententiousness and pomposity. One other passage by the Nun's Priest seems to apply unfavorably to the Monk. In his account of Samson, the Monk said:

> Beth war by this ensample oold and playn
> That no men telle hir conseil til hir wyves
> Of swich thyng as they wolde han secree fayn,
> If that it touche hir lymes or hir lyves.

Here, of course, is a typical antifeminist statement which a careful listener might well recall upon hearing the Nun's Priest's mock apology, quoted above, for speaking ill of "wommennes conseils." And the Nun's Priest seems eager to help his audience arrive at this connection when he shifts in his remarks from "reading" to "hearing" authors who have treated the woman question: "Read authors who treat such material, and you may hear what they say about women." Also, the Nun's Priest attributes the low opinion of women's counsel to Chanticleer, and thus once again equates the Monk with the cock, who, according to the Monk's words, should not have told Pertelote about his dream.

It seems clear, then, that in carrying out the Host's orders the Nun's Priest by the wonderful gaiety and charm of his story avoids any possible blame for not being merry, and that by the two implications present in his tale he goes further in his efforts to please, defend, and comfort the Host. Whether or not Harry understood these implications is not clear, but certainly he seems considerably mollified when he addresses the Nun's Priest in the "Epilogue" to the latter's tale.

Before we examine that Endlink, however, what of the claim by various editors of *The Canterbury Tales* that Chaucer meant to cancel it? This claim has been supported by three factors: first, the Endlink does not appear in most of the manuscripts; second, certain lines in the Endlink repeat matters present in the Host's remarks to the Monk in the "Prologue" to the "Nun's Priest's Tale;" and, third, as Manly and Rickert felt, cancellation seems "to be supported by the fact that the Host's words to the Priest after the tale suggest a different type of person from that suggested by his words [before the tale]..." But, as Tatlock argued, the manuscript situation may well result from patchwork by the scribes, and for Chaucer repetition of an idea is not infrequent, especially when as here actual verbal repetition is extremely limited. Further, the seeming conflict in the Host's comments as to the type of person addressed is present only if the Endlink is taken as straightforward description. Consequently, the claim for cancellation is not convincing, and, as we shall see, to throw away this "Epilogue" would be to lose its possibly ironic function and thus to rule out what may be one of Chaucer's carefully developed high points in the dramatic interplay among the Pilgrims. The Endlink in question may be quoted in full:

"Sire Nonnes Preest," oure Hooste seide anoon,
"I blessed be thy breche, and every stoon!
This was a murie tale of Chauntecleer.
But by my trouthe, if thou were seculer,
Thou woldest ben a trede-foul aright.
For if thou have corage as thou hast myght,
Thee were nede of hennes, as I wene,
Ya, moo than seven tymes seventene.
See, whiche braunes hath this gentil preest,
So gret a nekke, and swich a large breest!
He loketh as a sperhauk with his yen;
Him nedeth nat his coulour for to dyen
With brasile, ne with greyn of Portyngale.
Now, sire, faire falle you for your tale!"
And after that he, with ful merie chere,
Seide unto another, as ye shuln heere.

We see here that as a result of the gaiety of the Nun's Priest's "murie tale of Chauntecleer," the Host has lost much of the pique which he earlier felt because of the Monk's outdoing him. He therefore compliments the Nun's Priest for his narrative ability. But Harry still has not forgotten the rebuff dealt him by the Monk. To wipe away the memory of this loss of dignity, and to reestablish himself in the eyes of the company, he now directs at the Nun's Priest something of the same sexual jest at which the Monk earlier took offense. In so doing, Harry continues to use the second person singular familiar pronouns, a device he would surely not have employed if his intent here were solely to praise the Nun's Priest. It seems much more likely that this time his jest is ironically employed, in that the frail and timid Nun's Priest, of whom the Host feels not the least fear, lacks completely the appearance of vigorous manliness which Harry attributes to him in this "Epilogue." Thus the Host evens his score with the Monk, to his own satisfaction at least, at the expense of another churchman, and then condescends in the last line of his speech to address the Nun's Priest with a respectful "yow." Consequently, he is ready to call upon the next storyteller with his usual "ful merie chere."

My main contention, then, is that the dramatic interplay surrounding the Nun's Priest's performance depends upon a conception of this Pilgrim as frail, timid, and humble. Further, the Host plays a vital and consistent role in the interchanges which accompany the narratives presented in Fragment VII. A Nun's Priest fit to serve as a muscular bodyguard for the Prioress and the Second Nun would hardly have meekly suffered Harry's contemptuous attitude in calling upon him, or the Host's leering insinuations in commenting upon his story. Nor, in view of that attitude and those insinuations, is it likely that the physically impressive Nun's Priest who emerges if the "Nun's Priest's Epilogue" is taken as actual description would have been sufficiently eager to please the Host as to furnish him with a gay tale including implications which almost certainly represent retorts to Harry's most recent attackers—the Pilgrim Chaucer and the Monk—and which offer Harry some comfort for the female "maistrye" that he experiences at home. Finally, the interpretation set forth in this paper presents an explanation which in no way conflicts with Chaucer's usual method in handling his Pilgrims, and which accounts satisfactorily for the general similarity of the Host's remarks in the "Nun's Priest's Epilogue" and in his earlier address to the Monk.

Source: R. M. Lumiansky, "The Nun's Priest in *The Canterbury Tales*," in *P.M.L.A.*, Vol. 68, No. 4, September 1953, pp. 896–906.

Sources

Brewer, Derek Stanley, *Chaucer in His Time*, Thomas Nelson and Sons Ltd., 1963.

Chesterton, G. K., "The Greatness of Chaucer," in *Geoffrey Chaucer*, edited by Harold Bloom, Chelsea House Publishers, 1985.

Patterson, Lee, "'No Man His Reson Herde': Peasant Consciousness, Chaucer's Miller, and the Structure of *The Canterbury Tales*," in *South Atlantic Quarterly*, Vol. 86, 1987.

Stillinger, Thomas, Introduction, in *Critical Essays on Geoffrey Chaucer*, G. K. Hall, 1998, p. 2.

Further Reading

Cullen, Dolores L., *Chaucer's Host: Up-So-Doun*, Fithian Press, 1998.

Though many other books have been written about the other travelers, Cullen takes a rare book-length look at the Host of the trip, the innkeeper. Her study attempts to show him to be a Christ-like figure.

Lambdin, Laura C., ed., *Chaucer's Pilgrims: An Historical Guide to the Pilgrims in the "Canterbury Tales,"* Praeger Publishers, 1999.

This book assembles essays from experts in each field, explaining the social functions of the various pilgrims that Chaucer wrote about. Reading this book is a good way to get to know medieval England and *Canterbury Tales* at the same time.

Leiceister, H. Marshall, Jr., *The Disenchanted Self: Representing the Subject in the "Canterbury Tales,"* University of California Press, 1990.
> Marshall examines the question of whether *Canterbury Tales* has an overall narrative structure or are a collection of related, but not entwined, objects. The book's scholarly tone might be difficult for some students.

Loomis, Roger Sherman, *A Mirror of Chaucer's World*, Princeton University Press, 1965.
> This book tells the story of Chaucer, his age, and his acquaintances, making use of many illustrations to give readers a sense of what the land and life in general was like in the fourteenth century.

Patterson, Lee, *Chaucer and the Subject of History*, University of Wisconsin Press, 1991.
> Patterson is one of the world's great medievalists (scholars of the medieval era). This study of the time as it is reflected in Chaucer's work is solid and complete.

Robinson, Ian, *Chaucer and the English Tradition*, Cambridge University Press, 1972.
> Other studies show how English poetry evolved from Chaucer; this one puts his work into perspective with the works that were written before him and in his time. It also gives a good look at Chaucer's writings besides *The Canterbury Tales*.

Ruggiers, Paul G., *The Art of the "Canterbury Tales,"* The University of Wisconsin Press, 1965.
> Ruggiers, a Guggenheim Fellow, divides the tales into two functions, "comedy and irony" and "romantic," and he examines each in its designated category.

Climbing

Lucille Clifton
1993

"Climbing" is the first original poem in Lucille Clifton's collection *The Book of Light*, published by Copper Canyon Press, in 1993. It is in a section titled "Reflection," which comes directly after a found poem, "Light." In a lyric of twelve short lines, Clifton uses simple, accessible language to imagine what it would be like to be sixty years old. The speaker imagines herself in the future and uses that image to make statements to herself about what might have been different in her life. The poem's tone, however, is not one of despair but rather of achievement. The speaker doesn't really wish she had made other choices; rather, she seems proud of the decisions she has made and acknowledges the struggle ahead as she ages. Themes that the poem addresses include the relationship between ageing and desire, time and regret, and the ways in which self-image changes as human beings age. Clifton was in her mid-fifties when she wrote the poem, and there is much autobiographical material in it. The title of the collection could just as easily have been called *The Book of Lucille*, as Lucille derives from the Latin word *lucius*, meaning "light." Many of the poems in the collection address family members, both dead and alive, and a few poems address political figures, such as Senator Jesse Helms, and fictional figures, such as Clark Kent. Some are dramatic monologues, others confessional lyrics. All of the poems are marked by revelation and insight and evoke universal experiences to appeal to readers.

Author Biography

Born in 1936 to working-class parents Samuel Louis and Thelma Lucille Sayles, Lucille Clifton grew up in Depew, New York. She is descended from a long line of strong, resilient women who have battled and overcome adversity. Her great-great grandmother, Caroline Donald, whom Clifton cites as the inspiration for much of her poetry, was kidnapped from her home in Dahomey, West Africa, and brought to America along with her mother, sister, and brother. Clifton gives a full accounting of her family's story in her 1976 memoir *Generations*. After attending Howard University and Fredonia State Teachers College (now State University of New York College at Fredonia), Clifton worked as a claims clerk for the New York State Division of Employment and then as a literature assistant for the Central Atlantic Regional Educational Laboratory. She began teaching in 1971 at Coppin State College after winning the Discovery Award from the New York YW-YMHA Poetry Center and publishing *Good Times: Poems* in 1969, named by the *New York Times* as one of the year's ten best books. Since then, Clifton has garnered numerous other awards including National Endowment for the Arts awards, 1969, 1970, and 1972; the Juniper Prize for *Two-Headed Woman* from the University of Massachusetts in 1980; two Pulitzer Prize nominations for her poetry; the Lannan Literary Award for poetry in 1996 for *The Terrible Stories*; a 1999 Lila Wallace-Reader's Digest Writers' Award; and a National Book Award for poetry in 2000 for *Blessing the Boats: New and Selected Poems, 1988–2000*. Clifton is also an accomplished writer of children's books. Some of these include *My Brother Fine with Me* (1975), *Three Wishes* (1976), *Amifika* (1977), and *The Lucky Stone* (1979). She has also authored the popular Everett Anderson series of books for juveniles.

Her poetry is rooted in her experience as an African-American woman raised in an impoverished urban environment, who has a strong and enduring love for her family and community. Critics praise her work as fresh and honest and cite her ability to craft powerful, evocative images that express pride in her identity as a black woman. However, her most powerful poems, such as "Climbing," transcend gender and race to get at the heart of the human condition. Since 1990, Clifton has been St. Mary's Distinguished Professor of Humanities at St. Mary's College of Maryland.

Lucille Clifton

Poem Text

a woman precedes me up the long rope,
her dangling braids the color of rain.
maybe i should have had braids.
maybe i should have kept the body i started,
slim and possible as a boy's bone.   5
maybe i should have wanted less.
maybe i should have ignored the bowl in me
burning to be filled.
maybe i should have wanted less.
the woman passes the notch in the rope   10
marked Sixty. i rise toward it, struggling,
hand over hungry hand.

Poem Summary

Lines 1–2

In the first few lines of "Climbing," the speaker sets the tone of the poem by describing a ghostly apparition. By describing the woman on the rope as having "dangling braids the color of rain," the speaker signals that she is in the realm of the imagination. Rain is transparent and has no color *per se*. Rope, as a symbol, has many associations: it is both a form of transportation and a device used to pull things. It can also be used to hang people. The fact that it is a "long rope" implies that the speaker has a hard journey ahead of her.

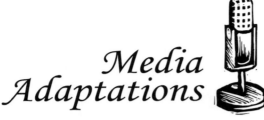

Media Adaptations

- New Letters on the Air distributes an audiocassette entitled *Lucille Clifton* with Clifton reading excerpts from her poetry (publication date unavailable).

- Clifton reads her poetry on *The Place for Keeping*, an audiocassette distributed by Watershed Tapes (publication date unavailable).

Lines 3–5

In these lines, the speaker begins the list of "maybe's" that structure the rest of the poem. By questioning whether she herself should have had braids, the speaker introduces the subject of regret. Braids themselves are decorative—and dangling braids more so—suggesting youth and vitality and a degree of sensuality. The speaker follows up this statement with a similar regret, this time wondering if she should have kept her younger body, which she describes as "slim and possible as a boy's bone." Young boys are still growing into their bodies, hence the idea of possibility, of something not yet completely formed. Readers can infer that the speaker no longer has this kind of body but also that it is an impossible desire. Bodies change with age. Although exercise, diet, and close attention to one's health can shape the way a body changes with time, a changing body is inevitable.

Lines 6–9

In these lines, the speaker reflects on the degree of desire she has had in her life. She uses the metaphor of the bowl inside of her to represent this desire. The image of the bowl is significant because it suggests food and the idea of hunger, which will reappear at the end of the poem. Clifton mixes her metaphors when she writes that the bowl is "burning to be filled," but the image works because it underlines the speaker's lust for life and love. Again the speaker presents an idea that may have nothing to do with choice. Can people really "choose" what they desire, or is desire itself so linked to the human body and identity that to ignore it would be to ignore oneself? Clifton repeats

the line "maybe I should have wanted less" to underscore the ruminative voice of the speaker as she climbs upward.

Lines 10–12

In these lines, the mystery of the rope is made clear. It symbolizes life itself and the way that human beings age. Another way to visualize the rope is to think of it as a timeline with a notch for each decade. The woman in front of the speaker "passes the notch in the rope / marked Sixty," meaning that she has turned sixty years old. The speaker's "struggling" to "rise toward it" means that she herself is approaching sixty, battling the processes of aging, yet still envisioning herself as a youthful woman full of life and the desire to live. This lust for life is embodied in the last image of the poem, which echoes the "bowl . . . / burning to be filled" described earlier in the poem. Hands can be hungry in the sense that they are always grasping for more and craving satisfaction. In this sense, they are metaphoric of the speaker's needs.

Themes

Transformation

There is an old adage that the only constant in life is change. Clifton emphasizes the idea of change by describing the desires of her present self in relation to versions of her past and future selves. The present self is the struggling self, full of anxiety and dread, the one who questions the life she has led. These doubts are underscored in the litany of "maybe's" the speaker rattles off. The past self is the one of the youthful body, as "slim and possible as a boy's bone." This self, like the present one, is full of desire and a lust for life, with a "bowl . . . / burning to be filled." The future self is more enigmatic, ghostly. She "precedes" the speaker on the rope, "her dangling braids the color of rain," and she "passes the notch in the rope / marked Sixty." Such a description suggests a woman who has come to terms with the changes in her life and who charges into the future, confident of who she is and the choices she has made. This version of the speaker's future self is still possible, and the speaker climbs towards her as she climbs towards her sixtieth year. The final image of the poem is one of a woman who reflects on her past while keeping an eye on a future ideal. Her continued hunger for life highlights the idea that she will weather coming changes.

Death

The very title of the poem emphasizes upward movement, often symbolically associated with growth. However, for a human being, the act of climbing also requires effort and a goal, something to climb toward. For the speaker of "Climbing," that goal isn't a chosen one but one that is built in, part of the natural process of ageing. The "goal," the culmination of aging, is death, and although the speaker never says the word, it hovers over the poem, the final notch in the rope. The woman who precedes the speaker on the rope is a future version of the speaker and someone closer to death than the speaker. She is "climbing" up the rope because aging also requires effort. One must battle feelings of regret both for things done and left undone, and one must continue to hope and to live in the face of a failing body and the imminence of death itself. Like a notch in the rope of ageing, "Sixty," for many people, signifies the end of middle age. Retirement is often a few years away, and people begin to think of how they will spend the rest of their lives. The speaker "struggles" towards this notch because she is both fearful of it and desirous of living more, of wanting more from life. She underscores that desire in the image of the "hungry hand."

Style

Lyric

"Climbing" is a lyric poem. Lyrics are short, first-person poems focusing on the speaker's emotional or mental state. They are often melodic and often based in the imagination rather than in the empirically verifiable real world. The word *lyric* derives from the Greek *lyre*, meaning a musical instrument once used to accompany poems. Clifton's poem stimulates the imagination when she describes her ghostly double preceding her on the rope of life. The poem's melody is due in part to its repetition of the phrase "maybe i should have." As one of poetry's oldest forms, the lyric has evolved into a variety of kinds including the ballad, the ode, and the sonnet. Most people today recognize the plural form of lyric as referring to a song's words. Well-known writers of lyric poetry include Emily Dickinson, William Shakespeare, and Robert Frost.

Punctuation

Clifton uses lower case throughout the poem, de-emphasizing the idea of new beginnings that

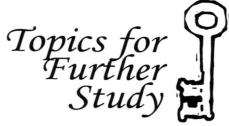

Topics for Further Study

- Write a descriptive essay speculating on what you will look like and how you will feel when you are sixty years old.

- Research the subject of body image and aging, then present your findings to your class. Make sure to address the following questions: What about their bodies do women most pay attention to when aging? Is this different from what men pay attention to? How is body image related to race?

- Take an informal poll of people over forty, asking them what they regret most in their lives. What similarities and differences do you see? Were most of the regrets for something they did not do or for something they did? What conclusions can you draw from your findings?

- Draw a time line running from your birth to the age at which you believe you will die, marking it in five-year increments. Under each five-year mark, write a short description of what you did that year or what you believe you will be doing. What does this time line tell you about how you think of your past and your future?

- Review three or four popular magazines such as *People*, *Cosmopolitan*, and *Ebony*, paying careful attention to women's hairstyles. Are there any connections you can make about hairstyle and age, hairstyle and body type?

- Research the cultural significance of hairstyles such as the Afro, the Mullet, the Mohawk, even the cleanly-shaved head, and report your findings to your class. Then lead a discussion on hairstyles, asking your classmates to explain what their hair says about who they are.

capital letters at the start of sentences mark. Using the small *i* throughout illustrates a speaker who, paradoxically, doesn't take herself too seriously. This is paradoxical because lyric poems are all about the "I." The single capitalized word is "Sixty," signifying the importance of that word relative to others in the poem.

Historical Context

In the early 1990s, when "Climbing"was written, the entertainment industry in the United States was coming to recognize the approximately 19 million black women as a lucrative market. The development of this market was helped in part by the phenomenal success of Oprah Winfrey's talk show, nationally syndicated in 1986 and widely recognized as the most popular talk show in the history of television. Winfrey's success provided a positive image of black women and helped to combat the racial and gender stereotypes of black women in American society. Through her book club and the book club segment on her show, Winfrey has also helped to popularize books by and about successful black women. For example, Winfrey has chosen books by Toni Morrison and Maya Angelou as book club selections, giving the works of these literary giants broad appeal. Terry McMillan's two blockbuster hit novels, *Waiting to Exhale* and *How Stella Got Her Groove Back*, capitalized on this market, and the films made from these novels have been critical as well as financial successes. With the growing audience for shows about African Americans and the increase in the number of black television executives, an all-black network was inevitable. Founded in the early 1990s, Black Entertainment Television (BET) runs sports shows, music videos, and reruns of series focusing on African Americans.

The status of American women in the 1990s was also changing. Feminist theorists refer to the 1990s as marking the advent of third wave feminism. Often defined in generational terms, third wave feminism refers to the response of younger women to feminist issues and other feminists. In "A Manifesto for Third Wave Feminism," Tamara Strauss writes:

> So an intergenerational struggle has sprung forth between mothers and daughters. On the one side are Second Wavers who lashed out against their sexually limiting roles as wives and mothers in exchange for equal pay and egalitarian partnerships. And on the other are Third Wavers who, perhaps dismissive of the battles fought and often won by their mothers, aspire to be Madonna, the woman who rose to fame as the ultimate virgin whore. Third Wavers . . . want to continue the fight for equal rights, but not to the detriment of their sexuality. They want to be both subject and object, when it comes to their sexual roles, their political power and their place in American culture.

These competing roles and conflicting desires are no doubt evident in Clifton's appraisal of her own life. As a prolific author of poetry and children's books, a wife, a professor, a mother of six, and a grandmother, Clifton has had to balance numerous demands on her time and attention. Rather than "wanting less," however, Clifton has always desired more for herself and her family. The fact that she is approaching the "end of her rope" occasions reflection and the sense that she could have done more. Statistically, Clifton has less than ten years of life left. For black women in the United States, life expectancy is 73.9 years, a little more than five years less than all American females.

Aging itself has become an international subject of research and concern. Paul Wallace, author of *Agequake*, writes about the world's population: "We have been remarkably young. Our average age has been around 20 or less. But in the current generation's lifetime, the average age of the world will nearly double from 22 in 1975 to 38 in 2050, according to the UN's latest projections issued at the end of 1998. . . . Many countries will reach average ages of 50 or more." Changes accompanying such a shift will include reassessing the future of the 9 to 5 work week, pension funds, and social security, providing health care for the aging, maintaining a stable and creative work force, and for rigidly patriarchal countries like Japan, re-thinking women's role in society, as the number of women in the world will increase.

Critical Overview

The book jacket of *The Book of Light* contains quotations from two prominent poets, Sharon Olds and Denise Levertov, that typify the critical response to the book. Olds writes, "These are poems of fierce joy, made as if under the pressure of passionate witness . . . They [the book's poems] have the exactness and authority of laws of nature—they are principles of life." Levertov is equally effusive in her praise, writing, "poem after poem exhilarates and inspires awe at the manifestation of such artistic and spiritual power." Reviewing the collection for *Poetry*, Calvin Bedient expresses reservations about Clifton's politics but commends her development as a poet, writing, "If this poet's art has deepened since her 1969 debut volume, *Good Times*, it's in an increased capacity for quiet delicacy and fresh generalization. *The Book of Light* contains several poems that show Clifton's penchant and gift for lucid self-assessment, indeed a forbearance toward herself and her family like that of the moon for the earth." In a review for *Belles*

Lettres, Andrea Lockett writes that the collection is "a gift of joy, a truly illuminated manuscript by a writer whose powers have been visited by grace."

Criticism

Chris Semansky

Semansky publishes widely in the field of twentieth-century poetry and culture. In the following essay, he considers how Clifton's poem uses the idea of doubling as a strategy for self-reflection.

Clifton uses the image of the doppelganger to reflect on the life that she's had and to envision her future life. *Doppelganger* is a German word for *alter ego*, or *other self*, and it marks just one of the "doubling" techniques Clifton uses in "Climbing." The doppelganger motif is popular in literature and has been used by many poets and writers, including Edgar Allen Poe, Octavio Paz, Robert Louis Stevenson, Oscar Wilde, and Charlotte Perkins Gilman. Writers often create versions of their other selves as mirrors of sorts to provide them with a clearer picture of their own lives. These representations are often either idealized or demonized projections of a part of the writer. For example, in Gilman's story "The Yellow Wallpaper," the woman the narrator sees in the yellow wallpaper is a symbolic projection of the speaker's self struggling to break free of patriarchal oppression.

Clifton's double is an idealized version of the self she wants to become. It "precedes" her on the rope of life because it exists only in the future. Many people imagine what they will be like in the future and attempt to gauge their progress in relation to that image. The problem, of course, is that the future is already here, and idealized versions of oneself must, by their very nature, remain unattainable. This is also the paradox of desire itself: it can only exist with an object; once that object is attained, there must be a new one. Significantly, Clifton never presents an image of this idealized self's body. It is represented only by "braids the color of rain." Braids, an interweaving of strands of hair, are themselves another image of doubling, a way in which many are made from one. As a trope—a figurative use of a word—the braids stand in for the many selves and bodies that proceed from the one body. Ropes themselves are braided strands of fiber, woven together to create a single, stronger thing. What, then, do braids signify? They signify the idea of youth itself: stylized and sensual, they

'The strong sense of general disappointment coupled with the sinking suspicion that one's life has missed the mark strikes responsive chords in many readers.'"

mark their wearer as "hip" and confident. That the speaker doesn't wear them tells readers she is, stylistically at least, perhaps more conventional in appearance.

The speaker's body is at the center of the poem, but readers are never given an explicit representation of her body. It's clear, however, that body image is at least a part of what the speaker battles as she ages. Her desire for a younger body and her second-guessing of her past both point to common issues people encounter in the ageing process. Rather than giving in to these doubts, however, Clifton's speaker goes forward in spite of them.

"Climbing" is as much a poem about falling as it is about rising. There can be no struggle to "rise" without the fear of falling. In this case, falling means giving up on life and on the object before her: her idealized self, the one she would grow into. To fall would be to settle for less, to ignore the "bowl . . . / burning to be filled." The speaker climbs because she envisions herself moving towards that future self and what it promises. That she never attains that self is irrelevant, for it is the climbing itself that is important, the desire to keep going. Rather than fearing the future, as Wilde's Dorian Gray might, Clifton embraces it.

Paralleling the idea of doubling is Clifton's use of repetition. The string of "maybe's" lengthens, as the years the speaker has lived and the notches she has already passed on the rope add up. Clifton's words also sonically embody "twosomeness," as in the alliterative phrases "boy's bone" and "bowl in me / burning." These images are themselves undergirded by the repetition of the phrase "maybe i should have wanted less," an inverted way of telling readers that she has wanted much.

The image of the other self provides a practical poetic vehicle for exploring the subject of regret, a common theme in Clifton's poetry. In the same collection as "Climbing" comes "it was a dream":

> in which my greater self
> rose up before me
> accusing me of my life
> with her extra finger
> whirling in a gyre of rage
> at what my days had come to.
> what,
> i pleaded with her, could i do,
> oh what could i have done?
> and she twisted her wild hair
> and sparked her wild eyes
> and screamed as long as
> i could hear her
> This. This. This.

The speaker's questioning of the "greater self" echoes the statements of regret in "Climbing," and, coincidentally, this self also has "wild hair." An observation that Wallace Peppers makes of poems from *An Ordinary Woman* can also be applied to those in *The Book of Light*: "The strong sense of general disappointment coupled with the sinking suspicion that one's life has missed the mark strikes responsive chords in many readers. And worse still, from the speaker's point of view, is the growing realization that this enormously unsatisfying condition is probably permanent." If regret is "terminal" in "it was a dream," it is ambiguous at best in "Climbing," for the "maybe's" don't ring true as missed opportunities. After all, how does one "want less," and how can anyone keep the body they started with? If anything, the speaker's tone in this poem is at once self-doubtful *and* defiant, the attitude like that of an athlete pushing forward toward the finish line. A poem closer in regret to "it was a dream" is the title poem of *An Ordinary Woman*, written when Clifton had almost hit the fortieth notch on the rope:

> Plain as cake
> an ordinary woman
> i had expected to be
> smaller than this,
> more beautiful,
> wiser in Afrikan ways,
> more confident,
> i had expected
> more than this.
> The sentiment is familiar.

Expectations, disappointment, acceptance: the stuff of an examined life. What was familiar at forty is familiar at sixty.

With aging comes reflection, and Clifton performs that act in both senses of the word: she looks back on her past and in that looking sees an image of herself in the future. The final image of doubling in the poem is the image of her "hungry" hands, the only body part of the present-tense speaker mentioned. Reflective readers, moved by Clifton's evocation of the struggle and joy that comes with desiring more from life, will see themselves in these hands.

Source: Chris Semansky, Critical Essay on "Climbing," in *Poetry for Students*, The Gale Group, 2002.

Joyce Hart

Hart is a freelance writer of literary themes. In this essay, she examines the ambiguity of the images in Clifton's poem and considers them as the meditations of one woman reflecting on her life, who, through the use of ambiguity, speaks to everyone.

At first reading, Lucille Clifton's poem "Climbing" seems to be made up of simple, seemingly non-complex words and fairly obvious images. Consisting of only twelve lines that create a single image of a woman climbing a metaphorical rope of time, "Climbing" could be read in a couple of minutes, smiled at, and then forgotten. But Clifton is a complicated woman, whose use of simple vocabulary and short-lined verse is not an indication of simple meaning or lack of depth. As Liz Rosenberg in her article in the *New York Times* puts it: "[W]hat may appear stylistically simple [in Clifton's poetry] is, upon close examination, an effort to free the true voice clear and plain."

In the poem "Climbing," Clifton raises her voice through metaphor, and upon closer reading, it becomes apparent that the images she creates are not so easy to define. However, it is through her use of simple vocabulary to create ambiguous imagery that Clifton draws her readers in and then opens her poem up to ever-expanding boundaries of definition. In this way, her poem becomes more than a meditation of one poet; it becomes a personal reflection for everyone who reads it.

With a very general sweep of the poem, anyone could define the basic element that exists here. This is a poem about a woman who is reflecting on her life. But what kind of woman is the speaker of this poem? Is she a general woman, symbolic of all womankind throughout history? Or is she more specific? Clifton has been described by some critics as a womanist writer. This term, allegedly coined by the writer Alice Walker, refers to a feminist point of view that targets the specific roles and circumstances of women of color. Besides the fact that Clifton herself is African American, there is a very strong possibility that this poem is purposely directed at African-American women and their needs.

The reader who looks closely might find implicit clues that refer to African-American women. For instance, Clifton begins her poem with a woman preceding the speaker of the poem "up a long rope." She describes this woman as having "dangling braids," which could be a possible reference to a popular hairstyle worn by African-American women. However, in the same line, she also gives these braids "the color of rain." So then the reader must ask, what is the color of rain? The color of rain is translucent, or is it? Rain is associated with dark, or black clouds, and overcast days that tone down colors into murky shades of gray. If rain is looked at through this lens, it may well be considered dark or even black. If the braids are considered black, then there is a hint, albeit slight, that this could be an image of a black woman.

But is it necessary to characterize or even identify this woman with braids? Clifton is ambiguous about this image, leaving it open for a broad range of interpretations. Readers can look at the clues, but even the clues are ambiguous, as ambiguous as the color of rain. In their ambiguity, Clifton expands her images, allowing all readers to claim the images for themselves.

If this image of the woman with the braids the color of rain is taken on a more emotional level, the reference to rain could also be an allusion to tears, which look like rain drops. Readers might then ask: Why would this woman be crying? If Clifton's allusion is to an African-American woman, it would be very easy to list reasons why she might be crying. History (something that Clifton is very aware of) reveals the cruelties of slavery that continue to affect African-American women. In modern times, despite many positive strides in society, there still remain injustices of racism in the United States, as well as in the rest of the world. But even if Clifton's allusion were to a less specific race of women, if she wrote this poem for all women without discriminating between whether this was a black woman or a white woman, there are many women, having lived their lives in a patriarchal society, who have suffered injustices. Clifton, then, could be speaking in a feminist voice. By taking the image a step further, if this image of a woman were merely the reflection of the speaker of the poem (who is a woman), the image could be looked at as a self-reflection, opening the allusion to include males or any other reader of the poem as well. Emotions and

> *She sets her poems up, exposing her concerns, empathizing with others who have experienced sadness and fears, but then she encourages movement, progression, even celebration."*

tears, suffering and pain, are universals, experienced by all humankind.

As the poem progresses, the woman in the poem climbs up the rope as Clifton gives further examples or explanations as to the source of the emotions and shedding of tears. Before proceeding with the rest of the poem and the possible emotions behind the images, there still remains the question of who this woman in braids might be. It has already been decided that her race is not clearly defined, but even her age is ambiguous. She wears braids, a hairstyle that is usually reflective of youth. If she is younger than the speaker of the poem, why is she preceding the speaker in terms of time? Why does she pass "the notch in the rope / marked Sixty" before the speaker. If the color of rain is taken to be transparent, is this indicative of the woman in braids herself? Is she also transparent, having no race, no age, no corporeal distinction? Could she be a mythical image of womanhood that the speaker holds in her mind? Is she the alter ego of the speaker, someone that the speaker once thought she might be? Is she the youth of the speaker? Is this woman in braids somehow not only representative of the speaker's past but also indicative of her future, climbing the rope of time in front of her, leading her in some metaphorical way? Is she a more generic symbol of time, of dreams unfulfilled? There's a lot to ponder in the broad spaces that Clifton has left surrounding her images. But the fascinating thing about the broad spaces and Clifton's ambiguity is that the more these questions are pondered, the more comfortable the poem feels. Although ambiguity can be confusing, it also can inspire readers to fill in the empty places with answers of their own.

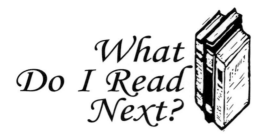
What Do I Read Next?

- The 1973 anthology *The Poetry of Black America: Anthology of the 20th Century*, edited by Adoff Arnold and introduced by Gwendolyn Brooks, contains poems by Clifton and many other prominent African-American poets, including Amiri Baraka, Sam Cornish, Countee Cullen, and Sterling Allen Brown.

- Clifton is also a writer of children's books. Her book, *Everett Anderson's 1–2–3* (1992), illustrated by Ann Grifalconi, tells the story of Everett Anderson, a young African-American boy living in the city, who comes to terms with his mother's new friend and grows up in the process.

- Terry McMillan's 1992 blockbuster novel, *Waiting to Exhale*, chronicles the lives of four thirty-something black women, their romantic adventures, and their deep emotional bonds with one another. Adapted into a popular movie, this novel, in part, examines how these women respond to ageing.

- Another popular McMillan novel, *How Stella Got Her Groove Back* (1996), explores the desires and choices of Stella Payne, a forty-something black woman who unexpectedly falls in love with a much younger man.

There may be many questions about who this woman in braids might be, but there are no questions that suggest that the speaker in this poem is reflecting on injustices in her life that have caused her pain. It is obvious that she is questioning the paths that she has chosen: "maybe i should have had braids. / maybe i should have kept the body i started / . . . maybe i should have wanted less." Clifton repeats this last line farther down in the poem, bringing home the sadness behind the statement. In wanting less, maybe she would not now feel so "hungry." In wanting less, maybe she would not be "struggling." She is full in the sense of no longer being slim, but the fullness comes from the "bowl in me" which remains empty. Readers do not know what the speaker wanted that she did not receive. They do not know what the speaker hungers for. But it is this indefiniteness that draws the reader in. By not filling in the spaces, Clifton touches the empty spaces in all women, in all readers, in spite of their gender. She touches everyone who has ever experienced failure, disappointment, or injustice. But Clifton does not leave her readers in this place. She does not leave them lost in self-pity. Although she has suffered and commiserates with others who have suffered, Clifton is a woman with a positive attitude.

This positive attitude is expressed in different ways. For instance, in another of her poems, "song at midnight," she writes: "come celebrate / with me that everyday / something has tried to kill me / and has failed." The "something" is not named, but it is defined as potentially lethal. Despite the potential danger that threatens her, she wants to celebrate. She focuses on the fact that she has survived, not on the something that has tried to kill her. This is a message that Clifton most likes to deliver. She sets her poems up, exposing her concerns, empathizing with others who have experienced sadness and fears, but then she encourages movement, progression, even celebration. In her poetry, there are often two elements at play: both the dangers and frustrations of life and the resiliency of the speaker. This resiliency is also apparent in the poem "Climbing." Regardless of the speaker's sorrows, her tears, her pain, she keeps on climbing.

Although Clifton's poetry often takes on the sadder elements of life, it has also been referred to as joyful. As Rosenberg writes, "Ms. Clifton's poetry is big enough to accommodate sorrow and madness and yet her vision emerges as overwhelmingly joyous and calm." Clifton describes her own positive outlook on life in her poem "hag riding":

> when i wake to the heat of morning
> galloping down the highway of my life
> something hopeful rises in me
> rises and runs me out into the road
> and i lob my fierce thigh high
> over the rump of the day and honey
> i ride i ride.

In her poem "Climbing," Clifton ends with her speaker rising, pulling herself up "hand over hungry hand." She is moving, despite her hunger, despite her struggles, despite her fear of death. She is moving, although she might not know where she is going or what is waiting for her along the way. In "Climbing," all she knows is that she is heading toward "Sixty," whatever that will mean. She does not know whether her hunger will be satisfied when she gets there. She does not know if her struggles will cease or become more difficult. She leaves many questions unanswered, as does this poem.

In another of her poems, however, she seems to console herself by hinting at a possible course of action in dealing with all those unanswered questions. In "evening and my dead once husband," she first ponders, "why cancer and terrible loneliness / and the wars against our people," but then she offers these lines in the same poem, as if in answer to all the questions that she has posed: "and out of the mist a hand / becomes flesh and i watch / as its pointing fingers spell / it does not help to know."

Maybe in Clifton's indefinite descriptions of race and age, or even in her uncertain allusions to earthly or mythical beings, she is saying that it is not in the knowing, it is not in the naming of specifics, it is not even in the naming of exact injustices or the pain caused by discrimination and unfairness and all the other frustrations and disappointments of life that one comes to accept human existence. In self-reflection it is not so important to second-guess what was not done, what could have been, what needs were never met. It's not about specifics at all. Life is vague, both in memories about the past and projected wishes for the future. Life is as vague and unanswerable as the images in Clifton's poetry.

One thing, however, that Clifton is not ambiguous about is her role as a poet. In an interview with Katie Davis on the radio program *All Things Considered*, Clifton had this to say: "I write about being human. If you have ever been human, I invite you to that place that we share." In the end, it does not matter who the images represent in the poem "Climbing." The poem is a meditation of a woman looking back on her life in an attempt to understand what waits for her in her future. In her meditation, the speaker beckons to everyone who reads this poem to follow, just as she is following the nondescript woman in braids. Do not forget what you have been through, the speaker seems to be saying, but don't ever let it stop you from climbing.

Source: Joyce Hart, Critical Essay on "Climbing," in *Poetry for Students*, The Gale Group, 2002.

Judi Ketteler

Ketteler has taught literature and composition. In this essay, she discusses Lucille Clifton's use of an extended metaphor to highlight the importance of both personal and political struggles of black women.

> *The presence of another climber also establishes that the speaker is not alone in her journey; there is a community of climbers.*

"Climbing," by Lucille Clifton, is a poem about possibility and about rising to meet the challenges that life presents. Clifton's poetics are down to Earth; her language is straightforward and her images are sharp. She uses an extended metaphor of climbing a rope to paint a vivid picture of the struggle, as well as the beauty, inherent in black womanhood as she has experienced it.

The title of the poem is key: It sets the mood. It is not called "To Climb" or "The Climb" but "Climbing." Climb*ing* creates motion, implying active movement in the present. This is more than a story of past climbs; it is about the everyday climb of the present moment and of the future, which lies stretched out before the speaker. "Climbing" is an action poem. Whereas "action" might be associated more closely with epic poems written by men about war and history, Clifton's poem is distinctly about women. As a poet and children's book author, she has written on many topics but has continually returned to women's issues. Literary critic Andrea Benton Rushing sees Clifton's writing as unique:

> Several things set Clifton apart from the strophes of others. First, she has written more poems about women's lives than any other African-American poet, except Gwendolyn Brooks. Second, she has consistently done so with sinewy diction, a confiding voice, and stark imagery.

The first words of the poem are, in fact, "a woman." From the beginning, the speaker has made a decision to focus the reader's attention on the woman, and in a larger sense, on womanhood. The speaker is observing the woman as she passes her on the climb: "a woman precedes me up the long rope." The speaker calls attention to the action of climbing by situating herself as a climber and naming the woman as a fellow climber. The woman is actively climbing, not just up any rope but a *long* rope. In the next line, the speaker offers a short, physical description of the woman climbing: "her dangling braids the color of rain." This description makes the woman sound unique; the word "dangling" suggests grace and beauty, and the image of rain is one of peace and tranquility. This woman doesn't seem to be in a hurry; she is slowly climbing up the long rope. The presence of another climber also establishes that the speaker is not alone in her journey; there is a community of climbers.

As the speaker progresses up the rope, she begins to doubt herself, to ask herself nagging questions: "maybe i should have had braids. / maybe i should have kept the body I started, / slim and possible as a boy's bone." This set of images is rich and suggestive. The line "maybe i should have kept the body I started" implies that the speaker is no longer a young woman. Her body has seen the battle scars of womanhood, and she is aging. In younger years, the speaker's body was full of possibility, "like a boy's bone," not totally grown to its full potential, but strong and confident. Women writers often address body issues; much poetry has been written about the female body as a site of struggle, and Clifton is echoing the sentiments expressed by many other women writers.

The self-doubt continues throughout the poem. The speaker's tone is a questioning one. Her voice is honest and sincere but not overconfident. As she climbs, she is looking back on her life, trying to decide if the struggle was worth it. "maybe i should have wanted less," she suggests to herself in line six. It is worth considering Clifton's personal politics, especially her involvement in the Civil Rights and Women's movements of the 1960s and 1970s. This line echoes the struggles of white women and African Americans in their fight for justice. "maybe i should have ignored the bowl in me / burning to be filled." The image of the empty bowl waiting to be filled is a vivid one, suggestive of many things: a thirst for knowledge, a desire to succeed and overcome obstacles, and a passion for creativity and self-expression.

In many ways, this is a poem about history—the history humankind carries in the struggle forward. As the speaker questions herself, repeating "maybe i should have wanted less," she is recalling her history. To celebrate history is important for all people, but it is especially important for minority groups and white women, who still face significant barriers in many cultures. In other words, there is strength in remembering where one started.

Critically acclaimed novelist and essayist Alice Walker writes about this in her landmark collection of essays entitled *In Search of Our Mothers' Gardens*. She describes teaching a group of underprivileged black women and struggling with this issue of valuing history: "How do you make them appreciate their own endurance, creativity, incredible loveliness of spirit? It should have been as simple as handing them a mirror, but it was not. How do you show a connection between past and present?" Clifton uses the extended metaphor of climbing to show a connection between past and present. She does not place the speaker in the poem alone on the rope; instead, she situates her within a community and a larger context. The struggle for freedom and for equal treatment and access to resources is more than an individual struggle; rather, it is a collective one.

"Climbing" is also a poem about ageing. Clifton is not a young woman when she writes this poem. It was included in a collection of poems entitled *The Book of Light*, published in 1993. (Clifton was born in 1936.) The words are not those of a young woman; instead, they are those of a woman who has lived several decades, whose life has followed a path and taken unexpected twists and turns, a woman who possesses the wisdom that comes along with a life well-lived. In the final lines of the poem, the speaker is looking toward something as she takes notice of her fellow climber: "the woman passes the notch in the rope marked Sixty."

It is worth noting that in the entire poem, "Sixty" is the only word capitalized, which makes it pop off the page. Clearly, Clifton is trying to emphasize turning sixty as a major milestone; she seems to approach it with both longing and apprehension. The two views on ageing are contradictory, yet intricately related. Simplistically speaking, each year older is another year of learning and wisdom to tack onto one's "resume" of life. But by the same token, each year lived also brings one closer to death, leading to careful introspection, which, in turn, brings more wisdom.

Ultimately, the speaker in "Climbing" embraces the idea of aging. The last line of the poem confirms this: "i rise toward it, struggling, / hand over hungry hand." The speaker is rising toward the future with no regrets. The shades of self-doubt melt away in this final declaration. Her history has been one of struggle, and she has no intention of giving up the fight now. This final image of the hungry hand is reminiscent of the image of the bowl inside, "burning to be filled." The speaker's bowl is not yet filled. This is not, however, a bad thing. This desire for fulfillment is the very thing that keeps the speaker constantly pushing forward, constantly climbing. To fight injustice, to demand change, and to live a life one can proud of when one dies is no easy task, but, as this poem points out, it is well worth the struggle.

Source: Judi Ketteler, Critical Essay on "Climbing," in *Poetry for Students*, The Gale Group, 2002.

Sources

Bedient, Calvin, Review of *The Book of Light*, in *Poetry*, 1994, pp. 344–50.

Clifton, Lucille, *The Book of Light*, Copper Canyon Press, 1993.

——, *Generations: A Memoir*, Random House, 1976.

——, *Good News about the Earth: New Poems*, Random House, 1972.

——, *Good Times: Poems*, Random House, 1969.

——, *An Ordinary Woman*, Random House, 1974.

Davis, Katie, "Poet Lucille Clifton Discusses Her Work and Her Life," on *All Things Considered (NPR)*, October 24, 1993.

Lockett, Andrea, Review of *The Book of Light*, in *Belles Lettres*, Summer 1993, p. 51.

"A Manifesto for Third Wave Feminism," http://www.alternet.org/story.html?StoryID=9986 (October 24, 2000).

Peppers, Wallace R., "Lucille Clifton," in *Dictionary of Literary Biography*, Vol. 41: *Afro-American Poets Since 1955*, edited by Trudier Harris and Thadious M. Davis, Gale Research, 1985, pp. 55–60.

Rosenberg, Liz, "Simply American and Mostly Free," in *New York Times*, February 19, 1989, p. 24.

Rushing, Andrea Benton, *Coming to Light*, edited by Diane Middlebrook and Marilyn Yalom, University of Michigan Press, 1985.

Walker, Alice, *In Search of Our Mothers' Gardens*, Harcourt Brace Jovanovich, 1983.

Wallace, Paul, *Agequake: Riding the Demographic Rollercoaster Shaking Business, Finance, and Our World*, Nicholas Brealey, 1999.

Further Reading

Brown, Fahamisha Patricia, *Performing the Word: African-American Poetry as Vernacular Culture*, Rutgers University Press, 1999.
    Poet and theorist Brown explores how poetry is a crucial agent for transmitting and preserving African-American vernacular culture.

Castells, Manuel, *End of Millennium*, Blackwell Publishers, 1998.
    Castells details the social trends of the 1990s that are changing the way people think about themselves and one another. He describes the collapse of the Soviet Union, the rise of "informational capitalism," and the increasing growth of a "Fourth World," arguing that the moral order of the world is rapidly being redrawn.

hooks, bell, *Feminism Is for Everybody: Passionate Politics*, South End Press, 2000.
    With accessible and concise language, hooks chronicles the feminist movement and explains how and why feminism struggles against patriarchal cultures. This is a passionate study that aims at unearthing the roots of gender oppression without gender bashing.

Roberts, Dorothy, *Killing the Black Body: Race, Reproduction, and the Meaning of Liberty*, Vintage Books, 1999.
    Roberts, a professor at Rutgers University School of Law, takes a historical approach to examining African-American women's fight to gain control of their reproductive choice. This is a challenging text at points, but it provides a theory of how black women's relationship to their bodies has been configured by oppressive laws and social institutions.

Courage

Anne Sexton
1975

"Courage" appears in Anne Sexton's eighth and last collection of original poems, *The Awful Rowing Toward God*, published by Houghton Mifflin, in 1975, a year after her suicide. It is the seventh poem in the collection, most of which were initially written to be a part of her 1974 collection, *The Death Notebooks*. The religious tone of the *Rowing* poems, however, dictated another book. Like many of the poems in the collection, "Courage" universalizes the speaker's experience, the "you" in the poem standing for everyone. Sexton marches the reader through the stages of life, detailing in a series of symbolic metaphors the courageous ways that human beings respond to adversity. In four free verse stanzas of crisp, fresh, sometimes surreal images, Sexton tells the story of a human being's life from childhood to old age, showing the resilience of the human spirit and underscoring human beings' power to endure even the most difficult circumstances.

Sexton wrote many of the poems in the collection when her mental health was deteriorating and her addiction to alcohol and tranquilizers was worsening. The forms of courage described in the poem were as much a part of Sexton's own life as they are symbolic of others'. "Courage" addresses such typical Sexton subjects as the death wish, loneliness, a search for meaning, and the body in pain. One of the last acts Sexton performed before killing herself was proofreading the galleys for *The Awful Rowing Toward God* with her friend, poet Maxine Kumin.

Author Biography

Anne Gray Harvey was born in 1928 in Weston, Massachusetts, the third of three daughters. Her father, Ralph Churchill Harvey, was a businessman and her mother, Mary Gray Staples, a socialite. Sexton conformed to the stereotype of a youngest child, often acting out and rebelling against her parents to get attention. Her frenetic activity and craving for attention continued through her high school years, which were otherwise unremarkable. Like many young women of her social class during mid-century, Sexton went to finishing school instead of college, and in 1948, she married Alfred Muller Sexton II, nicknamed "Kayo."

Sexton's engagement with poetry came only after she had given birth to her two children: Linda Gray Sexton in 1953 and Joyce Ladd Sexton in 1955. After the birth of her second child, Sexton was diagnosed with post-partum depression and prescribed medication. Over the next few years, she went in and out of hospitals and received regular psychiatric treatment. With the encouragement of her therapist, Dr. Martin Orne, Sexton began writing poetry, and in 1957, she enrolled in a poetry workshop with Beat writer John Clellon Holmes. During the next few years, she took part in workshops led by poets Robert Lowell and W. D. Snodgrass and met many of the writers who would help shape her career, including George Starbuck and Maxine Kumin. It was in Lowell's workshop that Sexton befriended poet Sylvia Plath. After her publication of *To Bedlam and Part Way Back* (1960), a collection of poems detailing her mental illness, Sexton developed a reputation as a confessional poet with a raw, fearless, often funny voice. Along with Plath, John Berryman, and Lowell, confessional poets who wrote during the 1950s and 1960s, Sexton made art out of mental and emotional anguish. Her poem "Courage," included in her last collection of poetry, *The Awful Rowing Toward God*, provides a glimpse into the pain—and the joy—of Sexton's struggles.

In the fifteen or so years that she wrote, Sexton published ten collections of poetry, a play, essays, and short stories. Her most popular collections include *All My Pretty Ones* (1963), *Live or Die* (1966), *Transformations* (1971), and *The Death Notebooks* (1974). She was also one of the most sought performers of her poetry on the college reading circuit, known for her dramatic presentation. For a short time, she even had her own rock group named Anne Sexton and Her Kind. A heavily decorated poet, Sexton won a Pulitzer

Anne Sexton

Prize, received the Shelley Memorial Award, and was named a Fellow of the Royal Society of Literature. She took her own life on October 4, 1974.

Poem Text

It is in the small things we see it.
The child's first step,
as awesome as an earthquake.
The first time you rode a bike,
wallowing up the sidewalk.   5
The first spanking when your heart
went on a journey all alone.
When they called you a crybaby
or poor or fatty or crazy
and made you into an alien,   10
you drank their acid
and concealed it.

Later,
if you faced the death of bombs and bullets
you did not do it with a banner,   15
you did it with only a hat to
cover your heart.
You did not fondle the weakness inside you
though it was there.
Your courage was a small coal   20
that you kept swallowing.
If your buddy saved you
and died himself in so doing,
then his courage was not courage,
it was love; love as simple as shaving soap.   25

Later,
if you have endured a great despair,
then you did it alone,
getting a transfusion from the fire,
picking the scabs off your heart,   30
then wringing it out like a sock.
Next, my kinsman, you powdered your sorrow,
you gave it a back rub
and then you covered it with a blanket
and after it had slept a while   35
it woke to the wings of the roses
and was transformed.

Later,
when you face old age and its natural conclusion
your courage will still be shown in the little ways, 40
each spring will be a sword you'll sharpen,
those you love will live in a fever of love,
and you'll bargain with the calendar
and at the last moment
when death opens the back door   45
you'll put on your carpet slippers
and stride out.

Poem Summary

First Stanza

Sexton uses the title "Courage" as a theme to be explained. The "it" in the first stanza is courage, and the items listed after "it" are examples of courage. Sexton likens a small thing such as a "child's first step" to a large thing, an earthquake, meaning that, both literally and metaphorically, taking a first step is a momentous occasion. In all of these examples, Sexton attempts to show the courageous aspect of everyday, often mundane, events. Being a confessional poet, Sexton is surely speaking to another part of herself; however, these events are universal as well, a point underscored by her use of the second person "we" and "you." Also, most of these examples are taken from childhood, a time of exploration and firsts. It is also human beings' most vulnerable time. This vulnerability often leads to suffering, something that Sexton points out as frequently repressed. This is what is meant by the lines "you drank their acid / and concealed it." The "they" are those who hurt others, the bullies and abusers of the world.

Second Stanza

The second stanza begins with the one-word line, "Later," signaling the time after childhood, late adolescence or early adulthood. The conditional "if" speaks to those who might have fought in the Vietnam War ("the death of bombs and bullets"). As in the first stanza, Sexton uses a series

of metaphors to develop the ways in which human beings are courageous at different times in their lives. Unlike the first stanza, which speaks to both men and women, this stanza seems primarily to address men (though it is important to note that women also fought in the Vietnam War). Lines 3–5 underline the idea of modesty, as the soldier does not face death with zeal and pride ("a banner") but with humility, signified by the hat-covered heart. Sexton highlights the idea of repression again, this time comparing courage to "a small coal / you kept swallowing." The last two lines show how courage can also be a form of love, which, like "shaving soap," is present every day.

Third Stanza

In this stanza, Sexton uses a series of images to describe the healing process after one has been emotionally hurt. The "fire" is the pain itself, the "coal" and "acid" swallowed in the first two stanzas, from which the speaker recovers by purging herself of pain through a symbolic transfusion of blood: "picking the scabs off your heart, / then wringing it out like a sock." The process of comforting oneself and letting time heal the pain is spelled out in how the speaker takes care of her sorrow: by powdering it, giving it a backrub, and letting it sleep. All of these actions suggest ways in which a baby is pampered and cared for. By extension, the speaker suggests that the self must also be shown the same kind of care and attention. The last image in the stanza alludes to the story of the phoenix, a mythical bird that lives 500 years, burns itself to ashes on a pyre, and rises from the ashes to live another 500 years. This image shows how human beings can also rise from the "ashes" of their own despair and pain if they are patient and take care of themselves.

Fourth Stanza

In the final stanza, Sexton describes the courage of people in old age and the ways in which they endure by finding hope in events such as spring, itself symbolic of renewal. The stanza begins with a euphemism, when the speaker describes death as the "natural conclusion" to old age. Euphemisms are understatements, more delicate ways of saying something difficult or offensive. The seemingly mundane image of "carpet slippers" underscores the heroic nature of the "everyman" (or woman), who goes through life largely unacknowledged and uncelebrated, yet who shows courage simply by enduring and continuing to hope. The last image is as much Sexton's own fantasy as it is a poetic representation of the common person. Sexton was well known for her death wish, and, in these lines, she visualizes her own death, a common feature of much of her poetry.

Themes

Change and Transformation

"Courage" argues the idea that it is only through fortitude and courage that human beings are able to survive and flourish. Such a notion effectively dismisses the notion that luck, genes, or destiny play the major role in determining the shape of a person's life. Sexton highlights this idea in the first stanza when her speaker describes childhood as a time of loneliness and despair, when people are ostracized from family and friends because of the way they look or behave. Making it through childhood, the speaker suggests, requires that response to pain be kept in, not expressed. The speaker symbolically describes this process in the last two lines of the first stanza: "You drank their acid / and concealed it" and in the second stanza in the lines, "your courage was a small coal / that you kept swallowing." Sexton's poem repeatedly makes the German philosopher Friedrich Nietzsche's point that "What doesn't kill you will make you stronger." In each stanza, she describes a kind of adversity and then shows how individuals deal with that adversity by integrating it into themselves. By becoming stronger, human beings can withstand pain, both physical and emotional, and live out their lives with grace and dignity. In the third stanza, in which Sexton again highlights the transformative power of suffering, she outlines the process through which people are changed by overcoming obstacles. This power is embodied in images suggested by words such as "transfusions," "wings," "spring," and "swords."

Individual and Society

Broadly conceived and applied to literature, romanticism emphasizes the individual's experience, with attention paid to expression of subjective emotion and feeling. Most confessional poetry, by its very nature, is romantic, and Sexton's poems are no different. "Courage" emphasizes the individual's journey through life, charting the self's tribulations and triumphs, while largely ignoring the relationship of the individual to society or, when the poem does allude to society, it does so in generalized and symbolic terms, as in her characterization of war in the second stanza. The "you" she addresses in the poem is at once another part of

Media Adaptations

- Harper Audio released a 60-minute audiocassette of Sexton reading her poems, called *Anne Sexton Reads* (1993).

- *Voice of the Poet* (2000), an audiocassette of Sexton reciting her poems, can be purchased from Random House.

- A documentary on Sexton's life was produced in 1966 as part of the public television series *USA Poetry* and is available at local libraries.

- *Sexton* is a documentary based on outtakes from the above film and is available from the American Poetry Archive at the Poetry Center, San Francisco State University, California.

- The Department of English at the State University of New York at Brockport has a videocassette of Art Poulin and William Heyen interviewing Sexton. *The Poetry of Anne Sexton* is included in their Writer's Forum Videotape Library.

- The Center for Cassette Studies has an audiocassette of Sexton, recorded in 1974: *A Conversation with Anne Sexton: The Late Pulitzer Prize-Winning Poet Talks with James Day.*

herself, and the reader. She universalizes her own feelings, making her experience representative of the human condition. Apart from using the second person "you" to mark this universalizing, the speaker uses terms such as "kinsman" in the third stanza to appeal to fellow sufferers, heroes, and heroines. The division of the poem into phases of life also emphasizes individual, as opposed to social, experience.

Style

Symbolic Metaphor

"Courage" is comprised largely of a list of metaphors and symbolic metaphors. Symbols are images or actions that can stand for something else,

Topics for Further Study

- Draw a time line ranging from your first memory to your current age. Then at the appropriate years mark events in your life when you behaved courageously. What do these events have in common? What do they tell you about yourself and your idea(s) of courage?

- Write an essay comparing a courageous deed of a public figure with a cowardly deed of a public figure. The figure may be a politician, a celebrity, a sports star. What does the comparison tell you about the pressures of living under public scrutiny?

- Ask at least a dozen people for their definitions of the word "courage"; then discuss features those definitions share. Discuss which features you agree with and which you disagree with.

often an idea or a related set of ideas. Metaphors are figures of speech that make associations and find similarities between two dissimilar things. Symbolic metaphors make associations between dissimilar things as well, but they do it in such a way that the vehicle of the metaphor represents something symbolically. The vehicle of a metaphor is that part that stands for something else. For example, in the last stanza, Sexton writes: "each spring will be a sword you'll sharpen." A sword is the image that represents spring. But a sword is also something associated with war, violence, and death—ideas not usually connected to spring. In this way the sword represents more than just spring; it represents a range of emotions and ideas.

Historical Context

Sexton believed that poems came from the unconscious and often meant more than the person writing them was aware of. Her poetry is full of imagery and details, not necessarily linked to a particular time or place but symbolic of the writer's own desires. "Courage" is typical of this kind of Sexton poem. In 1973, when this poem was written, Sex-

ton's mental health was deteriorating, and she was in and out of the hospital for suicide attempts. Her family and friends speculated that she killed herself (in 1974) largely because she feared spending the rest of her life in psychiatric institutions and hospitals like her great-aunt Nana. The 1970s was also the time when the dissolution of America's psychiatric institutions was gathering steam, and the mentally ill were released into the community, often without a sufficient support system in place. Many of these people developed drug and alcohol problems, fueled by their illnesses. Combined with a housing shortage in many of America's cities, the breakdown of institutions contributed to the exponential increase in homelessness in the 1970s.

Though Sexton took Thorazine, tranquilizers, and other prescribed drugs during the latter part of her life, critics and biographers often link her depression to societal oppression of women in general and the emotional battles that women fought for recognition and selfhood in a patriarchal society. Although Sexton was often reluctant to call herself a feminist, many women nonetheless saw her as a role model and an icon for the women's movement during the 1960s and 1970s. It was in 1966 that Betty Friedan, author of the 1963 bestseller, *The Feminine Mystique*, helped found the National Organization for Women (NOW), which fought for equal rights for women in the marketplace and in the home. In 1971, the National Women's Political Caucus was formed, and firebrand congressional representatives such as Shirley Chisolm and Bella Abzug helped to give women a greater say in national conventions. The percentage of female delegates in these conventions jumped from 10 percent in 1968 to 40 percent in 1972; in addition, from 1969 to 1981, the number of female state legislators tripled. It was also in the year 1972 that Congress passed the Equal Rights Amendment. However, the amendment failed to pass in the required number of states and failed to win ratification in 1982. Women gained a major victory in 1973 when the Supreme Court ruled in *Roe v. Wade* that state law prohibiting abortion during the first three months of pregnancy was unconstitutional.

The early 1970s saw the women's movement gain a foothold in academia as well, with the establishment of women's studies programs in various universities and courses devoted to women's issues in many humanities and social sciences departments. Poetry written by women became a vehicle through which women could express their discontent and argue for change. Anthologies of women's poetry such as the influential *No More*

Compare & Contrast

- **1974:** Battling mental illness, Anne Sexton commits suicide.

  Today: More than 30,000 people commit suicide in the United States.

- **1974:** Although drugs are sometimes prescribed for depression, psychotherapy remains a popular form of treatment.

  Today: Prescription drugs such as Prozac, Paxil, and Zoloft are advertised on television and routinely used to treat depression and other forms of mood disorder.

- **1974:** Publishing heiress Patty Hearst is kidnapped by the Symbionese Liberation Army, a left-wing underground organization dedicated to the overthrow of the United States government.

  Today: Sara Jane Olson, an alleged former member of the Symbionese Liberation Army, is arrested on a federal fugitive warrant that identified her as a member of the SLA who was wanted on charges of plotting to kill Los Angeles police officers by placing explosives under their patrol cars.

- **1974:** The average life expectancy for Americans is 72 years. For males it is 68.2, for females 75.9.

  Today: The average life expectancy for Americans is almost 77 years. For males it is 73.6, for females it is almost 80 years.

Masks, published in 1973, helped further this cause, as did groundbreaking work by poets such as Adrienne Rich, whose 1973 National Book Award–winning collection *Diving into the Wreck; Poems 1971–1972*, formed a manifesto of sorts for the women's movement.

Critical Overview

In the last three weeks of January 1973, Sexton wrote all of the poems in *The Awful Rowing Toward God*, including "Courage." Though many of her friends, including poet James Wright, made unfavorable comments about the manuscript as a whole, Sexton submitted it anyway, and it was accepted for publication. The collection received mostly negative reviews. Reviewing the book for *Modern Poetry Studies*, Steven Gould Axelrod writes, "These poems resemble episodes of consciousness rather than completed, unified objects." Axelrod, like many others, argued that the poems "should be seen as psychological jottings and prophetic notes." Sexton's close friend, poet Maxine Kumin, points out that the poems were written in an almost manic phase of Sexton's life and agrees with Axelrod, noting, "There is no psychic

distance between the poet and the poem." Critic Kathleen Nichols makes no judgment as to the aesthetic value of the poems; rather, she considers them as evidence of Sexton's "poetic descent into the unconscious." Nichols claims that "What she imaginatively attains at the end of the volume is a wish-fulfilling reunion with her lost soul or 'divine' father on a sigh-shaped island floating in and surrounded by the archetypal amniotic fluid of her preconscious, maternal origins." Caroline King Barnard Hall, in her book-length study of Sexton, notes that Sexton admitted in her letters that the poems in the collection are "raw" and "unworked." Hall notes, "Creation of a dramatic situation by which to realize theme is another strength of many of Sexton's best poems." However, Hall concedes that "Such strengths are largely absent from *The Awful Rowing Toward God*."

Criticism

Chris Semansky

Semansky has published widely in the field of twentieth-century poetry and culture. In the following essay, he considers the role "Courage" plays in the mythology of Anne Sexton's life.

> *She is born, suffers, is beaten down, is reborn, and dies again. This is not only Sexton's story but also the story of all human beings, of all life forms."*

Coming as it does in the middle of Sexton's collection *The Awful Rowing Toward God,* "Courage" is a fantasy of Sexton's own life and her future death. As such, it is part of the poet's personal mythology of self, the way in which she would have others think of her. For many confessional poets, such as Robert Lowell, John Berryman, and Sylvia Plath, the stories they tell about themselves become, in effect, the stories they come to believe. They construct personal mythologies of self, mining their own mental anguish for material. The psychoanalysis that these poets participated in helped them both to unearth and articulate many of their poetic themes. Hence, it is almost impossible to write about confessional poets' poetry without also discussing their lives, since they are inextricably entwined.

On the surface, "Courage" sets out to tell the story of a representative human being's life. In so doing, Sexton also attempts to tell the story of her own life, though it may be argued that her desires and gifts are anything but representative. Comparing the phases of life she symbolically describes—childhood, adolescence/early adulthood, middle age, and old age—with the phases of her own life, however, doesn't necessarily help to clarify the extent to which this poem is autobiographical, for Sexton was a complicated person. Sexton biographer Diane Wood Middlebrook writes about Sexton's relationship to the past: "One thing that became clear to her, since she spent so much time dwelling on it, was that the past exists only in versions, which differ according to our motives at the moment of recall." The version of the life described in "Courage," then, is an idealized version in which the individual is at once a martyr to and savior of herself.

In the opening stanza, Sexton describes childhood as a place of firsts, when the child realizes her aloneness in the world. Though she presents the

individual as a risk taker, the real emphasis is on the individual as a victim, someone that others pick on and ostracize. This victimization becomes internalized, figuratively described in the "acid" she drinks, and is carried with the individual throughout her life. Sexton develops the sense of victimization in the second stanza, as the individual courageously faces war. The metaphor becomes complicated midway through the stanza, however, when the speaker says:

> your courage was a small coal
> that you kept swallowing.
> If your buddy saved you
> and died himself in so doing,
> then his courage was not courage,
> it was love; love as simple as shaving soap.

Swallowing courage suggests resisting it, giving in to one's own fears. The sense of shame in doing this is underscored by the individual's characterizing his friend's sacrifice as an act of love, rather than courage. Explaining the world to themselves is how human beings survive. Sexton suggests that sometimes it is important to call things by different names for the sake of emotional and psychic survival. The image of "shaving soap" highlights the regularity with which this occurs.

The third stanza again begins with a statement about the individual's isolation, and readers can infer that a transfusion is needed because the individual is emotionally, spiritually exhausted. What is the fire, though? It is the resentment, bitterness, *and* courage that the individual has swallowed in the first two stanzas. Up until now, Sexton has characterized someone who has been victimized over and over but has done nothing about it. All of the pain has been endured alone. But in this stanza, representative of adulthood, the speaker has come to a crossroads. Her wounds have healed, and she is now "picking the scabs" from her heart. At age twenty-nine, after two years of psychotherapy and hospitalizations for depression, Sexton began writing poetry as a way of dealing with her demons. It's hard not to think of her life in this stanza, for poetry became a means by which she could indulge herself. Her transformation from a suburban housewife and mother of two to a nationally recognized and lauded poet came quickly. But this transformation didn't relieve Sexton of the pain and the sense of isolation; it merely gave her a way to express it. This expression, in turn, led to a great deal of attention, most of which Sexton craved and needed.

The last stanza is a variation on a theme that recurs throughout Sexton's work: the obsession with death. This representation of death is as part of the natural life cycle, a kind of quiet suburban death symbolized by the "carpet slippers." There's no raging against death, no spectacular violence, no dramatic suicide. Rather, it's an ordinary death, an image of death from the popular imagination. This everyday death can be seen as symbolic of the truth that Sexton sought in her poems. As critic Caroline King Barnard Hall and others note, Sexton threads the theme of death and rebirth throughout her poems. She does this as well in "Courage." She is born, suffers, is beaten down, is reborn, and dies again. This is not only Sexton's story but also the story of all human beings, of all life forms. In this sense, the poem is not confessional, as it contains no explicit details of the writer's own life but merely its outline. Looking outside herself for truth, then, Sexton here searches for what she has in common with others rather than for what sets her apart.

Sexton's poem is not only a symbolic version of the human journey but it is also the representative poem of *The Awful Rowing Toward God*, which tells the story of an individual's search for God and redemption. The two poems that bookend "Courage" are "The Earth Falls Down" and "Riding the Elevator into the Sky." The former is comprised of a litany of people, ideas, and things onto which the speaker attempts to cast blame for "conditions." At one point, the speaker asks, "Blame it on God perhaps?" then answers, "No, I'll blame it on Man, / for Man is God / and man is eating the earth up." This secular idea of god is also apparent in "Riding the Elevator into the Sky," a death fantasy ending with the speaker riding an elevator thousands of floors up, out of herself, to find a key "that opens something." Readers aren't told what the something is, and, indeed, Sexton herself didn't know. Her hunger for God and for death had merged. The story of Sexton's life by the time she wrote the poems in *The Awful Rowing Toward God* had become so entwined with her public persona that it was difficult for her to distinguish the difference. Her redemption, finally, wasn't in some god or death that she imagined existed outside of herself but in the very act of writing and rewriting her story. When she finally exhausted that story, she exhausted her will to live. She never got to battle against time and have the small ordinary death of old age that she described. Rather, she battled the very will to live and finally succumbed to a drive that haunted her a good part of her life, committing suicide at age forty-six. Whether this final act was one of courage or not is left for her readers to decide.

Source: Chris Semansky, Critical Essay on "Courage," in *Poetry for Students*, The Gale Group, 2002.

Adrian Blevins

Blevins is a writer and poet who has taught at Hollins University, Sweet Briar College, and in the Virginia Community College System. She is the author of The Man Who Went Out for Cigarettes, *a chapbook of poems, and has published poems, essays, and stories in many journals, magazines, and anthologies. In this essay, Blevins argues that "Courage" "suffers from a number of significant flaws."*

"Courage" is among the thirty-nine poems in the last book Anne Sexton wrote, *The Awful Rowing Toward God*. According to Diane Middlebrook's interesting and controversial biography of Sexton, *Anne Sexton: A Biography*, Sexton wrote the poems in this collection in less than a month. Middlebrook suggests that Sexton "knew the work was still fairly raw" after she finished it. She showed the manuscript to Maxine Kumin, George Starbuck, James Wright, and other friends and poets whose opinions she valued. Wright (quoted in Middlebrook) reportedly responded to Sexton's book by saying, "I have no intention of excusing your bad verse and your bad prose.... There are some good poems here that I think are fine. There are some that I think are junk. The choice between them is yours." Yet Kumin argues in favor of many of the poems Wright had found less than appealing, as have other critics. William Shurr, writing in *Soundings: An Interdisciplinary Journal*, strives valiantly to praise *The Awful Rowing Toward God*, suggesting that it is a book of "artistic vision and extraordinary beauty." Shurr, however, does not use "Courage" as an example of this vision and beauty. Perhaps he has good cause to comment that "like many of Sexton's poems in *The Awful Rowing*, 'Courage' suffers from a number of significant flaws."

Like other poems in *The Awful Rowing Toward God*, "Courage" is addressed to a specific reader, someone Sexton calls her "kinsman." If it were not for the references to "bombs and bullets" in the poem's second stanza, it might be possible to assume Sexton is addressing herself in "Courage"—telling herself in poetic terms what courage is in order to prepare herself (and her audience) for that final "stride out" into suicidal death. The war references, however, complicate this reading. It appears, instead, that Sexton is addressing a male reader in "Courage." In some

> *Though Anne Sexton's work illuminates some of the connections between mental illness and art and is for this reason alone worth investigating, some of it fails quite miserably."*

poems, the epistolary stance can be very moving—readers can experience the thrill of a private exchange, as is the case with Shakespeare's more moving sonnets. In "Courage," by contrast, there's too little information about the relationship between the speaker and the person she's addressing. Sexton has undercut her opportunity to give her readers the main pleasure of the point of view of direct address by being too mysterious about the affiliation between the poem's "I" and its "you."

"Courage" is organized chronologically, from "the child's first step" to "old age and its natural conclusion." The first stanza states matter-of-factly that we see the virtue of courage in "the small things"—in a "child's first step" or in "the first time you rode a bike." The poem turns in its sixth line from these picturesque images: we learn that courage might also be seen "in the first spanking when your heart / went on a journey all alone." The first stanza's last five lines implicate a child's caregivers or peers more directly, since they suggest that courage during this stage of life might be made from being called "crybaby / or poor or fatty or crazy." In other words, the sense of "despair" that is everywhere in Anne Sexton's poems begins to emerge in this section of the poem: the "you" of the poem must become an "alien"; he or she must "[drink] acid and [conceal] it."

The poem's second stanza moves to a war scene, with "bombs and bullets." Here, the unspecified "you" is reminded that he "faced death . . . with only a hat to / cover [his] heart." This makes the "you" of the poem very vulnerable, as does the beautiful line about "Courage" being "a small coal / that you kept swallowing." Yet it would probably be more moving if the *speaker* of the poem were the person who was made vulnerable—if the speaker of "Courage" were the person who "kept swallowing . . . a small coal," the poem might inspire more empathy. It's also worth noting that Sexton mentions love in this part of the poem, which she says is not courage but "simple as shaving soap." While it's interesting to note that Sexton makes a distinction between love and courage, the idea doesn't seem to serve the poem in any major way; it operates like a parenthetical observation.

The poem's third stanza is the most grotesque in Sexton's poem: here the unspecified person Sexton is addressing is told he has "[picked] scabs off [his] heart." Despite the ungainly image (which fails, because of its grotesque nature, to inspire empathy for the poem's "characters"), this line marks a shift from the poem's first two stanzas, since it suggests that courage comes from "[enduring] a great despair . . . alone," or from revealing the "acid" that was concealed in the poem's first stanza, turning it into "sorrow" and "wringing it out like a sock." These odd and illogical images point to Sexton's desire to transform her own "sorrow" into something more positive, as the rose image at the end of the stanza suggests. This "transformation" is death, as the poem's final stanza tells us.

The poem's final stanza moves to "old age" but repeats the idea that "courage will still be shown in little ways," as it was in the poem's first stanza. In this stanza, "each spring will be a sword you'll sharpen . . . those you love will live in a fever of love," and "when death opens the back door / you'll put on your carpet slippers / and stride out." This last gesture offers the poem's only surprise: if readers had thought previously that the courage of the "concealed acid" that turned into the courage of the "scabs [on the] heart" and then "transformed" into some untold other thing would save the "you" of the poem from death, they were mistaken.

Although the narrative structure just described may give the poem its accessibility by allowing the reader to follow Sexton's associations from first to last line, its risk is the flatness that chronological order sometimes produces. Because Sexton can rely on actual time to organize the poem, she need not bother with inventing her own methods of sequence or movement. The first lines of stanzas two, three, and four, each of which begins with the word "Later," reinforce the poem's structural flaws. The repeated use of the abstract term "later" does help Sexton leapfrog from segment into segment or stanza into stanza, but the lines themselves are uninteresting. They are utilitarian; Sexton is borrowing built-in structures rather than inventing them.

In writing workshops, teachers advise students to show rather than to tell in an effort to urge apprentice writers toward images, or mostly metaphorical word-combinations, that make usually visual but sometimes auditory and tactile sensual (and therefore emotional) sense. Sexton's topic in "Courage," is, of course, the *idea* of courage. Yet the poem is oddly unquestioning; "Courage" is very certain of itself. Sexton uses many images in this poem, as we shall see, but her overriding stance in "Courage" is an expository one. That is, she is not *showing* the reader what courage is metaphorically or by the use of image; rather she is *telling* the reader what courage is and using similes as examples. In this poem, Sexton is not so much wondering what courage is but is *telling* us what, in her opinion, courage is. Sexton's uncertainty regarding the answer to this philosophical question also undermines the poem's ability to move beyond itself, to transform everyday experience into art.

Sexton's indiscriminate use of simile also undermines the poem's power. The poem's last few lines suggest in the poem's most beautiful moment that "when death opens the back door / you'll put on your carpet slippers / and stride out." Sexton's view of death in these lines is everywhere in *The Awful Rowing Toward God* and is one of the book's few virtues. The accomplishment of these last lines has to do with the power of the final image; it is both unique and ironic. The comfort in "carpet slippers" destabilizes our more common vision of death, as does the power and strength in the phrase "stride out." Here and elsewhere in Sexton's final book is a statement about the beauty and power of death, and that is unusual enough to be interesting. In the image that ends "Courage," Sexton personifies death by suggesting it will "open the back door" (like a kind lover or friend). Then the person with courage will, Sexton suggests, go into that happy sleep, wearing "carpet slippers."

Yet other images and similes in the poem do not live up to the power and strength of this last image. Sexton says that a "child's first step" is "as awesome as an earthquake." This kind of statement fails because it's too obvious to be anything but common. Or perhaps the image fails because there is not much of a corollary between a child's first step and an earthquake. Sexton also says in "Courage" that if the person she's addressing will "powder" his or her "sorrow," "[give] it a back rub," and "[cover] it with a blanket," it—the sorrow—will "[wake] to the wings of the roses." Aside from the fact that roses don't have wings—not even imaginary or mythical ones—this image fails be-

cause it is shockingly sentimental—it's almost indistinguishable from a Hallmark card. The same might be said for "fever of love"; although the "e" sounds in this phrase are sonically pleasing, the image is ultimately cliché.

According to Sexton's biographer Diane Middlebrook, "[Maxine] Kumin remembered being worried about how agitated Sexton seemed [while she was working on the poems in *The Awful Rowing Toward God*] . . . [H]er friend's manic energy reminded her uncomfortably of the stories told about Sylvia Plath writing *Ariel* at white heat." Sexton killed herself the same day that she and Kumin met for lunch to correct the galleys of the book, so it seems Kumin was rightly concerned. Though Anne Sexton's work illuminates some of the connections between mental illness and art and is for this reason alone worth investigating, some of it fails quite miserably. Although Sexton's mental illness helped her produce many stunning and moving poems, the poems in *The Awful Rowing Toward God* are not as successful as some of her earlier poems, perhaps because she had already begun to move away from the hard labor of revising poems into the new labor of "[striding] out" toward death. Imagine what she could have done had she chosen to live instead.

Source: Adrian Blevins, Critical Essay on "Courage," in *Poetry for Students*, The Gale Group, 2002.

Carl Mowery

Mowery has a Ph.D. in literature and composition and has written extensively for the Gale Group. In the following essay, he considers the ironic twists that result when courage fragments into false heroism and bitterness in Anne Sexton's poem.

In an article for the *New Leader*, Pearl K. Bell said that Anne Sexton's collection *"The Awful Rowing Toward God* is sad reading, . . . because the poems are haunted by the self-destruction that was to be their terrible climax." In the first poem, "Rowing," she embarks on a voyage toward God that takes the reader through many disappointing and unsatisfying attempts to find Him. Another of these poems, "Courage," sets out a plan to examine courageous behavior in the face of unpleasantness. However, this poem takes the reader on a journey into a more unflattering aspect of courage: bluff, show, and resignation. It is not the heroic courage of bravery confronting adversity.

Indeed, "Courage" is a sad little poem. Its sadness comes from the internal conflict of someone ("you") summoning courage in an attempt to con-

> *One might expect a poem entitled 'Courage' to deal with one of the lofty concepts that ennoble and define human character. Here, however, this concept is used to hide the bitterness of the individual's experiences and tendencies towards self-destruction.'*

front a variety of issues at various stages of life. But the persona in the poem keeps coming up short. As a result, the courage in the poem fragments into false heroism and bitterness. The speaker in the poem, addressing "you," describes these two outcomes. As a result, the poem writhes with an irony coming from the contrast between them.

Images of heroism are scattered throughout the verse from the images of recent wars, "bombs and bullets," to the more ancient image of the sword in the last stanza. These images are caught up in a set of expectations in which boys were not allowed to cry, men went off to war to save a nation, husbands were taught to "suck it up and tough it out" in the face of marital difficulties, and even the specter of impending death was greeted with little more emotional investment than to put on one's slippers and trundle off into the abyss.

The surface images give off an air of familiarity, a feeling with which most people can identify from personal experiences. As Michael Lally claims, this is a poem "full of common things." But this is deceiving, because those familiar images hide something less noble: a willingness to hide from courageous behavior. In the poem, the speaker tries to invoke a strength of will in the "you." But by the end of each stanza, that will is subsumed by an attitude of resignation. The inevitable acquiescence results in a loss of self.

Joyce Carol Oates said that, in the search for a kind of self-immortality, Sexton had resigned herself to the idea that it could not be reached by "any remedy short of death." Sexton comments on this contradiction in many of her poems. In "The Poet of Ignorance," she says that she is trapped by her "human form. / That being the case / I would like to call attention to my problem." She suggests, although she does not say, that removing or being removed from that form is the answer. Here is the contradiction of trying to find a self-expression that can only be realized after death. She writes, "The place I live in / is a kind of maze / and I keep seeking / the exit or the home." These lines from the third poem of the volume, "The Children," are even more intense because that poem was published posthumously, one year after Sexton's suicide in 1974.

In "Courage," Sexton presents a similar contradiction. The efforts to maintain the self by drinking the acid of personal attacks, by transforming despair through "a back rub," or by sharpening the sword each spring are overwhelmed, and the self is lost in the attempt to be what others want "you" to be. Finally, when further attempts at courage are given up, "you'll put on your carpet slippers and stride out." This is not a courageous entrance through death's back door but rather resignation. Rather than being in charge of the self, "old age and *its* natural conclusion [italics added]" are in command and have made the decision for "you." Personal courage is given up through tacit compliance with outside decisions. In the poem "For Mr. Death Who Stands with His Door Open" (1974), she closes with these lines: "But when it comes to my death let it be slow, / let it be pantomime, the last peep show, / so that I may squat at the edge trying on my black necessary trousseau." This is in direct contrast with the persona in "Courage," who strides out quickly at the request of "old age."

The cycle of life, whether biological (birth, life, death) or temporal (hours, days, months), is a familiar thematic device many authors have used to tie their works together. Thoreau uses the circular nature of the seasonal changes to shape his *Walden*. In Sexton's volume, the first poem describes her rowing toward God as the symbolic searching for some theological purpose to life. The last poem closes with the mooring of the boat on the Island (God), the symbolic discovery of the God for whom she has been looking. These two poems complete the circle of the entire volume.

Sexton also uses the calendar as a unifying device. In her poem "Sermon of the Twelve Acknowledgements," she uses the months of the year to shape the poem. In "Courage," the human lifespan is the device that gives the poem its overall form. The child of the first stanza and the old person shuffling off through the back door wearing "carpet slippers" in the last are images that frame the poem. The reader is pulled through the poem and through the human life cycle by the repeated word "Later."

The cyclic nature of life's experiences is shown from "the child's first step" to the final striding out, in the "making into an alien" to the transformation, and in the eager anticipation of the child to the resigned capitulation of the old one at the end. The cycle of happiness returning to bitterness and back again in each stanza, the cyclic shifts of weakness in the face of the fury of war to the hidden strength of concealing the acid of the dehumanizing taunts of would-be friends create the irony that girds this poem. To these disappointments brought on by the loss of the self, add "the cruelty of life and the cruelty of people," as Robert Mazzocco noted in Sexton's poetry, and the easy resignation to the will of others is understandable. At the end of the poem, even the act of dying is cruel because there is no option, no choice for the individual, who acquiesces and merely steps through the open door.

Anne Sexton and Sylvia Plath both have written that there ought to be a choice. In her memoir of Plath, Sexton said (reprinted in Oates's article "On the Awful Rowing Toward God"), "We talked death, and this was life for us." For both poets, suicide was not a desperate last solution but a deliberate choice that was fed by a more heroic courage than that which is found in this poem. Readers may see that choice as a result of the loss of an individual's will to live. But for Sexton and Plath, it is a deliberate act of seeking God. In the last poem of the volume, she says, "I'm mooring my rowboat / at the dock of the island called God. / . . . and there are many boats moored / at many different docks. . . . I empty myself from my wooden boat / and onto the flesh of The Island." With these lines, she affirms her belief that it is her choice to row her boat to the Island (God); it is her choice to climb out of the boat; it is her choice to go to God when she wants. In "Courage," the "you" does not actively make the choice. That choice has been made for "you." It is this struggle that tormented Sexton for much of her life and which found expression in her poetry, especially her last volumes.

In seeking the courage to take full control of life, she rejects the attempts of some to define others as a "crybaby or poor or fatty or crazy" or to turn "you into an alien." These cruel and dehu-

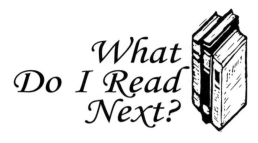

What Do I Read Next?

- "Courage" appears in Sexton's collection, *The Awful Rowing toward God*, published in 1975. Many of the poems in this book deal with the poet's quest for meaning in the form of religious understanding.

- *The Bell Jar* (1963), a novel by Sexton's friend and fellow tormented poet, Sylvia Plath, describes the fictional Esther Greenwood's descent into madness. Most critics see the novel as autobiographical.

- Noonday Press published Robert Lowell's *Life Studies* and *For the Union Dead* in 1967 in one volume. Lowell was Sexton's teacher and is considered to be one of the leading confessional poets of the 1950s and 1960s. These two critically acclaimed volumes are his most popular.

- Nicholas Mazza's 1999 text, *Poetry Therapy: Interface of the Arts and Psychology*, addresses the therapeutic use of creative writing including metaphor, narrative, journal writing, storytelling, bibliotherapy, and poetry. Sexton, who was in psychotherapy much of her adult life, considered the writing of poetry therapeutic. Mazza explicitly shows how to use poetry as part of a therapeutic program.

manizing attacks are often used by oppressors to control their subjects. The most egregious example of this is the manner by which the Nazis of the 1930s and 1940s turned the whole of European Jewry into aliens, people who were less than human. If one's victim is believed to be less than human, then there is no need for remorse. Sexton illustrates this remorselessness in her poem "After Auschwitz" when she writes, "And death [a Nazi] looks on with a casual eye / and picks at the dirt under his fingernail." In that poem, the oppressor is unmoved by the death of a baby he has just killed.

One might expect a poem entitled "Courage" to deal with one of the lofty concepts that ennoble and define human character. Here, however, this concept is used to hide the bitterness of the individual's experiences and tendencies towards self-destruction, as noted by Pearl K. Bell. Sexton has demonstrated how hard it is to maintain one's individuality and self-confidence in the face of life's difficulties. It is the struggle to find a resolution to this contradiction that haunted Sexton throughout her life, which found a voice in her poetry. The result is this bitterly ironic and sad poem.

Source: Carl Mowery, Critical Essay on "Courage," in *Poetry for Students*, The Gale Group, 2002.

Sources

Axelrod, Steven Gould, "Anne Sexton's Rowing towards God," in *Modern Poetry Studies*, Vol. 6, No. 2, 1975.

Bell, Pearl K., *New Leader*, May 26, 1975.

Bixler, Frances, ed., *Original Essays on the Poetry of Anne Sexton*, University of Central Arkansas Press, 1988.

Colburn, Steven E., ed., *Anne Sexton: Telling the Tale*, University of Michigan Press, 1988.

Davison, Peter, *The Fading Smile: Poets in Boston from Robert Lowell to Sylvia Plath*, W. W. Norton & Company, 1996.

George, Diana Hume, *Oedipus Anne: The Poetry of Anne Sexton*, University of Illinois Press, 1987.

Hall, Caroline King Barnard, *Anne Sexton*, Twayne, 1989.

Kumin, Maxine, "A Memorial for Anne Sexton," in *American Poetry Review*, edited by A. Poulin Jr., Vol. 4, No. 3, 1975.

Lally, Michael, "A Dark and Desperate Vision," in *Book World—The Washington Post*, May 25, 1975, p. 3.

Mazzocco, Robert, "Matters of Life and Death," in *New York Times Book Review*, April 3, 1975, pp. 22–23, reprinted in *Anne Sexton: The Artist and Her Critics*, edited by J. D. McClatchy, Indiana University Press, 1978.

McClatchy, J. D., ed., *Anne Sexton: The Artist and Her Critics*, Indiana University Press, 1978.

Middlebrook, Diane Wood, *Anne Sexton*, Random House, 1991.

Nichols, Kathleen, "The Hungry Beast Rowing toward God," in *Notes on Modern American Literature*, No. 3, 1979.

Oates, Joyce Carol, "On *The Awful Rowing toward God*," in *Private and Public Lives*, University of Windsor Press, Vol. 2, Spring 1970, pp. 107–08.

————, "Singing Pathologies of Our Time," in *New York Times Book Review*, March 23, 1975, pp. 3–4, reprinted in *Anne Sexton: The Artist and Her Critics*, edited by J. D. McClatchy, Indiana University Press, 1978.

Sexton, Anne, *The Awful Rowing toward God*, Houghton Mifflin Company, 1975.

————, *The Complete Poems*, Houghton Mifflin Company, 1981.

————, *45 Mercy Street*, edited by Linda Gray Sexton, Houghton Mifflin Company, 1976.

Sexton, Linda Grey, and Lois Ames, eds., *Anne Sexton: A Self-Portrait in Letters*, Houghton Mifflin Company, 1979.

Shurr, William, "Mysticism and Suicide: Anne Sexton's Last Poetry," in *Soundings: An Interdisciplinary Journal*, Vol. 68, No. 3, Fall 1985, pp. 335–56.

Stauffer, Donald Barlow, *A Short History of American Poetry*, E. P. Dutton & Company, 1974.

Wagner-Martin, Linda, ed., *Critical Essays on Anne Sexton*, G. K. Hall, 1989.

Further Reading

Davison, Peter, *The Fading Smile: Poets in Boston from Robert Lowell to Sylvia Plath*, W. W. Norton & Company, 1996.
    Davison recounts the Boston poetry world in this memoir and describes the complex relationships and behavior of such celebrated poets as Robert Lowell, Anne Sexton, Sylvia Plath, Richard Wilbur, and W. S. Merwin.

Middlebrook, Diane Wood, *Anne Sexton*, Random House, 1991.
    Diane Middlebrook's 1991 acclaimed biography is based on hundreds of hours of taped conversations between Sexton and her therapist. Middlebrook shows Sexton as representative of a generation of "broken" poets who fought alcohol and drug addiction, and were infatuated with the idea of celebrity.

Wagner-Martin, Linda, ed., *Critical Essays on Anne Sexton*, G. K. Hall, 1989.
    This study collects critical essays on Sexton's poetry from some of America's better known poetry critics such as Joyce Carol Oates, Paul Lacey, and Maxine Kumin. Almost all of the essays are accessible and useful and include further secondary sources.

Deep Woods

Howard Nemerov
1955

"Deep Woods" first appeared in *The Salt Garden*, Howard Nemerov's third collection of poetry, published by Little, Brown and Company, in 1955. Most critics agree that this book presented a turning point in the poet's focus and style, that it showed his poetic talent as unified and less rigid than the previous academic and heavily metered verse. "Deep Woods" is the final poem in the collection, and it aptly concludes a book in which the overall theme centers on Nemerov's fascination with how the human mind works, especially in comparison to the natural world. In his book, simply titled *Howard Nemerov*, critic Peter Meinke states that "Deep Woods" expresses the poet's "feeling about the hugeness and permanence of nature as against small impermanent man." This is a good description of the poem's central idea, but it does not address the manner in which Nemerov makes his point, and the manner is key to understanding it.

"Deep Woods" is a journey through history—mankind's history, as portrayed in literature, mythology, and factual accounts. At least half of the poem relies on allusions to events, both real and legendary, that occurred hundreds and thousands of years ago. Nemerov refers to fairy tales and forests where imaginary creatures live, to French painters and ancient Egyptian gods, even to Walt Disney, all to describe the difference between human activities and the deep woods of a New England forest. Other "characters" that crop up in the poem are minotaurs and unicorns, Jesus Christ, Hannibal,

Howard Nemerov

Old Testament folk such as Joseph, Mordecai, and Haman, and the allegorical figures Chaos and Pandemonium from Milton's *Paradise Lost*. In essence, "Deep Woods" is a smorgasbord of human history, all played against the backdrop of a quiet, dominating giant—nature in the form of deep woods.

Author Biography

Howard Nemerov was born in March 1920 in New York City. His parents were wealthy and influential in the city. His father served as president and chair of a prestigious retail store, and both parents were interested in art, theatre, philanthropy, and the social scenes of New York's finest. Nemerov was educated at the Society for Ethical Culture's Fieldstone School, where he excelled in academics and played on the football team's second string. Graduating from Fieldstone in 1937, Nemerov was accepted into Harvard University and earned a Bachelor of Arts degree in English four years later. Also in 1941, the United States entered World War II, and Nemerov joined a Royal Canadian unit of the American Army Air Force and then moved to the Eighth U. S. Army Air Force, based in Lincolnshire, England. He flew missions over the

North Sea throughout the war and was discharged in 1945 as a first lieutenant. While in England, Nemerov met and married Margaret Russel, and after the war, they returned to New York, where he began a college teaching career and completed his first collection of poetry.

Over the years, Nemerov taught on some of the best English faculties in the country, including Bennington College in Vermont and Brandeis University in Massachusetts. He was a visiting lecturer at the University of Minnesota and a writer-in-residence at both Hollins College in Virginia and Washington University in Missouri. In 1963 and 1964, Nemerov was a poetry consultant to the Library of Congress, and from 1988 to 1990, he served as the third Poet Laureate of the United States. His writing spanned the fields of poetry, novels, short stories, drama, nonfiction, and criticism, and he received numerous awards, including a Guggenheim, the Frank O'Hara Memorial Prize, and the Pulitzer. He died of cancer at his home in Missouri in July 1991.

Because Nemerov spent his working and writing life in universities, he has often been called an academic poet. His poems do tend to be philosophical and highly intellectual in nature, but they are also witty, satirical, and often humorous. Those who have been critical of his work, laden with historical and mythological allusions, have also recognized the sharp puns and sudden bursts of contemporary insight that many of his poems contain. "Deep Woods" is full of intellectual pondering and allusions, but it is also representative of some of Nemerov's best work—that addressing nature and man's relation to it—and it is one of his most anthologized poems.

Poem Text

Such places are too still for history,
Which slows, shudders, and shifts as the trucks do,
In hearing-distances, on the highway hill,
And staggers onward elsewhere with its load
Of statues, candelabra, buttons, gold;   5
But here the heart, racing strangely as though
Ready to stop, reaches a kind of rest;
The mind uneasily rests, as if a beast,
Being hunted down, made tiredness and terror
Its camouflage and fell asleep, and dreamed,   10
At the terrible, smooth pace of the running dogs,
A dream of being lost, covered with leaves
And hidden in a death like any sleep
So deep the bitter world must let it be
And go bay elsewhere after better game.   15

Even the restless eye, racing upon
Reticulated branch and vine which go
Nowhere, at last returns upon itself
And comes into a flickering kind of rest,
Being lost in the insanity of line.   20

Line, leaf, and light; darkness invades our day;
No meaning in it, but indifference
Which does not flatter with profundity.
Nor is it drama. Even the giant oak,
Stricken a hundred years or yesterday,   25
Has not found room to fall as heroes should
But crookedly leans on an awkward-squad of birch,
The tragic image and the mighty crash
Indefinitely delayed in favor of
Fresh weaving of vines, rooting of outer branches,   30
Beginning again, in spaces still more cramped,
A wandering calligraphy which seems
Enthralled to a magic constantly misspelled.

It is the same, they say, everywhere.
But that's not so. These here are the deep woods   35
Of now, New England, this October, when
Dry gold has little left to change, and half
The leaves are gone to ground, and half of those
Rained into the leaf-mold which tenses in
The fastenings of frost; where the white branches   40
Of birch are dry bones airborne in assaults
Which haven't worked yet. This unlegended land
Is no Black Forest where the wizard lived
Under a bent chimney and a thatch of straw;
Nor the hot swamp theatrical with snakes   45
And tigers; nor the Chinese forest on
The mountainside, with bridge, pagoda, fog,
Three poets in the foreground, drinking tea
(there is no tea, and not so many as three)—
But this land, this, unmitigated by myth   50
And whose common splendors are comparable only
           to
Themselves; this leaf, line, light, are scrawled
           alone
In solar definitions on a lump
Of hill like nothing known since Nature was
Invented by Watteau or Fragonard   55
In the Old Kingdom or the time of Set
Or before the Flood of Yao (or someone else
Of the same name) in the Fourth, or Disney,
           Dimension.

And this is yours to work; plant it to salt
Or men in armor who destroy each other,   60
Sprinkle with dragon's blood early in spring
And see what happens, epic or pastoral:
A sword in every stone, small minotaurs
Looking for thread, and unicorns for girls,
And Glastonbury thorns to make December   65
Bleed for the Saviour; the nightingale of Sarras
Enchants the traveler here three hundred years
And a day which seem but as a single day.
More probably nothing will happen. This
Place is too old for history to know   70
Beans about; these trees were here, are here,
Before king Hannibal had elephants
Or Frederick grew his red beard through the table
Or Mordecai hung Haman at the gate.

                                                                       75

The other Ahasuerus has not spat
Nor walked nor cobbled any shoe, nor Joseph
So much as dreamed that he will found the Corn
Exchange Bank in the baked country of Egypt.
Not even those burnt beauties are hawked out,
By the angry Beginner, on Chaos floor   80
Where they build Pandemonium the Palace
Back in the high old times. Most probably
Nothing will happen. Even the Fall of Man
Is waiting, here, for someone to grow apples;
And the snake, speckled as sunlight on the rock   85
In the deep woods, still sleeps with a whole head
And has not begun to grow a manly smile.

Poem Summary

Lines 1–5

These opening lines set the scene for "Deep Woods." The speaker is apparently walking through a forest within "hearing-distance" of a highway where trucks roll by with their heavy loads. Notice the clever use of metaphor here, however. At first, it reads as though the trucks are the ones moving on with their loads "Of statues, candelabra, buttons, gold," and so forth. But "trucks" is plural, and what "staggers onward" with "its" load is singular. The reference here is to "history, / Which slows, shudders, and shifts." Therefore, the first comparison between mankind's history and the natural world is that humanity has been volatile and restless and full of tangible objects (statues, candelabra, etc.,) but the deep woods are "too still" for all that.

Lines 6–10

These lines compare the body's response to the forest and the mind's response to it. The speaker's heart, although "racing strangely," is able to reach "a kind of rest," but his mind rests "uneasily." Recall the poet's fascination with how the human mind works, for here he claims it is so intimidated by the deep woods that it is like "a beast, / Being hunted down." The only way the mind can survive is to let its "tiredness and terror" act as a "camouflage" so that it can go to sleep—in essence, play dead.

Lines 11–15

When the mind goes to sleep, it dreams. Carrying on the hunted beast metaphor, these lines say that while the dogs run past, the mind dreams "of being lost, covered with leaves." As long as it is unconscious, it is safe in a deep, death-like sleep. The mind's dormancy is so deep that the "bitter world" that would hunt it down just runs on by, made to "go bay elsewhere after better game." In general, this metaphor simply means that the human intellect is not capable of understanding the true depth of unspoiled nature, and so, it protects itself by trying to ignore the magnitude of a pure forest.

Lines 16–20

Like the heart and the mind, the human eye is also "restless" in the deep woods. It attempts to get a grasp on nature by following the pattern of vines entwined with branches. The "branch and vine" are described as "Reticulated," meaning they form a network throughout the tree, but they appear to "go / Nowhere," and the eye cannot find a beginning or an end. Giving up, the eye "returns upon itself," the way the vines do, and comes to a "flickering kind of rest." Nature's patterns are impossible to trace, leaving the eye "lost in the insanity of line."

Lines 21–23

Line 21 begins with an alliterative phrase (each word beginning with an "L") that will be referred to again in line 52. "Line, leaf, and light" describe three aspects of the deep woods that may seem simple but that are actually incomprehensible to the human mind. This inability to understand is implied by the word "darkness" placed just after the word "light." Light is in the natural world, but "*darkness* invades *our* day" (italics added) because human intellect is limited in its comprehension of true light. As grand as this sounds on the part of nature, the deep woods are not arrogant about it, nor do they even care. Rather, nature is indifferent toward mankind's shortcomings and does not inflate the situation "with profundity"—that is, with a pretense of deep meaning or profound feelings.

Lines 24–27

These four lines compare nature's nonchalance toward natural occurrences and the human tendency to dramatize things. An oak tree that has been struck by lightning does not make a big to-do of collapsing in some emotional or theatrical fashion, as "heroes should." Instead, the big oak is content to let its fall be broken by a group of birch trees so that it leans on them, still alive.

Lines 28–31

Line 28 describes the way human beings would act if they were in the same situation as the "stricken" oak. Like a Hollywood movie, the scene would be "tragic" and there would be a "mighty crash" at the end, for a human hero could not simply fall over and lean against someone else for support. But in the deep woods, such shallow fanfare is "Indefinitely delayed" because there are more important things going on than a hero meeting death in a blaze of glory. Those things are a "Fresh weaving of vines" and the "rooting of outer branches" from the fallen, but still living, oak. The tree's life is "Beginning again," even though it does not have as much room as before and even though there is little drama, in human terms, involved.

Lines 32–33

The second stanza ends with another reference to the lines occurring in nature, and this time they are compared to fine handwriting. The new vines and roots sprouting from the oak form a "wandering calligraphy," happy to weave this way and that without regard for proper spelling or other such human constraints. Nature's untraceable patterns are like "magic," something people cannot fully understand.

Lines 34–42

The opening of the third stanza is a more detailed version of the opening of the first. The scene is clearer here, as the speaker is specific about place and time. It is October, and he is walking through the woods in New England. The "Dry gold" leaves have changed about as much color and texture as they are going to, and many have already fallen from the trees and begun to decompose into "leaf-mold." The compost of dried leaves sometimes "tenses," or stiffens, when frost covers the ground, and the birch tree branches become brittle in the cold, like dry bones protruding in the air. The human-like "assaults" that these stiff arms seem poised to carry out "haven't worked yet" because in the deep woods human behavior does not happen. Line 42 ends with a reference to the forest as an "unlegended land," meaning that it is so primitive and so untouched by man that not even any legends or tales have been created about it.

Lines 43–49

These lines are allusions to the magical forests and their odd inhabitants that make up many fairy tales and folk legends. Again, the speaker stresses what the *real* forest is *not* by listing creatures and things mankind has invented for its imaginary woods: wizards, straw thatches, snakes, tigers, a pagoda, some fog, and poets drinking tea. Where the speaker walks, "there is no tea," and the ending of line 49—"and not so many as three"—is a whimsical play on the style of writing often found in fairy tales.

Lines 50–54

These lines exalt nature to its supreme position over such supposed nonsense as folk stories. The woods are "unmitigated," or undiminished, "by myth," and nothing compares to their splendor except splendor itself. In line 52, the poet returns to the image of "leaf, line, light" to reiterate what is so splendid about the deep woods and he also returns to the metaphor of "line" as a type of calligraphy, this time "scrawled" in lines of sunlight ("solar definitions") across a hill.

Lines 55–58

The last four lines of the third stanza are filled with allusions in a kind of tongue-in-cheek jab at the human concept of man inventing nature. Jean Watteau and Jean Fragonard were eighteenth-century French painters known for their exotic landscapes and festive outdoor scenes. Further back in history, the "Old Kingdom" refers to Egypt around 2650–2134 B.C., when the great pyramids were built and "Set" was the ancient Egyptian god of chaos, sometimes synonymous with Satan. The "Flood of Yao" is said to have destroyed much of southern China in 2700 B.C., and "someone else of the same name" is perhaps a play on the pronunciation of "Yao," which is "you." The end of this stanza is definitely a play on contemporary mankind's superficiality with the sarcastic notion of nature being invented by Walt Disney. The "Fourth, or Disney, Dimension" implies that time itself—generally considered the fourth dimension—is also foolishly thought to be controllable by the human mind.

Lines 59–62

If the "Yao" is truly an inference to "you," then line 59 continues the second-person address by stating to the reader, "this is yours to work." And what is it that is ours? Presumably the deep woods themselves, the earth, the trees, all of nature. These lines provide a kind of recipe or instructions for "growing" the natural world into mankind's own creation. First, it must be planted "to salt," or to preserve it, unlike "men in armor who destroy each other." Then, in springtime, "Sprinkle it with dragon's blood"—yet another reference to creatures in fairy tales and folklore. Line 62 is important in understanding the gist of the entire poem, for the idea of "what happens" is central to the difference between the human mind and the deep woods. At this point,

Media Adaptations

- There have been several recordings of Nemerov taped by the Library of Congress, including "Language, Nonsense and Poetry" (1989), "The Poet and the Poem" (1990), and "Professor Gifford Interviews Howard Nemerov" (1990).

- Nemerov recorded a seventy-four-minute tape while reading at the New York Poetry Center in 1962. A two-cassette collection was also recorded in 1962 by Jeffrey Norton, simply titled "The Poetry of Howard Nemerov." These items most likely contain a good deal of material from *The Salt Garden* since the book was published only seven years earlier.

what happens will be either "epic"—celebrating the feats of a legendary hero in a grand, elevated fashion—or "pastoral"—idealizing the simplicity and serenity of rural life.

Lines 63–68

These lines (and most of those in the remainder of the poem) contain a potpourri of allusions to mythological and historical people, places, and events. The point is simply to emphasize the superabundance of mankind's activities throughout history, eventually going back to the biblical beginning of the human race. First, the "sword in the stone" refers to the legendary King Arthur who, after being raised in seclusion, has to retrieve a sword wedged in rock to prove his true birthright. "Minotaurs / Looking for thread" alludes to Theseus of Greek mythology who is able to slay the half-man/half-bull and then make his way out of the labyrinth by following the thread he had strung from the entrance. Unicorns look "for girls" because legend has it that the beautiful, virile horses with horns on their foreheads can be captured and tamed only by virgins. "Glastonbury thorns" are said to have grown from a staff that Joseph of Arimathea thrust into the soil when he arrived to Christianize England. The trees supposedly bloom each year on Christmas day, and their cuttings are believed to heal anyone who touches them on Christmas. Finally, the city of "Sarras," thought to be located in the Middle East, is where some believe the Holy Grail is hidden, and the town is often referred to as "Grail City." Many "travelers" have sought the Grail in Sarras and elsewhere.

Lines 69–74

The speaker here returns to the idea of something happening in the deep woods, something generated by man, and he concludes that "More probably nothing will happen." The reason is that the forest is older than history itself and has been left unscathed by human life. The "trees were here, are here" before the Carthaginian king Hannibal (c. 247–182 B.C.) led a pack of elephants along with his soldiers over the Alps to defeat a surprised Roman army. They were there before Emperor Frederick II of Germany is said to have gone to sleep in a cave and slumbered so long that his beard grew around a stone table in the cavern while he dreamed of bringing peace to a disorderly world. And the deep woods existed, too, before Mordecai, a servant of God recalled in the Book of Esther, had the evil Haman hanged at the gate leading to the palace of King Ahasueres, thereby saving the Jewish nation that Haman wanted to destroy.

Lines 75–78

Here are two more allusions to religious history. Although King Ahasueres is not mentioned by name in line 74, his relation to Mordecai and Haman is implied, and, therefore, the poet can now say the *other* Ahasueres in line 75. "The other Ahasueres" refers to the story of the Wandering Jew, who, as the story goes, was a cobbler named Ahasueres during the time of Jesus. The cobbler was the one who shouted, "Crucify him!" as Jesus bore his cross to Calvary. When Jesus stopped to rest in front of Ahasueres's door, the cobbler refused to let him stay, forcing him to keep walking. After that day, it is said the Jewish Ahasueres began to roam the world, unable to find a home, and so are continuously wandering. The images of Joseph, the Corn Exchange Bank, Egypt, and the word "dreamed" all refer to a story from Genesis in which Joseph is asked to interpret a dream that the Egyptian Pharaoh keeps having about seven ears of good corn and seven ears of thin corn. Joseph claims that it means Egypt will have seven years of bounty followed by seven years of famine. He advises the Pharaoh to develop a plan of stockpiling corn from the bountiful years so that it will be available to help people make it through the lean years.

Lines 79–81

The allusions here are to Milton's *Paradise Lost*. Perhaps "burnt beauties" refers back to the good kernels of corn in the "baked country of Egypt" or perhaps it implies beautiful Egyptian women. Regardless, they are not "hawked out," or sold aggressively, by one who has just begun his journey into hell. Chaos is a great, dark gulf that separates the underworld from the heavens and Earth in Milton's tale. "Pandemonium the Palace" refers to Satan's home in hell.

Lines 82–84

The third reference to something happening is in lines 82 and 83, and this time the speaker is surer of his conclusion. Now he says, "*Most* probably / Nothing will happen" (emphasis added). The deep woods are so pure, so untouched by human activity that they are like the Garden of Eden before "the Fall of Man." The well-known apple that Eve ate has not even been grown in this virgin environment.

Lines 85–87

The last three lines of "Deep Woods" complete the idea of nature's purity and its ability to ignore the entire history—real and fabled—of mankind. Here, the "snake," a symbol of Satan who entered the creature in order to tempt Eve, "still sleeps with a whole head / And has not begun to grow a manly smile." In other words, the snake is just a snake, sunning itself on a rock. In the deep woods, Satan, Eve, and the rest of humanity are nowhere to be found.

Themes

The Limits of Human Perception

The primary theme of "Deep Woods" is the shortfall of a human being's ability to perceive nature in its purest form. Although many people believe they are in tune with the natural world and can spiritually connect with animals, trees, oceans, stars, and so forth, this poem is about the more immediate response of an individual confronted with nature here and now. In the first stanza, the person walking through the woods must deal not only with the awe he feels in such overpowering surroundings but also with his physical reaction to it. His heart races, his mind feels like a hunted beast, and his eyes try desperately to trace the path of a vine winding through the branches, but they cannot. Instead, they become "lost in the insanity of line."

The idea of "line," along with "leaf, and light," represents nature's purity, beauty, and enigmatic qualities—those that make it difficult to understand and keep it out of reach of human perception. Adding to the perplexity of the observer in the woods is nature's "indifference." While humans insist on exact answers and clear motives, nature is content to have "No meaning in it." Whereas people seek drama and heroic actions, "the giant oak" is satisfied not "to fall as heroes should" but quietly to regenerate its life with new vines and branches, even as it leans among a group of birch trees. This behavior is puzzling to mankind. People find it difficult to go about their daily lives oblivious to their surroundings and the actions of loved ones, friends, neighbors, co-workers, government officials, movie stars, famous athletes, leaders of enemy nations, and any other human being capable of eliciting a response in the individual. In the quest to perceive nature as it really is, mankind keeps looking for the "tragic image and the mighty crash," but that is not how it really is in nature. Rather, the deep woods where the speaker walks is an "unlegended land," one that defies interpretation and is not diminished by past or present events. Perhaps the most compelling evidence of the human's limited perception is that nature's "common splendors are comparable only to / Themselves," leaving mankind in the dark, helpless to comprehend the deep woods.

Humanity's Troubled Past

A lesser, but still poignant, theme in "Deep Woods" is humanity's troubled past, presented in the poem in sharp contrast to nature's nonchalance and *un*troubled existence. The speaker that guides the reader through the deep woods also guides us through the travails of human history, both legendary and actual. Although some of the allusions are too benign or questionable entities—the wizard of the Black Forest, Chinese poets, French painters, Walt Disney, and unicorns—far more describe violent, often evil events and participants since the biblical beginning of mankind. The "flood of Yao" is likened to Noah's flood and supposedly killed thousands in southern China. The "time of Set" recalls a time when some people worshiped chaos and demonic power and perhaps reflects cults that have sprung up over the centuries adhering to black magic and Satanic ritual. Nearly all of Nemerov's allusions in "Deep Woods" have religious connotations, typically describing stories of pain and sorrow and sin. The poet was known to be of strong Jewish faith, and his high intellect complemented

Topics for Further Study

- Choose one person or event alluded to in "Deep Woods" and find out all you can about your subject. Write an essay explaining the person's or event's significance in history and tell why Nemerov may have selected the allusion for this poem.

- Write a poem from the perspective of the "giant oak" that leans against the birch trees instead of falling "as heroes should." What would the oak think of the human being passing by in the woods? How would it describe its own situation?

- Read Robert Frost's poem "Stopping By Woods on a Snowy Evening" and write an essay comparing it to "Deep Woods." Other than the obvious difference in length, how does the Frost poem contrast to Nemerov's? In what ways are the two similar?

- Howard Nemerov had a famous sister, also in the arts field. Find out who she was, what her profession was, and write a brief biography of her life.

profound meditations on the biblical past. He does not neglect the New Testament in this poem, referring to the crucifixion of Christ twice with the Glastonbury thorns that "make December / Bleed for the Saviour" and the "other Ahasuerus" who mocked Jesus on his way to Calvary. The story of Mordecai and Haman may be interpreted as a tale of the good guy coming out on top, but it is still a tale of violence and death, if not murder. As though thrown in for good measure, the reference to Hannibal points to historical events, without religious connotation but still reflecting mankind's history of war and aggression.

"Deep Woods" ends with an allusion to Satan's descent into hell, having lost his home in paradise after defying God, and with a final allusion to the biblical "Fall of Man." In the last two lines, the list of humanity's troubles is offset by the portrayal of nature's serenity and innocence. This scene is strikingly, and intentionally, different from all that comes before it.

Style

Blank Verse

Nemerov's "Deep Woods" is constructed in blank verse, with nearly every line written in unrhymed iambic pentameter. Though blank verse can generally refer to any unrhymed poem, most often the lines contain five two-syllable feet with the first syllable accented, the second unaccented. If the poem is read through slowly, tapping out each syllable with a finger, the number of syllables adds up to ten per line with an accent pattern of TA-da, TA-da, TA-da, and so forth. This poem is more relaxed in style than Nemerov's earlier work, and the ideas are presented in a more direct manner than those demonstrated through strict adherence to line number and rhyme scheme. Describing the poems in *The Salt Garden*, critic Ross Labrie, in his book *Howard Nemerov*, says the poems' "lines are less jagged than had been the case earlier as Nemerov begins to settle into a flexible blank verse, the frequent use of enjambment giving rise to the sort of graceful fluidity that is characteristic of his mature work." (In poetry, enjambment is the continuation of a syntactic unit from one line to the next, with no pause. For example, in "Deep Woods," there is no pause between lines 4 and 5, 6 and 7, 9 and 10, etc.). Considering the complexity of Nemerov's work, it is beneficial to the reader that the poet began to write in a more direct, loose manner so that the intellectual ideas are not made more elusive by a difficult style.

Historical Context

Written in the middle of one of the most kaleidoscopic decades in American history, "Deep Woods" includes almost as much hodgepodge reflecting on mankind's history as one would need to describe the 1950s—almost, but not quite. This decade is difficult to define in terms of any one great scientific invention, social movement, war, art or entertainment development, political action, or technological advancement. *All* these things and more occurred, causing the 1950s to stand alone in an era of innovation and changing attitudes.

After World War II, Americans in particular were anxious to keep the economic boom provided by the conflict growing ever stronger and to avoid the miserable conditions of the pre-war depression. World War II also taught Americans that science could have a greater impact on the lives of ordinary citizens than they had ever imagined. The atomic bomb brought a mixture of fear and pride to many individuals and would pave the way for the "Red Scare," McCarthyism, and air raid drills that all became a part of the culture of the 1950s.

The decade began with the United States involved in another overseas conflict, this time in Korea, where American and South Korean troops battled Chinese and North Korean troops over control of the entire country. At the end of the Second World War, Korea was divided at the 38th parallel, the northern half becoming communist, the southern half an ally of the United States. Although the division was intended to be temporary—only until a national election could be held—skirmishes began to break out along the dividing line, turning into all-out war by 1950. When an armistice was finally signed in 1953, a demilitarized zone was established at the 38th parallel, and the country remained divided. This confrontation with communism established America's role as the "policeman" for the world, with the determination to stop the spread of communism a rallying cry for American involvement in other nations' internal affairs. This, in turn, led to the arms race and the Cold War between the United States and the Soviet Union, points of contention that would last throughout the decade and beyond. For some, the fear of communism became fanatical, and Americans accused other Americans of being closet communists. Most famous was Senator Joseph McCarthy of Wisconsin who publicly announced the names of those he thought to be disloyal to the American government, including many Hollywood stars and other well-known people. The practice of publicizing accusations without regard for evidence became known as "McCarthyism."

The 1950s were not only tumultuous years on the political and military fronts, but also in health care, social reform, technology, and entertainment. In medicine, vaccinations for some of the deadliest childhood diseases, including polio and measles, were discovered, and birth control pills were introduced, although they were not available to women in the general population until 1960. Prior to the 1950s, segregation was common in schools, churches, public transportation, the work place—virtually all aspects of day-to-day living—but by the end of the decade, the federal government had adopted measures for desegregation, especially in

Compare & Contrast

- **1953:** Julius and Ethel Rosenberg, accused of cold war espionage, are executed. The Rosenbergs had been found guilty of conspiring to leak atomic bomb secrets to the Russians, but the accusations were controversial, and today many Americans believe their death sentences were a miscarriage of justice.

  Today: Robert Philip Hanssen, a counterintelligence specialist and FBI veteran, is accused of selling secrets to Russia for $1.4 million in cash, diamonds, and deferred money. If convicted, he could face the death penalty.

- **1955:** Disneyland, part of the empire that Walt Disney built, opens in California, the first theme park in America's history of leisure.

  Today: The Walt Disney Company is a multi-billion dollar entertainment giant, operating theme parks all over the world, including Great Britain, Japan, France, and Australia.

- **1959:** Anthropologist Louis Leakey finds the skull of "Nutcracker Man" in Olduvai Gorge, Tanzania, suggesting that human evolution began on the continent of Africa, not Asia.

  Today: In Ethiopia, a freshly unearthed skull and jawbone provide scientists with new details about the human ancestor called "Nutcracker Man"; other digs at the same site have turned up remains of a direct human ancestor, *Homo erectus*, suggesting that the two species may have coexisted in the same area.

schools. This movement, too, would find greatest impact in the next decade, but the seeds of sweeping changes in civil rights were sewn in the 1950s. Although television was already around prior to 1950, this was the decade that sent the new medium to incredible heights of popularity. Programs were broadcast nationally for the first time, and Americans flocked to stores to purchase TVs in much the same way that later generations would send computer sales skyrocketing. Jet airlines and turnpikes changed the way—and the speed—that Americans traveled, and microwave ovens and fast food became fashionable, although Mom's home cooking still topped the dinnertime list in the nuclear American household.

In entertainment, the 1950s saw the birth of rock and roll and a breakdown in the color barrier between musicians and their audiences. Young whites attended concerts and bought the records of black groups the same as they did for white groups, and there was an overall sense of independence, rebellion, and good times brought on by the music that kids loved and parents feared. In literature, "Beat" poets and storytellers read their stream-of-consciousness, off-the-wall work in smoky coffee shops and wine cafes, some, such as Allen Gins-

berg and Lawrence Ferlinghetti, becoming famous in the Beat generation. Painters, dancers, and photographers, too, embraced spontaneity in their art, throwing off traditional crafting and style much to the chagrin of the older followers of structured, well-defined art.

How Nemerov fit into this decade of James Dean, rock and roll, and poetry set to the beat of bongo drums is not easy to say. Evidence in his own work suggests he carried on as usual, probably not offended by the fast, unbridled turn of events, but not very strongly influenced by it either. He continued to produce highly intellectual poetry, fiction, and criticism while the tumultuous 1950s turned into the even more revolutionary 1960s. But in that decade, too, he maintained the Nemerov style.

Critical Overview

For some readers and critics of poetry, Nemerov's work has always been highly regarded, and for others it has taken awhile to get there. Those who received it well in the beginning only mildly complained that the poetry was a bit too derivative of earlier, popular poets, especially Robert Frost. But the harsher critics faulted it for a different reason, as Ross Labrie explains in his book *Howard Nemerov*: "A further reason for the belated recognition of Nemerov's worth can be found in his quiet and resolute resistance to sentimentality and in his forthright pursuit of complex forms." Labrie goes on to say that "his subject matter has appeared to many to be overly erudite and esoteric" and that his reputation "was of a cloistered academic who spent a lot of his time in trying to perfect obsolete forms of prose and verse."

By the mid-1950s, Nemerov had loosened his "obsolete forms" and gained more appreciative readers. As Peter Meinke notes in his own *Howard Nemerov*, "It is in *The Salt Garden* (1955) that Nemerov first unifies his talent.... This book, praised by virtually all critics, had the misfortune to run up against *The Collected Poems of Wallace Stevens*, which swept the literary awards of 1955." Of course, Nemerov went on to win his own literary awards and is today one of the most often anthologized poets in American collections.

Criticism

Pamela Steed Hill

Hill is the author of a poetry collection, has published widely in poetry journals, and is an associate editor for a university publications department. In the following essay, she argues that, while allusions are effective literary devices and can add much to a poem, "Deep Woods" is overdone with them, detracting from its quality and strength.

Howard Nemerov's "Deep Woods" may indeed be in keeping with the poet's profound, highly intellectual style and subject matter, but this time it appears he has "out-Nemerov'd" himself. This eighty-seven-line poem could end at line 42 and be much more effective in letting its remarkable early imagery stand alone to make the point. The addition of allusion after allusion piled on top of one another in the second half of the poem serves only to diminish the strong metaphors relied on in the first half. All the references to historical and legendary people, places, and events fall in such rapid succession that their placement seems helter-skelter, much overdone.

The first half of "Deep Woods" is both eloquent and unusual in its presentation of specific, physical imagery. How picturesque it is to describe something as ambiguous as history in terms of concrete objects, such as trucks passing by on a highway. The verb series "slows, shudders, and shifts" is accurate in describing a big, heavy rig moving down the road but remarkable in portraying humanity's past as unsettled and ominous. The metaphor continues with the word "staggers" and leads into the comparison of history to the reaction of the human body when faced with something completely non-historical. The speaker claims that the deep woods are "too still for history," but they certainly evoke a response in people. Nemerov calls out three poignant parts of a human being—the heart, the mind, and the eye—that are particularly affected by the quiet beauty and power of nature. The extended metaphor of the mind as a hunted beast is on target in describing the panic and confusion an individual feels in the midst of something too awesome to understand. This passage is easily understood, and many readers have probably known the feeling firsthand. Nemerov rounds out the first stanza with more strong imagery, and this time it is the eye that is restless and racing. Again, he uses a depiction of the natural environment to show the human response to it. The "Reticulated branch and vine which go / Nowhere" actually go *everywhere*, making their twining and meandering impossible to trace. In awe, the eye gives up, coming to "a flickering kind of rest" that really is not restful at all. Instead, it is in a suspended state of tension, much like the heart and mind, unable to grasp nature, and so becomes afraid of it.

Compare this first stanza to the third, beginning with line 43. Suddenly the imagery is not so concrete or easily understood. Now the references are to Black Forest wizards, something called the "hot swamp theatrical" with snakes and tigers thrown in, and a Chinese forest "with bridge, pagoda, fog," and three poets drinking tea in the foreground. As if this scene is not odd enough, line 49 adds further confusion by completely contradicting line 48—"(there is no tea, and not so many as three)." Starting with line 51, there is a promising return to good, clear imagery with the "common splendors" of the deep woods and their "leaf, line, light ... scrawled alone" in sunshine across a hillside. The promise, however, is unfulfilled because suddenly the allusions come back in full force. Crammed into the last four lines of the third stanza are references to French painters Watteau and Fragonard, Egypt's Old Kingdom, the god Set, the Flood of Yao, the Fourth Dimension, and Walt Disney. This motley list may contribute surprise to the poem, but it does nothing to complement the solid visual details of its beginning.

Going back to the second stanza, the reader can see how it continues the crisp imagery of the first. The initial mention of "Line, leaf, light" follows directly from the notion of seemingly endless vines woven into the branches of the trees and the brilliant patterns created by sunlight upon leaves in the forest. The highlight of this stanza is the comparison between a fallen human hero and a giant oak tree stricken, presumably, by lightning. Here again, the metaphor is impressive and highly comprehensible. The forest handles its wounded with beautiful, but tenacious, simplicity. The oak tree has a desire to carry on, even in less than heroic conditions, and is content to rejuvenate its life with a "Fresh weaving of vines, rooting of outer branches," all for the humble sake of "Beginning again." Human beings, on the other hand, would rather be dead than humble. Line 28, "The tragic image and the mighty crash," brings to mind scenes of noble heroes in movies, television shows, paintings, even epic novels and poems, as brave soldiers, kings, and lovers meet death gladly, falling as they "should." Contrasted against the depiction of the oak tree leaning "crookedly" but still alive, these images speak for themselves in getting the poet's message across: the gulf between the deep woods—one of nature's purest forms—and the human intellect is so great that they approach death, as well as life, very differently. Now move on to the fourth stanza and try to imagine the same, strong visuals based on the descriptions found there.

The last stanza, unfortunately, follows the pattern of the third in its series of allusions, some remotely related and others seeming to come out of nowhere. It begins with references to the King Arthur era, mentioning men in armor, dragons, and swords stuck in stone. Quickly, though, there is a shift to mythological beasts in the form of minotaurs and unicorns. Then, just as quickly, the allusions shift to religious history, mixing stories from both the New and Old Testaments. The connection between Glastonbury thorns, relating to the crucifixion of Jesus, and the city of Sarras, where some people say the Holy Grail is hidden, may not be far-fetched, but the next concrete allusion is to King Hannibal and his pack of elephants-turned-warriors. This "connection," the reader may rightfully think, *is* far-fetched.

In lines 73 through 78, the allusions change as much as they did in the last four lines of the third stanza, moving from Emperor Frederick II of Ger-

> *This motley list may contribute surprise to the poem, but it does nothing to complement the solid visual details of its beginning."*

many and his long, red beard to Mordecai and Haman from the Book of Esther to "The other Ahasuerus" who, at once, alludes to the king that Mordecai and Haman knew and to the man who became better known as the Wandering Jew. Next, the shift is to the Book of Genesis and the story of Joseph, an Egyptian Pharaoh, and a stockpile of corn. That this string of references is made up of such diverse people and events is further complicated by the fact that many readers are simply not familiar enough with them to understand who or what they were. While a serious reader of poetry may expect occasionally to pull out dictionaries, encyclopedias, or, nowadays, a computer connected to the Internet, most do not relish the idea of researching line after line of esoteric allusions. For the not-so-serious reader, a poem like "Deep Woods" is quite a turn-off—the second half, anyway.

Not surprisingly, the poem ends with yet another literary reference, this time to Milton's *Paradise Lost*. Evidently, the tie-in here is simply to the biblical story of the "Fall of Man," but the best part of the ending has nothing to do with this allusion. Instead, it is the portrayal of the snake, "speckled as sunlight on the rock / In the deep woods." This description is a return to strong, solid imagery, depicting a part of the natural environment in highly visible fashion. The reader can *see* the creature sleeping peacefully on a rock, much the same way one can see intertwining vines and branches, a giant oak leaning into a group of birch trees, and the dry, gold leaves of a New England October. These images are the strength of the poem. The god Set, Walt Disney, unicorns, and King Hannibal fall far short in evoking such vivid pictures in the mind. And "Deep Woods" would have been better without them.

Source: Pamela Steed Hill, Critical Essay on "Deep Woods," in *Poetry for Students*, The Gale Group, 2002.

What Do I Read Next?

- A *Howard Nemerov Reader*, published in 1991, is a collection that includes some of the writer's best poems, short stories, essays, and the comic novel *Federigo; or, the Power of Love*. For the full scope of Nemerov's writing talents, this book is an excellent source.

- Guy and Laura Waterman were known for their writings on preserving natural habitats and living in harmony with the environment. After her husband's death in 2000, Laura Waterman released a special edition of their book, *Wilderness Ethics: Preserving the Spirit of Wildness*. In this call-to-action book, the Watermans describe what they call nature's spiritual dimension, its fragile, untamed wildness, which is being destroyed by over-management and carelessness.

- There are many versions of John Milton's *Paradise Lost*, but for the average reader who is not an expert on religious history, the *Norton Crit-ical Edition* is one of the best. The full title of the paperback printing, published in 1993, is *Paradise Lost: An Authoritative Text, Backgrounds, and Sources Criticism (Norton Critical Edition)*, edited by Scott Elledge. This is a lengthy book, but more than half of it is a collection of various literature, excerpts, and footnotes that are vital to understanding this remarkable piece of literature.

- How the human mind works has been the topic of countless books and magazine articles, and psychologist Bernard Baars's *In the Theater of Consciousness: The Workspace of the Mind* is a recent example of an interesting approach to the subject. Published in 1997, the book shows how consciousness works like a theater stage in which thoughts and perceptions are examined by an inner audience. It is highly readable and contains exercises for the reader that demonstrate the phenomena he is explaining.

Carl Mowery

Mowery has a Ph.D. in literature and composition and has written extensively for the Gale Group. In the following essay he considers the tension that comes from creating an identity for the "Deep Woods."

"Nemerov is a very easy poet to read: you like him immediately. He always gives you something to think about," wrote James Dickey in 1961. Some of Howard Nemerov's earlier poems tended to be more abstract, but the later ones show a shift into what Peter Meinke calls "the simplicity of a highly educated man." These include the poems in the volume *The Salt Garden*, among them "Deep Woods."

At first the poem is reminiscent of the poetry of the New England poet Robert Frost, especially his "Stopping by a Woods on a Snowy Evening." In that Frost poem, the narrator stops in a quiet woods and watches the "woods fill up with snow." (The speaker or narrator in a poem is the persona, the voice telling the tale. It may or may not be the poet.) He wonders whether the owner will care if he watches. The only sound in these woods is the gentle wind and the sleigh bells shaken by his curious horse. For Frost, the woods were a very special place, well known by the narrator, a place he had visited often on his way home. The narrator takes a few moments to stop and enjoy the beauty of the dark woods before remembering that he has "Promises to keep." Frost's briefly descriptive approach to this poem is what some writers have called rustic. (In poetry this connotes a simple, unsophisticated approach to the wording but not necessarily to the meanings derived from them.) The editors of *The Literature of the United States* said, "For the most part, [the] bookish influences seem less important than those of the poet's inheritance and environment." Indeed, his poetry does have the feel of the country more than the library.

This is in strong contrast to the intensely descriptive poetry of Nemerov, whose works are filled with literary references and imagery from many facets of life and history. The combination of the images of kings, mythological creatures, and everyday events creates the impression that every event is significant no matter what it is. The falling oak in the woods and the Glastonbury thorn bush are equally important. (The latter is a famous thorn tree that stood for many years in front of St. John the Baptist's Church in Somerset, England. It was famous for its red Christmas blossoms, which, to some, were symbolic of the Blood of Christ.)

But this is not to say that Nemerov's poetry is too esoteric to be enjoyed. Peter Meinke said that Nemerov's poetry, especially that of *The Salt Garden*, is marked by the attempt "to convey the substance of his meditations clearly." As a result, some of Nemerov's work makes severe demands on the reader to assimilate large quantities of seemingly random information in order to come to an understanding of the poetry. Commenting on his own creative abilities, Howard Nemerov once said (as quoted in Perkins's "The Collected Nemerov"), "I hate intelligence, and have nothing else." His use of the intellectual imagery creates the unique impression of the woods in this poem. It is not a stuffy creation but one of craft and stimulating experiences. Julia Randall says in her article, "Nemerov does not seek to impose a vision upon the world so much as to listen to what it says. . . . [H]is . . . virtue . . . is not to diminish the mystery of the world but to allow it to appear without the interposition of a peculiar individuality."

In the two poems mentioned here, Frost's snow-filled woods is an unnamed yet well-known place in the countryside. Because Frost is spare in his descriptions, the reader is free to create an image of the woods depending on his or her own experiences and imagination. Therefore, these woods will seem more familiar to the reader.

Similarly, the "deep woods" is a place created by Nemerov in the reader's imagination, but it is drawn from "listening" to the many references to history and the arts. But this is an unknown place, a "mystery of the world" that remains without an identity. In spite of the attempts to create a specific image of the woods, including the lines "These here are the deep woods / Of now, New England, this October," these woods are an enigma, an "unlegended land." But it still is the task of the poet, through the narrator, to give the woods an identity, a legend.

Beneath the serene facade of "Deep Woods" is a restless and impatient narrator, whose "mind uneasily rests" dreaming of being lost, and whose "restless eye" scans the branches and vines trying

> " *Frost's woods are rustic, simple, snow-covered; Nemerov's are intellectually burdened, complex, noisy.* "

to read the misspelled calligraphy, yearning for a solution to the mystery of the tangled undergrowth. Nearby, the trucks struggle noisily to climb a hill on their way to deliver their load of trinkets. Elsewhere, dogs bay, running "after better game." Even when the "tragic image and the mighty crash" of the great oak are delayed by the birches, it waits impatiently "to fall as heroes should." This restlessness contrasts with the calm woods of Frost. There, the narrator watches snow fall before moving on to meet his schedule without any sense of urgency or impatience; here in Nemerov's poem, the combined events create a cacophony of urgent noises.

The result of impatience is an increase of tension. There is tension born of the conflict between the woods that "are too slow for history" and the frenetic attempts to decipher the riddles in the woods. The eye scans its surroundings trying to read a misspelled message and comes away with "No meaning in it, but indifference." It comes to a "flickering kind of rest." The woods are "yours to work" and after sprinkling it "with dragon's blood," "you" wait for something to occur, but "more probably nothing will happen." Even the efforts of the birch branches' "assaults which haven't worked yet" contribute to the frustration.

Moreover, there is a tension in the manner in which the speaker identifies the woods. It is a process of identification by negation: The reader is told what the woods are not. They are not the Black Forest; they are not Chinese fog-covered woods; they are not the woods waiting for someone to come along and plant apples in them. At the start of section three, there is a hint of the woods' identity: "It is the same, they say, everywhere. / But that's not so. These here are the deep woods / Of now, New England, this October." Nemerov hints that his woods are the same as the woods of Frost. "But that's not so." Frost's woods are rustic, simple, snow-covered; Nemerov's are intellectually burdened, complex, noisy.

> The woods are "yours to work," to sprinkle with blood and to wait see if anything will happen, "epic or pastoral." The multitude of images is symbolic of the mental processes of someone trying to find a solution to a puzzle of the definition of the woods. But the woods lack an identifying quality, as the Black Forest has. It is the goal of the search in the poem."

Frost's woods are well known to the narrator and, by implication, to the reader. The narrator seems to have passed through them many times. He knows who owns them. But Nemerov's woods are not known. They are "unlegended," "unmitigated by myth;" they are a "place [that] is too old for history to know beans about." It is a prehistoric place before apples grew and "the Fall of Man" occurred. In contrast to the simple ways Frost defined his woods, the woods in "Deep Woods" are described in the intellectual ways that Nemerov claimed to hate so much.

There is one final piece to the puzzle to help explain the process of defining the deep woods. Brian Jones said that "The theme of thought struggling continuously to master [the] world is a dominant one in his [Nemerov's] work." Combined with Meinke's remark that Nemerov was fascinated by the workings of "man's mind," it is an easy step to see the woods as a symbol for the ruminations of a human mind. A human being is born as a *tabula rasa*, a blank slate, on which will be written the sum of that individual's experiences. Out of those experiences then comes the identity of the person. Since everyone will have a different set of experiences, everyone will be unique. But the individual must act. For the woods of "Deep Woods," the speaker tries to identify the acts that will define them.

The speaker in "Deep Woods" makes many attempts to define the woods from the process of negation to claims that it is a New England woods. These attempts are massed in a free-association manner, drawing images from the arts, history, and theology. The woods may be "like nothing known since nature was invented by Watteau and Fragonard." They are "comparable only to themselves." The woods are older than Hannibal, or Frederick, or Mordecai. The woods are "yours to work," to sprinkle with blood and to wait see if anything will happen, "epic or pastoral." The multitude of images is symbolic of the mental processes of someone trying to find a solution to a puzzle of the definition of the woods. But the woods lack an identifying quality, as the Black Forest has. It is the goal of the search in the poem.

This is a fresh new place that will define its essence in terms of its own existence. Existentialist philosophy asserts that "existence precedes essence." Briefly, this means that an individual is nothing except what he or she makes of himself or herself through a series of choices of actions. Therefore, the individual's essence is the accumulation of those acts. Likewise, the final definition of "Deep Woods" depends solely on accumulation of the references the narrator makes and the active involvement of the reader with those references. The woods are not dependent on other places for identity, nor are they dependent on artists to give them an identity. They are the woods "whose splendors are comparable only to themselves" and whose identity is unique unto itself.

Source: Carl Mowery, Critical Essay on "Deep Woods," in *Poetry for Students*, The Gale Group, 2002.

Sources

Blair, Walter, et al., *The Literature of the United States*, Vol. 2, 3rd ed., Scott, Foresman and Company, 1953, pp. 915–17.

Dickey, James, "Howard Nemerov," in *Babel to Byzantium*, Farrar, Straus and Giroux, Inc. 1968, pp. 35–41.

Jones, Brian, in *London Magazine*, May 1968, pp. 75–7.

Labrie, Ross, *Howard Nemerov*, Twayne Publishers, 1980.

Meinke, Peter, *Howard Nemerov*, University of Minnesota Press, 1968.

Nemerov, Howard, *The Salt Garden*, Little, Brown and Company, 1955.

Perkins, David, "The Collected Nemerov," in *Poetry*, Vol. CXXXII, No. 6, September 1978, pp. 351–55.

Randall, Julia, "The Genius of the Shore: The Poetry of Howard Nemerov," in *Hollins Critic*, June 1969, pp. 1–12.

Further Reading

Duncan, Bowie, ed., *The Critical Reception of Howard Nemerov*, The Scarecrow Press, Inc., 1971.

This book contains an excellent collection of essays on both Nemerov and his work. The essays cover thirteen publications, including *The Salt Garden*, with an extensive bibliography at the end.

Harvey, R. D., "A Prophet Armed: An Introduction to the Poetry of Howard Nemerov," in *Poets in Progress*, edited by H. B. Hungerford, Northwestern University Press, 1967, pp. 116–33.

In this article, Harvey concentrates on the themes of war, nature, and city life, presenting an interesting discussion on the same themes found in "Deep Woods."

Mills, William, "Nemerov as Nature Poet," in *The Stillness in Moving Things: The World of Howard Nemerov*, Memphis State University Press, 1975, pp. 97–118.

In this essay, Mills explores the symbolism of the woods in "Deep Woods," especially their capacity as a "source of peace."

Nemerov, Howard, *The Collected Poems of Howard Nemerov*, University of Chicago Press, 1977.

Collected works always provide a good, thorough sampling of a writer's works, allowing readers to see changes in style, subject matter, and quality over the years.

————, *Figures of Thought: "Speculations on the Meaning of Poetry, and Other Essays,"* Godine, 1978.

Known as much for his thoughts on poetry as for writing it, Nemerov provides some interesting insight into his own work and others in this collection of essays. Although the theories here are accessible to any reader, the serious poetry student would find the book most helpful in getting to know the poet and his craft better.

————, *Journal of the Fictive Life*, Rutgers University Press, 1965.

This is as close to an autobiography as Nemerov wrote. It is actually a scribbled record of his thoughts as he tried to write a novel. The journal itself was a hit with readers for its humor, intellectual depth, and readability.

Elegy for My Father, Who Is Not Dead

Andrew Hudgins

1991

"Elegy for My Father, Who Is Not Dead" was published by Houghton Mifflin, in 1991, in *The Never-Ending*, Andrew Hudgins's third volume of poems. The poem calls itself an "elegy" in the first half of the title, and thus we expect to hear a poetic lament for someone who has died. But Hudgins puts a strange twist on the ancient genre, *elegia*. This poem is an elegy for someone who is not yet dead, namely, the poet's father. In the first two lines, Hudgins voices for many readers that secret dread of hearing that a parent has died. The poem anticipates mourning for his father, but because he is "not dead," another kind of elegy is also at work. Death will be one sort of distance eventually separating father from son; meanwhile, there are vast distances between them in life. His father, "in the sureness of his faith," is "ready . . . to see fresh worlds." The son is clearly not so sure and is instead "convinced / his ship's gone down." The poem is thus a kind of double elegy. It mourns both what is and what is not to be.

"Elegy for My Father, Who Is Not Dead" witnesses what numerous other poems and memoirs tell of Hudgins's relationship with both his father and his faith. When Hudgins speaks elsewhere of his father, it is with a complex mixture of fear, admiration, exasperation, awe, and sadness. An essay published in *The Washington Post* reconstructs a childhood that "belonged in some fundamental way to my father and the U.S. Air Force, not me." In his uniform, Hudgins's father "radiated authority, presence, a forceful place in the world"; in a suit,

"he looked strangely diminished." But for all its "authority," the uniform also became a symbol of the essential distance from his sons, none of whom Hudgins believes would have "flourished" in the military, "least of all me," he says. The pattern of "not following" his father is traced along yet another painful path in this quirky "elegy." This son has followed neither his father's path in life nor his contemplated route to death. The disjunctions between father and son, to borrow the book's title, appear "never-ending."

This poem is also characteristic of Hudgins's preoccupation with matters of religious faith. Biblical language, imagery, and characters appear frequently in Hudgins's writing, both poems and prose. But his expression of religious matters is hardly pious and never sentimental. On the contrary, his work has been called "grotesque," "violent," and "bawdry." The "stained glass" of his religious sensibility is more likely to be stained with compost, clay, and tobacco than with the usual jewel colors and pious figures of church windows. "Elegy for My Father" confesses his doubt that the hereafter is an adventure cruise and that the ultimate good-bye should be a cheery affair.

Like many Hudgins poems, this one locates death at the center of its verbal energy. But it is also characteristic of his style: short lines, accessible language, indelicate tone. It makes little difference whether one has a religious sensibility or shares Hudgins's southern or military upbringing; there is little distance, ultimately, between Hudgins and his readers. It is easy to recognize ourselves somehow in his poems' painful family scenes, humorous predicaments, and accounts of "sins" both contemplated and carried out. In the words of his first title, Hudgins emerges neither as "saint" nor "stranger" in the light of his earthy, accessible poems.

Author Biography

Andrew Hudgins was born in Killeen, Texas, on April 22, 1951. Between his birth and his entry into Sidney Lanier High School in Montgomery, Alabama, Hudgins and his family followed his father, a career Air Force officer, to New Mexico, England, Ohio, North Carolina, California, and France. Despite this apparent rootlessness, typical of the military lifestyle, Hudgins considers himself a Southerner and derives much of the material for his poems from the images, idioms, and folkways of the Deep South. The poet's parents, Andrew L. and

Andrew Hudgins

Roberta Rodgers Hudgins, both grew up in the cotton-mill town of Griffin, Georgia, and returned there often to visit their large, extended family.

Hudgins's father, a West Point graduate and a man of uncompromising moral uprightness and religious discipline, is an important influence on his son's work. He looms large in Hudgins's childhood memory and in numerous poems as a rather fearful figure, who "raised my three brothers and me as if we were recruits."

Hudgins's father was also a devout Christian, who grew up Methodist but "converted" to the Baptist church. The elder Hudgins required his sons to be present for nightly Bible readings and prayers, not to mention attendance at church on Wednesdays and Sundays. While the younger Andrew squirmed through the enforced devotionals, he nevertheless absorbed biblical language, images, and stories that his poems transform in often startling ways.

Hudgins's father, however, was not one to encourage his son's voracious reading habits, much less offer any aesthetic sympathies. He had no relationship with literature, per se, and only the most pragmatic attitude toward books. In his mind, the "good book," the Bible, was a guidebook for right living and devotion. For his son Andrew, the Bible became a rich source of stories and images for an art that strips away, poem by poem, every possible vestige of religious sentimentality and cliché.

By the time Hudgins was a teenager, his father "didn't want us to be uprooted once we entered high school," so he settled the family on the Air Force base near Montgomery, Alabama, in 1966, and then left for a year of duty in Vietnam. Hudgins says that his identity as a Southerner evolved from his high school and college years in Montgomery during a time when the city was the backdrop for critical events in the civil rights movement. Hudgins attended Sidney Lanier High School, the local public school named after the nineteenth-century, Georgia-born poet.

After completing a bachelor's degree in English at Huntingdon College in Montgomery, Hudgins married and earned a master's degree in arts at the University of Alabama. He never completed the Ph.D. in English that he began at Syracuse University, despite being the recipient of a fellowship and the Delmore Schwartz Award for Creative Writing. Instead, he returned to Montgomery to teach at a junior college. A divorce soon followed. Hudgins then applied successfully to the famed Iowa Writer's Workshop, receiving a masters degree in Fine Arts in 1983. His appointment to the faculty at the University of Cincinnati in 1985 coincided with the publication of his first volume of poetry, *Saints and Strangers*, a runner-up for the 1986 Pulitzer Prize. Hudgins has continued to receive awards for his writing: five volumes of poetry, a volume of essays, and numerous articles, short stories, and memoirs. *The Never-Ending* (1991), in which "Elegy for My Father, Who Is Not Dead" appears, was a finalist for the 1991 National Book Award in Poetry and received the Texas Institute of Letters Poetry Award. *After the Lost War* (1988), a poetic chronicle of the life of Sidney Lanier, received the Poets' Prize for the best book of poetry published in 1988. His most recent volume of poems is *Babylon in a Jar* (1998). Hudgins's work has been anthologized in such diverse collections as *The Best American Poetry, 1998, The Made Thing: An Anthology of Contemporary Southern Poetry*, and *Upholding Mystery: An Anthology of Contemporary Christian Poetry*.

Hudgins remarried in 1992 and continues to teach in the English department at the University of Cincinnati. The University recently awarded him the title "Distinguished Professor of Research," broadening the usual notion of "research" to embrace the poet's searches and re-searches into the work and power of words.

Poem Text

One day I'll lift the telephone
and be told my father's dead. He's ready.
In the sureness of his faith, he talks
about the world beyond this world
as though his reservations have   5
been made. I think he wants to go,
a little bit—a new desire
to travel building up, an itch
to see fresh worlds. Or older ones.
He thinks that when I follow him   10
he'll wrap me in his arms and laugh,
the way he did when I arrived
on earth. I do not think he's right.
He's ready. I am not. I can't
just say good-bye as cheerfully   15
as if he were embarking on a trip
to make my later trip go well.
I see myself on deck, convinced
his ship's gone down, while he's convinced
I'll see him standing on the dock   20
and waving, shouting, *Welcome back.*

Poem Summary

Lines 1–2

As though the reader were a listening friend, Hudgins's first two lines declare a personal "fact" in a simple sentence with plain words. "One day," he surmises, someone will call, and he'll hear that his father has died. It will be somewhat expected, however, because his father is elderly, and "he's ready." It's not unusual to hear aging or seriously ill people claim they're "ready" to die. The poem begins in familiar language with a familiar situation.

Lines 3–6

It is Hudgins's habit, however, to peel the layers off the familiar until it yields something more pungent and particular. In these lines, he begins to explore more precisely, and individually, just what "he's ready" means to his father. Here we learn that his father's religious faith is what enables this readiness to die. His faith has assured him that there is a "world beyond this world." Beyond death, there is something, not nothing. And the way his father talks about that next world has the tone of someone excited about a trip, a travel adventure. At least that's the way it strikes the ear of his son, and in the poem, it becomes a simile: "he talks . . . as though his reservations have / been made." It even sounds as though "he *wants* to go."

Lines 7–9

But after all, this is death, a serious sort of trip, so "I think he wants to go" is quickly qualified in the next line with "a little bit." The poem is written from the doubting son's point of view, and we can know about the father's attitude toward death only through the filter of what the son thinks and feels. Perhaps this qualifier emerges from the son's own position of doubt. Perhaps he reads into his father's "sureness" an occasional tentative undertone. Nevertheless, the travel metaphor continues as the son notices his father's desire to go elsewhere "building up," a kind of "itch," the poem calls it, colloquially. The son speculates that his father is looking forward to an eternity of "fresh" worlds, where all things are new, innocent, untainted. On the other hand, perhaps the landscape of the hereafter will be "older," akin to those times and places more proximate to Paradise. One thing seems sure: the aging man's vision of heaven scarcely resembles this present world.

Lines 10–13

Until now, the poem has spoken almost solely of the father's attitude toward his own death. At this point, the son enters, and the differences between their understandings of the "next life" emerge clearly. The father expects the son to "follow him" to that place, where their reunion will be full of affection and good humor. In fact, death will be much like birth, the poem implies. The son followed the father into life. Likewise, the assumption goes, he will follow him in death, another kind of passage like birth, to a new world. At least that is the optimism the father holds out. The son, in line 13, has a different position: "I do not think he's right."

Lines 14–17

In short bursts of contrast, line 14 declares simply: "He's ready. I am not." It is neither a simple, nor a "cheerful" matter for the son, this saying "good-bye." And he certainly feels no assurance that his father can make his own passage from life to death more comfortable simply by preceding him. The father's earlier "trip" will not of itself "make my later trip go well."

Lines 18–21

The "trip" metaphor culminates in the last lines with the image of both son and father traveling by sea. In the process, "sinking ship," a cliché for doom and death, recovers its original metaphoric freshness through the particulars of this father-son

relationship. The son sees himself "on deck" of his own ship, making his own journey in this life. But the poem clearly implies it is not the same ship as his father's. In fact, from his vantage point "on deck," the son is "convinced" his father's "ship's gone down." His father is not safe; he's submerged in something vast, cold, and deep.

Hudgins's father, however, is convinced of something quite different: in the next life, he'll be safely docked, and his son's ship will eventually arrive at the same port. "I'll see him standing on the dock," says the son, exuberant in his "*Welcome back*." The phrase could have ended simply in a *Welcome*, but the presence of *back* implies something of a return that cannot be ignored. What is it that the father believes his son will be returning to? His presence? That pure relationship that accompanied his birth? Or is it more complex, theologically speaking? Is he welcoming him "back" to something prior to both of their lives on Earth, something both fresh and old, something like heaven?

Themes

Parents and Children

Hudgins's elegy for his still-living father is certainly not the only poem that blends his preoccupation with his parents' death and dying. "My Father's Corpse" humorously reconstructs a memory from early childhood:

> [my father] lay stone still, pretended to be dead.
> My brothers and I, tiny, swarmed over him
> like puppies. He wouldn't move. We tickled him
> . . .
> . . . . We pushed small fingers up
> inside his nostrils, wiggled them, and giggled.
> He wouldn't move.

It wasn't until the little boys became alarmed that young Andrew himself aggressively tested the limits of his father's pretense:

> [and] slammed my forehead on his face. He rose,
> he rose up roaring, scattered us from his body
> and, as he raged, we sprawled at his feet—thrilled
> to have the resurrected bastard back.

It would be unfair to say that Andrew Hudgins is "obsessed" with his relationship to his parents and kin but not unreasonable to say that it occupies much of what we would call his "psychic space." Numerous poems throughout Hudgins's work recover some detail of clothing, a gesture, verbal habit, a scene or event from life, or death, for which his family, parents most often, are the focus. *The Never-Ending* contains unorthodox elegies for both father and mother, one for a father "Who is Not Dead" and one for a mother long ago "gone underground," mingled with the images of stubborn, dry flowers in "November Garden." Hudgins's autobiographical poems in *The Glass Hammer: A Southern Childhood* (1994) supply numerous family stories and images that help put the sad distance between father and son in "Elegy for My Father" in context.

The Glass Hammer opens with a passage from the Old Testament prophet Nehemiah: "both I and my father's house have sinned" and then begins immediately with a poem recalling a particular "sin" he commits as a curious child against his mother and her prized knickknack, a crystal hammer. The adults in Hudgins's life—father, mother, grandmother, aunts, uncles—appear in his poems as profoundly authoritative: "PUT THAT THING DOWN!," "*Shush, boy,*" "*Calm down! Sit still!,*" "Quit sniveling!" Constantly accountable for his behavior, the young Hudgins also feels completely accountable to his kin for what he does, and is. According to "Begotten":

> I've never, as some children do,
> Looked at my folks, and thought, I *must*
> Have come from someone else—
> I never had to ask, What am I?
> I stared at my blood-kin, and thought,
> So *this*, dear God, is what I am.

One has the sense that Hudgins has continued to "stare" at his kin and that poems are the result. He stares at them in all sorts of circumstances, letting the reader intimately into the four walls of a childhood that was less than ideal, sparing little of the daily cruelties and crudities that textured his family life. In "Dangling," Hudgins's father swings Andrew off the roof upside down, ankles cinched with rope, to paint the house. He also dangles his oldest son into "the darkness of the well," where Andrew recalls:

> [I] grabbled in black water till I found
> the rotting body of a cousin's dog.
> I hugged it to my chest and Daddy hauled
> the wet, gray rope. I vowed I'd always hate him.

There are poem-stories of raunchy joke-telling, ignorant, racist cousins, cursing uncles, and disheartening criticisms. Andrew announced at dinner one night:

> *I'd like to be a tree.* My father clinked
> his fork down on his plate and stared at me.
> "Boy, sometimes you say the dumbest things."
> *You ought to know*, I muttered, and got backhanded
> out of my chair.

Even as Hudgins tells these stories, says the poetic "Afterword" to *The Glass Hammer*, he realizes that "all telling's betrayal," not necessarily of his family in their unflattering portraits but of something larger—a betrayal of truth, which has been subject to his autobiographical "selection, rounding off, / interpretation and my failure / to stay as angry as I'd vowed." In the title essay of his most recent prose volume *The Glass Anvil* (1997), Hudgins remembers vowing as a fifteen-year-old with "plentiful rage and gravity" that "if I ever wrote about my life I'd do it while I was still angry and that my book would be brutal, ruthless, scorchingly honest. I'd blow the lid off the pot, dammit." "The Glass Anvil: 'The Lies of an Autobiographer'" confesses, describes, and ultimately accepts each of the eight "lies" that he had to tell in order to express what he "thinks his life means and how that life felt to the one who lived it."

Topics For Further Study

- Many people find it difficult to talk about death and dying and resort to using verbal alternatives, many of which are now stock expressions. List as many clichés or euphemisms for death as can you think of. Explain the purpose these expressions serve. What effects do they have, either intended or unintended? Write a poem, story, or essay in which you "unpack" a cliché or "translate" a euphemism for death.

- Do a research project in which you compare and contrast the burial rituals and attitudes toward death of two different cultures or religions. You may, for example, explore the differences between a contemporary Hindu and Buddhist burial ritual or between two ancient cultures such as the Incas and the Mayans. Or, study the differences between the practices of mainline Protestant denominations (Baptist, Methodist, Presbyterian, etc.) and that of a smaller group, such as the Quakers, Anthroposophists, or Nazarenes.

- Study a poem-elegy, either classical or contemporary, and interpret it musically by composing an instrumental piece that conveys the essence of the lament, without resorting to the words of the poem. What instrument(s), key, mode, rhythm, and style would you work with, for instance, to explore John Milton's "Lycidas" musically? What instruments and style does Hudgins's unorthodox elegy suggest?

- Write a poem in which you explore the ways in which you and one of your parents diverge, using a metaphor to express your differences, as Hudgins used a ship and a dock. Write a second poem in which you focus on some point of convergence or harmony, this time using a narrative form, a story or event that distills the essence of that meeting point.

- Visit a large graveyard. Record the styles and inscriptions of a sample number of headstones in some visual medium—photography, drawing, painting, and so on. Create an artistic or expressive "catalog of elegies" from your findings.

Perhaps Hudgins has "betrayed" his anger in "Elegy for My Father, Who Is Not Dead." It is not an angry poem. On the other hand, the Hudgins, in this poem, is grown up and has admittedly learned a few things about forgiveness: "How can you forgive your family?" he is asked at a reading. "By asking them to forgive me," he answers. This is the Hudgins who struggles in his weekly calls to his aging father "to say *I love you*, although it's true / and gets a little truer with each saying." There is less anger at his father in "Elegy" than sadness, for the inevitability in death, as in life, of absolute divergence. Hudgins's father would have liked his sons to follow his military career. They didn't. He would have liked them to follow his devotion to the Bible and the church in the way he did. They didn't. This elegy mourns a son's inability to "say good-bye as cheerfully / as if he were embarking on a trip / to make my later trip go well." There are no illusions of being ready to follow his father in life, or death.

Together, *The Glass Hammer* and *The Never-Ending* perform as a kind of poetic *bildungsroman*. A *bildungsroman* is a German term used for novels which reveal a character's trials in growing up, such as Charles Dickens's *David Copperfield* and James Joyce's *A Portrait of the Artist as a Young Man*. Hudgins's poems tell the story of a boy who becomes a man as he awakens to the truth of his upbringing and struggles to make sense of what's left in the wake of his necessary dis-illusionments. By the time Hudgins has written this poem, the energy once devoted to anger has found a better direction in the painful work of understanding, forgiveness, and acceptance. Although "convinced / his ship's gone down," the son has found ways to love his father anyway.

Death

According to its classical definition, an *elegy* is a poem written in honor of some loved or esteemed person who has died. John Milton's pastoral "Lycidas" is a good example of the classic elegy. John Donne, a contemporary of Milton in the seventeenth century, took more liberty with the genre. His elegies address matters of human love that, to his metaphysical bent of mind, often resemble death. In the hands of modern poets, the elegy has been re-imagined in both the subject and form. J. V. Cunningham, for instance, wrote a satirical "Elegy for a Cricket," and Alan Dugan, "the clown of nihilism," composed "Elegy for a Puritan Conscience." Both poems stray well outside the subject and form of a classical elegy. Yet there are also plenty of modern poems with traditional aims, such as William Carlos Williams's elegy for D. H. Lawrence, and W. H. Auden's elegiac memory of Irish poet William Butler Yeats.

Andrew Hudgins's curious elegy mourns the lonely gap that exists in the present between him and his still-living parent. In the original sense of the Greek word *elegeia*, the poem is a lament, in this case, for an irreparable disjunction in their belief in the hereafter. Father and son diverge in life; they will likely diverge in death. That emotional certainty is the cause for lament. The poem is full of the contrasts between the father's quite hopeful vision of life after death and the son's sad resignation to something more final. The elder Hudgins's firm orthodox Christian belief in the resurrection creates a happy prospect for this next journey, a continuation of life, not an end. The son is not so sure: "He's ready," but "I am not." According to the poem's final image, both father and son are on ships, but not aboard the same one. Their journeys may not bring them into the same port, finally, the last lines imply. The younger Hudgins is still working out his relationship to the eternal and the hereafter, largely through poems. At the moment, he is unable to greet the prospect of death, his father's or his own, with an "itch / to see fresh worlds."

Style

"Elegy for My Father, Who Is Not Dead" is written in free verse. Instead of adhering to an overtly formal pattern of meter or rhyme, it follows the path of the human voice. Hudgins's poems in general are quite conversational in tone and simple in word choice. He frequently includes snatches of overheard dialogue in his poems, capturing the raw, sometimes raunchy language of those around him.

While "Elegy" contains no such dialogue, it does witness and interpret in contemporary language the almost childlike conception of eternity his father holds: "he talks about the world beyond this world / as though his reservations / have been made."

This poem, like many others in *The Never-Ending* and his other volumes, consists of one long stanza and medium-length *enjambed* lines, lines that run on from one line into the next without punctuation or formal capitalization. Take lines 7–9, for example: "a new desire / to travel building up, an itch / to see fresh worlds." In free verse, the line breaks are quite important, not only because they help establish the poem's "melody," but also because they give special weight to the first and last words of the lines. In lines 7 and 8, "desire" and "itch" end the lines and thereby subtly offer themselves as synonyms. Together they intensify the impression of hope the father has in the "never-ending."

Within the twenty-one lines of this poem are eleven sentences, many of them quite short. Line 14 consists of two very short sentences and the pointed beginning of a third: "He's ready. I am not. I can't." Every sentence in the poem is declarative, stating a perception or a fact. There are no commands, questions, or exclamations. As a result, the poem speaks itself quietly and resignedly, as though there's nothing to rage about or praise, nothing to exhort or admonish, nothing to question or plead for. Furthermore, the words within these sentences are short themselves, consisting of only one or two syllables. These short words and spare sentences convey a simple grief, undecorated by pious words or euphemisms, undistracted by formal techniques. The textures of syllables, words, and lines work together to support the simple, stark realization at the heart of the poem that a separation has already begun.

Free verse is indeed free from the strictures of formal pattern, but it is not free of form. Hudgins's poems are often "formed" by an *iambic* meter. The *iambic foot* consists of an unstressed syllable, followed by a stressed syllable, as in line 4: "a*bout* the *world* be*yond* this *world*." The iambic foot comes closest to the natural rhythms of human speech. A scansion of "Elegy for My Father" reveals that the typical number of iambic "feet" per line is four, that is, *iambic tetrameter*. Iambic tetrameter is one foot shorter than the more common free verse meter, *iambic pentameter*. Poet Mary Oliver observes that iambic pentameter is "suitable to the construct of meditation," but that iambic tetrameter sustains the sense of strong emotion. We speak more briefly, breathe more quickly, "when we are pitched to some emotion sharper than contemplation," when, she says, "we reach, in emotion, for the succinct." Such is the emotion conveyed succinctly but urgently in Hudgins's elegy for his father. "Something wants to be resolved," says Oliver of poems written in iambic tetrameter. The meter of Hudgins's elegy is a revelation, in form, of the profound distances unresolved between father and son.

Historical Context

Andrew Hudgins's complex identity as a Southerner was formed primarily during his high school years in Montgomery, Alabama. Montgomery is often called the "cradle of the Confederacy" because it served, through 1861, as the first capital of the provisional government known as the Confederacy, the alliance of southern states that seceded from the Union. It was in Montgomery that the Confederacy's first constitution was drafted, which, while resembling the U.S. Constitution in many ways, also made provisions for states' rights and slavery.

A hundred years or so later, the city became nearly synonymous with the civil rights movement because so much of its tensions were embodied there. It was in Montgomery, on December 5, 1955, that Rosa Parks, a black woman, refused to give up her seat in the front of a bus to a white man and was arrested. Her individual protest rippled into a yearlong boycott of the Montgomery bus system and eventually into radical transformations effected by the civil rights movement and its leaders, foremost the Rev. Martin Luther King, Jr. Inspired by India's Mohandas Gandhi, King urged African Americans to protest the infringement of their rights peacefully. King himself participated in countless nonviolent protests and marches, even though many demonstrations were met with anger and violence on the part of their white detractors. It was during the peaceful march on Washington in 1963 that King delivered his famous "I Have a Dream" speech.

In "Letter from Birmingham Jail," King asserts that "We who engage in nonviolent direct action are not the creators of tension. We merely bring to the surface the hidden tension that is already alive." Tensions were quite high and alive in Alabama in 1965, just one year before Andrew Hudgins and his family moved to Montgomery. In February of that year, Rev. King and 770 others were arrested in Selma, Alabama, for protesting unjust voter registration laws. Another 2,000 were arrested in early March, prompting a march from Selma to Montgomery, the state capital. On their way, Alabama state police attacked marchers with tear gas, whips, and clubs. When Governor George C. Wallace refused to offer protection for another march, President Lyndon B. Johnson stepped in to provide three thousand National Guard members and military police. King then led the now-famous, five-day march from Selma to Montgomery, which began with 3,200 participants on March 21, 1965, and ended on March 25 with over 25,000 gathering in front of the state capitol building, further galvanizing the civil rights movement both in body and spirit. Meanwhile, the Ku Klux Klan, a white supremacist group, escalated their violence not only against blacks but against white civil rights activists.

The atmosphere of racial tension, human rights violations, and violence had a deep impact on the young Andrew Hudgins, who witnesses its horrors in many poems, especially from *The Glass Hammer: A Southern Childhood* but also in *The Never-Ending*. The first poem of that book, which also contains the elegy for his father, is called "How Shall We Sing the Lord's Song in a Strange Land?" The words of the title are taken from Psalm 137, in which David laments his people's captivity in Babylon: "there we sat down and wept when we remembered Zion." In Hudgins's poem, a childhood memory of a black man who was lynched and hung is jarringly juxtaposed with a scene of his cousin's maternal tenderness. We dwell in a world that "is home. But it / will never feel like home," the poem concludes.

Such images and memories helped form Hudgins's complex relationship with the South and civil rights, but so did his own father's "stubborn sense of rectitude" or justice. While that unwavering rectitude was often aimed at his sons in disciplinary actions, it also led the elder Hudgins into wider conflict on occasion. In one instance, son Andrew found his father's "mulish rectitude" especially "inspiring." The reporter who broke the story of the My Lai massacre in Vietnam to the nation was Wayne Greenhaw of the *Montgomery Advertiser*. In March of 1968, Lt. William Calley led U.S. troops into the South Vietnamese town of My Lai, an alleged Viet Cong stronghold, and shot 347 unarmed civilians, including many women and children. Following special investigations, Lt. Calley and four other soldiers were court martialed, and Calley was convicted and imprisoned. (His con-

Compare & Contrast

- **1951:** In response to the threat of a third world war, created by tensions between the United States, communist China, and the U.S.S.R., a huge increase in taxes is proposed in the United States and universal military training urged. U.S. armed forces number 2.9 million.

1969: In the midst of the Vietnam War and the beginning of the Nixon presidency, Congress votes for a $5 billion cut in military spending.

1990: In June, President George Bush and U.S.S.R. President Mikhail Gorbachev sign agreements whereby both countries would make large cuts in nuclear and chemical weapons, including missiles, submarines, and bombers. In November of 1990, the most extensive arms control treaty in history is signed in Paris by twenty European nations, the United States, and Canada.

1993: The Pentagon ends research on the military defense program known as "Star Wars," which was begun in 1983 at a cost of $30 billion. Star Wars, or the Strategic Defense Initiative, was intended to be an "outer space" shield against enemy missiles.

Today: Under the leadership of newly elected President Vladimir Putin, the Russian parliament ratifies the START II nuclear arms reduction treaty in April of 2000. Former president Boris Yeltsin had failed repeatedly to win approval for the treaty.

- **1638:** In Rhode Island, Roger Williams becomes the pastor of the first Baptist church to be established in America, but he actually remains in the church only a few months. Williams founds the Rhode Island colony as a haven for persecuted Christians.

1900: By the end of the nineteenth century, reformed and evangelical religious groups comprise the vast majority of Protestant denominations in the United States, with memberships of approximately 6 million Methodists, 5 million Baptists, 1.5 million Lutherans, and 1.5 million Presbyterians.

1989: In the United States, membership in the Roman Catholic Church numbers 54 million. The Southern Baptist Convention is the second largest religious denomination, with a membership of 14.8 million.

1992: Both the Southern Baptist Convention and the Roman Catholic Church make official statements of opposition to homosexuality. The Baptists vote to banish two churches that had accepted homosexuals and began the process of changing its by-laws to enable official exclusion of such churches. U.S. Catholic bishops are urged to oppose any laws that promote public acceptance of homosexual conduct.

1995: The Southern Baptist Convention votes "to repent racism of which we have been guilty," and to ask forgiveness of all African Americans. The Southern Baptist Convention was founded in 1845 in part for defense of slavery.

Today: The Southern Baptist Convention remains the largest Protestant denomination in the United States and has grown to over 18 million members. According to a *New York Times* article, the U.S. House and Senate were once dominated by a religiously liberal and moderate membership—mostly Presbyterians, Episcopalians, and Methodists. During President Bill Clinton's second term, the major government posts were, for a while, all occupied by Southern Baptists: Clinton himself, Vice-President Al Gore, House Speaker Newt Gingrich, Senate President Pro Tem Strom Thurmond, Senate Majority Leader Trent Lott, House Majority Leader Tom DeLay, and House Minority Leader Dick Gephardt.

viction was later overturned, and he was released in 1974). As Hudgins remembers it, "Alabama and the South rallied to Lt. William Calley's side," and letters to the editor excused Calley's action with such comments as "'Sure, it's sad, but collateral casualties just happen.'" Hudgins's father was outraged. In his father's own letter to the local paper, recalls Hudgins, his father said:

> … that he had served in the military for three decades, including a tour in Vietnam, and that as far as he was concerned there was never any reason for machinegunning unarmed women and children in a ditch. William Calley . . . deserved to be court-martialed.

The letter created a "big stink in our small, conservative military town," and "the paper was flooded with letters calling my father every kind of traitor and coward," writes Hudgins. But to his son, this father's sense of service to a higher authority with its unassailable justice was "inspiring" in the midst of daily violations, both local and global, of human worth, rights, and dignity.

Critical Overview

Andrew Hudgins's poems appear in such diverse anthologies as the annual volume *The Best American Poetry (1995, 1998)*, *The Literature of the American South: A Norton Anthology*, *The Columbia Book of Civil War Poetry*, and *Upholding Mystery: an Anthology of Contemporary Christian Poetry*. David Impastato, editor of the latter volume, notes Hudgins's "use of an iambic line . . . to sustain his intimate, colloquial voice" as well as his "link with a Southern Gothic tradition." However, Impastato's introduction gives a less compelling reason for including Hudgins in his collection of religious poetry than Richard Tillinghast does in a review of *The Never-Ending*, the volume in which "Elegy for My Father" appears. Tillinghast describes Hudgins's poems as "clear and accessible," humorous and bawdy, but that underneath the "disarming personal frankness [lies] a religious sensibility. . . . He may be praying drunk," comments Tillinghast, "but he is praying." To some, Hudgins may appear irreverent toward many hallowed religious images and figures, as one can see in numerous poems such as "Mary Magdelene's Left Foot," "Praying Drunk," "The Liar's Psalm," "An Old Joke," "Funeral Parlor Fan," and "Psalm Against Psalms," which begins:

> God had Isaiah eat hot coals,
> Ezekiel eat s—, and they sang
> his praises. I've eaten neither, despite
> my childhood need to test most things
> inside my mouth. My brothers and I
> would pop small frogs over our lips.

Tillinghast sees Hudgins's very earthy, candid approach to such matters as a sign of a sincere faith, the mark of one who will not separate his faith from the ordinary stuff of life.

Critic Clay Reynolds observes Hudgins's technique of bringing "the apparently insignificant elements of life" into the reader's awareness through a startling image of the ordinary, the shock of the commonplace. Hudgins studies intensely "how people react to experience," notes Reynolds. "Elegy for My Father, Who Is Not Dead" is the first-person study of a son's divergence from his father in matters of death, and life. In quite ordinary language, the relationship of an aging father and middle-aged son is evoked with simplicity and honesty. Though no mention of "Elegy" has been made specifically in reviews or criticism, its twist of wry humor in the title, its image of travel reservations as a way to speak of dying, and its frank expression of a universal emotion—grief—are the sorts of things critics find to praise in Hudgins's work. "It breathes," says reviewer Kevin McGowin of Hudgins's most recent book of poems, *Babylon in a Jar* (1998), because "he speaks our language," and this, McGowin says, "is why we bother to still read poetry."

Criticism

Adrian Blevins

Blevins is a poet and essayist who has taught at Hollins University, Sweet Briar College, and in the Virginia Community College system. She has published poems, stories, and essays in many magazines, journals, and anthologies. In this essay, Blevins views Andrew Hudgins's poem through a lens of what Donald Hall calls an "ethic of clarity."

In "Risk and Contemporary Poetry," Andrew Hudgins measures the success of eight volumes of poetry by focusing on what he calls "the risks of content," saying that "it is content that gives significance to form, that justifies form, and makes form worth looking at to see how it contributes to meaning." He also says that "like any performer the writer to some extent, large or small, puts himself or herself in jeopardy: a feat is worth praising

> *Poets must . . . work very hard to contain not only this emotion but all emotion. Indeed, it's possibly even more risky to express wonder or love in a sincere way than sorrow or grief."*

only if it runs the risk of failure too." Since it truly is a small accomplishment to succeed in writing an unambitious poem, we might also ask in our evaluations of poems about the risks the poet is confronting. Does the poet risk sentimentality by overstating his emotional response to a memory or observation that the memory or observation doesn't seem to warrant? Is he risking inscrutability by making associations he keeps private or by linking unrelated objects and impressions for reasons that seem to serve no aesthetic purpose? Is he exhibiting too much of his ego? Is he confessing so much that his lines embarrass rather than enlighten and surprise and delight? Or is the poem too accessible? Is it too easy to enter and process? Does it fail to defamiliarize the reader from the known world, to make the known world new and strange again? Has the poet missed his opportunity to deepen his meaning, to piece together the potential verbal layers like the various elements in one of the more exotic desserts?

While it is possible to argue that our more accessible poets are able to reach larger audiences because they are willing to risk appearing simple-minded, it is also true that our more *in*accessible poets—Jorie Graham and John Ashbury come immediately to mind—have been able to find readers and augment their reputations despite their antagonizing vagaries. Still, since Americans generally favor the plain-spoken over the obtuse, both in their poetry and their prose, it might be worthwhile to view Andrew Hudgins's "Elegy For My Father, Who Is Not Dead" through the lens of what Donald Hall, in the Introduction to his 1968 anthology *The Modern Stylists*, calls "an ethic of clarity."

Hudgins's poem "Elegy to My Father, Who Is Not Dead" comes from *The Never-Ending*, his third collection. "Elegy"is not a narrative: it does not tell a story. It is also not a dramatic monologue: it isn't written from an imagined point of view. Although it concerns itself with the differences between Hudgins's view of the afterlife and his father's view, it is not a prayer, as are many of the best poems in *The Never-Ending*. "Elegy" also makes no overt religious allusions; it uses no common Christian symbols, such as Christ or Mary Magdalene, as launching points for meditations that often bring these characters back to life in very stunning ways. For these reasons, "Elegy" is not as representative of the full body of Hudgins's work to date as are other poems in *The Never-Ending*. Yet there are a few constants—themes in the poem that were foreshadowed in *Saints and Strangers*, Hudgins's first book—that become downright preoccupations in *The Glass Hammer*, Hudgins's fourth.

The conflict Hudgins expresses in "Elegy" between his father's view of heaven and his own view of it is, in the poem, stated very directly: "He thinks that when I follow him / he'll wrap me in his arms and laugh, / the way he did when I arrived on earth." Then immediately he says: "I do not think he's right." At first it seems that "Elegy" works simply to reveal the tension inherent in a son's skepticism about his father's traditional view of the afterlife, striving merely to express the tension borne of the speaker's inability to accept his father's rather picturesque and even unimaginative belief in heaven. But a closer reading of the poem reveals that there are meanings beyond just this surface one, implications that do work to deepen a poem that risks—but overcomes—being one-dimensional or too accessible.

The speaker says he cannot "just say good-bye as cheerfully / as if he's embarking on a trip," revealing as a second tension the poet's fear of his father's death. When the speaker of the poem says he's not ready, he is telling us that he is not ready to let his father go, that he cannot accept his father's willingness to die. A third tension might be found in Hudgins's decision to use analogies to make more visible the differences between his views and his father's. Thus, "Elegy" articulates not only differences in belief but also an obvious difference in mood or inclination, and this difference might work to separate the two men even more than the religious difference we see on the poem's surface level. A desire to confess and then to mend this sense of being other than the people who "got me born and [taught] me how to read / and how to hold a fork," as he says in "Oh, Say, Can You See?" in *The Glass Hammer* is one of the most predominate struggles in the work of Andrew Hudgins.

Hudgins says that his father "talks / about the world beyond this world / as though his reservations have / been made." He says that his father is convinced he'll see Hudgins "standing on the dock / and waving, shouting, *Welcome back.*" The father's attitude toward death is obviously, thus, a positive one. Hudgins even tells us that he thinks his father "wants to go, / a little bit," that he's got a "new desire / to travel building up, an itch / to see fresh worlds." In comparison, Hudgins sees himself "on deck, convinced / [his father's] ship's gone down." Thus we can see a third tension in this relatively short poem: Hudgins has expressed in twenty-one lines not only the differences in religious views between his father and himself but differences in disposition, as well. He's also given us a sense of the grief that he knows accompanies a parent's death, but he has contained and controlled this grief, thus depersonalizing his subject matter for us, avoiding the risk of sentimentality inherent in any poem taking as its theme death and the afterlife.

Kevin McGowin, in a review of *Babylon in a Jar*, Hudgins's fifth collection of poems, says that the poems in *The Glass Hammer* "were at times flat, making an otherwise brilliant collection uneven and less passionate than I'd come to expect from his earlier work." "Elegy for My Father, Who Is Not Dead" is more closely akin in this way to the poems in *The Glass Hammer* than to many of the poems in *The Never-Ending*. But though it risks being too accessible, it does, in the end, work on more than one level.

In *Making Your Own Days: The Pleasures of Reading and Writing Poetry*, Kenneth Koch says:

> Along with its emphasis on music, poetry language is also notable for its predilection for certain rhetorical forms such as comparison, personification, apostrophe (talking to something or someone who isn't there), and for its inclinations toward the imaginary, the wished-for, the objectively untrue. Music either simply comes with these predilections or is a main factor in spiriting them. The sensuousness of music arouses feelings, memories, sensations, and its order and formality promise a way possibly to make sense of them.

A good poet's interest in the music of language comes, then, not from a desire to be obtuse or obscure or difficult, but from a knowledge of the ways in which the music of language inspires and

approximates human emotion. But un-contained grief that seems either out of step with the circumstances that has inspired it, as one might find in soap operas, or embellished by a trite, contrived, or predictable use of the language, as one might find in a Hallmark card, is both unbelievable and embarrassing. Poets must thus work very hard to contain not only this emotion but all emotion. Indeed, it's possibly even more risky to express wonder or love in a sincere way than sorrow or grief. Hudgins's choice in using the analogy rather than the image for a main method of comparison and his generally iambic cadence—that slow, steady heartbeat in many of the lines in "Elegy"—both work well to contain the grief at the heart of "Elegy," saving it from the sentimental risks it must naturally assume from the outset.

Other poems in *The Never-Ending*, though they are as accessible as "Elegy," adopt more musical devices: there are stunning images, emphatic repetitions, stories, alliterative accelerations, comparisons in neatly-packaged trinities, associative leaps, and gorgeous moments of imaginative fancy in which even Christ appears, wearing a "broad-brimmed hat / and muddy robe." For example, the first few lines in "The Liar's Psalm," one of the more complex poems in the book, illustrate this:

> Let us make homage to the fox, for his tail is as
>   lush
> as Babylon. His eyes, all glitter and distrust,
> are cruel as a Spanish crucifixion, and his paws so
>   subtle
> they can empty your refrigerator without the light
> coming on.

These lines show that Andrew Hudgins is in complete control of the devices at his disposal, further revealing that he is conscious of his own technique in each of his poems. If a reader thinks of "Elegy" as understated at first, or even as unmusical, it is only because the reader has not yet realized how the poem achieves its ambiguities or how its tone works to package and contain its emotion. "Elegy" is a statement of fact that becomes an unsentimental expression of sorrow. This sorrow, resting inside the incurable gap between two men's opposing views and moods and modes of being, succeeds in sidestepping the potential dangers it had to confront to get there.

In *Some Notes Towards the Definition of Culture*, T. S. Eliot says that "to be educated above the level of those whose social habits and tastes one has inherited may cause a division within a man which interferes with happiness." And, in *Three Steps on the Ladder of Writing*, Hélène Cixous says

What Do I Read Next?

- In response to the tragic shootings in April 1999 at Columbine High School in Littleton, Colorado, Hudgins wrote "When Bullies Ruled the Hallways," published in the Op-Ed section of the *New York Times*, May 1, 1999. In this brief essay, Hudgins recalls in graphic detail the various strategies of domination and torture the "jock-kings" used at his own high school in Montgomery, Alabama. Hudgins admits to having "nursed revenge fantasies against the jocks who tormented me" but "never came close to acting them out." He concludes, "I valued my life and theirs too much."

- "The Secret Sister" is a recent memoir in *The Hudson Review* (Winter 1999), which tells how, at age ten, Andrew Hudgins stumbles upon a well-kept family secret. An "error" on his birth certificate begins the process of revelation that ends in a startling fact: there had been a sister, Andrea, killed at age two in a car accident in which his mother, pregnant with Andrew at the time, was the driver. "The Secret Sister," like other Hudgins memoirs, radiates meaning from

a central fact into many other family dynamics and incidents and even into a "bone-deep understanding" of his own life.

- The religious matter in much of Hudgins's poetry is both strong and quite unorthodox. Two memoirs, "Half-Answered Prayers," published in *Southern Review* (Summer 1998) and "Born Again" published in *American Scholar* (Spring 1999), step outside the usual language and formulae of religious testimonies and into the flesh-and-blood accounts of Hudgins's own encounters with God.

- *A Summons to Memphis* (1986) by Tennessee-born Peter Taylor is a novel that revolves around the complex family relationships in a Southern family, especially between father and son. Like many of Andrew Hudgins's poems and memoirs, Taylor's story also deals with the power of childhood dislocations and the various ways memory is summoned to come to terms with the past.

---

that "the author writes as if he or she were in a foreign country, as if he or she were a foreigner in his or her own family." "Elegy For My Father, Who Is Not Dead" works beautifully to reveal in an unsentimental way the grief that may come when a man must move beyond the beliefs of the people who have loved and raised him. Other notable examples in *The Never-Ending*, such as "Hunting With My Brother," "The Adoration of the Magi," "In The Game," and "Suffer The Children," express the poet's recognition of the differences between himself and many of the members of his family. What is exceptional about this awareness is that, despite the differences, Hudgins has been able to stay connected with his family. He does not write as though he were a foreigner in his own family; he writes, rather, as though he were his family's very own personal scribe. For many a gorgeous example of the way he's managed to keep his heart affixed to the people and place that produced him,

all interested parties should look further into the work of Andrew Hudgins.

Source: Adrian Blevins, Critical Essay on "Elegy for My Father, Who Is Not Dead," in *Poetry for Students*, The Gale Group, 2002.

Bryan Aubrey

Aubrey holds a Ph.D. in English literature. In this essay, he considers "Elegy for My Father, Who Is Not Dead" in terms of many levels of gaps or distances: between the generations, between faith and doubt, and between belief and agnosticism or atheism.

Hudgins's reputation as a poet has been built in part on his concern with religion, especially the kind of fundamentalist Protestant Christianity that has a strong hold in the southern United States, where Hudgins spent much of his adolescence and early adulthood. Many of his most admired poems contain what Clay Reynolds describes in *Dictionary of Literary Biography* as a "sense of the grotesque," in which the reader is often shocked by horrific, morbid, or bizarre images intended to point attention to "the relationship between real behavior and religious conviction."

In many of Hudgins's poems, the poet steps outside accepted attitudes to biblical characters or objects of religious veneration (the figure of Christ as depicted in art, for example) and presents these objects in a fresh light. Often this is done through the eyes of a child who is contemplating them for the first time, without long years of religious training or indoctrination. In such poems, the poet stands outside the faith that he is examining. He sees it differently from its more enthusiastic and less reflective believers.

It is in this respect that "Elegy for My Father, Who Is Not Dead" reflects Hudgins's characteristic concerns. In many other respects, the poem is not typical of his work: the imagery is neither disturbing nor violent, and the poem does not shock or make the reader reflect with a sudden twist of thought at the end. The simplicity and apparent artlessness of the poem's language, scarcely distinguishable from prose, also mark it as different from much of Hudgins's other work. But the poem is clearly linked to Hudgins's favorite themes in that it presents widely different, irreconcilable points of view on matters of religion, especially relating to issues of life and death. The poem can be understood as a poem of gaps, of distances, of chasms, at a number of different levels, between different interpretations of life. There is the gap between father and son (although the speaker could also be the father's daughter), the gap between the generations, and the wide gulf that separates faith from doubt, belief from agnosticism or atheism.

This sense of distance is established in the first two lines: "One day I'll lift the telephone / and be told my father's dead." The speaker assumes that he will not be present at his father's death; he will receive the news from someone else, perhaps a relative or hospital official, and even then not in person but via the telephone. The hint of estrangement, of separation, is clear, although the poet offers no explanation of why he is so certain that this is the way events will unfold. Nor does he offer any information about whether his father is already ill and dying; the poet may simply be imagining what will happen at some undetermined point in the future. Certainly, the speaker does not sound concerned or distressed about the prospect; the matter-of-fact, in-

> *The son, of course, does not believe a word of this, quietly dissenting from his father's most deeply held beliefs."*

formal, somewhat detached conversational tone sets the mood of the poem as a whole. (The tone is quite different from the emotional intensity of another poem in which a son contemplates the death of his father, Dylan Thomas's "Do Not Go Gentle Into That Good Night.")

The poem is notable as much for what it does not say as for what it does say. The nature of the father's religious faith is approached obliquely, in terms of his basic, unquestioned assumptions, which are clearly those of the fundamentalist Christian. The father believes in the Christian doctrine of an afterlife: that those who have kept the faith in this life will be rewarded by admission to the community of the righteous in heaven, a paradise ruled by Christ, in which all pain and suffering have been banished and life continues forever. This is the "world beyond this world" referred to in the poem. The fortunate souls who inhabit it are the "saved," whose names are written in the "book of life" that is opened, according to the New Testament's book of Revelation, at the time of judgment.

Christian fundamentalist belief is characterized by two more elements that are clearly part of the belief system of the father in "Elegy for My Father, Who Is Not Dead." The first is that the conditions of salvation are unambiguous; a believer can know with absolute certainty that he is bound for heaven as long as he accepts that Christ is the Son of God and died for the sins of mankind, a doctrine that can be traced to the gospel of John 3:16: "For God so loved the world that he gave his only Son, that whoever believe in him should not perish but have eternal life." It is because the speaker's father accepts this belief that he can be so confident of his destination after death. He can make "reservations" for heaven, rather like a person might make flight reservations for a vacation (at least that is how the son sees it). For the religious fundamentalist, whether Christian, Muslim or adherent of another religion, there is never any room for doubt. For the Christian, doubting is considered the devil's work, and issues of faith and morality usually divide neatly into two categories: right and wrong, good and evil, salvation and damnation. Intellectual questioning is not encouraged.

The second element of fundamentalist belief relevant to the poem is the literal nature of the father's beliefs. He expects to live in heaven in the same physical form in which he lived on Earth. No doubt he has heard this preached from the pulpit on innumerable occasions. According to Christian doctrine, there is to be a resurrection of the body after the believer dies. In the Christian heaven, individuals are not transformed into disembodied spirits; souls still need bodies, even if the body concerned is, as St. Paul wrote in his first letter to the Corinthians (15:44), a "spiritual body." In the poem, the father clearly expects to be recognizably himself and to retain the same family ties that he had on Earth. He looks forward to the time when his son will join him and he is able to wrap him "in his arms and laugh, / the way he did when I arrived on earth." The image nicely links death with rebirth; the newly arrived soul in heaven is like a newborn baby on Earth. (There are hints here also of the fundamentalist belief that when a person accepts Jesus, he is "born again.")

The son, of course, does not believe a word of this, quietly dissenting from his father's most deeply held beliefs. He addresses his difference of opinion to the reader, rather than to his father, perhaps because the gap between the two men is so great he feels there is no point in discussing the subject directly with his father. There is no meeting point, no possibility of dialogue, between such radically divergent views, although the son puts forward no positive beliefs of his own; he is merely unconvinced by the faith into which he was born and appears to regard the prospect of death with some unease. Unlike his father, he is no happy voyager on the ship that sails to eternity. However, his trepidation stops far short of the blank terror of annihilation that is the theme of another contemporary poem about death, Philip Larkin's "Aubade."

The final four lines of the poem convey most starkly the chasm between the two attitudes being presented. These lines build on the poem's recurring image of the passage to death and beyond being like a sea voyage. Going to heaven is like being on a ship that docks in a harbor, finally safe on its journey home. This is a simple and universal image, but the speaker is clearly ready to deconstruct it. His choice of words suggests that both sets of beliefs, the faithful and the faithless, are no more than speculation in which the mind indulges:

> I see myself on deck, convinced
> his ship's gone down, while he's convinced
> I'll see him standing on the dock
> and waving, shouting, *Welcome back.*

Looking into the future, the poet is "convinced" that the ship (that is, his father's life) will go down, never to rise again, just as his father is "convinced" otherwise. To be convinced is simply to be persuaded of the truth of a certain statement or proposition. In this case, in the absence of any objectively verifiable proof—since death, as Hamlet famously said, is that "undiscover'd country, from whose bourn / No traveller returns"—neither statement can claim to be truer than the other. To adapt the ship image, father and son are like the proverbial two ships passing each other on a dark night; one is on a voyage of faith, the other on a voyage of doubt. They cannot see each other; they cannot exchange signals. They share no common language.

Source: Bryan Aubrey, Critical Essay on "Elegy for My Father, Who Is Not Dead," in *Poetry for Students*, The Gale Group, 2002.

Erik France

France is a librarian and teaches history and interdisciplinary studies at University Liggett School in Grosse Pointe Woods, Michigan. In the following essay, he considers how Hudgins's poem is a twentieth-century American variant on the elegiac tradition that emphasizes anxiety about death rather than consolation in its aftermath.

"Elegy for My Father, Who Is Not Dead" immediately suggests a twentieth-century tone that contrasts with earlier elegies. In previous centuries, elegies were usually meant to express lamentation, mourning, and praise for someone who had died. Like words spoken by a friend or relative of the deceased at a funeral, they often expressed sadness and feelings of loss but also provided consolation or comfort for the living. Two illustrative examples are Thomas Carew's "An Elegy Upon the Death of the Dean of St. Paul's, Dr. John Donne" (1633) and Walt Whitman's elegy for Abraham Lincoln, "When Lilacs Last in the Dooryard Bloom'd" (1865). In Hudgins's variation on the elegy, the speaker's father, as the title immediately announces, is not dead. Furthermore, once one reads or hears the poem, it becomes clear that the speaker does not provide any direct consolation to the audience. In fact, the speaker emphatically doubts the father's consoling notions. In contrasting the speaker's anxiety about death with the father's faith and belief in a cheerful afterlife, Hudgins inspires his audience to check on their own metaphysical beliefs: Why are we here, where did we come from, and where will we go next?

Hudgins's speaker's father takes a positive, even pleasant view of death. He conceives of death as a point of departure, as if what comes next will be as enjoyable and comfortable and fun as a luxury cruise with good friends. His images of travel are modern because luxury travel became practical and affordable to anyone but the wealthiest only in the twentieth century. The phrase "his reservations have / been made" suggests the modern transportation system in which one can go to a travel agent or make a phone call to make arrangements for a trip to any chosen destination. Near the end of the twentieth century, this system had become so automated that the speaker's father could have connected to the Internet and, using a credit card number, made the reservations himself. He is so convinced that the afterlife will be like a pleasant trip that he is almost eager to go. The idea of wanting to see "fresh worlds" suggests that he wants to move on from this one, almost like a futuristic astronaut heading out to explore another galaxy. The speaker is not entirely sure exactly where his father wants to go or where he thinks he is going, only that it is a worthwhile place. Perhaps it is rather "older" worlds he will see—the speaker is unsure. When Americans speak of "the old country," they are usually referring to the places from which they or their ancestors came. The phrase has been most often used by people of European descent in referring to some country or area of Europe, but it could just as well be any place of origin. In this case, the father is probably thinking in terms of the mystical place from which he came before he was born.

Hudgins leaves his speaker's father's age and state of health deliberately vague: he could be old or sick, but he may just as easily be healthy. There are clues that the father may be close to the end of his life in that he is "ready" for death, that the speaker "can't / just say good-bye." Nonetheless, "the sureness of his faith" and his belief in a positive afterlife are the most important things we learn about the speaker's father. This belief unsettles the speaker, makes the speaker anxious and gloomy. The speaker disbelieves the father's metaphysical views. The speaker takes a much more skeptical and negative view of things than the father does. The speaker sees technology, such as the telephone,

> *The speaker sees technology, such as the telephone, as a conveyor of bad news and dwells on the image of a ship that has sunk rather than afloat and smoothly cruising along."*

as a conveyor of bad news and dwells on the image of a ship that has sunk rather than afloat and smoothly cruising along. Whereas the father is calm about death, the speaker is terrified by the thought of it. This terror is made more understandable when one considers the history of the 1900s.

Technological innovations made life both easier and more terrifying during the twentieth century. Travel has been made easier, but disasters like the sinking of the passenger ship *Titanic* in 1912, the explosion of the space shuttle *Challenger* in 1986, and hundreds of airplane crashes dramatically showed that modern transportation technology did not guarantee safety. More terribly, much technology was used during the 1900s to deliberately kill civilians (as well as military personnel) on a vast scale. The use of railroads and poison gas to efficiently carry out the Holocaust in Europe and fast-flying airplanes to drop atomic bombs on Hiroshima and Nagasaki during the Second World War are particularly terrifying examples of how technology was used for extremely violent purposes. Over the course of the twentieth century, technology also dramatically changed the way people communicated and thought about life: it sped things up and loaded people's thoughts with huge amounts of information, leaving little time for quiet contemplation. News about disasters became harder to ignore as the century moved toward its end, giving many people a feeling of dread. This was largely due to the increasing availability, reach, and daily use of telephones, radios, televisions, and the Internet. All of these technologies changed from rare luxury items to seeming necessities. As 2001 approached, people anxiously coped with life-threatening issues such as AIDS, food-borne viruses, and random acts of terrorism. Without a calming belief system, one could easily be frightened by the thought of death in the twentieth century.

"Elegy for My Father, Who Is Not Dead" does not reveal how or when, in spite of the scarier aspects of the twentieth-century world, the speaker's father came to faith. Some people are more naturally optimistic whereas others remain pessimistic. Is the glass half full or half empty? Is the idea of traveling in space or at sea exciting or fraught with doom? The speaker's father comes across clearly as a person who prefers to think on the bright side. He seems like a happy, loving person. The speaker strongly suggests that "he'll wrap me in his arms and laugh, / the way he did when I arrived / on earth." Yet the father's love and affection do not bring consolation to the speaker, which leaves the latter feeling sad and hopeless.

The forcefulness of Hudgins's speaker's doubts—dwelling on fearful things like an imaginary telephone call announcing the father's death or a ship that has sunk with the father on board—emphasize how uneasy the speaker feels. As long as the speaker remains anxious and haunted by death, though, there remains the possibility that the speaker will find faith and hope. Southern Catholic novelist Flannery O'Connor, in her novel *Wise Blood* (1952), employed a protagonist named Hazel Motes to explore this theme. Like the speaker in Hudgins's poem, Hazel takes a deeply skeptical view of faith but can never shake the torment of anxiety or find happiness. The speaker becomes more anxious and tortured the more the speaker denies faith. Eventually, Hazel in *Wise Blood* comes to find faith with as much apparent conviction as the speaker's father has in "Elegy for My Father, Who Is Not Dead." Just as Hazel finds faith, there is hope that the speaker in "Elegy" will find it as well.

Source: Erik France, Critical Essay on "Elegy for My Father, Who Is Not Dead," in *Poetry for Students*, The Gale Group, 2002.

Sources

Carruth, Gorton, *What Happened When: A Chronology of Life and Events in America*, rev. ed., Harper Collins, 1996.

Cixous, Hélène, *Three Steps on the Ladder of Writing*, Columbia University Press, 1993, p. 20.

Eliot, T. S. *Notes towards the Definition of Culture*, Harcourt, Brace and Company, 1949.

Hall, Donald, ed., *The Modern Stylists: Writers on the Art of Writing*, Collier-Macmillan Ltd., 1968, pp. 1–7.

Hudgins, Andrew, *The Glass Anvil*, University of Michigan Press, 1997.

——, *The Glass Hammer: A Southern Childhood*, Houghton Mifflin, 1994.

——, *The Never-Ending*, Houghton Mifflin Company, 1991, p. 45.

——, "Risk and Contemporary Poetry," in *New England Review*, Summer 1986, p. 526.

——, "A Sense of Service," in *Washington Post*, Sunday, January 2, 2000, sec. W, p. 12.

Impastato, David, ed., Introduction, in *Upholding Mystery: An Anthology of Contemporary Christian Poetry*, Oxford University Press, 1997, pp. xxi–xxviii.

Koch, Kenneth, *Making Your Own Days: The Pleasures of Reading and Writing Poetry*, Scribner, 1998.

McGowin, Kevin, Review of *Babylon in a Jar*, in *Oyster Boy Review*, Vol. 10, January/March 1999.

Oliver, Mary, *Rules for the Dance: A Handbook for Writing and Reading Metrical Verse*, Houghton Mifflin, 1998.

Reynolds, Clay, "Andrew Hudgins," in *Dictionary of Literary Biography*, Vol. 120: *American Poets Since World War II, 3rd series*, edited by R. S. Gwynn, Gale Research, 1992, pp. 142–50.

Tillinghast, Richard, "The Everyday and the Transcendent," in *Michigan Quarterly Review*, Vol. 32, No. 3, Summer 1993, pp. 477–80.

Further Reading

Hudgins, Andrew, "A Sense of Service: As the Son of a Soldier . . ." in *Washington Post*, Sunday, January 2, 2000, sec. W, p. 12.

This prose memoir delivers a frank personal account both of Hudgins's relationship to his stern father and of growing up as a "military brat." Just as he does in his poems, Hudgins incorporates snatches of dialogue, details of daily life, and keen observations of character in his prose to bring the past, in all its humor and pain, candidly into the present. Although the poem "Elegy for My Father" can certainly stand on its own, this memoir supplies much biographical depth to the story of disparity so keenly rendered in the poem.

Jarman, Mark, and David Mason, eds., *Rebel Angels: 25 Poets of the New Formalism*, Story Line Press, 1996, pp. 102–21.

"Elegy for My Father, Who Is Not Dead" and thirteen other poems by Andrew Hudgins are included in this anthology, which represents the first wave of young poets writing in what is being called "the new formalism." New formalist poets retrieve the traditional tools of rhyme, meter, or narrative to achieve new results. Hudgins's skillful use of iambic meter and narrative are what earned him a place in this collection. Other poets included in the volume are Sydney Lea, Brad Leithauser, Molly Peacock, Rachel Hadas, Dana Gioia, and Julia Alvarez.

Rubin, Louis, ed., *The History of Southern Literature*, Louisiana State University Press, 1985.

Andrew Hudgins was just emerging as a poet when this definitive volume of regional literary history was published. Rubin solicited essays from a wide number of critics and literary historians in order to account for the development of Southern literature from its colonial beginnings to the present. It characterizes the significant movements and writers who represent the South's "story" in prose, fiction, and poetry. Readers may be particularly interested to learn about Sidney Lanier in Rayburn Moore's essay on "Poetry of the Late Nineteenth Century" before reading Hudgins's *After the Lost War*, a narrative poem-sequence based on the life of Lanier, a Georgia-born poet.

Stokesbury, Leon, ed., *The Made Thing: An Anthology of Contemporary Southern Poetry*, University of Arkansas Press, 1987, pp. 111–14.

If Hudgins's style allows him a place among the "new formalists," his subject matter grants him a solid place in Southern literature. Poems from his first volume, *Saints and Strangers* (1985), are included in this collection of over sixty poets from the American South, both men and women, many well known, such as James Dickey, Robert Penn Warren, and Alice Walker. Others such as Vassar Miller and Margaret Gibson are perhaps less familiar but important in editor Stokesbury's aim to profile the vitality of poetry in a region known primarily for such monumental fiction writers as Faulkner, Welty, and O'Connor.

The Fish

Marianne Moore
1921

Marianne Moore wrote "The Fish" in 1918 but it was published later in her first collection, *Poems*, in 1921. This collection was published, without her knowledge, in England by two of Moore's friends. An example of rhymed syllabic verse, "The Fish" highlights Moore's ability for precise visual description. Ironically, the poem is not about fish at all, but rather the relationship among a seaside cliff, sea life, and the sea itself. Sunlight acts upon the sea and its creatures, and the sea acts upon a cliff. Moore highlights the interdependence of these elements in the shape of the poem, which moves like a wave, surging towards a subject, then retreating from it. The narrator of the poem describes this interdependence in a hard, emotionally detached manner. Her images paradoxically suggest both fecundity and abundance and starkness and death. This dichotomy drives the poem, but Moore never resolves the paradox; rather, she suggests that it is a necessary part of the world. The processes of life and death are evident everywhere, and as much a part of the human as the natural landscape.

Moore was inspired by the natural world. She frequently wrote about animals, domestic and exotic, often preferring the non-human world over the human world. Moore was also interested in modern painting and studied color theory, which some critics mention as influencing "The Fish." Other possible influences were her brother Warner's passion for sailing and Moore's deep respect for him. When the poem was republished in her second collection, *Observations* (1924), Moore used six-line

stanzas instead of five. However, it is the five-line version that has been widely anthologized and written about.

Author Biography

Known for her precise and measured observations of insects and animals, an often ironic tone, and idiosyncratic form, Marianne Craig Moore offered modern poetry a compelling alternative to T. S. Eliot's fragmented universe of archaic allusions, William Carlos Williams's speech-based poetics, and Wallace Stevens's flowery meditations on reality and the imagination. A naturalist as much as a poet, Moore wrote poetry with a painter's eye, packing an entire world of meaning into a single image. Her quirky rhyme schemes, odd stanzaic patterns, and use of unconventional syllabic patterns caused some critics to ask if she was even a poet. Moore often asked the same question.

Moore was born in 1887 in Kirkwood, Missouri, to John Milton Moore, a construction engineer, and Mary Warner. Her parents separated before she was born and Marianne never saw her father, who was institutionalized after a nervous breakdown. She grew up in the house of her maternal grandfather, John Riddle Warner, the pastor of a Presbyterian church in Kirkwood. After graduating in 1909 from Bryn Mawr College in Pennsylvania with a degree in biology, Moore taught typing and bookkeeping while continuing her writing. The most influential person in Moore's life and on her writing was her mother, with whom she lived most of her life.

Though she began to publish poems in little magazines in 1915, Moore did not publish her first book until 1921 when her friends, H. D. (Hilda Doolittle) and Robert McAlmon, published, without her knowledge, a collection titled simply *Poems* in London. This volume contains "The Fish," her most anthologized poem. Moore developed her reputation as a poet when she became editor of the influential literary journal the *Dial* in 1925. During her four-year tenure at the *Dial*, Moore published many of the twentieth-century's most well-known writers such as Paul Valery, T. S. Eliot, Hart Crane, Ezra Pound, and Ortega y Gasset, and she corresponded extensively with many poets and writers.

Moore became somewhat of a celebrity in her old age. Photographs of her in a cape and tricorne hat often ran in newspapers and magazines, and she

Marianne Moore

even made an appearance on *The Tonight Show*. A lifelong fan of baseball, she was invited to throw out the first ball of the season at Yankee Stadium in 1967. In 1969, Moore was named "Senior Citizen of the Year" by the New York Conference on Aging. That same year, she received an honorary degree from Harvard.

In addition to the poetry collections published during the 1920s, Moore published *What Are Years?* (1941); *Nevertheless* (1944); the Pulitzer Prize-winning *Collected Poems* (1951), which was also awarded the 1952 National Book Award and the Bollingen Prize in 1953; a collection of essays, *Predilections* (1955); and *Idiosyncrasy and Technique: Two Lectures* (1958).

Moore died February 5, 1972, in New York City. She was 84 years old.

Poem Text

wade
through black jade.
   Of the crow-blue mussel-shells, one keeps
   adjusting the ash-heaps;
   opening and shutting itself like   5
an
injured fan.

The barnacles which encrust the side
of the wave, cannot hide
there for the submerged shafts of the   10

sun,
split like spun
    glass, move themselves with spotlight swiftness
    into the crevices—
    in and out, illuminating   15

the
turquoise sea
    of bodies. The water drives a wedge
    of iron through the iron edge
    of the cliff; whereupon the stars,   20

pink
rice-grains, ink-
    bespattered jelly-fish, crabs like green
    lilies, and submarine
    toadstools, slide each on the other.   25

All
external
    marks of abuse are present on this
    defiant edifice—
    all the physical features of   30

ac-
cident—lack
    of cornice, dynamite grooves, burns, and
    hatchet strokes, these things stand
    out on it; the chasm-side is   35

dead.
Repeated
    evidence has proved that it can live
    on what can not revive
    its youth. The sea grows old in it.   40

Poem Summary

First Stanza

The first line of "The Fish" syntactically belongs to the title. In an almost filmic manner, the speaker focuses on fish "wading" through "black jade." These words are telling because they suggest a heaviness and a slowness to the fish's movement. Jade is opaque and is not naturally associated with water. The darkness of the water underlines the mysteriousness of the sea, the difficulty of knowing it. By calling the sand disturbed by the opening and closing of one of the mussels "ash heaps," Moore underscores not only the physical appearance of this action but also how the sea floor looks "disposable" to human eyes. By singling out one of the shells, noting how it is "adjusting" the environment around it, Moore suggests how the movement of the smallest thing can have an effect on the larger world.

Second Stanza

The second stanza picks up from the last line of the preceding stanza. By running her lines over, a technique known as enjambment, Moore foregrounds her own composing strategy, which highlights the interdependence of words and lines. Formally, then, the poem parallels its subject: the interdependence of the living and the dead, the individual thing and the context in which it exists. Her composing strategy, then, is also a composting strategy. She finishes the simile she began in the first stanza by likening the opening and closing of the mussel to an "injured fan." The sea now begins to resemble nothing so much as a hospital ward for sick sea life.

In this stanza, Moore focuses on the sea, pointing out the vulnerability of barnacles. By writing that they "cannot hide," Moore humanizes these underwater creatures. Barnacles are marine crustaceans that are free-swimming as larvae but permanently fixed (as to rocks, boat hulls, or whales) as adults. In this case, they "encrust" a wave, which is unusual because we don't think of things being able to affix themselves to water.

Third Stanza

The sunlight is refracted ("split like spun / glass") and acts as a searchlight beaming into the nooks and crannies of underwater life. As narrator, Moore acts as the person holding the flashlight helping readers *see* what they could not without her help. The "spotlight swiftness" of the sun suggests that it may be a cloudy day, as the sun comes out, then falls behind clouds.

Fourth Stanza

In this stanza, the water acts upon a cliff. Moore underscores the force and relentlessness of the sea's actions with the verb "drives" and the repetition of "iron." Iron is meant both figuratively and literally. Figuratively, it suggests the power of the waves; literally, it describes the iron deposits on the cliff from previous waves. The sea is no longer "black jade" but "turquoise" thanks to the sun's transformative action.

Fifth Stanza

The action of the waves wreaks havoc on the sea life on the cliff, as jellyfish, crab, and starfish "slide each on the other." Moore describes sea life here as land life—lilies, toadstools, grains, rice. Her precise descriptions of these animals highlight the sea's fecundity, reminding readers that all life came from the sea. The profusion of colors in this stanza marks it as the visual center of the poem. Also, it is interesting to note that, apart from the last stanza, this is the only stanza that does not run over to the next. After spending five stanzas describing the movement of the sea, Moore spends three commenting on that movement.

Sixth Stanza

The "abuse" comes from the waves' repeated striking of the cliff. However, the cliff is "defiant," meaning that it stands up in the face of such abuse. As she did with the sea, Moore personifies the cliff. By using the word "external," however, Moore implies that there is something internal that may not be known.

Seventh Stanza

By making the first syllable of "accident" the first line, Moore sticks with the syllabic pattern she has established for the poem. The break also underlines the idea of an accident (in which something is broken). The list of "the physical features of / ac- / cident" are graphic. The violence of the marks also denotes human, as opposed to natural, action. Hatchet strokes, burns, and dynamite grooves all point to things done to the cliff by people who are never explicitly mentioned in the poem.

Eighth Stanza

This stanza is perhaps the most enigmatic in the entire poem. The "chasm side" of the cliff is "dead," suggesting that it might not contain sea life. However, it continues to live, evidence of its power to endure with little sustenance. The sea itself is that which "can not revive / its youth," and "the sea grows old" in the chasm. These last lines describe an interdependent relationship between the cliff and the sea, how they define and are defined by each other.

Themes

Nature

Moore's poem attests to the fact that although humanity may attempt to shape nature to fit its needs, it is ultimately a futile endeavor. Time itself effaces humanity's attempt to control nature. Moore threads images of the human world—culture—throughout the poem. In almost all cases they are negative images, suggesting the worst that human beings have to offer. In the opening stanza, she refers to the ocean's sand as "ash heaps," creating the sense, ironically, of a landscape decimated by

Media Adaptations

- Moore reads her poems on *Caedmon Treasury of Modern Poets Reading Their Own Poetry*, released by Caedmon/HarperAudio in 1980.

- Caedmon/HarperAudio also carries *Marianne Moore Reading Her Poems & Fables from La Fontaine* in 1984.

- In 1987, The Annenberg/CPB Project produced *Voices and Visions*, a series of documentaries on modern American poetry that appeared on Public Television. A segment is devoted to Moore titled *Marianne Moore: In Her Own Image*. Many libraries and video stores carry this series.

fire. Later, she describes the sun as moving with "spotlight swiftness" as it slices through the water. By comparing the sun to a man-made object (that is, a spotlight), Moore highlights not only the human drive to "know" nature but the intrusive quality of that drive. More violent images of human presence occur in the seventh stanza, where Moore lists "marks of abuse" found on the seaside cliff. These marks include "dynamite grooves, burns, and / hatchet strokes." A human being, however, appears nowhere in the poem, testament to humanity's failure to change nature and to nature's capacity to endure long after human beings have gone.

Order versus Disorder

"The Fish" symbolically illustrates humanity's desire to impose order on experience and to make meaning out of a world in flux. The very opening of the poem attests to the elusiveness of meaning as the fish "wade / through black jade." Jade is a dark stone and, used here, underscores the absence of visibility in the sea. It is so difficult to see, in fact, that the fish can become lost, figuratively, and Moore focuses instead on the mussels. The shifting subject of the poem—from fish to mussel, to light, to cliff—underscores the axiom attributed to Heraclitus, that you can never step in the same river twice. Change is constant and everywhere, and Moore's description of sea creatures colliding into

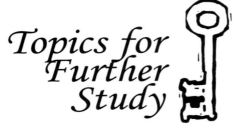

Topics for Further Study

- Research the history of the world's oceans, paying particular attention to how long certain species of fish have existed. Then pick one species and describe how it has adapted to its changing environment. What effects can be attributed to human beings (overfishing or pollution) and to natural changes (climate or non-human predators)? Report your findings to your class.

- Write a descriptive poem on some natural phenomenon other than the sea. Concentrate on describing parts of this phenomenon that echo or parallel the processes of human life. Do you find any similarities between your poem and Moore's? What are they?

- Research a local topic in which human beings are attempting to control or alter nature in some way and describe what is at stake and for whom. Possible topics might include development, pollution, and species preservation.

- Compare the first version of "The Fish" from *Poems*, which has six-line stanzas, with the later version, which has five-line stanzas. What is gained and lost in the changes? Which format do you prefer and why? Can you think of other formats that may have suited the poem better?

one another in the fifth stanza points to the impossibility of "fixing" the world in place or time. Instead of human-made order, the sea, and by extension all of nature, has its own order that, in Moore's poem, is ever changing and inscrutable to human beings, regardless of their desire to understand it.

Style

Syllabic Verse

"The Fish" is written in rhymed syllabic verse: organized in eight five-line stanzas, the poem is rhymed a-a-b-b-c. The syllabic pattern for each stanza is 1, 3, 9, 6, 8. In addition to end rhymes, Moore uses a variety of internal rhymes including slant rhyme, off rhyme, consonance, and alliteration. The sound of her poem mimics its subject matter. In the second through fourth stanzas, for example, the "s" sound dominates, echoing the ripple and splash of water itself. Her organization of the poem into syllabic units also provides the poem with its visual shape. Like the sea it describes, the poem ebbs and flows, the number of syllables expanding and contracting with each line.

Concrete Imagery

The poem looks like it does on the page because of its syllabic structure. However, the concrete visual imagery *in* the poem constructs another "look" in readers' imaginations. Images are concrete when they refer to one of the senses. Imagism was a movement popular at the beginning of the twentieth century. Imagists rejected sentimentalism and believed that poetry should create new rhythms, use precise, clear images, and address any subject the poet desired. Other imagists writing during Moore's time include Amy Lowell, William Carlos Williams, H. D. (Hilda Doolittle), and Ezra Pound.

Historical Context

In his biography of Moore, Charles Molesworth speculates that "The Fish" was influenced by the poet's interest in color theory and in writing a poetry that was unsentimental and "critical," as opposed to flowery and expressive. Molesworth notes that, while studying at Bryn Mawr College, Moore would take out books on art and art theory and spend much of her time visiting galleries and discussing art and literature with her friends.

In the second decade of the twentieth century, when this poem was written, the world of art and literature was changing dramatically. Taking the lead from painters Paul Cézanne and Georges Seurat, Pablo Picasso and Georges Braque experimented with increasingly more abstract compositions. Their cubist paintings broke down a subject, analyzed it, then reconstructed it in abstract form. Picasso's painting *Les Demoiselles d'Avignon*, considered by many to be the first Cubist painting, depicted five nude women in an angular and distorted way, destroying the continuity of the human body and creating an almost three dimensional ef-

Compare & Contrast

- **1920:** Grand Canyon National Park is dedicated.

  1980: Environmental and conservationist groups find that, over the last 200 years, the lower 48 states have lost an estimated 53 percent of their original wetlands.

  Today: Before leaving office, President Clinton signs a parks bill designed to protect lands in forty-one states, including the Presidio in San Francisco, the country's oldest continuously operated military post.

- **1921:** U.S. President Harding issues an executive order transferring management of the Navy's emergency oil field deposits at Teapot Dome to the Department of the Interior. The deal is thought to be a win-win situation, allowing developers to profit from the oil while setting aside part of it in reserve for naval emergencies.

  1980: The price of crude oil peaks at thirty-six

dollars per barrel as the Organization of Petroleum Exporting Countries exercises its power to control oil production.

Today: President Bush pushes to open Alaska's pristine Arctic National Wildlife Refuge for oil drilling.

- **1920:** The Nineteenth Amendment gives American women the right to vote.

  1984: Congress passes the Women's Economic Equity Act in 1984, which ends pension discrimination against women, provides job options for displaced homemakers, and enables homemakers to open Individual Retirement Accounts (IRAs).

  Today: The Supreme Court rules that college athletics programs must actively involve roughly equal numbers of men and women to qualify for federal support.

---

fect. Cubism, and other art movements such as futurism, surrealism, and dadaism have since become part of the history of modernism itself, their emergence both effect and cause of how human beings perceived the world. The reconfiguration of space in the new art was part of the changing ideas of time and space in the early part of the century. In America, Daylight Savings Time, radio, shorter work weeks, and the explosion in the number of automobiles on the streets all helped to create the sense of a much smaller world, yet one that was moving faster. Albert Einstein provided the theoretical foundation for thinking about this new world when he published what became known as the theory of relativity in a series of papers in the first fifteen years of the twentieth century. Einstein's theories dramatically altered ideas about time, space, and gravitation by challenging the Newtonian physics upon which so much science was built.

Poets responded to the changing world by rethinking what was possible in verse. In the second decade of the century, Wallace Stevens, Ezra

Pound, and T. S. Eliot all published works that would launch their reputations as distinctly modern poets interested in exploring new forms and subject matter. Moore herself was part of the move away from emotionalism and convention in poetry and towards a more precise description of the physical world that was dense with images and borrowings from other texts. Though initially she had little success in publishing with established magazines, she was successful with smaller, newer journals such as *Poetry*, established in 1912; the *Egoist*, a magazine of imagist verse; and *Others*. Moore was influenced as much by her study of biology and histology in college as she was by other writers. Joseph Parisi, writing in *Voices and Visions Viewer's Guide*, quotes Moore as saying this about the creative process: "Precision, economy of statement, logic employed to ends that are disinterested, drawing and identifying, liberate—at least have some bearing on—the imagination." Moore's success in the smaller journals and her correspondence with Eliot, Stevens, Williams, and Pound helped her to acquire the editorship of the *Dial*, a prestigious literary journal of the 1920s. Her four-year tenure there solidified her reputation as someone with discriminating taste and critical acumen, a reputation that would only grow in the years to come.

Critical Overview

"The Fish" has been a popular poem ever since its publication. Biographer Charles Molesworth notes in his book *Marianne Moore: A Literary Life* that early responders to the poem such as Moore's good friend Winifred Ellerman (also known as Bryher) considered it an example of Moore's "otherworldliness." Molesworth writes,

> Moore's poetry was increasingly to concern itself with . . . the struggles of perdurability. This subject is part of her interest in museums, in the forms of animal life, and in the intersections of nature and culture.

Critic Laurence Stapleton, writing in his book *Marianne Moore: The Poet's Advance,* makes a connection between the poem and Moore's interest in art. According to Stapleton, "The Fish" is notable "for intensity in the use of color." Stapleton, however, insists that it cannot be considered a "complex" poem. Bernard Engel locates the otherworldliness of the poem in the image of the cliff, which he claims represents "an ideal . . . the capacity of the courageous in spirit to triumph." George Nitchie finds the poem difficult, however, noting: "a rich and controlled confusion characterizes both the poem and the method." Writing in 1977, Pamela White Hadas remains fascinated by Moore's poem, calling it "immensely powerful and bitter." More recently, Cristanne Miller praises the poem for its formal qualities, its "ability to lace words appropriately within the severe limits of . . . a logically unpredictable form." Moore's poem appears in a number of anthologies on modern poetry, most notably *The Norton Anthology of Modern Poetry*, signalling its continued popularity.

Criticism

Chris Semansky

Semansky publishes widely in the field of twentieth century poetry and culture. In the following essay, he considers how Moore's poem is both a Romantic poem and a modern one.

Presented as a description of the sea's power and beauty, "The Fish" presents a Romantic subject in a modern way. Like so much Romantic poetry, it deifies nature; however, with its hard-edged imagery, its shifting subject, and its odd syllabic construction, it belongs to modernism. Occupying the middle ground between these two "isms," Moore's poem is a bridge of sorts between new and old ways of thinking about nature.

Writing some two hundred years ago, Romantic poets such as William Wordsworth represented humanity's response to the grandeur of nature as one of awe and terror. This feeling is called the sublime. In 1757, Edmund Burke drew a distinction between the sublime and the beautiful in his treatise *A Philosophical Inquiry into the Origin of Our Ideas of the Sublime and the Beautiful.* Burke argues that the sublime is one of the most powerful human emotions and links it to ideas of infinity; beauty, he argues, belongs to the temporal, finite world. For Wordsworth and other Romantics, experiences of the sublime come out of immersing oneself in the processes of nature, melding with the object beheld. This is different than simply observing nature's beauty. In the former experience, one participates in nature; in the latter, one is merely a tourist, marveling at the sites.

In her poem, Moore simultaneously underscores humanity's distance from the natural world and its participation in it. Like the adjustment one of the mussel shells makes in the first two stanzas, Moore's narrator adjusts her own gaze throughout the poem, as her "eye" shifts from sea to land to sea again. This searching but thwarted desire to know the sea highlights both humanity's drive to be lord of creation and nature's essentially mysterious and transcendent quality, its "unwillingness" to be dominated. The split between nature and humanity is evident in the poem's metaphors, which underline the incapacity of words to adequately name the natural world. Moore's speaker cannot describe the sea without comparing it to human-made things. Comparing natural processes or actions of the sea to "ash heaps," "injured fans," and "spotlights" demonstrates that the narrator is locked within the human world of perception, though she tries to break free from it and be a part of nature's processes.

The speaker's attempts to break free of the human world can be seen in the sympathetic description of the sea and, later, the seaside cliff. Moore presents both as objects that have been acted upon by malicious human forces. The seaside cliff, appearing in the last three stanzas, shows "marks of abuse," though those marks are also described as "ac- / cident[s]." Moore doesn't attempt to reconcile this apparent contradiction; rather, she focuses on the cliff's ability to withstand any and all assaults, to persevere *even in death*. Moore personifies the cliff by calling it "defiant," and she also martyrs it, giving the cliff a kind of supernatural identity, a common poetic gesture in Romantic poetry. The cliff endures beyond all earthly limits. After writing that the "chasm side is / dead," the speaker states, "Repeated / evidence has proved that it can live / on what can not revive / its youth. The sea grows old in it." Critics grapple with the meaning of these last lines, some calling them incomprehensible. How should readers understand the youth of the chasm side? And to what does "what" refer? These vague references and obscure descriptions only highlight the natural world's inscrutability. There is a moral in Moore's poem, but what is it? Moore scholar Taffy Martin asks:

> Why does the sea, clearly the most active and powerful force in this scene, grow old within this teeming shelter? Moore not only does not answer these questions, she does not even admit that she has asked them. The poem pretends that it works visually, whereas it should warn readers that images in poems are not always what they seem to be.

Obscurity itself became a hallmark of modern poetry. Poets such as Wallace Stevens and T. S. Eliot, though widely celebrated in literary circles, were often considered elitist, their work dense with allusions and full of poetic techniques that were beyond the ken of the average reader, if there ever were such a creature. Moore certainly became a part of this tradition, though her work was never seen as elusive as that of either Stevens or Eliot. Indeed, she is considered to be one of the more accessible of America's modern poets. But by writing a poetry that, in many cases, didn't even look like poetry, and by constructing poems whose subject was the form of the poem itself, Moore helped to change the way people read poetry and thought about their surroundings.

Just as the sublime became a staple of Romantic verse, changes in human perception became a staple of modern poetry. Moore contributed to that in her acute observations of the natural world and her visual display of poems. "The Fish," for example, a rhymed syllabic poem, uses a rigidly fixed form to describe organic natural processes. However, connections can be made between the two. For example, from the first to the second stanza, Moore runs over the words "an / injured

> *The speaker's attempts to break free of the human world can be seen in the sympathetic description of the sea and, later, the seaside cliff. Moore presents both as objects that have been acted upon by malicious human forces."*

fan." Visually, this looks like the very thing she describes. Similarly, the dominance of particular sounds helps to draw attention to her subject. The "k" sounds throughout the seventh stanza, for instance, give the poem a choppy and rough sound as well as look. This is appropriate for describing an edifice that has literally been attacked and scarred by the violent sea that surrounds it. Ultimately, the artificiality of the form for its subject asks readers to more carefully consider *how* the poem says what it does. This technique helps focus readers' attention on the relationship between sea and cliff, rather than on any one thing. By doing so, readers see the interrelationships of all things and processes in the natural world: animals (for example, the sea creatures); sea, sun, gravity, etc. By concentrating so much on how the poem means, rather than what it means, Moore participates in the twentieth century's obsession with epistemology, which asks the question: "How do we know what we know?"

Critic Pamela White Hadas sees in "The Fish" an allegory of sorts, a myth that Moore wrote to understand her own life's story. Hadas writes, "This strange poem is the work of a thirty-year-old woman whose rather unnervingly cool sympathies lie with a battered and violated nature. It is a poem about injury of wholeness, resentful but resigned deprivation." Ironically, Moore sees herself in this violated nature. Her attempt to understand it is also an attempt to understand herself and her relationship to the natural world. That her attempt results in both insight *and* confusion attests to its success. In the end readers understand that it is not a question of whether or not human beings are part of or separate from nature, but rather to what extent are we part of and separate from it? By focusing on the process of knowing as well as its product, Moore creates a distinctly modern poem from a conventionally Romantic subject.

Source: Chris Semansky, Critical Essay on "The Fish," in *Poetry for Students*, The Gale Group, 2002.

Jerrald Ranta

In the following essay, Ranta examines Moore's "The Fish" and her other "sea" poems, emphasizing the role of the wave and rhythm in her poetic expression.

Marianne Moore's poetic depiction of the sea offers special challenges to her readers. For one, there is a disparity between the largeness of the subject "the sea" and the specificity of Moore's formal methodology in treating it; the connection between the two is subtle and generally difficult to apprehend. We see this when we realize that, despite the attention given to her poems of the sea, we are left with an interesting, unanswered question: What is Moore's sea as sea and as poetic construction? For a second, no single verbal formulation seems satisfactory for the many features of the sea that Moore treats when she writes about it. Her focus is constantly shifting and the reader is hard pressed to keep up with her. In "The Fish," for instance, she successively glimpses so many things—the fish, water like black jade, an injured mussel, barnacles, a wave, the sunlight, a cliff, etc.—that she hardly seems to be writing about the sea itself. Indeed, of this poem Bonnie Costello says, "We are not interested in the sea as such." (As we shall see below, however, this is not the case.) Finally, the challenge derives in part from Moore's method, which is sufficiently subtle and mystifying that she is sometimes able to represent the sea formally even if she is not saying anything directly about it in the content of the poem. This is the case in "Sojourn in the Whale," which—as far as I can tell—has not hitherto been recognized as being significantly about the sea, among other things. No doubt related to the difficulties of reading Moore's poems in general, such things almost convince one that her sea is inaccessible.

Faced with such difficulties, it has proven expedient for Moore's critics to generalize her sea and, all too often, to settle for assigning abstract and/or symbolic meanings and values to it. Bernard Engle, for example, says that "in 'The Fish' the sea [is] a challenge and threat, a symbol of forces to be resisted with bravery and independence. The ever-present perils of existence are the subject of her poem on the sea, significantly entitled 'A Grave.' In it the sea is beautiful, tempting, and challenging. But it concedes nothing; it is totally inhuman; and, more than impersonal, it is malign." And George Nitchie says that "the sea in 'A Grave,' 'Novices,' or 'The Fish' . . . exempli[fies] the essential nonhumanness of the nonhuman." Finally, without trying to assimilate all of the tags put on Moore's sea in the various discussions of this or that poem, we can note that Pamela White Hadas has reached the furthest in trying to grasp Moore's writing about the sea as a subject possessing larger meanings and values. For Hadas, Moore's sea is many things—"an image of language," an analog of "all that has been written before one," an example of freedom gained by surrendering, an analog for "unconscious force," an analog for poetry itself, and even an analog for Moore's conversational style.

It is not that Engle, Nitchie, Hadas, and others who have taken this approach are wrong in their choice of labels. Rather, it is that they do not show us exactly what it is that Moore treats when she writes of the sea—what her sea is as sea—nor how she constructs it. There is need for further analysis and elucidation in this connection. In particular, it is important to note that, whether Moore writes about the sea at length or alludes to it in passing, the central thing she keeps returning to is the wave—water rising or surging. Sometimes the wave breaks, "turn[s] and twist[s]", and there is even the "drama of water against rocks," but her recurring point of focus is the wave. Moreover, her wave is generally built up by an accumulation of small, measured, formal units. Geometric patterns are at the heart of the representation of water in motion in all four of her extended sea-poems, although they are more pronounced—and apparently more crucial to her sense of how to represent a wave—in "Sojourn in the Whale," "The Fish," and "A Grave," than in "Novices." They are also evident in the poems where she treats the sea less lengthily. Finally, these patterns are generally consistent with Moore's notion of prosody. "Prosody," she says, "is a tool; poetry is 'a maze, a trap, a web'—Professor Richards' epitome." Of importance here are the metaphors of maze, trap, and web, for Moore's prosody is often complicated by the extension of syntactical structures into geometric patterns.

More often than not, Moore's geometric waves are couched in syntactical constructions—

particularly, the sentence—and in manipulations of a sequence of sentences, rather than in line and stanza arrangements. In keeping with her own sense of her work, the shape and rhythm of her waves is "governed by the pull of the sentence"; the rhythm is "built in" the sentence. As the analyses below will show, we begin to understand her work with water in the sea-poems better, and to understand the poems themselves better, when we examine their sentences. Then we discover that her sentences—what she does in them individually and with them collectively—are not only syntactic but prosodic undertakings. They are more or less loosely measured units whose lengths and masses and movements she manipulates—often syllabically—for the purpose of creating and shaping space, motion, rhythm, and design. Relevant here is W. S. Merwin's observation that, "in a world of technique," which is at least a partially accurate description of Moore's world in the sea-poems, "*motions* tend to become methods" (his italics). This handling of the sentence (or any syntactical unit) as a syllabic *unit of motion* would seem to constitute a new—a modern—variation of syllabic metrics.

Then, too, particularly among the four sea-poems, Moore's waves are more often than not prosodically or formally implied rather than directly described or stated; the action—the rhythm—is deemed sufficient in itself without the reiterated statement of wave as subject. The statement might treat something else—the fate of Ireland, the repetitive movements of an injured mussel, the grave-like nature of the sea, the failings of certain "good and alive young men." Nevertheless, the formal implication of wave brings meaning into the poem. This is deliberate, according to principle: "With regard to form," Moore wrote in 1934, "I value an effect of naturalness and feel that the motion of the composition should reinforce the meaning and make it cumulatively impressive." "An effect of naturalness" and "the motion of the composition": in large part, this is what her wave-making is about; hers is something of a craftish wave, an aesthetic wave.

This quality notwithstanding, in "The Fish" and "A Grave" there is a definite attempt to give the movement and rhythm of the poem over as much as possible to the naturalistic action of the sea. The same holds true for "Sojourn in the Whale" and "Novices." Indeed, one could argue that the attempt to do this increasingly dominates the four poems as a sequence—a sequence that runs from "Sojourn in the Whale" (1917) to "The Fish" (1918) to "A Grave" (1921) to "Novices" (1923).

> *In 'The Fish' and 'A Grave' there is a definite attempt to give the movement and rhythm of the poem over as much as possible to the naturalistic action of the sea."*

What is being pursued in this sequence is the effect of contact with, or a verbal embodiment of, water-in-motion, the wave. Moreover, since Moore's chief means of achieving this effect is by formal implication as opposed to descriptive statement, we could say that her formal means—her syntax and prosody—perform a naturalistic function in these poems. With them, she makes her waves. As she said in "Things Others Never Notice" regarding one of William Carlos Williams' water passages: "With the bee's sense of polarity he searches for a flower, and that flower is representation. Likenesses here are not reminders of the object, they are it." That her main primary work with this particular naturalistic representation engaged Moore throughout four poems and over a period of some half dozen years is evidence of both the inexhaustible variety inherent in it and of the strength of her attraction to it.

The importance of the effect of contact with physical reality—and the representation thereof—cannot be over-emphasized. Insofar as the waves in the sea-poems are concerned, this is the central, recurring "truth" among all of the others; without it, perhaps the others would not be possible; certainly, they would be presented very differently from how they are. Rhythm is at the heart of this effect, the rhythm of water in motion. However, this is never the burden of the statements in the poems but the means, the vehicle, for conveying them. Again, Moore's waves are structural-metaphoric waves that speak of other things—the fate of Ireland, the rule of age-old accident over natural phenomena, the limits of "volition" and "consciousness," a language that can stand on equal terms with the potentially overwhelming forces of the physical world. Perhaps this use of metaphor is something of what Robert Duncan had in mind when he said in "Ideas of the Meaning of Form" that Moore's "metaphor is never a device but a meaningful disclosure."

In section three of "Novices," Moore comes closest to *saying* directly what she herself is doing in and with her verse about the sea, but then, that poem is not about her own work with representation but about the failings of the "good and alive young men." Nevertheless, it is the case that she succeeds where they fail. Here, too, she seems to suggest that expressing themselves well of the sea, whether as fact or as metaphor, is a test of the powers of language and art. That she kept coming back to this test, handling it differently—yet similarly—each time, suggests its importance to her. Indeed, writing of T. S. Eliot's poems, Moore says that "correspondences of allusion provide an unmistakable logic of preference," an idea that applies directly to her work with the sea, where a "logic of preference" for the geometric-syntactic-rhythmic representation of waves is displayed.

Indeed, the range of writing in which she cultivated this "preference" is larger than the poems. In her unpublished notebooks and in her criticism, Moore frequently refers to the sea and to writing about it. Of the former, Bonnie Costello says that Moore's "notebooks are filled not only with long, detailed presentations of 'facts' but with quotations about the need for the factual in art" and that the "notebooks [are] full of passages about the sea." As for her criticism, in her reviews Moore's discussion of her contemporaries' writing frequently includes illustrative quotations from their work that pertain to the sea, or to water in other bodies and forms, and these are often associated with the notion of the value of faithful, effective representation of physical reality. The comment cited above regarding one of Williams' water passages is an excellent example of this kind of thing. Such observations are critical-theoretical echoes of what she herself is engaged with in the sea-poems. They constitute another form as well as further instances of the "correspondences of allusion [that] provide an unmistakable logic of preference"—a "logic of preference" for a certain event in the experience of natural phenomena, for a certain rhythm and subject matter in writing, for a certain kind and quality of representation, for a certain moment in the act of writing, for a certain moment in the act of reading.

On first reading, the statement that "correspondences of allusion provide an unmistakable logic of preference" might seem flat and mechanical. Reflecting on it, however, we realize that "cor-respondences" are not identical but diverse and that a "logic of preference" that would either satisfy or describe Marianne Moore would not be rigid and closed but variable and open. Reconsidering, then, that Moore presented the combination of the principle of representation and water-in-motion in various ways in her writing over the years, we begin to notice a quality of this writing in general that is important to her work with waves in the sea-poems. This is its projective transformational quality—the fact that over a period of several years it variously depicts and embodies and represents something (water-in-motion, in general, and waves, in particular) that, in itself, constantly changes as it exists in time and space, and in our experience of it. Now and then, this quality is expressed directly in the poems. In the words of "A Grave," "the ocean . . . / advances as usual." And in the closing lines of "Novices," there is an image of a seemingly perpetually moving ocean eternally "crashing itself out in one long hiss of spray." Or, or borrow some lines from Wallace Stevens's poem, "That Which Cannot Be Fixed," which Moore cites in the review "A Bold Virtuoso", and which work very well to describe her own sea: "there is / A beating and a beating in the centre of / The sea, a strength that tumbles everywhere." These are all images of something that, the longer it stays the same, the more it changes: the inexhaustible variety of forms in flux that waves, or the sea in motion, take. And for Moore, the proper rendering of this matter seems to have required a new and slightly different reenactment of its wave-ness, along with others of its recurrent actions, each time she came to it. Hence, the projective-transformational quality of the sea-poems—the sense that they constitute a sequence of representations of waves projected through four transformations. This quality is visible in the poems at least partly in the different prosodic-syntactic ways in which they embody waves, in their different geometrical features, and perhaps even in their different tones and points of view and subjects and larger meanings. Moreover, it allows us to recognize that in each of the poems a wave is "held up for us to see," that in each of them the sea "advances as usual," and that in each of them there is abundant evidence in both form and content of that "strength that tumbles everywhere." In short, it allows us to see in these poems a great deal of the uniformity in variety, and variety in uniformity, that is a fact of the sea. But, as an illustration of these ideas, let me make a few observations about three of the sea-poems—"Sojourn in the Whale," "The Fish," and "A Grave."

Initially, Moore pinpoints her interest regarding the sea and water in "Sojourn in the Whale" (1917) as "water in motion." But while the statement of subject is general, the prosodic and formal construction that embodies the activity of "water in motion" is specific and detailed; in particular, the last few lines of the poem are made to do what they say. The effect is as if obstructed water suddenly rose "automatically." A major source of this effect, a pivot or reversal mechanism is built around the penultimate sentence of the poem: "Water in motion is far / from level." Structure and rhythm and meaning pivot geometrically around this sentence.

Visually and prosodically, the effect of the last stanza is like that of a wave or a swell, first building and spreading, then overflowing at the end. This effect is paralleled in the pattern achieved with the lengths of the six sentences in the poem. There is a fairly regular reduction of the number of syllables per sentence—from sentence to sentence—through the pivotal fifth sentence. Then, in the last sentence—in accord with the idea of obstructed water suddenly rising "automatically" and surprisingly, the syllable count per sentence suddenly increases, approximately to what it was in the fourth sentence. At the same time, this effect is further particularized by variations in the syllable-counts (the lengths) of—and by the pauses among—the phrases and clauses of the last three sentences. Altogether, these things take us past the pivot so that we experience the lift as Moore's "water in motion" "rise[s] automatically." The implication is that the rising of the water, and the formal building capable of reenacting it, continues after the ending of the poem. This work in and with the six sentences makes the effect of the poem, and illustrates something of what Moore meant when she remarked to Donald Hall that she was "governed by the pull of the sentence." To repeat, this is a key notion with respect to all of the sea-poems.

What Moore did in "Sojourn in the Whale" was to reenact the movement of a trough followed by a mounting swell or wave. This is to say that she gave the rhythm of the poem over to the embodiment of that action. Similarly, her concern in "The Fish" (1918) was to reenact the action of a wave as it builds, crashes into a cliff, then recedes. Again, too, the mechanisms that give the poem over to the activity of the sea are caught up in the syllabics, the syntax, and a geometrical formal design.

We sight the line of the wave, so to speak, if we notice the relative syllabic lengths of the seven sentences in the poem. There are 6, 28, 57, 49, 54, 20, and 6 syllables per sentence. The design embodied here becomes more obvious if the sentences are typed out at full length across an extrawide page; then they make a visual pattern that looks like this:

```
Sentence 1: ———.
        2: ——————————————.
        3: ————————————————.
        4: ——————————————————.
        5: ————————————————————.
        6: —————————.
        7: ———.
```

Syllabically, or visually, this is a palindromic pattern in that, like a palindrome (*e.g.,* deified), it starts at a certain point (sentence 1), progresses through a series of steps (sentences 2 and 3) to a middle point (sentence 4), then reverses itself and progresses backwards through the aforementioned series of steps (sentences 5 and 6) to its beginning point (sentence 7). In both form and content, sentences one through three incorporate the approaching-building of the wave. The fourth or middle sentence—slightly shorter than the ones on either side of it—likewise incorporates the impact of the wave on the cliff and the subsequent backwash. And sentences five through seven, whose content is not directly about the wave, formally present the receding-diminishment of the wave. Like a similar pattern in her poem "To a Chameleon," this wave is illustrative of Moore's self-proclaimed liking of symmetry.

Like the pattern among the sentences of "Sojourn in the Whale," this wave is not an incidental feature of the poem but the very essence of its heard, formal design—the primary shape of the sound and rhythm that address the ear. Moore's remark that she was "governed by the pull of the sentence" is especially relevant here. The individual and cumulative "pull" of the seven sentences of the poem is this wave; to read the poem properly is—among other things—a matter of recognizing and accounting for the sentences as wave. In that sense, the whole poem is a process of wave-building, wave-impacting, and wave-diminishing, which should not be ignored. Nor should it matter that only two of the seven sentences (three and four) directly refer to and enact the wave in their content inasmuch as each of the seven sentences formally holds its own unique place in the poem; once the wave's shape and path are perceived, we see that its activity can be and is formally implied as well as directly stated. Indeed, Moore's formally implying this activity becomes another means by which she can and does allow meaning to enter the poem. We can—and apparently should—read the poem which such formally induced meaning in mind.

To do so is to recognize that—in addition to everything else they say and do—the seven sentences bespeak moments in time and locations in space germane to the approaching-building, impacting-backwashing, receding-diminishing of the wave. The changes in the lengths and masses of the sentences parallel changes in the size of the wave. Contrary to Bonnie Costello's notion that "we are not interested in the sea as such" in this poem, the poem is the story of a wave. Thus, the first sentence—*"The Fish / wade / through black jade"*—bespeaks that moment when the wave, still small, begins to take shape and that location, at some distance from the shore, where it begins to form. This sentence's elliptical, compressed quality is perhaps intended as metaphor for the power that generates the wave. In sentence two, closer to the shore and increasing in size, the wave in passing imparts motion to an injured mussel in a heap of mussels; moved by successive waves, the mussel keeps "opening and shutting itself like / an / injured fan." Still closer to the shore—and still greater in body, the wave is directly mentioned in sentence three. Now, it is perceived as carrying barnacles, and its mass and motion refract and give motion to the sunlight in the water. At the beginning of sentence four (the middle sentence), the wave is again mentioned directly—as it impacts on the cliff: "The water drives a wedge / of iron through the iron edge / of the cliff." The rest of this sentence appropriately treats the immediate backwash effect. The wave has begun to recede and diminish, and in their progressively shorter lengths and lighter masses, the remaining three sentences provide formal metaphors for the measured termination of this action. The separation between the content and the formal "pull" in these three sentences is interesting; perhaps it is intended as metaphor for the diminishing power of the wave. The poem does not resolve the observations and apparent paradoxes of the last three sentences but recedes out of them with the wave. The last sentence suggests a lifted gaze and a look at the broad expanse of the sea—at a distance in space from the shore—and, unlike the highly compressed first sentence, it makes a general statement about the sea as a whole: "The sea grows old in it." Appropriately, this expansive but weary-sounding statement parallels the disappearance of the wave.

"A Grave" (1921), the next extended sea-poem Moore composed, has no tightly constructed syllabic stanzas like the two preceding poems but is all of a piece in free verse, and while it too possesses geometrical qualities of design, it lacks the neat, symmetrical kind of form of "The Fish." Perhaps Moore was interested in giving a poem over still further to the naturalistic action of water in motion, and sought a different way to do this in the syntactic manipulations, the free verse, and the less rigid structuring of "A Grave." Be that as it may, the poem conveys a greater sense of the threatening, unpredictable, indifferent nature of the sea in relation to human life than does "The Fish."

Subtle though they are, the geometrical formal features of "A Grave" are crucial to the poem, and have to do with the way in which Moore creates and utilizes space in it. For instance, the poem is divided into two large halves of eleven lines each by lines one and twelve, which are syllabically the same (7 syllables) and are the two shortest lines in the poem. These halves are used differently, the first dominated by stasis and the second by action, motion. Among the ideas of the poem, the stasis of the first half, which is characterized by the standing, looking, and wearing of a look of the man who has taken the view from others, is synonymous with the "volition" and "consciousness" mentioned in the last line, while the action or motion of the second half, which is characterized by the activities of the fishermen, the wrinkles, the birds, the tortoise shell, and the ocean itself, is synonymous with the "turn[ing] and twist[ing]" mentioned in that line. Altogether, Moore transforms the space in stasis of the first half of the poem into the space in motion of the second half, simultaneously giving the movement and rhythm of the poem over to the inhuman action of the sea.

An important element of this undertaking is a building-pattern that goes from less to more in the measures of the poem. With line lengths varying between 7 and 24 syllables in the poem, there is no clear dividing point between long and short lines. Rather, counting syllables per line, we notice that the first half is dominated by shorter lines and the second half by longer lines, with a syllable difference between the two halves of 168 syllables (first half) and 197 syllables (second half). An important part of this building, the last eight lines are some of the longest in the poem, both sonically and syllabically. The building is also reflected in the lengths of the four sentences of the poem, which contain 68, 67, 92, and 138 syllables, respectively—another instance of Moore's working with "the pull of the sentence." Necessarily, the effect of the shorter lines of the first half of the poem, together with the first two shorter sentences, is synonymous with the stasis and the "volition" and "consciousness" of that half, while the effect of the longer lines of the second half, together with the last two longer sentences, is synonymous with the action or motion—essentially, the "turn[ing] and twist[ing]"—of that half. This is to say that a characteristic effect of the whole poem is generated at its very beginning by the transition from the first line (a shorter line) to the second line (a longer line). You can hear the stasis of the first line give way to the "turn[ing] and twist[ing]" of the second line: "Man looking into the sea / taking the view from those who have as much right to it as you have to it yourself." Significantly, the second half of the poem begins with two pairs of lines which repeat this pattern and effect twice—in itself a building or increase.

In general, if the purpose of the building in the poem is to increase the space in the lines and sentences toward the end of the poem, then the use of this space is to increase both the allusions to the sea's dangerous nature *and* the reenactment of its inhuman activity. We see Moore creating and using space in this way, when we look at what she does inside her sentences. This is still another aspect of her work with "the pull of the sentence" in this poem. In several respects, the key point of her sentences—at least the first three of them—is their middles, and what she does there.

In the first one, the line, "it is human nature to stand in the middle of a thing," is both the middle line and the middle clause of the sentence. It is also syllabically at the middle of the sentence, with 27 syllables before it and 26 after it. Not only is it a line whose content emphasizes standing in the middle of things, but it stands in the middle of things itself. Moreover, near or at its middle—and therefore at the middle of the sentence—is the infinitive "to stand," which is the syllable and word middle not only of the line but of the whole, centered and balanced sentence. Then, immediately after this centering of things—and the effect of stasis that comes with it—we have the exception which undercuts it (my emphasis): "*but* you cannot stand in the middle of this; / the sea has nothing to give but a well excavated grave." At this point, with this first reference to the inhuman nature of the sea, the poem suddenly opens up—expands—to include the terrible consequences of someone's tumbling into that "turn[ing] and twist[ing]" grave. Or, to put it differently, the shift from less to more space, from stasis to motion, from "volition" and "consciousness" to the mindless "turn[ing] and twist[ing]" of the sea, begins here.

A similar thing happens in sentence two, where the tonally heightened exception, "repression, however," marks the line and word and syllable middles of the sentence, and initiates the expansion of the sentence and a repetition of the aforementioned shift.

Things change subtly in sentence three, which is—suddenly—a longer, more spacious sentence. While a colon marks the line middle of this sentence, dividing it into two three-line units, there is no stated exception that generates space here, and the word and syllable middles, which come in the line after the colon, do not seem to matter very much tonally or quantitatively. However, with the abrupt quality of extension signaled by the colon, there is a sense that additional space is simply taken, assumed—as if the sea-grave suddenly opened up beneath one. Moreover, allusions to the threatening, grave-like sea, and (implicitly) embodiment of the sea's action into the rhythm of the poem, are not reserved for the second half of the sentence but pervade the whole thing. In both content and syntax, the poem's embodiment of the nature and action of the sea increases.

The increase continues in sentence four, which abruptly assumes still more space to itself. With no particular tonal or quantitative or descriptive emphasis placed on its middle—certainly no strong emphasis as in sentences one and two—*all* of its seven lines treat the "beautiful" but dangerous world of the sea. The birds and the tortoise shell replace the man and the fishermen of the preceding sentences, as possible representatives of some degree of "volition" and "consciousness," but even they are subject to the power of the sea. Altogether, sentence by sentence, any human attempt "to stand in the middle" of things—whether the poem or the sea—is rendered increasingly impossible as, sentence by sentence, the "turn[ing] and twist[ing]" action of the sea is increasingly embodied in the poem.

The form this embodiment takes is that of an incoming wave. As Moore says in sentence four, "the ocean . . . / advances as usual." Also, as in "The Fish," the construction of the wave occurs syntactically and is formally implied rather than directly stated; it is embodied in those lines and clauses that make direct reference to the sea. The prototype of the building-mechanisms in the poem, the wave starts out small in sentence one, with one line: "the sea has nothing to give but a well excavated grave." This increases to two lines in sentence two: "repression, however, is not the most obvious characteristic of the sea; / the sea is a collector, quick to return a rapacious look". In sentence three, which is less amenable to counting in this way, the cumulative reference to the sea's nature or action is something like three to four lines. And in sentence four, if we choose to omit the lines about the birds and the tortoise shell, at least five of the seven lines embody the wave. Altogether throughout the poem, there is increasing direct reference to the sea's nature or action, and increasing formal representation of the approaching-building action of a single wave. Subtler than "The Fish" in its representation of water in motion, "A Grave" reaches further with its ability to touch the heart of the reader with the inhuman "turn[ing] and twist[ing]" of that motion or action.

Apart from the general ideas summed up earlier, the chief revelation of these analyses is the extent of Moore's work with the sentence, and with a larger, sentence-based, geometrical form, in the sea-poems. As it has been described here, this work involves at least three kinds of manipulations of the sentence: one having to do with content and/or form, including rhythm, *inside* a sentence; one having to do with the *length* of a sentence; and one having to do with the *placement* of a sentence in a geometrical sequence of sentences. These manipulations describe or apply to all of the sentences in the three poems, although some of the sentences are more striking in certain respects than others. Whatever might have been the case in the writing, all three manipulations register simultaneously in reading. It is when we examine the poems that we discern the manipulations. To mention some of the more striking sentences: in the diminishing-then-building sentence pattern of "Sojourn in the Whale," there is the pivotal fifth sentence with its important pronouncement about "water in motion." In "The Fish," there are the first and the last sentences, with their identical lengths, their contrasting contents and rhythms, and their associations with the beginning and the ending of the wave. Also in this poem, there is the brilliant middle sentence, which is slightly shorter than the sentences before and after it (a consequence of the impact), and in which the wave crashes into the cliff in the first half of the sentence, and the consequent backwash is registered in the second half of the sentence. And in "A Grave," there is the subtly centered and balanced first sentence with its attention to the middle of things—and its sudden "twist and turn," or expansion, via exception. Perhaps it is significant that these sentences all mark turning points and boundary lines (beginnings and endings). In sum:

with these manipulations, Moore implicitly and explicitly states and / or reenacts sea-water-in-motion—chiefly, waves—in the form and content of the three study poems. Among other things, this work is ample testimony to her admission that she was "governed by the pull of the sentence." At the same time, this work is an excellent illustration of Ron Silliman's observation in "The New Sentence" that

> it is at the level of the sentence that the use value and the exchange value of any statement unfold into view.
>
> As such, the sentence is the hinge unit of any literary product.
>
> Larger literary products, such as poems, are like completed machines. Any individual sentence might be a piston. It will not get you down the road by itself, but you cannot move the automobile without it.

My sense is that Moore's phrase "the pull of the sentence" refers to the same subtle complex of language and literary phenomena as Silliman's phrase "the use value and the exchange value of any statement."

Although a more thorough examination of these phenomena lies outside the scope of this essay, a crucial question that must be asked—an ideal one—is: How do the main elements of Moore's sentence in the sea-poems participate in the determination of the poems' "use value" and "exchange value"? In a highly relevant passage that focuses directly on the function of sentence elements in modern poetry, Roland Barthes characterizes modern poetry in "Is There Any Poetic Writing?" as "an explosion of words" and says that it

> destroys the spontaneously functional nature of language, and leaves standing only its lexical basis. It retains only the outward shape of relationships, their music, but not their reality. The Word shines forth above a line of relationships emptied of their content, grammar is bereft of its purpose, it becomes prosody and is no longer anything but an inflexion which lasts only to present the Word.

While this might be true for some modern poems, we are on more solid ground with the sea-poems if we take them not as "explosion[s] of words" (a questionable metaphor) but as reenactments of water activity, and if we make their sentences the focus of our reading. Taking this approach, we see that Moore does not destroy "the spontaneously functional nature of language," but that she calculatedly heightens it, or gives it more to do, by making it state and/or reenact the activity of water-in-motion. As we have seen, the syntax carries the burden of this reenactment in the content, the length, the location, the form, and the function of the sentence, individually and as a unit in a larger, geometrical form. At the same time, her "lexical basis" is given over to making images and abstract statements—and even rhythmic constructions—that complement, extend, and deepen the effect of the reenactment. So, while it is true that "grammar . . . becomes prosody" in the sea-poems, this is not done at the expense of its function but as a more complete utilization of it, and rather than reducing grammar to "an [empty] inflexion which lasts only to present the Word," it gives grammar the much more lively and demanding task of appropriately carrying rhythm and image and abstract statement. Rhythm here, we should note, is a two-sided thing, including the rhythm of wave and the rhythm of a natural speaking voice, both of which Moore achieves in the sea-poems.

We see the central role of rhythm in this context still more clearly, when we note that—at the level of the sentence as well as at the level of the poem's overall form—it is *the* basis of correspondence in the "correspondences of allusion [to the sea, which] provide [the] unmistakable logic of [Moore's] preference" for wave. (Similarly, in her criticism rhythm is the basis of her interest in many of her citations of her contemporaries' writing about the sea, or water in other bodies or forms, which I have commented on above.) As we have seen, when it comes to waves and what is done with them in the sentences and the overall forms of the sea-poems, the "allusions" might appear at times in the content, or in the form, or in both, making for some variety of "correspondences." And underlying all of them is the one thing: rhythm. Although much of the "logic of preference" has vanished with Moore because she never explained it, the one thing she did say something about is rhythm. For instance, her self-announced "passion for rhythm" is well-known, as is her statement that she preferred to think of her poems as "experiments in rhythm." These emphases take on new meaning here. Similarly, she says in "Poetry and Criticism," "Rhythm was my prime objective. If I succeeded in embodying a rhythm that preoccupied me, I was satisfied." Obviously, the wave was such a rhythm. Then, there is also her notion of a *personal* relation to rhythm: "You don't devise a rhythm," she says in "Feeling and Precision," "the rhythm is the person, and the sentence but a radiograph of personality." Finally, going a step further with respect to the possibility of a special connection between the person and the rhythm of the sea, there is her observation that, "The many water metaphors in the work of Wallace Stevens are striking evidence . . .

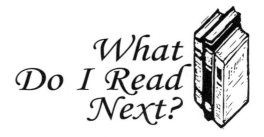

What Do I Read Next?

- Moore's collection of essays *Predilections*, published in 1955, contains essays on major poets such as Wallace Stevens, William Carlos Williams, and Ezra Pound, as well as Moore's own idiosyncratic views on poetry and nature.

- Mark Kurlansky's 1998 book, *Cod: A Biography of the Fish That Changed the World*, tells the story of the cod, a fish that contributed to the economic development of New England and contributed words such as "codpiece" to the English language. Kurlansky also includes a dozen recipes for cod dishes.

- Lyla Foggia's 1995 study, *Reel Women: The World of Women Who Fish*, explores the history of women who love to fish. Foggia's book is also an excellent resource guide listing organizations, clubs, and businesses for and about women who fish.

- Craig Lesley's novel *The Sky Fisherman* (1995), tells the story of a rugged small town Oregon family and their trials and tribulations in a sometimes harsh, sometimes beautiful landscape. The novel includes lyrical insights into the joys of flyfishing.

of his affinity—say, synonymity—with rhythm." Here she quotes the lines cited earlier from Stevens' "That Which Cannot Be Fixed"—with their unique image of wave-action: "there is / A beating and a beating in the centre of / The sea, a strength that tumbles everywhere." The evidence suggests that Moore herself possessed a similar "affinity—say, synonymity—with rhythm," one associated with the sea generally, and with waves specificially. And so, the sentences in the sea-poems are "radiograph[s] of [her] personality," and in them we find "a strength that tumbles everywhere," a strength that is hers, as well as the sea's.

Source: Jerrald Ranta, "Marianne Moore's Sea and the Sentence," in *Essays in Literature*, Vol. 15, No. 2, Fall 1988, pp. 245–57.

Taffy Martin

In the following essay excerpt, Martin comments on contradiction and false images in "The Fish."

In "The Fish," for instance, Moore employs a typically intricate stanzaic pattern along with evocative, sensual language to create a scene as unfathomable as it initially seems specific. The first three sentences are clear enough. The fish "wade through [the] black jade" of a sea where "submerged shafts of the / sun … move themselves with spotlight swiftness." Nevertheless, even within those sentences, Moore has hinted at the broken vision to follow. She describes the movement of one of the "crow-blue mussel-shells" with curious indirection. The movement of the sand helps a viewer to infer rather than to observe directly the broken movement of the shells. We know only that "one keeps / adjusting the ash heaps, / opening and shutting itself like / an / injured fan." The rest of the poem develops this hint of submerged movement and emphasizes its potential for violence: "The water drives a wedge / of iron through the iron edge / of the cliff" and the cliff itself shows "external / marks of abuse," both natural and deliberately inflicted. Having developed the apparent specificity of the poem to this point, Moore dissolves the scene in a flood of ambiguity. One side of the cliff provides a sheltered pool for sea life. In describing it, Moore begins a new stanza with a new sentence, a technique which, in her poems, often foretells dissolution.

All
external
marks of abuse are present on this
defiant edifice—
all the physical features of
accident—lack
of cornice, dynamite grooves, burns, and
hatchet strokes, these things stand
out on it; the chasm side is
dead.
Repeated
evidence has proved that it can live
on what it can not revive
its youth. The sea grows old in it.

Contradiction dominates these images. "Lack of cornice," if it means a natural curve to the edge of the cliff, is certainly a physical feature of accident; but "dynamite grooves, burns, and / hatchet strokes" are just as surely not accidental. They are human interventions that "stand out" on the cliff. Thus, it should not be surprising that "the chasm side is dead." That announcement, however, makes the next two sentences entirely incomprehensible.

If the chasm side is dead, ravaged as it clearly has been by the force of the water it contains, how does it *live* on the barnacles that adhere to its surface, on the shifting mussel shells that may or may not contain live mussels, and on the rest of the sliding mass of sea life that it shelters? Finally, why does the sea, clearly the most active and powerful force in this scene, grow old within this teeming shelter? Moore not only does not answer these questions, she does not even admit that she has asked them. The poem pretends that it works visually, whereas it should warn readers that images in poems are not always what they seem to be.

Source: Taffy Martin, "Craftsmanship Disfigured and Restored," in *Marianne Moore: Subversive Modernist*, University of Texas Press, 1986, pp. 92–112.

Elizabeth Phillips

In the following essay excerpt, Phillips analyzes "The Fish," calling it "both imagist and extra-imagist."

"The Fish" (1918) are among the poems responsible for association of Moore's verse with the seminal movement of the Imagists in the pre-World War I period. She said simply, "I like to describe things."

Moore correctly insisted that she was not one of the Imagists. They, of course, had no monopoly on a tenet essential to their poetry: language "should endeavor to arrest you, and to make you see a physical thing, and prevent your gliding through an abstract process." On that basis alone, however, they could claim Moore's work. She said simply, "I like to describe things."

She was a fine descriptive poet whose keen sense of the visual and shifting images is perfected in "The Fish." The initial perspective is that of an observer looking down into the sea as she stands on the coast. The words of the title, "The Fish," run over to the opening lines:

wade
through black jade.

The typography is not mimetic, as it was for "Chameleon"; spacing, on first glance, is more jagged and seems to contradict the expectations of the movement of fish. The space between the lines, between the verb "wade" and the phrase "through black jade" (preceded by the use of the title as the subject of the poem's first verb), prevents one from darting through inattentively. The almost startling image depicts the slow motion of the fish and the stillness of the water, its resistance, color, sheen, and polish. Both literal and figurative, the image is not only powerful in itself, but prepares the reader for the poem's final subject—the "defiant edifice." The eyes move down to see crow-blue mussel shells: "one keeps / adjusting the ash-heaps; / opening and shutting itself like / an / injured fan." Again, the singular images are visually interesting and anticipate the conclusion—the seascape is both beautiful and treacherous.

The scene quickens. There is a succession of changing actions:

> The barnacles which encrust the side
> of the wave, cannot hide
> there for the submerged shafts of the
>
> sun,
> split like spun
> glass, move themselves with spotlight swiftness
> into the crevices—

The barnacles play tricks on the eyes. The sense of the water's stillness has been dissipated. Nothing is inert; the poet's eyes, the water, the light—all are fluid. The color changes; there is a "turquoise sea / of bodies." The coast is rocky.

> The water drives a wedge
> of iron through the iron edge
> of the cliff; whereupon the stars,
>
> pink
> rice-grains, ink-
> bespattered jelly-fish, crabs like green
> lilies, and submarine
> toadstools, slide each on the other.

The effect is kaleidoscopic, but the precision of the images gives one the experience of standing alongside the sentient poet. Then the action of the eyes is arrested by the wrecked ship:

> All
> external
> marks of abuse are present on this
> defiant edifice—
> all the physical features of
>
> ac-
> cident—lack
> of cornice, dynamite grooves, burns, and
> hatchet strokes, these things stand
> out on it; the chasm-side is
>
> dead.
> Repeated
> evidence has proved that it can live
> on what can not revive
> its youth. The sea grows old in it.

The ocean, the source of life, is also a place of conflict, danger, and destruction. The sense of dying life within the sea garden hovers over the poem in much the same way that a theme hovers over a Picasso painting without being articulated. The poem's final statement, "The sea grows old in it

> *She was a fine descriptive poet whose keen sense of the visual and shifting images is perfected in 'The Fish.'"*

[the damaged and deteriorating vessel]," is similar to the "barnacles which encrust the side / of the wave" in reversing the usual habit of "saying and thinking," but different in the fact that the old sea is no illusion. The complexity of the statement stimulates a meditation on time and change in "the world's body" that the dissolving images clearly define.

The typography delineates the music of the poem. On a minor scale, the hard rhymes are dominant: "wade . . . jade," "keeps . . . heaps," "side . . . hide," "pink . . . ink-," "ac- . . . lack"; but the sibilants in "keeps" and "heaps" introduce the words that also mimic the sound of the sea: "swiftness" and "crevices," "the" and "sea," "this" and "edifice." The old-fashioned word "edifice" attracts attention to itself and contrasts with "spotlight swiftness" at the same time that the language echoes the slapping and shishing of the waves. Alternations in stress patterns of syllables for pairs of rhyming words, "an" and "fan," "green" and "submarine," "all" and "external" or "dead" and "repeated" lighten the music; and the unrhymed last line of each stanza points up the subtle discordant tones. The final eye rhyme is a musical pun: "it can live / on what cannot revive . . ." The form is synonymous with the content.

The modulations of sound and images, the expressive use of space in the line and stanzaic arrangements—all work together in the contemplation of a scene to which the fish alert the observer. In the poem, Moore's vision is both imagistic and extra-imagist. By describing movement in space she was able to escape the Imagists' tendency toward stasis; this tendency was frustrating, for example, to Williams because it limited the choice and development of subjects. The major reason she was not a "pure" Imagist, however, is apparent in the "vivid exposition consonant with the best use of metaphor," as Moore said of Eliot's verse. Fascinated as she was with the visual object and the phenomenal world, she always respected the natural shapes, colors, textures, and autonomous physical values of what she saw. In this she was like the modern painters she admired, was aligned with Williams, and was not a visionary or mystic; but her penchant for exposition was strong and seldom denied in the poems, as the commentary beginning with "All" in "The Fish" indicates.

Source: Elizabeth Phillips, "The Art of Singular Forms," in *Marianne Moore*, Frederick Ungar Publishing Co., 1982, pp. 21–68.

Sources

Abbott, Craig S., *Marianne Moore: A Descriptive Bibliography*, University of Pittsburgh Press, 1977.

Burke, Edmund, *A Philosophical Enquiry into the Origin of Our Ideas of the Sublime and Beautiful: And Other Pre-Revolutionary Writings*, edited by David Womersley, Penguin USA, 1999.

Engel, Bernard F., *Marianne Moore*, Twayne Publishers, 1989.

Foggia, Lyla, *Reel Women: The World of Women Who Fish*, Beyond Words Publishing Company, 1995.

Hadas, Pamela White, *Marianne Moore: Poet of Affection*, Syracuse University Press, 1977.

Martin, Taffy, *Marianne Moore: Subversive Modernist*, University of Texas Press, 1986.

Miller, Cristianne, *Marianne Moore: Question of Authority*, Harvard University Press, 1995.

Molesworth, Charles, *Marianne Moore: A Literary Life*, Atheneum, 1990.

Moore, Marianne, *Predilections*, Viking, 1955.

Nitchie, George W., *Marianne Moore: An Introduction to the Poetry*, Columbia University Press, 1969.

Parisi, Joseph, *Voices and Visions Viewer's Guide*, American Library Association, 1997.

Stapleton, Laurence, *Marianne Moore: The Poet's Advance*, Princeton University Press, 1978.

Further Reading

Allen, Frederick Lewis, *Only Yesterday: An Informal History of the 1920's*, HarperPerennial Library, 2000
    Originally published in 1931, *Only Yesterday* traces the rise of post–World War I prosperity up to the Wall Street crash of 1929 and against the backdrop of flappers, Prohibition, and the rise of the women's suffrage movement.

Molesworth, Charles, *Marianne Moore: A Literary Life*, Atheneum, 1990.
    Molesworth's biography is the best so far on Moore's life. Using Moore's correspondence and diaries, he deftly makes connections between the poet's work and her life.

Stapleton, Laurence, *Marianne Moore: The Poet's Advance*, Princeton University Press, 1978.
    Stapleton's critical study of Moore's poetry contains a good deal of biographical information, and makes connections between her work and other poets and poetry. This is a very accessible study.

Incident in a Rose Garden

Donald Justice
1967

Donald Justice included "Incident in a Rose Garden" in his 1967 collection of poems, *Night Light*, and revised the poem for his *Selected Poems*, published by Atheneum, in 1979. Unlike most of Justice's other poems, "Incident in a Rose Garden" tells a story. The three characters, the Gardener, the Master, and Death, play out a familiar scene in which Death, whom Justice describes in stereotypical fashion as adorned in black and being "thin as a scythe," mistakes the identity of one character for another. The language is simple, yet formal, the dialogue straightforward, the theme clear: Death may come when least expected; live life with that thought in mind. Other themes addressed include the relationship of human beings to nature, self-deception, and fate versus self-creation. In its use of stock characters and situation and its obvious moral, the poem resembles a medieval allegory.

In the revised version of "Incident in a Rose Garden," Justice moves from an objective point of view, which contains only the dialogue of the characters, to a first person point of view in which the Master relates the story. This change allows for a more detailed description of the Gardener and Death and gives the surprise ending more bite. The relationship between a consciousness of death and an appreciation of life is a theme in Wallace Stevens's poetry, which Justice notes as a primary influence on his own writing. Justice dedicates the poem to poet Mark Strand who, like Justice, writes about the presence of death in everyday life and the ways in which the self responds to and is shaped

Donald Justice

by that presence. Strand was a student of Justice's at the University of Iowa.

Author Biography

Donald Rodney Justice was born in Miami, Florida, in 1925 to Vascoe J., a carpenter, and Mary Ethel Cook Justice, both of whom had moved to Florida from Georgia in the early 1920s. His mother encouraged Justice's interest in the arts early in his life, providing him with piano lessons, and Justice has remained passionate about music and art throughout his life. In Miami, Justice studied with composer Carl Ruggles, one of the first professional artists he ever met, and poet George Marion O'Donnell, who taught him how to read poets such as Thomas Hardy in a new way. After earning his bachelor's degree in English from the University of Miami, Justice moved to New York City for a year before resuming his studies at the University of North Carolina at Chapel Hill, where he earned a master's degree in 1947. Although enrolled in Stanford's doctoral program for a year, Justice felt the pace of the program was too slow. He left to study in the Writing Workshop at the University of Iowa, where he received his Ph. D.

in 1954. As student and teacher, Justice has worked with many well-known writers including Yvor Winters, Robert Lowell, William Logan, Karl Shapiro, and Charles Wright. One of his students at Iowa, Mark Strand, to whom Justice dedicates "Incident in a Rose Garden," was poet laureate for the United States from 1990 to 1992.

Justice is known as a technician of poetry, an accomplished technician who describes himself as "a rationalist defender of the meters." His work is as much influenced by William Carlos Williams as by Wallace Stevens. Though critics sometimes fault his poetry for being too restrained, Justice has developed a reputation as a craftsman who has influenced a good number of younger poets. His poetic output has not been prolific, but it has been steady. His poetry collections include *The Summer Anniversaries* (1960), *Night Light* (1967), *Departures* (1973), and *Selected Poems* (1979). Justice's collection of prose and poetry, *The Sunset Maker: Poems/Stories/A Memoir*, was published in 1987, and his collection of essays, *Oblivion: On Writers and Writing* came out in 1998. In addition to writing poems, Justice has edited a number of books, including *The Collected Poems of Weldon Kees* and *Contemporary French Poetry*, and has written a libretto *The Death of Lincoln*. His awards include a Rockefeller Foundation fellow in poetry, Lamont Poetry Award, a Ford Foundation fellowship in theater, National Endowment for the Arts grants, a Guggenheim fellowship, and the Pulitzer Prize in poetry for *Selected Poems*. A professor for most of his adult life, Justice retired from the University of Florida in 1992.

Poem Text

Gardener: Sir, I encountered Death
    Just now among our roses.
    Thin as a scythe he stood there.

    I knew him by his pictures.
    He had his black coat on,   5
    Black gloves, a broad black hat.

    I think he would have spoken,
    Seeing his mouth stood open.
    Big it was, with white teeth.

    As soon as he beckoned, I ran.   10
    I ran until I found you.
    Sir, I am quitting my job.

    I want to see my sons
    Once more before I die.
    I want to see California.   15

Master: Sir you must be that stranger
    Who threatened my gardener.
    This is my property, sir.

    I welcome only friends here.

Death: Sir, I knew your father.   20
    And we were friends at the end.

    As for your gardener
    I did not threaten him.
    Old men mistake my gestures.

    I only meant to ask him   25
    To show me to his master.
    I take it you are he?

Poem Summary

Title

The title of the poem makes use of understatement in the same way as the poem. By titling the poem "Incident in a Rose Garden" instead of, for example, "Death Visits the Master," Justice creates a sense of mystery, of suspense. Readers are never told directly the significance of what is happening but must make the connections themselves. Setting the poem in a rose garden underscores the relationships among death, nature, and human beings and shows the folly of human beings in thinking that they are somehow not a part of the natural world, which includes death.

Gardener

In the first stanza of "Incident in a Rose Garden," the Gardener addresses his Master, telling him that he "encountered Death" in the garden. The Gardener recognized him "through his pictures," meaning the stereotypical ways that death has been personified in painting and illustrations: all in black and "thin as a scythe." This description evokes death's identity as the grim reaper. A scythe is an instrument with a long blade used to cut crops or grass. It belongs in a garden. The personification of death, however, is as old as humankind and forms a part of every culture. The image of Death's wide-open mouth evokes the devouring void, the very nothingness that comes with the cessation of consciousness. His teeth are predatory, and the end rhymes of "open / spoken" have a hypnotic effect. The formality of the Gardener's language belies his experience. Readers wouldn't expect someone who just encountered death to respond with such a restrained tone. It is this restraint, however, helped by the formal restraint of three-line stanzas and three-beat lines, that gives the poem its shape.

The Gardener relates his fear that Death had come for him. Readers can infer that he is quitting because he believes that he has only a short time to live. It is common for people, when told they are going to die, to put their affairs in order and to prioritize what is important to them. The Gardener wants to see his sons and to see California before he dies, which are understandable desires. The introduction of California, however, seems anachronistic for this poem, whose word choice and setting seem to predate the discovery of the New World. In this instance, California is a promised land, an exotic place of fantasy, which readers can assume the Gardener has thought about visiting before.

Master

In between dialogue, readers can assume that the Master went to the rose garden to see Death, from whom his Gardener had run. Although the Master addresses Death as "Sir," as his Gardener had addressed him, his words suggest a restrained anger. He accuses Death, whom he refers to as a "stranger," of "threatening" his Gardener, and warns him off his property, which is ironic since Death has the final say over who and what gets to live in the rose garden. The Master assumes an adversarial stance towards Death, treating him as an intruder when he tells him, "I welcome only friends

Topics for Further Study

- Interview your classmates, family, and friends about a time when they had a premonition of death. What similarities do you see in their stories?

- Justice dedicated this poem to poet Mark Strand. Read Strand's collection of poems *Darker*. Discuss similarities between the two poets' representation and awareness of death.

- Brainstorm a list of ways in which death is visually represented in contemporary art, film, writing, and culture. What gender is death? How old? Where and when does death usually appear? What can you conclude from these facts about society's relationship with death?

- Research what happens to the brain in the last minutes before death. Report your findings to your class.

- Research the stories of those who have had near-death experiences. How have these people changed their lives as a result of the experience?

- If you were told that you were going to die tomorrow, how would you spend your last day? Make an itinerary, right down to your last minute.

- Continue the poem, writing one or two three-line stanzas in which the master replies to death. Then write another stanza or two in which Death responds. Try to get as close to Justice's tone and style as possible.

here." The Master's restraint is heightened by the end rhyme of all of his lines.

Death

Death responds to the Master, telling him, ironically, that he was a friend of his father. Readers can deduce from this that the Master's father is dead. Again, the use of such understatement, a feature of the poem as a whole, is part of the formal speech of the characters and belies the significance of what is actually happening. When Death tells the Master that the reason the Gardener was afraid was that "Old men mistake my gestures," he means that older people live closer to death, believing that it may come at any moment.

In the last three lines of the poem, readers learn that Death's intention for coming to the rose garden was not to take the Gardener but to take the Master. This reversal is an example of situational irony, in which there is a contradiction between expectation and reality.

Themes

Death

"Incident in a Rose Garden" underscores the arrogance of human beings and how they mistakenly assume they are beyond the rules and processes of the natural world. The relationship between the Gardener and the Master parallels the relationship between the Master and Death. In the first relationship, the Gardener treats his Master with the deference and civility of an inferior, even though he quits his job. He comes running to the Master after he sees Death in the garden. The Master, believing that Death has come for the Gardener, in his arrogance refuses to recognize Death's power, calling him a "stranger" and telling him he is not welcome. He assumes that, because he is the owner of the rose garden, he owns death as well and can order him about the same way he orders his servants about. Such hubris is common for many who see themselves as existing separate from the natural world. Many religions warn against making oneself into a god. In the Bible, for example, Proverbs 16.18 says, "Pride goes before destruction, / and a haughty spirit before a fall." Proud human beings sometimes believe that the world somehow exists for them and not the other way around. Death's response to the Master, his measured coolness, and his own extension of "friendship" show who the real Master is, and Death, quite literally, puts the Master in his place.

Nature

The fact that Death appears in the rose garden underscores the place of death in the order of the natural world. He not only encounters the Gardener there but the Master as well, emphasizing that death's dominion is nature itself. A rose garden is a place of great beauty, but that beauty is seasonal. When the season changes, the roses wither and die. So, too, with human beings. Justice, however, shows how death can come unexpectedly and out of season. Although the Gardener is older than his Master and thinks that Death has come for him, in fact, Death has come for the younger man. A rose garden is also a cultivated place, man-made, ordered to human desire. Death's appearance upsets that order, suggesting that humanity's attempt to control nature, like the Master's attempt to order Death out of his garden, is doomed to fail. Death's confidence in the face of the Master's impoliteness, highlights this.

Style

Narrative

"Incident in a Rose Garden" is a dramatized narrative poem. Narrative poems are stories, with characters, a plot, and action, as opposed to lyric poems, which are the utterance of one speaker, often describing or explaining an emotion or thought. This poem is all dialogue and is presented from an objective point of view. This means that the narrator never intrudes to comment on the action or to explain or describe what is happening. In this way, the poem resembles a very short play. Readers have to infer from the dialogue the theme of the story. The organization of the poem into three-line stanzas, whose lines have three beats apiece, makes the work look and sound like a poem.

Personification

When ideas or inanimate things are given human qualities, they are personified. Justice personifies death by drawing on traditional depictions of death and by packing his description with symbolic imagery appropriate to the idea of death. He is dressed in black and is "thin as a scythe" and his mouth "stood open. / . . . with white teeth"—all images we associate with the grim reaper, a popular depiction of death. The Gardener and the Master obviously cannot be personifications, but they do represent two very different social strata.

Historical Context

The time period of "Incident in a Rose Garden" isn't explicit, though its themes, structure, and diction suggest the Middle Ages. Justice's poem evokes the idea of *danse macabre*, or the dance of death, a notion that grew out of Western Europe's response to the bubonic plague, which killed millions of people beginning in the fourteenth century. In paintings and poems, the allegorical concept of danse macabre depicted a procession of people from all walks of life, both living and dead. One of the earliest representations of the dance of death is in a series of paintings (1424–1425) formerly in the Cimetière des Innocents, a cemetery in Paris that was moved in the eighteenth century. These paintings depict a procession of living people from the church and state being led to their graves by corpses and skeletons. The living are arranged according to their rank so as to present an inclusive representation of humanity. This scene is meant to underscore the leveling power of death and the idea that death can come at any time. The earliest use of the term danse macabre occurs in 1376 in a poem by Jean Le Fevre. The obsession with death also found expression during this time in the morality play. Morality plays were allegories in dramatic form, performed to teach viewers the path from sin to salvation and the fragility of earthly life. Justice's poem does not include a procession like the dance of death, but it does include a personification of death and the character types of Master and Gardener, who stand for social classes, and it does emphasize the idea that death does not discriminate based on social status. A few of the more popular morality plays include *Mankind* and *Everyman*.

The rate at which the bubonic plague spread and the fact that no one knew what caused it, created a heightened anxiety and uncertainty. Theories were bandied about, including one put forth by scholars at the University of Paris, who held that a combination of earthquakes and astrological forces were responsible for the plague. Many believed that the plague was God's punishment for humanity's sins and that extreme penitence was required to appease God's wrath. Groups of people known as flagellants paraded through towns whipping themselves and criticizing the Catholic Church for not following God's law. Jews also became the scapegoat for the disease, as people frantically sought someone to blame for the epidemic. Thousands of Jews were persecuted and slaughtered by hysterical mobs during this time.

In the mid-1960s, when this poem was written, the United States was becoming more deeply involved with the war in Vietnam. Televised images of the war, including footage of dead soldiers, became a staple of the nightly news. In 1968, shortly after the Tet offensive, American photographer Eddie Adams caught a South Vietnamese security official on film executing a Viet Cong pris-

Compare & Contrast

- **1967:** The life expectancy for Americans is 70.5 years.

  Today: The life expectancy for Americans is almost 77 years.

- **1967:** International Treaty bans weapons of mass destruction from space, and the United Nations approves a nuclear non-proliferation treaty.

  Today: Arguing that rogue states could still compromise the United States security and put millions of citizens at risk during a nuclear attack, the Bush administration argues for continuing development on a national missile defense shield.

- **1967:** The World Health Organization begins a program to get rid of the smallpox virus completely, which has killed millions of people in its history. Although the virus had been stamped out in Europe and North America, it still exists in poorer regions of the world. In May 1980, WHO formally announces that smallpox has been eliminated.

  Today: More than 33 million people worldwide have been infected with the HIV virus, which can lead to Acquired Immunodeficiency Syndrome (AIDS). More than two and one half million people die from the virus.

---

oner. For Vietnam War protestors, this photograph served as evidence of the brutalities of the war and undermined American assumptions about the South Vietnamese themselves.

The presence of death and mortality is evidenced throughout *Night Light*. In 1965, Justice himself turned forty years old. "Men at Forty," one of the heavily anthologized poems from the collection, describes Justice's sentiment about this milestone, and other poems in the collection address the idea of mortality and aging and of regret for a life unlived.

Critical Overview

The collection in which "Incident in a Rose Garden" appears, *Night Light*, was Justice's second full-length collection and contains some of his best-known works, including "Men at Forty," "The Man Closing Up," and "The Thin Man." Reviewing the collection, Robert Pawlowski stresses that Justice is more than simply a technically brilliant poet but is "a good poet who is as interested in life, death, hate, love, fun, and sorrow as anyone." Noting the sadness of the poems in the volume, William Pritchard was not as flattering, writing that "the best line in the book is an epigraph" from someone else.

In *Shenandoah*, critic Joel Conarroe praises Justice for bringing "a controlled, urbane intensity to his Chekhovian descriptions of loss and the unlived life." Conarroe notes that Justice's poems "are all fairly accessible on one or two careful readings." James McMichael agrees, writing, "Justice is tightly in charge of everything that goes on within his poems, so much so that very few of them are not almost totally accessible after careful reading." William Hunt considers Justice's poem a conservative response to the often hyper-emotionalism of romanticism, writing, "Mr. Justice's poems are eloquent replies in a classical mode to the all or nothing element in romanticism. The best poems in the book are closest to this anachronistic struggle." Such a struggle expectedly contains a barely restrained tension between "message" and form. Richard Howard notes that the collection emits "a kind of vexed buzz close to the fretful."

Criticism

Chris Semansky

Semansky publishes widely in the field of twentieth-century poetry and culture. In the following essay, he considers what is gained and what is lost in Justice's revision of his poem.

Many reasons can dictate why writers revise their work after it has been published: psychological distance from subject matter, a change in aesthetics, a belief that a poem is never finished. Donald Justice is an inveterate reviser of his own writing. Like Yeats, he believes that revising is a lifelong process and that his poems can always be better. For his *Selected Poems*, Justice revised a number of poems and "Incident in a Rose Garden" substantially. The changes Justice made, however, effectively create a new poem.

The first version of the poem is written as a mini-drama. Three characters interact with one another through dialogue. No narrator intervenes to comment on the action or to describe the setting. It is a spare, elliptical poem, which succeeds because it shows rather than tells the reader what to see. The revised version changes to the master's first person point of view, adds a little explanatory apparatus to the dialogue, and deepens a secondary theme. The poem opens now with these new lines:

> The gardener came running,
> An old man, out of breath.
> Fear had given him legs.

Adding this information allows readers to see the gardener as an old man before Death mentions this fact in his own speech. It also adds action, something the previous version of the poem didn't have. Readers can see the old man running, afraid. After the gardener's words, the master says, "We shook hands; he was off." This revision tells readers that the poem is told from the master's point of view. All subsequent information must be evaluated in light of this detail. The revised version demands that readers be aware that everything they see is seen through the master's eyes. Not only does the master want others to see him as an understanding person, who can empathize with his gardener, but we must also now see Death through the master's eyes as well. The revised version prefaces the master's dialogue with these eleven lines:

> And there stood Death in the garden,
> Dressed like a Spanish waiter.
> He had the air of someone
> Who because he likes arriving
> At all appointments early
> Learns to think himself patient.
> I watched him pinch one bloom off
> And hold it to his nose—
> A connoisseur of roses—
> One bloom and then another.
> They strewed the earth around him.

These changes have several effects: they deepen the characterization of both Death and the master, and they make what was previously a sec-

> *By providing more details about Death, Justice creates a character who transcends type. He is almost a dandy here, an aesthete, with an inflated sense of himself.*"

ondary theme—the relationship of death to beauty—a primary one. By providing more details about Death, Justice creates a character who transcends type. He is almost a dandy here, an aesthete with an inflated sense of himself. But the master's psychological insight into Death's behavior also tells us something about himself. By describing Death as someone "Who because he likes arriving / At all appointments early / Learns to think himself patient," the master shows his ability to read others. This is significant because it makes the reversal at the end of the poem all the more poignant. His insight into Death's demeanor doesn't make him any less vulnerable to Death; it merely makes the fact that he is not Death's master, as he assumes, more ironic. Death's preoccupation with the roses also highlights the idea that beauty only exists because death exists. The very temporal nature of life enables people to experience beauty. Wallace Stevens, whose own poetry influenced Justice's, sums up this thought in these lines from his famous poem "Sunday Morning":

> Death is the mother of beauty; hence from her,
> Alone, shall come fulfilment to our dreams
> And our desires. Although she strews the leaves
> Of sure obliteration on our paths,
> The path sick sorrow took, the many paths
> Where triumph rang its brassy phrase, or love
> Whispered a little out of tenderness,
> She makes the willow shiver in the sun
> For maidens who were wont to sit and gaze
> Upon the grass, relinquished to their feet.

For Stevens, Death has a feminine character. "She" gives birth to beauty, to all the moments of inspiration and feeling human beings experience. For Justice, Death is a male who arrives for appointments early. He is all business, and he takes pleasure in that business. His smelling of the roses is rife with allusions and meaning. It plays off the popular saying that people should "stop and smell the roses," meaning that people should not be all about work but should take time to enjoy the good things in life. Justice's depiction of Death here also underscores Stevens's notion that without death, there could be no beauty. Like human beings, roses die.

The last revision Justice made also deepens a reader's image of Death. Before Death is allowed to speak, the master reports his depiction of it:

> Death grinned, and his eyes lit up
> With the pale glow of those lanterns
> That workmen carry sometimes
> To light their way through the dusk.
> Now with great care he slid
> The glove from his right hand
> And held that out in greeting,
> A little cage of bone.

These details are true to type. Death appears, as the gardener says, like he does in his pictures. Many of the conventional personifications of death, such as the grim reaper, depict him as an emaciated figure or a skeleton either with black hollow eyes or with eyes that burn. Personifications of death appear in almost all cultures and religious traditions. In the Judeo-Christian-Islamic world, the Angel of Death was called Azrael. Seker was the name for death in ancient Egypt. The Greek personification of death, known as Thanatos, had a twin brother, Morpheus, the god of sleep, while the Romans had Orcus, a thin, pale figure with huge black wings.

The added detail of Death reaching out to shake the master's hand links the revised version of the poem to stories about how death takes his victims. Sammael, the Angel of Death in Jewish folklore, stands above the victim's head, a sword with a suspended drop of poison at its tip, poised to strike. In other incarnations Death carries a rod of fire, a shaft of light, a knife or, like Justice's Death, a scythe. Death in Justice's poem, however, isn't violent, just matter of fact. His demeanor is gentlemanly, almost businesslike. His handshake, not his scythe, is his weapon. A significant detail in Justice's description is that Death wears gloves. Gloves are a marker of the dress of aristocrats, of people of privilege. This detail highlights the fact that Death is more like the master than not.

The revised version of the poem not only adds more information about the characters and changes the emphasis of the poem's theme, but it also establishes a more personal tone. The voice of the master knows Death more intimately, as do readers. By drawing out the encounter between the master and Death, Justice creates a kind of slow-motion scene. The "care" with which Death attempts to physically befriend the master, presages the master's own death. The problem with this revision, of course, is the same as the problem with the movies *Sunset Boulevard* and *American Beauty*: it is narrated by a dead man.

Justice himself was more than a decade older when he revised "Incident in a Rose Garden," so readers might legitimately infer that his revisions are informed, at least in part, by the writer's own experience and growing intimacy with the encroaching inevitability of death. The changes in the poem, then, reflect Justice's own creeping mortality.

Source: Chris Semansky, Critical Essay on "Incident in a Rose Garden," in *Poetry for Students*, The Gale Group, 2002.

Joyce Hart

Hart is a freelance writer of literary themes. In this essay, she analyzes the carefully chosen language that Justice uses to produce the variations in attitudes of the three main voices in his poem.

Donald Justice is often referred to as the poet's poet. This title refers to the fact that many poets know and respect his work, many of them having had him as their teacher, but few critics pay much attention to his work because he does not draw the attention of a large, general audience. Although they have won many prestigious awards, his published works are few. He is, in other words, a poet who cherishes quality over quantity. He concentrates on the specifics, carefully choosing his words, filling each one with as much meaning as possible, and then saying no more. And although his words carry much weight, they do not feel heavy. They feel quite ordinary, as a matter of fact. They feel so ordinary that the art behind them, the carefully constructed picture they display, the economy with which the few words say so much in so little time is almost lost if the poem is read only once. To do justice to Justice's work, his poems should be read several times. They should be as read as slowly as the slow, sure pace of Death in Justice's poem "Incident in a Rose Garden."

In "Incident in a Rose Garden," Justice has placed three voices: the Gardener, the Master, and Death, in juxtaposition with one another. The Gardener, the most humble of the three voices, begins the poem with the word "Sir." He is addressing his Master, although the reader does not know this until later. But, by the use of the word "Sir," the reader is immediately confronted with the concept of hierarchy. The Gardener is using very polite language, and he is probably talking to someone he considers of higher rank than himself. He quickly moves past this first word, having completed the required social convention, and by the end of the first line, the Gardener's heart is beating fast out of fear. He has, after all, just encountered Death. Justice writes this first line in language that is clear and simple. He grabs the attention of his readers just as Death has grabbed the attention of the Gardener. Justice is not writing in obscure metaphor or allusion. There is no mistaking that the Gardener has "encountered Death." This being said, the poem moves on.

The second line of this poem conjures up memories of one of the most often quoted first stanzas of poetry ever written. The stanza comes from Robert Herrick (1591–1674). The poem is titled "To the Virgins, to Make Much of Time." The lines go like this:

> Gather ye rosebuds while ye may
> Old Time is still a-flying
> And this same flower that smiles today
> Tomorrow will be dying.

Justice appears to have been thinking about Herrick's poem, for he has set his own poem in a rose garden. By doing this and without having to say anything more, Justice puts this well-established image of the rose as the symbol of life right in the face of his readers. He has stated the entire theme of his poem in two lines: the fear of death and the transitory nature of life. But the poem, of course, does not end here. Justice has much more to say.

Next, the poem goes into a description of death. It is through the description that the reader feels the racing heart of the Gardener. He is excited by the experience but not to the point of wordlessness. The phrase "Thin as a scythe" is as sharp and as threatening as a well-honed butcher's blade. But it is interesting to note that the Gardener recognizes Death not through a personal reference but rather through a picture he has seen. This removes the Gardener, at least by one step, from personal knowing. By distancing the Gardener in this way, Justice makes the Gardener somewhat less mesmerized by Death. He creates the idea, in a very well-planned way, that the Gardener has not known anyone who has died. The Gardener has not really witnessed mortality. As a matter of fact, Justice makes it sound as if this might be the Gardener's first encounter, and although it frightens him, it does not immobilize him. Instead, the Gardener's

> " *But the last joke is yet to come. And of course Justice portrays it so simply and so powerfully that the last line turns the whole poem inside out.* "

confrontation with Death has given him an instant epiphany of understanding: he does not want to waste any more time.

The difference between the picture of Death that the Gardener has seen and the image that stands before him is that Death has opened his mouth. And it is in the opening of his mouth that the Gardener sees something he had not seen in the picture: Death's mouth is big "with white teeth." Because Death is dressed all in black, these white teeth must stand out. Having Death open his big mouth and show his teeth is reminiscent of the wolf in "Little Red Riding Hood" saying, "The better to eat you with." This is no quiet picture, and neither is it a fairy tale. This is the real thing. This Death has teeth, and the Gardener is not sticking around to find out who Death is looking for.

With this thought, the Gardener then again politely addresses his Master: "Sir, I am quitting my job." And again, Justice seems to be referring back to Herrick's *carpe diem* ("seize the day") poem, for the Gardener no longer worries about his job; all he wants is to leave. He wants to do the things that he has been putting off, things that he thought he would always have time for later. And then with a little hint of comedy, Justice writes that the Gardener not only wants to see his sons, but he also wants to see California—America's version of the mythological Garden of Paradise.

With the departure of the Gardener, the first half of Justice's poem is complete. And in the next line, once again the word "Sir" is used; only this time it is spoken by the Master, and it is spoken in a voice quite a bit less humble than the Gardener's. The Master is, after all, the master. He is the master of the Gardener and the Garden itself. These are his roses (although earlier the Gardener referred to the flowers as "our roses," using this phrase to imply that he was as protective and caring of them as

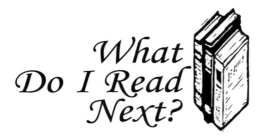

What Do I Read Next?

- Justice dedicated "Incident in a Rose Garden" to poet, friend, former student, and former Poet Laureate of the United States, Mark Strand. Like Justice, Strand frequently writes about the absence of the self and the sadness of human life. His *Selected Poems* (1979) is a good introduction to his work.

- Philip Ziegler's *The Black Death* (1998) details the plague that gripped Europe from the fourteenth to the seventeenth centuries. Ziegler notes that plague probably cost Europe between 12.5 and 70 percent of its population according to region, population density, hygiene, and other factors.

- Justice's *New and Selected Poems* (1997) updates his Pulitzer Prize-winning 1979 *Selected Poems* by changing the previous volume's selection and adding many poems written in the intervening fifteen years.

---

the Master was—except when it was time for the Gardener to make a neat and abrupt departure to save his own skin). "This is my property, sir," the Master tells Death, and you are not welcome. Why is Death not welcome here? Because he is a "stranger." How unfortunate for the Master that he does not recognize Death. Not only does he not recognize Death, he disbelieves his own gardener's recognition. What could a gardener know? He is merely a superstitious fool who is easily spooked. And Justice says all this in such few words. How does he do it?

One thing that Justice does is create a tone of voice that is filled with obvious psychological implications. For instance, the tone of his words gives away the psychology of the Master. "You must be that stranger," he says. He does not ask, "Who are you?" Neither does he ask anything else of him. Instead, he attempts to tell Death who he is, and he does this in a tone of admonishment: not only are you a stranger but you have "threatened my [note the possessive pronoun] gardener." Then the Mas-

ter more or less points out the no trespassing signs that he has posted around the periphery of his private estate, saying, "I welcome only friends here." There is a guest list implied here. This is a private club, and no one enters without the Master's permission. All this Justice says in four lines.

Now for the climax: Death also begins his part of this poem with the word "Sir." But here Death mocks not only humility but also the Master. Death knows who the real Master is, even if the Master is ignorant of his place in life's hierarchy. Death mocks the Master first with the honorific salutation; then he mocks him by turning the Master's list of friends on its proverbial head. I was a friend of your father's, Death states. "We were friends," he says, but then cleverly adds, "at the end." Here Justice makes several points: First he has Death put the Master in his place. This Master might own the garden, and he might have the right to keep anyone he chooses outside its gates, but he cannot avoid facing Death. And by using the phrase "at the end," Justice is also, in three little words, exposing the identity of Death to the Master. Another interesting thing that is going on here is that this so-called Master, who has witnessed the death of his father, does not recognize Death. Why is that, and what is Justice saying here?

Whereas the Gardener immediately recognized Death and found a way to escape, stating that he has more to do with his life and is not ready to face him, the Master is clueless. Where was the Master when his father died? Is Justice implying that the death of the Master's father was not enough to wake him up to fear Death enough to make the most of his life? Is that why the Master is caught off guard? Was his arrogance his own undoing? Did he think he could live forever? In his statement, "I welcome only friends here," is he repeating a remark that his father once said, and is that why Death counsels him with "we were friends at the end?" Was the Master's father also as arrogant as his son?

Death, in this poem, now controls the stage. He explains himself as humbly as Death can. He did not mean to frighten the gardener. "Old men mistake my gestures." This statement is close to being read as a private joke. The Gardener mistook his gestures to mean that Death was coming for him, whereas the Master mistook his gestures to mean that he was some stranger come to try to win favors. But the last joke is yet to come, and of course Justice portrays it so simply and so powerfully that the last line turns the whole poem inside out. Justice makes fools of everyone, the Master as well as everyone who reads this poem. Of course that is why Death allowed the Gardener to leave. Of course Death knew exactly what he was doing. Of course the Master did not know what was going on, but neither did any of the readers. "I only meant to ask him / To show me to his master. / I take it you are he?"

Source: Joyce Hart, Critical Essay on "Incident in a Rose Garden," in *Poetry for Students*, The Gale Group, 2002.

Sources

Conarroe, Joel O., "Five Poets," in *Shenandoah*, Vol. 18, No. 4, Summer 1967, pp. 87–88.

Howard, Richard, "Donald Justice," in *Alone with America: Essays on the Art of Poetry in the United States since 1950*, Atheneum, 1980.

Hunt, William, "The Poems of Donald Justice," in *Poetry*, Vol. 112, No. 4, July 1968, pp. 272–73.

Justice, Donald, *A Donald Justice Reader*, Middlebury College Press, 1991.

———, *Night Light*, Wesleyan University Press, 1967.

———, *Oblivion*, Story Line Press, 1998.

———, *Selected Poems*, Atheneum, 1979.

———, ed., *The Collected Poems of Weldon Kees*, Stone Wall Press, 1960.

Justice, Donald, and Alexander Aspel, eds., *Contemporary French Poetry*, University of Michigan Press, 1965.

Malkoff, Karl, *Escape from the Self: A Study in Contemporary American Poetry and Poetics*, Columbia University Press, 1977.

McMichael, James, "Justice," in *North American Review*, Vol. 252, No. 6, November 1967, pp. 39–40.

Pawlowski, Robert, Review of *Night Light*, in *Denver Quarterly*, Vol. 2, No. 2, Summer 1967, pp. 175–77.

Pritchard, William H., "Poetry Chronicle," in *Hudson Review*, Vol. 20, No. 2, Summer 1967, pp. 309–10.

Further Reading

Gioia, Dana, "Interview with Donald Justice," in *American Poetry Review*, Vol. 25, No. 1, January/February 1996, p. 37.

Justice discusses the influence of music on his poetry and comments on the proliferation of creative writing programs.

Gioia, Dana, and William Logan, eds. *Certain Solitudes: On the Poetry of Donald Justice*, University of Arkansas Press, 1998.

This book collects essays and reviews written on Justice's poetry. It remains the single best source of criticism on the poet.

Howard, Richard, *Alone with America: Essays on the Art of Poetry in the United States since 1950*, Atheneum, 1969.

This collection of essays on post–World War II American poetry by one of America's most insightful critics is useful for those who want to locate Justice's work among his contemporaries.

In the Suburbs

Louis Simpson
1963

"In the Suburbs" can be considered a representative poem of Louis Simpson's, both in subject matter and style. Following in the footsteps of his literary idol, Anton Chekhov, Simpson has fashioned a career of chronicling the mundane lives of ordinary people. However, his descriptions of middle-class life are not without thorns. Undergirding his poems about suburbia and small talk lurks a pervasive sense of gloom and despair. The very collection in which the poem appears, *At the End of the Open Road*, published in 1963 by Wesleyan University Press, is itself an extended and complicated evaluation of American society in the middle of the twentieth century. The title is a response to Walt Whitman's vision of America as a place of endless possibility, described in his poem "Song of the Open Road." Simpson considers the country a hundred years after Whitman wrote, when its geographical, and by implication spiritual, frontiers have been exhausted. Simpson asks, what's next?

"In the Suburbs" is the second poem in the collection, following "In California," a dark piece about what happens when a dream has gone bad. "In the Suburbs" is only six lines long and comprised of just three sentences, each a separate statement about the emptiness of suburban life. Using the second person "you," Simpson pronounces both the meaninglessness of this existence and the futility of attempting to escape. In its evocation of a life that needs to be changed, it echoes both Rilke's poem "Archaic Torso of Apollo" and James

Wright's poem "Lying in a Hammock on William Duffy's Farm in Pine Island, Minnesota." Statement poems like these are frequently anthologized because they are short and considered "easy" to understand. "In the Suburbs" is no exception, having appeared in a number of introductory poetry texts, including *The Norton Anthology of Modern Poetry* and Michael Meyer's *Poetry: An Introduction.*

Author Biography

Louis Aston Marantz Simpson was born in 1923 in Kingston, Jamaica, West Indies, to Aston Simpson, a lawyer, and Rosalind Marantz Simpson, an Eastern European emigré and beauty queen. The Simpsons lived in the suburbs of Kingston and were quite well off. Simpson describes his family during that time as "well-to-do colonials" and solid members of the upper middle class. Rosalind Simpson was a major influence on her son's literary development, keeping the young Louis entertained with fairy tales and tales of her life in Poland. When he turned nine years old, Simpson enrolled in Munro College, an elite preparatory school. He began to write poems and stories in earnest in his early adolescence and even won an essay competition when he was fourteen. His article on the coronation of George VI was printed in the *Daily Gleaner*, a Kingston newspaper.

After graduating from Munro, Simpson left Jamaica for America, where his mother had moved after his parents had divorced. Simpson studied literature at Columbia University in New York City but interrupted his studies in 1943 to join the United States Army. He returned to Columbia after the war and graduated with a bachelor of science degree in 1948. A few years later he received a master's degree in English from Columbia and his doctorate degree in comparative literature from Columbia in 1959.

Simpson's career as a poet and critic was helped by his teaching career, as the latter provided him time and money to write. He taught literature, first at the University of California at Berkeley, then at the State University of New York at Stony Brook, from which he retired in 1993. In all of his writing, Simpson's dry wit and humor is evident, as is his attention to the lives of his subjects. His many books include poetry collections including *The Arrivistes: Poems 1940–1949* (1949), *A Dream of Governors* (1959), *At the End of the Open Road*

Louis Simpson

(1963), *Caviare at the Funeral*, and *Selected Poems* (1988); an anthology, *An Introduction to Poetry* (1972); criticism, *A Revolution in Taste: Studies of Dylan Thomas, Allen Ginsberg, Sylvia Plath and Robert Lowell* (1979), *Three on the Tower: The Lives and Works of Ezra Pound, T. S. Eliot and William Carlos Williams* (1975), and *The Character of the Poet* (1986); a novel, *Riverside Drive* (1962); and memoirs, *North of Jamaica* (1972), and *The King My Father's Wreck*, (1995). His many awards include a Pulitzer Prize for *At the End of the Open Road*, which includes the poem "In the Suburbs," an American Academy of Arts and Letters Rome Fellowship, two Guggenheim Fellowships, an American Council for Learned Societies grant, and Columbia University's Medal for Excellence. Simpson lives and writes in Setauket, New York, on Long Island.

Poem Text

There's no way out.
You were born to waste your life.
You were born to this middleclass life

As others before you
Were born to walk in procession   5
To the temple, singing.

Media Adaptations

- Watershed Tapes released an audiocassette, titled *Physical Universe*, of Simpson reading his poems in 1985. Watershed Tapes are distributed by Inland Book Company, P. O. Box 120261, East Haven, CT 06512.

- In 1983, New Letters on the Air released an audiocassette of Simpson reading his poems on National Public Radio. To obtain a copy of this tape, contact New Letters at the University of Missouri at Kansas City, 5100 Rockhill Rd., Kansas City, MO 64110.

- *Wonderland*, released in 2001, is director John O'Hagan's documentary of Levittown, Long Island. The film explores the idea that 1950s suburban developments were part of the baby boomers' quest for middle-class bliss.

Poem Summary

Lines 1–3

"In the Suburbs" is a small poem about a big topic. Its title announces its subject. For Americans, the idea and image of the suburbs is mixed. On the one hand, many consider it a welcome refuge from the congestion, noise, and crime of the city. On the other hand, it has the reputation as a place marked by conformity, conservative values, and stodginess. In the first stanza, the speaker adopts the latter point of view, presenting the suburbs as a prison of sorts. The tone is harsh and accusatory, as the speaker equates the suburbs with middle-class life, both of which he sees as meaningless. The important word in this stanza is "born." Being born into a situation or identity suggests that one has little or no choice in the matter, that he or she acts according to a path already laid out. By using the second person "you," Simpson suggests that he is addressing another part of himself. This is a standard use of the second person in contemporary poetry.

The idea that one is born into a way of life over which one has no control is embodied in naturalism, a way of representing the world that emerged in the nineteenth century, largely as a result of the theories of Charles Darwin and Sigmund Freud. Naturalist writers, like realist writers, focus on the observable world, paying close attention to those forces that limit human desire or will, such as nature, one's genetic inheritance, or economic conditions. American naturalist writers include Stephen Crane and Theodore Dreiser. In Simpson's poem, these forces are implied rather than explicitly described.

Lines 4–6

This stanza completes the third sentence of the first stanza. By running the sentence over into the next paragraph, Simpson emphasizes the idea of "procession," which he introduces in the fifth line. A procession is a group of people moving along in a systematic and orderly manner. The word also suggests ritual, which is embodied in the image of people walking to church.

This last image is key for understanding the poem. Linking suburban, middle-class life to churchgoing makes sense, as church life was a conventional and regular part of American life when Simpson wrote the poem in the early 1960s. However, Simpson's tone is ironic. By using a religious image to describe suburban, middle-class life, he is saying that this group of people holds their way of life sacred, even though they are largely powerless to change it and, Simpson suggests, unconscious of its effect on them.

Themes

American Dream

Since the country was established in 1776, the United States has offered the promise of freedom, freedom not only to worship one's own God but freedom also to pursue material wealth. When Walt Whitman wrote "Song of the Open Road" in the middle of the nineteenth century, he represented America as a place of brotherhood and expansiveness, where each person was a cosmos unto him or herself. Possibility was limited only by what one could dream. Simpson takes that vision of America and the American Dream and shows its tawdry underbelly. He suggests that the achievement of the Dream leads not to untold happiness and communion with one's countrymen and women but to a life of monotony, where the pursuit of pleasure and convenience outweighs any desire to pursue the higher good. Rather than saying these things outright, Simpson implies them by depicting the middle-class life as one of waste, where its inhabitants can only blindly chase what they have been told is the "good" life. This blind pursuit is summed up in the image of people walking in procession "To the temple, singing." The suggestion here is that middle-class life itself is a form of religion with its own gods and rituals. Though Simpson doesn't draw out his analogy, readers understand that these gods are security and material wealth and that the rituals of the middle class include the "daily grind" of a 9 to 5 job and, for many suburbanites, the traffic-clogged commute.

Class

By linking social class with the suburbs, Simpson's poem perpetuates stereotypes both of people who live in the suburbs and of those who inhabit the middle class. Equating a middle-class life with a "wasted" life, the speaker draws on popular assumptions about what constitutes the middle class. These assumptions include a certain income, conventional tastes, conformity, an aversion to risk and, paradoxically, a feeling of hopelessness. A life can be wasteful, however, only if there exists an idea of a productive life. Although Simpson never explicitly describes what such a life might look like, he suggests that it would not include middle-class "virtues." A "productive" life might be one in which the individual values risk over security, adventure over stability, the exotic over the mundane, the very kind of life that Walt Whitman explored in his poems more than a hundred years ago.

Style

Analogy

"In the Suburbs" is one short analogy, comparing middle-class life to a form of unconscious devotion. Analogies are similar to similes (they both may use "as" or "like") but often extend the terms of comparison. They also frequently attempt to explain the abstract in terms of the concrete. In this case, the middle-class is the abstraction, and people walking to the temple singing is the concrete term.

Tone

The tone of the poem is both accusatory and despairing. The speaker establishes the accusatory tone through the use of the second person "you,"

Topics for Further Study

- Compare Simpson's poem to John Ciardi's poem "Suburban." How does Ciardi's poem support or contradict Simpson's assumptions about the suburbs?

- Interview people in your neighborhood about how they perceive their own class status. Does their description of themselves match the way you perceive them? Why or why not?

- Class in America is a contentious subject, with some people even claiming that America is a "classless" society. Make a list of the criteria you would use to determine a person's or a group's class. How widely do you believe other people share these same criteria?

- Do you consider yourself a part of the middle class? Another class? On what do you base your inclusion?

- Compare the caste system of India to the class system of America. What similarities and differences do you notice? What does this tell you about your own country?

- Write an essay about how the suburbs are depicted in popular films. Consider the movies *Edward Scissorhands*, *Truman*, *Pleasantville*, and *Wonderland*.

- Simpson's poem suggests that people are born into their class and that there is little hope of changing one's desires. Write an essay addressing the idea of history as a constraining force.

and he establishes the despairing tone through his insistence that nothing can be changed and that belonging to the middle class is only the most recent form of self-imprisonment. Underlying the tone is the image of the last stanza, an image Simpson critic Ronald Moran would argue belongs to the "emotive imagination." According to Moran, such an image creates "a muted shock effect insofar as the reader's expectations are concerned."

Compare & Contrast

- **1963:** United States unemployment stands at 6.1 percent.

  Today: A decade-long economic expansion lowers the United States unemployment rate to 4.1 percent.

- **1961:** In the United States, 87.5 percent of all families are married couple families, and 10 percent are headed by females.

  Today: Married couple families account for 79.2 percent of all families in the United States, and 16.5 percent of all families are headed by females.

- **1967:** In his book *The Medium Is the Message*, writer Marshall McLuhan introduces the idea of the Global Village, claiming that advances in transportation and communication enable people to live as if time and space had vanished. People now communicate as if they lived in the same "village."

  Today: The World Wide Web collapses time and space even further, enabling people simultaneous, ubiquitous and, for those in economically developed countries, inexpensive communication with others throughout the world.

Historical Context

R. W. Flint notes that Simpson once told an interviewer that "[i]t's the timidity of suburban life that is so limiting." Timidity aside, Simpson has become a poet of the middle class, at times even heroizing the characters that people his poems. These characters shop, gossip, commute, and go on summer vacations. It is a life Simpson knows well. While contemporaries like Allen Ginsberg were composing loud, often surrealist, poems that screamed out against the conformity of middle-class, mid-century suburban American life, Simpson was busy crafting quiet poems of understatement and wit. At the time Simpson was writing the poems that make up *At the End of the Open Road*, the United States was in the midst of a post-war economic expansion.

Beginning in the late 1940s, returning World War II veterans flooded the country and helped to create a new market for inexpensive housing. The overwhelming majority of these veterans wanted their own land and their own *new* house. Using less than top-shelf materials, developers such as William J. Levitt began building on the outskirts of large cities, converting farmland into sprawling housing tracts. Levitt factored the cost of elementary schools into the price of the houses, helping to create genuine communities. Built on fifteen hundred acres of

potato fields on Long Island, the first Levittown is often credited with being the model for thousands of suburban developments of the 1950s and 1960s. The uniformity of these developments helped to create the image that many Americans have about suburban life: that it is a place of conformity and blandness, devoid of the rich cultural opportunities and diversity that define many big cities.

A certain conservative ideology also came to be associated with the suburban mindset. As American cities fought poverty, crime, congestion, and general unrest, more and more people fled to the suburbs for peace and security. Historians and social critics termed this phenomenon "white flight" because most of those fleeing cities for the suburbs were Caucasian. Popular television shows of this period, such as *Ozzie and Harriet*, *Dennis the Menace*, and, later, *The Brady Bunch*, underscore the mainstream middle-class values that came to be associated with the suburban life.

The conservative nature of the suburbs stood in stark contrast to what was taking hold in America's cities in the early 1960s. In 1960, John F. Kennedy, a Democrat, was narrowly elected president. Though remarkably passive at first—considering that Kennedy received more than 70 percent of the Black vote—the Kennedy administration helped to further the cause of civil rights, creating the Commission on Equal Employment Opportunity in 1961 and ending segregation in interstate travel and in federally funded housing the same year. In 1963, Civil Rights leader Martin Luther King's Southern Christian Leadership Council began a sustained campaign against racial segregation in Birmingham, Alabama. Sit-ins and marches antagonized white leadership and law enforcement, and Birmingham police chief "Bull" Connor unintentionally helped galvanize protesters by turning loose police dogs, fire hoses, and his force on the peaceful demonstrators. In August 1963, a quarter million protesters marched on Washington D. C. to urge Congress to pass Kennedy's civil rights bill and to hear King deliver his famous "I Have a Dream" speech.

Critical Overview

Like many of the poems in *At the End of the Open Road*, "In the Suburbs" explores the contradictions between America's promise and its reality. Reviewing the collection for *Southern Review*, Ronald Moran writes that although he does not believe that Simpson's longer poems succeed, he enjoys his shorter ones. "In the Suburbs" works because it is a "statement poem" that relies on "a quiet power generated through restrained diction, loose rhythms, and an imaginative interplay between subject and attitude." Commenting on the sadness of the poem, poet and critic James Dickey says that "In the Suburbs" underscores the impoverished inner life of the American individual in the mid-twentieth century, living in a landscape of used-car lots and suburbs. "Nothing can be done," Dickey writes. "The individual has only what he has, only what history has allowed him to be born to." While praising Simpson's poetry in general, R. W. Flint finds the poem confusing, unsure of its meaning. Flint writes, "The ending is unsatisfactory. Does he mean there is a religious temple-haunting dimension to suburbia? The John Cheever gospel? Or does he only mean that things have gone rapidly downhill, that *homo medius americanus* can but dimly understand what he has lost?" The poem's brevity and very American-ness make it a popular choice for anthologies.

Criticism

Chris Semansky

Semansky is an instructor of English literature and composition and publishes frequently on Amer-

> " *Unlike Whitman, whose vision of the American people transcends class, Simpson sees America in the middle of the twentieth century hemmed in by class, by the dictates of a society that provides ready-made dreams, which can't possibly be fulfilled.*"

ican literature and culture. In this essay, he compares Simpson's vision of America in the 1950s to Walt Whitman's vision of it in the middle of the nineteenth century.

"In the Suburbs" is a sour little poem, full of disappointment and unfulfilled expectations. It is, like many of Simpson's poems in his collection *At the End of the Open Road*, a confrontation with the self as much as it is with an America who does not measure up to the writer's expectations. To see America as Simpson does, however, it is necessary to imagine it as he initially did through the eyes of Walt Whitman, whose poem "Song of the Open Road" "In the Suburbs" responds to.

Writing a hundred years before Simpson, Whitman saw America as a land of opportunity and untapped potential, which he expresses in his poem, itself a long, loose catalogue of America's promise. Using the open road as a symbol of life's journey, Whitman focuses on the individual, the single person's experience. His is a romantic vision of the individual's relationship to society and nature. He begins the poem:

> Afoot and light-hearted I take to the open road,
> healthy, free, the world before me,
> The long brown path before me leading wherever I
>   choose.

In contrast, Simpson focuses on the group, categorized by social class. Unlike Whitman, whose vision of the American people transcends class, Simpson sees America in the middle of the twentieth century hemmed in by class, by the dictates of a society that provides ready-made dreams that can't possibly be fulfilled. Whereas Whitman begins his journey on the open road "healthy" and "free, the world before me," Simpson opens his poem on a dead end street with "no way out." Simpson's vision of the middle class draws on stereotypes of a class-bound society marked by its pursuit of material wealth. The middle-class life, for Simpson, is marked by "waste," because it neglects the spirit. Whitman's vision, on the other hand, is of a people whose very nature is spiritual. Speaking of life on America's open road, Whitman writes:

> I believe that much unseen is also here.
> Here the profound lesson of reception, nor
> preference nor denial,
> The black with his wooly head, the felon, the
> diseas'd, the illiterate
> person, are not denied;
> The birth, the hasting after the physician, the
> beggar's tramp, the
> drunkard's stagger, the laughing party of
> mechanics,
> The escaped youth, the rich person's carriage, the
> fop, the eloping
> couple, . . .
> None but are accepted, none but shall be dear to
> me.

Whitman cultivated his reputation as a man of the people. His vision of inclusion, of a society where everyone, regardless of race, gender, class, or profession is accepted, defines the very essence of a progressive politics where worth is determined by one's very existence, not by one's work or possessions. This is the vision of America to which Simpson's poem cynically replies. It inverts Whitman's world. In his autobiography, *North of Jamaica*, Simpson writes about his response to Whitman's poetry when he emigrated to the United States from Jamaica in 1940:

> I found Whitman's poetry almost intolerable; celebrating progress and industry as ends in themselves was understandable in 1879, for at that time material expansion was also a spiritual experience, but in the twentieth century, the message seemed out of date. The mountains had been crossed, the land had been gobbled up, and industry was turning out more goods than people could consume. Also, the democracy Whitman celebrated, the instinctive rightness of the common man, was very much in doubt. Now, we were governed by the rich, and the masses were hopelessly committed to an economy based on war. It was a curious thing that a man could write great poetry and still be mistaken in his ideas.

Because Simpson expected so much from America, it's understandable that when he arrived he would be disappointed. The optimism Whitman expressed for the country's future no longer seemed possible or, rather, seemed possible only in a lim-

ited, economic sense. The vision of America in the 1950s when Simpson wrote most of the poems in *At the End of the Open Road* is one of a country that had traded its soul for material success. Suburbs had sprouted everywhere, as developers rushed to build cheap housing for World War II veterans and their families. These cookie-cutter neighborhoods gave the impression (which was often right) of a people who were not as interested in defining their own individuality as they were of acquiring things that would make their lives easier and provide them with the social status they sought.

The 1950s was also the age of the "corporation worker." After the war, the country turned to private corporations to help rebuild the economy. Big business successfully lobbied the government to lift wartime regulations. They bought up government wartime plants and shouldered out many smaller businesses. Millions of people went to work for transnational corporations, which were redefining not only the American economy but the world economy as well. Living in the suburbs, these newly minted "corporate drones" commuted to their 9 to 5 jobs. To do this comfortably, they needed comfortable cars, which they also had to buy, thereby cementing their relationship to their work even more strongly.

Simpson's friend, Allen Ginsberg, a Beat poet who had also been strongly influenced by Whitman, similarly lamented America's sad state of affairs at mid-century in his poem "A Supermarket in California." Like Simpson, Ginsberg questioned the deterioration of American values, its obsession with money and security, its neglect of the greater good and of self-enlightenment. But whereas Ginsberg questioned the country as a whole and the direction in which it was headed, Simpson singles out the middle class as his target of disdain, claiming that "There's no way out" of the endless cycle of consumption and production the middle class had brought into the country. For Simpson, America's future had arrived; there was no going back.

Simpson echoes Ginsberg's concern about America's lack of spirituality, but he does so ironically by comparing middle-class life to ritualized religion itself. Addressing himself as much as he is those among whom he lives, Simpson writes:

> You were born to this middle-class life
> As others before you
> Were born to walk in procession
> To the temple, singing.

The comparison is odd, but right. It also tells readers that for Simpson ritualized religion is *as* imprisoning as a middle-class life. Where, then, one might ask, does Simpson see hope? The answer is nowhere. In this poem and others in the collection, middle-class life is accepted at the same time it is scorned. The characters and speakers of Simpson's poems not only inhabit the middle class, but they are aware of what this means—to their relationships, to their desires, to their tastes. They are imprisoned not only by their class but by their awareness that there is no hope. At the end of Whitman's and America's open road in the middle of the twentieth century, Simpson sees a vapid land of wasted potential, a land for which there is no redemption. The only "choice" left is to make a religion of it, to embrace one's misery. Simpson has made a career out of just such an embrace.

Source: Chris Semansky, Critical Essay on "In the Suburbs," in *Poetry for Students*, The Gale Group, 2002.

Adrian Blevins

Blevins is a writer and poet who has taught at Hollins University, Sweet Briar College, and in the Virginia Community College System. She has published poems, essays, and stories in many magazines, journals, and anthologies. In this essay, Blevins examines how Simpson uses free verse or open form as opposed to fixed verse.

Louis Simpson's "In the Suburbs" is a criticism of American suburban life—an expression of the poet's feelings of hopelessness about a country of people who "are too slow for death, and change / to stone." Simpson expresses this same sentiment about more specific Americans in another poem included in his Pulitzer Prize-winning book, *At The End of the Open Road*, which also contains "In the Suburbs." In its criticism of middle-class America, "In the Suburbs" is akin to many poems of the 1950s and 1960s, recalling the opinions of other poets of Simpson's generation who struggled valiantly to discover new poetic forms in an effort to more accurately record the country's changing attitudes and moods.

James Wright's "Lying in a Hammock in William Duffy's Farm in Pine Island Minnesota," which was published five years after Simpson's *At the End of the Open Road*, is among the most famous of poems expressing the view that man leads a pointless life, though its main rhetorical device is a comparison between the natural world and the self rather than the present period in cultural history and a more ancient one. Wright also implicates *himself* in "Lying in a Hammock," whereas Simpson implicates American culture in "In the Sub-

> *By investigating the devices at work in this poem, we can uncover the way the poem's form mimics or gives birth to its meaning."*

urbs." In this poem, Simpson is certain he is powerless to change and alter his own circumstances. Unlike Wright, who ironically claims to have "wasted his [own] life," Simpson tells us that he "was *born* to waste [his] life," suggesting that he was—as by implication we all are—destined to live meaningless lives. The similarity of feeling in a good many poems written by poets of Simpson's generation reveals the cultural unease many American poets of the period experienced and articulated. This unease ultimately served to transform American poetry formally, as a close look at the composition of "In the Suburbs" will reveal.

In "In the Suburbs," Simpson moves from making a series of statements to a single image, while Wright moves "Lying in a Hammock" from a whole series of images to his famous last statement, "I have wasted my life." The movement or tension in Simpson's poem between the first stanza—which is very direct and plainspoken—and the second stanza—which is almost pure image—reenacts the comparison that is being made between what the speaker feels he was "born" to do and what "others before" him did. By investigating the devices at work in this poem, we can uncover the way the poem's form mimics or gives birth to its meaning. Since Simpson moves away in *At the End of the Open Road* from the more traditional forms and meters he used in his earlier books to free verse, investigating the way "In the Suburbs" reveals what it says, by looking at how it says what it says, might be the best method of testing the vitality of Simpson's use of free verse or open (as opposed to fixed) form.

"In the Suburbs" is, first of all, a comparison. That is, its rhetorical stance is a comparison between the way the speaker lives (and feels he has no choice but to live) and the way people used to live. The use of the second person "you," which is the point of view of direct address, suggests that

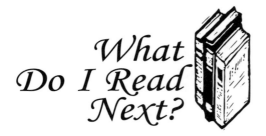

What Do I Read Next?

- *Ships Going into the Blue: Essays and Notes on Poetry* collects Simpson's own iconoclastic views on poetry, both his own and others. It was published in 1994 by the University of Michigan Press.

- Story Line Press issued an anthology of critical essays on narrative poetry in 1991 titled *Poetry after Modernism*, which discusses, among other subjects, the "New Narrative." Simpson is often cited as a major voice of "New Narrative" poetry.

- Jerome Klinkowitz's *The American 1960s: Imaginative Acts in a Decade of Change* (1980), makes intriguing connections between the political life of the country and the imaginative lives of artists during the 1960s.

- In *The Levittowners: Ways of Life and Politics in a New Suburban Community* (1982), Herbert Gans offers a historical look at the original inhabitants of America's most celebrated suburban development.

---

the speaker of the poem is addressing a specific person unknown to us, or, following the conventions of self-address, is speaking to himself. Although it is impossible to know for sure who the speaker in "In the Suburbs" is addressing, the mystery makes little difference to the poem's effect, since the immutability of the statements Simpson makes controls the poem's tone. That is, the emphatic nature of "There's no way out" and "You were born to this middle-class life" takes precedence over the issue of who's speaking to whom because it is so solidly closed to options: it does not matter if Simpson is addressing himself, the entire world, or a friend: by implication, it is clear that Simpson is suggesting in this poem that those "born to" the middle class have no way out.

One of the poem's mysteries, though, is Simpson's use of the same phrase—"born to"—in the poem's second stanza. Since this phrase suggests

that the people who came before present generations were also predestined to live the lives they lived, it's possible to read the second stanza as a statement much like the first: perhaps Simpson is suggesting that "others before" him were "born to waste" their lives, as well. Simpson's use of the word "procession" leans toward this meaning as it undercuts the sense of individual purpose that most Americans (and poets) value. Yet the way the poem opens up *formally* in its second stanza suggests a more positive reading of the poem. This opening or expansion toward the poem's closure is what the poem's form contributes to how the poem is read in this essay and reveals the famous inseparability of form and content.

The second stanza in "Suburbs" is partly achieved because the poem's first stanza is so plain-spoken and unadorned. That is, the poem's first lines are so closed (rhetorically) that any change of pattern or mode in the second stanza would be pleasurable. Here again we see a comparison at work, but this time the comparison is not rhetorical but musical. That is, Simpson's use of line and line-break contributes to the way the poem gradually opens up. The poem's first two lines are completely end-stopped—"There's no way out. / You were born to waste your life." That these two lines come to complete stops reinforces how emphatic Simpson's statements are. They enact the feeling of being trapped—of being born to something like waste. In comparison to these lines, the lines in the poem's second stanza are enjambed, or break at more unexpected places. The lines "As others before you / Were born to walk in procession / To the temple, singing" explain formally or *musically* the difference between life in the American suburbs and life in more spiritual times. The hesitation created by the end-stopped lines at the ending of the first two lines in the last stanza actually produce space, implying in this formal way the emotional differences between the feelings of entrapment expressed in the first stanza and the far more divine feeling of walking to a temple with others "singing" in the second.

It's also worth noting that the poem's one-stanza break is not end-stopped. That is, the shift from end-stopped line to enjambed line begins at the end of the first stanza rather than at the beginning of the second. The use of the enjambed line in this section of the poem also contributes to the feeling of expansion in the second stanza. We might also notice that Simpson's use of syntax in this poem contributes to the feeling of expansion. The poem's first two sentences are very short: the first is only four words long while the second is seven. The poem's last sentence is much longer, however—it's twenty-one words long. That gradual syntactical expansion of phrase also helps the poem spread out in its last three lines.

The way the poem expands in its second stanza is also partly achieved because of the way Simpson has used the image. That is, Simpson's *image-restraint* in his first stanza contributes to the differences he wishes to express between life in suburban America and life in simpler, more spiritual times. In his second stanza, Simpson is using the comparison, too: he *tells* readers what he wants them to *think* in his first stanza and *shows* them what he wants them to *feel* in his second. The sense of community in this image—the idea of a community of people who "were born to walk in procession / to the temple, singing"—produces pleasure partly because it's a shift from the imageless pattern established in Simpson's first stanza and partly because it actually acts out a kind of walking toward something. In comparison to the first stanza made up of ideas that are not even substantiated with examples, the second stanza produces the physical sense of movement with the word "walking" and of sound with the word "singing." The only comma in Simpson's poem shows up in his last line. This comma, or little half-stop, produces a break in the middle of the poem's last line and contributes to the feeling of joy in the last stanza because it suspends that final word—"singing"—for a brief moment. That feeling of joy chimes at the end of the poem because it is so noticeably unlike the feeling produced in the poem's first stanza. But it also contributes to the poem's sense of closure, finalizing Simpson's argument in a way that is as musically unchallengeable as was the poem's use of rhetoric in its first stanza.

And yet there is an undercurrent of irony in Simpson's poem in that he has even *expressed* his disappointment in American culture in this short poem. In *How to Read a Poem and Fall in Love with Poetry*, the American poet Edward Hirsche says:

> The lyric poem is a highly concentrated and passionate form of communication between strangers— an immediate, intense, and unsettling form of literary discourse. Reading poetry is a way of connecting— through the medium of language—more deeply with yourself even as you connect more deeply with another.

The major irony of Simpson's argument against middle-class suburban life is that there is this *poem* in the world—this statement on record of one poet's

take on life in the suburbs of America, circa 1963. Thus, despite how solidly the poem expresses the feeling of hopelessness and entrapment, there is an odd feeling of hope seeping out of it, inspiring us to behave and believe as though we were born to infuse our lives with some kind of meaning and purpose. Perhaps it's Simpson's use of free verse or open form that really lets this hope release, since by its various techniques of comparison it points ironically toward the alternative to waste, which is song.

Source: Adrian Blevins, Critical Essay on "In the Suburbs," in *Poetry for Students*, The Gale Group, 2002.

Sources

Bradley, Sculley, and Harold W. Blodgett, eds., *Walt Whitman: "Leaves of Grass,"* Norton, 1973.

Dickey, James, Review of *Selected Poems*, in *American Scholar*, Vol. 34, Autumn 1965, p. 650.

Ellman, Richard, and Robert O'Clair, eds., *The Norton Anthology of Modern Poetry*, 2nd ed., Norton, 1983.

Flint, R. W., "Child of This World," in *Parnassus*, Vol. 11, No. 2, Fall/Winter 1983–Spring/Summer 1984, pp. 302–17.

Gans, Herbert, *The Levittowners: Ways of Life and Politics in a New Suburban Community*, Columbia University Press, 1982.

Hirsche, Edward, *How to Read a Poem and Fall in Love with Poetry*, Harcourt, 1999, pp. 4–5.

Horowitz, David A., Peter N. Carroll, and David D. Lee, eds., *On the Edge: A New History of Twentieth-Century America*, West Publishing Company, 1990.

Howard, Richard, *Alone with America*, Atheneum, 1961, pp. 451–70.

Hungerford, Edward, ed., *Poets in Progress: Critical Prefaces to Thirteen Modern American Poets*, Northwestern University Press, 1967.

Klinkowitz, Jerome, *The American 1960s: Imaginative Acts in a Decade of Change*, Iowa State University Press, 1980.

Lazer, Hank, ed., *On Louis Simpson: Depths beyond Happiness*, University of Michigan Press, 1988.

Moran, Ronald, *Louis Simpson*, Twayne, 1972.

———, Review, in *Southern Review*, Spring 1965, pp. 475–77.

Rosenthal, M. L., *The New Poets: American & British Poetry since World War II*, Oxford, 1967, pp. 323–24.

Simpson, Louis, *The End of the Open Road*, Wesleyan University Press, 1960.

———, *North of Jamaica*, Harper, 1972.

———, *Ships Going into the Blue: Essays and Notes on Poetry*, University of Michigan Press, 1994.

Stitt, Peter, *The World's Hieroglyphic Beauty: Five American Poets*, University of Georgia Press, 1985.

Wright, James, *Above the River: The Complete Poems*, Farrar, Straus and Giroux, 1990.

Further Reading

Baxandall, Rosalyn Fraad, and Elizabeth Ewen, *Picture Windows: How the Suburbs Happened*, Basic Books, 2000.
    The authors, academics who commute from Manhattan to Old Westbury, Long Island, explore the stereotypes of suburban life, concluding that it is not the cultural wasteland or place of privilege that others have often described.

Lensing, George S., and Ronald Moran, *Four Poets and the Emotive Imagination: Robert Bly, James Wright, Louis Simpson, and William Stafford*, Louisiana State University Press, 1976, 2000.
    Moran and Lensing argue that these poets constitute a school of poetry in that their work is defined by what they call the "emotive imagination." Their poetry relies on associative leaps of logic and is linked to deep image poetry.

Simpson, Louis, *The King My Father's Wreck*, Story Line Press, 1995.
    Simpson's memoir recounts the poet's childhood in Kingston, Jamaica, his expectations in coming to America, and the reality of living in the United States.

Stepanchev, Stephen, *American Poetry since 1945*, Harper, 1965.
    Stepanchev's literary history is a highly readable account of the aesthetic and ideological movements in American poetry after World War II.

Kilroy

Peter Viereck
1948

Peter Viereck's "Kilroy" appeared in his first collection of poetry, *Terror and Decorum: Poems 1940–1948*, published in 1948. The poem's title is taken from the phrase "Kilroy was here," popularized during World War II to draw attention to the wide scope of territory on which American soldiers landed or which they occupied during the conflict. The name "Kilroy" represented every GI from the United States, and thousands of soldiers scrawled the phrase on walls, tanks, latrines, train cars—virtually anything that would accept a marking. The graffiti's appearance in so many likely and unlikely places made a loud statement about the mighty American presence in Europe, Asia, and the South Pacific islands where GIs fought, killed, died, and were held captive. Soldiers from all the enemy nations were familiar with the phrase and, obviously, were not too happy to see it turn up nearly everywhere they looked.

Viereck's poem emphasizes not only the daunting American presence in World War II, but also the spirit of adventure with which the culture hero Kilroy was associated. Through allusions to several historical and mythical figures who were widely traveled and gallantly successful in one way or another, Viereck portrays the World War II American soldier as a courageous, romantic globetrotter—a swashbuckling daredevil unafraid of strange lands and a far greater man than the sedate suburbanite who was not up to the same noble challenges. "Kilroy" incorporates legendary adventures from Roman mythology, Marco Polo's travels,

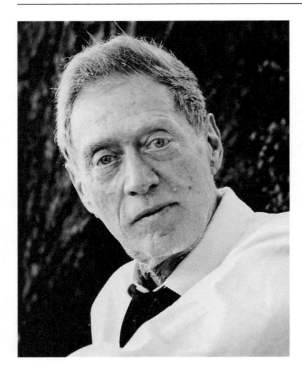

Peter Viereck

even Chaucer's *Canterbury Tales* and Dr. Faustus. These heroes (or anti-heroes) are compared to allegorical figures with negative names—Can't, Ought, But, and so forth—as a form of praise and admiration for the soldier who did his duty not with blind submission and formality but with a flare for the exotic experience and a hearty appetite for both danger and victory.

Author Biography

Peter Viereck was born in New York City in August 1916, the second son of well-to-do and well-educated German-American parents. Several of his relatives in both the United States and Germany were writers, including his father, who wrote poetry mostly in the period before World War I and prose later in life. Viereck's literary heritage inspired his own writing, and his powerful intellect enabled him to produce highly prolific works in history, politics, philosophy, and verse.

Viereck earned a bachelor of science in literature and history in 1937 and a master of arts in history in 1939, both from Harvard. Three years later, he was awarded a Ph.D. in history from Harvard. He had been writing and publishing both po-

etry and political essays throughout his academic career. Even before earning his bachelor's degree, he had written much of what would become his first book, *Metapolitics*, which was published in 1941. His interest in politics and history was fed by his coming of age in the tumultuous period before World War II, as well as by his father's pro-Nazi beliefs, which Viereck abhorred and which created a rift in the family that would last throughout the war. The older Viereck underestimated Hitler's power and intentions, believing the dictator was a positive influence and that he could bring peace and prosperity to the Germans. The younger Viereck, however, was a fiercely proud American, and he wrote scathing essays against the rise of Nazi Germany and against all Nazi sympathizers in America.

In 1943, Viereck was drafted into the army and sent to Italy and Africa, where he served in the Psychological Warfare Intelligence Branch, analyzing anti-Allied radio broadcasts. In 1944, his brother was killed in action in Anzio, Italy—an extremely distressing event for Viereck that inspired poems in memory of his fallen brother. While serving overseas, Viereck also met and married Anya de Markov, a Russian emigrant, and began his teaching career as an instructor in history at the United States Army University in Florence, Italy. Upon returning to America in 1946, Viereck taught history and German literature at Harvard for a year, then moved to Smith College. After a year at Smith, he moved in 1948 to Mount Holyoke College, where he taught until his retirement in 1987. He continued to teach a survey of Russian history until 1997 and now remains at Mount Holyoke College as professor emeritus in Russian history.

Over the decades following World War II, Viereck continued to publish both poetry and prose. Although he never attended writing classes or had any formal instruction in verse, he has been one of the most highly praised and widely published poets in modern America. Believing that too much creative training can stifle the creative spirit, Viereck chose to concentrate his studies in the disciplines he would teach and leave his poetic efforts solely up to inspired imagination, free of any rules or standards. While many academic poets disdain that attitude, Viereck has won numerous prestigious awards for his poetry, including his first volume, *Terror and Decorum: Poems 1940–1948* (1948), which won the Pulitzer Prize for Poetry in 1949. "Kilroy" is included in this collection.

Poem Text

1

Also Ulysses once—that other war.
  (Is it because we find his scrawl
  Today on every privy door
  That we forget his ancient rôle?)
Also was there—he did it for the wages—   5
When a Cathay-drunk Genoese set sail.
Whenever "longen folk to goon on pilgrimages,"
Kilroy is there;
  he tells The Miller's Tale.

2

At times he seems a paranoiac king   10
Who stamps his crest on walls and says, "My
    own!"
But in the end he fades like a lost tune,
Tossed here and there, whom all the breezes sing.
"Kilroy was here"; these words sound wanly gay,
  Haughty yet tired with long marching.   15
He is Orestes—guilty of what crime?—
  For whom the Furies still are searching;
  When they arrive, they find their prey
(Leaving his name to mock them) went away.
Sometimes he does not flee from them in time: 20
"Kilroy was—"
  (with his blood a dying man
  Wrote half the phrase out in Bataan.)

3

Kilroy, beware. "HOME" is the final trap
That lurks for you in many a wily shape: 25
In pipe-and-slippers plus a Loyal Hound
  Or fooling around, just fooling around.
Kind to the old (their warm Penelope)
But fierce to boys,
  thus "home" becomes that sea,   30
Horribly disguised, where you were always
    drowned,—
  (How could suburban Crete condone
The yarns you would have V-mailed from the
    sun?)—
And folksy fishes sip Icarian tea.

One stab of hopeless wings imprinted your   35
  Exultant Kilroy-signature
Upon sheer sky for all the world to stare:
  "I was there! I was there! I was there!"

4

God is like Kilroy; He, too, sees it all;
That's how He knows of every sparrow's fall;   40
That's why we prayed each time the tightropes
    cracked
On which our loveliest clowns contrived their act.
The G.I. Faustus who was
  everywhere
Strolled home again. "What was it like outside?"   45
Asked Can't, with his good neighbors Ought and
    But
And pale Perhaps and grave-eyed Better Not;

For "Kilroy" means: the world is very wide.
  He was there, he was there, he was there!

And in the suburbs Can't sat down and cried.   50

Poem Summary

Line 1

The first line of "Kilroy" is rather odd in starting with the word "Also," as though the reader is already in the midst of the poem. However, it serves to set the tone for the series of allusions to both legendary and historical adventurers—allusions that follow one another in rapid succession and sometimes become entwined. All the heroic explorers and travelers referred to are compared to Kilroy, the "everyman" American GI of World War II, and the first comparison is to Ulysses. In Roman mythology, Ulysses (called Odysseus in Greek mythology) was the creator of the giant wooden horse that was used to trick the Trojans and allow the Greek army to enter the city of Troy. The Trojan War left Troy in shambles, and its destruction angered the gods. As punishment, Poseidon sentenced Ulysses to ten years traveling the treacherous seas, suffering misfortune after misfortune but eventually making his way back home.

Lines 2–4

These parenthetical lines refer to the overall prevalence of the "Kilroy" graffiti in the Second World War. The scrawl of the name is so common that it appears on restroom doors like common inscriptions, making one forget the namesake's connection to the heroic Ulysses—Kilroy's "ancient role."

Lines 5–6

Two different references may be inferred from these lines. Cathay is the name Italian explorer Marco Polo gave to the country of China during his travels there in the thirteenth century. Polo was from Venice, and in 1298, he participated in a battle between Venice and Genoa, Italy. Polo was taken prisoner by the Genoese, and, while he was in prison, he told a fellow inmate about the things he saw and experienced while on his travels to China. The other prisoner wrote down the account and it became the The Travels of Marco Polo, one of the most famous adventure books in history.

The other possible reference in lines 5 and 6 is to Christopher Columbus. He was a Genoese who enjoyed sea excursions and who was hired by

Queen Isabella and King Ferdinand of Spain to explore the possibility of reaching Asia by sailing westward across the Atlantic rather than trying to sail around Africa into and across the Indian Ocean. On October 11, 1492, Columbus and his ships reached North America, landing on an island he named San Salvador (Holy Savior).

Lines 7–9

These lines refer to Chaucer's *Canterbury Tales*. Written during the 1380s, this first collection of short stories in the English language is about a group of pilgrims who pass time telling stories on their way to Canterbury, the site of the shrine dedicated to Thomas à Beckett, who was martyred for his Catholic faith in 1170. Line 7 is specifically from the prologue of Chaucer's tales and translates as "Then do folk long to go on pilgrimage." Their journey, then, is in keeping with Kilroy's spirit of adventure and his willingness to travel to strange lands for a cause. Line 8 confirms that wherever pilgrims go, Kilroy has already been there. Had he been on the trip to Canterbury with Chaucer's travelers, he would tell "The Miller's Tale" because it is bawdy, raucous, and full of untamed characters who apparently share some of the reckless abandon that fuels Kilroy's adventures.

Lines 10–13

At the beginning of the second stanza, Kilroy is now like a "paranoic king," or one who is powerful and glorious but not too secure about it. And like a king lacking assurance who "stamps his crest on walls" to show everyone his importance and might, Kilroy tags walls and fences and such with his own name to exhibit the same thing. However, even epic heroes run the risk of fading "like a lost tune" and being "Tossed here and there" after all the glory days are over.

Lines 14–15

Continuing the idea of the more somber side of an adventurer's life, these lines reflect the weariness that sets in, making the words "'Kilroy was here'" now sound "wanly gay," or weakly happy. Though the phrase is still "Haughty" with self-confidence, it is also tiring of the journey. The words "long marching" here keep Kilroy the soldier in the picture, as well as Kilroy the adventurer.

Lines 16–19

The allusion in these lines is again to Greek mythology, and Kilroy is now compared to Orestes, the son of King Agamemnon and his wife Clytemnestra. In their tale, Agamemnon is murdered by Clytemnestra's lover, Aegisthus, when Orestes was just a boy. Upon reaching manhood, Orestes avenges his father's death by killing both his mother and her lover. Afterwards, the Furies, who are powerful goddesses personifying conscience that punish those who commit crimes against their own families, pursue him. In the poem, Viereck seems to justify Orestes's act of revenge, asking "guilty of what crime?" and showing the young man's victory over the Furies by noting that when they think they have found him, all they really find is his name scrawled somewhere "to mock them." This, of course, is a direct reference to Kilroy leaving his own name wherever he has been—to the delight of some, the frustration of others.

Lines 20–23

There are two allusions in these lines. Kilroy is still Orestes running from the Furies, but in line 20—when he "does not flee from them in time"—Kilroy becomes the American soldier captured by the enemy. Lines 22 and 23 confirm this, for the "dying man" who passes away before completing the popular scrawl represents the troops who became prisoners of war or were killed on the island of Bataan during World War II. Between Manila Bay and the South China Sea, Bataan was the site of one of the Allies' losses. American and Filipino soldiers were overwhelmed by a Japanese invasion of the island, and thousands perished during the long, infamous Bataan Death March on the way to a prison camp erected by the Japanese.

Lines 24–25

Here, the poet warns his hero of what lies ahead after all the globe-trotting is done. For the free-spirited wanderer, "'HOME'" is not a good place to be. It is much too confining and restraining, much like a "trap." Kilroy is also warned that confinement may come in "many a wily shape," so he must beware of alluring places and people that would rob him of his freedom without his even knowing it at first.

Lines 26–29:

These lines give examples of the ways that "home" may disguise itself and, therefore, trick the traveler into settling down. The allusion goes back to Ulysses, whose "Loyal Hound," Argos, is the only one who recognizes him when he returns from his ten years at sea. The comfort of a "pipe-and-slippers" or "just fooling around" are attractive to a tired wanderer, as is Penelope, the faithful wife of Ulysses who fends off would-be lovers and waits a decade for her husband to return. These sedate scenes may be "Kind to the old," but they are "fierce to boys" who should see and do all that is possible while they can.

Lines 30–31

During Ulysses's ten-year voyage, he suffers mishap after mishap, often at the hands of some devious god or goddess who uses charming disguises to tempt the weary hero in various ways. Ulysses is "always drowned" on the seas because he falls for these tricks and pays both mentally and physically.

Lines 32–34

Here, the poem shifts allusion to another mythological figure, Icarus, for whom the Icarian Sea (a part of the Aegean) is named. Icarus, the son of Daedalus, goes with his father to Crete where they both become trapped in a labyrinth. To free them, Daedalus constructs wings out of feathers and wax that they use to fly out of the maze. Ignoring his father's warnings, Icarus flies too close to the sun, and the wax holding his wings melts, sending him plummeting into the sea below. The young Icarus, then, is like Kilroy—daring, foolhardy, and willing to tempt fate. The mention of "suburban Crete" and "folksy fishes" sipping tea ties the myth to the reality of suburban America, which is one of the "home" traps Kilroy has avoided to this point. The idea that Icarus could have "V-mailed" his adventure stories "from the sun" links him to a soldier of the Second World War who really did use this type of correspondence to write home. Because the load of letters from soldiers overseas was so overwhelming to the postal system, the United States Post Office adopted the V-mail system to use during the war. V-mail consisted of photographing correspondence and then transferring the photographs to microfilm for shipping. In terms of numbers, it took nearly forty mail bags to carry 150,000 one-page letters, but only one bag to carry the same amount of V-mail.

Lines 35–38

The final lines of the third stanza wrap up the exuberant joy of the daredevil spirit and of the thrill of going places where no one else has been just for the sake of shouting "'I was there! I was there! I was there!'" Sadly, of course, not all adventures end well, as with the high-flying Icarus who is on "hopeless wings" when he starts out.

Media Adaptations

- In 1963, Peter Viereck recorded two poems— "Obsessed by Her Beauty" and "Which of Us Two?"—on a 12-inch album entitled *Nine Pulitzer Prize Poets Read Their Own Poems*. This recording is difficult to find but may be available through the University of Minnesota library.

Lines 39–42

Line 39 of "Kilroy" has been given much attention by readers and critics because of its unlikely irony. Here, Kilroy is not like God; rather "God is like Kilroy," exalting the free-spirited individualist to the higher position. Both God and Kilroy have seen it all—the latter in his worldly adventures and God in his awareness of every "sparrow's fall" and of every mishap that befalls people, including clowns on tightropes.

Lines 43–45

The final comparison between Kilroy and a legendary figure is in line 43, and this time his counterpart is Dr. Faustus, or "G.I. Faustus." The Faustus character has appeared in a variety of tales over the centuries, most notably in Christopher Marlowe's dramatic play *Dr. Faustus*, published in the early seventeenth century. Faustus is a well-trained scholar in both religion and the "sciences" of astrology, sorcery, and necromancy, as well as medicine and mathematics. Bored with normal human life, Faustus enters into a pact with Satan who offers him all the luxuries and excesses he desires, including the ability to travel through space and to give horoscopes that never fail to be correct. In exchange for these powers and pleasures, Faustus must agree to renounce his Christian faith and surrender himself—body and soul—to the devil after a period of twenty-four years. The deal made, Faustus lives a life of comfort, luxury, adventure, and perversion for two-and-a-half decades before it is time to keep his end of the bargain. At that point, of course, he regrets ever having made the pact.

Though there is no evidence that Kilroy the soldier ever sold his soul to the devil, he does exhibit the same lust for fast living that Faustus had. Unlike the doomed doctor, however, Kilroy has been "everywhere" and now has "strolled home again." Upon arriving, the first question he is asked is "'What was it like outside?'"

Lines 46–49

Viereck ends the poem with an allegory, or a representation of ideas through characters who symbolize them. In this case, Kilroy is met by his neighbors who remain in the suburbs while he is away at war, and their names imply their attitudes toward living the kind of life that Kilroy has lived: Can't, Ought, But, Perhaps, and Better Not. In spite of the more cautious mindset of the neighbors, however, they still display an envious excitement in considering what Kilroy's name implies—adventure, freedom, travel, for "He was there, he was there, he was there!"

Line 50

The final line of "Kilroy" sums up the feelings of those who have opted for the safety and security (as well as dullness and boredom) of life in the suburbs as opposed to taking chances on a few adventures. Apparently, those who "Can't" end up regretting that they never tried.

Themes

Spirit of Adventure

The most prevalent theme in Viereck's "Kilroy" is praise for the spirit of adventure, particularly that of soldiers trekking through foreign lands with eagerness and bravado. The phrase "Kilroy was here" symbolizes the American GI's vitality during World War II and his widespread presence in cities and jungles, deserts and islands. The poem celebrates—ironically perhaps—a soldier's sense of liberation and desire to follow gut instinct. It turns the common soldier into an epic hero, comparing him to such historical adventurers as Christopher Columbus or Marco Polo and the mythological figures Ulysses, Orestes, and Icarus. Each of these characters brings an essential ingredient to the whole idea of spirit. Columbus and Polo bring the desire for discovery and the willingness to travel great lengths to find new places, new people, and new things. Ulysses has no choice in his ten-year voyage since he was sentenced to it by Poseidon as

punishment for his part in the Trojan War; however, he makes the best of it by surviving devious tricks, alluring monsters, and dangerous waters. Therefore, Ulysses represents sheer willpower in the spirit of adventure. Orestes brings a sense of self-justification and belief in his own actions, even when it means avenging his father's death by killing his adulterous mother. The narrator asks "guilty of what crime?" implying there really is no crime because Orestes is justified in his revenge. Finally, Icarus brings youthful foolhardiness to the spirit. He dares to zoom toward the sun on wings held together by wax and pays dearly for the thrill, but his attempt is passionate and wild, as well as regrettable.

All these attributes—travel and discovery, willpower, self-justification, and foolish, youthful passion—make up the mindset of the legendary Kilroy during the Second World War. The lines from the poem that best sum up this spirit are the repetitive cries "'I was there! I was there! I was there!'" and "He was there, he was there, he was there!" If the point has not been clear enough, the poet throws in an allegory at the end to show how weak and mundane the anti-Kilroy citizen of the suburbs is—"Can't sat down and cried" because he either has no sense of adventure or lacks the guts to act.

The Anonymous Soldier

Obviously, not all is upbeat and exhilarating for soldiers gone to war, and some would understandably say there are no positive feelings associated with battle at all. Viereck's poem avoids the horrible realities of bloodshed and death in favor of highlighting travel opportunities and the chance to experience new ways of life. However, there is a subtle, underlying theme that is unavoidable in any writing with war as its subject—the anonymous soldier; the lonely GI who tires of long days in strange lands and who really misses his home even if he refuses to admit it.

The story of Ulysses is the most prevalent allusion in "Kilroy," and this legendary hero is an adventurer who is *forced* to go on his journey, much like a young man drafted into the service and sent overseas. Although Ulysses is victorious in the end and manages to return home, his travels are anything but free-spirited and thrilling. So, too, a soldier at times feels as though he has faded "like a lost tune" and that he has been "Tossed here and there" like a trivial pawn in someone else's game. The most direct description in the poem of how devastating war really is appears at the end of the second stanza with its reference to soldiers who perished on the island of Bataan during World War

II. Unable to complete the scrawl "Kilroy was here," "(with his blood a dying man / Wrote half the phrase)." This is hardly the portrayal of a daring, young swashbuckler enjoying a new adventure. Rather, it is sadly much more representative of the real GI's experience.

Style

Near-Lyric Poetry

Viereck's style of verse is generally considered lyric poetry, but the description does not end there. Lyric poets use a melodic rhythm and rhyme to write subjectively and personally about feelings and events that most human beings experience. Viereck may do just this with his poems, but he often throws the melody off-key and the rhyme scheme askew by using coarse, unrhymed words and comedic imagery that surprise the reader, sometimes pleasantly, sometimes not.

"Kilroy" is an example of what may be called *near*-lyric poetry. It is filled with commentary on the life of a soldier—something that has been written about by thousands of writers for centuries. But Viereck's style is unorthodox in its glorification of a warrior's day-to-day activities. Here, the images shift quickly from one allusion to another, taking the reader from ancient mythology ("Ulysses once— that other war") to the mid-twentieth century when World War II found American soldiers scrawling the Kilroy signature "on every privy door," and then back several hundred years to the travels of Marco Polo and Christopher Columbus, and back further to Chaucer's *The Canterbury Tales*. All of this is in the first stanza of "Kilroy"—the first nine lines— and it sets the tone for the rest of the fifty-line poem.

The first stanza is also a mixture of exact-rhyme and near-rhyme. Lines 1 and 3 end in "war" and "door" and lines 6 and 9 end in "sail" and "Tale," which are both examples of exact-rhyme. But lines 2 and 4 end in "scrawl" and "role" and lines 5 and 7 end in "wages" and "pilgrimages," which are both examples of near-rhyme. Again, these pairings are from the first nine lines, but one can go through the rest of the poem and find similar examples.

While typical lyric poetry is not immune to addressing comedic situations, "Kilroy" suddenly takes a turn for the absurd just when the subject seems wholly serious. Viereck travels quickly from a dying soldier in Bataan to "pipe-and-slippers plus a Loyal Hound / Or fooling around, just fooling

Topics for Further Study

- If you were the originator of a catch-phrase that became popular during the Gulf War, which began in 1991 between the United States and Iraq, what would your phrase be and how would it capture the essence of the conflict?

- Write a poem from the perspective of the allegorical character "Can't" in the "Kilroy" poem. How would Can't defend his behavior as described at the end of Viereck's poem and what would be the major theme of your poem?

- Most people never knew about the systematic destruction of Jews in wartime Germany until after the conflict and the remains in concentration camps such as Auschwitz were discovered. Some people still refuse to believe that the Holocaust ever happened. Why do you think this belief exists and what does historical research say about it?

- Read the story of Orestes in Greek mythology and write an essay on whether you would find him guilty or innocent if you were sitting in judgment of the crime he was accused of committing.

around." He moves the last stanza from religious imagery to suburban America, noting first that "God is like Kilroy" and then describing how the GI "Strolled home again" only to face his envious neighbors who were too scared to follow the soldier into battle. Finally, Viereck resorts to allegory to end the poem, still using off-beat rhythm and coarse rhyming, but capping it off with the personification of negative attitudes and spiritless personalities.

Historical Context

The social, cultural, and historical events that surround the time "Kilroy" was written and the time it takes place are some of the most studied, re-

Compare & Contrast

- **1940s:** The Nuremberg Trials condemn twelve Nazis to death, including Hermann Goering, founder and leader of the Gestapo. Goering commits suicide in his cell before he can be hanged.

  Today: Neo-Nazi groups, consisting mostly of young males, still plague Germany, particularly after the unification of East and West Germany in 1990. These groups have been responsible for killing, injuring, and threatening foreigners in their country, including the 1996 fire-bombing of a house for immigrants, killing ten and injuring several others.

- **1940s:** President Harry Truman abolishes racial segregation in the United States military.

  Today: The military's policy of "don't ask, don't tell" in regard to homosexuals serving in the armed forces has come under severe scrutiny since its adoption in 1993. Many opponents argue that it is a policy based on contradiction since service personnel may still be legally discharged for engaging in homosexual activity.

- **1940s:** The Soviet Union conducts A-bomb tests, creating more tension with the United States in the Cold War arms race.

  Today: While leaders of the United States and the Soviet Union hailed the end of the Cold War with the break-up of the latter in 1991, today tension has mounted with the election of Vladimir Putin as president of Russia in 2000. Putin's election has brought mixed international reaction because some fear he favors a more authoritarian and expansionist Russia.

---

searched, and talked about happenings in history. The 1940s literally erupted onto the planet, spurred by Germany's invasion of Poland in 1939 and the beginning of World War II. But the war's real origins preceded that invasion by a decade and had a direct tie to America. Although the United States remained out of the conflict until Japan's attack on Pearl Harbor in 1941, the seeds of worldwide unrest were sown in the Great Depression that rocked the American economy after the stock market crash in 1929. Devastating economic conditions in the United States meant even more devastating economic conditions in other countries, both industrial and Third World. Production levels dropped dramatically in America and elsewhere, causing world trade to plummet and unemployment to skyrocket. Governments in Europe, Asia, and Africa tried to protect their nations by becoming isolationists and adopting anti-free trade policies, thereby worsening tensions with other countries and creating fear within the minds of their own citizens. Throughout the 1930s, political and social changes took place, particularly in Europe, that carried those seeds of American economic depression into the winds of all-out war.

"Kilroy" may have a naive reader believing that war for the American GI was a great adventure, full of excitement and exotic travel, and it is true that the cartoon character with a long nose peering over a wall was a favorite graffiti symbol for American servicemen during World War II. While there are various accounts of who, if anyone, the real Kilroy was, the most accepted story is that he was James J. Kilroy, a shipyard inspector from Massachusetts. After he had looked at tanks, ships, and airplanes, the inspector scrawled "Kilroy was here" in chalk on the side of each one. Servicemen who saw the markings when the military transports reached them overseas helped spread the phrase, and somewhere along the way, the little cartoon face was added to it.

But the portrayal of a real soldier's life is hardly represented by this poem, regardless of his or her nationality. Both military personnel and innocent citizens of all the countries involved felt the terrible forces of death and destruction as the Second World War escalated. In Japan, the 1930s saw the return to power of imperialistic and military leaders after the assassination of liberal Prime Minister Yuko Hamaguchi. This created tension between Japan and China, leading to the second Sino-Japanese war even before World War II began. In Italy, fascist leader Benito Mussolini invaded Ethiopia in a move to fuel his nation's spirit and economy, taking control of the African country with little resistance. Meanwhile, in France, a coalition of socialists and communists seized control of the government after democratic French leaders were accused of corruption and murdering their opponents. And in Spain, a civil war between left-wing liberals and right-wing fascists left dictator Francisco Franco in charge of the country in 1939.

While all this turmoil played out in Europe, Asia, and Africa, Germany was quietly building its Nazi government, poising itself for the invasion of Poland—the first step in Hitler's pursuit of world domination. Within a year of that invasion, Norway, Denmark, the Netherlands, Belgium, Luxembourg, and France—the major prize—all fell to German forces. In 1941, Romania, Bulgaria, Hungary, and Yugoslavia were added to the list. Throughout this time, the United States remained on the sidelines, except for supplying the Allies with military equipment. But things changed on December 7, 1941, when Japan attacked America, and the United States entered the war. The accounts of American involvement in World War II are well known, from the decisive battle of Midway in 1942 to the Allies' victory on the beaches of Normandy—known as "D-Day"—and the Battle of the Bulge in 1944. Battered and worn down, Germany finally surrendered in May 1945, and Japan, reeling from atomic blasts on Hiroshima and Nagasaki, surrendered in September.

By the latter part of the 1940s, a conflict between the former allied countries who then controlled Germany turned into a "cold" war, particularly between the United States and the Soviet Union. The conquered nation was officially separated into the republics of East and West Germany, and they would remain divided for over forty years. Economically, the United States came out of the war more sound than it went in, and the Marshall Plan—named for Secretary of State George C. Marshall and enacted in 1947—channeled billions of American dollars into war-devastated Europe to aid its economic recovery. The post-war years were both prosperous and technologically significant for the United States. Between 1946 and 1950, the television boom was under way with close to one million households having TV sets, and the invention of the transistor allowed for miniaturization in science and technology. On Long Island, builders erected "Levittown," noted as the first middle-class

suburb, and the first freeway system in Los Angeles opened. At the end of the decade, the United States Gross National Product (GNP) had nearly tripled since 1940, reaching $284 million. In spite of the growth and good times, however, one would have had difficulty finding veterans of the war who would have described their experiences as Viereck describes Kilroy's. The poet, of course, knows this, as evidenced in his allusion to the horrors of Bataan and in his admission that Icarus flew on "hopeless wings."

Critical Overview

Viereck's poetry was not initially as well received as his nonfiction books and essays. The poems, critics said, were lively and experimental for the time but that usually translated into overwritten and insignificant. Set against the erudite composition of his historical and political writings, the poetry seemed immature and unfinished. In spite of the negative comments, however, Viereck's first full-length collection of poems, *Terror and Decorum: Poems 1940–1948*, including "Kilroy," was received well enough to win the Pulitzer Prize for Poetry in 1949.

Reviewing *Terror and Decorum*, many critics still noted mixed feelings toward its content although the favorable outweighed the not so favorable. In the *Dictionary of Literary Biography*, Idris McElveen says the book shows Viereck's "energetic control of language for purposes of wit and variety in tone and subject matter," then goes on to note that "The volume presents a full view of his art at its best and worst." Addressing "Kilroy" specifically, McElveen calls it "one of Viereck's most daring poems" and "perhaps the best example among all his poems of the kind of circus act that he alone would risk." In her book of biographical material and criticism simply titled *Peter Viereck*, critic Marie Henault is not as kind to the poem in question. She writes that

> In the early 1940s, 'Kilroy was here' meant no more than that American soldiers had been at the place so labeled. This connotation, now partly lost, makes this robust and technically adept poem diminish with the passage of time.

Henault goes on to say that, "joyfully as it begins, 'Kilroy' also becomes a despairing and somewhat cliché-ridden poem."

Over the years, Viereck has continued to write "robust" poetry that has been more widely appreciated by critics and scholars today than in the past. He has won additional awards for his work, including a Guggenheim fellowship and the Poetry Award of the Massachusetts Artists Foundation. But most of Viereck's career has been spent in academic history departments, and his name is not as recognizable to students and general readers as other more highly anthologized poets' may be. Still, Viereck's poems are often surprisingly fresh—even funny—and it is too bad that they frequently go unnoticed outside the circle of scholarly, academic works.

Criticism

Pamela Steed Hill

Hill is the author of a poetry collection, has published widely in poetry journals, and is an associate editor for a university communications department. In the following essay, she argues that praise for the American spirit of adventure may have great merit in certain circumstances but is misleading and inappropriate set against a backdrop of war.

"Kilroy" is a poem that could not have been written about the War in Vietnam, the more recent Gulf War, or even earlier conflicts such as World War I and the American Civil War. Its cavalier treatment of a soldier's experience (on the surface, at least—obviously, the poet is familiar with the actual horrors of battle) reflects Americans' overwhelming support of the government's declaration of war on Japan after its attack on Pearl Harbor. Shocked and angered by this act of aggression, young men were happy to sign up for the armed forces, not only to protect their own nation, but also to help rid the world of Nazism, Fascism, and any other governing system considered evil by most of the free world. Likewise, American citizens were happy to support them. But even in the midst of gung ho patriotic fervor and feelings of justification in fighting for a worthy cause, real combat is anything but glorious victories, conquering heroes, and exotic travel.

Adolph Hitler was one of the most feared and despised men in the history of the human race. As obvious as his unquenchable thirst for power and territory was, the full terror of his inhumane plans was not completely recognized by people outside the target groups—Jews, people of color, homosexuals, and others deemed unsuitable—until the

war was over. Even so, the "Final Solution" was understood well enough by Hitler's enemies to know it was a threat to democracy and individual rights everywhere. Americans who may have felt isolated or protected from Germany's aggression changed their tunes in 1941, realizing Hitler's push to conquer the world was supported by nations hoping to gain more territory for themselves by supporting Germany—in particular, Japan and Italy. But a newly enlisted soldier who suddenly found himself in boot camp and weeks later in some distant land a world away from family and friends must have felt fear and confusion, if not panic and regret. Many who wound up in Europe, Africa, or the South Pacific islands had probably never ventured far from their quiet homes in the suburbs, that place considered a "final trap" in the poem. But how likely is it that a GI trying to fall asleep in a tent somewhere with death a possibility at every moment would be thinking of his home in America as a trap?

Throughout "Kilroy" the hero is compared to figures who are not even fighting a war when they go on their adventures. Only Ulysses has a connection to battle, but the accounts of his journeys make it clear that he would have preferred to go home to his wife after the Trojan War instead of being sentenced to ten years traveling dangerous seas. Marco Polo and Christopher Columbus were not warriors, but explorers. Their agenda was obvious and a great spirit of adventure came with the territory. In the tale of Icarus, the point is clear that he is a victim of youthful abandon and too immature to appreciate a need for caution. And Orestes is hardly a swashbuckling soldier; rather he is an accused killer on the run. So what do these mythological and historical figures really have in common with Viereck's concept of the American GI in World War II? The most likely answer is that the overwhelming feeling of patriotism that permeated soldiers and citizens alike during this war is easily translated into a high-spirited sense of duty and self-righteousness. Kilroy is a man on a mission—one that not only provides an opportunity to see the world, but that may also save it from destruction.

Consider a poem written about a soldier's experience in the American Civil War. Most likely a "Kilroy" in this conflict would have had a Blue or Gray counterpart just as heroic. Supporters of both the Confederacy and of the Union considered themselves "Americans," and, therefore, each side considered themselves patriotic and justified. But this war tore the United States apart, and a poet would have difficulty singling out any one particular trait of the real American soldier—especially a free-wheeling spirit and lust for adventure since many men were fighting against their own brothers.

The same doubtful scenario may be assumed for a poem about World War I. Americans did not enter this war until the tail-end of it, and then had little difficulty helping defeat a battered German military. What may have been most difficult was grasping the full scope of "world war," the first one of its kind, leaving many Americans fearful, disillusioned, and angered by the seeming madness of politics and territoriality. While the "doughboys" were heralded as heroes in many accounts, there was not a representative figure like Kilroy that marked the spot of all the wondrous places where American soldiers had turned up. Most were stunned to have turned up at all in such unlikely foreign lands, and many did not understand for what they were fighting.

By the time World War II rolled around, Americans were in dire need of a hero. A decade of a depressed economy and a continued gloomy outlook was soon reversed by the nation's need to pull together to fight a common enemy. Japan had had the audacity to attack American ground, and that was enough provocation to muster wholesale support for entering the war. As men left for overseas, women went to work in factories, and many companies altered their normal production to manufacture war materials. It seemed that every American had an opportunity to do something for the war effort, and millions took advantage of it. This kind of support back home bolstered GI spirit around the world and made possible a poem like Viereck's "Kilroy." Many young soldiers surely did land in Europe and the South Pacific with dreams of being heroes and thoughts of how envious those who did not or could not fight would be. They likely had many "yarns" that they "would have V-mailed from the sun," and they would not have considered their wings "hopeless." Not in the beginning, anyway. But the poem does not venture into the dark, despairing side of being an American GI in a foreign world. It does not show that the same soldier who scrawls an "Exultant Kilroy-signature / Upon sheer sky for all the world to stare" is the same frightened young man who hunkers down in the trenches praying for the bullets and bombs to miss him. It does not say that the same godlike conqueror who "sees it all" is the same lonely cadet who longs to see his loved ones back home. Probably the most misleading notion in this poem is implied in the phrase "Strolled home again," specifically the word "Strolled." Few, if any, real soldiers have returned

> *But how likely is it that a GI trying to fall asleep in a tent somewhere with death a possibility at every moment would be thinking of his home in America as a trap?"*

to the United States with casual, carefree steps. Even those fortunate enough to have remained unharmed during their service and to have participated in victorious battles still suffered the emotional trauma of combat. Given the atrocities witnessed in the war, it is doubtful that anyone *strolled* home again, regardless of how happy he was to be there.

Even if one could make a case for Kilroy-like adventurism occurring in conflicts previous to World War II, it would be pure fantasy to claim it for any war after. The Korean War is often called the "forgotten" war because it occurred between the more memorable conflicts of World War II and Vietnam. Throughout the 1980s, 1990s, and even today, American soldiers have had a presence in the Persian Gulf, Bosnia, and the Middle East, among other areas, and American citizens hold mixed feelings about these conflicts. Some argue that Americans should stay out of countries fighting their own wars, while others say leaders like Saddam Hussein are just as threatening as Hitler and need to be stopped. With this division, no cult hero has emerged from the ranks of the modern-day soldier. But it was the Vietnam War that truly brought an end to the American war spirit, and Viereck's Kilroy could not have arisen from this strife.

The televised Vietnam War brought the massacre of thousands of people into American living rooms. Evening newscasts alternated between scenes of the bloodshed in Southeast Asia and scenes of riots on American streets and college campuses. The GI in Vietnam had little public support from home to take comfort in, and many soldiers contended with guilt over their own presence there as well as the hatred and accusations of anti-war protesters back in the United States and across the world. In short, Kilroy was *not* there. After the conflict ended, there were few hero welcomes, and most veterans were content to return home quietly and try to pick up the pieces of shattered illusions and lingering doubts. Ironically, many were probably elated to live sedate lives in the suburbs, unlike Kilroy, who felt superior to his neighbors Can't, Perhaps, Better Not, and so forth. During Vietnam, Can't turned into Won't, and most often it was the spirit of adventure that sat down and cried—a spirit broken by the realities of war.

Source: Pamela Steed Hill, Critical Essay on "Kilroy," in *Poetry for Students*, The Gale Group, 2002.

Peter Viereck

In the following essay, Viereck discusses his poetry and describes a need for clarity and form in contemporary poetry.

I

Right from the start, I must disappoint many readers by the unexciting conservatism of my poetic techniques. After experimenting with more easy-going prosodies, I've found it more effective to adhere to the admittedly arbitrary laws of conventional rhyme and meter. In the history of English literature these have again and again been discarded as "outworn" but have returned to outwear the discarders. Irregular scansion can be useful onomatopoeia to bring out a jolt in the mood or the narrative. But as Amy Lowell's revolt illustrated, this is a habit-forming drug. Used once too often in poetry, irregularity becomes just another kind of regularity, that of prose.

Equally conservative is my passionate conviction that the time is now ripe for a frontal assault on obscurity as inartistic—*provided* the assault is not allowed to play into the hands of those who want a pretext for being lazy about poetry. The time is ripe for poets and readers, both making sincerer efforts at mutual understanding, to end the schism between them by restoring communication. The eighteenth-century motto "be thou clear!" expresses the timeliest need of American poetry in 1949.

It's not enough to say a poet must belong to none of the arty coteries. It's essential that he actively sin against their rituals. *My own sin is twofold.* (1) I've content—something to say about the profane world they scorn—and not only form; this makes me an "impure" poet. (2) I try to communicate to the qualified layman also, instead of only to fellow poets and critics; this makes me a philistine.

My style has been ironically summarized as "Manhattan classicism." In case labels are necessary at all, that's as accurate a label as any. Mine is not the arcadian escapism of an aloof anti-urban classicism but a classicism of the industrial age, with an ivory tower built where the subway rumbles loudest. Being classicist means that my poetry is equally interested in shaking off the vague sentimentalities of the pre-Eliot romanticism and the hermetic ingenuities of the post-Eliot version of neo-classicism. The latter contains (1) no fun and (2) no humanness, two "vulgar" qualities that are the lifeblood of art. What was new and imaginative in the master becomes a slot-machine stereotype in the disciples, who thereby create a new and more insidious type of Babbitt: the highbrow Babbitt-baiting Babbitt. Thus does an exciting literary movement age into a cocktail-party clique, a mutual admiration pact, a pressure group upon college English departments and Little Magazines. Think ye, because ye are virtuosos, there shall be no more cakes and ale?

In my book *Conservatism Revisited: The Revolt Against Revolt* I've already defined my humanist and classical credo. Here I shall try instead to be more specific about concrete examples of my poetry. When they violate my conservative working principles, as they sometimes do, this is occasionally done on purpose, using disharmony to bring out the harmony by contrast. More often it may pretend to be on purpose but is really done out of insufficient competence, in which case: so much the worse for me and my writings rather than so much the worse for the principles.

Just as political liberty is not based on a radical smashing of traffic lights but on law and traditional established institutions, so poetry must be subjected to the challenge of form, the more rigorous and traditional and conservative the better, to bring out the response of beauty—if one may apply Toynbee's "challenge and response" to art. For my own poems, form—Toynbee's "challenge"—always means rhythm and usually means rhyme. I try to avoid those fraudulent rhymes that change the *consonants;* the rhyming of "thornbush" and "ambush" in my long poem "Crass Times" is an exception that I now regret. But for certain purposes, my rhymes use slightly different vowel sounds with the same consonants. An example is stanza two of "Crass Times." In his essay "Peter Viereck: the Poet and the Form" Professor John Ciardi of the Harvard English department analyzes my characteristic use of rhyme vowels more ably than I ever could. Therefore, I quote from him (in condensed form):

"Viereck has what Eliot has called 'the audio-imagination,' with a sure sense of how rhyme can function to punctuate, emphasize and resolve the flow of the poem. The reader who has thought of rhyme only as a regularly arranged ornamentation will do well to underscore this point in his mind. Skillfully used, rhyme is a rich device for controlling the reader's voice, teaching him to hear the poem as the poet heard it.

"For example, *"Crass Times Redeemed By Dignity Of Souls."* This is an incantatory poem. The poet wants the poem read in a mechanical, litanized way. Such a reading requires a full voice stop at the end of each line. But normally, if the meaning does not pause, the voice continues on to the next line. You then have a run-on or *enjambement*. The first three lines in this passage do not provide a pause in meaning. Here, the poet makes rhyme function. The triple use of the strong 'oals' rhyme demands stress. Thus, despite the run-on, the rhyme produces the desired voice-stress. In the subsequent lines, this device is not needed since there is a meaning-pause at the end of each line with the exception of the next to the last. And there again you will note the rhyme of 'knives' becomes heavy, again requiring a stress. By 'heavy' I mean closely positioned as the second rhyme of a couplet, a strong 'ives' sound and a literal rhyme as opposed to the approximate rhyme of 'are' and 'hear' that precedes:

"'The weight that tortures diamonds out of coals
Is lighter than the skimming hooves of foals
Compared to one old heaviness our souls
Hoist daily, each alone, and cannot share.
To-be-awake, to sense, to-be-aware.
Then even the dusty dreams that clog our skulls,
The rant and thunder of the storm we are,
The sunny silences our prophets hear,
The rainbow of the oil upon the shoals,
The crimes and Christmases of creature-lives,
And all pride's barefoot tarantelle on knives
Are but man's search for dignity of souls.'"

Rhyme and meter are the unchanging stage on which the changing actors stumble or dance. By keeping rhyme regular, I can provide a background which, by contrast, makes more effective the utmost variety, change, and imaginative flight. When rhyme and rhythm become too irregular, there is no contrast to spotlight the goings-on of the actors on the stage. This regularity demands that the vowels of full-voweled rhymes be the same. But in the case of rhymes whose vowels are short, quick, and inconspicuous (e.g., rhyming "heard" with "stirred"), I shall continue to use rhymes of slightly different vowels in order to increase the speed and to force the reader into *enjambement* (by not lingering over the rhyme) even when the line ends with a punctuation mark.

It would distract from a slow, strong, open-voweled rhyme to repeat the same vowel in the mid-

> *By keeping rhyme regular, I can provide a background which, by contrast, makes more effective the utmost variety, change, and imaginative flight."*

dle of the same or following line. So I usually avoid this. For example, if the rhyme-word is "mood," I should not in the same line or following line use any word with an "oo" sound. This would distract the ear of the reader from doing what I will it to do: namely, to remain in unconscious suspense waiting for the second half of the rhymed pair. If the end-word "viewed" is to rhyme with the earlier end word "mood," I don't want any intervening non-end-word like "cruel" or "blue." If I find that, for the sake of lilt or meaning, I must repeat the rhyme-vowel inside the line, then I try to repeat it twice. Thereby the two repetitions, by pairing with each other, cease to distract the ear from the third repetition in the rhyme-word at the end of that same line. I try to have strong, open vowel-sounds occur an odd number of times in a line (once, three times, five times), never an even number of times, except in unrhymed poems (Alcaic or Sapphic odes or blank verse), where I prefer even to odd. I make no fetish of this or any other rule, the total effect of a poem being more important than any single detail.

II

Free verse I write not at all: on principle. Unrhymed metrical verse only rarely. Almost all my poems are rhymed. For me the most difficult verse-form is the form that glib or sloppy craftsmen deem easiest: unrhymed iambic pentameter. I've begun many poems in this blank-verse form but not one have I been able to finish. The exception—"A Walk on Snow"—proves the rule: except for some 1947 interpolations about art, it was written so long ago (in 1932 in high school when I was 15) that I cannot even remember what sort of person or poet I then was. Since then, no luck.

I don't mean I've given up attempting blank verse. But I've destroyed all the attempts because they all bogged down into pale reflections of the blank verse style of either the Elizabethans or Milton or Swinburne. "A Walk on Snow" I included in my *Terror and Decorum* collection (against the advice of so fine a critic as I. A. Richards) because, no matter how redolent of juvenilia, it at least has a personal blank verse style: a poor thing perhaps but all my own. Even here I stuck to my typical pattern, later exemplified once in each stanza of "Poet" and "Kilroy" and in the final stanza of "For Two Girls," of breaking the pentameter monotony with an occasional tetrameter of emphatic meaning.

Alliteration as a working principle? For me, definitely yes. If done not too unobtrusively, a poet can use it triply instead of doubly; and triply is to my ear more effective. More than triply is too obvious. Doubly, by a mathematical paradox, sounds more crudely obvious than triply. Triply can or cannot be obvious, depending on how it's handled. It is only effective when the reader hears it unawares. Shakespeare was not afraid to use alliteration, not only doubly as in: "Ruin hath taught me thus to ruminate" but even in three successive words: "To leap large lengths of miles." In the nineteenth century, alliteration was overused and used too mechanically by Poe and Swinburne. It became discredited after such mechanical usage as Poe's "Came out of the lair of the lion / With love in her luminous eyes." That fourth "l" ("luminous") is just too much of a good thing and becomes farce.

Wearing their heartlessness on their sleeve, modern poets go to the opposite extreme. Just as they are afraid to let themselves go emotionally and be wild, for fear of seeming ridiculous, with the result that their lyrics are unlyrical, so likewise are they afraid to let themselves go in alliteration, for fear of seeming crude, with the result that they lack lilt and music. They should take to heart the very wise words of a very vulgar song of the 1920's:

"It don't mean a thing
If it ain't got the swing."

My practice is to be both lyrically wild and musically alliterative when the meaning and mood of the poem are enhanced thereby, but never otherwise, never mechanically, never too frequently. Never alliteration for its own sake but only for the poem's total effect. In the following couplet, the purpose of the two triple-alliterations ("f" and "m") is not lilt or music, their usual purpose, but a heightened emotional emphasis to signalize the climax and turning-point of the whole poem:

Then, with a final flutter, philomel—
How mud-splashed, what a mangy miracle!—etc.
(from "Some Lines In Three Parts")

It might be interesting to have each poet of the '40's name what poet influenced him most. Our answers might be wrong because we would not know of unconscious influences. Consciously, I'm most influenced by Yeats. In rhythmic technique his "Cold Heaven," published 1914, seems to me the greatest lyric in our language. Yeats is the poet whose rhythms I most imitate, especially his habit of a quick extra unaccented syllable amid an iambic or trochaic line. For example, the second syllable of "ignorant" when he speaks of "beauty's ignorant ear."

I've imitated this mannerism, though with a different purpose, in part III, line four of "Some Lines." The same type of quick extra unaccented syllable recurs in "cartilaginous": "A cártiláginous, móst rheumátic squéak." Were every alternating syllable in "cartilaginous" accented, as might normally be expected, then there would be no room for the word "most," and the line would read: "A cártiláginóus, rheumátic squéak." Contrasting the two readings, it will be noted that the latter is correct in iambics but pedestrian while the former gives the needed onomatopoeia of a rheumatic hobble and also the necessary ironic tone for describing owlish-pedantic wisdom in its painful effort to become the singing beauty of philomel, the nightingale.

Recently I heard an appeal for "liberating" poetry from the "tyranny of iambic pentameter"; but who will liberate poetry from such self-appointed liberators? My *typical* poem is a moderately long poem, often of several pages, in rhymed iambic pentameter, in which lyrical emotions and philosophical ideas are equally present and are fused into unity by expressing the ideas in sensuous metaphors. For variety or special emphasis, I periodically alternate the five-beat line with a shorter line, four-beat or three-beat. The shorter line occurs several times per stanza in "Kilroy" but, more typically, once only per stanza in "Poet," "Some Lines," "A Walk on Snow," etc. When long, this "typical" poem of mine is divided into stanzas of varying length, coinciding with changes of mood. "Crass Times," otherwise typical, omits the shorter line from all stanzas because, when a sound of steady incantation is desired, then monotony becomes for once desirable and variety undesirable.

Stanza two of "Poet" expresses my insistence on making intellectual concepts sensuous. In a prose essay, rhymes are rhymes, exclamation marks are exclamation marks, nouns are nouns. This being poetry, they become three-dimensional physical creatures with lives of their own. The passage describes the revolt of the outworn romantic clap-trap against the dead classical poet who has hith-erto tamed them:

> "Words that begged favor at his court in vain—
> Lush adverbs, senile rhymes in tattered gowns—
> Send notes to certain exiled nouns
> And mutter openly against his reign.
> While rouged clichés hang out red lights again,
> Hoarse refugees report from far-flung towns
> That exclamation marks are running wild
> And prowling half-truths carried off a child."

Mine is a poetry of ideas. Above all, ideas con-nected with ethics or with the search for ethical val-ues. Often my poems use history as grist for their mill, not only history of the past but of the future (chapter five of *Terror and Decorum* is called "News From the 60th century"). Ideas are the he-roes, villains, and agonisants of an unusually large number of my poems. Unlike the arid didacticism of some eighteenth-century poetry of ideas, my ideas are presented not abstractly but sensuously: lyrical and philosophical at the same instant. Lyri-cism teaches ideas to dance rather than to plod along like a Ph.D. thesis:

> "Here abstractions have contours; here flesh is
>   wraith;
> On these cold and warming stones, only solidity
>   throws no shadow.
> Listen, when the high bells ripple the half-light:
> Ideas, ideas, the tall ideas dancing."
> (from "Incantation.")

III

Poets pretend to ignore their critics with lordly dandyism. In truth, I've constantly learnt from hos-tile critics and am grateful to them for my most valuable revisions and deletions. Intelligent hostile criticism is all the more important to me, indeed indispensable, in view of my inability to discrimi-nate between my worse and better poems. I agree with Professor D. C. Allen's strictures:

> "This deliberate effort to ruin a poem by what seems a consciously chosen unpoetic word or phrase is Viereck's main weakness as a poet. As there are scars that disfigure individual poems, so there are poems that disfigure the collection. I wish they had never been written or, having been written, destroyed. One can hope that the next collection will be smaller and more selective."

In turn, some of my non-hostile critics have succeeded in explicitly and consciously summariz-ing those of my working principles which I follow only implicitly and semiconsciously and am unable to summarize competently. An example of such summarizing is Louis Fuller in the *Antioch Review*:

"What has not been sufficiently noted by those who have a corner on modern poetry is that this book may be read and enjoyed *without any special key,* and without serving any *special novitiate.* Mr. Viereck doesn't write down, or up; he simply writes as person to person. If there is any misunderstand-ing of meaning or intention, it is not because he has tried to create it." Another example is Selden Rod-man writing in the *Saturday Review*:

> "He is never trying to bait and hence is never delib-erately elusive. Indeed, one of the qualities that make *Terror and Decorum* more of a *break with the Eliot-dominated past* than any recent book is this very pas-sion to communicate. The soldiering has contributed to his verse as a whole its racy colloquialism and its sense of identity with ordinary people. Academic training has given him a working knowledge of the styles of a half dozen literatures and a familiarity with cross-reference almost Joycean in scope. . . . Out of extreme complexity, simplicity. From sophistication beyond cleverness, innocence. In Shakespeare, Donne, Blake, Hopkins, the later Yeats, perhaps in all of the greatest poetry, it is the 'formula' toward which Viereck, more than any contemporary poet, seems to be moving."

The above "formula" of a difficult simplicity, though unattainable for my practice, is the truest summary of the ideal behind all my "working prin-ciples."

Several critics of *Terror and Decorum* beamed upon what they called "its wit"; others frowned upon "its frivolous clowning around." Both were referring to the same element; both misconstrued its aim. The element of so-called wit or buffoon-ery is a means, not an end. Usually it is found con-cerning things that are "no laughing matter." It is my means of expressing the tragedy inseparable from living and the terror inseparable from the shock of beauty. Tragedy is brought out better by wit—through incongruity and grotesque under-statement—than by the lurid overstatement of po-ems like Poe's "Ulalume" that are forever saying "Boo!" to the reader.

This double-talk use of frivolity is the basis of section II of *Terror and Decorum* entitled "Six The-ological Cradle Songs." Their motto might have been "Six cradles make six coffins." These songs are to be read simultaneously on two levels: (1) hu-morous nursery rhymes for children; (2) sinister al-legories for adults. The same sinister-naïve, double-level technique recurs in many of my other poems, such as the concluding dialogue between man and a sadistic reality ("sky," nature, God) in "From Ancient Fangs." This method is no new-fangled affectation but inherent in nursery rhymes, fairy tales, myths, and the language of childhood; for example, the *frisson* of so familiar a Mother Goose couplet as: "Here comes a candle to light you to bed, / And here comes a chopper to chop off your head." In this connection David Daiches wrote of *Terror and Decorum*:

> "When the wit is wholly absorbed in the form, we get something quite distinctive in modern poetry—witty, but not with the wit of the early Auden; subtle, but not with the subtlety of the neo-Yeatsians; speculative, but still and essentially lyrical . . . 'Better Come Quietly' and 'Exorcism' have an admirable sardonic humor which is positively terrifying."

"Better Come Quietly," the example cited by Mr. Daiches, is the first of the "Six Theological Cradle Songs." It is meant to be chanted with a childishly over-obvious stress on the accented words, just as a child jumping rhythmically on the springs of its crib might chant. The overstress is indicated here and in other poems of mine by capital letters. As used by me, this typographical device does not mean "more important" (though capital letters often are used to mean this) but means: "read this at a raucous shout." The same voice function of capitals occurs in "Exorcism" in the Athos And Assisi chapter. On the allegorical level of its double-talk, "Better Come Quietly" is a medieval morality play of the four ages of man from embryo into afterlife. In each age, the questioning demand for consolation receives the same answer from the triple chorus that haunts us all:

> *Baby John:* O kinsfolk and gentlefolk, PLEASE be forgiving, But nothing can lure me to living, to living. I'm snug where I am; I don't WISH to burst through.

> *Chorus of Nurses, Furies, and Muses:* That's what YOU think. If only you KNEW!

> *Baby John:* Well then YES, I'll be BORN, but my EARTH will be heaven; My dice will throw nothing but seven-eleven; Life is tall lilacs, all giddy with dew.

> *Chorus of Nurses, Furies, and Muses:* That's what YOU think. If only you KNEW!

> *Baby John:* Well then YES, there'll be sorrows, be sorrows that best me; But these are mere teasings to test me, to test me. We'll ZOOM from our graves when God orders us to.

> *Chorus of Nurses, Furies, and Muses:* That's what YOU think. If only you KNEW!

> *Baby John:* Well then YES, I'll belie my belief in survival. But IF there's no God, then at least there's no devil: If at LAST I must die—well, at LEAST when I do, It's clear I won't sizzle.

> *Chorus of Nurses, Furies, and Muses:* If only you KNEW!

IV

There's an essential element I haven't discussed so far and am unable to define. Yet I am dedicated to it side by side with my classicism in a synthesis of antitheses. The title *Terror and Decorum* and lines like "What terror crowns the sweetness of all song?" formulate this dualism of what Nietzsche called the Dionysian and the Appolonian; also the dualism of the primordial "dark gods" of the unconscious and the more rational, civilized conscious mind. The creative tension of these antitheses is in the shiver of holy dread, the tragic exaltation which makes the hair stand on end and is the difference between poetry and verse.

My nearest approach to catching this element is in "Some Lines In Three Parts." The poem describes the attempt of the ego, trapped in its vulnerable mortal skull, to burst free by means of song. Completed after *Terror and Decorum* and appearing in *Harper's* magazine this poem is (I believe) my best so far. Part III of the poem photographs the ego in the fleeting moment of metamorphosis from owl, the bird of wisdom, into philomel, the bird of song. This moment of "holy dread," being as unbearably ugly as birth and creativity always are, is the moment of the birth of beauty:

> "What hubbub rocks the nest? What panic-
>   freighted
> Invasion—when he tried to sing—dilated
> The big eyes of my blinking, hooting fowl?
> A cartilaginous, most rheumatic squeak
> Portends (half mocks) the change; the wrenched
>   bones creak;
> Unself descends, invoked or uninvited;
> Self ousts itself, consumed and consummated;
> An inward-facing mask is what must break.
> The magic feverish fun of chirping, all
> That professorial squints and squawks indicted,
> Is here—descends, descends—till wisdom, hoarse
> From bawling beauty out, at last adores,
> Possessed by metamorphosis so strong.
> Then, with a final flutter, philomel—
> How mud-splashed, what a mangy miracle!—
> Writhes out of owl and stands with drooping wing.
> Just stands there. Moulted, naked, two-thirds dead.
> From shock and pain (and dread of holy dread)
> Suddenly vomiting.
> Look away quick; you are watching the birth of
>   song."

Yet even here, I can only grope. I am unable to say more or to see deeper because I don't understand enough about the all-important night-side of art, its magic. I can only repeat falteringly that its magic contains "more things between heaven and earth, Horatio, than are dreamt of" in the dayside of "your philosophy." Who does understand it? Perhaps Robert Graves in *The White Goddess* or the Yeats of "Ego Dominus Tuus"? Perhaps Lowes in *The Road To Xanadu*, Frazer in *The Golden Bough*, or Jessie Weston in *From Ritual To Romance?* Or is the answer in Schopenhauer, Freud, Orpheus, Icarus, Kilroy? I don't know. I wish I did.

Different poets take such different attitudes towards poetic magic that it is helpful for each to clarify his attitude for the reader. In *Terror and Decorum* the "Author's Note on Marabouts and Planted Poets" and the poems "The Killer and the Dove," "Poet," "A Walk on Snow," "Africa and My New York," and my mock-archaic "Ballad of the Jollie Gleeman" together give a composite picture of the artist as culture-hero, the showman as shaman, the clown as priest. Uneasy lies the clown that wears a head, according to "A Walk on Snow":

> Not priest but clown, the shuddering sorcerer
> Is more astounded than his rapt applauders:
> "Then all those props and Easters of my stage
> Came true? But I was joking all the time!"
> Art, being bartender, is never drunk;
> And magic that believes itself, must die . . .
> Unfrocked magicians freeze the whole night long;
> Holy iambic cannot thaw the snow
> They walk on when obsessive crystals bloom.

A key word is "obsessive." This is true in the lines above. It is true in "Dolce Ossessione," where the beauty left by the artist (is it lies? is it truth?) remains to be picked up not by the lean-ribbed scavenger cats (just who are *they?*) but by the child, the future:

> "I'll urge Obsession on: an eel, I'll swim
> To every far Sargasso of my whim . . .
> A flame-scaled trout, I'll shimmer through your
>   nets—
> Like lies?, like truth?—and gasp on fatal sands.
> Trailed fawning by lascivious hungry cats,
> What child will scoop me up, what pudgy hands?"

V

Many poets wince automatically whenever any critic paraphrases their poems, as if an elephant were trampling on butterfly wings. The "heresy of paraphrase" it is called. To be sure paraphrase is helpful only in conjunction with the other tools of criticism. By itself, paraphrase is inadequate because it gives only the What of a poem, not the How. Nevertheless, a lucid rendering of the What can usually throw a little more light on the How, form and content being inseparable. Even a little light helps inasmuch as our new credo must be that communication is artistic, obscurity inartistic, and a deep simplicity the first virtue.

What Do I Read Next?

- Peter Viereck's first published work was actually his doctoral dissertation *Metapolitics: From the Romantics to Hitler*, which came out in 1941. In this book, he explores his conservative political beliefs, most of which stem from his father's support of Nazism. While it may be considered "dry" by readers not interested in history or political thought, *Metapolitics* is actually an interesting look at what Viereck calls the theory of "revolt against revolt."

- Edith Hamilton's *Mythology* is a classic retelling of the stories of Greek and Roman mythology. Originally published in 1942, it has gone through numerous reprints and is readily available in both libraries and bookstores. The book is divided into sections on the gods and early heroes, love and adventure stories, heroes before and during the Trojan War, and lesser myths.

- Published in 1977, Guy Sajer's *The Forgotten Soldier* is an autobiographical account of a young German's experience on the Eastern Front during World War II. The book has been called shocking, horrifying, and difficult to put down as Sajer relates the story of bloody battles, miserable living conditions, cruel Russian winters, and even falling in love with a young woman from Berlin.

- In 1991, Jim Nye published a collection of poems and essays written by soldiers who fought in Vietnam. *Aftershock: Poems and Prose from the Vietnam War* depicts the horror and grief of those who went to war and the loved ones they left behind. Most of these works present a striking contrast to those written about World War II, including "Kilroy."

The use of words like "heresy" in current criticism is typical. It is a hierarchical word, deriding the non-élite reader. It helps show how pontifical discussions of poetry have become since the triumph of the Eliotizing epigones. Such ruling trends (penny-wise but Pound-foolish in the case of the

1949 Bollingen Prize) explain the awe of the fancier critics for the 98 per cent incoherent, 2 per cent lovely, and persistently fascist and anti-semitic *Pisan Cantos* of the man who has done so much to establish the Eliot movement. Does this imply fascist sympathies (as has been overhastily alleged) in either the New Critics or in Eliot? Emphatically not! Rather, their attitude toward Pound implies an untenable doctrinaire attempt to separate form from content and to separate poetry from its inextricable moral and historical context. One should feel a deep pity for those poor reviewers who struggled so painfully to praise the *Pisan Cantos* because they dared not, for reasons of *avantgarde* prestige, admit they couldn't make head or tail out of them.

Eliot is a great poet, who happens also to be a brilliantly self-contradictory critic. Not he so much as his ungreat imitators are to blame for the fact that their cult of his criticism and their accompanying cult of studied obscurity are stifling the growth of poetry today. Charming and velvet-gloved, this dictatorship is based not on coercion but on an ambiguous mixture of snobbism and real excellence.

Fresh air? No hope for that yet. Not until a new generation of poets and critics—honest enough not to crave praise from the precious, courageous enough not to fear the sarcasm of the pretentious—throws open the windows in the hermetic house.

With their tone of "we the mandarins," the "heresy"-scorning exquisites forbid anybody except crossword-puzzle decoders to get fun out of poetry, not to mention beauty. The poetry-murdering vocabulary to which this has ultimately led is the "Glossary of the New Criticism" published in *Poetry* magazine. Originally the New Criticism was a needed liberating revolution. It produced such masterpieces as Ransom's "Painted Head" and Tate's "Mediterranean." It freed our metrics from the sloppy, smug clichés of the nineteenth century. Today, the New Criticism, already a very old criticism, has become a bar to further esthetic progress, producing nimble imitative pedants and enslaving our metrics with its own twentieth-century clichés. Read a fresh and joyous poem like Ransom's "Armageddon"; then contemplate the "Glossary of the New Criticism." So doing, you will feel like an enthusiast of the early idealistic phase of the French Revolution contemplating the intolerant "Committee of Public Safety"—or, to draw a more accurate parallel, contemplating the dictatorship of the stale and unimaginative Directorate.

Every poet should read that unbelievably humorless "Glossary" to learn why twenty years of brilliant nonsense have helped alienate the general public from poetry and its critics. No wonder all modern poetry is dismissed (unjustly) as a snore and an allusion by that audience of intelligent non-experts who are neither professional poets nor professional critics. It is precisely this lost audience to whom my own poetry is directed, which is why these remarks are not irrelevant to a discussion of my working principles.

Such an audience can be seduced only temporarily by snob appeal or by acrobatics. It can be intimidated only temporarily by being told to admire—or else be damned as philistine—the poetic reputations created synthetically with an almost convincing air of authority by the too-clever-to-be-true jargon of coteries. Critics and poets will not win back the intelligent general reader until they speak to him humanly and clearly—in the truly classic sense—instead of more royally than the king, more classically than the Greeks, and more pontifically than any pope. This is the assumption on which all my poetry and criticism are written: *"En ceste foy"* (to recall the Villon refrain) *"je vueil vivre et mourir."*

Source: Peter Viereck, "My Kind of Poetry," in *Mid-Century American Poets*, edited by John Ciardi, Twayne Publishers, Inc., 1950, pp. 16–30.

Sources

Henault, Marie, *Peter Viereck*, Twayne Publishers, Inc., 1969, p. 60.

McElveen, Idris, "Peter Viereck," in *Dictionary of Literary Biography*, Vol. 5: *American Poets since World War II, Part II: L–Z*, Gale Research, 1980, pp. 340–48.

Viereck, Peter, *New and Selected Poems 1932–1967*, The Bobbs-Merrill Company, Inc., 1967.

Further Reading

G.I.: American Soldier in World War II, Warner Books, 1987.

This account covers a soldier's experience from boot camp to military discharge. It includes such minute details as what GIs ate as well as a broad discussion on the mental and emotional states of American soldiers fighting in Europe, Asia, and the South Pacific.

Osgood, Charles, ed., *Kilroy Was Here: The Best American Humor from World War II*, Hyperion, 2001.

This is television journalist Charles Osgood's collection of some of the best humor writing to come out of the Second World War. It has been said that much of the tragedy of battle is made bearable by trying to find things to laugh at, and this is a wonderful look at everything from veterans' funny memoirs to classic lines which helped buoy the American spirit through one of history's darkest times.

Viereck, Peter, *Tide and Continuities: Last and First Poems, 1995–1938*, University of Arkansas Press, 1995.

Like the poem "Kilroy," much of the poetry in this recent publication of Viereck's is philosophical and filled with allusions to Greek and Roman mythology. The works included span much of the poet's career, and, although it is lengthy and at times over-laden, it is worth at least a partial read for one interested in his writing.

———, *The Unadjusted Man: A New Hero for Americans*, Capricorn Books, 1956.

This is one of Viereck's most important nonfiction works. Its subtitle is "Reflections on the Distinction between Conforming and Conserving," and it helps shed light on the nature of Viereck's politics—the driving force behind his poetry.

Last Request

Joel Brouwer

1999

When Joel Brouwer's "Last Request" was published in his first (and only, to date) collection *Exactly What Happened* in 1999, it was one among many poems that surprised readers with a macabre subject and somewhat bizarre humor. With poem titles such as "Former Kenyan Parliament Member Arrested for 'Imagining the Death' of President Daniel Arap Moi," "Astronomers Detect Water in Distant Galaxy," and "Locking Up the Russian," Brouwer shows his audience up front that he is not afraid to break the rules of formal or "expected" poetry. His work tackles any and all topics, and "Last Request" is a good example. Its subject is not only strange and funny but frightening and tragic as well.

In this poem, the speaker requests that, after he dies, his body be entombed in a cardboard pyramid and placed in the backyard at first, then taken to a dump and left among the stench of spoiled food and hungry flies buzzing about the piles of garbage. As odd and deplorable as this sounds, the speaker presents a good case for his request and does so in simple, honest, perfectly sane language—in spite of his obviously crazy desire. "Last Request" is funny in places, sad in others, and always surprising. This mixture of intriguing qualities is what makes Brouwer's work stand out among the throng of young, contemporary American poets, and it is what makes this poem both delightful and depressing at the same time.

Author Biography

Joel Brouwer was born in Grand Rapids, Michigan, in 1968. He earned his bachelor's degree from Sarah Lawrence College in 1990 and a master's degree from Syracuse University in 1993. He was a visiting assistant professor in the creative writing department at the University of Alabama in Tuscaloosa for the 2000–2001 academic year. Though his poems are anything but typical contemporary mainstream works, they have been published in several of America's most prestigious journals, including the *Boston Review*, *Harvard Review*, *Paris Review*, *Ploughshares*, and *Southwest Review*. In addition to his teaching position, he is also a freelance writer and critic and has written reviews for the *Progressive* and the *Harvard Review*.

The poem "Last Request" appears in Brouwer's first collection of poetry, *Exactly What Happened*, published in 1999. The manuscript was awarded the 1998 Verna Emery Prize by Purdue University Press and was published by Purdue the following year. In 2000, *Exactly What Happened* won the Larry Levis Reading Prize, awarded by Virginia Commonwealth University. Brouwer's often uncanny presentation of subject matter in his poetry, as well as his quirky sense of humor and tendency to pull poem titles directly from newspaper headlines, have gotten his work much attention from readers in both academic and nonacademic settings. He is currently at work on a collection of prose poems entitled *Centuries* and a collection of his more typically styled poems tentatively called *Reproductions of the Masters*. A prolific writer, Brouwer is also currently compiling essays for a book on the uses of history in contemporary poetry.

Joel Brouwer

Poem Text

A pine box for me. I mean it.
My father.

For the record, friends and family,
I'd like a pyramid when I go.

A small one is fine: build it   5
out of cardboard in the backyard.

For mortar use duct tape
or school glue: nothing strong enough

to make it sturdy. I want it
to fall down a lot. Lay me in there naked   10

on the shadowed grass and,
whatever the weather,

wait outside all night.
No beer, no burgers or dancing,

no horseshoes. You may smoke. Talk quietly   15
if you must talk. Be very sad.

the wind will push the pyramid over often.
Grumble as you set it back up.

Let it be a hard night. Be bored
and edgy. Snap at each other. Yawn.   20

And just before dawn toss me and my pyramid
in the back of a pickup, drive us

to the dump, and dump us
on the tallest garbage mountain

you can find. It will be repulsive: flies   25
on my lips, old spaghetti sauce smeared

in my hair. Let it smell terrible.
Then go home. Quickly, before the cops show up

with their plastic bags and notebooks.
And on your way home, please   30

accept from me the only gift
I'll have to give: relief

You're not me. That even if this world
is a stagnant ditch between nothing

and nothing, you may at least   35
sip from it a little longer. Be glad,

and because I loved you,
forget me as fast as you can.

Poem Summary

Lines 1–2

Brouwer prefaces the poem "Last Request" with a line he attributes to his father speaking about his own burial: "A pine box for me. I mean it." Apparently, the older man would be content with a very simple, inexpensive interment, and he is adamant about it. The opening lines of the poem, then, present a stark contrast to the father's request. The speaker, or son, does not want a pine box but "a pyramid" when he dies, and he informs his "friends and family" about his request "for the record." Lines 1 and 2 provide the basis for a poem that becomes a list of instructions on how the speaker wants to be buried.

Lines 3–4

The pyramids of ancient Egypt represent a glorification of life after death, in particular the lives and deaths of pharaohs. Pyramids were built as monuments to house the tombs of the powerful, beloved kings, and death was seen as merely the beginning of a journey to the other world. In ancient Egypt, an individual's eternal life depended on the continued existence of the king, making the pharaoh's tomb a vital concern for the entire kingdom. But the speaker in "Last Request" is not a powerful ruler, and he humbly acknowledges this by asking for a modest pyramid: "A small one is fine," and it is all right to "build it / out of cardboard."

Lines 5–8

If the poem has not seemed bizarre enough at this point, these four lines are convincing of its odd subject. Here, the speaker admits that he does not want a sturdy, permanent burial place but rather one that will "fall down a lot." He okays the use of "duct tape / or school glue"—again two common, meager products that are in direct contrast to what one normally thinks of when considering a real pyramid. The Great Pyramid of Giza, today a part of Greater Cairo, Egypt, is the oldest yet only surviving "wonder" of the Seven Ancient Wonders of the World. This pyramid houses the tomb of Khufu (Cheops) and took over twenty years to build—hardly in line with the cardboard structure the poem's speaker requests. It is doubtful, too, that King Khufu went to his grave unclothed, for pharaohs were buried with most of their royal possessions to use in the afterlife. The speaker, however, humbly states, "Lay me in there naked."

Lines 9–11

These lines indicate a slight turn in the speaker's modest, obliging request to his family and friends. He is making his funeral and burial cheap for them, but "whatever the weather," he wants them to "wait outside all night." The thought here is both humorous and horrifying, as one pictures a group of mourners huddled throughout the night—in rain, snow, sleet, whatever—around a poor cardboard pyramid with their loved one lying naked inside "on the shadowed grass."

Lines 12–14

The speaker's tone grows a bit more forceful and obstinate in these lines as he makes his instructions very clear in a no-nonsense manner. He dictates what the mourners may not eat or drink as well as what forms of entertainment they must not engage in. He reluctantly allows them to talk to each other if they "must," and he goes so far as to instruct them on their emotional mindset: "Be very sad."

Lines 15–18

The speaker predicts that "The wind will push the pyramid over often," just as he wants it to do, and he seems to enjoy the idea of having his friends and family "Grumble" each time they must set it upright. Lines 17 and 18 reflect more selfishness than humility in the speaker's request, as he wants it to "be a hard night" for those gathered around, and he wants them to be "bored / and edgy," hateful and tired.

Lines 19–20

As though to soften the harshness of the previous lines, the speaker now appeases his audience by allowing them to pay their respects to him by entering his "rickety tomb" and saying goodbye. Unable to let it go at that, however, he adds a further instruction: visit "one at a time."

Lines 21–24

Now the poem takes an even more peculiar turn as the speaker's request list becomes more outlandish and macabre. He apparently believes his dead body will be no different from garbage, and so he wants it taken, along with his pyramid, to a dump where it should be placed "on the tallest garbage mountain" his mourners can find.

Lines 25–27

The key word in these lines is "repulsive," for that is exactly the kind of scene they describe. The image of a dead loved one with flies on his lips and spaghetti sauce in his hair is obviously shocking and sickening. Adding to the visuals, Brouwer does not want readers to forget what this scene must smell like, too, and so, the reminder that it will "smell terrible."

Lines 28–29

Nearing the end of the to-do list for his friends and family, the speaker now allows them to go home. With tongue-in-cheek caution, he warns them against being caught dumping a dead body on a trash heap—an act that homicide detectives "with their plastic bags and notebooks" would hardly believe had been requested by the deceased.

Lines 30–32

Here, the poem begins to reveal its true meaning. This is the first mention of a "gift" that the speaker wants to leave for those he loved. After requesting such a gruesome funeral, the idea of telling his mourners to accept "the only gift" he will be able to give seems as strange as all the other orders he has given them. Line 32 ends with the revelation of the gift, but it is ambiguous at this point. Is his gift "relief" that the terrible night is over? Is it "relief" that his loved ones managed to honor his requests without getting arrested? Or is it something else—something even more unexpected?

Lines 33–36

In keeping with a typical Brouwer poem, yes, it is something even more unexpected. The speaker's gift to his friends and family is the relief they will find in knowing it was he who died and not they. Regardless of how saddened the loved ones are by his passing, they still relish their own lives, and the speaker readily acknowledges that fact. These lines contain the only true metaphor in this poem, and it is a powerful one. Calling the world "a stagnant ditch between nothing / and nothing," he inflicts a hard sentence on human society and yet determines that living in a bad world is still better than not living at all. In contrast to line 14 in which the speaker instructs his mourners to "Be very sad," he now tells them to "Be glad."

Lines 37–38

The poem ends with what is essentially the speaker's last request. While most dying people would want to be remembered—hopefully in a good way—by their friends and family, this potential dead man wants to be forgotten as quickly

Media Adaptations

- There are several Joel Brouwer poems posted on the Internet, although "Last Request" is not one of them at this time. Doing a general search under the poet's name brings up sites where the poems reside, as well as some reviews Brouwer has written for various publications.

as his loved ones can manage to do so. The last two lines present an odd juxtaposition of emotions. To say "because I loved you" makes the speaker seem gentle and kind in stating his heartfelt affection for those he will leave behind, but finishing the phrase with the abrupt, rather crude comment "forget me as fast as you can" offsets the softer tone with yet a final bizarre twist.

Themes

Macabre Humor

Brouwer uses macabre humor in "Last Request" not only as a device to grab and keep the reader's attention but also as a set-up for the more somber—and separate—theme of the human will to live in spite of the world's problems. One's asking for his body, after death, to be placed in a pyramid is strange enough, but to want the pyramid constructed out of cardboard, duct tape, and school glue takes *strange* to a new level. The request is truly morbid and weird, but it is also funny. And as the speaker moves through his list of do's and don'ts for proper behavior at his odd funeral, the items become progressively more ghoulish, as well as more humorous. He does not mind if the wind blows the flimsy pyramid from his naked body, but he wants to be sure no one is eating hamburgers or playing horseshoes. He is adamant that friends and family members mourn him all night long, but he hopes they have a bad time while doing so. And as if they have not endured enough throughout the night, he adds to their anguish—and to the reader's delight—by asking them to "toss" him and his pyra-

Topics for Further Study

- Write a poem about the kind of funeral you would prefer for yourself with as many details as possible and including descriptions of how friends and loved ones may respond to your ceremony.

- Why do you think the speaker in Brouwer's poem selects a pyramid for his tomb? What connection might he feel with these ancient structures, and why would he want his own tomb to be so flimsy?

- James Randi is an outspoken commentator on fraudulent psychics, magicians, and so forth. Read some of his research and write an essay on whether you agree or disagree with his controversial claims.

- Pretend you are one of the onlookers at the speaker's all-night funeral in "Last Request" and that you are keeping a journal of the events. What would your entry include about the other people there, the weather, the pyramid itself, the mood of the evening, and so on. Be specific and feel free to quote the other mourners.

---

mid in a truck and take him to the dump for his final resting place. Brouwer paints a particularly gruesome scene at the dump, with flies stuck to the dead man's lips, rancid tomato sauce strung in his hair, and, of course, the horrible odor. This disgusting picture is softened somewhat by the offhand comment to hurry home "before the cops show up," but the reader is still left with a very ugly, very disturbing image in mind as the poem draws to a close. The ending, however, shifts away from both morbidity and humor, as the speaker requests something even more unexpected than any other item on his ghastly list.

The Will to Live

Although only a few lines in "Last Request" are dedicated to this theme, the idea of the human will to live, which comes in at the end, jolts the intellect harder than the exaggerated imagery and hu-

mor do. The final eight lines of the poem express a sentiment far different from the first three-quarters of it, and the startling turnaround is what affords this theme such a powerful effect. After requesting friends and family to perform bizarre, disrespectful, and illegal acts, the speaker asks an even more dismaying favor—that each accepts the feeling of relief that comes with knowing he or she is still alive. While this feeling is certainly not unheard of—many people probably sit through funerals happy not to be the one the ceremony is *for*—it occurs in this poem at a point when human life and human dignity have just been dragged through some deep mud. Juxtaposed against a grotesque setting of an all-night funeral and a horrible garbage dump, the serene, calming notion of being able to "sip" from life a little longer takes on even greater significance. The water in the "stagnant ditch" of the world is still drinkable to the living, and the desire to be able to partake of it—no matter how filthy or vile—is a testament to the human will to hold on to life under any circumstances.

Style

Free Verse

"Last Request" is written in free verse with very little attention to any literary devices or poetic elements. If not for the line breaks dividing the work into couplets, one could hear it read and could think it was written as a simple prose paragraph. It is this simplicity of language and curt, direct sentences that enhance the poem's shocking subject. Using obvious, flowery meter or contrived metaphors to describe a dead body in a cardboard pyramid with family members standing around "bored / and edgy" would not be nearly as effective as Brouwer's somber, clear address. The speaker gives startling, to-the-point instructions throughout the poem, leading to the most surprising—and most disturbing—request at the end. Note the simple language, yet horrific meaning, in such lines as: "For mortar use duct tape," "Lay me in there naked," "No beer, no burgers or dancing," "You may smoke," "Be very sad," "Yawn," "Then go home," "Be glad," and, finally, "forget me as fast as you can."

While the visual images evoked by "Last Request" are precise and easy to picture throughout the poem, Brouwer throws in an intriguing metaphor toward the end that conjures a mixed bag of dreary images. He likens the world to "a stagnant ditch between nothing / and nothing" that the

---

living "may at least / sip from . . . a little longer." This analogy may be more poetic than anything else in the poem, but the fact that it stands alone makes it all the more important in the work. After reading through a string of direct, brief instructions, the reader is suddenly hit with a powerful, provocative metaphor that may elicit sadness and fear or even anger and shame. The point is that *some* emotion is called out, and it is a very effective way to end the poem.

Historical Context

Since Brouwer's first published book is only two years old as of this writing, a true historical perspective on his work, when it can be measured against the events of its time in a broader scope, is several years away. However, one can speculate fairly safely on the cultural, political, and social occurrences, as well as on the acts of some now notorious individuals, that could cause a poet to refer to the world in which he lives as a "stagnant ditch between nothing / and nothing." The last few years of the twentieth century were filled with news stories of unprecedented violence on American soil as well as continued conflicts in timeworn trouble spots across the globe. Problems between Israel and Palestine were nothing new in 1995, but in that year, Israel was shocked by violence within its own ranks when a young Jewish student assassinated Prime Minister Yitzhak Rabin. The student was angry with his leader for "giving" Israel to the Arabs. Although the Hebron Accord was designed to promote peace between Arabs and Jews, the pact was undermined by both sides when renewed terrorist acts broke out in 1997 and both sides tried to establish new settlements in spite of the non-expansionist agreement. In 1999, Israel elected its most decorated soldier, Ehud Barak, prime minister, and he has since come under fire for having no success in promoting peace in the Middle East.

But Israel and Palestine were hardly the only warring factions in the late 1990s. In Africa in 1997, Rwanda collapsed into civil war as violence between the ethnic groups Hutus and Tutsis tore the country apart. In 1998, the United States and Great Britain launched air strikes against Iraq in retaliation for Saddam Hussein's refusal to allow representatives from the United Nations access to Iraq's weaponry arsenals. And in 1999, Russia launched a major offensive against Chechnyan sep-

aratists, the second time in a decade that the Russians attempted to bring the rebels under control with warfare. The *threat* of war and unscrupulous power was also distressing in this period: France angered the international community by detonating five underground nuclear devices on two South Pacific atolls in 1995, and longtime enemies India and Pakistan both conducted underground nuclear tests in 1998, to the chagrin of the Western world.

Perhaps the most dismaying acts of violence in this decade came in the form of terrorism, both overseas and in the United States. In 1996, nineteen American servicemen were killed and hundreds were wounded in Saudi Arabia when a bomb planted in a fuel truck exploded in front of an apartment complex housing military personnel. Two years later, 258 people were killed when American embassies were destroyed by terrorist bombings, allegedly instigated by Islamic radical Osama bin Laden. The United States retaliated with air strikes against Afghanistan and Sudan. But no overseas terrorist act had as far-reaching and sobering effect on Americans as did the 1995 bombing of the Murrah Federal building in Oklahoma City. Timothy McVeigh was arrested for causing the deaths of 168 children and adults in the worst terrorist attack to that date on American soil. McVeigh, scheduled for execution in May 2001, missed his first date with death when the FBI revealed that not all records had been turned over to the defense during the investigation; he was later executed in June 2001. Only a year after the Oklahoma bombing, the summer Olympic games were underway in Atlanta when a bomb exploded in the city's Centennial Park, killing 1 and injuring 111. It was the one-hundredth anniversary of the Olympics, a celebration cut short by terrorism. Also in 1996, the FBI received a tip from a terrorist's brother, leading to the arrest of Theodore Kaczynski, wanted for murdering three people and injuring twenty-three by sending mail bombs. Kaczynski had been on the run for seventeen years.

Not all the horrendous acts of violence committed during the time that Brouwer was writing poems for his first collection were politically motivated. Individuals also made decisions that would shock society for their barbarism and cruelty, seemingly based on personal agendas only. In 1995, in Union, South Carolina, Susan Smith was found guilty of drowning her two young sons in order to gain the affection of a man who did not want children. In 1997, thirty-nine members of the Heavens Gate cult committed suicide in California, believing that was the only way to get on board a spaceship supposedly following the path of the Hale-Bopp comet. Even more shocking was the 1999 slaughter at Columbine High School in Littleton, Colorado, when two teenage students went on a shooting spree, killing fifteen and wounding twenty-three. The Columbine shooting was only one of a series of school violence incidents that has plagued the United States in recent years, furthering the fear, cynicism, doubt, and anger that many Americans contend with in their daily lives.

Reporting only the bad news from the past several years may be an unfair assessment of the historical and cultural events that occurred during this time. Surely, good things happened, too, and one could provide a list just as long on the accomplishments in medicine, civil rights, international relations, and many other venues that the world witnessed at the close of the twentieth century. The task, though, to provide a possible impetus for the dark conclusion that one young poet draws in one of his poems dictates a rundown of the just as dark events he read about, heard about, and saw on television while composing his work. All *bad* things considered, it is no wonder that Brouwer finds his world a "stagnant ditch," but, even so, he still admits it is best to "sip from it" as long as one can.

Critical Overview

Brouwer is a young poet whose first book has not yet had time to elicit a great deal of published criticism. Considering, however, that *Exactly What Happened* has already won two distinguished awards for poetry, one can safely assume that Brouwer's work has received favorable recognition from critics and readers in general. Brouwer was selected for one of the awards, the Verna Emery Poetry Prize sponsored by Purdue University, by Lucia Perillo, herself a former Emery winner in 1996. Writing for the university's press, Perillo describes *Exactly What Happened* as "both canny and innocent, hopeful one minute and bleak the next, and always mordantly funny." She goes on to say that the poems "are spoken in the voice of the guy on the corner, without any poetic curlicues" and that their subjects "will make you think that you can feel the poet's hand tipping your head so that the world came into focus at an angle slightly different from the way that you are used to seeing it."

Pleasant surprise is probably the most likely response among readers who are doubtful of contemporary poetry's merits, or of poetry as a whole.

Critic Kevin Sampsell, writing for the online magazine *theStranger.com*, admits that he has "a bias against books published by university presses . . . . which are usually as dry and lifeless as a Christmas tree in January." After reading *Exactly What Happened*, Sampsell changed his mind, stating that "Brouwer's work does the opposite of what I expect from an academic press. It sparkles, hypnotizes, connects, and squeezes juice out of the poet's life and into your funny bone." This admitted about-face from a critic who does not mince words is one of the highest compliments a young poet could be handed.

Criticism

Pamela Steed Hill

Hill is the author of a poetry collection, has published widely in poetry journals, and is an associate editor for a university publications department. In the following essay, she addresses the humorous irony in the speaker's last request, claiming he has intentionally made the wish impossible to grant.

A cardboard pyramid instead of a satin-lined coffin. A naked body instead of one dressed in its best, or brand new, suit. An outdoor, all-night gathering of dubious mourners in bad weather instead of a quiet indoor vigil and service for loved ones. A clandestine drive in a pick-up truck to a garbage dump instead of a somber procession with a hearse carrying the dead to a pretty, well-manicured cemetery lawn. And, finally, an attempt to honor the last request of the dearly departed whose remains have just been left on a pile of garbage with flies on his lips and spaghetti sauce in his hair: you must forget him as fast as you can.

It is only fitting that a poem made up of brief, prosy couplets, each progressively more bizarre than the previous in meaning, and a wonderfully dry tone on the part of the speaker should end with a quick punch in the gut—and in the funny bone. Brouwer's "Last Request" does not disappoint. Even so, the last line—the *last request*—is still unexpected, for the reader is waiting for one more gruesome, off-the-wall solicitation from a speaker who has already put friends and family through unspeakable horrors regarding his burial preferences. But the poem ends with a seemingly loving touch, and the operative word here is *seemingly*. The next-to-last line implies a tender, emotional moment as the speaker at last admits his feelings toward his mourners: "because I loved you" resonates with affection, sweetness, and sincerity. What it leads into, however, is a bit puzzling. Does he love them so much that he cannot bear the thought of the pain and grief his death will cause and therefore he unselfishly gives them permission to forget him quickly and spare themselves the agony? Is this not an act of complete, altruistic love?

Hardly. It is, rather, a hilarious, ironic, and somewhat cruel joke on the "loved ones" left behind. After what they will have been through—should they even decide to grant the speaker's wishes after he has actually died—how can they possibly forget him *ever*, much less *quickly*? The speaker has set up an intentional impasse for his friends and family. If they do not carry out his requests, they are guilty of denying a dead man his final wishes. If they do carry them out, they will certainly never be able to forget him. And that, of course, means they will never be able to carry out the last request.

All this may simply lead to the question, what's the point? Why make a final will and testament so difficult for those left behind to carry out, and, more so, why make the requests so weird? Brouwer's poem is a conundrum of sorts. It appears the speaker is just a self-centered, crude individual who wants to get the last laugh on his friends and family even after he is dead. But perhaps he is a frantic, despairing man, so desperate to hold on to life that he creates a panorama of sensory events—granted, both strange and disgusting—to keep himself in the tangible world as long as possible. And perhaps this explains why his to-do list becomes increasingly bizarre and offensive to the senses as one reads it from beginning to end. This progression into total repulsion is worth examining.

The first hint of oddness, of course, is the notion of being laid to rest in a cardboard pyramid so rickety and fragile that it keeps falling down. But it is a funny notion, one that is amusing to picture, not gruesome. Unfortunately, the humor is darkened somewhat by knowing that when the pyramid falls over, it exposes the *naked* body of a dead loved one. It is bad enough that his mourners have to keep getting glimpses of him at all, but to see the body in such a vulnerable—and embarrassing—state is particularly painful. But for the speaker, perhaps this is just a good way of staying in direct physical contact with the tangible world. Lying completely unclothed "on the shadowed grass" in "whatever the weather" is a purely sensory experience, something very attractive to one who is contemplating death.

> *It is only fitting that a poem made up of brief, prosy couplets, each progressively more bizarre than the previous in meaning, and a wonderfully dry tone on the part of the speaker should end with a quick punch in the gut—and in the funny bone."*

Stanzas 6–9 contain a conglomeration of words describing things one can taste, smell, hear, and physically do: beer and burgers, dancing and playing horseshoes, smoking and talking, grumbling, snapping at each other, and yawning. The speaker has become very specific about the human activity he wants to control in the onlookers, but it is also the human activity that he will not be alive to participate in. This fact alone makes the senses of taste, smell, and hearing all the more vital, and being specific about them allows him to enjoy them a little longer. While there is nothing particularly ghoulish or disgusting about the activities and food he mentions in this list, the items do imply a growing desperation to be near what is *real*. His frenzy takes a big leap forward in the latter part of the poem when the speaker resorts to the truly revolting notion of having his dead, naked body dumped on a pile of garbage. Nevertheless, he still concentrates on the sensory experience it will evoke—the horrible sight of flies and spoiled food, the terrible odor, even an allusion to the sound of approaching sirens as the police arrive on the scene. The final sensory description is in the metaphor at the end. It, too, is repulsive—drinking stagnant water from a ditch—but it drives home the speaker's most important point: any kind of life is better than none at all.

Whether Brouwer's persona in "Last Request" is just a cruel, gross individual with a warped sense of humor or a thoughtful man desperate to point out the sanctity of life to his friends and family can-

What Do I Read Next?

- Reading Brouwer's book reviews of other contemporary poets' works provides insight on what he looks for in poetry and the elements he finds least appealing. He has written various reviews—two in *Progressive* (Vol. 63, No. 8, August 1999; Vol. 63, No. 12, December 1999 respectively), for example.

- *The Complete Pyramids: Solving the Ancient Mysteries* by Mark Lehner, published in 1997, is a thorough, fully illustrated compilation of every major pyramid of ancient Egypt. Lehner is a leading Egyptologist, and in this book he surveys the history, building, and purpose of the pyramids in extensive detail.

- Brouwer's *Exactly What Happened* deals heavily with the concepts of illusion and truth and how a magician's work depends on the audience believing that what just happened really did happen. Harry Houdini is one of the most popular illusionists and escape artists in history, and many books have been written about him. *The Secrets of Houdini* by John Clucas Cannell, published in 1975, is one of the better books. It covers Houdini's life, the details of his famous escapes (except the water torture cell), and his fight against fraudulent mediums.

- Albert Goldbarth has been writing poetry much longer than Brouwer, but the two poets' styles and quirky subject matter are similar. In 1990, Goldbarth released a collection called *Popular Culture*, including poems about Donald Duck being lost and trying to read Egyptian hieroglyphs to get back to Duckberg, and Orphan Annie and her dog passing by a line of people from Oklahoma waiting to eat at a soup kitchen.

not be determined once and for all. Perhaps he is both. But one thing is certain: his last request cannot be honored by a normal-thinking human being. No one in his right mind could forget a friend—or a funeral—like this one.

Source: Pamela Steed Hill, Critical Essay on "Last Request," in *Poetry for Students*, The Gale Group, 2002.

Sources

Brouwer, Joel, *Exactly What Happened*, Purdue University Press, 1999.

Perillo, Lucia, *Purdue University Press: Publishing the Best!*, http://www.thepress.purdue.edu/New_Books_for_Spring_1999/Exactly_What_Happened/exactly_what_happened.html (May 10, 2001).

Sampsell, Kevin, *theStranger.com*, http://google.yahoo.com/bin/query?p=joel+brouwer&hc=0&hs=0, (May 10, 2001).

Further Reading

Brouwer, Joel, *This Just In*, Beyond Baroque Literary Arts Center, 1998.
　　This is a chapbook of poems published by Brouwer while he was completing his first full-length manuscript, *Exactly What Happened*. The chapbook may be difficult to find without ordering it from the publisher, but it would be interesting to read the precursor to the intriguing full-length collection.

McDaniel, Jeffrey, *The Forgiveness Parade*, Manic D Press, 1998.
　　McDaniel is a contemporary poet to whom Joel Brouwer is sometimes compared. Like Brouwer, McDaniel is noted for his witty, uncanny presentations of subject matter and bizarre humor, and this collection is a good example of that.

Prufer, Kevin, ed., *The New Young American Poets: An Anthology*, Southern Illinois University Press, 2000.
　　Prufer was born in 1969 and grew up in Cleveland, Ohio, making him a close contemporary of Joel Brouwer in both time and place. This collection of young American poets does not include Brouwer's work, but the poems presented offer a good complement to his bold style and offbeat topics.

Sewell, Lisa, *The Way Out: Poems*, Alice James Books, 1998
　　This fascinating first collection by a young poet has been called both strange and beautiful, reflecting the more daring side of contemporary poetry, as does Brouwer's. Sewell's poems are sometimes quirky, sometimes bold, and always provocative. This collection is essentially a record of what it means to be an American living in the last years of the twentieth century.

The Nymph's Reply to the Shepherd

Sir Walter Raleigh
1600

"The Nymph's Reply to the Shepherd" is Sir Walter Raleigh's response to a poem written by Christopher Marlowe, "The Passionate Shepherd to His Love." In the Marlowe poem, the shepherd proposes to his beloved by portraying their ideal future together: a life filled with earthly pleasures in a world of eternal spring. Raleigh's reply, however, debunks the shepherd's fanciful vision. While Marlowe's speaker promises nature's beauty and a litany of gifts, Raleigh's nymph responds that such promises could only remain valid "if all the world and love were young." Thus, she introduces the concepts of time and change. In her world, the seasons cause the shepherd's "shallow rivers" to "rage," rocks to "grow cold" and roses to "fade." The shepherd's gifts might be desirable, but they too are transient: they "soon break, soon wither" and are "soon forgotten." In the end, the nymph acknowledges that she would accept the shepherd's offer "could youth last" and "had joys no date." Like the shepherd, she longs for such things to be true, but like Raleigh, she is a skeptic, retaining faith only in reason's power to discount the "folly" of "fancy's spring."

Author Biography

One of the most colorful and politically powerful members of the court of Queen Elizabeth I, Raleigh has come to personify the English Renaissance.

Sir Walter Raleigh

Born at Hayes Barton, Devonshire, most likely in 1554, Raleigh came from a prominent family long associated with seafaring. In his mid-teens, Raleigh interrupted his education to fight with Huguenot forces in France. Upon his return to England in 1572, he attended Oxford University for two years and left, without earning a degree, to study law in London. One of the first examples of his poetry appeared in 1576 as the preface to George Gascoigne's satire *The Steele Glas*. Two years later, Raleigh and his half-brother Sir Humphrey Gilbert sailed to North America in an unsuccessful attempt to find the Northwest Passage. In 1580, Raleigh took part in the English suppression of Ireland, earning a reputation as a war hero primarily for leading a massacre of unarmed Spanish and Italian troops. Upon his return to England, Raleigh was summoned by Queen Elizabeth to serve as an advisor on Irish affairs. Elizabeth was taken with Raleigh's personal charm, and he soon became one of her court favorites. In addition to lucrative royal commissions and grants, he was knighted in 1585, and in 1587, he was named captain of the Queen's personal guard. The majority of Raleigh's poetry was written during this period, much of it designed to flatter Elizabeth and secure her royal favor. He was able to use that influence to ensure the Queen's favorable reception of his friend Edmund Spenser's

The Faerie Queen (1590). Raleigh also used his influence to gain the Queen's support for his plan to establish the first English colony in North America, on Roanoke Island, in what is now North Carolina. Established in 1587, the colony was soon abandoned, and its inhabitants vanished without a trace, presumed to have been massacred by members of Chief Powhatan's tribe.

In 1592, Elizabeth discovered that Raleigh had secretly married Elizabeth Throckmorton, a member of the royal court, sometime during the late 1580s. Furious over what she believed to be their betrayal, Elizabeth ordered the couple imprisoned in separate cells in the Tower of London. Although Raleigh was released within months, he was stripped of many of his privileges and exiled from the court. In February of 1595, Raleigh sailed to the Orinoco River in Guiana (now Venezuela) in search of gold. He regained Elizabeth's favor in 1597 by taking part in a daring raid on the Spanish at Cadiz. He was reappointed captain of the Queen's Guard, named governor of the Isle of Jersey, and in 1601, he put down a rebellion led by his longtime rival, the earl of Essex.

Elizabeth's successor, James I, disliked and mistrusted Raleigh, and brought charges of treason against him in November, 1603. Convicted and sentenced to death, Raleigh was again imprisoned in the Tower of London, where he spent the next thirteen years. During this time, he wrote *The History of the World*, considered a literary, if not a historical, masterpiece. Raleigh eventually convinced James to release him to lead an expedition to find gold and silver in South America. Spain had become rich and powerful from the gold it had taken from the New World, and with England's treasury nearly depleted, James reluctantly agreed to back the plan. As a result of his earlier voyage to the Orinoco River, Raleigh knew that there was little chance that gold would be found there; he instead planned to capture Spanish ships carrying gold back to Spain. Although James had ordered Raleigh not to tempt war with Spain, Raleigh believed that if he could pirate enough gold, the king would overlook his disobedience. Unfortunately, the expedition was a disaster. Raleigh encountered and attacked Spanish forces near Santo Tomé, and in the ensuing battle, his eldest son was killed. Upon his return to England, Raleigh was again imprisoned and his order of execution reinstated. He was beheaded outside the Palace of Westminster on October 29, 1618.

Poem Text

If all the world and love were young,
And truth in every shepherd's tongue,
These pretty pleasures might me move
To live with thee and be thy love.

But time drives flocks from field to fold,   5
When rivers rage and rocks grow cold,
And Philomel becometh dumb;
The rest complain of cares to come.

The flowers do fade, and wanton fields
To wayward Winter reckoning yields;   10
A honey tongue, a heart of gall,
Is fancy's spring, but sorrow's fall.

Thy gowns, thy shoes, thy beds of roses,
Thy cap, thy kirtle, and thy posies
Soon break, soon wither, soon forgotten,   15
In folly ripe, in reason rotten.

Thy belt of straw and ivy buds,
Thy coral clasps and amber studs,
All these in me no means can move
To come to thee and be thy love.   20

But could youth last and love still breed,
Had joys no date nor age no need,
Then these delights my mind might move
To live with thee and be thy love.

Poem Summary

Lines 1–8

The nymph's reply begins in the subjunctive—the grammatical mood used to convey hypothetical or contingent action. The subjunctive is commonly expressed with the "if . . . were" construction: "If I were king," for example, or, in the first line of the poem, "If all the world and love were young." This usage sets up the primary rhetorical structure of the entire poem: the speaker is going to contrast the shepherd's vision, his hypothetical world, with the realities introduced by the word "but" in the second stanza. While the second part of the "if" statement—"And truth in every shepherd's tongue"—may seem the more biting, the nature of the contrast exists in the first part. What renders the shepherd's vision false, the nymph says, is time: the world and love do not remain young. Thus, while she finds lovely the shepherd's evocation of spring, shallow rivers, flocks of sheep and rocks that exist merely so lovers can sit on them, in reality these ideal images are time-bound, subject to change and decay. Thus, "time drives flocks from field to fold," "rivers rage" from rainy weather, "rocks grow cold" with winter, and even the nightingale—the timeless symbol of beauty unmentioned in the Marlowe poem—becomes "dumb" with the change in seasons. In contrast with the nightingale are "the rest"—those who do not become dumb but who instead "complain of cares to come." By this, the nymph means human beings who, burdened with the consciousness of passing time, are subject to the anxiety of future misfortunes. In the shepherd's evocation, no such anxieties can exist because no such timeless world can exist: his vision, like Keats's Grecian urn, is only a product of the imagination.

Lines 9–16

Raleigh makes frequent use of the poetic devices that give Marlowe's poem its musicality. Yet the reader cannot help but sense the mockery in end-rhymes like "gall"/"fall" and "forgotten"/"rotten," especially since they follow couplets in which Raleigh exactly duplicates Marlowe's rhymes: "fields"/"yields" and "roses"/"posies." It is as if the nymph adheres to the shepherd's style one moment only to undermine it the next. The same is true for the way Raleigh mimics Marlowe's overuse of alliteration, or the repetition of initial consonant sounds: "flowers" and "fade," "wayward" and "winter," "spring" and "sorrow," "fancy" and "fall." But the slyest form of mockery occurs in lines 9 and 10. Here, Raleigh imitates the glaring grammatical mistake found in the Marlowe poem: just as Marlowe fails to match the singular verb "yields" with its plural subjects in the first stanza of "The Passionate Shepherd to His Love," so Raleigh mismatches the same singular verb in line 10 with its plural subject "fields" in line 9. But there are also bits of original trickery in the Raleigh poem. In the last line of the second stanza the reader might find a clever double-meaning for the words "spring"—meaning either "source" or the season—and "fall"—an allusion both to autumnal death and the to the "fall of man." This last meaning refers to the creation story: living in the timeless Garden of Eden and unaware of death or change, man fell prey to the "honey tongue" of Satan, who convinced man to eat the fruit of God-like knowledge. The consequence of such knowledge is, of course, the awareness of death. After Eden, one cannot live in "fancy's spring" as the shepherd pretends one can. With human consciousness, one instead must suffer the burden of foreknowledge. Thus, the nymph reminds him, his gifts only symbolize decay and the passing of time: they "soon break, soon wither," and are "soon forgotten." While "in folly" such gifts may seem to exist always in their perfect, "ripe" state, to a reason-possessing and time-

Media Adaptations

- A 1999 audiocassette of Professor Elliot Engel's lecture entitled "Sir Walter Raleigh, Renaissance Man" is available from Author's Ink of Raleigh, North Carolina.

- Sir Walter Raleigh is one of the authors included on Spoken Arts' audiocassette *Elizabethan Love Poems*, presented by Arthur Luce Klein and published in 1969.

- The videocassette *English Explorers*, released by Schlesinger Media in 2000, has an actor as Sir Walter Raleigh narrating the stories of explorers such as himself, John Cabot, and Sir Francis Drake.

- *Sir Walter Raleigh and the Orinoco Disaster* is the fourth tape in a six-tape videocassette series from Kulter, Inc., called "Great Adventurers," released in 1999.

- A 1987 videocassette from Films for the Humanities entitled *Medieval to Elizabethan Poetry* covers poems and songs from England, 1400–1600, including Raleigh's poetry.

- This poem and Marlowe's "The Passionate Shepherd" are also included on *The Poetry Hall of Fame*, originally part of the Public Broadcasting System's "Anyone for Tennyson?" series. This videocassette was released by Monterey Home Video in 1993.

- Raleigh is one of the characters in the English-language opera *Gloriana*, about life in the court of Elizabeth I. A videocassette from 1984 is available on Thorn EMI/HBO Video.

haunted human like the nymph, they are already "rotten" with the foreknowledge of change.

Lines 17–24

In the final two stanzas, the nymph shifts back to the subjunctive mood of the opening lines. Listing the last of the shepherd's gifts, she says, "All these in me no means can move / To come to thee and be thy love." This seems her final word: her rejection. Yet the last stanza offers a twist—a "but." "[C]ould youth last," she says, and "Had joys no date"—if the world were as the shepherd has promised, in other words, then indeed she would be "moved" by his offer and become his love. Although reason prohibits her belief in his promises, she nevertheless wishes such belief were possible. Thus, the nymph admits to the human need to believe in timelessness and immortality. At the same time, however, she must acknowledge that reason prohibits such belief, which it dismisses as "folly."

Themes

Skepticism

This poem is a response to Christopher Marlowe's "The Passionate Shepherd to His Love," written in 1599. In Marlowe's poem, the shepherd asks the woman that he loves to run away with him and live the simple life outdoors, where he will make her clothes from flowers and shells and the wool of their sheep, and life will be a celebration of their youthful love. In her response, Raleigh has the nymph list reasons why the ideal life that the shepherd describes is unlikely to happen. The shepherd emphasizes his love, as if love alone can conquer any problems, and he lists the things that he is willing to do for her as well as the splendors of the simple country life. The nymph, on the other hand, looks at the darker side of human nature. In the second line, she brings up the idea that shepherds do, in fact, lie sometimes, implying that she would be foolish to believe everything that he claims. Throughout the rest of the poem, she explains reasons why, whether he is sincere or not, she has to be skeptical that their life together would be as the shepherd describes it. Her main point is that the shepherd's plans do not account for the changes that are inevitable over time, and so the future that he foresees will almost certainly not come to pass. Her skepticism is based on the fact that she understands his hopeful vision, but that she also sees that he does not understand the world well enough to make an accurate prediction.

Abstinence and Chastity

An element that is important to understanding the nymph's reluctance, but that is never explicitly stated in the poem, is the value she places on her chastity. Her main argument is that the young lovers will probably, over time, lose interest in one another as youthful beauty fades and eventually part. To readers who assume that the two could then go on with their lives separately, this might seem unimportant. This view, however, does not take into account how much would have changed in the nymph's life by the sheer fact of having lived with the shepherd. To a young lady of the sixteenth century, the importance of retaining her chastity and the circumstances under which she would give it up could not be overstated. There would be no going back to the person she was before once she decided to live with the shepherd. To the strong Christian sensibilities of Elizabethan England, living and sleeping with the shepherd would constitute a serious sin. To a great extent, modern social mores are so different from the nymph's that today's readers cannot feel the enormity of what the shepherd is asking her to give up with such a faint possibility that their love will last. On the other hand, readers who are aware of the immense importance earlier generations put on a woman's chastity might be surprised to hear the nymph say she actually would be willing to run off with the shepherd if she thought that their youthful enthusiasm could last.

Decay

The aging process can sometimes be seen as a period of growth and refinement. The examples that the nymph uses in this poem, however, all present aging as decay. Rivers run dry, plants shrivel, and birds die and fall silent. The nymph uses these examples to show what must inevitably become of youthful love over the course of time. In line 16, she discusses the flowers that the shepherd has offered to weave into clothes for her, and explains their eventual decay with the words, "In folly ripe, in reason rotten." Her point is that the flowers can only be thought to stay their best, "ripe," through mistaken thinking. Reason is the process of seeing the shepherd's offer through to its inevitable solution and, as this nymph sees it, all of the things that the shepherd promises, as well as all things in nature, inevitably lead to decay.

The examples that she uses to show decay, just as the examples that Christopher Marlowe previously had the shepherd use to show the vibrancy of his love, are all physical symbols from nature. This poem does little to address the issue of whether love can grow and adapt—whether it can, as line 21 puts it, "still breed." Like Marlowe, Raleigh draws a connection between love and the worldly things found in nature. The difference is that Marlowe's shepherd points out that love is as wonderful as the nature images he describes, while

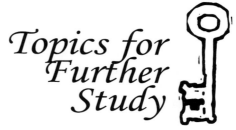

Topics for Further Study

- In the last stanza of the poem, what does the Nymph mean by age having need? How does this stand in the way of her relationship with the shepherd?

- In this poem, the Nymph counters the shepherd's request to live with him and be his love. Rewrite the argument in prose, in modern language, so that it could be used by any young person today as a defense against pressure from a lover.

- Compare the style of this poem to Christopher Marlowe's style in writing "The Passionate Shepherd to His Love." In what ways has Raleigh matched Marlowe's style exactly? What clues can you find to indicate that the two works are by separate authors?

- William Shakespeare wrote at the same time that Raleigh did. Choose a character from Shakespeare's plays that you think is most like the Nymph portrayed here. Why do you think so?

- Write a short story about the Nymph in her old age. Would she be satisfied with her decision to refuse the shepherd's offer, or would she regret having let him get away? Why?

Raleigh's nymph points out how love eventually will be as decayed as those natural objects.

Lies

The nymph in this poem briefly mentions the possibility of the shepherd being untrue, in the second line, but for the most part she examines his offer to her as if he is being sincere. She does not seem to think that the flowery prose Christopher Marlowe gave the shepherd to say is a trick to get her to run away with him. Instead, she briefly passes over the fact that people generally have the capacity to lie, as just one minor consideration. Contemporary readers are used to seeing writers present their works with some sort of falsehood embedded within them. The post-modern, ironic sensibility gives readers more than the surface situation that is presented, often giving the narrator a hidden, secret idea as well. In a case like Marlowe's poem, a contemporary poet would be more likely to hint that the shepherd is just using poetic language to trick the nymph into sleeping with him. The fact that the nymph only mentions this possibility in passing indicates that she probably thinks he is not lying, or, if he is, he is lying to himself as much as to her. Dramas from the Elizabethan era often present deceptive characters, indicating that lying was not unusual when Raleigh wrote this poem, only that it was not assumed in love poetry of the day.

Style

In structure, "The Nymph's Reply to the Shepherd" mimics Marlowe's "The Passionate Shepherd to His Love." Like the latter poem, it consists of six four-line stanzas, or quatrains, with each stanza the fusion of two rhymed couplets. Also like Marlowe's poem, the predominant meter of "The Nymph's Reply to the Shepherd" is iambic tetrameter. This means each line contains four iambs, or two-syllable units of rhythm in which the first syllable is unstressed and the second is stressed. As an example of iambic tetrameter, consider the following line from the poem:

If all the world and love were young ...

If we divide the iambs from one another and distinguish unstressed from stressed syllables, the line appears like this:

If all / the world / and love / were young ...

Reading the line naturally, note the emphasis on the four stressed syllables. Throughout the poem, Raleigh seems to mock Marlowe's strict adherence to iambic tetrameter, even going so far as to mimic many of Marlowe's end-rhymes ("roses" and "posies," for example). This is appropriate to the nature of the response: Raleigh is replying in Marlowe's own terms, eliminating the chance that the superiority of the his argument might be taken as purely rhetorical.

Historical Context

One of the most important aspects of Sir Walter Raleigh's adult life was his close relationship with Queen Elizabeth I. Their close friendship gave him access to many opportunities that he might never have had otherwise, and it eventually put him on the wrong side of the queen's successor, James I, who had Raleigh beheaded.

Elizabeth was the last of the Tudor dynasty, which ruled England from 1485 to 1603. She was the daughter of King Henry VIII and the second of his eight wives, Anne Boleyn. In 1547, when Henry died, Elizabeth's ten-year-old half-brother, Edward, became king. Edward became ill and died six years later, and Mary Tudor, another of Henry VIII's children, ascended to the throne. Mary was a Catholic, and she did not trust Elizabeth's strong Protestantism, so she had Elizabeth locked up in the Tower of London in 1553 until she signed a document swearing her allegiance to the Catholic Church. Mary's marriage to the King of Spain, himself a devout Catholic, acted as encouragement for her to commit English forces to joining Spain in a war against France, during which England suffered great losses. When Mary died in 1558, there were suspicions that she had been poisoned by her many political opponents, who arranged for Elizabeth to take the throne, thinking that she would be a weak ruler that would follow their orders. In fact, Elizabeth turned out to be strong-willed and decisive, ruling for the next forty-five years, leaving the impression of her personality forever on English political and social life.

It was during Elizabeth's reign that England achieved a golden age, with its influence as a world power taking shape for years to come. She calmed the domestic strife between Catholics and Protestants that had torn the country apart for decades by imposing harsh penalties against Catholics and Puritans, uniting the country under the Church of England. She took steps to address the growing problems of urban poverty that arose as the country's population shifted from rural to more urban areas. Through shrewd diplomacy, including a courtship with King Philip of Spain, she was able to raise the country's influence around the world. Elizabeth saw the importance of a strong navy, and built up the British naval fleet, leading to Sir Francis Drake's 1588 defeat of the Spanish Armada, which established England's dominance of the oceans. It was her interest in world expansion that led her to support many naval expeditions to the Western Hemisphere, including Raleigh's voyages to North America (where he founded Virginia, named after Elizabeth, the Virgin Queen) and to Trinidad and Venezuela, in pursuit of the legendary City of Gold, El Dorado.

During Elizabeth's reign, the literary scene in England blossomed. The list of writers active at that time included Raleigh, Christopher Marlowe, Edmund Spenser, Francis Bacon, and the greatest

Compare & Contrast

- **1600:** England is experiencing one of the greatest eras of literary growth that it has ever known. Theater, in particular, is popular, with artists such as Christopher Marlowe (*Dr. Faustus, Tamburlaine*) and William Shakespeare, whose *As You Like It* and *Julius Caesar* both appear this year. Poets of the time include George Herbert, John Donne, and Ben Jonson, who is so popular that he has his own group of followers, who call themselves the Tribe of Ben.

  Today: The works of the Elizabethan playwrights are still held up as examples of craftsmanship and word artistry and are performed frequently.

- **1600:** The queen of England, Elizabeth I, is the country's political, spiritual, and social leader. Her personal relationships with suitors like Raleigh are kept out of the public eye.

  Today: The British royal family has hardly any political authority. Newspapers regularly expose scandals about the personal lives of the royals.

- **1600:** Tobacco, recently imported from North America, is popular among the elite of London. Although a tradition that Sir Walter Raleigh is the first person to import tobacco into Europe develops, tobacco is really introduced by John Hawkins in 1565.

  Today: Tobacco use in third world countries continues to rise, while use in industrialized nations is decreasing due to a greater access to information detailing tobacco's inherent health risks.

- **1600:** America is a land occupied by its native inhabitants. Sir Walter Raleigh's attempt to start a colony in Virginia in 1585 failed, as did several other expeditions. French traders have been able to live peaceably with the Indians, but the English are not able to spread their civilization to this continent until the founding of Jamestown in 1607.

  Today: Because England was the dominant colonizing force in America throughout the seventeenth century, it is the country that America is most closely linked to culturally.

English poet and playwright of all, William Shakespeare. As a poet, Raleigh was associated with a small, loose-knit group of writers that was dubbed the "School of Night" for their critical skepticism and refusal to accept religious doctrines that did not make logical sense. "The Nymph's Reply to the Shepherd" is considered one of the most notable examples of this group's philosophical approach to life. Other members of the group included Christopher Marlowe, George Chapman, and Thomas Harriot, who was Raleigh's tutor.

Critical Overview

Rather than a simple song, "The Nymph's Reply to the Shepherd" is considered an example of Raleigh's skepticism. "Memento mori," or recog-

nition of death, and "tempus edax," or "devouring time," are important concepts for understanding Raleigh. He questioned everything, including the religious and political ideas of his time and the premises of the courtly love tradition. Many have contrasted Christopher Marlowe's "The Passionate Shepherd to His Love" with "The Nymph's Reply to the Shepherd." Jerry Leath Mills has called it a "witty and sardonic" response to Marlowe's poem, by pointedly demonstrating "the human propensity for self-delusion." While Marlowe emphasizes the pleasures of "living and loving" and presents the shared life as a "garden of earthly delights," Raleigh emphasizes the inevitability of change. And while Marlowe presents nature as a place for seduction and pleasure, Raleigh depicts the grim fact of decay. Raleigh is thought by critics such as M. C. Bradbrook to have been part of an antireligious philosophical movement, the "School of

Night," that studied occult science and necromancy and defied conventional Christianity. However, his awareness of mortality is evocative of the Christian concept of the fall of man—the reminder that it is delusional to think of Eden without the concept of redemption.

Criticism

David Kelly

Kelly is an instructor of literature and creative writing at two colleges in Illinois. In the following essay, he explains how, even though poetry was not the primary interest of Sir Walter Raleigh or Christopher Marlowe, they were able to touch on universal truths about humanity by examining the pastoral tradition in poetry.

Most of what has been written about Sir Walter Raleigh focuses, for good reason, on his fascinating life as a suitor of Queen Elizabeth I, an adventurer and a scoundrel, a slayer of indigenous peoples and, overall, as an opportunist who several times slipped out of the clutches of defeat to redefine his own fortune. He founded colonies, named the territory of Virginia, led an expedition to the fabled City of Gold, and spent thirteen years in the Tower of London, where he wrote a million-word-long history of the world. Of course, he is an important historic figure. Little, though, is written about his poetry. Raleigh was a talented writer in a time when gentlemen generally wrote poetry; his work is generally considered adept, but none too remarkable.

Of the few poems of Raleigh's that are even mentioned today, it is "The Nymph's Reply to the Shepherd" that is most often reprinted. The poem is almost always printed with its companion piece, Christopher Marlowe's "The Passionate Shepherd to His Love." Readers might find it a bitter piece of irony that Raleigh as a poet is best remembered for what is in effect a novelty piece, an experiment in team writing. If you consider him mainly as an explorer though, it is amazing that any sample of his verse should have stayed in print consistently throughout these past four hundred years.

Neither Marlowe nor Raleigh built his reputation primarily on poetry. Marlowe is, and was then, best known for the writing he did for the stage. Among Elizabethan playwrights, he is considered second only to Shakespeare himself, which is no light feat considering that no playwright in all of history exceeds Shakespeare's reputation. Today, Marlowe's *Tamburlaine* is constantly revived, while his *Dr. Faustus* is likely to run in most major cities in any given month. Raleigh is, as mentioned, remembered as an explorer, but he also has more legendary anecdotes told about him than most figures of the times. The story of him taking off his cloak and throwing it over a puddle that the queen was about to step in is probably untrue, but it stands today as an unforgettable example of the gallantry of a bygone era. The legend that Raleigh was the individual who brought American tobacco to Europe, and turned the plant into a commercial product, is certainly false, but generations have associated Sir Walter Raleigh with tobacco to such an extent that a popular brand of cigarettes bore his name and likeness, a strange distinction that no other poet can claim.

In life, they were friends, but their different career paths make Marlowe and Raleigh an interesting pair to be linked through time by their poems. The secret to the longevity of these two works seems to be not in the skill of the poets, which, even if combined, would not add up to the skill of many poets who have ended up forgotten ten years after their deaths. Instead, the secret is in the subject matter that these two poems cover so thoroughly. It would be a mistake to think that these are poems about love, even though that is what most schoolroom discussions probably make of them. They are only about love in the most general sense. More specifically, Marlowe's "Shepherd" poem is about the idealism that either causes or is caused by love, while Raleigh's "Nymph" addresses the sorrow of harsh reality. Together, these poems give readers a brief but thorough tour of all that is best and worst of the pastoral tradition in poetry.

In their book about Raleigh entitled *Shepherd of the Ocean*, J. H. Adamson and H. F. Folland discuss the interest that the poet and Queen Elizabeth took together in "the new vogue of pastoralism." Poems from ancient Greece, recently discovered at that time, stirred up interest in the pastoral convention, which

> describes life through an image of the idealized existence of literate and artistic shepherds in a lovely landscape of timeless spring, [and] is the playful wish-fulfillment of a sophisticated and complex culture, an imaginative vision of something like an unspoiled Eden, a Golden Age of simple purity and beauty.

Over the centuries, the pastoral convention has arisen regularly in complex societies looking for the quiet serenity of rolling fields, gentle sheep, and honest shepherds who were as close to nature as humans can get. The Elizabethans amused themselves with this sort of idealism; the romantics made it their lives; the moderns were nostalgic, as if they had just missed it. To this day, farmers enjoy idealized associations with soil, sunshine, and seeds, while popular culture tends to forget the cold reality of their lives involving machinery, chemicals, and contracts.

The shepherd that Marlowe presented sprang directly from the tradition of the ancient Greeks, with shallow rivers and singing birds presenting a perfect setting for the noble, optimistic lover who was a popular figure at the time. Half of the poem is about the clothes the shepherd promises to make out of flowers and wool, gold and coral: the appeal these gifts held for the nymph would presumably not be the thrill of having clothes made by a shepherd but wearing things so freshly part of nature. The shepherd does not spend much time proclaiming the intensity of his love for the nymph, instead letting nature make his emotional appeal for him. If anything, that appeal is felt more strongly today. Since Marlowe's time, the world has only gotten more crowded, polluted, and impersonal, as cities have grown to hold larger populations than the entire continent had then. Now, like never before, the rolling hills that Marlowe's shepherd offered trigger a longing for love.

It was not exactly genius that gave Sir Walter Raleigh his insight that the pastoral vision was founded on wishful thinking. The purity and innate wisdom and dignity and all that Adamson and Folland described so well can be mesmerizing to readers when they let themselves become immersed in a pastoral poem, but the same conventions become easy to mock once the reader is out from under the poet's spell. Raleigh's genius was that he wrote his response so immediately, and that he mirrored Marlowe's writing so closely. He provides the yin to Marlowe's yang (opposite principles), the night to Marlowe's day: together, these two poems add up to a whole that says much more about human hopes and fears than the sum of its parts.

Marlowe's shepherd seems sincere in his claims of love, even though the nymph in Raleigh's poem makes a point of mentioning that shepherds are sometimes untrue. A lesser poem might have made more of the fact that lovers can lie to get what they want, using the very strength of the shepherd's claims as evidence that he is trying too hard, that he is hiding his real agenda. The problem with this is that it would mean raising doubts about the na-

> " *The secret to the longevity of these two works seems to be not in the skill of the poets, which, even if combined, would not add up to the skill of many poets who have ended up forgotten ten years after their deaths. Instead, the secret is in the subject matter that these two poems cover so thoroughly.* "

ture of love itself, making all lovers subject to suspicion. When the nymph passes so quickly over this possibility of dishonesty, Raleigh can address pastoralism itself without having to bring all lovers into question.

Rather than assault the basic trust that love relies on, the nymph's reply takes on the pastoral tradition. The weakness with this idealized vision is that it focuses on the good things in the world, ignoring the rest. The wrong way to go about countering this idealism would be to argue that there are bad things, too: such an argument would go on to infinity, with good point matching bad. Instead, Raleigh has the nymph take a philosophical approach to pastoralism. She cannot prove that the bad aspects of the life that the shepherd has proposed would be more common or powerful than the good ones, but she can prove that all of the wonders of nature that the shepherd has offered her will eventually go bad.

Time is the key to the nymph's reply. It is time that turns ripeness into rot: not because the universe is bad or love is an illusion, but simply because it is not the nature of things to stay the same. The nymph offers every possible concession to the shepherd's argument. She accepts his sincerity, she admits that the pastoral life is lovely, and she even agrees that she would be glad to live with him in such a beautiful place. Her objection is that it would eventually have to quit being the beautiful place that he has described. There is no arguing against the fact that time changes things.

Between the two poems, "The Passionate Shepherd to His Love" and "The Nymph's Reply to the Shepherd," a whole range of human beliefs is covered. The shepherd is right to stand in awe of the magnificent world that surrounds him, and readers cannot help but feel empathy for his powerful love, which drives him to promise his service and devotion. But the nymph has a good point, too, in showing that the circumstances that the shepherd offers her are bound to change. Each person should be able to understand and agree with each of these views, although, deep down, each person probably leans toward one more than the other. With these two poems, Raleigh and Marlowe created a sort of personality test that helps people understand their own basic beliefs. It is a feat that some poets strive to achieve for a lifetime.

Source: David Kelly, Critical Essay on "The Nymph's Reply to the Shepherd," in *Poetry for Students*, The Gale Group, 2002.

Daniel Moran

Moran is a secondary school teacher of English and American literature. In this essay, he examines the ways in which Raleigh's poem satirizes the sentiments found in Marlowe's poem.

In his collection of interviews, *Strong Opinions*, Vladimir Nabokov remarks, "Satire is a lesson; parody is a game." In other words, the aim of satire is to point out some fault in human nature that the artist feels needs to be remedied, while the aim (or "game") of parody is to imitate the form and style of the original work as closely as possible. Well-crafted parodies are often amusing, but when an artist combines the playful game of parody with the weighty lessons of satire, the result can be a work more intense and thought-provoking than one that only mimics or instructs. Jonathan Swift's "A Modest Proposal" is one of the most forceful examples of what happens when parody (in this case, an imitation of the language used by "proposers" who offer their solutions to social ills) is combined with a "lesson" (the English are responsible for the terrible poverty in Ireland): the result is Swift's unforgettable essay. Other writers have merged satire and parody with similarly impressive results. Lawrence Sterne's *Tristam Shandy*, Alexander Pope's "The Rape of the Lock" and Nabokov's own *Pale Fire* all amuse their readers by imitating existing literary forms (for example, diaries, epics, and criticism) while simulta-

neously "teaching" their readers some "lesson" about human failings. All satirists must, in part, assume the role of teacher, since they speak from a position from which they can identify the shortcomings of others. The humor inherent in parody, however, makes these lessons more palatable.

Sir Walter Raleigh's "The Nymph's Reply to the Shepherd" is a work that, like the previously mentioned examples, combines the lesson of satire and the game of parody to point out the silliness of the promises being made in Christopher Marlowe's "The Passionate Shepherd to His Love" and, by extension, the promises of all young, eager lovers. The vows of the shepherd—a stock character in pastoral poetry known for his innocence—are dead-on-arrival when they reach the ears of Raleigh's nymph, who speaks from experience and with a sense of worldliness that her suitor does not anticipate and presumably cannot understand. The artistry and fun of Raleigh's poem lies in the way that it parodies Marlowe's original to, ultimately, teach the shepherd (and the reader) a lesson about the effects of time on promises made in youth.

The nymph's intention to teach the shepherd a lesson is evident in the fact that she does not refuse him outright until almost the end of the poem. Instead, she speaks of hypothetical possibilities that, if true, would lead her to accept his invitations. By withholding her refusal until the end of the poem, however, the nymph ensures that the shepherd understands, or at least considers, why she is refusing him at all. Perhaps she has encountered such passionate shepherds before and this most recent invitation to "live with me and be my love" has unleashed this didactic reply. At any rate, her lesson is a forceful one whose humor is only apparent to the reader—certainly not to the shepherd, who, one imagines, listens to the nymph's reply in stunned silence.

The nymph begins her lesson with a hypothetical premise, the first of several in the poem: "If all the world and love were young," she states, she "might" be moved to love him. The tone of the opening seems polite ("I would love you, of course, except for this one small thing") but the "if," in this case, presents an impossible situation: "all the world and love" are not "young." The planet has existed for eons, and her understanding of love has matured with time and experience. Hers is not a "young" heart, easily won by poetry. This tone of polite refusal coupled with an impossibility is the first sign that she has no intention of succumbing. Her second hypothetical situation: "if" there were "truth in every shepherd's tongue," does the same rhetorical office as the first: if shepherds taken as a type were all honest, she would be moved to love him—but she is too wise to take stock in such a naive notion. Her calling his offers of pastoral paradise "pretty pleasures" adds to the sense of sarcastic scorn covered by a thin layer of ostensible politeness.

The next two stanzas elaborate upon the nymph's first hypothetical premise about the age of the world. Unlike *carpe diem* poems in which a young woman is urged to love her suitor before, as Andrew Marvell calls it, "time's winged chariot" has run its course, the nymph's words argue that the passing of time is the reason why she will not love the shepherd. Raleigh's poem can thus be read as the counterpart, or complement, of Marvell's "To His Coy Mistress" or Herrick's "To the Virgins." All of the enticements offered by the shepherd will be affected for the worse by time: the flocks will move "from field to fold"; the "rocks," upon which they will presumably sit, will "grow cold"; the nightingale will become "dumb" and "the rest"—a group in which they are presumably included—will "complain of cares to come." With the passing of time, the passion of youth must, she argues, give way to the worries inherent in old age—something that Marlowe's shepherd innocently, or conveniently, fails to mention in his appeal. "Flowers do fade" and so will their passion. Even worse, "wanton fields / To wayward winter reckoning yields": even the most lively and lusty lovers must pay the reckoning of winter, when fields and feeling grow fallow.

Marlowe's shepherd may be an innocent bumpkin (who simply has no idea that his gifts have become empty clichés) or a conniving lothario (who adopts the pose of a simpler man to seem less threatening). Marlowe never tells the reader and so both interpretations are valid. As the poem proceeds, however, the nymph seems to assume the worst about her would-be country husband. Her epigram, or witty remark, "A honey tongue, a heart of gall, / Is fancy's spring, but sorrow's fall" implies that the shepherd is consciously using "honeyed" words to disguise his inner "gall": what sounds sweet only covers a bitter truth. The parallel structure of these lines helps the nymph emphasize her distance in age and worldliness from those who may fall prey to such promises. A "honey tongue" is "fancy's spring" because sweet words excite the imagination; such words, however, always lead to "sorrow's fall" and disillusionment. Of course, "spring" and "fall" are words that refer not only to figurative physical actions but to the seasons as well: just as in springtime, when

> *The content of the nymph's attack on the shepherd is obviously severe; what makes it even more biting is her parody of the shepherd's style."*

new life (and love) is in bloom, fall always arrives to undo the fruits of nature and promises made in the spring of youth.

The content of the nymph's attack on the shepherd is obviously severe; what makes it even more biting is her parody of the shepherd's style. Marlowe's poem is written in iambic tetrameter, a light and singsong meter (associated with simple, honest speakers) used to complement the images of the pleasant pastoral life that will be the nymph's, should she accept the shepherd's offer. Likewise, Raleigh's poem is written in iambic tetrameter, as if the nymph is mimicking the "honey tongue" of the shepherd. As Marlowe's poem features several alliterative phrases (words that begin with the same sound or type of sound, again to reflect the "honey tongue"), Raleigh's abounds in them. The nymph of Raleigh's poem speaks of "pretty pleasures," how "rivers rage and rocks grow cold," how many will "complain of cares to come," how "flowers fade" and "wanton fields" fall to "wayward winter," and how the shepherd's promises are "ripe" in one way yet "rotten" in another. The difference is that Marlowe's shepherd uses alliteration to please the nymph's ear and, by extension, her heart, while Raleigh's nymph uses them to mock the very notion that she can be taken in by poetry, however pleasant it may sound. More importantly, the nymph parodies the very quality of the shepherd's presumed love by listing all the things promised to her ("Thy gowns, thy shoes, thy beds of roses," etc.); she implies that such easily "withered" and "forgotten" things are, in essence, a joke. These unsubstantial trifles are, as Polonius in *Hamlet* calls them, "springes to catch woodcocks"—little traps used to catch unsuspecting birds. This bird, however, has been through the forest of love and found it to be a rough place; things weightier than "ivy buds" and "amber studs" are needed if she is to consider his offer and if love is to endure.

What Do I Read Next?

- To fully appreciate this poem, it should be read in conjunction with Christopher Marlowe's poem, "The Passionate Shepherd to His Love," which can be found in *Christopher Marlowe: The Complete Poems*, edited by Mark Thornton Burnett and published by Tuttle Publishing in 2001.

- One of Raleigh's most famous poems is "A Vision upon the Conceit of the Faerie Queene." It is his response to the book-length poem, "The Faerie Queene," by his friend and protégé Edmund Spenser.

- John Keats's "Ode on a Grecian Urn" is one of the greatest poems from the romantic period, two hundred years after this poem was written. It addresses the same themes Raleigh addressed, looking with sorrow at the youthful figures painted on the urn of the title, who can enjoy their youth forever. It is in most standard poetry anthologies, as well as Modern Library's *The Complete Poems of John Keats* (1994).

- The case that Raleigh makes here about the consequences of present actions would also apply to another famous poem, Robert Herrick's "To The Virgins, to Make Much of Time," which was published in 1648. Like Marlowe's poem, Herrick's presents a suitor pressuring the woman he loves to take advantage of youth, en-

couraging her to forget the effects of time that are the focus of Raleigh's poem. Robert Herrick's poetry is available in an Everyman's Paperback Classic edition, edited by Douglas Brooks-Davies and published in 1997.

- A new book about Raleigh's tragic exploration of the Orinoco River to find the City of Gold, El Dorado, is Charles Nicholl's *The Creature in the Map: A Journey to El Dorado*, reprinted in 1997 by University of Chicago Press. Nicholl, a travel writer and English literature scholar, traces the trip step-by-step.

- Readers can see the spirit of Raleigh in one of Edgar Allan Poe's most moving poems, "The Road to El Dorado," which does not mention Raleigh but focuses instead on the excitement of knights seeking the city of legend. It is in many poetry anthologies, and can also be found in Doubleday Press's *Complete Stories and Poems of Edgar Allan Poe* (1966).

- Seamus Heaney is a Nobel Prize–winning Irish poet. In 1990, Sidney Burris did a study of Heaney that connected his themes to those explored in this poem. The book, *The Poetry of Resistance: Seamus Heaney and the Pastoral Tradition*, Ohio University Press, shows his work to be like Raleigh's in its insistence on reality over idealism.

By the last stanza, the nymph's tone and dismissal of the shepherd is unmistakable, yet she reverts to the tone of "polite indignation" found in the opening lines and again offers a hypothetical situation in which she would reciprocate the shepherd's passion. But "could youth last and love still breed, / Had joys no date nor age no need," then she would consider his offer. As before, she offers imaginary impossibilities to suggest the real impossibility of her giving in to his offers: youth does not last, love does not always grow, the joys of life do end, and old age is a time of tremendous need. Her final couplet, therefore, features a per-

fectly reasonable tone that both completes the game of parody (by imitating the shepherd's final couplet) and the lesson of satire (anyone who assumes that an intelligent woman can be easily moved with material things is a fool). Marlowe, alas, never composed "The Shepherd's Reply to the Nymph," so readers can only assume that after hearing her speak, the shepherd walked back to his fields, scratching his head and wondering what he said that could have sparked such a reply—or that he sought out another nymph less experienced and more easily swayed by promises of pastoral pleasures.

Source: Daniel Moran, Critical Essay on "The Nymph's Reply to the Shepherd," in *Poetry for Students*, The Gale Group, 2002.

Erika Taibl

Taibl has published widely in poetic studies. In the following essay, she explores Raleigh's poem as a companion poem exposing the conventions and escapism of the pastoral form and questioning the romanticized notion of the simple life.

Sir Walter Raleigh's poem, "The Nymph's Reply to the Shepherd," is one of the most celebrated companion poems in all of English literature as it responds to and challenges Christopher Marlowe's poem, "The Passionate Shepherd to His Love." Raleigh's poem engages the earlier poem in a dialogue that challenges the validity of the Elizabethan romantics' preoccupation for the pastoral, or the idyllic, simple life. Raleigh points toward a more complex and realistic understanding of life that is subject to darkness and the inevitable progression of time. Raleigh uses the conventions of Marlowe's poem to mock the idealized picture of nature for which Marlowe argues. By subverting the content of Marlowe's poem, Raleigh follows the prescriptions for a companion poem, which critic Steven May, in his article, "Companion Poems in the Raleigh Canon," describes as "one poem that may answer another, usually in a contradictory fashion," or as "two or more poems that may begin with similar themes and wording what appear to be exercises in literary collaboration." Following May's definition, Raleigh accomplishes both of these tasks as his nymph contradicts Marlowe's shepherd using pastoral conventions and direct allusions to Marlowe's poem to do so. Raleigh is not alone in his use of "The Passionate Shepherd to His Love." Other poets to use Marlowe's lines either through direct quotation, or allusion, include: John Donne, Robert Herrick, C. Day Lewis, and even Shakespeare in his "Merry Wives of Windsor." Raleigh's effort is perhaps the most famous, and was almost as popular as Marlowe's poem in the sixteenth century. Raleigh pays tribute to the loveliness of "The Passionate Shepherd to His Love" as he constructs a parallel vision more prone to questions concerning the validity and possibility of the shepherd's idyllic portrait.

Raleigh and Marlowe wrote at the height of the Renaissance, which came to England in the sixteenth century under the rule of Queen Elizabeth. The era was marked by an urgent sense of the meaning of the word Renaissance, or "rebirth," as

> *The 'pretty pleasures' are not enough for Raleigh because they do not last. In the poem, he suggests the futility and meaninglessness of ornaments and unattainable musings."*

artists worked with and through one another to discover new artistic forms and make old forms new. The companion poem is a fine example of the ways in which artists, as May suggests, were working in dialogue with one another to create deep, lasting impressions with their audiences. Raleigh worked in dialogue with many of his Elizabethan romantic contemporaries including Sir Philip Sidney, Edmund Spenser, and Christopher Marlowe. Critic C. F. Tucker Brooke, in his article "Sir Walter Raleigh as Poet and Philosopher," claims that Raleigh "shares Sidney's courtly brilliance and chivalry, Spenser's political imagination, and Marlowe's luminous independence of mind. He is more like each of the three than any of them was like another." Such a variety of literary skills coupled with his political and practical talents made Raleigh a truly Renaissance, or "complete," "well-rounded" man. Raleigh brings his diverse talents to "The Nymph's Reply to the Shepherd" as he uses the pastoral lyric to reveal a darker future than was generally explored using the form.

Throughout "The Nymph's Reply to the Shepherd," Raleigh employs allusion, or direct literary reference, to Marlowe's poem. The singsong, "To live with thee and be thy love," is taken directly from Marlowe's poem. Instead of a wistful dreaming, with it, Raleigh employs more pessimism and caution. Where Marlowe sings of loveliness and inflated possibility, Raleigh claims implausibility. Raleigh's "pretty pleasures" in the third line of the poem refer to the ornaments of the pastoral lyric form and the pretty surface of Marlowe's idealized natural world. The "pretty pleasures" are not enough for Raleigh because they do not last. In the poem, he suggests the futility and meaninglessness of ornaments and unattainable musings.

The use of the pastoral form dates to the third century B.C., and was, even then, a conventional poem celebrating the simplicity and peace of a shepherd's life in an idealized natural setting. The word "pastoral" comes from the Latin, "pastor" for "shepherd," thus the preponderance of shepherd characters in the examples of the form. The word "idyl," is used synonymously with "pastoral," and is connected to the romanticized notion of the shepherd's "idyllic" life roaming through perfected nature. The form worked for the Elizabethan romantic whose goal was, as Brooke explains, to "expand the world in which men live—the world of the senses and the world of the spirit." Marlowe's poem does this through idealization of the natural world. Raleigh addresses such an expansion of mind and ideas by questioning the idyl. In the sixteenth century, "idyl" would also be used to describe the life of the high-ranking gentry, who led idle lives and were exempt from the physical work of the shepherd, but whose role suggested a similar romanticized and idealized state. It is this romanticized notion of life as a gentleman and courtier that Raleigh deems unrealistic in the face of changing times.

Marlowe and Raleigh's dialogue pits the simple pastoral life against the influence of a more complex existence where dark shadows reside alongside the bright meadows of the shepherd's home. Pastorals, including Marlowe's, favor the simple. Raleigh uses the form to expose the rudimentary and short-sightedness of the simple. Where Marlowe escapes from the court and society and flees to nature, Raleigh argues that such escapism, such simplicity is unattainable. In Marlowe's opening if/then statement, there is a sense of certain romance and possibility. Raleigh's opening if/then statement is more cautious, uncertain. He seems to suggest that if such an idealized life were possible, he would embrace the romantic, but his "if" is much more uncertain. His uncertainty stems from questioning the truth the shepherd tells. Is there "truth in every shepherd's tongue?" the nymph seems to ask. Is there any truth, or any possibility of such a simple life? The nymph and Raleigh are not at all certain. Where Marlowe's "melodious birds sing madrigals," Raleigh's nightingale, his "Philomel," ceases singing and becomes "dumb," solidifying the implausibility of the romantic. Where Marlowe sees only the positive future, Raleigh sees and understands a future fraught with difficulty as much as with ease.

Raleigh's second stanza introduces the element of time that so permeates and clouds his romantic visions. Time "drives flocks from field to fold" and turns "the rest" to the cares and burdens of the future. Joyce Horner, in "The Large Landscape: A Study of Certain Images in Raleigh," discusses Raleigh's tendency to expose the trappings of the ideal through a look at the power and fluctuations of time. Often, Horner notes, Raleigh's work addresses "the erasing, effacing power of time, the vanity of human effort." Raleigh's contemporary, Spencer, called Raleigh the "Shepherd of the Ocean," as he tackled the vastness, the "ocean," of the historical and human landscape. Raleigh's poetic voice is not content in the clean, conventional, and idealistic pastoral lyric unless it is exposing and subverting its conventions in an attempt to discuss the larger picture of human history. Where Marlowe's imagery offers a contained and tamed nature, Raleigh acknowledges "wanton," or rebellious fields and "wayward Winter." Here, the poet does not control the image of nature. Nature is ruler. Time progresses through the seasons and carries humanity with it. In this stanza, we cannot trust a "honey tongue" because it may hide "a heart of gall." Idyllic portraits, Raleigh suggests, are not to be trusted. To trust in the image and the ideal is to miss meaning. Horner notes in Raleigh's lyrics, "the small, enclosed world of the pastoral keeps cracking," and where "life-giving streams overflow," Raleigh also recognizes that "they have the power to drown." That life exists next to death, for Raleigh, is the point. That the romantic must exist next to the realistic is a fact with which the poet, the courtier, and the shepherd ultimately must contend.

In the fourth stanza of "The Nymph's Reply to the Shepherd," the trifles of language, the masks of idealism, which deal with nothing but self-delusion are "In folly ripe, in reason rotten." Raleigh does more than suggest the pastoral lyric's lack of real power. For Raleigh, challenging the delusion is what creates meaning, and he is looking beyond the conventions of the form, the folly and fun, to address the greater human story, which is one of struggle and "Winter" as much as it is one of romance in "May." The shepherd's "belt of straw and ivy buds," his "coral clasps and amber studs" become the frivolous ornaments of the pastoral lyric, the elements of superficial living. For Raleigh, the trifles of language and convention, these elements and visions of a shallow life, cannot move him to believe in the romantic. The need for a deeper love is implied, a relationship with society and lover that has the ability to transcend the beautiful ideal by questioning its validity and living fully in the darkness as much as the light. But, Raleigh needs the ideal to fully see and write the contradiction. Raleigh's nymph is as wrapped up in the thought of the ideal as Marlowe's shepherd, if not more so. For the nymph, the romantic ideal is the ultimate prize, made even more beautiful for its illusiveness and the yearning it creates with its distance and impossibility. If it were possible to harbor a constant joy, if youth was endless and love boundless, then perhaps, Raleigh suggests, he would be able to live and love the shepherd's passionate vision. But, only if . . . therefore, never.

The ideal cannot exist without the contradiction of that ideal, and herein lay the strength of this companion poem. In the sixteenth century, audiences seemed to recognize, as Brooke notes, "The forces of Elizabethan romanticism are seen in him [Raleigh] not fused, but in divergence, not in harmony, but in conflict. Raleigh's imagination destroyed nearly as much as it created." Together Raleigh's destruction and Marlowe's creation present a whole picture. Raleigh's vision balances Marlowe's and allows for the questioning that becomes the basis for a fully realized experience. In "The Nymph's Reply to the Shepherd," Raleigh harbors a yearning for the ideal that would make it possible to live and love as the shepherd, a yearning that is not quite belief, but a yearning that can be in itself a kind of rebirth. Raleigh's questions and dark predictions stem from this yearning, creating a deep impression and invitation to the reader to consider the many complex implications of what it means "To live with thee and be thy love."

Source: Erika Taibl, Critical Essay on "The Nymph's Reply to the Shepherd," in *Poetry for Students*, The Gale Group, 2002.

Sources

Adamson, J. H., and H. F. Folland, *The Shepherd of the Ocean: Sir Walter Raleigh and His Times*, Gambit, Inc., 1969.

Bradbrook, M. C., *The School of Night*, Cambridge University Press, 1936.

Brooke, C. F. Tucker, "Sir Walter Raleigh As Poet and Philosopher," in *ELH*, Vol. 5, Issue 2, June 1938, pp. 93–112.

Horner, Joyce, "The Large Landscape: A Study of Certain Images in Raleigh," in *Essays in Criticism*, Vol. 5, No. 3, July 1955, pp. 197–213.

Marlowe, Christopher, "The Passionate Shepherd to His Love," in *The Norton Anthology of English Literature*, edited by M. H. Abrams, W. W. Norton & Company, 1993.

May, Steven, "Companion Poems in the Raleigh Canon," in *English Literary Renaissance*, Vol. 13, No. 3, 1983, pp. 260–73.

Mills, Jerry Leath, "Sir Walter Raleigh," in *Concise Dictionary of British Literary Biography*, Vol. 1: *Writers of the Middle Ages and Renaissance*, Gale Research, 1992, pp. 235–50.

Nabokov, Vladimir, *Strong Opinions*, McGraw-Hill, 1973, p. 75.

"Old Arcadia" (For a discussion of Raleigh, Christopher Marlowe, Shakespeare and other Elizabethan poets), http://www.oldarcadia.com (August 6, 2001).

Further Reading

Aronson, Marc, *Sir Walter Raleigh and the Quest for El Dorado*, Houghton Mifflin Co., 2000.

Although written for a young adult audience, this recent biography gives a good sense of Raleigh's life as an explorer, especially in his vain journey to Venezuela to find the fabled Land of Gold.

Beer, Anna R., *Sir Walter Raleigh and His Readers in the Seventeenth Century: Speaking to the People*, Macmillan Press, 1997.

This historical study gives a better sense of the time that Raleigh wrote in, giving students an idea of the relationships between poets and of Raleigh's relationship with the English court.

Irwin, Margaret, *That Great Lucifer: A Portrait of Sir Walter Raleigh*, Chatto & Windus, 1960.

This book is not a comprehensive biography, but rather, as its title declares, a "portrait." It is divided into two parts, focusing on Raleigh's relationship with Elizabeth and then with James, her successor on the throne.

Latham, Agnes, and Joyce Youings, eds., *The Letters of Sir Walter Raleigh*, University of Exeter Press, 1999.

Although Raleigh's output as a poet was meager, he was a tireless letter writer, and some of his best literary output can be found here.

Remember

Christina Rossetti
1862

When the sonnet "Remember" first appeared in *"Goblin Market" and Other Poems* in 1862, it was both warmly and sadly received by readers. A mixture of happiness and depression tends to run throughout many of Christina Rossetti's poems, and this one, which begins "Remember me when I am gone away," implies immediately a loving, yet sad, request. How Rossetti resolves the conflict she presents in the poem reflects the way she handled similar dilemmas in her own life—emotionally and philosophically, always letting her devout Christian beliefs be the deciding factor.

Whether it was her struggle with debilitating illnesses or a desire to meet her maker, Rossetti appears to have been obsessed with her own pending death. "Remember" couples this persistent thought with an awkward love affair, one in which the speaker, presumably the poet herself, confesses that she may not be as passionately in love with her suitor as he is with her. But since she believes she is going to die anyway, her ambivalence toward him is not the most important issue. Instead, the dominant concern becomes how he will remember her when she is gone. Will he think of her and recall the pain of not knowing whether she truly loved him or will he remember, rightly or wrongly, that she adored him as much as he adored her?

In his book, *Christina Rossetti in Context*, author Antony H. Harrison discusses the poet's work and the "dominant tensions upon which it is constructed: between beauty and death; between love of man and love of God; between the ephemeral

and the eternal; between the sensory and the transcendent." "Remember" is very much concerned with these tensions, especially those between the ephemeral, or short-lived, and the eternal and between beauty and death, which the poet seems often to confuse in her work as well as in her life.

Author Biography

Christina Rossetti was born in London, England, in December 1830 and died in London in December 1894. Although she was of Italian descent, Rossetti never lived outside Great Britain because her father had moved to London where he was a professor of Italian at King's College. Rossetti's mother was also a teacher, and she schooled her own children at home. All four Rossetti children were artistically inclined—the two sons, William Michael and Dante Gabriel, were poets and painters; the older daughter, Maria, was a writer; and the youngest, Christina, became one of Victorian England's most prominent poets of both adult and children's verse.

Her brother, Dante Gabriel, probably had the greatest influence on Rossetti's early work. Dante was one of the founders of the Pre-Raphaelite Brotherhood, an artistic group whose objective was to recapture the more natural creative spirit of art before the renowned Renaissance painter Raphael (1483–1520) suggested restrictions on how a painting "should" look. When Dante started the Pre-Raphaelite movement in 1848, he and other members declined to attend any formal classes, essentially snubbing the Royal Academy and the fine-tuned artists it turned out. He also started a Pre-Raphaelite journal called The Germ, and this journal is where Rossetti published many of her first poems. Her first book, *Goblin Market and Other Poems*, was a collection of both adult and children's verse published in 1862. It includes the sonnet "Remember." Its symbolism and religious allegories are evidence of the Pre-Raphaelite influence on her work.

In spite of her association with this artistic movement of the mid-nineteenth century, Rossetti's life was governed more by her strict religious beliefs than by poetry, paintings, or famous siblings. She was a devout member of the Anglican Church, and she turned down two marriage proposals because the would-be husbands did not share her faith. Although she had apparently fallen in love both times, Rossetti declined her first suitor's proposal because he became a Roman Catholic and the second because he claimed to follow no faith at all.

Christina Rossetti

As a result, she remained single all her life. The tension brought about by conflicts between loving a man and loving God haunted Rossetti continuously. It is a theme played out in much of her poetry, including the sonnet sequence "Monna Innominata" (Unnamed Lady), which appears in *A Pageant and Other Poems*, published in 1881. At that point, the poet was in ill health and turning more toward writing religious essays than verse. Many of Rossetti's sonnets portray her consistent belief that she was close to death, and "Remember" is an excellent example of this belief.

Poem Text

Remember me when I am gone away,
   Gone far away into the silent land;
   When you can no more hold me by the hand,
Nor I half turn to go yet turning stay.
Remember me when no more day by day   5
   You tell me of our future that you planned:
   Only remember me; you understand
It will be late to counsel then or pray.
Yet if you should forget me for a while
   And afterwards remember, do not grieve: 10
   For if the darkness and corruption leave
   A vestige of the thoughts that once I had,
Better by far you should forget and smile
   Than that you should remember and be sad.

Media Adaptations

- Visit the "ArtMagick" web site at http://www. artmagick.com/index.asp (last accessed August, 2001), a "virtual museum displaying paintings and poetry from art movements of the nineteenth and twentieth centuries" (for example: romantic, symbolist, Pre-Raphaelite and art nouveau). The site includes dozens of paintings by the Pre-Raphaelites, as well as twenty poems by Christina Rossetti.

Poem Summary

Lines 1–2

The opening two lines of Rossetti's sonnet "Remember" introduce the idea of separation, but whether the speaker's eminent departure is because she has chosen to leave her lover or because she is dying is not immediately clear. As the poem unfolds, the reader understands that death will divide the couple, and the initial hint of that is the phrase "silent land" to describe the place the speaker is going. The words seem to define a cemetery or individual grave more than heaven, and "silent," in particular, implies a dormant state—an existence and a place that are neither joyous nor painful, pleasant nor sad. The opening lines also portray the speaker's desire to be remembered, and she requests her lover to do just that. This request will become more significant at the end of the poem when the dying woman appears to do an about-face with what she asks of him.

Lines 3–4

Line 3 simply furthers the idea of the couple's time together coming to an end, describing their physical separation when death will remove her from his touch. Line 4, however, presents an interesting twist in the situation. If Rossetti is writing only about the sadness of a loving man and woman being torn apart by one's actual death, then the woman—the one dying—would not have the option of turning "to go yet turning stay." The implication here is that the death theme is not the only

one at work. Caught between two opposites, going and staying, the speaker reveals her uncertainty in whether she really loves the man to whom she is speaking. Her unsure feelings become clearer in the latter part of the poem.

Lines 5–6

In line 5, the woman once again requests that her lover remember her "when no more day by day" he can talk to her about the future he was planning for the both of them. Notice here that the speaker says "*our* future that *you* planned," implying that she may not have given as much thought to staying together for the rest of their lives as he had.

Lines 7–8

These are the last two lines of the "octave," or a sonnet's first eight lines that generally follow a specific rhyme scheme and present a question or dilemma to be resolved in the "sestet," or final six lines. This poem's resolution—if there is one—is not quite as satisfying or conclusive as most. Lines 7 and 8 present the third time the speaker uses the word "remember," and it seems almost like a plea now. She essentially tells her lover that the only way to keep her with him is in his memory because, as her death approaches, it will be too late to discuss or pray about anything.

Lines 9–10

The beginning of the sestet is also the beginning of the about-face in the speaker's instructions to her lover. For the first time, she uses the word "forget," obviously the opposite of everything she has said to this point. Now she admits the possibility that the memory of her may slip from the man's mind from time to time, and she tells him not to worry about this or "grieve" over it. Suddenly, she seems more realistic about their relationship and the likelihood that her lover will go on with his own life, not dwelling on the memory of a woman he once had and lost.

Lines 11–12

In these lines, the speaker explains why she has granted permission for her lover to forget her as well as remember her. The revelation here is further evidence that the woman has had doubts about her love for this man throughout their relationship. She acknowledges that her death will leave "darkness and corruption" in his life, and that in this state of grief, he may actually recall the bad as well as the good. That is, he may remember that the thoughts the woman once had were about leaving him, ending their relationship before death had the chance to end it. A "vestige," or trace, of the doubt she sometimes felt would only bring him pain in remembering her after she is dead. With that in mind, the woman comes to the conclusion that she reveals in the final two lines of the sonnet.

Lines 13–14

Lines 13 and 14 present what feminist writer and critic Dolores Rosenblum calls an "equipoise," or an equilibrium as a means of resolution. In *Christina Rossetti: The Poetry of Endurance*, Rosenblum states:

> the young poet has already grasped the possibilities of the valediction of holding opposites in balance, for keeping and letting go.... If opposites cannot be reconciled, if self-division cannot be healed, then at least one can imagine the perfect equipoise.

The decision, or balance, in "Remember" is that it is better for the man to forget his dead lover if remembering her will only bring him pain. Keep in mind that it is not the normal pain that comes along with grieving for a lost loved one that the speaker wants him to avoid. Rather, it is the pain of remembering that she may not have really loved him, and their relationship would not have been a lifelong one even if she had lived into old age.

Themes

Imperfect Love

The theme of imperfect love in Rossetti's "Remember" is an idea based on the more obvious and often used theme of religion in her work. To a poet so devoutly centered on her Christian faith and love of God, the love of a man must seem second-rate, at best. A question, therefore, arises about her sincerity in the relationship she has with her lover— on one hand, she seems honestly to love him and begs him to remember her when she is dead; on the other hand, she appears a bit nonchalant in her willingness to tell him to forget her just the same.

In the beginning of the poem, the love between the couple seems strong, and the overtone of sadness and grief stems from the notion that death is about to tear them apart. But is this notion a fact? Is the woman really dying and, if so, how much time does she have left—a few hours, a few weeks, a year? There is no indication of a time limit, nor is there any reference to what she is dying from.

Topics for Further Study

- Try writing a Petrarchan sonnet. Remember that there is a general expectation of what the content in the octave and in the sestet should provide, as well as strict meter and rhyme schemes throughout.

- Read as much information as you can on Queen Victoria of Great Britain and then write an essay on some of the likely reasons that she was the longest reigning monarch in European history (besides Louis XIV).

- The Pre-Raphaelite art movement was a short-lived one, but it paved the way for other "rebellious" styles of painting, sculpting, writing, and so forth. What twentieth-century art movements have also been controversial and considered out of the mainstream? How have they been received by the general public and other artists?

- The Industrial Revolution brought swift changes to manufacturing, production, and communication capabilities throughout the world. What do you think was the most significant invention of the age and why?

All the reader knows is that the speaker is urgent in her message, and her message is based on love. But the last line of the octave, line 8, implies a higher love than the secular one shared by man and woman. Here, the speaker seems to tell her lover that once she is with God, he may as well not bother seeking help or praying because she will be far beyond his feeble and imperfect love. Only God's love is perfect.

In the latter part of the poem, the woman relinquishes her lover from his duty to remember her, acknowledging that, still on earth, he will encounter the "darkness and corruption" that befalls human beings on a regular basis. Feeling sorry for him, she frees him from any painful memories of her, particularly the recollections of how his love could never measure up to her expectations. In light of her strict faith, it would seem that no mortal man's ever could.

Balance and Contradiction

"Remember" is an exercise in opposites—a poem made up of a back-and-forth shift between balance and contradiction. This theme echoes Rossetti's own life, which often found her pulled between two poles, usually in regard to religion and worldly passion. This tension is reflected in the sonnet in both the speaker's indecision on whether to "turn to go" or "turning stay" and in her initial request to be remembered and her final request to be forgotten.

In her book, *Christina Rossetti Revisited*, critic Sharon Smulders says this of "Remember": "Poised between going and staying, between life and death, the speaker inhabits a subject position that is rife with indeterminacy." And in an article for *Victorian Poetry*, critic Thom Dombrowski notes that in Rossetti's religious poems in general "the torment is especially intense because the speaker . . . seems torn between longing and loathing, hope and despair, resolution and weariness." The contradicting emotions and pull in opposite directions essentially pave the way for the balance that Rossetti provides at the end of the poem. Although the speaker appears unsure of whether to go or stay, in the end she has no choice. If her death is real, then she must leave her lover behind. But the conflict does not end there. Instead, the man's memory of her will carry on the duality she posed to him when she was alive. Will it be a good memory or a bad memory? The speaker's answer does not actually resolve the problem, but, rather provides an "out" for either result: if the memory is good, remember her; if it is bad, forget her.

Style

The Sonnet

In Victorian England and centuries prior, writing poetry meant writing with formality, adhering to a specific line length, rhyme scheme, meter, and so forth. The sonnet is one of the most popular styles of formal verse, and there are two main types of sonnets—the Shakespearean (English) and the Petrarchan (Italian). In its structure, "Remember" most closely follows the Petrarchan style, named for the Italian poet Petrarch Francesco (1307–1374) who made it popular. This type of sonnet contains fourteen lines, divided into an octave (the first eight lines) and a sestet (the last six lines). Usually, the octave acts as a kind of rising action, presenting a question, vision, or desire that becomes the subject of the poem. The sestet is typically the resolution section, providing an answer to the question, bringing the vision into full view, or satisfying the desire expressed in the octave. A Petrarchan sonnet generally follows the rhyme scheme a-b-b-a-a-b-b-a for the first eight lines and c-d-e-c-d-e for the final six.

Rossetti's "Remember" follows precisely the Petrarchan rhyme scheme for the octave, but offers a slight variation in the sestet, which rhymes c-d-d-e-c-e. One cannot be certain why the poet strayed from the usual form, and perhaps it was simply because she liked the sound of it better this way. Some speculation has also suggested that rhyming lines 12 and 14 gives greater emphasis to the poem's ending, in which the speaker's final decision is revealed. As far as the use of the octave and sestet to present typical Petrarchan dilemma and resolution is concerned, this sonnet also runs off course, especially in the sestet. Rather than expanding on the idea of remembrance presented in the octave or bringing a satisfying closure to the speaker's assumed last request, the final lines in "Remember" speak of even grimmer "darkness and corruption" and jump from remembering to forgetting. As such, Rossetti's poem shows mastery of the formal style, but also demonstrates how slight deviations can provide greater impact for the work.

Historical Context

While the Rossetti family was gaining prominence in literary and artistic circles throughout England, Queen Victoria was in the early years of her long reign over the country, lasting from 1837 until her death in 1901. Because the Victorian era spanned much of the nineteenth century, it encompassed some of the greatest changes the world had witnessed up to that time. Foreign trade agreements, cultural expansion, the Industrial Revolution, widespread civil unrest, and a profusion of creative outlets all represented the social and political atmosphere of the times. This era also encompassed two prominent "ages" that occurred in the 1800s—the Age of Liberalism (1826–1850) and the Age of Imperialism (1875–1900). The former was characterized by social class battles and an effort by millions of citizens to secure a more democratic government, and the latter established empires for countries who were able to dominate small nations and gain control of world markets and raw materials. While emerging middle classes throughout the world struggled for greater

Compare & Contrast

- **1850s:** American social reformer and feminist Amelia Jenks Bloomer initiates "bloomer" fashion when she starts wearing full-cut pants under skirts. Bloomers enable women to move more freely and comfortably than did petticoats.

  Today: Just about anything goes in the world of fashion for women—from conservative business suits and low heels to revived mini-skirts and tall black boots to the ever-present blue jeans, sweat shirts, and sneakers. "Bloomers" are an option, not a must, for some.

- **1850s:** Florence Nightingale takes London nurses to the battlefields of the Crimean War, a conflict pitting Britain, France, and Turkey against Russia when the latter tries to advance into Turkey. Nightingale organizes a barracks hospital in a war that will claim more lives through disease than combat.

  Today: Women still make up the great majority of the nursing field, but they are also in-

creasing their numbers as physicians. Approximately twenty-five percent of doctors today are women, and forty-three percent of all medical students are female.

- **1850s:** The first Women's Rights Convention in the United States, led by Elizabeth Cady Stanton and Lucretia Mott, opens at Seneca Falls, New York in 1948. In 1953, seventy-three women present a petition to the Massachusetts Constitutional Convention urging women's right to vote.

  Today: The League of Women Voters, begun in 1920 as an advocate for citizen education, has seen its numbers steadily decrease over the years, mostly because women are more concerned about juggling careers and family responsibilities and young adults are not particularly interested in civic participation. Ironically, though, the number of women voters has been higher than their male counterparts for the past two decades.

---

recognition and independence, large governments exerted their imperialistic powers over weaker nations. Under Victoria, Great Britain expanded its colonial holdings in Africa and, in 1877, the queen was made Empress of India, thereby strengthening Britain's presence in Asia.

The term "Victorian" often carries a negative connotation because the queen to whom it refers was a rather dowdy, pretentious woman who gave new meaning to extremely high—and often hypocritical—moral standards and proper conduct, especially for women. In spite of Victoria's title of Queen of Britain, she allowed her prime minister and other male members of Parliament to run the government. Victoria believed a woman's place was in the home, and during her reign, women took over the duties of running their households, spurred on by the establishment of many clothing and home furnishings retailers. But Queen Victoria was also widely respected for her strength of character and tact, and her reign was the longest in European his-

tory, except for King Louis XIV of France. Under her rule, Britain saw unprecedented industrial and commercial prosperity, and several reform acts enfranchised the new middle class and the working class, as well as millions of new voters. Legislators passed humanitarian laws that eliminated some of the worst abuses in workplaces, and, toward the end of the century, the labor party grew strong, a regular civil service was established, and more children had greater opportunities to receive an education.

The Rossetti children were not poor, but the family did suffer financial hardship after the death of the father in 1854. Everyone pitched in to find various sources of income, the most successful being William Michael, who was employed by the Excise Office and also made money as a literary journalist. It was his income that supported the Rossetti family throughout much of the mid-nineteenth century. Having established the Pre-Raphaelite Brotherhood in 1848, Dante Gabriel and other members of the movement were viewed by the well-schooled, formal artists and critics of the time as impertinent young men who wanted to make a name for themselves by rebelling against the cultural norm. The "norm" in question was that established more than three centuries earlier by Raphael who suggested proper guidelines for paintings, such as one-seventh of the canvas should be in bright light and one-third in shadow, and the human figures used as subjects should represent ideal beauty. The Pre-Raphaelite movement began small but its influence was widespread in the art world, as well as the literary. The return to more natural subjects and less structured canvases paved the way for the loose, informal creativity that took hold in the mid-1800s and can still be seen today.

Critical Overview

Rossetti's poetry was widely accepted and appreciated from the beginning. Since her work, on the surface at least, was largely a reflection of Victorian primness and Anglican faith, it had no trouble making its way into the hearts and the libraries of the literary highbrows of the times. She was regarded as an important figure in the Pre-Raphaelite movement, and even those who criticized the rebellious nature of the brotherhood's painters turned a kinder eye toward the gentle, shy, and extremely pious poet.

In his article, "Christina Rossetti: A Reconsideration," critic Robert N. Keane notes that Rossetti "has been regarded by many as Britain's finest poet, yet her work has seldom been studied for its own sake." Instead, it was often thought of only in terms of its relationship to the Pre-Raphaelite movement, or in comparison to possibly the most popular female Victorian poet, Elizabeth Barrett Browning. But with Browning's death in 1861, Rossetti rose to the top of the list in many literary circles. Still, her work tended to be qualified by many readers and critics who studied it for its religious messages or its lessons in morality. Others searched it for hidden clues to the true nature of a fanatically devout and presumed lonely woman who devoted herself to church and family at the expense of personal happiness in an intimate relationship. When more recent researchers began looking at female Victorian poets for hints of early feminist views, Rossetti's work was heralded as a voice secretly crying out for independence and freedom while remaining obediently within the

strictures of the Victorian woman's place. As Keane points out, however, "In the last few years . . . there has been some movement toward studying her poetry for its own sake."

Whether the reviews have been based on fair terms or not, the overall consensus of critics is that Rossetti was one of the nineteenth century's best poets. She has consistently been praised for her ability to master formal verse, and the simple, honest voices of the speakers in her poems give authority to the tone, the subject matter, and the sometimes odd perspectives of the speakers themselves.

Criticism

Pamela Steed Hill

Hill is the author of a poetry collection, has published widely in poetry journals, and is an associate editor for a university communications department. In the following essay, she discusses the lack of sincerity in the poem's speaker and why it results from an inner conflict between worldly desires and religious fervor.

When it comes to poetry, many readers assume that the "I" in a poem must be the voice of the poet him or herself. While it is often true that at least a glimmer of the author's own beliefs, experiences, and perspectives show up in any creative work, one should not take for granted that a first-person narrative is always an autobiographical account. All that being the case, however, Christina Rossetti and her sonnets are hard to separate. That is, because her pious, reserved lifestyle is so heavily reflected in her work, a reader can safely make the assumption that was just warned against. Rossetti usually *is* the "I" in her sonnets, and "Remember" is a good example. Just like the poet, the speaker in this poem wages a war of conscience, one side leaning toward human love, the other toward divine love. And in this case, it is a struggle that renders her feelings on the human side hypocritical and false.

The title of the sonnet seems appropriate, at least through the octave. Beyond that, there is room for debate, but even in the first eight lines there are hints foreshadowing the abrupt change of heart that occurs in the sestet. It appears the speaker cannot make up her mind about whether she should stay with her lover or "turn to go." This would be an odd hesitation if she were describing only her impending death, but the dilly-dallying has more to do with living than with dying. A part of her wants to remain with the man she addresses and to enjoy a loving relationship as a typical couple. Another part denies worldly pleasure by placing God at the center of her attention, and, therefore, death, since that is the vehicle to heaven in the Christian faith. Rossetti forfeited two romantic relationships in her lifetime because the suitors fell short of the religious fervor she expected in them. The speaker in "Remember" opts to give up hers as well, supposedly because she is dying, but that notion turns out to be a facade for something all too commonly human.

The last three lines of the octave are nonchalant at best, callous at worst. If the reader accepts that the male companion here is truly in love with a dying woman—and there is no evidence suggesting otherwise—then imagine his emotion upon hearing her say what amounts to, "Yes, I know you were planning on a future together, but all you will have is your memory because I'm going to meet God. You're too late." This sentiment, of course, implies that there have been false feelings on the woman's part long before the impasse she and the man now face. Apparently, the speaker has always had hidden doubts about her love for him. She has never denied her love for God though, and given that she cannot resolve loving a human being and a supreme power at the same time, it must be the commitment to her suitor that does not quite ring true.

The speaker finally comes clean in the sonnet's sestet. Here, she reveals an opposing, and apparently more accurate, sentiment toward her lover's memory of her. She now gives him permission to forget. At first, this may seem to be a noble, selfless gesture, one reflecting such strong love for the man that she is making decisions to benefit his best interest even after she is gone. And perhaps her motive *is* charitable and devoted, but she also points out that her lover's pending grief will stem from a "vestige of the thoughts that once" she had— thoughts about leaving him because she did not love him or because her attraction to him interfered with her religious faith. He may likely look back on their relationship and recall that it was not as secure and loving as he had imagined and hoped for. In that case, he should put the painful memories out of his mind and go on with his life, presumably with another woman who really loves him. If he accepts this instruction as selfless on the woman's part, then all is well and the poem ends resolutely, if not happily. But can the man over-

> *Just like the poet, the speaker in this poem wages a war of conscience, one side leaning toward human love, the other toward divine love. And in this case, it is a struggle that renders her feelings on the human side hypocritical and false."*

look the fact that the speaker states her case in such a nonchalant, carefree manner?

An abrupt change of heart or mind often implies falseness in whatever notion is suddenly altered. Three times in the first eight lines of Rossetti's sonnet she uses the phrase "remember me." Include the title and the context is fairly solid: this poem reflects a longing to be remembered by a loved one. The sestet, of course, indicates this is not so. The constant pull between opposites has resulted in the speaker's inability to be completely sincere in either direction. Whatever initial appeal she may find in a man is quickly thwarted by her tendency to see him as less than perfect, less than godly. On the other hand, as devoted as she is to her church and her God, she nonetheless admits a longing for human intimacy. While obviously the vast majority of individuals who are just as devout in their religious faith have no problem carrying on long-lasting, loving marriages at the same time, the speaker in "Remember" cannot. Rossetti died a single woman, perhaps making this poem an eerie foreshadowing of her own circumstance at the end of her life.

Some readers will find this criticism harsh or overstated, and one could make a good argument in either case. The problem often faced with sonnets in which there is an "I" addressing a "you" is that subtlety far outweighs concrete description. This leaves the poet's history, a good knowledge of the poet's other work, and much implication as the starting point for comments and critique. Whether one views "Remember" as a flippant poem about a woman who has been a wishy-washy lover with a neurotic hang-up on religion or as an honest outpouring of true love and devotion from the lips of a dying woman, one point is clear: the circumstance is unfortunate for both the speaker and the man she addresses. Even if she has been insincere in the relationship, she at least attempted; the hypocrisy and falseness are not necessarily intended. She is caught between two opposing forces and appears helpless in standing firm for one or in finding a way to resolve a conflict that does not need to exist in the first place. Therefore, blame is not the issue here. While there may be room for a bit of guilt on the part of the speaker, she is a victim as much as is her companion.

Source: Pamela Steed Hill, Critical Essay on "Remember," in *Poetry for Students*, The Gale Group, 2002.

Susan Conley

In the following essay excerpt, Conley compares and contrasts "Remember" with "After Death," a poem Rossetti wrote around the same time.

In the sonnet "Remember" (1849) the speaker addresses a lover concerning her imminent death, with the repeated imperative to "remember me." Unlike "Song" ("When I am dead, my dearest") (1848), in which the speaker withdraws from the beloved into the indifference of death, "Remember" presents a speaker who at least appears to engage with the beloved and offer remembrance as the possibility of continuity between life and death. However, while adopting a different strategy to that of "Song," in which death renders null and void the terms "remember" and "forget" through an equivocating diction of indifference—"Haply I may remember, / And haply may forget"—"Remember" privileges first one term and then the other, until their independent value is eroded.

Death is never named in "Remember," but is invoked in the opening lines through the common conceit of the distant, "silent land", and elaborated in lines 3–6 in a description of a future of loss, of a negation of the lovers' present happiness. Yet what is the nature of their present relationship—why does the speaker vacillate between going and staying; why is it "*our* future that *you* planned" (my emphasis)? The subtle suggestion through these details of a problematic love relationship retrospectively undermines even the apparently easy intimacy of line 3—"when you can no more hold me by the hand"—until it hints at coercion: unlike the lover, death at least lets her "turn [and] go." As in "Song," the desire for death rather than the

beloved speaks loudest in the poem; death as an escape from a life that is enigmatically unsatisfactory, from an intimate relationship that mysteriously falls short.

Why, then, the repeated exhortations to "remember me"? The phrase occurs three times in the octave, becoming urgent in the final repetition, "Only remember me." The addition of the adverb here is further highlighted by its inverted stress, and the phrase as a whole is isolated by the caesura which follows, the only mid-line break in the whole poem. Yet the ambiguous syntax—"remember me alone" or "simply remember me"—undermines the very urgency of her plea; and the value of remembrance itself is in turn made dubious by what follows—"you understand / It will be late to counsel then or pray"—which implies that remembrance is what is left when it is too late to do something more effective. So even before we reach the sestet and the sonnet's turn, the rubric "remember me" appears to be virtually emptied of its literal meaning. While in one way a talisman *against* death, the realm of forgetting, its repetition creates a somnolent refrain where sound overwhelms sense, until it proleptically signifies the dissolution of meaning and the speaker's own forgetting in death. Its loss of proper meaning conjures its opposite: the void of forgetting.

Nevertheless, after the entreaties to "remember me," the turn at line 9 is still unsettling, especially due to the ease with which the speaker permits the lover to forget her. Lines 9–10 illustrate the paradoxical nature of the relationship between remembering and forgetting, acknowledging as they do that the lover will grieve only when he remembers he has forgotten; that remembering depends for its meaning on, and is only kept alive by, the possibility of forgetting: "Yet if you should forget me for a while, / And afterwards remember, do not grieve." As the dialectic of remembering and forgetting becomes more intricate, Rossetti takes bold license with the rhyme scheme in the sestet, with a nonsymmetrical pattern, *cddece*. One way in which the subtle and subversive effects of this poem are achieved can be observed by noting that the lines in which the word "forget" appears (once in the first line of the sestet and once in the penultimate line) also contain the most widely spaced of the poem's five end rhymes, forming thus the subtlest of alliances: "while" and "smile" link the passing of time with the passing of grief, suggesting the inevitable passage from remembrance to forgetting.

Such an inevitable progression, or perhaps regression, is suggested more directly in lines 11–12:

"For if the darkness and corruption leave / A vestige of the thoughts that once I had." These lines seem to reveal the poem's real interest, which revolves less around whether the lover remembers or forgets, than around the "darkness and corruption" of the grave and the fate of human "thoughts" therein. By projecting the speaker into the grave, rather than into an identifiably Christian afterlife, these lines could be read, like many of Rossetti's poems on the death-state, as a virtual denial of such an afterlife in their exclusive focus on the grave, the place of the body. The vision of death is especially bleak in these lines, with their metonymic extension of the literal destruction of the dead body to the figurative destruction of her "thoughts" of the lover, and, vice versa, their extension of a figurative, that is, metaphysical "darkness and corruption" to the "thoughts that once I had." Further, the use of the neutral "thoughts," rather than the expected "love," creates an emotional detachment consonant with the speaker's ambivalence toward the lover detected in the octave. As in "Song," the speaker seems to become absorbed into the indifferent world of the dead during the course of the poem. Thus, by the closing lines—"Better by far you should forget and smile / Than that you should remember and be sad"—the poem has achieved a complete *volte-face,* from imploring remembrance, to preferring that the lover forget her. Rossetti has employed the form of the Petrachan sonnet with a sinister logic. The binary thematics of the poem, based on both stated and implicit pairs of terms—living/dead, stay/go, past/future, smile/sad, remember/forget—are completely realigned by the end: life is linked with remembrance and sorrow, while death is linked with the smile of forgetfulness.

As I have suggested, these lyrics are the basis on which Rossetti's work has been characterized solely and often dismissively in terms of a lyric spontaneity and simplicity. Even in a recent critical anthology on Rossetti, a prolific critic of Victorian poetry writes that by the end of "Remember," "tactful concern for the lover ... displaces any self-centred desire to live on in his memory." Such a reading is clearly overdetermined by the prevalent biographical myth of Rossetti as a meek, deferential Victorian spinster, "tactfully" self-renouncing. By contrast, I am arguing for a reading that hears a skeptical, ironic female voice.

"Remember" and "After Death" (1849) were copied into Rossetti's notebook within three months of each other; and in *Goblin Market and Other Poems* she placed "After Death" immediately following "Remember." This latter fact at

least invites comparison between the two; at most, it suggests that "After Death," in which we hear the voice of a woman now dead, may be read as the sequel to "Remember." "After Death," however, establishes an altogether different mood from that of "Remember." This is partly due to its different use of the sonnet form. Unlike the unbroken lines and verbal echoes of "Remember," contributing to its dreamy melodiousness—"gone away / Gone far away"; "turn ... turning"; "day by day"— "After Death" breaks up the line more often than not with increased punctuation and enjambment. In addition, the octave, consisting of the speaker's description of the scene in the room where she has just died, has less of a lyric and more of a narrative structure than "Remember":

> The curtains were half drawn, the floor was swept
> And strewn with rushes, rosemary and may
> Lay thick upon the bed on which I lay,
> Where thro' the lattice ivy-shadows crept.
> He leaned above me, thinking that I slept
> And could not hear him; but I heard him say:
> "Poor child, poor child:" and as he turned away
> Came a deep silence, and I knew he wept.

The first quatrain suggests an archaic, perhaps medieval setting—the rushes, herbs, and flowers, and the ivy-covered lattice window—and this, as part of a deathbed scene, immediately conjures the world of Pre-Raphaelite gothic. Enhancing this is the effect of the uncanny, produced by the contrast between the speaker's straightforward, nonemotive reportage, and the awareness that she is dead.

The next quatrain introduces the would-be mourner of her death, an unnamed "he." The speaker appears at pains to display her superior

What Do I Read Next?

- In 1994, editor and poet Linda Hall put together a remarkable collection of women's poetry, including works from both the nineteenth and twentieth centuries. Called *An Anthology of Poetry by Women: Tracing the Tradition*, this book contains poems by such notable Victorian poets as Christina Rossetti and Elizabeth Barrett Browning, as well as contemporary American poets, including Sylvia Plath and Anne Sexton.

- *The Language of Exclusion*, written by Sharon Leader and published in 1987, is a feminist critical study of the nineteenth century's two most puzzling and shy female poets—Christina Rossetti and Emily Dickinson. Leader argues that most studies of women poets written before 1960 simply perpetuate the spinster/recluse view of these two women instead of highlighting their public significance and the impact that history and environment had on their demeanor.

- British scholar Christopher Hibbert's *Queen Victoria: A Personal History* (2000) is one of the most refreshing biographies of the prim, somewhat pompous, ruler of England because he explores a side of her that is rarely shown. This book describes the queen's relationship with her husband, children, and members of government and portrays her as a fun-loving, passionate woman who was madly in love with her partner and was sometimes a difficult, overbearing mother.

- The 2000 publication of Elizabeth Prettejohn's *The Art of the Pre-Raphaelites* provides readers a look at a much-studied subject. This book is considered the most comprehensive view of the movement to date, and it shows why Pre-Raphaelite art is still one of the most fascinating, sometimes shocking styles that never seems to lose popularity with museum-goers worldwide.

---

vantage point over this man; for while "He leaned above me" connotes a figuratively superior position, this is quickly shown to be falsely assumed, both by him and us: "but I heard him say." The speaker's ascendancy over him is heightened here by the simple, monosyllabic diction and balanced syntax of line 6, as she coolly negates his presumption of her deathly insentience. The inclusion of direct speech ("'Poor child, poor child'") is unusual among these death lyrics, in giving the lover a voice, however small, in the poem. Yet it is not a voice in dialogue with the speaker, but a solitary voice on which she eavesdrops; further, his words sound merely patronizing, his pity ironically undercut, placed as it is within her knowing narrative, in which she demonstrates the supreme vantage point of death.

The sestet abandons the narrative mode in which the speaker has quietly established her authority over the living, and offers instead a catalogue of omitted actions through which "he" is judged and found wanting. Here is an ironic vari-

ation on the litany of worldly rejection usually uttered by Rossetti's dying speakers ("Sing no sad songs," "Wreathe no more lilies in my hair" ["'The Summer is ended'"]). Speaking "after death," rather than before, the woman rebukes "his" stance of denial or rejection toward her. The object of the actions listed in lines 9–11 is the dead body, so these are symbolic ministrations, signifying an intense emotional attachment to the physical person of the beloved—the passionate bereavement she would have him feel, if he was the lover she wishes he were. The parallel syntax of lines 9 and 12—"He did not touch," "He did not love"—reinforces the equation offered between these sins of omission and the absence of love.

The final lines of "After Death" have been conventionally read as granting "his" redemption through his pity, the poem ending on a note of self-effacing generosity (not unlike the "tactful" renunciation of "Remember") or, alternatively, of "immature self-pity." Yet to what extent pity redeems him, if at all, depends on the worth assigned it by the poem. Pity is distinguished from love, clearly to its detriment:

> He did not love me living; but once dead
> He pitied me.

Firstly, "He pitied me" is isolated by enjambment, to parallel "He did not love me living"; secondly, there is an alignment through alliteration between "love" and "living," and through consonance between "dead" and "pitied." The apparent self-effacement of the closing words—

> . . . and very sweet it is
> To know he still is warm tho' I am cold.

—is in one sense real. For when for the first time in the poem the speaker expresses emotion, she effaces herself, as subject, from the utterance. This is in marked contrast to the sprinkling of simple verb phrases in which she has so far presented herself—"I lay," "I slept," "I heard," "I knew"—that collectively emphasize her heightened awareness "after death," even as such emotionally neutral verbs sustain an impression of aloofness and self-control. This leads me to suggest that the speaker attaches herself only obliquely to "very sweet" because of the emotional freight of this moment, and instead lends weight to her final words, "I am cold." Abandoning the prose syntax of the rest of the poem, these closing words promote ambiguity, as they simultaneously uncover and obscure the intense feeling they bear. "Sweet" is the only significant term in the last three lines without a companion word: there is "love" and "pitied," "living" and "dead," "warm" and "cold." In such a context, "sweet" invokes "bitter," and indeed *bittersweet* seems to capture precisely the conclusion to this poem.

The words "warm" and "cold" in the final line clearly operate metonymically for "the living" and "the dead." Yet, in addition, their several literal and figurative meanings flicker retrospectively over the poem. The word "cold" is given structural prominence both by being the final word of the poem, and by forming part of a rhyme ("cold"/"fold") that is so widely spaced it is barely heard. This near-dissonance contributes to the unsettling effect of the final line. "Cold" has resonances throughout the poem, from the creeping "ivy shadows," to the dead body whose hand is not held, to "his" tears of chilly pity. "Cold" also is the speaker's voice, a voice that reveals little emotion as she turns a cold, judging eye on the scene of her death and on "him." Such all-pervasive coldness enhances the irony of the final line, in which the epithet "warm" resonates with all that the poem shows to be lacking—life, love,

and passionate emotion. And while replete with irony, the final line is, at the same time, sincerely spoken; for, as with almost all of Rossetti's dead or dying, death *is* to be preferred over life, and for this speaker in particular, death is a bittersweet victory over the unloving living.

Source: Susan Conley, "Rossetti's Cold Women: Irony and Liminal Fantasy in the Death Lyrics," in *The Culture of Christina Rossetti*, edited by Mary Arseneau, Antony H. Harrison, and Lorraine Janzen Kooistra, Ohio University Press, 1999, pp. 260–84.

Sources

Dombrowski, Theo, "Dualism in the Poetry of Christina Rossetti," in *Victorian Poetry*, Vol. 14, No. 1, Spring 1976, pp. 70–76.

Harrison, Antony H., *Christina Rossetti in Context*, University of North Carolina Press, 1988, p. 21.

Keane, Robert N., "Christina Rossetti: A Reconsideration," in *Nineteenth-Century Women Writers of the English-Speaking World*, edited by Rhoda B. Nathan, Greenwood Press, 1986, pp. 99–106.

Rosenblum, Dolores, *Christina Rossetti: The Poetry of Endurance*, Southern Illinois University Press, 1986, p. 209.

Rossetti, Christina, *The Complete Poems of Christina Rossetti*, Vol. 1, edited by R. W. Crump, Louisiana State University Press, 1979, p. 37.

Smulders, Sharon, *Christina Rossetti Revisited*, Twayne Publishers, 1996, p. 125.

Further Reading

Jones, Kathleen, *Learning Not to Be First: The Life of Christina Rossetti*, St. Martin's Press, 1992.
    This biography of Rossetti is comprehensive and easy to read. It takes a sensitive look at the poet, based on the humble, pious, and selfless life she lived.

Lootens, Tricia A., *Lost Saints: Silence, Gender, and Victorian Literary Canonization*, University Press of Virginia, 1996.
    Lootens presents an interesting look at how and why many Victorian female writers were thought of as "saints," often at the expense of seeing them for who they really were. With such chapter titles as "Poet Worship Meets 'Woman' Worship" and "Canonization of Christina Rossetti," this book is a good read for those who want a better grasp of the environment in which Victorian women wrote and lived.

Rossetti, Christina, *The Letters of Christina Rossetti*, edited by Antony H. Harrison, University Press of Virginia, 1997.
    Reading the correspondence that Rossetti sent to her family and friends is beneficial in understanding the

poet's mindset. The letters confirm her devout Christian faith and help the reader understand why she would have written poems with themes of imperfect love, religion, and death.

———, *A Pageant and Other Poems*, Roberts Brothers, 1881.

Original copies of this book are likely to be housed in "rare books" sections of libraries and must be read there. However, later editions are available, and it is worth the read, especially for the "Monna Innominata" (Unnamed Lady) sonnet sequence.

———, *Selected Prose of Christina Rossetti*, edited by David A. Kent and P. G. Stanwood, St. Martin's Press, 1998.

Any reader who is seriously interested in understanding Rossetti's poetry and the perspective from which she wrote should read her prose as well. This book provides generous excerpts of both her short stories and religious writings, along with helpful introductions, publication histories, and synopses of the entire works. In general, Rossetti's prose is more revealing of her powerful intellect and keen perception of theological issues than her poetry is.

She Walks in Beauty

Lord Byron
1815

Written in 1814, when Byron was twenty-six years old, and published in *Hebrew Melodies* in 1815, the poem of praise "She Walks in Beauty" was inspired by the poet's first sight of his young cousin by marriage, Anne Wilmot. According to literary historians, Byron's cousin wore a black gown that was brightened with spangles. This description helps the reader understand the origin of the poem, and its mixing together of images of darkness and light, but the poem itself cannot be reduced to its origins; its beauty lies in its powerful description not only of a woman's physical beauty, but also of her interior strengths. There is no mention in the poem of spangles or a gown, no images of a woman actually walking, because the poet is after something larger than mere physical description.

Author Biography

Byron was born in 1788 in London to John Byron and Catherine Go a descendant of a Scottish noble family. He was born with a clubbed foot, with which he suffered throughout his life. Byron's father had married his mother for her money, which he soon squandered and then fled to France, where he died in 1791. When Byron was a year old, he and his mother moved to Aberdeen, Scotland, and Byron spent his childhood there. Upon the death of his great uncle in 1798, Byron became the sixth Baron Byron of Rochdale and inherited the ances-

Lord Byron

Following his separation, which had caused something of a scandal, Byron left England for Europe. In Geneva, Switzerland, he met Percy Bysshe Shelley and his wife Mary Wollstonecraft Shelley, with whom he became close friends. The three stayed in a villa rented by Byron. During this time, Mary Shelley wrote her famous novel *Frankenstein*, and Byron worked on Canto III of *Childe Harold* (1816). In 1817, Byron moved on to Italy, where he worked on Canto IV, which was published the next year. For several years, Byron lived in a variety of Italian cities, engaging in a series of affairs and composing large portions of his masterpiece *Don Juan* (1819–1824) as well as other poems. In 1823, he left Italy for Greece to join a group of insurgents fighting for independence from the Turks. On April 9, 1824, after being soaked in the rain, Byron contracted a fever from which he died ten days later.

Poem Text

She walks in beauty, like the night
Of cloudless climes and starry skies;
And all that's best of dark and bright
Meet in her aspect and her eyes:
Thus mellowed to that tender light   5
Which heaven to gaudy day denies.

One shade the more, one ray the less,
Had half impaired the nameless grace
Which waves in every raven tress,
Or softly lightens o'er her face;   10
Where thoughts serenely sweet express
How pure, how dear, their dwelling-place.

And on that cheek, and o'er that brow,
So soft, so calm, so eloquent,
The smiles that win, the tints that glow,   15
But tell of days in goodness spent,
A mind at peace with all below,
A heart whose love is innocent!

Poem Summary

Lines 1–2

Readers of poetry often get confused because they stop when they reach the end of a line, even if there is no mark of punctuation there. This could be the case with this poem, which opens with an enjambed line, a line that does not end with a mark of punctuation. The word enjambment comes from the French word for leg, "jamb"; a line is enjambed when it runs over (using its "legs") to the next line

tral home, Newstead Abbey in Nottingham. He attended Harrow School from 1801 to 1805 and then Trinity College at Cambridge University until 1808, when he received a master's degree. Byron's first publication was a collection of poems, *Fugitive Pieces* (1807), which he himself paid to have printed, and which he revised and expanded twice within a year. When he turned twenty-one in 1809, Byron was entitled to a seat in the House of Lords, and he attended several sessions of Parliament that year. In July, however, he left England on a journey through Greece and Turkey. He recorded his experiences in poetic form in several works, most importantly in *Childe Harold's Pilgrimage* (1812–1818). He returned to England in 1811 and once again took his seat in Parliament. The publication of the first two cantos of *Childe Harold* in 1812 met with great acclaim, and Byron was hailed in literary circles. Around this time, he engaged in a tempestuous affair with Lady Caroline Lamb, who characterized Byron as "mad—bad—and dangerous to know." Throughout his life, Byron conducted numerous affairs and fathered several illegitimate children. One of his most notorious liaisons was with his half-sister, Augusta. Byron married Annabella Millbank in 1815, with whom he had a daughter, Augusta Ada. He was periodically abusive toward Annabella, and she left him in 1816. He never saw his wife and daughter again.

Media Adaptations

- Learning Corp. of America has a video, released in 1971, entitled *Romanticism: The Revolt of Spirit*. It is a part of their "Shaping of the Western World" series, and examines the breadth of romanticism in music, art, and literature.

- A video called *The Bad Lord Byron* examines the poet's life through a mock trial. This 1949 feature film was released on videocassette in 1994 by Hollywood Select Video. It stars Dennis Price, Mai Zitterling, and Wilfred Hyde-White.

- *Byron: Mad, Bad, and Dangerous to Know* is a documentary based on the poet's correspondences with his publisher. It was released on videocassette in 1993 by Films for the Humanities and Sciences.

- Monterrey Home Video's 1993 title *The Glorious Romantics: A Poetic Return to the Regency* has actors playing Byron, Keats, Shelley, and others. It is part of the Public Broadcasting System's "Anyone for Tennyson?" series.

- "She Walks in Beauty" is included with other love poems on a compact disc from Naxos Audiobooks called *A Lover's Gift from Him to Her*, released in 1999.

- HarperCollins Audio Books released an unabridged selection of *Lord Byron's Poetry* on audiocassette in 1999, read by Linus Roache.

- Frederick Davidson reads Byron's poetry on *Lord Byron: Selected Poems*, a two-cassette package released by Blackstone Audio Books in 1992.

- "She Walks in Beauty" is one of the love poems included on the Capitol Records compact disc *Beauty and the Beast: Of Love and Hope*. Based on the television program of the same name, it was released in 1989.

- Dove Audio has a number of famous actors reading on a 1997 cassette entitled *The Poetry of the Romantics*. It includes works by Keats, Byron, Shelley, Wordsworth, Coleridge, and Blake.

---

without a pause. If read by itself, the first line becomes confusing because the reader can only see a dark image, almost a blank image. If "she walks in beauty, like the night," a reader might wonder how she can be seen. But the line continues: the night is a cloudless one and the stars are bright. So immediately the poem brings together its two opposing forces that will be at work, darkness and light.

Lines 3–4

These lines work well because they employ an enjambed line as well as a metrical substitution— a momentary change in the regular meter of the poem. When poets enjamb a line and use a metrical substitution at the beginning of the next line, they are calling attention to something that is a key to a poem. Here Byron substitutes a trochaic foot (an accented syllable followed by an unaccented one) for the iambic foot at the start of the fourth line. Why? Because he is putting particular em-

phasis on that word "meet." He is emphasizing that the unique feature of this woman is her ability to contain opposites within her; "the best of dark and bright / meet" in her. In the same way that enjambment forces lines together, and a metrical substitution jars the reader somewhat, this woman joins together darkness and light, an unlikely pair. They "meet" in her, and perhaps nowhere else besides a starry night. It's also important to note that the joining together can be seen in her "aspect," or appearance, but also in her "eyes." A reader might think of the eyes simply as a feature of beauty, but the eyes also have been associated in literature with the soul, or the internal aspect of the person: the eyes reveal the heart.

Lines 5–6

The emphasized word "meet" is here again echoed with the initial "m" sound in "mellowed." This woman joins together what is normally kept separate, but there is no violent yoking going on here; instead, the opposites meld together to form a mellowed, or softened, whole. By joining together the two opposing forces, she creates a "tender light," not the gaudiness of daytime, but a gentler light that even "heaven" does not bestow on the day. If a reader were to think of night in terms of irrationality and day in terms of reason—as is implied by the term enlightenment—that would not be apt for this poem. Neither night nor day seem pleasing to the speaker; only the meeting of those two extremes in this woman pleases him. She is a composite, neither wholly held by rationality nor by irrationality.

Lines 7–10

Once again the opposites are combined here. "Shade" or darkness is combined with "day" or light, and "raven tress" or dark hair is linked with a lightened face. The speaker suggests that if the woman contained within her and in her appearance either a little bit more of darkness or a little bit more of light, she would be "half impaired." A reader might expect the speaker to say she would be totally ruined or impaired, but if things were not just in the right proportion, she'd be half impaired, but still half magnificent. A key word in this section is "grace." Although the poet is seemingly talking about appearances, in actuality he is referring to the "nameless grace" that is in her hair and face. Once again, it is something internal as well as external that is so attractive about this woman.

Lines 11–12

Although this poem begins with the image of a woman walking, the reader should notice by now that no images are given of her legs or arms or feet; this is a head poem, confined to hair and eyes and face and cheeks and brows. The conclusion to the second stanza emphasizes this. The reader is given an insight into the "dwelling place" of the woman's thoughts, an insight into her mind. The repetition of the "s" sounds is soothing in the phrase "serenely sweet express"; because the poet is referring to her thoughts, and her thoughts are nothing but serene, readers may infer how pure her mind is.

Lines 13–18

Byron concludes the poem with three lines of physical description that lead to the final three lines of moral characterization. The soft cheeks, the winning smile, the tints in the skin eloquently express not only physical beauty, but they attest to her morality. The physical beauty, the speaker con-

cludes, reflects days spent doing good, a mind at peace, and "a heart whose love is innocent." Whether Byron would have preferred a less innocent cousin, someone with whom he could enjoy Byronic passions, is left unspoken for the reader to decipher.

Themes

Beauty

Lord Byron's poem "She Walks in Beauty" was written in praise of a beautiful woman. History holds that he wrote it for a female cousin, Mrs. Wilmot, whom he ran into at a party in London one night when she was in mourning, wearing a black dress with glittering sequins. The poem uses images of light and darkness interacting to describe the wide spectrum of elements in a beautiful woman's personality and looks.

Unlike common love poetry, which makes the claim that its subject is filled with beauty, this poem describes its subject as being possessed by beauty. This woman does have beauty within her, but it is to such a great degree that she is actually surrounded by it, like an aura. To some extent, her positive attributes create her beauty, and so the poem makes a point of mentioning her goodness, her serenity, and her innocence, which all have a direct causal effect on her looks. There is, though, another element: the "nameless grace" that is a type of beauty bestowed by heaven, as in the common expression "she is graced by beauty." The woman described in this poem is so completely beautiful, inside and out, that Byron goes out of his way to mention all of the various possible sources, to show that he appreciates her beauty to its fullest.

The beauty described here is a result of the woman being well-rounded, to such an extent that the second stanza notes how the very slightest difference—a shade or a ray—would alter her beauty drastically, cutting it in half. While a more conventional sense of beauty might list only the woman's positive attributes, it is typical of Byron's romantic sensibilities to see beauty as a mixture of light and darkness, admitting that the sinister, mysterious darkness of night has as much to do with a woman's appeal as the positive aspects associated with light. Pure light, according to this vision, is so limited in its relation to beauty as to be "gaudy."

Harmony

In this poem, Byron balances light and dark within the personality of one beautiful woman. If any two concepts can be recognized as being mutually exclusive, it would be these; light does not exist where there is darkness, and darkness does not exist in light, even though they can exist next to one another, with darkness taking up where light ends and vice versa. In some cases, the two are thought of as struggling against one another, but in the case of a beautiful woman, as Byron explains it here, light and dark can exist together, at the same time, in harmony.

Harmony is more than different things existing together. In music, which is where the word is most often used, it refers to a special, third tone that occurs when two tones work together with each other and make a new, pleasing sound. Similarly, Byron implies in "She Walks in Beauty" that the convergence of light and dark within this woman creates a new thing that is greater than the sum of the two. The darkness of her "raven tresses" and the lightness of her skin do not contrast with each other, they create a well-rounded whole that is great enough to hold contrasting elements.

Flesh versus Spirit

This poem raises the issue of the mind-body duality that has concerned philosophers for centuries. The most puzzling thing about this concept is the fact that the mind, or spirit, is definitely not a physical thing that anyone would ever be able to point to, but it definitely responds to changes in the body. Even today, when science can identify electrochemical reactions in the brain that seem to be direct responses to physical stimulation, there is no clear way of showing how what happens in the brain translates into the immaterial world of thoughts.

The version of the mind-body duality that Byron presents in this poem is the opposite of the one that measures neural reactions. To him, the woman's beauty originates in her thoughts, and the innocence and purity of her mind manifest themselves on her face, to create the beauty that he sees there. The third stanza states this process directly. The first three lines of this stanza catalog the parts of the woman's face that the poet finds beautiful, listing her cheek and brow, her smile, and her complexion. In the last three lines, the cause of this beauty is linked to what goes on inside of her mind. It is her goodness, her peacefulness, her love and innocence that are all "told of" in the woman's features. Because of the fact that this romantic view

Topics for Further Study

- Can a person's spiritual goodness make them physically beautiful? Give examples of qualities you feel would make a person beautiful and explain why.

- Try to draw a picture of what you imagine the woman in this poem to be like, taking care to include what details Lord Byron gives about her, but also giving your own interpretation of her beauty.

- This poem is written in a very common metric scheme, iambic tetrameter. Try to find a contemporary song that you like that fits this meter and sing this poem to that music.

- Find pictures of a male and female from the early nineteenth century. How have standards of beauty changed from Byron's time to our own?

- In his lifetime, Byron was notorious for his love affairs and for flaunting the conventions of society in the name of art. Read some biographical material about him, then write a paper comparing him to someone who is in the news today.

of love has prevailed throughout Western society, modern readers often fail to appreciate the fact that beauty does not necessarily have to be caused by purity of spirit. Byron's poem claims that the woman's virtues are the cause of her external beauty, but there is no real proof of any link between the spirit and the flesh.

Perfection

There are several places that "She Walks in Beauty" implies that it is giving an image of womanly perfection. In line 3, for instance, the poem describes how this woman's eyes contain "all that's best of dark and bright." Lines 7–8 explain that the slightest variance of light or dark would cut in half the indescribable grace that gives her the great beauty she wears. As Byron describes this woman, there is nothing that could be better about her and much that could be lost if things were not exactly as they are. All elements about her must be kept in exactly the present proportions for her beauty to remain. This is perfection.

Because the poem draws a connection between the woman's finely-balanced features and her personality, readers can assume that this woman is not only perfect in her looks, but in her personality as well. She is perfect through-and-through. It is fitting for a romantic expression of love that Byron's claims about her should be so extreme as to say that she is not just good, not great, but perfect. In poetry, the device of overstating things with great exaggeration is called hyperbole. Lovers often make such exaggerated claims about those who are the objects of their affections, driven by the excitement of their emotions. It is typical of Byron to casually shower such praise on a woman with whom he had no direct romantic involvement at all.

Style

The three six-line stanzas of this poem all follow the same rhyme scheme and the same metrical pattern. There are only six rhyming sounds in this eighteen-line poem because the poem rhymes *ababab, cdcdcd, efefef.* The pairing of two rhyming sounds in each stanza works well because the poem concerns itself with the two forces—darkness and light—at work in the woman's beauty, and also the two areas of her beauty—the internal and the external. The rhyming words themselves, especially in the first stanza, have importance: notice how "night" rhymes with its opposites, "light" and "bright," in the same way that this woman contains the two opposing forces in her particular type of beauty. Oftentimes poets use their poetic structures to mirror what the poem's chief concerns are. Poetic form—stanzas and meter—and content—what the poem's subject is—are almost always related.

The meter is also very regular—iambic tetrameter. This means there are four—"tetra" is Greek for four—iambs per line. An iamb means that the line is divided into units, or feet, of two syllables, and each unit has an unaccented syllable followed by an accented syllable. This can be clearly seen if you look closely at the construction of a particular line:

She <u>walks</u> / in <u>beau</u> / ty <u>like</u> / the <u>night</u>.

This poem was included in Byron's 1815 book, *Hebrew Melodies,* which included poems written

to be set to adaptations of traditional Jewish tunes. This very regular iambic line is very suitable for being set to music because of its strong rhythm.

Historical Context

Lord Byron is considered one of the most important and interesting poets of the romantic movement in England, and "She Walks in Beauty" is frequently considered one of his most powerful works. In the late eighteenth and early nineteenth centuries, romanticism swept across the world, affecting the sensibilities of artists and philosophers in a number of countries. Like any social movement, it was not the result of any kind of structured effort on the parts of its adherents so much as it reflected a response to the times they lived in and the problems that they found with the work of artists that came before them.

The last half of the 1700s represented a time of great social unrest in Western society. In the United States, this era is best remembered for the American Revolution, which was fought from 1776 to 1783, leading to the adoption of the Constitution in 1789. Even more compelling to the people of Europe was the French Revolution, which lasted from 1789 to 1799. While the American Revolution freed a new colonial country from the country that ruled it, establishing a democratic government of the people, by the people, and for the people, the revolution in France overturned the government of a political structure that had existed for hundreds of years. Both revolutions reflected the same basic principles, supporting the rights of individuals to control their own fates and rejecting the previous order that gave the aristocratic ruling class the power to establish laws and levy taxes without holding its members responsible. Although the ruling monarchies were shocked by the unruliness of the American rebels and their methods of defying the existing social order, such as the Boston Tea Party, these actions paled when compared with the widespread bloody chaos that took place throughout France during the revolution there. The French government ordered massive executions to frighten the revolutionaries, and when they gained power, the revolutionaries put hundreds of members of the nobility to death at the guillotine.

These political upheavals encouraged the sense of freedom that characterized the romantic movement. Earlier generations had focused attention on using order, reason, and scientific exploration to

Compare & Contrast

- **1815:** The world's political powers are in a state of change. The French army of Napoleon Bonaparte is defeated by the British at Waterloo, ending his dominance of Europe, while the British army is defeated in the Battle of New Orleans, establishing America's control of the continent.

  Today: The major military powers seldom come into direct conflict with each other, although they do take sides in the conflicts of smaller nations.

- **1815:** A woman in mourning for a dead relative is expected to wear black for at least a year and to stay out of public social situations for at least that long.

  Today: Social conventions for how a person should express her or his grief have less stringent rules.

- **1815:** A London banker is able to get news of Napoleon's defeat days before the newspapers have the information because he has associates send the report by carrier pigeon.

  Today: Cell phones and e-mail transmit information around the globe instantly.

- **1815:** Sources of artificial light are gas lanterns (in the wealthier homes) and candles.

  Today: Most homes and streets are lit with electrical light.

---

address the world's problems. During the Age of Enlightenment, which is measured from roughly the year 1700 to the start of the French Revolution in 1789, philosophers such as Jean Jacques Rousseau, Voltaire, and Denis Diderot published works that promoted humanity's ability for self-improvement and were influential throughout Europe and North America. This faith in the social and physical sciences was reflected in literature in greater attention to studying the styles and themes of ancient writers, so that in the early to mid-1700s neoclassicism flourished. The Enlightenment's support of reason can be said to have created a revolutionary spirit, as people around the world began questioning the qualifications of aristocrats, who had power only because their parents had power. The spirit of revolution led to the romantic movement, which shifted emphasis from rationality toward spirituality.

The romantic movement in literature developed gradually in different places, but most historians agree that it came into focus with the introduction that William Wordsworth wrote for the 1800 edition of *Lyrical Ballads*, a book of poems that he and Samuel Taylor Coleridge wrote. In this introduction, Wordsworth described poetry, using a much-quoted phrase, as "the spontaneous overflow of powerful feelings." This emphasis on spontaneity and feeling gave romanticism its defining characteristics: a focus on beauty, insistence on the importance of the writer's sensibilities, and an emphasis on the non-rational that eventually developed into an interest in the occult. The early English romantic poets included Wordsworth, Coleridge, and William Blake.

Lord Byron belongs to the second phase of romanticism in England, which began early in the nineteenth century. This new wave included an appreciation of history, but not the ancient history of Western civilization that was popular with the neoclassicists. As it went along, romanticism picked up an interest in folk arts and national history, giving a social context to the "powerful feelings" that Wordsworth emphasized without shackling romanticism to social tradition. The poets of this period—most notably Byron, John Keats, and Percy Bysshe Shelley—are the ones that modern students most often associate with the romantic movement. Their works are sensual and patriotic, mysterious and mournful. The stereotype of the poet as a young man, struggling feverishly with the unnamed inspiration that he is compelled to follow, consumed by love and doomed to a tragic end, is based almost entirely on the lives of Keats, Shelley, and Byron, who lived and loved heartily and all died young.

Critical Overview

Although Byron is known as one of the major poets of the Romantic period, his work has been faulted by a number of famous writers. According to the poet W. H. Auden in his book *Dyer's Hand and Other Essays*, Byron's poems need to be "read very rapidly" because if one slows down the "poetry vanishes—the feeling seems superficial, the rhyme forced, the grammar all over the place." While nineteenth-century British poet Matthew Arnold considers Byron, along with Wordsworth, "first and pre-eminent in actual performance . . . among the English poets of this century," he holds a similar opinion of Byron's technical merit. Writing in a preface to *Poetry of Byron*, Arnold states: "As a poet, he has no fine and exact sense for word and structure and rhythm; he has not the artist's nature and gifts."

Other critics have disagreed with such negative assessments of Byron's worth. In response to the first appearance of *Hebrew Melodies*, a British critic writes in a 1815 *Augustan Review* critique that "there are traits of exquisite feeling and beauty" in the collection; the poetry itself was considered by this nameless critic to be of "superior excellence." Other critics in this century have likewise praised *Hebrew Melodies* and specifically "She Walks in Beauty." L. C. Martin admires "the generous allowance of long vowels, the variety of vowels and consonants, and the likeness within the differences effected by internal rhymes or other devices" in the poem. He suggests that Byron should be taken "with some seriousness as a technician in verse." Another critic, Frederick W. Shilstone, also applauds *Hebrew Melodies*, calling it "an important experiment in genre" that prepared the way for "more elaborate volumes like Robert Lowell's *Notebook* and John Berryman's *Dream Songs*."

Criticism

David Kelly

Kelly is an instructor of creative writing and composition at Oakton Community College and the College of Lake County. In the following essay, he examines how the concept of the Byronic hero applies to "She Walks in Beauty."

Modern appreciation of the poetry of Lord Byron is focused mainly on his works about male characters who in some ways represent the poet, or at least the person the poet liked to think he was. Like the Hemingway hero, who embodied manly ideals that biographers can show novelist Ernest Hemingway was trying to incorporate into his way of life, the Byronic hero had elements of genius, tragedy, and sex appeal that set the standard for the poet, as well as for generations of would-be misunderstood poets for years to come. There were, in fact, several Byronic heroes, from the intensely silent man of action to the sensitive *artiste* to the brash, unwavering lover, who provides the sensibilities for a poem like "She Walks in Beauty," even if he does not appear in it directly. P. L. Thorslev, in his book *The Byronic Hero: Types and Prototypes* (quoted in Jump, p. 76) gives a list of basic heroic types that were popular in Byron's time:

> the Child of Nature; the Gothic Villain (unregenerated, as in the novel, or remorseful, as in the drama or in [Sir Walter] Scott's romances); the accursed Wanderer; the Gloomy Egoist, meditating on ruins, death, or the vanity of life; and the Man of Feeling, suffering from a lost love, or philanthropically concerned with the suffering caused by war or oppression.

In "She Walks in Beauty," there is no particular narrator referred to, no mention of an "I" or "me" that would tell readers they are supposed to think about the person who is telling them about this beautiful woman. Still, it is rare that there is ever a poem where the persona of the speaker is not a central concern. Prose is for conveying information; when one writes poetry, the words are arranged on the page in a highly stylized fashion, and readers are bound, eventually, to question the personality that this arrangement reveals. Often, the personality of the speaker is that of the poet, but it would be a mistake to assume that this is always the case. As the list above indicates, Lord Byron projected a number of various personalities through his poetry. Readers cannot just assume that "She Walks in Beauty" is a revelation of Byron himself; instead, they have to ask just what kind of character is behind the words of this particular poem, implied but not examined, almost hidden within the attempt to throw attention onto the beautiful woman of the title.

The little that is known about how this poem came into being seems to give it some sort of basis in real life, although this simple conclusion is not as simple as it seems at first. The story of its genesis is told over and over again, with no more details than Leslie A. Marchand gave in his 1970 biography of Byron. In his summary of the festive

London social scene at the end of the Napoleonic Wars in 1814, when the city was overrun with returning army officers and alive with the thrill of victory, Marchand writes:

> One evening [James Wedderburn] Webster dragged him against his will to a party at Lady Sitwell's, where they saw Byron's cousin, the beautiful Mrs. Wilmot, in mourning with spangles on her dress. The next day he wrote a gemlike lyric about her.

Many readers assume from this snippet of Byron's life a background context for "She Walks in Beauty." They find it to be about the chaste love of a man for his relative, or they add the element of Mrs. Wilmot's grief to her beauty and speculate on whether the magic surrounding her is in spite of or because of it. It provides a sense of the poem's speaker as a Hopeless Romantic, using the word in the modern sense, as it has come down to current times with associations that it picked up from the age of romanticism. This poem presents itself as a work of pure love and intellectual appreciation for the object of desire that Byron had no interest in pursuing as a lover.

While it is fine to know the circumstances under which a work of art first appeared, it can sometimes be a distraction. Examining this poem without considering the poet or the little that is known about his inspiration for it reveals a slightly different personality for the speaker: one still mostly hidden behind the grandeur of the woman being discussed, but one who exists nonetheless. For the sake of discussion, and for no other reason, this speaker can be referred to as "he," although there is really no strong evidence that links it to either gender once the author's identity has been removed from the equation. He appears to be sensitive, intelligent, smitten, and respectful, swept off of his feet by the sheer elegance of the lady being described. These aspects projected in the poem are all consistent with various versions of the Byronic hero. It is obvious that this speaker is meant to be admired and respected for the admiration and respect that he extends toward the beautiful woman, and it is this that qualifies him for the label of "hero."

A significant part of this hero's profile is the knowledge that he claims to have about the woman's personality. He knows, according to the poem, that she has "thoughts serenely sweet" and "a heart whose love is innocent." How would he know these things? It is a small point, but one that colors the whole message of the poem, and therefore one that gives many students their entire understanding of the spirit of romanticism.

> *The speaker of this poem knows things about the woman that he would not know if he existed in the real world."*

Looking at the matter biographically, one could say that Byron was familiar with Mrs. Wilmot, that he knew her personality and chose to characterize it as such. This explanation misses the point; however, no matter how well he knew the woman (and indications are that they were not very close at all), it is impossible to know any other person's soul with the certainty that the speaker claims in this poem. The other option that is drawn from reality would be that the poem's speaker might be understood as seeing the purity of the woman's heart through the purity of her face. The poem certainly leans readers toward this interpretation at the end, when it lists several of the aspects of her face and then explains that they "tell of" the goodness of her spirit. This sort of interpretation of physical clues, of saying that a person's psyche must be a particular way to have caused her face to come out the way it has, is well within the responsibility of poetry. But "She Walks in Beauty" is inconsistent in its method of interpreting personality. Lines 10–12 have "thoughts" expressing purity and dearness on her face, which seems to explain how the face reflects personality but actually confuses the issue by claiming that this woman has thoughts on her face. So common is the language that people use when telling about how they can "read" emotions that Byron almost gets away with putting a non-physical idea in a physical place.

There is a jump in logic required to understand the speaker of the poem as he is presented. It is this logical jump that takes him beyond the logical, measurable, knowable world and gives him almost supernatural ability to know the woman's soul that makes this poem's speaker heroic. As an actual human being, Byron may have been incredibly sensitive to the physical characteristics of people he encountered, and he may have shown great intuition in guessing their personalities from the traits that he observed. Still, he could not have seen this deeply into the spiritual realm, to know the immeasurable aspects that they might not have even known about themselves. Though, as a hero, he could. There are many traits associated with the word "hero," and the variations on the "Byronic hero" are almost too numerous to be useful anymore, but one thing stays consistent: the word "hero" is almost always used for a person who achieves things that ordinary people cannot. The speaker of this poem knows things about the woman that he would not know if he existed in the real world. The fact that he uses this power selflessly, to shower praise on another, is what makes him "heroic" in the conventional sense of the word.

When a poet lives an interesting life, as Lord Byron did, there is a great temptation to read his work in terms of his life. This is especially true when there is at least a little bit known about the inspiration for the poem, as is the case with "She Walks in Beauty." Often, the knowledge about Byron's life is mixed with the concept of the hero that he often projected in his work, and critics will understand a piece of literature through that double filter. Because there is no semblance of the author or of a heroic character in this poem, readers too often tend to interpret it as if it came from outside of the normal range of Byron's work, instead of looking for the ways that it fits in. In fact, "She Walks in Beauty" is as interesting for the things that are not explicitly mentioned, that are only implied, as it is for the technical brilliance and passion it conveys.

Source: David Kelly, Critical Essay on "She Walks in Beauty," in *Poetry for Students*, The Gale Group, 2002.

Daniel Moran

Moran is a secondary school teacher of English and American literature. In this essay, he examines the ways in which Byron's poem presents its subject as aesthetically perfect and as a reminder of Byron's own lost innocence.

In Orson Welles's *Citizen Kane*, Mr. Bernstein, a one-time associate of the enigmatic title character, is interviewed by Thompson, the reporter whose quest for the meaning of Kane's final word ("Rosebud") propels the film. Bernstein suggests to Thompson that perhaps "Rosebud" refers to "some girl" from Kane's "early days," only to be told by Thompson that "'it's hardly likely . . . that Mr. Kane could have met some girl casually and then, fifty years later, on his deathbed,'" recall her during his last moments on earth. Bernstein, however, offers an example from his own life to suggest the power of a moment spent in the presence of a certain type of beauty:

A fellow will remember things you wouldn't think he'd remember. You take me. One day, back in 1896, I was crossing over to Jersey on a ferry and as we pulled out there was another ferry pulling in—and on it there was a girl waiting to get off. A white dress she had on—and she was carrying a white parasol—and I only saw her for a second and she didn't see me at all—but I'll bet a month hasn't gone by since that I haven't thought of that girl.

What specifically fascinated Bernstein about this girl is never revealed, but if the details he offers are to be trusted, her complete innocence (suggested by her white dress and parasol) had something to do with the force of her vision on Bernstein's mind—surely he does not recall her month after month as "the one that got away," or as the fuel for licentious imaginings. The very fact that the girl was completely oblivious to the eyes of men is part of what made her so attractive; had she flirted with Bernstein or otherwise shown her approval of his adoration, the spell would have broken.

A similar phenomenon is dramatized in Byron's "She Walks in Beauty," where the title figure (Byron's cousin by marriage, Mrs. Robert John Wilmot) has no idea she is being watched so attentively or producing a reaction of such intensity. Byron is fascinated by the vision of Wilmot for reasons similar to why Bernstein was fascinated by the girl on the ferry: she is beautiful and her beauty is enriched by her innocence.

The poem presents Wilmot as a woman made beautiful by a perfect combination of opposites, the foremost being that she appears so striking while in mourning, as Wilmot was when Byron had his now famous glimpse of her. Wilmot's grace in mourning only heightens her beauty and ignites Byron's eye, rather than turning it away with the solemnity and sobriety one would expect from a woman in mourning dress. (Funerals, of course, are not thought of as breeding grounds for beauty, nor are mourning clothes worn to accentuate one's physical charms.) Her striking appearance is also the result of perfectly blended opposites: in this case, shades of light and dark. Her dress and "raven" hair are black, yet her skin and eyes are fair, so that "All that's best of dark and bright / Meet in her aspect and her eyes." These contrary attributes are ones not even found in nature (a longtime poetic standard for beauty), for here they are "mellowed to that tender light / Which heaven to gaudy day denies." The "day" is "gaudy" because it lacks the perfect balance of light and dark that is found in Wilmot—instead, the heavens simply dump an unmeasured heap of light onto the sky and do the opposite with darkness a few hours later. The person with the loudest voice is not, of course, the greatest singer, just as the thing with the greatest amount of light is not the most beautiful. In fact, the combination of light and dark is so perfect in Wilmot that "One shade the more, one ray the less" would destroy the totality of her beauty.

Aesthetically, therefore, she is perfect—but the world is full of beautiful girls whose beauty has been painted by artists even more carefully than by Byron. What makes Wilmot so alluring is the fact that her beauty is the direct result of her purity. Her face is one shaped by a number of "thoughts serenely sweet" that reflect the "pure" and "dear" mind from which they spring; similarly, her "smiles that win" and "tints that glow" are not ones that reveal her desire to capture the hearts of leering men, but instead "tell of days in goodness spent." Just as the physical deformity of Shakespeare's Richard III is meant to suggest his twisted, vile heart, Wilmot's physical beauty is indicative of her moral perfection. Although Wilmot's angelic appearance and soul elevate her to the point where people like Byron are "below" her, she does not find her admirers bothersome: instead, she is "at peace" with her worshippers because of her "heart whose love is innocent"—jealousy, envy, and cunning are not a part of her heart and therefore do not mar her appearance.

Had "She Walks in Beauty" been written by a different poet, the analysis here would most likely be finished. However, the identity of the author complicates matters because of what the world has learned about his mind and passions. Byron was widely described as mad, bad and dangerous to know—an apt description, for Byron stood in his own time (and certainly stands today) as the embodiment of rebellion and dismissal of conventional moral codes—so much so that the term "Byronic hero" has been coined to describe a moody, dark figure without roots or respect for those values held dear by his contemporaries. Byron's promiscuity has been well documented and endlessly discussed by himself and others: his sleeping with his half sister, bisexuality, and (by his own count) over two hundred affairs may shock a reader, but also make "She Walks in Beauty" more moving and complex.

Consider the speaker, then, not only as one who is particularly sensitive to beauty but as Byron, the licentious literary legend. Why would a man so consumed by his own insatiable sexual appetites pause to ponder such a woman? The answer lies in the attraction of the impure for the pure. Now

> *The person with the loudest voice is not, of course, the greatest singer, just as the thing with the greatest amount of light is not the most beautiful."*

the combinations of light and dark take on added meaning: she possesses a "heart whose love is innocent" but he sees her walking "like the night"— that is, like a woman *of* the night. Her black mourning dress now takes on a significance that she cannot understand (because of her "thoughts serenely sweet") but that he, as one who has lost the capacity or inclination for such "sweet" thoughts, finds alluring. The very fact that the innocent Wilmot could not begin to fathom a mind that would connect the darkness of mourning clothes with the dark thoughts of sexuality makes her all the more rare and alluring to Byron. Unlike Vladimir Nabokov's heroine Lolita, who is quite aware of her own desirability yet teases men with a pretense of innocence, Wilmot is (at least in Byron's eyes) genuinely innocent and this innocence is what sparks Byron's attraction, fuels his fascination, and elicits his worship.

To appreciate such innocence, the speaker must therefore acknowledge that he has lost this same quality in himself—which Byron did in a number of letters and poems. Abandoning oneself to hedonistic impulses may be liberating or exhilarating, but "She Walks in Beauty" suggests the price of such liberation through its tone of longing and implicit regret for the speaker's own immoral ways. He has been removed forever from the Wilmots of the world. She walks in beauty while he slouches in corruption.

The poem's iambic tetrameter is a meter commonly found in hymns and associated with "sincerity" and "simplicity" (consider Marlow's "The Passionate Shepherd to His Love," for example), as opposed to iambic pentameter, which is usually used to depict more complex emotions (consider the blank verse of Shakespeare or Milton). Byron's choice of meter reflects his yearning for the simplicity embodied in Wilmot but absent in himself. Here, the wistful longing of the bad for the good carries with it the sweetness of lyric verse, a sweetness that both praises the observed while condemning the observer.

In his book *Byron and the Spoiler's Art*, Paul West remarks that "Byron's only sincerity seems to be toward emotions he has lost and tries to recapture." Read in this light, "She Walks in Beauty" is both a catalog of aesthetic wonders as well as a psychological study of a person who weeps for the innocence he knows he has lost, and who therefore seeks relief from the pain of such knowledge in his public affirmation of the desirability of purity. His meditation on "A heart whose love is innocent" serves as a means by which a reader can examine his or her own heart and ponder the degree to which it is as innocent as Wilmot's, fouled like Byron's, or somewhere in between.

Source: Daniel Moran, Critical Essay on "She Walks in Beauty," in *Poetry for Students*, The Gale Group, 2002.

Uma Kukathas

Kukathas is a freelance writer and editor. In this essay, she argues that Byron's poem is more complex than previous critics have allowed and that it is a poem not only about a beautiful woman but about the power of art to render worldly things immortal.

"She Walks in Beauty" is counted among the best known of Byron's lyrics, and is the most famous of the verses published in his 1815 volume, *Hebrew Melodies*. While critics have admired the poem for its gracefulness, lyricism, and masterful use of internal rhyme—William Dick, for example, writing in *Byron and His Poetry*, calls it a work of "peculiar sweetness and beauty"; in his essay "George Gordon, Lord Byron," Northrop Frye remarks on the work's "caressing rhythm"; and Thomas L. Ashton in *Byron's Hebrew Melodies* points out that it is the "most enjoyed" of all the verses in that early volume—commentators have generally regarded it as a pleasing "mood" piece of no particular intellectual interest. Frye, writing about Byron's lyrical poetry in general, claims that it "contains nothing that 'modern' critics look for: no texture, no ambiguities, no intellectualized ironies, no intensity, no vividness of phrasing, the words and images being vague to the point of abstraction." The poetic emotion in Byron's lyrics, according to Frye, is made out of "worn," "ordinary" language, and he singles out "She Walks in Beauty" for its "flat conventional diction" whose strength lies in its musicality and not its language or ideas. Herbert Read, in *Byron*, offers a similar

criticism of the poem, claiming that Byron uses words that are apt to express his thoughts but which lack "originality of . . . application . . . or collocation" and hence do not produce "an essentially somatic thrill of appreciation." Read points out that the poem's references to "cloudless climes" and "starry skies" are obvious clichés, and concludes from this that Byron "was not in the fundamental sense poetic," and certainly not on a par with other "major" English poets.

While it is easy on the one hand to see why these critics regard the poem as they do—it is, after all, a work much of whose charm lies in its simplicity of diction, gentle musical rhythms, and singularity of concern as its offers lavish praise of a beautiful woman—on the other hand, they do not do justice to the subtle complexity of the piece. They overlook the fact that, with his straightforward hymn of adulation to a beautiful woman, Byron might be saying much more—for example, about the nature of art, reality, and immortality—than at first would be suspected. The critics ignore, too, that the poem manifests the impulse, common among romantic writers, to avoid didacticism, or overt instructional intent, and to communicate human concerns not in the language of reason but of feeling. It is not that the poem does not convey subtle and complex ideas, but rather this is done not in intellectual terms but by calling upon the emotional responses of the reader. Thus it seems unfair and incorrect to regard Byron as "unpoetic" because of the simplicity of expression used in these verses. Although the poem is certainly set forth in the words of plain speech, it can be argued that what Byron does in "She Walks in Beauty" is present in simple, immediate form a wealth of ideas that could not be done justice to in more ambiguous, intellectualized, intense, or vivid language.

The poem, as is well known, was written by Byron after seeing for the first time his cousin, the beautiful Mrs. John Wilmot, at a party. She appeared in a black mourning gown decorated with spangles. The verses, written by Byron the next day, describe and praise a beautiful woman, shrouded in the beauty of the starry night, in idealized, other-worldly terms. It is not just her physical beauty that is exalted, but her "nameless grace," or inner beauty, that is glorified. In the poem, she is associated immediately with a more exotic locale than England, a place of "cloudless climes." The most intense image in the poem is that of light, but it is a different sort of light than is normally associated with heavenly beauty; it is muted or "tender," not the light of "gaudy day," but a light that is fused with darkness. Byron overturns the reader's expectations by associating beauty with darkness rather than light and also by showing how light and darkness merge to create a perfect harmony. The woman's dark hair "lightens o'er her face," and the poet suggests that if she contained within her more darkness or more light, she would be "half impaired," or less than perfect as she is now. She also exudes a nameless grace or indescribable inner loveliness that matches her exterior perfection.

At first reading, it might seem that the poem *is* merely a beautiful tribute to a lovely woman, a poem that is perhaps exceptional because of the interesting use of the images of darkness and light, the harmony of inner and outer beauty, and the rhythmic musicality of the lines, but which does not offer much else of intellectual interest. But, upon closer examination and especially when considered in the context of the volume of verses in which it first appeared, another interpretation suggests itself that shows the poem to be far richer and subtler than most critics have allowed.

Byron certainly thought of the work as significant in some way, as he requested of the songwriter Isaac Nathan, who composed the musical accompaniment for the verses in the *Hebrew Melodies*, that it be the opening poem in any edition of the volume. The *Hebrew Melodies* were not a project that Byron conceived of himself, but the poet was asked by his friend Douglas Kinnaird to collaborate on a volume of verses set to "ancient" Jewish melodies that Nathan would arrange for contemporary performance. "She Walks in Beauty" was actually written in the summer of 1814, some months before Byron was commissioned to write the pieces for Nathan's volume, and its subject matter is certainly not biblical in any way. But, for some reason, Byron considered the poem to be a fitting overture to the volume of poems. One possible reason for this, suggested by Frederick W. Shilstone in *Byron and the Myth of Tradition*, is that Byron considered the *Hebrew Melodies* to be more than simply a work about the history of the Jews, but also about the mystical power of music and, ultimately, of art. The poems in that volume, according to Shilstone, are very different, some treating biblical and other purely secular themes, but what they have in common is a concern with earthly life, immortality, and art—especially how poetry takes the materials of the real and physical world and renders them immortal.

> *[W]hat Byron does in 'She Walks in Beauty' is present in simple, immediate form a wealth of ideas that could not be done justice to in more ambiguous, intellectualized, intense, or vivid language."*

If Byron considered "She Walks in Beauty" to be so central to the *Hebrew Melodies* that he insisted it be the lead poem in every edition of the work, it seems reasonable to suppose that he thought it embodied many of that volume's most important ideas. And, if Shilstone is correct and a concern with the power of art is at the heart of the work, this suggests an interpretation that in describing the idealized "she" of the poem, Byron was not merely honoring a beautiful woman but also offering a hymn of praise to a personification of art, and of poetry in particular. That is, Byron, in praising and describing the lovely Mrs. Wilmot, is also praising and describing what he thinks of as the power of art and poetry. This is certainly supported by the text itself if art (or poetry) is thought of as being something that is not only bright and illuminating but also dark and mysterious. Poetry is not only beautiful for what it shows but for what it hides, as it casts light on certain ideas but also leaves some things up to the imagination of the reader. Poetry too can be thought of as having the internal and external beauty that is mentioned in the poem as well as a perfect balance of what is revealed (light) and what is concealed (darkness) to convey meaning. It has a "nameless grace" that would be impaired if the combination of illumination and concealment of ideas were different than it is. All art has an inner quality that cannot be described and that would be impaired if the artist were to have made any part of it differently. If art and poetry are seen in this way, they clearly fit in with and may be seen as being personified by the beautiful woman of Byron's poem.

In his description of Mrs. Wilmot, Byron takes a character from real life and, with his words, ele-

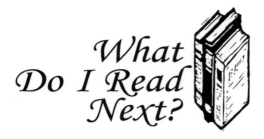
What Do I Read Next?

- Oxford World's Classics has an affordable, scholarly paperback edition of Byron's poetry published under the title *Lord Byron: The Major Works* (2000).

- Byron's friend Percy Bysshe Shelley wrote an essay that captured the artistic theory of that whole age of romantic poets. Entitled "A Defence of Poetry," the essay examines the various functions of reason and imagination in the poet's work. It was originally published in 1821 and is reprinted at http://www.library.utoronto.ca/utel/rp/criticism/shell_il.html (last accessed August, 2001).

- Harvard University Press has collected the poet's most important personal writings in the 1984 collection *Lord Byron: Selected Letters and Journals*, edited by Leslie A. Marchand.

- One of the most influential recent books about romanticism is by influential critic Northrop Frye, whose short 1968 book *A Study of English Romanticism* gives an excellent quick background to the cultural movement that is almost always mentioned along with Keats's name.

- Fact and fiction are mixed together in Tom Holland's imaginative 1998 novel *Lord of the Dead: The Secret History of Byron*. Lord Byron is presented as a vampire.

vates her until she becomes immortal. He describes her in terms that are not of this world, declaring that "all that's best" of dark and bright meet in her person, that she displays a perfect balance of darkness and light, that her mind is pure and at peace, and that her heart is innocent. This, then, is the power that poetry has, as it takes something from the earthly world and renders it immortal. A mortal woman is described in the words of the poet and is elevated to a divine status. In the same breath, Byron uses the poem in which the woman is immortalized by poetry to offer his own hymn to poetry.

According to this reading of "She Walks in Beauty," most critics have been too dismissive of the lyric as being one-dimensional when it can be seen to have considerable depth of meaning. Some might complain that the reading presented here is not plausible, and that to see the poem as being a praise of poetry itself is not suggested by the simple language and thoughts presented in it. However, if it is remembered that one of the goals of the romantic poets was to convey ideas not only through rational means but by conveying feelings and moods, offering insights into the world of nature and art through the most simple aspects of human experience, it seems entirely possible that with his straightforward, plainly written poem, Byron was calling upon the emotional response and imagination of the reader to see beyond the description of other-worldly beauty and recognize the force that renders such things immortal. Indeed it is by using the simplest of words and ideas, unhindered by intellectualized concerns, that the poet can convey such pure emotion and invite the reader to move beyond the overt description of the poem and recognize its other possibilities.

Source: Uma Kukathas, Critical Essay on "She Walks in Beauty," in *Poetry for Students*, The Gale Group, 2002.

Sources

Arnold, Matthew, Preface to *Poetry of Byron*, Macmillan, 1881, reprinted as "Byron," in *Essays in Criticism*, Dutton, 1964, pp. 312–30.

Ashton, Thomas L., *Byron's "Hebrew Melodies,"* University of Texas Press, 1972, p. 21.

Auden, W. H., "Don Juan," in *The Dyer & Other Essays*, Random House, 1962, pp. 386–406.

Dick, William A., *Byron and His Poetry*, Haskell House Publishers, 1977, p. 81.

Frye, Northrop, "George Gordon, Lord Byron," in *Major British Writers*, Vol. II, Harcourt, Brace and Company, 1959, pp. 152–53.

Jump, John D., *Byron*, Routledge & Kegan Paul, 1972.

Mankiewicz, Herman J., and Orson Welles, *The Shooting Script: Citizen Kane*, in *The Citizen Kane Book*, Atlantic Monthly Press, 1971, pp. 153–55.

Marchand, Leslie A., *Byron: A Portrait*, Alfred A. Knopf, 1970.

Martin, L. C., in *Byron's Lyrics*, University of Nottingham, 1948, p. 25.

Read, Herbert, *Byron*, The British Council, 1951, p. 24.

Review of "Hebrew Melodies," in *Augustan Review*, Volume 1, July, 1815, reprinted in *The Romantics Reviewed*,

Contemporary Reviews of British Romantic Writers: Byron and Regency Society Poets, edited by Donald H. Reiman, Garland Publishing, 1972, pp. 57–60.

Shilstone, Frederick W., *Byron and the Myth of Tradition*, University of Nebraska Press, 1988.

West, Paul, *Byron and the Spoiler's Art*, Lumen Books, 1992, p. 23.

Further Reading

Bernbaum, Ernest, *Guide through the Romantic Movement*, The Ronald Press Co., 1949.

> Bernbaum's work includes many minor figures from the Age of Romanticism, giving readers a better sense of the time than they might have gotten from just reading the standard synopses of the age.

Bostetter, Edward E., *The Romantic Ventriloquists: Wordsworth, Coleridge, Keats, Shelley, and Byron*, University of Washington Press, 1963.

> The tone of this study is a little dry, but Bosetter captures the important details of Byron's life.

Christensen, Jerome, *Lord Byron's Strength: Romantic Writing and Commercial Society*, Johns Hopkins University Press, 1995.

> Christensen presents a study of the poet's career using modern marketing theory.

Levine, Alice, "Byron and the Romantic Composer," in *Lord Byron and His Contemporaries*, edited by Charles E. Robinson, University of Delaware Press, 1982, pp. 178–203.

> Since this poem was originally published with others that were to be put to music, Levine's detailed search for musical inspirations and derivations is entirely relevant.

Rutherford, Andrew, *Byron: A Critical Study*, Stanford University Press, 1961.

> Rutherford looks at Byron's life and works simultaneously as a career, breaking it into two at the year 1817. Much of this complex work gives background that readers of this poem might find too detailed.

Wain, John, "The Search for Identity," in *Byron*, edited by Paul West, Prentice-Hall, Inc., 1963, pp. 157–70.

> The author examines the poet's persona and the underlying psychology of his most famous works.

Song of the Chattahoochee

Sidney Lanier

1877

Sidney Lanier composed "Song of the Chattahoochee" in November 1877 for a small paper in West Point, Georgia; nonetheless, at the time he considered it the best poem he had ever written, and critics have generally agreed that it is one of his finer efforts. Originally from Macon, Georgia, Lanier travelled much in Georgia, Maryland, Florida, and North Carolina for employment and for his health. He fought for the Confederacy in the Civil War and was eventually captured by Union troops. He spent the rest of the war in prison, where he relieved his own sufferings and those of his fellow prisoners with melodious tunes on the flute he had taught himself to play when he was younger. But unfortunately, he contracted tuberculosis, and he spent the rest of his life trying unsuccessfully to restore himself to good health. These circumstances—travel, flute-playing, military discipline, and a keen awareness of his own mortality—may account for the major elements of his poetry : nature, music, moral duty, and religion. Lanier was able to see much of the South's natural beauty, and he found much religious and spiritual significance in it. As a poet, he is regarded as a minor writer in American literature whose prime contribution was to lyrical or musical poetry in the tradition of the American poet Edgar Allan Poe and the English poet Alfred Tennyson. "Song of the Chattahoochee" is primarily a musical poem whose words flow very much like the river that is its speaker. The river's aim is to do its duty, answering the call of God.

Author Biography

Lanier was born in 1842 and raised in Macon, Georgia, the son of R. Sampson Lanier, a lawyer, and Mary Jane Anderson Lanier. His family enjoyed a long tradition of involvement in music and the arts, and Lanier read much of his family's extensive library before attending Oglethrope College, a local Presbyterian institution, in 1857. At school he came under the tutelage of Professor James Woodrow, a natural scientist educated at the University of Heidelberg, Germany. Woodrow encouraged his protege's interest in the German Romantic writers and fostered in Lanier an enthusiasm for nature and science that would inform his poetry and criticism. Following graduation, Lanier first wanted to earn a doctorate at Heidelberg University, but the outbreak of the Civil War obliged him to join the Macon Volunteers, a company of Confederate Army soldiers. During his service, Lanier developed tuberculosis, a condition that left him in poor health for the rest of his life.

In 1873, concerned that his life would be shortened by illness and convinced that, for aspiring writers in the South, "the whole of life had been merely not dying," Lanier resolved to move to the North and dedicate his life to music and literature. He went to Baltimore and began writing poetry that embodied some of his ideas about the relationship between music and verse. His interest in music—Lanier played several instruments—led him to join the Peabody Orchestra as their first flutist. Lanier also wrote numerous pieces for flute. In 1876, he was commissioned to write the text for a cantata to be composed by Dudley Buck and performed at the opening of the national Centennial Exposition at Philadelphia. From 1878 to 1881, Lanier gave a series of lectures at Johns Hopkins University in Baltimore on such topics as the works of William Shakespeare and the development of the English novel. Because of recurring financial problems, Lanier also wrote a travel guide to Florida and edited four books for boys. In August 1881, seeking relief from recurring attacks of tuberculosis, Lanier moved to Lynn, North Carolina, where he died later that year.

Sidney Lanier

Poem Text

Out of the hills of Habersham,
Down the valleys of Hall,
I hurry amain to reach the plain,

Run the rapid and leap the fall,
Split at the rock and together again,   5
Accept my bed, or narrow or wide,
And flee from folly on every side
With a lover's pain to attain the plain
    Far from the hills of Habersham,
    Far from the valleys of Hall.   10

    All down the hills of Habersham,
    All through the valleys of Hall,
The rushes cried, *Abide, abide,*
The willful water weeds held me thrall,
The laving laurel turned my tide,   15
The ferns and the fondling grass said, *Stay,*
The dewberry dipped for to work delay,
And the little reeds sighed, *Abide, abide,*
    Here in the hills of Habersham,
    Here in the valleys of Hall.   20

    High o'er the hills of Habersham,
    Veiling the valleys of Hall,
The hickory told me manifold
Fair tales of shade, the poplar tall
Wrought me her shadowy self to hold,   25
The chestnut, the oak, the walnut, the pine,
Overleaning, with flickering meaning and sign,
Said, *Pass not, so cold, these manifold*
    Deep shades of the hills of Habersham,
    These glades in the valleys of Hall.   30

    And oft in the hills of Habersham,
    And oft in the valleys of Hall,
The white quartz shone, and the smooth
    brook-stone

Did bar me of passage with friendly brawl,
And many a luminous jewel lone   35
—Crystals clear or a-cloud with mist,
Ruby, garnet, and amethyst—
Made lures with the lights of streaming stone
    In the clefts of the hills of Habersham,
    In the beds of the valleys of Hall.   40

    But oh, not the hills of Habersham,
    And oh, not the valleys of Hall
Avail: I am fain for to water the plain.
Downward the voices of Duty call—
Downward, to toil and be mixed with the main,   45
The dry fields burn, and the mills are to turn,
And a myriad flowers mortally yearn,
And the lordly main from beyond the plain
    Calls o'er the hills of Habersham,
    Calls through the valleys of Hall.   50

Poem Summary

Lines 1–10

The Chattahoochee River begins in the Blue Ridge Mountains of northeast Georgia, in Habersham County, and flows into Hall County (where the Buford Dam has since created Lake Lanier—named for the poet). From there, it flows southwest through Atlanta to Alabama, where it turns south, forming the Georgia-Alabama border. It ends at the southwest corner of Georgia bordering Florida, in another recently created lake, Lake Seminole, having watered the East Gulf Coastal Plain. Naturally, during its course, the river includes rapids and waterfalls, and its bed narrows and widens.

Line 3

The "I" of line 3 is the river itself. Lanier uses personification to turn the poem into an allegory of a person motivated by love ("a lover's pain") to resist temptations ("flee from folly") and do his duty, which is to water the plain. Lanier thus gives the river's flow moral significance and provides a lesson for human readers. The music of the poem echoes its sense here in that "Hurry amain" can be read hurriedly. Additional music is added by the internal rhyme of "amain" with the end rhyme "plain."

Line 4

This line is a masterful example of onomatopoeia, the sound of words imitating their sense. The alliteration of the r's mimics the roughness of rapids. Also, after the word "run," a slight pause slows the line to imitate hitting a rock, and "the rapid and leap" can be read rapidly to mimic

the water returning to its uninterrupted course. A short pause at "leap" imitates an actual leap as the water goes over a waterfall. Soundwise, the line leaps from an initial "l" and high pitched "e" sound in "leap" to the lower "a" sound (as in a sigh: "Aaaaah") and concluding "l" sound of "fall."

Line 6

"Or narrow or wide" is an old-fashioned poetic way of saying "whether narrow or wide."

Lines 11–20

One of the major features of allegories is that the main character overcomes obstacles and temptations to achieve virtue. The first set of obstacles are literally various plants growing or trailing their branches in the river. But allegorically, they refer to the pleasures of the senses. Whatever the specific meaning of each plant (assuming meant it to have one), the foliage are those common to the river; they do interfere with the river's duty, and they demonstrate Lanier's tendency to see spiritual meaning in nature.

Line 13

Rushes are grasses with hollow stems that grow mostly in marshy areas. Being a flute player who made his own flutes, Lanier may mean these plants and the reeds in line 18 to suggest the pleasures of music.

Line 14

The "willful water weeds" hold the river "thrall" (that is, in slavery). Weeds are traditionally reputed to be stubborn and unwanted plants, and they may be clogging the river's bed.

Line 15

The laurel is a small evergreen tree. The ancient Romans crowned victors of battles and athletic contests with its branches as a sign of honor. The temptation here may be to rest on one's laurels (that is, to be satisfied with what one has already achieved).

Line 16

Ferns are plants common to warm, moist, or swampy areas, with long triangular fronds. The grass, which is said to be "fondling," may represent sensual or carnal pleasures.

Line 17

The dewberry is a kind of blackberry and may represent the pleasures of food.

Media Adaptations

- Lanier's serious involvement in musical composition can be examined in his musical scores, published under the title *The Sidney Lanier Collection: Music for Solo Flute and Flute with Piano Accompaniment Composed by the American Flutist and Poet*. This work, with an introduction by Paula Robison and poems by Lanier between the scores, was published by Universal Edition in 1997.

- Southern Film Lab Inc. is the distributor for a 16 mm film by the University of Georgia called *Sidney Lanier: Poet of the Marshes*, produced in 1983.

- Lanier, along with Henry Timrod and Paul Hamilton Hayne, is included on Pacifica Tape Library's 1975 cassette called *Southern Poets*.

- The poet's flute compositions are featured on a 1996 compact disc entitled *By the Old Pine Tree*, from Arabesque Records of New York.

- Lanier's poem "The Marshes of Glynn" is included on the Harper Audio 2-cassette collection called *Great American Poetry: 3 Centuries of Classics*.

- The condition of the Chattahoochee River is monitored today by the Upper Chattahoochee Riverkeeper, a non-profit organization. Their web page, found at http://www.ucriverkeeper.org (last accessed August, 2001), keeps people aware of the river's condition and new legislative actions that might affect it.

- The full text of the 1884 edition of *The Poems of Sidney Lanier*, edited by his wife, is available online at http://docsouth.unc.edu/lanier/menu.html (last accessed August, 2001) on a page sponsored by the "Documenting the American South" project at the University of South Carolina.

Lines 19–20

Lanier does in these two lines what he tries to do with each of the Habersham and Hall refrains; he uses alliteration, the repetition of initial consonant sounds in "Here," "Habersham," and "Hall." And he uses consonance, the repetition of other consonants such as the "l" sound in "hills," "valleys," and "Hall." And he uses assonance such as "a" sounds in "Habersham" and "valleys." Together, they create an effect called syzygy, when the poet tries to put as many similar sounds as possible into the lines without disturbing the sense with tongue twisters such as "she sells seashells by the seashore."

Lines 21–30

The next group of obstacles are trees common to the region. Georgia was and still is a major lumber producing state. The literal image here is of light and shadow among the branches, along the bank, and in the reflection of the trees on the waters (the "shadowy self" the river is "to hold"). The allegorical image is of the trees as persons distracting the speaker with imagined pleasures.

Lines 23–25

The hickory tells many ("manifold") beautiful stories about resting. The poplar invites an embrace, not of her real self, but of her image, the reflection in the water.

Lines 26–28

The other trees make other indefinite suggestions inviting the speaker not to be "so cold" but to be warm, perhaps, and friendly. "Flickering meaning and sign" may literally refer to the lights and shadows created by the trees blowing in the wind and reflecting on the surface of the river's waves.

Lines 29–30

"Shades" can be used to refer to ghosts, but here it may merely suggest the ghostly nature of tales, reflections, and images of light and shadow.

Lines 31–40

The final group of obstacles are literally minerals common to the region—quartz, rubies, garnets, and amethyst—all used as gemstones. Rubies and garnets are red, and amethyst is frequently a deep purple. Allegorically, they are temptations to be greedy and may illustrate Lanier's dislike of trade and materialism.

Line 34

"Friendly brawl" is an oxymoron since a brawl is a fight and cannot normally be said to be friendly. Lanier may mean to refer to the conflict in capitalism between the friendly manner of salespeople and their competitive aim to profit from a good trade.

Lines 35–41

The image in the last two lines to cleavage ("clefts") and "beds" may read as a euphemism for the seductive powers of wealth, with the "streaming stones" being a necklace dangling upon a woman's breast as a "lure" to pleasure. "Lure" also suggests fishing; she may be baiting the river.

Lines 41–50

The river overcomes its obstacles and flows over Georgia's East Gulf Coastal Plain. At this point, the Chattahoochee becomes known as the Apalachicola River, flowing into the Gulf of Mexico and then into the ocean.

Line 43

"Fain" is an ambiguous word here since it can mean both "glad" and "forced."

Line 44

"Downward" can have two senses here: the voices are from above calling down, and the voices call the river to flow down, as all waters do because of gravity. The voices of the personification of Duty overcome the earlier voices of the rushes, reeds, and trees.

Lines 45–48

The waters of the river do the work of watering the fields and the flowers so that they do not burn in the hot, Georgia sun and die of thirst, and turning the waterwheels of mills. A waterwheel has paddles that make cups which fill with water, and the weight of the water pulls one side of the wheel down so that other cups at the top turn up to fill with water while cups at the bottom turn down to empty back into the river.

Lines 48–50

The last three lines indicate another calling voice, usually interpreted as that of the ocean, "the lordly main from beyond the plain," but also as God, due to the word "lordly" and because the poem is often read as an allegory of the soul's progress to reunion with the deity. The repetition of the word "calls" is a particularly effective use of onomatopoeia and repetition, since the two "calls" suggest the sound of calls echoing through the valley.

Themes

Nature

In "Song of the Chattahoochee," the Chattahoochee River in Georgia describes for readers its journey, from its headspring in Habersham county to its end in Georgia's East Gulf coastal plains, where, in Lanier's time, it fed into another river that led to the Gulf of Mexico. Lanier's style in this poem copies the rushing, shifting, gurgling motion of a true river, giving readers a little bit of the experience of following the water on its journey. He gives the river a human personality, ascribing to it human motivation. This helps to make this natural phenomenon more understandable to people who are not familiar with it and to make readers who are familiar with rivers experience the feeling of them anew.

The river is introduced as being on a mission, to water the dry fields of Georgia and to turn the water wheels that power the grain mills. Similarly, the other natural objects that the Chattahoochee passes seem to have a human motivation. They all want the river to stop, or "abide." Most of the natural objects in the poem are presented as calling for the river to stop its motion. The waterweeds hold the river, the trees command "pass not," the gemstones try to lure it to stay with them, etc. Nature, in general, is presented as favoring passive behavior over action. The river is presented here as an exception to nature, as being almost unnatural in its rush to keep on moving. This idea is supported by the fact that the river's "Duty" (which is capitalized in the poem, to show its connection to God's will) is not to aid nature, but to aid humanity in the commercial enterprises of farming and milling. The river, though natural, rushes like a human in order to fulfill its human responsibilities.

Music

One of the aspects of Lanier's poetry that is most often mentioned is his devotion to the idea of a poem's musical nature being used to capture the natural world in words. This is very evident in "Song of the Chattahoochee." His repetition of specific phrases, rhythms, and sounds is used to connect the motion of a flowing river to the way the human mind understands the harmonies and melodies of music. Lanier was a composer who wrote music for different instruments, but in particular he worked with the flute, and it is the sound of the flute that this poem most resembles: there are individual syllables, like notes, but they flow together fluidly, just like the tone of a flute or the motion of a river.

Like a piece of music, "Song of the Chattahoochee" has a refrain that is repeated often, with only slight variation. In instrumental music, which does not use words to completely show its ideas, the use of a refrain helps to keep listeners aware of one outstanding mood, even while other thoughts are explored. Lanier uses the refrain for a similar effect here. There is no concrete, definable significance to the poem's constant reminder that the river begins in the hills of Habersham and the valleys of Hall. The mention of these facts at the beginning and end of each stanza serves to balance the rest of the poem. This is a poem about motion, about the river's inability to remain in any one place, and Lanier uses the refrain (repetition) to bring readers back to the river's original source, even as a musical refrain might be used to take listeners back to a composition's main idea.

Quest

This poem presents the idea that the river might travel from its source to its end to reach its final goal when it finally arrives. The river knows that at the end there are dry fields, parched flowers and mills that cannot be set into motion without its powerful force. Lines 48 and 49 reveal how the Chattahoochee would know that it must go on this journey, and what lies at the end. The "lordly main," presumably the ocean, has called out to it over the miles that separated them. Lanier presents the river's journey as a quest (pursuit) to bring water to those suffering in the dry plains of the south.

Like most quests in literature, the one the river undergoes takes it through a series of obstacles that try to distract it from its goal. Some offer only mild resistance, like the rushes that gently call "abide." As the river progresses, however, and its force increases, the strength of the opposition increases too.

Topics for Further Study

- Two poetic techniques used frequently in this poem are alliteration—the repetition of the first sound in words, such as "flee from folly" and "laving laurel"—and internal rhyme, which places rhyming words inside of lines instead of at the end, as in "pain" and "plain" in line 8 or "sighed" and "abide" in line 18. Write a few stanzas, speaking from the point of view of some natural phenomenon, emphasizing these two techniques.

- Choose a street or highway that passes near where you live and write a description of its journey from the road's perspective.

- Investigate the history of modern irrigation methods that have taken over the responsibilities the Chattahoochee claims for itself in this poem.

- Walt Whitman wrote around the same time as Lanier, but his poems about the American landscape were more free-flowing, less stylized. Read some of Whitman's poetry and explain which poet you prefer and why.

- Report on the condition of the Chattahoochee River today and what Lanier would think of efforts to conserve it.

The trees of the third stanza stand more firmly than the various soft plants that precede them in the poem, and the stones in the stanza that follows are even more resistant to the river's force. In the ordinary, everyday way of looking at things, water running over stones is a passive event, but as Lanier presents it here the river urgently needs to reach its final destination, in fulfillment of its quest.

Permanence

In addition to the two lines that, with some variation, begin and end each stanza, the one phrase that is repeated in this poem is "abide, abide." It is spoken twice in the second stanza, by the rushes and the reeds, and it is the feeling that is expressed in different words by all of the other natural patterns that the Chattahoochee passes. It is as if the other parts of nature, lacking human consciousness as they are, have no fonder wish than to freeze time. It is only the river that acts as an agent of change in this poem.

In the larger sense, though, the river's situation is also frozen in time because it is forever flowing from Habersham to the "main" that is mentioned in the final stanza. While any particular portion of water keeps in motion, the river as a whole retains the same shape year after year. This is an aspect of the river that is not examined in this poem, though. Lanier presents the theme of change versus permanence as being one of the river in conflict with the various aspects of the surrounding countryside, not as the different aspects of the river in conflict against each other.

Style

"Song of the Chattahoochee," as the title suggests, is a song. Lanier tries to make the sounds of words have the rhythm and tonal qualities of musical notes. Soon after completing "Song of the Chattahoochee," Lanier wrote a book on poetic theory called *The Science of English Verse* (1880). In this volume, he embraces a poetry based on time and rhythm rather than one based on accented and unaccented syllables. He scanned lines of poetry using musical notes to indicate the length of each syllable. Lanier broke up his lines into measures or bars, which he further broke down into groups of three or four notes. The musical nature of "Song of the Chattahoochee" is enhanced by the repetition of a slightly varying phrase at the beginning and end of each stanza. This phrase, or refrain, refers to the hills of Habersham and the valleys of Hall and frames the middle six lines of each stanza. These six lines describe the various natural things that the river encounters, including weeds, trees, and rocks. Lanier also uses rhyme to give the poem a musical sound. If we diagram the pattern of rhymes created by the last words in each line of the stanzas, the rhyme scheme appears as *abcbcddcab*. In addition to this intricate pattern, Lanier also employs internal rhyme, meaning that words within a single line rhyme with one another. An example of this occurs in line 3:

I hurry amain to reach the plain,

The words "amain" and "plain" create an internal rhyme, and the repeating sound is further am-

plified because "plain" is an end-rhyming word that will be echoed in other lines in the stanza.

Historical Context

"Song of the Chattahoochee" was published in 1877, just twelve years after the end of the Civil War. As for Sidney Lanier, who contracted tuberculosis while being held prisoner by the Union Army, the effects of the war were felt throughout the rest of his life.

Most history books explain the Civil War in terms of the differing attitudes that the two sides had regarding the enslavement of black people. It is true that the Confederacy of the South wished to continue slavery and that the Union of the North wished to abolish it, but that is just one of the relevant differences that led the two sides to violent conflict. Many Northerners opposed slavery, but even more did not care about the rights of black people, or at least did not care enough to engage in a war over the issue. Slavery was just the most visible issue to force an open conflict over the different lifestyles led in the two sections of the country.

Slavery existed in the American colonies for more than two hundred years before the war. In 1641, Massachusetts became the first colony to recognize slavery. The continent was settled with the labor of slaves brought from other countries, primarily Africa, specifically to be sold to landowners as laborers. By 1750, when Georgia, the last of the British colonies, was established, slavery was legal in all thirteen of them. After the American Revolution ended in 1783, the movement to abolish slavery gained momentum in the North, especially around Massachusetts. One noticeable reason was that the Northern states had more of an influence from the Puritans, who had left England to avoid religious persecution. Their religious heritage left a small amount of moral discourse in the way political issues were addressed. A more compelling reason why the North turned against slavery had to do with geography and basic economics. Northern states, more rocky and cold, did not have the land for huge farms that the South did. The Northern economy came to be based on factory production and small farms, neither of which benefited from unskilled slave labor.

As the country expanded west, the two sides of the slavery issue became more and more firm in

Compare & Contrast

- **1877:** The Chattahoochee River flows freely across the northern part of Georgia.

  Today: A dam constructed near Atlanta in the 1950s has created Lake Sidney Lanier, a popular spot for boaters and fishers.

- **1877:** The South's agrarian tradition is changing as traditional plantation owners cannot afford to keep their farms any longer, and Northern industries move in.

  Today: The South's economy has grown tremendously since the 1870s as high-tech industries have left the North to open manufacturing plants in the Sun Belt.

- **1877:** Individual mills for grinding grain into meal can operate on the power of a water wheel, turned by a flowing river.

  Today: The explosion of consumer electronics at the end of the twentieth century has made it difficult for the world's producers of petroleum, coal, nuclear, and hydroelectric energy to keep up with demand.

- **1877:** People in rural areas like Georgia's Appalachian Mountains live in relative seclusion from the rest of the world.

  Today: More than ninety-three percent of U.S. households have at least one telephone, and approximately ninety-nine percent of U.S. households have televisions.

- **1877:** After the Civil War (1861–1865) drains the country's population, measures are taken to encourage immigrants to move from Europe to America.

  Today: Because of limited resources, immigration laws are becoming increasingly strict.

---

their convictions. In the Northern states where slavery had been abolished, generations of white families grew up outraged at the way they saw black people being treated by slave owners. In the South, however, generations of whites grew up among the black families that they owned, and they resented Northerners for trying to butt into their way of life. As each new state was added to the United States, the question came up again about whether slavery would be permitted there or not.

The country split apart in 1860, after South Carolina seceded from the United States to protest the election of Abraham Lincoln, who opposed slavery. It was joined the following year by several other Southern states, and they combined to form the Confederate States of America. Lincoln was unwilling to let these states form a new country, leading to four years of armed conflict. Most of the battles of the Civil War were fought in the South. Before the South surrendered, the losses were heavy: not only had 134,000 Southern soldiers died (as compared to 646,000 deaths on the Northern, Union side), but the plantations were destroyed in battle and the economic structure was decimated by the loss of slavery. It is only in recent decades that the South has become powerful again, as industries flocked to the Sun Belt to take advantage of inexpensive labor during the economic recession of the 1970s.

After the Civil War, Southern culture was largely nostalgic for the splendor of the days gone by, and this nostalgia or home-sickness is reflected in the tone of "Song of the Chattahoochee." To this day, the huge plantation houses built during the booming Southern economy of the early 1800s are referred to as reflecting or mirroring the "antebellum" style. The word technically refers to the period before any war, but it is most associated with the South of nearly a century and a half ago.

To Lanier's generation, the South's glory days were just a memory. Poverty replaced splendor, and those who once held political power were forced to take orders from poor, ignorant opportunists from the North, called "carpetbaggers" because they arrived in the South with cheap luggage looking for political appointments that would give them power over the defeated Confederates. In focusing on the willfulness and unstoppable force of the Chattahoochee River, Lanier focused on one of the few things that had not been destroyed by the war: nature itself. The personality that he gives the river reflects prewar Southern boldness, giving this poem special significance to his contemporaries.

In the 1950s, the U.S. Army Corps of Engineers built a dam across the Chattahoochee near Atlanta to hold back its water and irrigate the nearby valley. The water that is held back formed a lake, which in 1957 was named Lake Sidney Lanier, in honor of the poet. Today, the lake is one of the area's most popular recreation attractions, with 30,000 surface acres of water and 540 miles of shoreline.

Critical Overview

Sidney Lanier's literary reputation rises and falls to the degree that critics value musical poetry. The criticism on "Song of the Chattahoochee" illustrates this battle of fashions. Critics at the end of the nineteenth century valued Lanier's melodious verse highly. Asserting that Lanier wrote better when he wrote unself-consciously, Edmund Clarence Stedman says that "Song of the Chattahoochee" is one of the poems that show Lanier's poetic gifts "unadulterated by meditations on rhythmical structure," and he calls it "almost as haunting as [Edgar Allan Poe's] 'Ulalume.'" Charles Kent calls the poem "one of the most musical of English poems," remarking on the frequent use of alliteration, internal rhyme, and syzygy, or the repetition of similar sounds, both consonants and vowels, throughout neighboring words. He concludes that "The effect of the whole is musical beyond description. It sings itself and yet nowhere sacrifices the thought."

Twentieth-century critics are not always so generous. When they concentrate on Lanier's imagery and technical skills, they tend to find the images and the thought unclear, and the quality of the music uneven. Lanier disappoints those who expect highly intellectual poetry. Lanier's most definitive biographer, Aubrey Harrison Starke, says that "Song of the Chattahoochee" is "far from a great poem." He points out the poem's weaknesses: too little variation in music and rhythm, some awkwardly constructed sentences, and the word "brawl" in the fourth stanza used in an unusual way. He also comments, "Nor is the apparent fact of

gravitation a fitting symbol of devotion to duty and of the sacrifice of individuality in merging it in a larger individuality." Critics often wish to apologize for Lanier. Richard Webb writes that Lanier might have written better if his health were not so bad and his need for money so pressing in the devastated economy of the post-Civil War South, but he nonetheless finds Lanier's imagery unclear and his musical effects strained.

The more positive critiques of the poem concentrate on its musical and spiritual effects. Lincoln Lorenz reads the poem as an appreciation of the harmony of nature inspired by the friendly Creek Indians, who "bequeathed to the Georgia settler something of both [their] religious veneration for the forces of nature and [their] musical names for her rivers." Jay B. Hubbell says that "Song of the Chattahoochee" is one of "a handful of poems which give [Lanier] a secure place among American poets," and he ranks Lanier third in importance behind Walt Whitman and Emily Dickinson in post-Civil-War, nineteenth-century American poetry.

Criticism

David Kelly

Kelly is an English instructor at two colleges in Illinois. In the following essay, he explores Lanier's poem as a sad reminder of man's dominance over nature that remains effective to this day.

At the turn of the nineteenth century, Sidney Lanier was one of America's best-known poets, included in all of the standard poetry collections. Even during his lifetime, he had been a controversial choice, mocked by critics almost as much as he was admired, but he was never left out. Fashions change, however; today, only a couple of Lanier's poems are likely to be remembered or studied. "Song of the Chattahoochee" is probably his most lasting work. This would be a surprise to his harshest critics, who from its first publication found the poem to be both light in ideas and heavyhanded in its performance. But it is the poem's simple obviousness, to a large extent, that has enabled it to survive. One does not have to be a specialist in reading poetry to understand it. New readers do not need to know of Lanier's musical experience to appreciate the musicality of his words, and most will, even without explanation, catch the way that the poetic lines resemble the flow and eddy of run-

The Chattahoochee River

ning water. "Song of the Chattahoochee" is a good poem for people to practice on as they are learning what poetry can do, but it is generally not considered important for what it has to say.

It is unlikely, though, that the poem would have endured into the twenty-first century on just the basis of its clever imitation of river sounds. The story that it tells should be given more credit than it generally receives. It has the elements of drama and suspense that keep the most compelling stories alive for generation after generation. The river keeps pushing forward, the Georgian region keeps pulling at it, and readers are left interested in seeing how this conflict will turn out. The poem has a sense of homesickness for a slower, sleepier time, a time that becomes more lost to humanity (and therefore more nostalgic) with every passing day. Both of these elements, suspense and nostalgia, add up to a pronounced struggle between the pre-industrial world and the busy world as it stands right now. As long as there is some sense of nature, visible from a car window or on the Nature Channel, this is a struggle that people will understand deep in their souls.

The misleading thing about "Song of the Chattahoochee" is that, even though the river is a natural thing, and even though Lanier's musical awareness caused him to portray its old-fashioned

style, the river does not function as a thing of nature. In fact, in this poem, it functions as nature's antithesis, the social force that overcomes nature. A look at the final stanza reveals that the river's great hurry is to water the fields, turn the mills, and raise up drying flowers. Today, these are recognized as society's functions. The business that compels the Chattahoochee to race through the countryside in the poem is agribusiness and food processing. People no longer expect nature to take care of these tasks anymore.

This is not a prophetic poem that claims to foretell the future, but it is hardly likely that Sidney Lanier did not see the new world that was coming. He was a wistful, (yearning, melancholy) backwards-looking writer at a most interesting time in American history. Raised in the calm, solemn old South that was comfortable with centuries of tradition, he was painfully familiar with the changes brought on by the Civil War. His year as a prisoner of war left Lanier a broken man with ruined health, just as the terms of the Surrender at Appomattox left the South weak, helpless, and at the mercy of the Industrial Age.

In his 1933 biography of Lanier, Aubrey Harrison Starke pointed out that the poet was one of many who, in 1877, believed that industrialization had been the South's "undoing." The industrial

" *This is not a prophetic poem that claims to foretell the future, but it is unlikely that Sidney Lanier did not see the new world that was coming.*"

craze that swept across the globe in the last half of the nineteenth century was basically a Northern concern: the South's economy was mostly agricultural. The different views eventually led to war, and the South lost, leaving no choice but to accept the new values of the victors. Industrialization meant timetables, increases in production expectations, and a fast-paced but dissatisfying lifestyle. It meant a step away from nature.

If one judged only by the last stanza, then it might be considered a bit of a stretch to claim that the Chattahoochee River represents industrialization in this poem. The opposite interpretation could also be drawn from this stanza. It could be argued that, in having the river irrigate or water the fields and power the mill, Lanier was pointing out how nature was better than industry at being able to take care of itself. This theory does not hold, though, when the rest of the poem is taken into account.

The single clearest idea imparted by "Song of the Chattahoochee" is that the river is racing past the wonders of the natural world. The verbs that Lanier uses in the first stanza alone show the river breezing along recklessly: "hurry," "run," and "flee." Critics have pointed out that Lanier chose many of his words because of their sound. It is true that the stanza has several other verbs, such as "split" and "attain," that do not show this sense of furious motion. Still, there is no denying the feeling that the river in this poem is too busy to focus on anything besides its business. Readers can speculate about what the calling "voices of Duty" in line 44 might represent, but it is clear that the river is following some kind of call. It is not self-motivated, but is instead pushed into action by some outside force. Given the changes happening in the South during Lanier's time, it does not take much of a stretch to relate this outside force to the Industrial Revolution.

The poem is able to tap into true emotion, even for modern readers, with its melancholy descriptions of the things of nature being left behind. It constantly brings up hills and valleys, calling for an open view of the natural landscape, reminding readers of nature's majesty. Between the hills and valleys, though, Lanier provides details about the river's bed that stir up a sense of loss as the river rushes by them. He builds up from the simplest (the reeds) to the most enduring (the stones). He colors his descriptions with reminders of the Bible, such as the rushes (which figure into the story of Moses) and the archaic phrase "abide," and the river's Duty to toil in the plain. And through it all, Lanier packs a tremendous amount of detail into each line, naming specific plants and trees and shrubs, causing one to have a sense of a real place.

What is surprising in a poem that speaks so lovingly about stationary objects is that it does not show faith in them to capture readers' hearts on their own. This is not a poem that asks its readers to drink in, savor, or appreciate the experience of the places to which it takes them. It is instead a poem that uses all of its mental pictures in the course of making a higher point, much as the river passes by all of these natural objects in the course of fulfilling its higher Duty.

Lanier has constructed "Song of the Chattahoochee" in the shape of a classical, five-paragraph essay, the type that teachers have beginning composition students use to present their thoughts. The introductory and concluding stanzas raise and then repeat the thematic (topic) idea that the river is rushing to fulfill its responsibility, and the three "body" stanzas that fall in between build one upon the other, each adding new evidence to make the author's point clearer. The supreme balance of using three developmental stanzas—not two or four—gives a sense of order, implying that all that is going on in nature is intentionally organized, presumably by God. Critics often examine the word choices that Lanier used, and their criticisms of him have often pointed out the fact that mimicking the sound of a flowing river, though a nice little trick, is not necessarily what a poem should be trying so hard to do. They seldom give appreciation for the control that the poet exercises over the structure of the entire piece, from the first word to the last.

It is entirely possible that Lanier was not even conscious of the parallels between "Song of the Chattahoochee" and his society's preoccupation with the start of the fast-paced Industrial Age. He may have just meant to write a nice poem about a nice river, showing it flowing because that is just what rivers do. If this is the case, then he stumbled into something that is bigger than for what he hoped. The poet's musical language gathers all of the attention in poetry classes, but it is the poem's view of nature developing the duty-bound values of a modern executive that make it something that readers can relate to, right up to the present day.

Source: David Kelly, Critical Essay on "Song of the Chattahoochee," in *Poetry for Students*, The Gale Group, 2002.

Jack De Bellis

In the following essay excerpt, De Bellis analyzes "The Song of the Chattahoochee," asserting that "the music rather than the idea controls the poem."

Lanier's guidebook, *Florida* (1876), commissioned, ironically enough, by a railroad owner who had liked "Corn," served as a transition from his earlier attitudes toward nature. Naturally the *Nation* attacked it for its "rhetorical-poetical foible of seeing 'God in everything,'" as is shown in some similes. But Lanier had begun to express a new idea in this book; nature is an "everlasting Word" which reveals God is everything. In his wild river and in his mysterious marshes, Lanier adds to the beneficence, purposiveness, and harmony of nature a sublimity, while he continues the idea dramatized in *Tiger-Lilies* of nature as guide. His travel book had guided him toward a new handling of nature, one partly heralded by "Corn" and "The Symphony" but one incorporating the idea of the regeneration of nature and man that he had sporadically used for many years.

"The Song of the Chattahoochee" is a sharp departure from "Clover" and "The Waving of the Corn" of 1876. In the blank-verse "Clover" an ox, "Course of things," grazes on clover made of the heads of Keats, Chopin, and others—a strained allegorical attack on boorish society that Lanier concludes serenely with the assertion that "The artist's market is the heart of man." In "The Waving of the Corn," the narrator desires to "Suck honey summer with unjealous bees" in a pastoral retreat from the "terrible Towns." Lanier's habitual opposition of God's nature and man's town receives nearly no development and perhaps causes the eccentric imagery. But in "The Song of the Chattahoochee" the symbolic meaning arises through onomatopoetic representation of the physical sublimity of the river. The movement of the river through the romantic landscape to the sea is the moral imperative of responsibility. But the moral is mainly implied, and

> *An improvement on the sentimental piety of 'seeing God in everything,' Lanier found his true voice again in this poem."*

the music rather than the idea controls the poem. An improvement on the sentimental piety of "seeing God in everything," Lanier found his true voice again in this poem.

Since the poem was not in the first person in the first draft, Lanier may have recognized that the poem would gain immediacy if the river narrated its own trip. In his revision, he also chose present over past tense, and he reinforced his action verbs and long prepositional phrases to give the river a swooping speed:

> Out of the hills of Habersham,
> Down the valleys of Hall,
> I hurry amain to reach the plain,
> Run the rapid and leap the fall,
> Split at the rock and together again,
> Accept my bed, or narrow or wide,
> And flee from folly on every side
> With a lover's pain to attain the plain
> Far from the hills of Habersham,
> Far from the valleys of Hall.

In this stanza and throughout the poem, Lanier outdoes himself in his ability to vary the meter, match and clash tone colors, create structural effects, and link the movement of the river to his special effects. Perhaps the first thing to notice is the exceptional ease or "fluidity" with which the lines move through their four feet of mainly anapestic substitution (line 8). Yet pulling against this is the frequent trochaic substitution (lines 3, 4, 5, 9, and 10) and the successive stresses of line 7, in which even "on" takes at least a secondary stress. Facilitating this fluid movement are the use of duosyllables or polysyllables often broken by the foot stresses (of Hab/ersham), the lack of caesuras (line 6 is the exception), and the lack of hiatus (vowels or consonants the same in successive syllables: "a army"; "lone neck"). Alliteration (lines 4 and 5) and internal rhyme (line 8) also give propulsion to the lines. But it should be understood that these devices only assist the semantic meaning in the lines, for semantic meaning guides us to locate the prosodic elements which account for the speed with which we read. Because all his poetic devices help to give a kinesthetic sense of the river's movement, we could say that the river is physically represented through the onomatopoeia created by all those elements. For this reason the poem is a classic example of a perfect blending of sound and sense.

Some of the tone color is especially good. We notice how the staccato rhythm of "run the rapid" echoes the rapids themselves. A linkage between the phrases could easily have been made ("rapids"), but this would diminish the effect. The graceful but dissonant phrase "leap the fall" balances its alliterative cluster against "run the rapid." Additionally, *p* and *f* are consonantal cousins related to the *p* of "rapid." The two phrases are thus separated but subtly joined.

Lanier's rhymes show great ingenuity. The refrains that form opening and closing couplets of each stanza are naturally perfect rhymes. Lines 3 and 8 of each stanza are rhymed with the same words, and in these lines Lanier rhymes a medial word with the rhyme word in nine out of ten places in the poem. In line 8 of stanza four, there is no medial rhyme; but Lanier uses all vowels (*a-u-i-e-o*), substituting variety for the expected pattern. In the second stanza for additional variety he uses three consecutive rhyme words (two of which are the same) in lines 3 and 7—the same pattern used in line 7 of the first stanza. When Lanier discards one device, he usually emphasizes another: in stanza three, for example, at the turning of the poem, he uses internal rhyme in lines 3, 6, 7, 9, and 10 (the last one is an interlinear rhyme). But in stanza four there is no internal rhyme, while in the final stanza nearly every line has internal rhyme. A comparison with the rhyme of "The Symphony" shows how Lanier's penchant for rhyme had led him into a playfulness early in the strings section which underminded his serious thoughts. But in "The Song of the Chattahoochee" the rhyme is exactly right; though the theme of the poem is serious—the obedient response of nature to its higher commands—the eagerness and excitement of the river as it fulfills that theme are the real center of interest.

It has been observed that, although the anapestic meter gives speed and urgency to the line (perhaps because we instinctively read over unstressed syllables quickly in order to find the stresses), Lanier had also employed frequent trochaic substitutions which tended to slow the line by placing the stress early in the foot. Thus a resistance is created

to the river's movement; and, as we would expect, the resistance becomes actively embodied in the imagery of the poem, as well as in other musical devices.

For in the second stanza as the idea of resistance enters the poem, Lanier uses such a line as this to slow the line with caesura, long vowels and hiatus: "And the little reeds sighed *Abide, abide.*" In addition, every line in the stanza is end-stopped; it is the only stanza without any enjambment. But in the third and fifth stanzas, to increase the pace of the river's movement, Lanier uses enjambment three times. To give some idea of the circuitous route of the river in the third stanza, Lanier uses eight caesuras to fragment the line; but the sense of the stanza is still a forward movement because of the many other sound devices at work. The refrain must not be overlooked as a source of that speed and fluidity; for, once we anticipate its position in the stanza, we gain a sense of direction and "purpose." The first line of the refrain is exactly one syllable longer than the second line in each of its ten appearances, thereby giving a slightly top-heavy momentum to the first line. Twice the eighth lines of the stanza run directly into the refrain, in the first and fifth stanzas, and thus seemingly pours the river into the sea. The prepositional phrases in the final stanza beginning "Downward" carry greater weight than the lines in the same position of previous stanzas. The trochees seem to suggest not only determination but also that the journey of the river to its Lord the sea is rapidly coming to its conclusion.

By such careful handling of poetic devices as these, Lanier shows that his reputation for musical verse is so well deserved as to assure him of continued attention. And the success of this poem ought not to be minimized, for Lanier found a way to educate feelings through the music of verse in many ways more effectively than he had in "The Symphony." For one thing, he was able to insert detailed descriptions of nature, as he had in "The Symphony," but without letting the general direction of the poem become lax. He could imply the idea of the importance of feeling and of love through the river's obedient response to its Lord the sea without being excessively didactic. The poem easily admits the symbolic meaning of the soul's journey through a turbulent life toward peace or God. It is possible that the poem reflects Lanier's own growth of confidence and direction.

Source: Jack De Bellis, "The Poetry of Freedom," in *Sidney Lanier*, Twayne Publishers, Inc., 1972, pp. 97–125.

Charmenz S. Lenhart

In the following essay excerpt, Lenhart examines the rhythmic quality of "Song of the Chattahoochee."

"Song of the Chattahoochee" has been universally accepted as one of the most unusual poems in American poetry. Most of the inherent musicality does not stem from repetitive consonants or rhyme or alliteration; it is not, in short, melodious—but it has a structure that is repetitive, impetuous, and ideally suited to the subject. Half of the wonder in Lanier's verse surely grows from the unmusical subjects of which he makes a kind of pure music. His similarity to Whitman can be noticed in the construction of prepositional phrases in "Song of the Chattahoochee," written in 1877 after his ideas on music and poetry had crystallized:

> Out of the hills of Habersham,
> Down the valleys of Hall . . .
> In the clefts of the hills . . .
> In the beds of the valleys . . .

This parallelism of pattern is borne out in the rest of the structure, where even many of the lines attain a singular balance.

The most important thing about "Song of the Chattahoochee," and the quality which differentiates it from all previous nature writing, is the poet's approach to the river itself, which approach is extremely personal, and yet altogether lacking in any ordinary descriptiveness on the poet's part. Here the verse lines become the river's voice, just as Debussy's music became the wind's voice. This is an "impression" of the river told in the flow and ebb of rhythm. The poem excels in its rhythmic freedom. While the larger foot patterns may be thought of as running dactyls, there is a constant releasing of sounds through these, followed by a springing return to the shorter leaps of trochees, interrupted at points by sluggish spondees, etc., so that the poet is obviously more interested in the movement to the two repetitious lines at the end of each stanza than he is concerned with foot patterns. He is writing in musical or (rather here) in poetic phrases—prepositional and verbal—and balanced clauses.

Both his alliterative patterns and the use he made of equal time units rather than foot patterns are everywhere noticeable. The important concern of the poet was with the rush and flow of the river, and his effort was expended to keep the stanza in a fluid shape, with occasional little springing phrases to push the metrical pattern down the page. His use of parallel structure, alliteration, and logi-

> *The important concern of the poet was with the rush and flow of the river, and his effort was expended to keep the stanza in a fluid shape, with occasional little springing phrases to push the metrical pattern down the page."*

cal syllabic groupings can be seen in this stanza as well as any other:

> I *hurry amain* to *reach the plain,*
> *Run the rapid* and *leap the fall,*
> *Split at the rock* and *together again,*
> *Accept my bed,* or narrow or wide,
> And flee from folly on every side
> *With a lover's pain* to *attend the plain*
> Far from the hills of Habersham,
> Far down the valleys of Hall.

The series of verb phrases culminating in "and flee," move the poem downward to the completion of that stanza. The alliterative devices in "run the rapid and leap the fall," and "flee from folly" are only the apparent links in the stanza; not quite so obviously alliterative is "hurry amain" and "reach the plain," and "lover's pain," "narrow or wide," etc. The rhyming device, suspending a return to "fall" until the last word in the stanza, moves through a pattern inverted from -am, -all, -ain, to -ain, -am, -all. This pattern of rhyme inversion works in every stanza. Lanier was fond of varying rhythms from iambs:

> The rushes cried *Abide, abide,*
> The willful waterweeds held me thrall

to dactyls. Note also his consciousness of a choral element in nature.

Another device used here is that of making the first stanza the voice of the Chattahoochee, and the second and third the voices, successively, of the rushes and reeds, and the various "overleaning" trees. The fourth strophe introduces not only colors and gem-like minerals, but spondaic rhythms which lengthen the line and widely space the em-

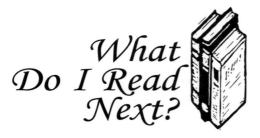

What Do I Read Next?

- Some academic libraries still have available copies of Lanier's influential collection of theoretical essays, *The Science of English Verse*, which was first published in by Scribners 1880.

- This poem is included on the collection *The Poems of Sidney Lanier*, most recently reprinted by the University of Georgia Press in 1999.

- The musical nature of Lanier's poetry reminds some readers of the works of Edgar Allan Poe. "Annabel Lee" and "The Bells" are two of Poe's poems that rely on sound in a way similar to "Song of the Chattahoochee."

- Lanier's poetry reminds readers of the mournful work of Walt Whitman, one of America's greatest poets, who wrote at about the same time. Whitman's finest work is in his collection *Leaves of Grass*, first published in 1855.

- The twentieth-century poet Karl Shapiro admired Lanier's poetic theory and noted how his theories continue to be appropriate and have influence. Interested readers can read Shapiro's poetry in *Collected Poems, 1940–1978*, and read his own theories of poetry in *The Poetry Wreck: Selected Essays, 1950–1970*.

---

phases; these really slow down the flow of the movement and impede, just as the sense of the poem signifies:

> The white quartz shone, and the smooth
> brook-stone
> Did bar me of passage with friendly brawl,
> And many a luminous jewel lone
> —Crystals clear or a-cloud with mist,
> Ruby, garnet and amethyst—
> Made lures with lights of streaming stone
> In the clefts of the hills of Habersham,
> In the beds of the valleys of Hall.

The imagery here is sharply cut, clear, sparkling. Then the final strophe occurs with the voice of the Chattahoochee saying that all depends upon the call of the lordly "main." Here all of the

lines point in the direction of the verb "calls" and fall from "downward" and "and":

> But oh, not the hills of Habersham,
> And oh, not the valleys of Hall
> Avail: I am fain for to water the plain.
> Downward the voices of Duty call—
> Downward, to toil and be mixed with the main,
> The dry fields burn, and the mills are to turn,
> And a myriad flowers mortally yearn,
> And the lordly main from beyond the plain
> Calls o'er the hills of Habersham,
> Calls through the valleys of Hall.

All the rhythms are alternately bound and released, caught, and sprung free. Parallelisms, short internal rhymes, and a certain ebbing and flowing from the initial line repetitions are caught in successive and alternate rhyme endings. The poem is, of course, a slight one, lacking many of the graver overtones so often found in Lanier's work. But it is a little art-work, not simple, delighted in for its tiny and perfectly wrought mosaic rhyme scheme.

Source: Charmenz S. Lenhart, "Sidney Lanier," in *Musical Influence on American Poetry*, University of Georgia Press, 1956, pp. 210–92.

Aubrey Harrison Starke

In the following essay excerpt, Starke speculates on the date of composition of "The Song of the Chattahoochee," and points out numerous "defects in the poem."

One other poem by Lanier may have been written in 1877, "The Song of the Chattahoochee," a poem so successful in onomatopœia that it early caught the popular fancy and has become perhaps the best known of all Lanier's poems. In the 1884 volume of collected poems Mrs. Lanier gives the date of composition as 1877, and in the table of contents notes the original publication as "*Scott's Magazine*, 1877." But *Scott's Magazine* had ceased existence in 1869. Inasmuch as the poem was printed in the *Independent* for December 20, 1883, exactly as given in the collected poems, one might guess that the poem had not been published during Lanier's lifetime, and that the date of composition may well have been 1877. However, at least one poem, "A Song of Eternity in Time," was twice published by Lanier himself in only slightly different versions, in 1870 and again in 1881; so posthumous publication in the *Independent* is no proof of original publication. Furthermore, F. V. N. Painter gives in his little volume, *Poets of the South*, published in 1903, a version of "The Song of the Chattahoochee" that differs from the 1883 *Independent* version. The first stanza is not written in the first person, so that the poem is not, therefore, the song of the Chattahoochee but a description of the river with a transcript of its song. Painter states in a note: "This poem was first published in *Scott's Magazine*, Atlanta, Georgia, from which it is here taken. It at once became popular, and was copied in many newspapers throughout the South. It was subsequently revised . . . "

But a careful search of files of *Scott's Magazine* has so far failed to reveal any version of "The Song of the Chattahoochee" or any poem by Lanier (or ascribable to Lanier) except those discussed in an earlier chapter. Unfortunately there is absolutely no reference to the poem in any of Lanier's published correspondence or in any of the unpublished letters available, and all those who have written on Lanier except Painter (whose book, it should be noted, preceded the appearance of Professor Mims's official biography by two years) have accepted 1877 as the date of composition. It probably is the date of the revised version, and Lanier probably revised it for inclusion in one of the several volumes of poetry he was preparing for publication as the time of his death. This version shows a change from the third person to the first in the first stanza, a change in four lines of the fourth, and a few verbal changes elsewhere. The changes are with two exceptions improvements, but they are not drastic. The poem in the early version is essentially the same as the poem in the later version.

It is, surely, the most popular of all Lanier's poems but, as is so often the case, popularity is no sign of excellence, and "The Song of the Chattahoochee" is far from being a great poem. Still, like Tennyson's "Brook," with which it must inevitably be compared, it deserves a recognition greater than that accorded it by frequent inclusion in grammar school readers. Any child can hear in it the music of the water, but the child who has heard this too often, may fail later to note the varied meter of the poem, the use of short vowels, liquid consonants, alliteration, internal rhyme, and skillful repetition by means of which the music is recorded. Nor does early familiarity with the poem make for intelligent appreciation of its central idea, the river's swift answer to the call of duty.

But defects in the poem are numerous. The rhythm is monotonous; the music is not varied enough; the style is not always transparent, for some of the sentences are awkwardly constructed and some of the words—such as "brawl," in the fourth stanza—are used in an unfamiliar way; and the thought is not always clear; what, for instance,

> *The rhythm is monotonous; the music is not varied enough; the style is not always transparent, for some of the sentences are awkwardly constructed . . ."*

does the river mean in saying "I . . . flee from folly on every side"? Nor is the apparent fact of gravitation a fitting symbol of devotion to duty and of the sacrifice of individuality in merging it in a larger individuality. Still, without "The Song of the Chattahoochee" American literature would be the poorer, and the American literary landscape the less pleasing.

Source: Aubrey Harrison Starke, "Ephemerae," in *Sidney Lanier: A Biographical and Critical Study*, University of Carolina Press, 1933, pp. 290–93.

Sources

Hubbell, Jay B., "The New South, 1865–1900: Sidney Lanier" in *The South in American Literature: 1607–1900*, Duke University Press, 1954, pp. 758–76.

Kent, Charles W., "A Study of Lanier's Poems" in *PMLA*, Vol. VII, No. 2, April–June, 1892, pp. 33–63.

Starke, Aubrey Harrison *Sidney Lanier: A Biographical and Critical Study*, Russell & Russell, Inc., 1964, p. 290.

Stedman, Edmund Clarence, "The Outlook," in *Poets of America*, Houghton Mifflin, 1885, pp. 435–76.

Webb, Richard, and Edwin R. Coulson, *Sidney Lanier: Poet and Prosodist*, University of Georgia Press, 1941.

Further Reading

Coughlin, Robert D., *A Storybook Site: The Early History and Construction of the Buford Dam*, Russell & Russell, Inc., 1933.
    This self-published book tells the history of the dam that now backs the Chattahoochee into Lake Sidney Lanier, with many pictures of how the river looked before the dam was built.

Debellis, Jack, *Sidney Lanier: Poet of the Marshes*, University of Georgia Press, 1991.

    This newer biography of the poet takes into account his reduced reputation as a serious poet and looks at him as an interesting regional writer.

Lanier, Sidney, *Music and Poetry: Essays upon Some Aspects and Inter-Relations of the Two Arts*, AMS Press, Inc., 1977.

    This collection of Lanier's essays, currently out of print, makes interesting reading, but is by no means necessary for understanding his poetry.

Mims, Edwin, *Sidney Lanier*, Kennikat Press, Inc., 1968.

    First published in 1905, Mims's book is considered to be the standard in Lanier studies. It suffers from not knowing how the poet's reputation stood up throughout the twentieth century, and modern readers might find Mims's language a little hard to follow.

Starke, Aubrey Harrison, *Sidney Lanier: A Biographical and Critical Study*, Robert D. Coughlin, 1998.

    Although this book is one of the most thorough studies of Lanier ever done and despite the title and the author's stated intention to emphasize the critical aspect, the work passes by many of Lanier's works without much commentary on them.

There Will Come Soft Rains

In 1950, noted science fiction writer Ray Bradbury published his popular collection of futuristic short stories called *The Martian Chronicles*. That book contains a story called "There Will Come Soft Rains," and it is not by accident that the title is the same as Sara Teasdale's poem published in *Flame and Shadow* thirty years earlier, in 1920, by MacMillan. Bradbury borrowed the name directly from the poet's work and based his story on a theme similar to the poem's, the senseless destruction of humankind by their own hands through war. In the story, a talking house is left confused and devastated by the loss of its masters, who vanished in an atomic blast. At one point, the house, lonely for its mistress, reads aloud one of the dead woman's favorite poems—"There Will Come Soft Rains" by Sara Teasdale.

Teasdale's poem is a response to her disdain for and disillusionment over World War I. When the United States became involved in the conflict, Teasdale turned some of her creative attention to writing anti-war lyrics, and when this poem appeared in *Flame and Shadow*, it carried the subtitle "War Time." The poem addresses the atrocity of battle from the perspective of nature—of birds and frogs and trees whose lives will go on even if human beings obliterate themselves from the planet. It is interesting to note that in Bradbury's short story based on the poem, nature and non-human objects do not fare quite as well, eventually succumbing to their own deaths without people around to support them. But Teasdale takes per-

Sara Teasdale

1920

Sara Teasdale

haps a more cynical approach in that nature will not only endure but will carry on without even noticing "that we were gone."

Author Biography

Sara Teasdale was born in St. Louis, Missouri, in August 1884 and committed suicide in New York City in January 1933. She was the youngest child of a prim middle-class family and grew up believing she was a fragile, helpless girl, vulnerable to a variety of undetermined illnesses, both physical and emotional. Her perceived frailty resulted in lifelong bouts of nervous exhaustion and chronic weakness, and she remained dependent upon her parents until she married at age thirty. After being schooled at home, Teasdale ventured out of the house long enough to become acquainted with a local women's poetry group and began writing poetry in her early twenties. Her fondness for music was reflected in the lyric poems she wrote, most very rhythmic and many of which ended up set to musical scores. Her work at the time centered primarily on love from a woman's perspective, and its childlike innocence was widely acclaimed, be-

ing published in major poetry journals in Chicago, New York, and Europe.

As well liked as Teasdale's poetry was, the poet herself became just as admired, and she was welcomed into the circles of America's most esteemed early-twentieth-century writers. But in spite of the popularity, Teasdale was her own worst enemy. She often lapsed into depression without a definable cause and suffered a consistent lack of self-confidence, believing she would never be independent or able to live on her own. In the early 1910s, she fretted over finding a husband but worried that the bliss of marriage might dash her inspiration for creativity, which usually derived from sadness and despair. By 1914, she had at least two adoring suitors: Vachel Lindsay, an eccentric, unemployed poet, who spent years walking through the United States trading poems for room and board, and Ernst Filsinger, a St. Louis businessman, savvy in his profession and respectful of the creative arts. Opting for a safer, more sensible environment, Teasdale married Filsinger in 1914 and eventually moved to New York with him where his business expanded into foreign trade.

It did not take long for Teasdale to realize that her marriage was anything but blissful. Although Filsinger was a loving, faithful husband, she could not get beyond her own depression, and she spent many months at sanatoriums in New England. The love lyrics she had initially been so highly praised for turned darker in theme and expression, even though she still attempted to present a woman's perspective and involved the idea of love as much as possible amidst more somber subjects. World War I especially disillusioned her, and both she and her husband maintained pacifist positions throughout the conflict. In 1920, she published her fifth collection of poetry, *Flame and Shadow*, which contains "There Will Come Soft Rains," and which demonstrated her turn toward philosophical and socially conscious themes, while still including love lyrics. But whether it was the turmoil of world events and the changing, conflicting roles of women in society or something deeply personal and emotionally debilitating inside the poet, Teasdale never overcame her sense of hopelessness and despair. In 1929, she divorced her husband against his will and lived alone for the first time in her life. In 1933, she took an overdose of sedatives in her New York apartment and lay down in a tub of water where her nurse found her body the next morning.

Poem Text

There will come soft rains and the smell of the
ground,
And swallows circling with their shimmering
sound;

And frogs in the pools singing at night,
And wild plum-trees in tremulous white;

Robins will wear their feathery fire   5
Whistling their whims on a low fence-wire;

And not one will know of the war, not one
Will care at last when it is done.

Not one would mind, neither bird nor tree
If mankind perished utterly;   10

And Spring herself, when she woke at dawn,
Would scarcely know that we were gone.

Media Adaptations

- Many of Teasdale's lyric poems have been set to music and recorded by numerous individual singers and groups. A general Internet search under "Sara Teasdale recordings" brings up over fifty pages of information on song titles, the artists who recorded them, and, in some cases, where they are available for purchasing or borrowing.

Poem Summary

Lines 1–2

The verb phrase "will come" in both the title and the first line of "There Will Come Soft Rains" indicates that the poem takes place in the future, but whether the future is an hour away, a day away, or many years away is not clear. Not until the end of the poem is there an implication that the time the poem looks forward to is actually a season away—a time when spring comes around again. The "soft rains" are the gentle showers of springtime that dampen the ground and bring out its earthy scents of wet grass and mud. Spring also means the return of birds, and "swallows" are a good choice to describe as making a "shimmering sound" because of their graceful, swift movements in the air.

Lines 3–4

Lines 3 and 4 introduce more elements of nature in the form of frogs, pools, and plum trees. The frogs are depicted "singing at night" to show their nonchalance toward the world around them. They go about their merry business completely oblivious to what is happening in the human world, which is not revealed until line 7. The plum trees are "wild," implying carefree and natural, but they are also "tremulous," or fearful and timid. The latter description is a foreshadowing of the revelation of war and death in the poem. Although the animals and plants are safe from the madness of humankind, they still reflect the fear and insecurity that people have brought into the environment.

Lines 5–6

Line 5 also contains a foreshadowing image, as the robins are wearing "their feathery fire." While the reddish orange color of robins' breasts may resemble the color of fire, there is likely more to the word choice here than an attempt to match hues. Fire is a part of war. Whether it refers to gunfire itself or to actual fires that often result from hand grenades, cannon balls, or bombs, the intention is to portray the beauty and peacefulness of nature against the horrific imagery of battle. Line 6 reinforces the idea of innocent animals' playfulness and nonchalance amidst human chaos. The robins sit on a fence wire "Whistling their whims" because they do not have the same worries and fears that humans do.

Lines 7–8

Here, the poem reveals its theme. Lines 7 and 8 make an abrupt change in the tone and subject matter, shifting from pastoral scenes of animals enjoying a spring day to the recognition of a war going on. These lines also explain why the poet has been so careful to portray the wild life as completely happy and carefree. Showing them circling and singing and whistling drives home even harder Teasdale's contention that the natural world is not as foolish as the human world has become. Blissfully ignorant of the destruction and devastation the humans are suffering, the animals do not "know of the war" and "not one / Will care" what the outcome is, for the swallows, frogs, robins, and so forth will remain unaffected.

Lines 9–10

These two lines are perhaps the most dismal in the poem and the most revealing of the poet's true disdain for the act of war. Although there were no atomic or hydrogen bombs used in World War I—the only world war Teasdale lived through—she still seems to recognize the possibility of mankind's total self-annihilation through large-scale violence and bloodshed. The phrase, "If mankind perished utterly," parallels the theme of much of the science fiction stories and novels that would become popular over the decades after the poem was published. Teasdale would be long dead before Ray Bradbury published *The Martian Chronicles* and before World War II would end with the U.S. obliteration of Hiroshima and Nagasaki, Japan. But the ability to destroy places and people "utterly" is obviously something she could foresee and chose to warn against in her poetry.

Lines 11–12

Line 11 now reveals the time in the future when the soft rains will come. "Spring herself" will show no more concern for human war than do the birds, frogs, and trees. Instead, when the season arrives again, it will not even notice that mankind is no longer around.

Themes

Death and Meaninglessness

World War I brought an entirely new meaning to the idea of conflicts between nations. While thousands of patriots from each of the countries involved went eagerly and confidently into battle, thousands more were shocked by the massive undertaking, never before having witnessed such large-scale political participation in warfare. For many, that shock led to disillusionment with their own governments and depression over the loss of so many young men who fought and died without fully understanding why they were fighting and for whom they were dying. Sara Teasdale was one of the latter.

For years, the poet had used her creativity to write love poems. Her style was simple, elegant, and innocent, expressing feminine sensitivity to romantic relationships, marriage, loss of love, and the beauty of finding it again. Addressing the brutality of physical battle and warring nations did not enter her work until her own emotional response to World War I forced her into it. This was new territory for Teasdale, but she ventured into it with the same simple yet imposing style, changing only her themes to reflect the dark mood and nagging fear that plagued her own mind and her environment. Suddenly, life seemed meaningless. With so many people willing to take up arms and march into strange lands ready to kill or be killed, Teasdale found it difficult to maintain any sense of decency or order in the world, to hold onto a belief in a gentle and peaceful human nature. Both her anger and pessimism are evident in "There Will Come Soft Rains."

The first half of the poem—with its pastoral scenes and pretty depiction of animals and trees in their natural states—is a set-up for the second half when suddenly the tone turns bitter, admonishing mankind's absurd and chaotic behavior. The total disappearance of human beings from the earth is not as far-fetched an idea as it once may have been, and "If mankind perished utterly," it would be by his own hands, a notion the poet believes is evidence of the meaninglessness and disorder in human life. Death is no longer personal and tragic, but impersonal and cursory. A war between several different nations implies dubious reasoning and reckless action, leaving little room to be passionate about life or show respect for individuals. "There Will Come Soft Rains" is a poem that calls out for orderly design and meaning in everyday living, but in this work, only the animals and trees can answer the call.

Detachment

Many writers who address the issue of war and all of its results include the obvious destruction of property and loss of human life as well as the sometimes neglected mention of harm done to wildlife and the natural environment. Novels, short stories, and poems typically portray flora and fauna as helpless, unavoidable bystanders during battle, victims of violence among people and incapable of getting out of the way. Teasdale's "There Will Come Soft Rains" puts a different spin on the role of nature during wartime, affording it not only the ability to stay alive but to distance itself distinctly and nonchalantly from the entire debacle.

The first six lines of the poem may appear innocent and even childlike in their description of birds and frogs going happily about their day, which consists of sailing through the air, singing by the waterside, and whiling away time on a fence wire, whistling a tune. But the simplicity is both intentional and powerful in providing a foundation for the comparison Teasdale eventually makes between man and nature—man, violent and foolish; nature, beautiful and content. Neither animals nor "wild plum-trees" will fall victim to human violence, for they can and do remain detached from it all. So the first half of the poem illustrates an especially peaceful day among wildlife to make a more compelling, stark contrast to human behavior.

The indifference of nature to mankind's self-destruction is a theme borne out of disgust with the human race as well as disappointment. Teasdale's well-documented pacifism made her particularly vulnerable to the human tendency to settle disagreements through physical combat, and she was both hurt by it and angered. This poem conveys a point that Teasdale made regularly in her war poetry—that while human beings may destroy themselves one day, nature will prevail. In a poem also included in *Flame and Shadow* called "In a Garden," she describes the peaceful beauty of apple trees, purple phlox, asters, and roses all offset by the hysteria of a regiment of soldiers suddenly marching nearby. The poem ends with much the same sentiment as "There Will Come Soft Rains," its final line declaring: "Earth takes her children's many sorrows calmly / And stills herself to sleep."

Style

Lyric Poetry

Lyric poetry is poetry that expresses subjective thoughts and feelings in a songlike style, often using both rhythm and rhyme. It is not a coincidence that people who write words to songs are writing "lyrics," but lyric poetry does not necessarily imply a simple, unsophisticated style that must appeal to a mass audience to be considered popular. Truly, many of Teasdale's poems were set to music, especially the early ones in which the themes were lighter and more concerned with love and relationships than depression and war. "There Will Come Soft Rains" is lyrical and the couplets do rhyme, but its dark, cynical subject keeps the poem from falling into a simplistic, naïve category that describes some short, rhyming poems.

The obvious end-rhyming of the lines in this poem is offset by very effective alliteration within the lines. Alliteration is a poetic device used to emphasize the sound of a poem or the way individual words work together to create interesting patterns of repetition. There are two types of alliteration: consonance, which means a repetition of like-sounding consonants, and assonance, which means

Topics for Further Study

- Lyric poetry encompasses a wide range of styles and presentations, although it does prescribe certain guidelines. After familiarizing yourself with those guidelines and with the work of various lyric poets, compare Sara Teasdale's poetry to Walt Whitman's. How are they similar and how do they differ?

- Read Ray Bradbury's short story, "There Will Come Soft Rains" and write an essay explaining why you think his interpretation of the world's future—in a science fiction sense—is more or less frightening than Teasdale's.

- World War I was called "the war to end all wars." Why do you think this phrase came about, and how do you believe people interpreted it as the conflict was going on? Why did the First World War *not* end all others?

- "Lost Generation" was the nickname of Americans in their twenties and thirties during the 1920s. In particular, it described those who felt disillusioned with their own government and society, so not everyone who fit the age category would have appreciated the term. What is the nickname of your generation, or what would you call it if it were up to you? What does the name say about your generation, and how do you reflect it or reject it?

a repetition of like-sounding vowels. Notice the *s* sound in the first couplet, using the words "soft," "smell," "swallows," "circling," "shimmering," and "sound." In only two lines, Teasdale manages to use six words alliteratively without lapsing into overdone poetics or forced intonation. The third couplet also employs very impressive consonance with the *w* sound. The words "will," "wear," "whistling," "whims," and "wire" are, again, effective without being trite. Although "There Will Come Soft Rains" does not contain as much assonance as consonance, there is one example of the repetition of the *long-i* vowel sound in lines 3 and 4 in the words "night," "wild," and "white."

The rhythm of lyric poetry derives from its methodic use of meter throughout. In this poem, each line in the first couplet contains eleven syllables, each line in the second couplet contains nine syllables, as do those in the third, and so forth. The final three couplets have differing syllable counts within their lines, but lines 8–12 follow an 8, 9, 8, 9, 8 syllabic pattern. But in spite of Teasdale's careful attention to poetic style, "There Will Come Soft Rains" is stronger in its meaning than in its form. This helps to make the poem more appealing, as well as more credible, to readers.

Historical Context

Living and writing during the 1910s, Teasdale was exposed to and inspired by some of the most dramatic changes American life had ever encountered. By the time "There Will Come Soft Rains" was published in 1920, the United States had risen to the status of world power, and mass production had made the nation the most highly industrialized in the world. Henry Ford's one millionth Model T had rolled off the newly invented assembly line, selling for a little over $300. Social attitudes loosened remarkably, compared to the previous Victorian era, and women became more outspoken about voting rights, better job opportunities, and greater freedom and independence. In the same year that Congress passed the Nineteenth Amendment, 1919, granting women the right to vote, Prohibition was also enacted, a law that would prove futile and pave the way for bootlegging gangsters such as Al Capone and Dutch Schultz. In response to the illegality of alcohol sales, clandestine speakeasies cropped up, providing throngs of customers a place to have a drink and listen to jazz, the music that became increasingly popular during the period.

The decade of the 1910s also saw the rise of labor unions, mostly because of widespread unsafe working conditions. Children were hired for low wages to work long hours in mills, mines, and factories, and the Triangle Shirtwaist Factory fire, a result of hazardous workplace conditions, took the lives of 145 female employees. By the middle of the decade, every state had passed a minimum age law for employment, but a federal law with the same restrictions had failed. One of the most remarkable, as well as saddest, occurrences of the 1910s was the sinking of the *Titanic* on April 15, 1912, drowning more than fifteen hundred people after the mighty "unsinkable" ship was ripped apart by an iceberg. But regardless of all the unprece-

dented social, political, and personal changes that Americans witnessed and endured during this decade, none surpassed the "war to end all wars" in its lasting effect on individual perspective and human life in general.

World War I was the impetus behind Teasdale's writing "There Will Come Soft Rains." When the conflict erupted in 1914, pitting Germany and Austria-Hungary against Great Britain, France, and Russia, American President Woodrow Wilson took a position of neutrality. He insisted, however, on maintaining full trading rights with all the countries on both sides of the battle, a proposal that both Germany and Britain tried to use to its own advantage. While Britain enacted commercial regulations and trade restrictions to try to entice the United States into the war on its side, the Germans resorted to attacking merchant ships with U-boat torpedoes. In May 1915, a submarine torpedoed the British passenger liner *Lusitania*, killing 128 Americans, but still Wilson refused to enter the campaign. Two years later, the U-boats sank several American merchant vessels, and, at about the same time, Americans learned of German foreign minister Arthur Zimmermann's proposal to bring Mexico into the war against the United States. The foreign minister's promise to return Texas, New Mexico, and Arizona to the Mexican government in return for its help in defeating the Americans was essentially the final straw for Woodrow Wilson. Although he had won reelection to the presidency in 1916 on the slogan "He kept us out of the war," on April 17, 1917, he asked Congress for a declaration of war against Germany and received it.

For the United States, World War I lasted only a year and a half. The massive onslaught of American troops to the western front proved too much for Germany and Austria-Hungary—the "Central Powers"—to withstand. Although Germany had been spurred on by the separate peace it had concluded with Russia in March of 1918, the continued efforts of Great Britain, France, and, now, the United States eventually wore down their enemies. On November 11, 1918, the Central Powers surrendered, leaving 112,432 Americans dead, more than half having died of disease.

Because this was a relatively brief encounter for the United States, history does not record it as having as great an impact on American society as other conflicts, in particular, the Civil War, World War II, and Vietnam. However, the effect was deep and indelible for some, including Teasdale. Her anti-war poems reflect not only a sadness and depression over the horrors of battle, but also anger

Compare & Contrast

- **1917:** The Selective Service Act is passed, forcing men between twenty and thirty to enlist for military service. The first drafted American troops arrive in France in October to begin America's involvement in World War I.

  Today: The Center on Conscience and War continues its struggle to end funding for draft registration. The organization made progress when the House of Representatives agreed and voted to end government financial support of selective service. However, the Senate voted to restore funding and, today, males between the ages of eighteen and twenty-five are required to register for the draft.

- **1921:** President Warren G. Harding pardons Socialist Labor Party candidate Eugene V. Debs, allowing for his release from prison. Debs had been sentenced to ten years behind bars for his controversial anti-war speeches delivered during World War I.

  Today: Before leaving office, President Bill Clinton announces controversial pardons of several convicted white-collar criminals. Perhaps the most disturbing was his pardon of fugitive financier Marc Rich, who was indicted in 1983 on charges of tax evasion, fraud, and participation in illegal oil deals with Iran. Before he could face trial, Rich left the country and settled in Switzerland.

- **1924:** Nellie Ross of Wyoming and Miriam Ferguson of Texas become the first female governors in the United States.

  Today: A record five women hold positions as governors in the states of New Hampshire, Montana, Delaware, Arizona, and New Jersey. In addition, there are twelve female senators and a record fifty-nine female members of the House of Representatives.

---

and cynicism toward, in her opinion, such a senseless loss of life. "There Will Come Soft Rains" stresses the beauty and peacefulness of nature in contrast to the foolish brutality of mankind. Many other poets, writers, and artists of the period also felt disillusionment with the American government, as well as a stifling of their creative arts by the authorities. During the 1920s, a group of writers from the "Lost Generation" left the United States to live and write in France. These self-exiled expatriates sought freedom to write what they wanted, which was realistic fiction, uncensored in its use of profanity and sexual content and more reflective, they believed, of the world around them. This group included such Teasdale contemporaries as Ernest Hemingway, F. Scott Fitzgerald, Gertrude Stein, Henry Miller, and John Dos Passos.

Back in the United States, the Roaring Twenties were underway with a boom in automobile sales and the increasing popularity of radios and movies. Women's fashion was out of control during the "Flapper Age," named for a style of sack-like dress with no bosom, no waistline, and lots of feathers and silky fringe. This was also the decade when cosmetic manufacturing took off, and women flocked to stores for powder, rouge, lipstick, eye shadow, and nail polish. Another dubious practice that became fashionable during this time was buying on credit, leading to a very active stock market and rising economy. By the end of the decade, however, the party was over. On October 24, 1929, the stock market crashed, resulting in closed banks and widespread panic among consumers. Black Thursday, as the day was called, was the beginning of an economic depression that would last throughout most of the 1930s. Teasdale would not live to see the recovery nor the beginning of a second world war, more lengthy, more devastating than the first.

Critical Overview

Teasdale's early popularity is reflected in her winning the first Columbia Poetry Prize in 1918, an

Sara Teasdale contrasts the ugliness of World War I with the beauty of Nature

award that would later be called the Pulitzer Prize for Poetry. Her work was especially liked for its lyrical style and musical rhythm, and it was received equally well by male critics as well as by female critics, even though the subjects were often sensitive and sentimental. At least two critics who reviewed *Flame and Shadow* shortly after it was published found the collection stronger than her previous work, although similar in theme and tone. Writing for *The Bookman*, reviewer Louis Untermeyer claims the book

> is by no means a series of facile melodies that live only to be set to music or to fill a page. . . . Here are new rhythms, far more subtle than those she has ever employed; here are words chosen with a keener sense of their actual as well as their musical value.

Mark Van Doren, writing for the *Nation*, admonishes Teasdale for still being tempted "to deal exclusively in stock love-lyric materials," but praises the poems that go beyond her typical theme: "Sara Teasdale only reaches her perfection when, defeating her temptations, she interpenetrates pain with metaphor and metaphor with pain, when she finds the proper balance between fire and form."

Because *Flame and Shadow* contains a section of poems addressing World War I and such meditative themes as human self-destruction and nature's beauty versus mankind's ugliness, critics claimed that this book demonstrated a growth in Teasdale's intellectual work and philosophical thought. Ironically, the development of her artistry paralleled her deepening depression, and the more she centered her poetry on pessimistic themes, the more her own self-examination left her distraught and disillusioned. After Teasdale's suicide in 1933, her work eventually faded from academic venues, and critics simply moved on to other poets. However, she was still popular with nonacademic audiences, and *The Collected Poems*, which came out four years after her death, went through more than twenty printings before 1966, when it was republished in paperback. Her work was kept alive in the 1970s when the feminist movement came about. Many contemporary women regarded her as one who struggled valiantly with the revolutionary changes that swept society during the early twentieth century, revamping the roles of females and yet still placing on them demands and restrictions that were confusing at best, debilitating at worst. Today, critics maintain a fair amount of attention on Teasdale's work, and there are many volumes of criticism available that address it along with other poetry of the period. Most textbooks and anthologies, however, neglect to include her poems in their publications.

Criticism

Pamela Steed Hill

Hill is the author of a poetry collection, has published widely in poetry journals, and is an associate editor for a university communications department. In the following essay, she contends that the peacefulness and beauty of nature described in the poem serve as evidence of Teasdale's acute cynicism toward humankind.

For as long as human beings have been writing poetry, fiction, and philosophical or religious essays, they have addressed the conditions of the world around them. Some writings have tried to teach moral lessons through everything from didactic preaching to ribald comedy, and some have simply presented themselves as lamentations on hopeless situations and the downfall of man. Still other writings have celebrated the human condition, telling stories of great achievements, great romances, and great friendships. Of course, most writers prior to the nineteenth century were men, and much of the poetry and other writing that addressed one major phenomenon unique to humans in the animal kingdom—war—did so in terms of glory and grandeur. Themes centered on valor and victory, pride and strength, and nobility in dying for a cause. More recent writers have been wondering just what the "cause" is, and Sara Teasdale is one of them. That notion—coupled with the fact that she was a woman—makes "There Will Come Soft Rains" all the more intriguing and forceful in its portrayal of humankind's bleak future.

The most powerful statement in this poem is Teasdale's claim that neither animals nor plants "would mind . . . / If mankind perished utterly." Many other futuristic poems and fictional accounts tell the story of a total destruction of life as a result of wars started by human beings—total in that the demise of man also means the demise of dogs and cats and elephants and geraniums and roses and so on. The rationale behind this dismal prediction is that domesticated animals have become dependent on human masters for survival and that wild animals and plants will die out because the aftermath of radiation or other bomb residue is sure to poison the air and water or block out the sun's rays. Teasdale paints a different picture in "There Will Come Soft Rains." She steps back from the conclusion that everything will perish in favor of the more cynical view that all living things other than humans will carry on as normal, not even noticing our absence.

> *Even 'Spring herself' will be ambivalent about mankind's departure, for the seasons of the year hardly need people around to keep time and the earth turning as usual."*

When Ray Bradbury adopted the name of Teasdale's poem for his short story about a thinking, talking, fully-automated house of the future (2026, to be exact), he also adopted the idea of man's self-destruction through all-out war. Briefly, this tale is told from the house's point of view—the reader is unaware in the beginning that the people who lived there are all dead because the house still rings bells to awaken them, calls out for them to get up, makes breakfast for them, and so forth. Not until Bradbury describes the eerie silhouettes of a man, woman, and two children imprinted on an outside wall of the house does the reader understand what has happened. The family was apparently caught off-guard by an attack that occurred in their small California town, and only the charred outlines of their bodies remain as evidence of their existence. The shadowy figures are still posed as the humans' last moments on earth were spent—mowing grass, picking flowers, playing ball. The family dog, trapped inside the house with no one to feed him or free him, wanders aimlessly for several days before dying of starvation and madness. Eventually, the house catches fire when cleaning liquid spills across the kitchen stove, and it, too, "dies."

Again, this scenario is a familiar one in futuristic writing. It foretells a complete loss of life in a nuclear war. Even if the thing lost is inhuman, such as the dog or the house in the Bradbury tale, it is all a part of the belief that humankind rules the earth and nothing can survive without us. It is interesting that the science fiction writer of the mid-twentieth century took a poignantly different approach from the poet of the early-twentieth century who originated the title of both pieces—interesting and ironic. Because Teasdale's animals and plants live happily on after man is gone, the reader

What Do I Read Next?

- World War I is explored from an interesting perspective in Gary Mead's *The Doughboys: America and the First World War*, published in 2000. Readers may be surprised to learn about how the United States's own allies tried to use American involvement in favor of their respective nations as well as against the enemies. This book is lengthy but reads more like a novel than a history text.

- Richard Rhodes's 1995 publication of *Dark Sun: The Making of the Hydrogen Bomb* gives readers an inside look at "super" science, postwar politics, espionage, and moral challenges all rolled into one. This book is different in its account of the bomb's creation in that it not only provides the facts of scientific discovery, but also the personality quirks and sometimes odd details of the physicists who brought it about.

- Most people recall the photograph taken during the Vietnam War of a young girl running nude down a road amid a throng of other horrified people, her body seared in a napalm attack. That child was nine-year-old Kim Phuc whose biography is told in Denise Chong's *The Girl in the Picture: The Story of Kim Phuc, the Photographer and the Vietnam War*, published in 2000. The book recounts her amazing survival, her relationship with both Americans and the North Vietnamese, and her present life in Canada with her husband and two sons.

- First published in 1937, *The Collected Poems of Sara Teasdale* has been through numerous editions and reprinting and is easily available in libraries. This is an excellent compilation of her work, including many of the simple love lyrics that made her famous, as well as the darker poems that she wrote in the years before her suicide.

- During World War I, Vera Brittain volunteered as a nurse in military hospitals in England and France. Like so many others, Brittain was horrified by the magnitude of the war, and she lost her boyfriend, a brother, and two close friends on the battlefields. Their stories are told around a collection of letters they wrote to one another during the war in a book called *Letters from a Lost Generation* (1999), edited by Alan Bishop and Mark Bostridge.

---

is tempted to think that hers is the more positive outcome. After all, the death of everything must be more distressful and ominous than a war that eliminates people but mercifully leaves the rest of Mother Nature alone. Not necessarily. Teasdale's theme is actually more disturbing than Bradbury's because it demonstrates a wholesale disregard for mankind's coming and going. Man is not so evil that everything we have touched will die; instead, man is so evil that our self-destruction is not worthy of noticing.

The first half of "There Will Come Soft Rains" does not even mention human beings. It reads like an exaltation of nature with its placid descriptions of gentle rains, the smell of the earth, swallows flying about, frogs singing, and robins whistling. This scene sets the stage for Teasdale's sudden ironic turn. Juxtaposing the beauty of the natural world against the sudden mention of "the war" convinces the reader that there is more going on here than a pretty little poem about birds and trees. But even though the subject changes, the perspective is still nature's. While human calamity rages on, the animals and plants are oblivious to it—"not one will know" that the conflict is even happening. But Teasdale does not stop with nature's lack of knowledge, for that could be interpreted as simple ignorance or the absence of intellectual ability. Rather, she makes sure the point is not missed by bringing attitude into the picture. Not only will birds and trees not know of the war but "not one / Will care." Furthermore, "Not one would mind." The words "care" and "mind" are actually human attributes, so applying them to non-human beings adds deeper insult to the race that is supposed to be superior to all else. Even "Spring herself" will be ambivalent about mankind's departure because the seasons of the year hardly need people around to keep time and the earth turning as usual.

It may be argued that the poet's cynical approach really is not cynicism at all; rather, she contends that animals and plants will survive human war only because she cannot know of a weapon so massive and so destructive that anything in its vicinity will perish—people, animals, trees, buildings, automobiles, virtually everything. The atomic bomb had not yet been invented. The language of this poem, however, still suggests disdain for and anger toward man's participation in deadly combat. Had she portrayed an outcome that claimed the natural world would not know of the war and left it at that, perhaps the reader could accept her obvious lack of knowledge of what would occur in the next world war, one she did not live to see. But the fact that nature will neither care nor mind in this poet's calculation suggests something much more cynical, much darker, than simply not being able to predict the real future.

Source: Pamela Steed Hill, Critical Essay on "There Will Come Soft Rains," in *Poetry for Students*, The Gale Group, 2002.

Doreen Piano

Piano is a Ph.D. candidate in English at Bowling Green State University. In the following essay, she analyzes how Teasdale's lyric poem reflects the indifference of the natural world to the destruction of humanity during war time.

During World War I, many American and British poets expressed through their poetry their feelings of outrage and horror about the loss of a generation of young men killed in the fields of Northern Europe. Sara Teasdale, a young American poet known more for her love poetry than political statements, contributed to these anti-war sentiments in her lyric poem "There Will Come Soft Rains." As defined by literary critic M. H. Abrams in *A Glossary of Literary Terms*, a lyric poem is "any fairly short poem, consisting of the utterance by a single speaker, who expresses a state of mind or a process of perception." Written in the lyric tradition, this poem illuminates a brief but startling picture of the natural world's indifference to the foibles and follies of humankind. Teasdale does this by creating an extended description of the natural world as being completely involved in its own cycle of life while war rages on in another part

> *Thus, a portrait of pastoral tranquility set up early in the poem becomes a moment of meditating on the futility of war later on. It is this tension that creates the drama in the poem."*

of the world. Impervious to humankind's ability to destroy itself, the natural world exists in an untouched parallel universe. Most intriguing about this poem is its ability to contrast the timelessness of the natural world with the transience of humanity to reveal an utterly devastating point: regardless of the destructive impulse that impels nation-states to destroy each other, the natural world continues to exist. Thus, this poem sends a poignant message about how little affected the natural world would be by the destruction of human life.

Although Teasdale's poetry may lack an extensive use of literary devices, such as similes and tropes, it is important not to dismiss her work as simplistic or sentimental. Her direct use of language and her song-like verse contain deep and hidden meanings that may take more than one reading to discern. As many of her critics and admirers note, Teasdale's popularity as a poet was based on the appearance of a simple style that often hid complex meanings. In *The New Era in American Poetry*, critic Louis Untermeyer notes that Teasdale had "a genius for the song, for the pure lyric in which words seem to have fallen into place without art or effort." However, her ability to write a poem that adeptly moves from a feeling of peaceful, rustic tranquility to a searing critique of the futility of war in only twelve lines is no easy achievement.

The deceptive quality of Teasdale's art lies in her subtle use of description to set a particular mood that changes in tone throughout the poem. For example, the opening lines of this poem create a sense of beauty and peacefulness in the natural world, of gentle rain and the fresh smell of earth, of birds flying and trees blooming. It is spring time, a time of new life and new beginnings. This extended description of the natural world views life as active and vibrant, as well as undisturbed, because it is night time when most humans are asleep. Although a portrait of tranquility, these lines set up the rest of the poem's overriding idea that the natural world is impervious to humans and could easily exist without them. The suggestion is that the tranquility of this rustic tableau is partially due to the lack of human interference.

The poem creates a constant movement between the natural world and that of humans through its tonal shifts. Thus, a portrait of pastoral tranquility set up early in the poem becomes a moment of meditating on the futility of war later on. It is this tension that creates the drama in the poem. For example, in the first two stanzas, the natural world has its own rhythms and sense of time. The frequent use of the conjunction "and" and the verb ending "-ing" reveals this sense of natural time as being continual and undisturbed by human activity. Moreover, the use of end rhymes in the beginning two stanzas, such as "ground" and "sound" and "night" and "white," contribute to the notion of a world that is able to sustain itself without the influence of humans. However, the consistent use of the conjunction "and" also creates a subtle sense of suspense as if something is about to happen. However, nothing really changes in the scene of nature; the timing is cyclical and continual rather than linear. Thus, the suspenseful use of "and" indicates a change of tone in the poem similar to a break in a song.

In the third stanza, the natural world is once again described, only this time the poet focuses on robins to reveal the natural world's isolation from humanity. Here a close-up view is given of robins "whistling their whims on a low fence-wire." Although it appears like a seemingly innocuous description, this stanza conveys a strong sense of detachment from human concerns. In particular, the excessive use of *alliteration*, such as "feathery fire" and "whistling their whims," reinforces the feeling of a world in tune with its own rhythm and far removed from that of humans. The subtle change in tone that occurs in this stanza is noted by the use of off-rhymes, such as "fire" and "fence-wire," rather than the end rhymes that preceded this stanza. This change in rhyme pattern prepares the reader for another disruption in the poem's mood. The fourth stanza reveals this mood change as the poem leaves the natural world momentarily to contemplate the separation of the human and natural worlds through direct reference to the war and the sobering fact that "not one / Will care at last when it is done."

In the "Introduction" to *Mirror of the Heart: Poems of Sara Teasdale*, critic and biographer William Drake claims that "for Teasdale the point of a lyric was not merely to state an emotion . . . but to clarify and analyze, to coax it from the dim regions of disquiet into consciousness." Thus, the rest of the poem reflects on how the natural world co-exists with the human world, yet ultimately humanity's despairing moments, such as during times of war, have little or no effect on it. Although the ravages of war seem to loom large in the speaker's mind, in the natural world the war does not even exist. A wistful feeling is expressed here that being as divested of human matters as the natural world is a desirable state. Although the natural world can be indifferent to human foibles, it is impossible for humans to be because of their consciousness.

The last two stanzas examine the insignificance of war in light of the natural world's response to it. As the speaker makes clear, the negation of human existence would have little effect on the natural world's cyclical and enduring concept of time. The movement from the future to subjunctive tense makes the last two stanzas speculative. If it were to happen that "mankind perished utterly," then "Spring herself / Would scarcely know that we were gone." This grim prognosis gives the reader an opportunity to reflect on how destructive impulses that propel humans to announce war on each other have little resonance in the natural world. Although a disturbing thought, it points to the egocentric and self-motivated will of humankind to see themselves as the center of the universe. From this unusual point of view, Teasdale suggests that humankind's concept of time that privileges the temporal over the cyclical contributes to our ability to destroy each other. The dissonance between these two worlds, that of humans and the natural world, is linguistically noted by Teasdale's subtle but exquisite use of the slant rhyme, "dawn" and "gone," that ends the poem's last stanza.

Source: Doreen Piano, Critical Essay on "There Will Come Soft Rains," in *Poetry for Students*, The Gale Group, 2002.

Sources

Abrams, M. H., *A Glossary of Literary Terms, Sixth edition*, Harcourt Brace, 1993, p. 108.

Drake, William, "Introduction," in *Mirror of the Heart: Poems of Sara Teasdale*, edited by William Drake, Macmillan, 1984, pp. xxxviii–xxxxix.

Teasdale, Sara, *Flame and Shadow*, The Macmillan Company, 1935.

Untermeyer, Louis, in *Bookman*, Vol. LII, No. 5, January 1921, pp. 361–64.

———, *The New Era in American Poetry*, H. Holt, 1919, p. 267.

Van Doren, Mark, in *Nation*, Vol. 112, No. 2896, January 5, 1921, p. 20.

Further Reading

Drake, William, *Sara Teasdale: Woman and Poet*, Harper and Row, 1979.
    This biography of Teasdale is one of only a handful that have been written. Drake is the first biographer to gain permission from the poet's literary executor, Margaret Conklin, to quote directly from Teasdale's letters and other unpublished materials. As he notes in the book's preface, his intent was to "reconstruct the tragic history of a vivid and sensitive personal-ity, with respect and sympathy." That makes this bi-ography an excellent read.

Schoen, Carol B., *Sara Teasdale*, Twayne Publishers, 1986.
    This is a critical study of Teasdale's poetry, cover-ing all her works and including aspects of her per-sonal life that had a direct bearing on her subjects and themes. Schoen considers her one of the best lyric poets in history and one who has been overlooked too long by critics favoring more controversial or mil-itant female poets.

Teasdale, Sara, *Sonnets to Duse, and Other Poems*, Poet Lore Company, 1907.
    While this first collection of Teasdale's may be avail-able for reading only in the library, it is worth being acquainted with the poet's beginnings and the work she was doing at age twenty-three. Eleonora Duse was a famous actress whom Teasdale idolized but never met.

———, *Strange Victory*, Macmillan, 1933.
    This is a collection of the last poetry Teasdale wrote before killing herself in 1933. On instructions the poet had left in her notebooks, literary executor Mar-garet Conklin gathered the poems and had them pub-lished with the title that Teasdale had chosen.

Glossary of Literary Terms

A

Abstract: Used as a noun, the term refers to a short summary or outline of a longer work. As an adjective applied to writing or literary works, abstract refers to words or phrases that name things not knowable through the five senses.

Accent: The emphasis or stress placed on a syllable in poetry. Traditional poetry commonly uses patterns of accented and unaccented syllables (known as feet) that create distinct rhythms. Much modern poetry uses less formal arrangements that create a sense of freedom and spontaneity.

Aestheticism: A literary and artistic movement of the nineteenth century. Followers of the movement believed that art should not be mixed with social, political, or moral teaching. The statement "art for art's sake" is a good summary of aestheticism. The movement had its roots in France, but it gained widespread importance in England in the last half of the nineteenth century, where it helped change the Victorian practice of including moral lessons in literature.

Affective Fallacy: An error in judging the merits or faults of a work of literature. The "error" results from stressing the importance of the work's effect upon the reader—that is, how it makes a reader "feel" emotionally, what it does as a literary work—instead of stressing its inner qualities as a created object, or what it "is."

Age of Johnson: The period in English literature between 1750 and 1798, named after the most prominent literary figure of the age, Samuel Johnson. Works written during this time are noted for their emphasis on "sensibility," or emotional quality. These works formed a transition between the rational works of the Age of Reason, or Neoclassical period, and the emphasis on individual feelings and responses of the Romantic period.

Age of Reason: See *Neoclassicism*

Age of Sensibility: See *Age of Johnson*

Agrarians: A group of Southern American writers of the 1930s and 1940s who fostered an economic and cultural program for the South based on agriculture, in opposition to the industrial society of the North. The term can refer to any group that promotes the value of farm life and agricultural society.

Alexandrine Meter: See *Meter*

Allegory: A narrative technique in which characters representing things or abstract ideas are used to convey a message or teach a lesson. Allegory is typically used to teach moral, ethical, or religious lessons but is sometimes used for satiric or political purposes.

Alliteration: A poetic device where the first consonant sounds or any vowel sounds in words or syllables are repeated.

Allusion: A reference to a familiar literary or historical person or event, used to make an idea more easily understood.

Amerind Literature: The writing and oral traditions of Native Americans. Native American literature was originally passed on by word of mouth, so it consisted largely of stories and events that were easily memorized. Amerind prose is often rhythmic like poetry because it was recited to the beat of a ceremonial drum.

Analogy: A comparison of two things made to explain something unfamiliar through its similarities to something familiar, or to prove one point based on the acceptedness of another. Similes and metaphors are types of analogies.

Anapest: See *Foot*

Angry Young Men: A group of British writers of the 1950s whose work expressed bitterness and disillusionment with society. Common to their work is an antihero who rebels against a corrupt social order and strives for personal integrity.

Anthropomorphism: The presentation of animals or objects in human shape or with human characteristics. The term is derived from the Greek word for "human form."

Antimasque: See *Masque*

Antithesis: The antithesis of something is its direct opposite. In literature, the use of antithesis as a figure of speech results in two statements that show a contrast through the balancing of two opposite ideas. Technically, it is the second portion of the statement that is defined as the "antithesis"; the first portion is the "thesis."

Apocrypha: Writings tentatively attributed to an author but not proven or universally accepted to be their works. The term was originally applied to certain books of the Bible that were not considered inspired and so were not included in the "sacred canon."

Apollonian and Dionysian: The two impulses believed to guide authors of dramatic tragedy. The Apollonian impulse is named after Apollo, the Greek god of light and beauty and the symbol of intellectual order. The Dionysian impulse is named after Dionysus, the Greek god of wine and the symbol of the unrestrained forces of nature. The Apollonian impulse is to create a rational, harmonious world, while the Dionysian is to express the irrational forces of personality.

Apostrophe: A statement, question, or request addressed to an inanimate object or concept or to a nonexistent or absent person.

Archetype: The word archetype is commonly used to describe an original pattern or model from which all other things of the same kind are made. This term was introduced to literary criticism from the psychology of Carl Jung. It expresses Jung's theory that behind every person's "unconscious," or repressed memories of the past, lies the "collective unconscious" of the human race: memories of the countless typical experiences of our ancestors. These memories are said to prompt illogical associations that trigger powerful emotions in the reader. Often, the emotional process is primitive, even primordial. Archetypes are the literary images that grow out of the "collective unconscious." They appear in literature as incidents and plots that repeat basic patterns of life. They may also appear as stereotyped characters.

Argument: The argument of a work is the author's subject matter or principal idea.

Art for Art's Sake: See *Aestheticism*

Assonance: The repetition of similar vowel sounds in poetry.

Audience: The people for whom a piece of literature is written. Authors usually write with a certain audience in mind, for example, children, members of a religious or ethnic group, or colleagues in a professional field. The term "audience" also applies to the people who gather to see or hear any performance, including plays, poetry readings, speeches, and concerts.

Automatic Writing: Writing carried out without a preconceived plan in an effort to capture every random thought. Authors who engage in automatic writing typically do not revise their work, preferring instead to preserve the revealed truth and beauty of spontaneous expression.

Avant-garde: A French term meaning "vanguard." It is used in literary criticism to describe new writing that rejects traditional approaches to literature in favor of innovations in style or content.

B

Ballad: A short poem that tells a simple story and has a repeated refrain. Ballads were originally intended to be sung. Early ballads, known as folk ballads, were passed down through generations, so their authors are often unknown. Later ballads composed by known authors are called literary ballads.

Baroque: A term used in literary criticism to describe literature that is complex or ornate in style or diction. Baroque works typically express tension, anxiety, and violent emotion. The term "Baroque Age" designates a period in Western European literature beginning in the late sixteenth century and ending about one hundred years later.

Works of this period often mirror the qualities of works more generally associated with the label "baroque" and sometimes feature elaborate conceits.

Baroque Age: See *Baroque*

Baroque Period: See *Baroque*

Beat Generation: See *Beat Movement*

Beat Movement: A period featuring a group of American poets and novelists of the 1950s and 1960s—including Jack Kerouac, Allen Ginsberg, Gregory Corso, William S. Burroughs, and Lawrence Ferlinghetti—who rejected established social and literary values. Using such techniques as stream-of-consciousness writing and jazz-influenced free verse and focusing on unusual or abnormal states of mind—generated by religious ecstasy or the use of drugs—the Beat writers aimed to create works that were unconventional in both form and subject matter.

Beat Poets: See *Beat Movement*

Beats, The: See *Beat Movement*

Belles-lettres: A French term meaning "fine letters" or "beautiful writing." It is often used as a synonym for literature, typically referring to imaginative and artistic rather than scientific or expository writing. Current usage sometimes restricts the meaning to light or humorous writing and appreciative essays about literature.

Black Aesthetic Movement: A period of artistic and literary development among African Americans in the 1960s and early 1970s. This was the first major African American artistic movement since the Harlem Renaissance and was closely paralleled by the civil rights and black power movements. The black aesthetic writers attempted to produce works of art that would be meaningful to the black masses. Key figures in black aesthetics included one of its founders, poet and playwright Amiri Baraka, formerly known as LeRoi Jones; poet and essayist Haki R. Madhubuti, formerly Don L. Lee; poet and playwright Sonia Sanchez; and dramatist Ed Bullins.

Black Arts Movement: See *Black Aesthetic Movement*

Black Comedy: See *Black Humor*

Black Humor: Writing that places grotesque elements side by side with humorous ones in an attempt to shock the reader, forcing him or her to laugh at the horrifying reality of a disordered world.

Black Mountain School: Black Mountain College and three of its instructors—Robert Creeley, Robert Duncan, and Charles Olson—were all influential in projective verse. Today poets working in projective verse are referred to as members of the Black Mountain school.

Blank Verse: Loosely, any unrhymed poetry, but more generally, unrhymed iambic pentameter verse (composed of lines of five two-syllable feet with the first syllable accented, the second unaccented). Blank verse has been used by poets since the Renaissance for its flexibility and its graceful, dignified tone.

Bloomsbury Group: A group of English writers, artists, and intellectuals who held informal artistic and philosophical discussions in Bloomsbury, a district of London, from around 1907 to the early 1930s. The Bloomsbury Group held no uniform philosophical beliefs but did commonly express an aversion to moral prudery and a desire for greater social tolerance.

Bon Mot: A French term meaning "good word." A *bon mot* is a witty remark or clever observation.

Breath Verse: See *Projective Verse*

Burlesque: Any literary work that uses exaggeration to make its subject appear ridiculous, either by treating a trivial subject with profound seriousness or by treating a dignified subject frivolously. The word "burlesque" may also be used as an adjective, as in "burlesque show," to mean "striptease act."

C

Cadence: The natural rhythm of language caused by the alternation of accented and unaccented syllables. Much modern poetry—notably free verse—deliberately manipulates cadence to create complex rhythmic effects.

Caesura: A pause in a line of poetry, usually occurring near the middle. It typically corresponds to a break in the natural rhythm or sense of the line but is sometimes shifted to create special meanings or rhythmic effects.

Canzone: A short Italian or Provencal lyric poem, commonly about love and often set to music. The *canzone* has no set form but typically contains five or six stanzas made up of seven to twenty lines of eleven syllables each. A shorter, five- to ten-line "envoy," or concluding stanza, completes the poem.

Carpe Diem: A Latin term meaning "seize the day." This is a traditional theme of poetry, especially lyrics. A *carpe diem* poem advises the reader or the person it addresses to live for today and enjoy the pleasures of the moment.

Catharsis: The release or purging of unwanted emotions—specifically fear and pity—brought about by exposure to art. The term was first used by the Greek philosopher Aristotle in his *Poetics* to refer to the desired effect of tragedy on spectators.

Celtic Renaissance: A period of Irish literary and cultural history at the end of the nineteenth century. Followers of the movement aimed to create a romantic vision of Celtic myth and legend. The most significant works of the Celtic Renaissance typically present a dreamy, unreal world, usually in reaction against the reality of contemporary problems.

Celtic Twilight: See *Celtic Renaissance*

Character: Broadly speaking, a person in a literary work. The actions of characters are what constitute the plot of a story, novel, or poem. There are numerous types of characters, ranging from simple, stereotypical figures to intricate, multifaceted ones. In the techniques of anthropomorphism and personification, animals—and even places or things—can assume aspects of character. "Characterization" is the process by which an author creates vivid, believable characters in a work of art. This may be done in a variety of ways, including (1) direct description of the character by the narrator; (2) the direct presentation of the speech, thoughts, or actions of the character; and (3) the responses of other characters to the character. The term "character" also refers to a form originated by the ancient Greek writer Theophrastus that later became popular in the seventeenth and eighteenth centuries. It is a short essay or sketch of a person who prominently displays a specific attribute or quality, such as miserliness or ambition.

Characterization: See *Character*

Classical: In its strictest definition in literary criticism, classicism refers to works of ancient Greek or Roman literature. The term may also be used to describe a literary work of recognized importance (a "classic") from any time period or literature that exhibits the traits of classicism.

Classicism: A term used in literary criticism to describe critical doctrines that have their roots in ancient Greek and Roman literature, philosophy, and art. Works associated with classicism typically exhibit restraint on the part of the author, unity of design and purpose, clarity, simplicity, logical organization, and respect for tradition.

Colloquialism: A word, phrase, or form of pronunciation that is acceptable in casual conversation but not in formal, written communication. It is considered more acceptable than slang.

Complaint: A lyric poem, popular in the Renaissance, in which the speaker expresses sorrow about his or her condition. Typically, the speaker's sadness is caused by an unresponsive lover, but some complaints cite other sources of unhappiness, such as poverty or fate.

Conceit: A clever and fanciful metaphor, usually expressed through elaborate and extended comparison, that presents a striking parallel between two seemingly dissimilar things—for example, elaborately comparing a beautiful woman to an object like a garden or the sun. The conceit was a popular device throughout the Elizabethan Age and Baroque Age and was the principal technique of the seventeenth-century English metaphysical poets. This usage of the word conceit is unrelated to the best-known definition of conceit as an arrogant attitude or behavior.

Concrete: Concrete is the opposite of abstract, and refers to a thing that actually exists or a description that allows the reader to experience an object or concept with the senses.

Concrete Poetry: Poetry in which visual elements play a large part in the poetic effect. Punctuation marks, letters, or words are arranged on a page to form a visual design: a cross, for example, or a bumblebee.

Confessional Poetry: A form of poetry in which the poet reveals very personal, intimate, sometimes shocking information about himself or herself.

Connotation: The impression that a word gives beyond its defined meaning. Connotations may be universally understood or may be significant only to a certain group.

Consonance: Consonance occurs in poetry when words appearing at the ends of two or more verses have similar final consonant sounds but have final vowel sounds that differ, as with "stuff" and "off."

Convention: Any widely accepted literary device, style, or form.

Corrido: A Mexican ballad.

Couplet: Two lines of poetry with the same rhyme and meter, often expressing a complete and self-contained thought.

Criticism: The systematic study and evaluation of literary works, usually based on a specific method or set of principles. An important part of literary studies since ancient times, the practice of criticism has given rise to numerous theories, methods, and "schools," sometimes producing conflicting, even contradictory, interpretations of literature in general as well as of individual works. Even such basic issues as what constitutes a poem or a novel have been the subject of much criticism over the centuries.

D

Dactyl: See *Foot*

Dadaism: A protest movement in art and literature founded by Tristan Tzara in 1916. Followers of the movement expressed their outrage at the destruction brought about by World War I by revolting against numerous forms of social convention. The Dadaists presented works marked by calculated madness and flamboyant nonsense. They stressed total freedom of expression, commonly through primitive displays of emotion and illogical, often senseless, poetry. The movement ended shortly after the war, when it was replaced by surrealism.

Decadent: See *Decadents*

Decadents: The followers of a nineteenth-century literary movement that had its beginnings in French aestheticism. Decadent literature displays a fascination with perverse and morbid states; a search for novelty and sensation—the "new thrill"; a preoccupation with mysticism; and a belief in the senselessness of human existence. The movement is closely associated with the doctrine Art for Art's Sake. The term "decadence" is sometimes used to denote a decline in the quality of art or literature following a period of greatness.

Deconstruction: A method of literary criticism developed by Jacques Derrida and characterized by multiple conflicting interpretations of a given work. Deconstructionists consider the impact of the language of a work and suggest that the true meaning of the work is not necessarily the meaning that the author intended.

Deduction: The process of reaching a conclusion through reasoning from general premises to a specific premise.

Denotation: The definition of a word, apart from the impressions or feelings it creates in the reader.

Diction: The selection and arrangement of words in a literary work. Either or both may vary depending on the desired effect. There are four general types of diction: "formal," used in scholarly or lofty writing; "informal," used in relaxed but educated conversation; "colloquial," used in everyday speech; and "slang," containing newly coined words and other terms not accepted in formal usage.

Didactic: A term used to describe works of literature that aim to teach some moral, religious, political, or practical lesson. Although didactic elements are often found in artistically pleasing works, the term "didactic" usually refers to literature in which the message is more important than the form. The term may also be used to criticize a work that the critic finds "overly didactic," that is, heavy-handed in its delivery of a lesson.

Dimeter: See *Meter*

Dionysian: See *Apollonian and Dionysian*

Discordia concours: A Latin phrase meaning "discord in harmony." The term was coined by the eighteenth-century English writer Samuel Johnson to describe "a combination of dissimilar images or discovery of occult resemblances in things apparently unlike." Johnson created the expression by reversing a phrase by the Latin poet Horace.

Dissonance: A combination of harsh or jarring sounds, especially in poetry. Although such combinations may be accidental, poets sometimes intentionally make them to achieve particular effects. Dissonance is also sometimes used to refer to close but not identical rhymes. When this is the case, the word functions as a synonym for consonance.

Double Entendre: A corruption of a French phrase meaning "double meaning." The term is used to indicate a word or phrase that is deliberately ambiguous, especially when one of the meanings is risque or improper.

Draft: Any preliminary version of a written work. An author may write dozens of drafts which are revised to form the final work, or he or she may write only one, with few or no revisions.

Dramatic Monologue: See *Monologue*

Dramatic Poetry: Any lyric work that employs elements of drama such as dialogue, conflict, or characterization, but excluding works that are intended for stage presentation.

Dream Allegory: See *Dream Vision*

Dream Vision: A literary convention, chiefly of the Middle Ages. In a dream vision a story is presented as a literal dream of the narrator. This device was commonly used to teach moral and religious lessons.

E

Eclogue: In classical literature, a poem featuring rural themes and structured as a dialogue among shepherds. Eclogues often took specific poetic forms, such as elegies or love poems. Some were written as the soliloquy of a shepherd. In later centuries, "eclogue" came to refer to any poem that was in the pastoral tradition or that had a dialogue or monologue structure.

Edwardian: Describes cultural conventions identified with the period of the reign of Edward VII of England (1901–1910). Writers of the Edwardian Age typically displayed a strong reaction against the propriety and conservatism of the Victorian Age. Their work often exhibits distrust of authority in religion, politics, and art and expresses strong doubts about the soundness of conventional values.

Edwardian Age: See *Edwardian*

Electra Complex: A daughter's amorous obsession with her father.

Elegy: A lyric poem that laments the death of a person or the eventual death of all people. In a conventional elegy, set in a classical world, the poet and subject are spoken of as shepherds. In modern criticism, the word elegy is often used to refer to a poem that is melancholy or mournfully contemplative.

Elizabethan Age: A period of great economic growth, religious controversy, and nationalism closely associated with the reign of Elizabeth I of England (1558–1603). The Elizabethan Age is considered a part of the general renaissance—that is, the flowering of arts and literature—that took place in Europe during the fourteenth through sixteenth centuries. The era is considered the golden age of English literature. The most important dramas in English and a great deal of lyric poetry were produced during this period, and modern English criticism began around this time.

Empathy: A sense of shared experience, including emotional and physical feelings, with someone or something other than oneself. Empathy is often used to describe the response of a reader to a literary character.

English Sonnet: See *Sonnet*

Enjambment: The running over of the sense and structure of a line of verse or a couplet into the following verse or couplet.

Enlightenment, The: An eighteenth-century philosophical movement. It began in France but had a wide impact throughout Europe and America. Thinkers of the Enlightenment valued reason and believed that both the individual and society could achieve a state of perfection. Corresponding to this essentially humanist vision was a resistance to religious authority.

Epic: A long narrative poem about the adventures of a hero of great historic or legendary importance. The setting is vast and the action is often given cosmic significance through the intervention of supernatural forces such as gods, angels, or demons. Epics are typically written in a classical style of grand simplicity with elaborate metaphors and allusions that enhance the symbolic importance of a hero's adventures.

Epic Simile: See *Homeric Simile*

Epigram: A saying that makes the speaker's point quickly and concisely.

Epilogue: A concluding statement or section of a literary work. In dramas, particularly those of the seventeenth and eighteenth centuries, the epilogue is a closing speech, often in verse, delivered by an actor at the end of a play and spoken directly to the audience.

Epiphany: A sudden revelation of truth inspired by a seemingly trivial incident.

Epitaph: An inscription on a tomb or tombstone, or a verse written on the occasion of a person's death. Epitaphs may be serious or humorous.

Epithalamion: A song or poem written to honor and commemorate a marriage ceremony.

Epithalamium: See *Epithalamion*

Epithet: A word or phrase, often disparaging or abusive, that expresses a character trait of someone or something.

Erziehungsroman: See *Bildungsroman*

Essay: A prose composition with a focused subject of discussion. The term was coined by Michel de Montaigne to describe his 1580 collection of brief, informal reflections on himself and on various topics relating to human nature. An essay can also be a long, systematic discourse.

Existentialism: A predominantly twentieth-century philosophy concerned with the nature and perception of human existence. There are two major strains of existentialist thought: atheistic and Christian. Followers of atheistic existentialism believe that the individual is alone in a godless universe and that the basic human condition is one of suffering and loneliness. Nevertheless, because there are no fixed values, individuals can create their own characters—indeed, they can shape themselves—through the exercise of free will. The atheistic strain culminates in and is popularly associated with the works of Jean-Paul Sartre. The Christian existentialists, on the other hand, believe that only in God may people find freedom from life's anguish. The two strains hold certain beliefs in common: that existence cannot be fully understood or described through empirical effort; that anguish is a universal element of life; that individuals must bear responsibility for their actions; and that there is no common standard of behavior or perception for religious and ethical matters.

Expatriates: See *Expatriatism*

Expatriatism: The practice of leaving one's country to live for an extended period in another country.

Exposition: Writing intended to explain the nature of an idea, thing, or theme. Expository writing is often combined with description, narration, or argument. In dramatic writing, the exposition is the introductory material which presents the characters, setting, and tone of the play.

Expressionism: An indistinct literary term, originally used to describe an early twentieth-century school of German painting. The term applies to almost any mode of unconventional, highly subjective writing that distorts reality in some way.

Extended Monologue: See *Monologue*

F

Feet: See *Foot*

Feminine Rhyme: See *Rhyme*

Fiction: Any story that is the product of imagination rather than a documentation of fact. Characters and events in such narratives may be based in real life but their ultimate form and configuration is a creation of the author.

Figurative Language: A technique in writing in which the author temporarily interrupts the order, construction, or meaning of the writing for a particular effect. This interruption takes the form of one or more figures of speech such as hyperbole, irony, or simile. Figurative language is the opposite of literal language, in which every word is truthful, accurate, and free of exaggeration or embellishment.

Figures of Speech: Writing that differs from customary conventions for construction, meaning, order, or significance for the purpose of a special meaning or effect. There are two major types of figures of speech: rhetorical figures, which do not make changes in the meaning of the words; and tropes, which do.

Fin de siecle: A French term meaning "end of the century." The term is used to denote the last decade of the nineteenth century, a transition period when

writers and other artists abandoned old conventions and looked for new techniques and objectives.

First Person: See *Point of View*

Folk Ballad: See *Ballad*

Folklore: Traditions and myths preserved in a culture or group of people. Typically, these are passed on by word of mouth in various forms—such as legends, songs, and proverbs—or preserved in customs and ceremonies. This term was first used by W. J. Thoms in 1846.

Folktale: A story originating in oral tradition. Folktales fall into a variety of categories, including legends, ghost stories, fairy tales, fables, and anecdotes based on historical figures and events.

Foot: The smallest unit of rhythm in a line of poetry. In English-language poetry, a foot is typically one accented syllable combined with one or two unaccented syllables.

Form: The pattern or construction of a work which identifies its genre and distinguishes it from other genres.

Formalism: In literary criticism, the belief that literature should follow prescribed rules of construction, such as those that govern the sonnet form.

Fourteener Meter: See *Meter*

Free Verse: Poetry that lacks regular metrical and rhyme patterns but that tries to capture the cadences of everyday speech. The form allows a poet to exploit a variety of rhythmical effects within a single poem.

Futurism: A flamboyant literary and artistic movement that developed in France, Italy, and Russia from 1908 through the 1920s. Futurist theater and poetry abandoned traditional literary forms. In their place, followers of the movement attempted to achieve total freedom of expression through bizarre imagery and deformed or newly invented words. The Futurists were self-consciously modern artists who attempted to incorporate the appearances and sounds of modern life into their work.

G

Genre: A category of literary work. In critical theory, genre may refer to both the content of a given work—tragedy, comedy, pastoral—and to its form, such as poetry, novel, or drama.

Genteel Tradition: A term coined by critic George Santayana to describe the literary practice of certain late nineteenth-century American writers, especially New Englanders. Followers of the Genteel

Tradition emphasized conventionality in social, religious, moral, and literary standards.

Georgian Age: See *Georgian Poets*

Georgian Period: See *Georgian Poets*

Georgian Poets: A loose grouping of English poets during the years 1912–1922. The Georgians reacted against certain literary schools and practices, especially Victorian wordiness, turn-of-the-century aestheticism, and contemporary urban realism. In their place, the Georgians embraced the nineteenth-century poetic practices of William Wordsworth and the other Lake Poets.

Georgic: A poem about farming and the farmer's way of life, named from Virgil's *Georgics*.

Gilded Age: A period in American history during the 1870s characterized by political corruption and materialism. A number of important novels of social and political criticism were written during this time.

Gothic: See *Gothicism*

Gothicism: In literary criticism, works characterized by a taste for the medieval or morbidly attractive. A gothic novel prominently features elements of horror, the supernatural, gloom, and violence: clanking chains, terror, charnel houses, ghosts, medieval castles, and mysteriously slamming doors. The term "gothic novel" is also applied to novels that lack elements of the traditional Gothic setting but that create a similar atmosphere of terror or dread.

Graveyard School: A group of eighteenth-century English poets who wrote long, picturesque meditations on death. Their works were designed to cause the reader to ponder immortality.

Great Chain of Being: The belief that all things and creatures in nature are organized in a hierarchy from inanimate objects at the bottom to God at the top. This system of belief was popular in the seventeenth and eighteenth centuries.

Grotesque: In literary criticism, the subject matter of a work or a style of expression characterized by exaggeration, deformity, freakishness, and disorder. The grotesque often includes an element of comic absurdity.

H

Haiku: The shortest form of Japanese poetry, constructed in three lines of five, seven, and five syllables respectively. The message of a *haiku* poem usually centers on some aspect of spirituality and provokes an emotional response in the reader.

Half Rhyme: See *Consonance*

Harlem Renaissance: The Harlem Renaissance of the 1920s is generally considered the first significant movement of black writers and artists in the United States. During this period, new and established black writers published more fiction and poetry than ever before, the first influential black literary journals were established, and black authors and artists received their first widespread recognition and serious critical appraisal. Among the major writers associated with this period are Claude McKay, Jean Toomer, Countee Cullen, Langston Hughes, Arna Bontemps, Nella Larsen, and Zora Neale Hurston.

Hellenism: Imitation of ancient Greek thought or styles. Also, an approach to life that focuses on the growth and development of the intellect. "Hellenism" is sometimes used to refer to the belief that reason can be applied to examine all human experience.

Heptameter: See *Meter*

Hero/Heroine: The principal sympathetic character (male or female) in a literary work. Heroes and heroines typically exhibit admirable traits: idealism, courage, and integrity, for example.

Heroic Couplet: A rhyming couplet written in iambic pentameter (a verse with five iambic feet).

Heroic Line: The meter and length of a line of verse in epic or heroic poetry. This varies by language and time period.

Heroine: See *Hero/Heroine*

Hexameter: See *Meter*

Historical Criticism: The study of a work based on its impact on the world of the time period in which it was written.

Hokku: See *Haiku*

Holocaust: See *Holocaust Literature*

Holocaust Literature: Literature influenced by or written about the Holocaust of World War II. Such literature includes true stories of survival in concentration camps, escape, and life after the war, as well as fictional works and poetry.

Homeric Simile: An elaborate, detailed comparison written as a simile many lines in length.

Horatian Satire: See *Satire*

Humanism: A philosophy that places faith in the dignity of humankind and rejects the medieval perception of the individual as a weak, fallen creature. "Humanists" typically believe in the perfectibility of human nature and view reason and education as the means to that end.

Humors: Mentions of the humors refer to the ancient Greek theory that a person's health and personality were determined by the balance of four basic fluids in the body: blood, phlegm, yellow bile, and black bile. A dominance of any fluid would cause extremes in behavior. An excess of blood created a sanguine person who was joyful, aggressive, and passionate; a phlegmatic person was shy, fearful, and sluggish; too much yellow bile led to a choleric temperament characterized by impatience, anger, bitterness, and stubbornness; and excessive black bile created melancholy, a state of laziness, gluttony, and lack of motivation.

Humours: See *Humors*

Hyperbole: In literary criticism, deliberate exaggeration used to achieve an effect.

I

Iamb: See *Foot*

Idiom: A word construction or verbal expression closely associated with a given language.

Image: A concrete representation of an object or sensory experience. Typically, such a representation helps evoke the feelings associated with the object or experience itself. Images are either "literal" or "figurative." Literal images are especially concrete and involve little or no extension of the obvious meaning of the words used to express them. Figurative images do not follow the literal meaning of the words exactly. Images in literature are usually visual, but the term "image" can also refer to the representation of any sensory experience.

Imagery: The array of images in a literary work. Also, figurative language.

Imagism: An English and American poetry movement that flourished between 1908 and 1917. The Imagists used precise, clearly presented images in their works. They also used common, everyday speech and aimed for conciseness, concrete imagery, and the creation of new rhythms.

In medias res: A Latin term meaning "in the middle of things." It refers to the technique of beginning a story at its midpoint and then using various flashback devices to reveal previous action.

Induction: The process of reaching a conclusion by reasoning from specific premises to form a general premise. Also, an introductory portion of a work of literature, especially a play.

Intentional Fallacy: The belief that judgments of a literary work based solely on an author's stated or implied intentions are false and misleading. Critics who believe in the concept of the intentional fallacy typically argue that the work itself is sufficient matter for interpretation, even though they may concede that an author's statement of purpose can be useful.

Interior Monologue: A narrative technique in which characters' thoughts are revealed in a way that appears to be uncontrolled by the author. The interior monologue typically aims to reveal the inner self of a character. It portrays emotional experiences as they occur at both a conscious and unconscious level. Images are often used to represent sensations or emotions.

Internal Rhyme: Rhyme that occurs within a single line of verse.

Irish Literary Renaissance: A late nineteenth- and early twentieth-century movement in Irish literature. Members of the movement aimed to reduce the influence of British culture in Ireland and create an Irish national literature.

Irony: In literary criticism, the effect of language in which the intended meaning is the opposite of what is stated.

Italian Sonnet: See *Sonnet*

J

Jacobean Age: The period of the reign of James I of England (1603–1625). The early literature of this period reflected the worldview of the Elizabethan Age, but a darker, more cynical attitude steadily grew in the art and literature of the Jacobean Age. This was an important time for English drama and poetry.

Jargon: Language that is used or understood only by a select group of people. Jargon may refer to terminology used in a certain profession, such as computer jargon, or it may refer to any nonsensical language that is not understood by most people.

Journalism: Writing intended for publication in a newspaper or magazine, or for broadcast on a radio or television program featuring news, sports, entertainment, or other timely material.

K

Knickerbocker Group: A somewhat indistinct group of New York writers of the first half of the nineteenth century. Members of the group were linked only by location and a common theme: New York life.

Kunstlerroman: See *Bildungsroman*

L

Lais: See *Lay*

Lake Poets: See *Lake School*

Lake School: These poets all lived in the Lake District of England at the turn of the nineteenth century. As a group, they followed no single "school" of thought or literary practice, although their works were uniformly disparaged by the *Edinburgh Review*.

Lay: A song or simple narrative poem. The form originated in medieval France. Early French *lais* were often based on the Celtic legends and other tales sung by Breton minstrels—thus the name of the "Breton lay." In fourteenth-century England, the term "lay" was used to describe short narratives written in imitation of the Breton lays.

Leitmotiv: See *Motif*

Literal Language: An author uses literal language when he or she writes without exaggerating or embellishing the subject matter and without any tools of figurative language.

Literary Ballad: See *Ballad*

Literature: Literature is broadly defined as any written or spoken material, but the term most often refers to creative works.

Lost Generation: A term first used by Gertrude Stein to describe the post-World War I generation of American writers: men and women haunted by a sense of betrayal and emptiness brought about by the destructiveness of the war.

Lyric Poetry: A poem expressing the subjective feelings and personal emotions of the poet. Such poetry is melodic, since it was originally accompanied by a lyre in recitals. Most Western poetry in the twentieth century may be classified as lyrical.

M

Mannerism: Exaggerated, artificial adherence to a literary manner or style. Also, a popular style of the visual arts of late sixteenth-century Europe that was marked by elongation of the human form and by intentional spatial distortion. Literary works that are self-consciously high-toned and artistic are often said to be "mannered."

Masculine Rhyme: See *Rhyme*

Measure: The foot, verse, or time sequence used in a literary work, especially a poem. Measure is often used somewhat incorrectly as a synonym for meter.

Metaphor: A figure of speech that expresses an idea through the image of another object. Metaphors suggest the essence of the first object by identifying it with certain qualities of the second object.

Metaphysical Conceit: See *Conceit*

Metaphysical Poetry: The body of poetry produced by a group of seventeenth-century English writers called the "Metaphysical Poets." The group includes John Donne and Andrew Marvell. The Metaphysical Poets made use of everyday speech, intellectual analysis, and unique imagery. They aimed to portray the ordinary conflicts and contradictions of life. Their poems often took the form of an argument, and many of them emphasize physical and religious love as well as the fleeting nature of life. Elaborate conceits are typical in metaphysical poetry.

Metaphysical Poets: See *Metaphysical Poetry*

Meter: In literary criticism, the repetition of sound patterns that creates a rhythm in poetry. The patterns are based on the number of syllables and the presence and absence of accents. The unit of rhythm in a line is called a foot. Types of meter are classified according to the number of feet in a line. These are the standard English lines: Monometer, one foot; Dimeter, two feet; Trimeter, three feet; Tetrameter, four feet; Pentameter, five feet; Hexameter, six feet (also called the Alexandrine); Heptameter, seven feet (also called the "Fourteener" when the feet are iambic).

Modernism: Modern literary practices. Also, the principles of a literary school that lasted from roughly the beginning of the twentieth century until the end of World War II. Modernism is defined by its rejection of the literary conventions of the nineteenth century and by its opposition to conventional morality, taste, traditions, and economic values.

Monologue: A composition, written or oral, by a single individual. More specifically, a speech given by a single individual in a drama or other public entertainment. It has no set length, although it is usually several or more lines long.

Monometer: See *Meter*

Mood: The prevailing emotions of a work or of the author in his or her creation of the work. The mood of a work is not always what might be expected based on its subject matter.

Motif: A theme, character type, image, metaphor, or other verbal element that recurs throughout a single work of literature or occurs in a number of different works over a period of time.

Motiv: See *Motif*

Muckrakers: An early twentieth-century group of American writers. Typically, their works exposed the wrongdoings of big business and government in the United States.

Muses: Nine Greek mythological goddesses, the daughters of Zeus and Mnemosyne (Memory). Each muse patronized a specific area of the liberal arts and sciences. Calliope presided over epic poetry, Clio over history, Erato over love poetry, Euterpe over music or lyric poetry, Melpomene over tragedy, Polyhymnia over hymns to the gods, Terpsichore over dance, Thalia over comedy, and Urania over astronomy. Poets and writers traditionally made appeals to the Muses for inspiration in their work.

Myth: An anonymous tale emerging from the traditional beliefs of a culture or social unit. Myths use supernatural explanations for natural phenomena. They may also explain cosmic issues like creation and death. Collections of myths, known as mythologies, are common to all cultures and nations, but the best-known myths belong to the Norse, Roman, and Greek mythologies.

N

Narration: The telling of a series of events, real or invented. A narration may be either a simple narrative, in which the events are recounted chronologically, or a narrative with a plot, in which the account is given in a style reflecting the author's artistic concept of the story. Narration is sometimes used as a synonym for "storyline."

Narrative: A verse or prose accounting of an event or sequence of events, real or invented. The term is also used as an adjective in the sense "method of narration." For example, in literary criticism, the expression "narrative technique" usually refers to the way the author structures and presents his or her story.

Narrative Poetry: A nondramatic poem in which the author tells a story. Such poems may be of any length or level of complexity.

Narrator: The teller of a story. The narrator may be the author or a character in the story through whom the author speaks.

Naturalism: A literary movement of the late nineteenth and early twentieth centuries. The movement's major theorist, French novelist Emile Zola, envisioned a type of fiction that would examine human life with the objectivity of scientific inquiry. The Naturalists typically viewed human beings as either the products of "biological determinism," ruled by hereditary instincts and engaged in an endless struggle for survival, or as the products of "socioeconomic determinism," ruled by social and economic forces beyond their control. In their works, the Naturalists generally ignored the highest levels of society and focused on degradation: poverty, alcoholism, prostitution, insanity, and disease.

Negritude: A literary movement based on the concept of a shared cultural bond on the part of black Africans, wherever they may be in the world. It traces its origins to the former French colonies of Africa and the Caribbean. Negritude poets, novelists, and essayists generally stress four points in their writings: One, black alienation from traditional African culture can lead to feelings of inferiority. Two, European colonialism and Western education should be resisted. Three, black Africans should seek to affirm and define their own identity. Four, African culture can and should be reclaimed. Many Negritude writers also claim that blacks can make unique contributions to the world, based on a heightened appreciation of nature, rhythm, and human emotions—aspects of life they say are not so highly valued in the materialistic and rationalistic West.

Negro Renaissance: See *Harlem Renaissance*

Neoclassical Period: See *Neoclassicism*

Neoclassicism: In literary criticism, this term refers to the revival of the attitudes and styles of expression of classical literature. It is generally used to describe a period in European history beginning in the late seventeenth century and lasting until about 1800. In its purest form, Neoclassicism marked a return to order, proportion, restraint, logic, accuracy, and decorum. In England, where Neoclassicism perhaps was most popular, it reflected the influence of seventeenth-century French writers, especially dramatists. Neoclassical writers typically reacted against the intensity and enthusiasm of the Renaissance period. They wrote works that appealed to the intellect, using elevated language and classical literary forms such as satire and the ode. Neoclassical works were often governed by the classical goal of instruction.

Neoclassicists: See *Neoclassicism*

New Criticism: A movement in literary criticism, dating from the late 1920s, that stressed close textual analysis in the interpretation of works of literature. The New Critics saw little merit in historical and biographical analysis. Rather, they aimed to examine the text alone, free from the question of how external events—biographical or otherwise—may have helped shape it.

New Journalism: A type of writing in which the journalist presents factual information in a form usually used in fiction. New journalism emphasizes description, narration, and character development to bring readers closer to the human element of the story, and is often used in personality profiles and in-depth feature articles. It is not compatible with "straight" or "hard" newswriting, which is generally composed in a brief, fact-based style.

New Journalists: See *New Journalism*

New Negro Movement: See *Harlem Renaissance*

Noble Savage: The idea that primitive man is noble and good but becomes evil and corrupted as he becomes civilized. The concept of the noble savage originated in the Renaissance period but is more closely identified with such later writers as Jean-Jacques Rousseau and Aphra Behn.

O

Objective Correlative: An outward set of objects, a situation, or a chain of events corresponding to an inward experience and evoking this experience in the reader. The term frequently appears in modern criticism in discussions of authors' intended effects on the emotional responses of readers.

Objectivity: A quality in writing characterized by the absence of the author's opinion or feeling about the subject matter. Objectivity is an important factor in criticism.

Occasional Verse: Poetry written on the occasion of a significant historical or personal event. *Vers de societe* is sometimes called occasional verse although it is of a less serious nature.

Octave: A poem or stanza composed of eight lines. The term octave most often represents the first eight lines of a Petrarchan sonnet.

Ode: Name given to an extended lyric poem characterized by exalted emotion and dignified style. An ode usually concerns a single, serious theme. Most odes, but not all, are addressed to an object or individual. Odes are distinguished from other lyric poetic forms by their complex rhythmic and stanzaic patterns.

Oedipus Complex: A son's amorous obsession with his mother. The phrase is derived from the story of the ancient Theban hero Oedipus, who un-

knowingly killed his father and married his mother.

Omniscience: See *Point of View*

Onomatopoeia: The use of words whose sounds express or suggest their meaning. In its simplest sense, onomatopoeia may be represented by words that mimic the sounds they denote such as "hiss" or "meow." At a more subtle level, the pattern and rhythm of sounds and rhymes of a line or poem may be onomatopoeic.

Oral Tradition: See *Oral Transmission*

Oral Transmission: A process by which songs, ballads, folklore, and other material are transmitted by word of mouth. The tradition of oral transmission predates the written record systems of literate society. Oral transmission preserves material sometimes over generations, although often with variations. Memory plays a large part in the recitation and preservation of orally transmitted material.

*Ottava Rima***:** An eight-line stanza of poetry composed in iambic pentameter (a five-foot line in which each foot consists of an unaccented syllable followed by an accented syllable), following the *abababcc* rhyme scheme.

Oxymoron: A phrase combining two contradictory terms. Oxymorons may be intentional or unintentional.

P

Pantheism: The idea that all things are both a manifestation or revelation of God and a part of God at the same time. Pantheism was a common attitude in the early societies of Egypt, India, and Greece—the term derives from the Greek *pan* meaning "all" and *theos* meaning "deity." It later became a significant part of the Christian faith.

Parable: A story intended to teach a moral lesson or answer an ethical question.

Paradox: A statement that appears illogical or contradictory at first, but may actually point to an underlying truth.

Parallelism: A method of comparison of two ideas in which each is developed in the same grammatical structure.

Parnassianism: A mid nineteenth-century movement in French literature. Followers of the movement stressed adherence to well-defined artistic forms as a reaction against the often chaotic expression of the artist's ego that dominated the work of the Romantics. The Parnassians also rejected the moral, ethical, and social themes exhibited in the works of French Romantics such as Victor Hugo. The aesthetic doctrines of the Parnassians strongly influenced the later symbolist and decadent movements.

Parody: In literary criticism, this term refers to an imitation of a serious literary work or the signature style of a particular author in a ridiculous manner. A typical parody adopts the style of the original and applies it to an inappropriate subject for humorous effect. Parody is a form of satire and could be considered the literary equivalent of a caricature or cartoon.

Pastoral: A term derived from the Latin word "pastor," meaning shepherd. A pastoral is a literary composition on a rural theme. The conventions of the pastoral were originated by the third-century Greek poet Theocritus, who wrote about the experiences, love affairs, and pastimes of Sicilian shepherds. In a pastoral, characters and language of a courtly nature are often placed in a simple setting. The term pastoral is also used to classify dramas, elegies, and lyrics that exhibit the use of country settings and shepherd characters.

Pathetic Fallacy: A term coined by English critic John Ruskin to identify writing that falsely endows nonhuman things with human intentions and feelings, such as "angry clouds" and "sad trees."

Pen Name: See *Pseudonym*

Pentameter: See *Meter*

Persona: A Latin term meaning "mask." *Personae* are the characters in a fictional work of literature. The *persona* generally functions as a mask through which the author tells a story in a voice other than his or her own. A *persona* is usually either a character in a story who acts as a narrator or an "implied author," a voice created by the author to act as the narrator for himself or herself.

Personae: See *Persona*

Personal Point of View: See *Point of View*

Personification: A figure of speech that gives human qualities to abstract ideas, animals, and inanimate objects.

Petrarchan Sonnet: See *Sonnet*

Phenomenology: A method of literary criticism based on the belief that things have no existence outside of human consciousness or awareness. Proponents of this theory believe that art is a process that takes place in the mind of the observer as he or she contemplates an object rather than a quality of the object itself.

Plagiarism: Claiming another person's written material as one's own. Plagiarism can take the form of direct, word-for-word copying or the theft of the substance or idea of the work.

Platonic Criticism: A form of criticism that stresses an artistic work's usefulness as an agent of social engineering rather than any quality or value of the work itself.

Platonism: The embracing of the doctrines of the philosopher Plato, popular among the poets of the Renaissance and the Romantic period. Platonism is more flexible than Aristotelian Criticism and places more emphasis on the supernatural and unknown aspects of life.

Plot: In literary criticism, this term refers to the pattern of events in a narrative or drama. In its simplest sense, the plot guides the author in composing the work and helps the reader follow the work. Typically, plots exhibit causality and unity and have a beginning, a middle, and an end. Sometimes, however, a plot may consist of a series of disconnected events, in which case it is known as an "episodic plot."

Poem: In its broadest sense, a composition utilizing rhyme, meter, concrete detail, and expressive language to create a literary experience with emotional and aesthetic appeal.

Poet: An author who writes poetry or verse. The term is also used to refer to an artist or writer who has an exceptional gift for expression, imagination, and energy in the making of art in any form.

Poete maudit: A term derived from Paul Verlaine's *Les poetes maudits* (*The Accursed Poets*), a collection of essays on the French symbolist writers Stephane Mallarme, Arthur Rimbaud, and Tristan Corbiere. In the sense intended by Verlaine, the poet is "accursed" for choosing to explore extremes of human experience outside of middle-class society.

Poetic Fallacy: See *Pathetic Fallacy*

Poetic Justice: An outcome in a literary work, not necessarily a poem, in which the good are rewarded and the evil are punished, especially in ways that particularly fit their virtues or crimes.

Poetic License: Distortions of fact and literary convention made by a writer—not always a poet—for the sake of the effect gained. Poetic license is closely related to the concept of "artistic freedom."

Poetics: This term has two closely related meanings. It denotes (1) an aesthetic theory in literary criticism about the essence of poetry or (2) rules prescribing the proper methods, content, style, or diction of poetry. The term poetics may also refer to theories about literature in general, not just poetry.

Poetry: In its broadest sense, writing that aims to present ideas and evoke an emotional experience in the reader through the use of meter, imagery, connotative and concrete words, and a carefully constructed structure based on rhythmic patterns. Poetry typically relies on words and expressions that have several layers of meaning. It also makes use of the effects of regular rhythm on the ear and may make a strong appeal to the senses through the use of imagery.

Point of View: The narrative perspective from which a literary work is presented to the reader. There are four traditional points of view. The "third person omniscient" gives the reader a "godlike" perspective, unrestricted by time or place, from which to see actions and look into the minds of characters. This allows the author to comment openly on characters and events in the work. The "third-person" point of view presents the events of the story from outside of any single character's perception, much like the omniscient point of view, but the reader must understand the action as it takes place and without any special insight into characters' minds or motivations. The "first person" or "personal" point of view relates events as they are perceived by a single character. The main character "tells" the story and may offer opinions about the action and characters which differ from those of the author. Much less common than omniscient, third person, and first person is the "second-person" point of view, wherein the author tells the story as if it is happening to the reader.

Polemic: A work in which the author takes a stand on a controversial subject, such as abortion or religion. Such works are often extremely argumentative or provocative.

Pornography: Writing intended to provoke feelings of lust in the reader. Such works are often condemned by critics and teachers, but those which can be shown to have literary value are viewed less harshly.

Post-Aesthetic Movement: An artistic response made by African Americans to the black aesthetic movement of the 1960s and early 1970s. Writers since that time have adopted a somewhat different tone in their work, with less emphasis placed on the disparity between black and white in the United States. In the words of post-aesthetic authors such as Toni Morrison, John Edgar Wideman, and Kristin Hunter, African Americans are portrayed as

looking inward for answers to their own questions, rather than always looking to the outside world.

Postmodernism: Writing from the 1960s forward characterized by experimentation and continuing to apply some of the fundamentals of modernism, which included existentialism and alienation. Postmodernists have gone a step further in the rejection of tradition begun with the modernists by also rejecting traditional forms, preferring the antinovel over the novel and the antihero over the hero.

Pre-Raphaelites: A circle of writers and artists in mid nineteenth-century England. Valuing the pre-Renaissance artistic qualities of religious symbolism, lavish pictorialism, and natural sensuousness, the Pre-Raphaelites cultivated a sense of mystery and melancholy that influenced later writers associated with the Symbolist and Decadent movements.

Primitivism: The belief that primitive peoples were nobler and less flawed than civilized peoples because they had not been subjected to the corrupt influence of society.

Projective Verse: A form of free verse in which the poet's breathing pattern determines the lines of the poem. Poets who advocate projective verse are against all formal structures in writing, including meter and form.

Prologue: An introductory section of a literary work. It often contains information establishing the situation of the characters or presents information about the setting, time period, or action. In drama, the prologue is spoken by a chorus or by one of the principal characters.

Prose: A literary medium that attempts to mirror the language of everyday speech. It is distinguished from poetry by its use of unmetered, unrhymed language consisting of logically related sentences. Prose is usually grouped into paragraphs that form a cohesive whole such as an essay or a novel.

Prosopopoeia: See *Personification*

Protagonist: The central character of a story who serves as a focus for its themes and incidents and as the principal rationale for its development. The protagonist is sometimes referred to in discussions of modern literature as the hero or antihero.

Proverb: A brief, sage saying that expresses a truth about life in a striking manner.

Pseudonym: A name assumed by a writer, most often intended to prevent his or her identification as the author of a work. Two or more authors may work together under one pseudonym, or an author may use a different name for each genre he or she publishes in. Some publishing companies maintain "house pseudonyms," under which any number of authors may write installations in a series. Some authors also choose a pseudonym over their real names the way an actor may use a stage name.

Pun: A play on words that have similar sounds but different meanings.

Pure Poetry: poetry written without instructional intent or moral purpose that aims only to please a reader by its imagery or musical flow. The term pure poetry is used as the antonym of the term "didacticism."

Q

Quatrain: A four-line stanza of a poem or an entire poem consisting of four lines.

R

Realism: A nineteenth-century European literary movement that sought to portray familiar characters, situations, and settings in a realistic manner. This was done primarily by using an objective narrative point of view and through the buildup of accurate detail. The standard for success of any realistic work depends on how faithfully it transfers common experience into fictional forms. The realistic method may be altered or extended, as in stream of consciousness writing, to record highly subjective experience.

Refrain: A phrase repeated at intervals throughout a poem. A refrain may appear at the end of each stanza or at less regular intervals. It may be altered slightly at each appearance.

Renaissance: The period in European history that marked the end of the Middle Ages. It began in Italy in the late fourteenth century. In broad terms, it is usually seen as spanning the fourteenth, fifteenth, and sixteenth centuries, although it did not reach Great Britain, for example, until the 1480s or so. The Renaissance saw an awakening in almost every sphere of human activity, especially science, philosophy, and the arts. The period is best defined by the emergence of a general philosophy that emphasized the importance of the intellect, the individual, and world affairs. It contrasts strongly with the medieval worldview, characterized by the dominant concerns of faith, the social collective, and spiritual salvation.

Repartee: Conversation featuring snappy retorts and witticisms.

Restoration: See *Restoration Age*

Restoration Age: A period in English literature beginning with the crowning of Charles II in 1660 and running to about 1700. The era, which was characterized by a reaction against Puritanism, was the first great age of the comedy of manners. The finest literature of the era is typically witty and urbane, and often lewd.

Rhetoric: In literary criticism, this term denotes the art of ethical persuasion. In its strictest sense, rhetoric adheres to various principles developed since classical times for arranging facts and ideas in a clear, persuasive, appealing manner. The term is also used to refer to effective prose in general and theories of or methods for composing effective prose.

Rhetorical Question: A question intended to provoke thought, but not an expressed answer, in the reader. It is most commonly used in oratory and other persuasive genres.

Rhyme: When used as a noun in literary criticism, this term generally refers to a poem in which words sound identical or very similar and appear in parallel positions in two or more lines. Rhymes are classified into different types according to where they fall in a line or stanza or according to the degree of similarity they exhibit in their spellings and sounds. Some major types of rhyme are "masculine" rhyme, "feminine" rhyme, and "triple" rhyme. In a masculine rhyme, the rhyming sound falls in a single accented syllable, as with "heat" and "eat." Feminine rhyme is a rhyme of two syllables, one stressed and one unstressed, as with "merry" and "tarry." Triple rhyme matches the sound of the accented syllable and the two unaccented syllables that follow: "narrative" and "declarative."

Rhyme Royal: A stanza of seven lines composed in iambic pentameter and rhymed *ababbcc*. The name is said to be a tribute to King James I of Scotland, who made much use of the form in his poetry.

Rhyme Scheme: See *Rhyme*

Rhythm: A regular pattern of sound, time intervals, or events occurring in writing, most often and most discernably in poetry. Regular, reliable rhythm is known to be soothing to humans, while interrupted, unpredictable, or rapidly changing rhythm is disturbing. These effects are known to authors, who use them to produce a desired reaction in the reader.

Rococo: A style of European architecture that flourished in the eighteenth century, especially in

France. The most notable features of *rococo* are its extensive use of ornamentation and its themes of lightness, gaiety, and intimacy. In literary criticism, the term is often used disparagingly to refer to a decadent or overly ornamental style.

Romance:

Romantic Age: See *Romanticism*

Romanticism: This term has two widely accepted meanings. In historical criticism, it refers to a European intellectual and artistic movement of the late eighteenth and early nineteenth centuries that sought greater freedom of personal expression than that allowed by the strict rules of literary form and logic of the eighteenth-century Neoclassicists. The Romantics preferred emotional and imaginative expression to rational analysis. They considered the individual to be at the center of all experience and so placed him or her at the center of their art. The Romantics believed that the creative imagination reveals nobler truths—unique feelings and attitudes—than those that could be discovered by logic or by scientific examination. Both the natural world and the state of childhood were important sources for revelations of "eternal truths." "Romanticism" is also used as a general term to refer to a type of sensibility found in all periods of literary history and usually considered to be in opposition to the principles of classicism. In this sense, Romanticism signifies any work or philosophy in which the exotic or dreamlike figure strongly, or that is devoted to individualistic expression, self-analysis, or a pursuit of a higher realm of knowledge than can be discovered by human reason.

Romantics: See *Romanticism*

Russian Symbolism: A Russian poetic movement, derived from French symbolism, that flourished between 1894 and 1910. While some Russian Symbolists continued in the French tradition, stressing aestheticism and the importance of suggestion above didactic intent, others saw their craft as a form of mystical worship, and themselves as mediators between the supernatural and the mundane.

S

Satire: A work that uses ridicule, humor, and wit to criticize and provoke change in human nature and institutions. There are two major types of satire: "formal" or "direct" satire speaks directly to the reader or to a character in the work; "indirect" satire relies upon the ridiculous behavior of its characters to make its point. Formal satire is further divided into two manners: the "Horatian," which ridicules gently, and the "Juvenalian," which derides its subjects harshly and bitterly.

Scansion: The analysis or "scanning" of a poem to determine its meter and often its rhyme scheme. The most common system of scansion uses accents (slanted lines drawn above syllables) to show stressed syllables, breves (curved lines drawn above syllables) to show unstressed syllables, and vertical lines to separate each foot.

Second Person: See *Point of View*

Semiotics: The study of how literary forms and conventions affect the meaning of language.

Sestet: Any six-line poem or stanza.

Setting: The time, place, and culture in which the action of a narrative takes place. The elements of setting may include geographic location, characters' physical and mental environments, prevailing cultural attitudes, or the historical time in which the action takes place.

Shakespearean Sonnet: See *Sonnet*

Signifying Monkey: A popular trickster figure in black folklore, with hundreds of tales about this character documented since the nineteenth century.

Simile: A comparison, usually using "like" or "as," of two essentially dissimilar things, as in "coffee as cold as ice" or "He sounded like a broken record."

Slang: A type of informal verbal communication that is generally unacceptable for formal writing. Slang words and phrases are often colorful exaggerations used to emphasize the speaker's point; they may also be shortened versions of an often-used word or phrase.

Slant Rhyme: See *Consonance*

Slave Narrative: Autobiographical accounts of American slave life as told by escaped slaves. These works first appeared during the abolition movement of the 1830s through the 1850s.

Social Realism: See *Socialist Realism*

Socialist Realism: The Socialist Realism school of literary theory was proposed by Maxim Gorky and established as a dogma by the first Soviet Congress of Writers. It demanded adherence to a communist worldview in works of literature. Its doctrines required an objective viewpoint comprehensible to the working classes and themes of social struggle featuring strong proletarian heroes.

Soliloquy: A monologue in a drama used to give the audience information and to develop the speaker's character. It is typically a projection of the speaker's innermost thoughts. Usually delivered while the speaker is alone on stage, a soliloquy is intended to present an illusion of unspoken reflection.

Sonnet: A fourteen-line poem, usually composed in iambic pentameter, employing one of several rhyme schemes. There are three major types of sonnets, upon which all other variations of the form are based: the "Petrarchan" or "Italian" sonnet, the "Shakespearean" or "English" sonnet, and the "Spenserian" sonnet. A Petrarchan sonnet consists of an octave rhymed *abbaabba* and a "sestet" rhymed either *cdecde, cdccdc,* or *cdedce*. The octave poses a question or problem, relates a narrative, or puts forth a proposition; the sestet presents a solution to the problem, comments upon the narrative, or applies the proposition put forth in the octave. The Shakespearean sonnet is divided into three quatrains and a couplet rhymed *abab cdcd efef gg*. The couplet provides an epigrammatic comment on the narrative or problem put forth in the quatrains. The Spenserian sonnet uses three quatrains and a couplet like the Shakespearean, but links their three rhyme schemes in this way: *abab bcbc cdcd ee*. The Spenserian sonnet develops its theme in two parts like the Petrarchan, its final six lines resolving a problem, analyzing a narrative, or applying a proposition put forth in its first eight lines.

Spenserian Sonnet: See *Sonnet*

Spenserian Stanza: A nine-line stanza having eight verses in iambic pentameter, its ninth verse in iambic hexameter, and the rhyme scheme *abab-bcbcc*.

Spondee: In poetry meter, a foot consisting of two long or stressed syllables occurring together. This form is quite rare in English verse, and is usually composed of two monosyllabic words.

Sprung Rhythm: Versification using a specific number of accented syllables per line but disregarding the number of unaccented syllables that fall in each line, producing an irregular rhythm in the poem.

Stanza: A subdivision of a poem consisting of lines grouped together, often in recurring patterns of rhyme, line length, and meter. Stanzas may also serve as units of thought in a poem much like paragraphs in prose.

Stereotype: A stereotype was originally the name for a duplication made during the printing process; this led to its modern definition as a person or thing that is (or is assumed to be) the same as all others of its type.

Stream of Consciousness: A narrative technique for rendering the inward experience of a character. This technique is designed to give the impression of an ever-changing series of thoughts, emotions, images, and memories in the spontaneous and seemingly illogical order that they occur in life.

Structuralism: A twentieth-century movement in literary criticism that examines how literary texts arrive at their meanings, rather than the meanings themselves. There are two major types of structuralist analysis: one examines the way patterns of linguistic structures unify a specific text and emphasize certain elements of that text, and the other interprets the way literary forms and conventions affect the meaning of language itself.

Structure: The form taken by a piece of literature. The structure may be made obvious for ease of understanding, as in nonfiction works, or may be obscured for artistic purposes, as in some poetry or seemingly "unstructured" prose.

Sturm und Drang: A German term meaning "storm and stress." It refers to a German literary movement of the 1770s and 1780s that reacted against the order and rationalism of the enlightenment, focusing instead on the intense experience of extraordinary individuals.

Style: A writer's distinctive manner of arranging words to suit his or her ideas and purpose in writing. The unique imprint of the author's personality upon his or her writing, style is the product of an author's way of arranging ideas and his or her use of diction, different sentence structures, rhythm, figures of speech, rhetorical principles, and other elements of composition.

Subject: The person, event, or theme at the center of a work of literature. A work may have one or more subjects of each type, with shorter works tending to have fewer and longer works tending to have more.

Subjectivity: Writing that expresses the author's personal feelings about his subject, and which may or may not include factual information about the subject.

Surrealism: A term introduced to criticism by Guillaume Apollinaire and later adopted by Andre Breton. It refers to a French literary and artistic movement founded in the 1920s. The Surrealists sought to express unconscious thoughts and feelings in their works. The best-known technique used for achieving this aim was automatic writing—transcriptions of spontaneous outpourings from the unconscious. The Surrealists proposed to unify the contrary levels of conscious and unconscious, dream and reality, objectivity and subjectivity into a new level of "super-realism."

Suspense: A literary device in which the author maintains the audience's attention through the buildup of events, the outcome of which will soon be revealed.

Syllogism: A method of presenting a logical argument. In its most basic form, the syllogism consists of a major premise, a minor premise, and a conclusion.

Symbol: Something that suggests or stands for something else without losing its original identity. In literature, symbols combine their literal meaning with the suggestion of an abstract concept. Literary symbols are of two types: those that carry complex associations of meaning no matter what their contexts, and those that derive their suggestive meaning from their functions in specific literary works.

Symbolism: This term has two widely accepted meanings. In historical criticism, it denotes an early modernist literary movement initiated in France during the nineteenth century that reacted against the prevailing standards of realism. Writers in this movement aimed to evoke, indirectly and symbolically, an order of being beyond the material world of the five senses. Poetic expression of personal emotion figured strongly in the movement, typically by means of a private set of symbols uniquely identifiable with the individual poet. The principal aim of the Symbolists was to express in words the highly complex feelings that grew out of everyday contact with the world. In a broader sense, the term "symbolism" refers to the use of one object to represent another.

Symbolist: See *Symbolism*

Symbolist Movement: See *Symbolism*

Sympathetic Fallacy: See *Affective Fallacy*

T

Tanka: A form of Japanese poetry similar to *haiku*. A *tanka* is five lines long, with the lines containing five, seven, five, seven, and seven syllables respectively.

Terza Rima: A three-line stanza form in poetry in which the rhymes are made on the last word of each line in the following manner: the first and third lines of the first stanza, then the second line of the first stanza and the first and third lines of the second stanza, and so on with the middle line of any stanza rhyming with the first and third lines of the following stanza.

Tetrameter: See *Meter*

Textual Criticism: A branch of literary criticism that seeks to establish the authoritative text of a literary work. Textual critics typically compare all known manuscripts or printings of a single work in order to assess the meanings of differences and revisions. This procedure allows them to arrive at a definitive version that (supposedly) corresponds to the author's original intention.

Theme: The main point of a work of literature. The term is used interchangeably with thesis.

Thesis: A thesis is both an essay and the point argued in the essay. Thesis novels and thesis plays share the quality of containing a thesis which is supported through the action of the story.

Third Person: See *Point of View*

Tone: The author's attitude toward his or her audience may be deduced from the tone of the work. A formal tone may create distance or convey politeness, while an informal tone may encourage a friendly, intimate, or intrusive feeling in the reader. The author's attitude toward his or her subject matter may also be deduced from the tone of the words he or she uses in discussing it.

Tragedy: A drama in prose or poetry about a noble, courageous hero of excellent character who, because of some tragic character flaw or *hamartia*, brings ruin upon him- or herself. Tragedy treats its subjects in a dignified and serious manner, using poetic language to help evoke pity and fear and bring about catharsis, a purging of these emotions. The tragic form was practiced extensively by the ancient Greeks. In the Middle Ages, when classical works were virtually unknown, tragedy came to denote any works about the fall of persons from exalted to low conditions due to any reason: fate, vice, weakness, etc. According to the classical definition of tragedy, such works present the "pathetic"—that which evokes pity—rather than the tragic. The classical form of tragedy was revived in the sixteenth century; it flourished especially on the Elizabethan stage. In modern times, dramatists have attempted to adapt the form to the needs of modern society by drawing their heroes from the ranks of ordinary men and women and defining the nobility of these heroes in terms of spirit rather than exalted social standing.

Tragic Flaw: In a tragedy, the quality within the hero or heroine which leads to his or her downfall.

Transcendentalism: An American philosophical and religious movement, based in New England from around 1835 until the Civil War. Transcendentalism was a form of American romanticism that had its roots abroad in the works of Thomas Carlyle, Samuel Coleridge, and Johann Wolfgang von Goethe. The Transcendentalists stressed the importance of intuition and subjective experience in communication with God. They rejected religious dogma and texts in favor of mysticism and scientific naturalism. They pursued truths that lie beyond the "colorless" realms perceived by reason and the senses and were active social reformers in public education, women's rights, and the abolition of slavery.

Trickster: A character or figure common in Native American and African literature who uses his ingenuity to defeat enemies and escape difficult situations. Tricksters are most often animals, such as the spider, hare, or coyote, although they may take the form of humans as well.

Trimeter: See *Meter*

Triple Rhyme: See *Rhyme*

Trochee: See *Foot*

U

Understatement: See *Irony*

Unities: Strict rules of dramatic structure, formulated by Italian and French critics of the Renaissance and based loosely on the principles of drama discussed by Aristotle in his *Poetics*. Foremost among these rules were the three unities of action, time, and place that compelled a dramatist to: (1) construct a single plot with a beginning, middle, and end that details the causal relationships of action and character; (2) restrict the action to the events of a single day; and (3) limit the scene to a single place or city. The unities were observed faithfully by continental European writers until the Romantic Age, but they were never regularly observed in English drama. Modern dramatists are typically more concerned with a unity of impression or emotional effect than with any of the classical unities.

Urban Realism: A branch of realist writing that attempts to accurately reflect the often harsh facts of modern urban existence.

Utopia: A fictional perfect place, such as "paradise" or "heaven."

Utopian: See *Utopia*

Utopianism: See *Utopia*

V

Verisimilitude: Literally, the appearance of truth. In literary criticism, the term refers to aspects of a work of literature that seem true to the reader.

Vers de societe: See *Occasional Verse*

Vers libre: See *Free Verse*

Verse: A line of metered language, a line of a poem, or any work written in verse.

Versification: The writing of verse. Versification may also refer to the meter, rhyme, and other mechanical components of a poem.

Victorian: Refers broadly to the reign of Queen Victoria of England (1837–1901) and to anything with qualities typical of that era. For example, the qualities of smug narrowmindedness, bourgeois materialism, faith in social progress, and priggish morality are often considered Victorian. This stereotype is contradicted by such dramatic intellectual developments as the theories of Charles Darwin, Karl Marx, and Sigmund Freud (which stirred strong debates in England) and the critical attitudes of serious Victorian writers like Charles Dickens and George Eliot. In literature, the Victorian Period was the great age of the English novel, and the latter part of the era saw the rise of movements such as decadence and symbolism.

Victorian Age: See *Victorian*

Victorian Period: See *Victorian*

W

Weltanschauung: A German term referring to a person's worldview or philosophy.

Weltschmerz: A German term meaning "world pain." It describes a sense of anguish about the nature of existence, usually associated with a melancholy, pessimistic attitude.

Z

Zarzuela: A type of Spanish operetta.

Zeitgeist: A German term meaning "spirit of the time." It refers to the moral and intellectual trends of a given era.

Cumulative Author/Title Index

McGinley, Phyllis
    The Conquerors: V13
    *Reactionary Essay on Applied
      Science:* V9
McKay, Claude
    The Tropics in New York: V4
Meeting the British (Muldoon): V7
Mending Wall (Frost): V5
Merriam, Eve
    Onomatopoeia: V6
Merwin, W. S.
    Leviathan: V5
Midnight (Heaney): V2
The Milkfish Gatherers (Fenton): V11
Millay, Edna St. Vincent
    *The Courage That My Mother
      Had*: V3
Milton, John
    [On His Blindness] Sonnet 16: V3
Mirror (Plath): V1
Miss Rosie (Clifton): V1
The Missing (Gunn): V9
Momaday, N. Scott
    Angle of Geese: V2
    *To a Child Running With
      Outstretched Arms in Canyon
      de Chelly:* V11
Montague, John
    A Grafted Tongue: V12
The Moon Glows the Same (Bashō):
    V7
Moore, Marianne
    The Fish: V14
"More Light! More Light!" (Hecht):
    V6
Mother to Son (Hughes): V3
Muldoon, Paul
    Meeting the British: V7
Mueller, Lisel
    Blood Oranges: V13
    The Exhibit: V9
Musée des Beaux Arts (Auden): V1
Music Lessons (Oliver): V8
My Last Duchess (Browning): V1
*My Life Closed Twice Before Its
    Close* (Dickinson): V8
My Mother Pieced Quilts (Acosta):
    V12
My Papa's Waltz (Roethke): V3

N

Names of Horses (Hall): V8
A Narrow Fellow in the Grass
    (Dickinson): V11
The Negro Speaks of Rivers
    (Hughes): V10
Nemerov, Howard
    Deep Woods: V14
    The Phoenix: V10
Neruda, Pablo
    Tonight I Can Write: V11
Not Waving but Drowning (Smith): V3

Nothing Gold Can Stay (Frost): V3
Nowlan, Alden
    *For Jean Vincent D'abbadie,
      Baron St.-Castin:* V12
Noyes, Alfred
    The Highwayman: V4
The Nymph's Reply to the Shepherd
    (Raleigh): V14

O

O Captain! My Captain! (Whitman):
    V2
Ode on a Grecian Urn (Keats): V1
Ode to a Nightingale (Keats): V3
Ode to the West Wind (Shelley): V2
O'Hara, Frank
    Having a Coke with You: V12
    Why I Am Not a Painter: V8
old age sticks (cummings): V3
Old Ironsides (Holmes): V9
Oliver, Mary
    Music Lessons: V8
[On His Blindness] Sonnet 16
    (Milton):V3
Ondaatje, Michael
    To a Sad Daughter: V8
On Freedom's Ground (Wilbur): V12
Onomatopoeia (Merriam): V6
On the Pulse of Morning (Angelou):
    V3
Ortiz, Simon
    Hunger in New York City: V4
Out, Out— (Frost):V10
Overture to a Dance of Locomotives
    (Williams): V11
Owen, Wilfred
    *Dulce et Decorum Est:*V10
Oysters (Sexton): V4

P

Paradoxes and Oxymorons
    (Ashbery): V11
Pastan, Linda
    Ethics: V8
Paul Revere's Ride (Longfellow): V2
The Phoenix (Nemerov): V10
Piano (Lawrence): V6
Piercy, Marge
    Barbie Doll: V9
Plath, Sylvia
    Mirror: V1
A Psalm of Life (Longfellow): V7
Poe, Edgar Allan
    Annabel Lee: V9
    The Bells: V3
    The Raven: V1
Pope, Alexander
    The Rape of the Lock: V12
Pound, Ezra
    In a Station of the Metro: V2
    *The River-Merchant's Wife: A
      Letter:* V8

Psalm 8 (King James Bible): V9
Psalm 23 (King James Bible): V4
Purdy, Al
    Lament for the Dorsets: V5
    Wilderness Gothic: V12

Q

The Quaker Graveyard in Nantucket
    (Lowell): V6
Queen-Ann's-Lace (Williams): V6

R

Raine, Craig
    *A Martian Sends a Postcard
      Home:* V7
Raleigh, Walter, Sir
    *The Nymph's Reply to the
      Shepherd:* V14
Randall, Dudley
    Ballad of Birmingham: V5
The Rape of the Lock (Pope): V12
The Raven (Poe): V1
*Reactionary Essay on Applied
    Science* (McGinley): V9
A Red, Red Rose (Burns): V8
The Red Wheelbarrow (Williams): V1
Reed, Ishmael
    Beware: Do Not Read This Poem:
      V6
Remember (Rossetti): V14
Revard, Carter
    Birch Canoe: V5
Richard Cory (Robinson): V4
The Rime of the Ancient Mariner
    (Coleridge): V4
Ríos, Alberto
    Island of the Three Marias: V11
The River-Merchant's Wife: A Letter
    (Pound): V8
The Road Not Taken (Frost): V2
Robinson, E. A.
    Richard Cory: V4
Roethke, Theodore
    My Papa's Waltz: V3
Rose, Wendy
    *For the White poets who would be
      Indian:* V13
Rossetti, Christina
    *A Birthday:*V10
    Remember: V14
Rukeyser, Muriel
    *Ballad of Orange and Grape:*V10

S

Sailing to Byzantium (Yeats): V2
Saint Francis and the Sow (Kinnell):
    V9
Sandburg, Carl
    Chicago: V3
    Cool Tombs: V6

Y

Cumulative Nationality/Ethnicity Index

Acoma Pueblo

Ortiz, Simon
    Hunger in New York City: V4

African American

Angelou, Maya
    Harlem Hopscotch: V2
    On the Pulse of Morning: V3
Baraka, Amiri
    In Memory of Radio: V9
Brooks, Gwendolyn
    The Bean Eaters: V2
    The Sonnet-Ballad: V1
    Strong Men, Riding Horses: V4
    We Real Cool: V6
Clifton, Lucille
    Climbing: V14
    Miss Rosie: V1
Cullen, Countee
    Any Human to Another: V3
Dove, Rita
    This Life: V1
Hayden, Robert
    Those Winter Sundays: V1
Hughes, Langston
    Harlem: V1
    Mother to Son: V3
    The Negro Speaks of Rivers: V10
    Theme for English B: V6
Johnson, James Weldon
    The Creation: V1
Komunyakaa, Yusef
    Facing It: V5
Madgett, Naomi Long
    Alabama Centennial: V10
McElroy, Colleen

    A Pièd: V3
Randall, Dudley
    Ballad of Birmingham: V5
Reed, Ishmael
    Beware: Do Not Read This Poem:
      V6

American

Acosta, Teresa Palomo
    My Mother Pieced Quilts: V12
Angelou, Maya
    Harlem Hopscotch: V2
    On the Pulse of Morning: V3
Ashbery, John
    Paradoxes and Oxymorons: V11
Auden, W. H.
    As I Walked Out One Evening:
      V4
    Musée des Beaux Arts: V1
    The Unknown Citizen: V3
Bishop, Elizabeth
    Brazil, January 1, 1502: V6
    Filling Station: V12
Blumenthal, Michael
    Inventors: V7
Bly, Robert
    Come with Me: V6
Bradstreet, Anne
    To My Dear and Loving Husband:
      V6
Brooks, Gwendolyn
    The Bean Eaters: V2
    The Sonnet-Ballad: V1
    Strong Men, Riding Horses: V4
    We Real Cool: V6
Brouwer, Joel

    Last Request: V14
Clifton, Lucille
    Climbing: V14
    Miss Rosie: V1
Crane, Stephen
    War Is Kind: V9
Cullen, Countee
    Any Human to Another: V3
cummings, e. e.
    l(a: V1
    i was sitting in mcsorley's: V13
    maggie and milly and molly and
      may: V12
    old age sticks: V3
Dickey, James
    The Heaven of Animals: V6
    The Hospital Window: V11
Dickinson, Emily
    Because I Could Not Stop for
      Death: V2
    The Bustle in a House: V10
    "Hope" Is the Thing with
      Feathers: V3
    I felt a Funeral, in my Brain: V13
    I Heard a Fly Buzz—When I
      Died—: V5
    My Life Closed Twice Before Its
      Close: V8
    A Narrow Fellow in the Grass:
      V11
    The Soul Selects Her Own
      Society: V1
    There's a Certain Slant of Light:
      V6
    This Is My Letter to the World: V4
Dove, Rita
    This Life: V1
Dubie, Norman
    The Czar's Last Christmas Letter.

Subject/Theme Index

Boldface denotes dicussion in
Themes section.

A

Abandonment
  Bidwell Ghost: 2, 4, 7–8
Abstinence
  The Canterbury Tales: 59–63
Abstinence and Chastity
  *The Nymph's Reply to the
    Shepherd:* 242
Abuse
  The Fish: 173
Adultery
  The Canterbury Tales: 77–78, 80
Adventure and Exploration
  The Canterbury Tales: 34–35, 37,
    39–40
  Kilroy: 211, 213–218, 220–222
Africa
  The Canterbury Tales: 64–66, 68,
    73
  Deep Woods: 141–142, 145
  Last Request: 232, 235
Alcoholism, Drugs, and Drug
  Addiction
  Courage: 124, 128–129
Allegory
  The Canterbury Tales: 89–90
  Incident in a Rose Garden: 189,
    193
  Kilroy: 212, 216–217
  Song of the Chattahoochee:
    284–286
Alliteration
  Kilroy: 224

Song of the Chattahoochee:
    284–285, 290, 295
  There Will Come Soft Rains: 303
Ambiguity
  Climbing: 119
American Dream
  In the Suburbs: 202
American Northeast
  Song of the Chattahoochee: 282,
    288–289
American South
  *Elegy for My Father, Who is Not
    Dead:* 159, 161
  Song of the Chattahoochee: 282,
    284–286, 288–290
Anger
  The Canterbury Tales: 65–66, 68
  *Elegy for My Father, Who is Not
    Dead:* 156–159
  Last Request: 235–236
The Anonymous Soldier
  Kilroy: 216
Anti-Semitism
  The Canterbury Tales: 28–31,
    33–34
Arthurian Legend
  Deep Woods: 141–142
Asia
  Deep Woods: 141, 143–145
  Kilroy: 211, 213–214, 218–222
Atonement
  The Canterbury Tales: 36–39
Authoritarianism
  Kilroy: 218–219

B

Balance and Contradiction
  Remember: 258

Beauty
  The Canterbury Tales: 17–18,
    20–22, 25
  Courage: 131–133
  Incident in a Rose Garden:
    195–196
  Kilroy: 222, 224–228
  *The Nymph's Reply to the
    Shepherd:* 246–248
  She Walks in Beauty: 267,
    269–280
  There Will Come Soft Rains:
    301–303, 305–306

C

Change and Transformation
  Courage: 127
Charity
  The Canterbury Tales: 86
Childhood
  Courage: 124, 126–127
  *Elegy for My Father, Who is Not
    Dead:* 152, 156–157, 159, 161
Christianity
  The Canterbury Tales: 20–21,
    24–25, 29–33, 58, 60, 62–63
  *Elegy for My Father, Who is Not
    Dead:* 164–166
City Life
  Bidwell Ghost: 6–7
Civil Rights
  *Elegy for My Father, Who is Not
    Dead:* 159
Class
  In the Suburbs: 203

Cumulative Index of First Lines

A

A brackish reach of shoal off Madaket,— (The Quaker Graveyard in Nantucket) V6:158

"A cold coming we had of it (Journey of the Magi) V7:110

A line in long array where they wind betwixt green islands, (Cavalry Crossing a Ford) V13:50

A narrow Fellow in the grass (A Narrow Fellow in the Grass) V11:127

A pine box for me. I mean it. (Last Request) V14: 231

A poem should be palpable and mute (Ars Poetica) V5:2

A wind is ruffling the tawny pelt (A Far Cry from Africa) V6:60

a woman precedes me up the long rope, (Climbing) V14:113

About me the night moonless wimples the mountains (Vancouver Lights) V8:245

About suffering they were never wrong (Musée des Beaux Arts) V1:148

Across Roblin Lake, two shores away, (Wilderness Gothic) V12:241

After you finish your work (Ballad of Orange and Grape) V10:17

"Ah, are you digging on my grave (Ah, Are You Digging on My Grave?) V4:2

All Greece hates (Helen) V6:92

All night long the hockey pictures (To a Sad Daughter) V8:230

All winter your brute shoulders strained against collars, padding (Names of Horses) V8:141

Also Ulysses once—that other war. (Kilroy) V14:213

Anasazi (Anasazi) V9:2

And God stepped out on space (The Creation) V1:19

Animal bones and some mossy tent rings (Lament for the Dorsets) V5:190

As I perceive (The Gold Lily) V5:127

As I walked out one evening (As I Walked Out One Evening) V4:15

At noon in the desert a panting lizard (At the Bomb Testing Site) V8:2

Ay, tear her tattered ensign down! (Old Ironsides) V9:172

As virtuous men pass mildly away (A Valediction: Forbidding Mourning) V11:201

B

Back then, before we came (On Freedom's Ground) V12:186

Bananas ripe and green, and ginger-root (The Tropics in New York) V4:255

Because I could not stop for Death— (Because I Could Not Stop for Death) V2:27

Before the indifferent beak could let her drop? (Leda and the Swan) V13:182

Bent double, like old beggars under slacks, (Dulce et Decorum Est) V10:109

Between my finger and my thumb (Digging) V5:70

Beware of ruins: they have a treacherous charm (Beware of Ruins) V8:43

Bright star! would I were steadfast as thou art— (Bright Star! Would I Were Steadfast as Thou Art) V9:44

By the rude bridge that arched the flood (Concord Hymn) V4:30

C

Celestial choir! enthron'd in realms of light, (To His Excellency General Washington V13:212

Come with me into those things that have felt his despair for so long— (Come with Me) V6:31

Composed in the Tower, before his execution ("More Light! More Light!") V6:119

D

Darkened by time, the masters, like our memories, mix
(Black Zodiac) V10:46

Death, be not proud, though some have called thee (Holy
Sonnet 10) V2:103

Devouring Time, blunt thou the lion's paws (Sonnet 19)
V9:210

Do not go gentle into that good night (Do Not Go Gentle
into that Good Night) V1:51

Do not weep, maiden, for war is kind (War Is Kind)
V9:252

(Dumb, (A Grafted Tongue) V12:92

E

Each day the shadow swings (In the Land of Shinar) V7:83

Each night she waits by the road (Bidwell Ghost) V14:2

F

Falling upon earth (Falling Upon Earth) V2:64

Five years have past; five summers, with the length
(Tintern Abbey) V2:249

Flesh is heretic. (Anorexic) V12:2

From my mother's sleep I fell into the State (The Death
of the Ball Turret Gunner) V2:41

G

Gardener: Sir, I encountered Death (Incident in a Rose
Garden) V14:190

Gather ye Rose-buds while ye may, (To the Virgins, to
Make Much of Time) V13:226

Go down, Moses (Go Down, Moses) V11:42

Gray mist wolf (Four Mountain Wolves) V9:131

H

"Had he and I but met (The Man He Killed) V3:167

Had we but world enough, and time (To His Coy
Mistress) V5:276

Half a league, half a league (The Charge of the Light
Brigade) V1:2

Having a Coke with You (Having a Coke with You)
V12:105

He clasps the crag with crooked hands (The Eagle)
V11:30

He was found by the Bureau of Statistics to be (The
Unknown Citizen) V3:302

Hear the sledges with the bells— (The Bells) V3:46

Her body is not so white as (Queen-Ann's-Lace) V6:179

Her eyes were coins of porter and her West (A Farewell
to English) V10:126

Here they are. The soft eyes open (The Heaven of
Animals) V6:75

Hog Butcher for the World (Chicago) V3:61

Hope is a tattered flag and a dream out of time. (Hope is
a Tattered Flag) V12:120

"Hope" is the thing with feathers— (Hope Is the Thing
with Feathers) V3:123

How do I love thee? Let me count the ways (Sonnet 43)
V2:236

How shall we adorn (Angle of Geese) V2:2

How would it be if you took yourself off (Landscape with
Tractor) V10:182

Hunger crawls into you (Hunger in New York City) V4:79

I

I am not a painter, I am a poet (Why I Am Not a Painter)
V8:258

I am the Smoke King (The Song of the Smoke) V13:196

I am silver and exact. I have no preconceptions (Mirror)
V1:116

I am trying to pry open your casket (Dear Reader) V10:85

I cannot love the Brothers Wright (Reactionary Essay on
Applied Science) V9:199

I felt a Funeral, in my Brain, (I felt a Funeral in my
Brain) V13:137

I have just come down from my father (The Hospital
Window) V11:58

I have met them at close of day (Easter 1916) V5:91

I hear America singing, the varied carols I hear (I Hear
America Singing) V3:152

I heard a Fly buzz—when I died— (I Heard a Fly Buzz—
When I Died—) V5:140

I know that I shall meet my fate (An Irish Airman
Foresees His Death) V1:76

I sit in the top of the wood, my eyes closed (Hawk
Roosting) V4:55

I'm delighted to see you (The Constellation Orion) V8:53

I've known rivers; (The Negro Speaks of Rivers) V10:197

I was sitting in mcsorley's. outside it was New York and
beautifully snowing. (i was sitting in
mcsorley's) V13:151

If all the world and love were young, (The Nymph's
Reply to the Shepard) V14:241

If ever two were one, then surely we (To My Dear and
Loving Husband) V6:228

If I should die, think only this of me (The Soldier) V7:218

"Imagine being the first to say: *surveillance*," (Inventors)
V7:97

In 1936, a child (Blood Oranges) V13:34

In China (Lost Sister) V5:216

In ethics class so many years ago (Ethics) V8:88

In Flanders fields the poppies blow (In Flanders Fields)
V5:155

In the groves of Africa from their natural wonder (An
African Elegy) V13:3

In the Shreve High football stadium (Autumn Begins in
Martins Ferry, Ohio) V8:17

In Xanadu did Kubla Khan (Kubla Khan) V5:172

Ink runs from the corners of my mouth (Eating Poetry)
V9:60

It is an ancient Mariner (The Rime of the Ancient
Mariner) V4:127

It is in the small things we see it. (Courage) V14:125OOO

It little profits that an idle king (Ulysses) V2:278

It looked extremely rocky for the Mudville nine that day
(Casey at the Bat) V5:57

It seems vainglorious and proud (The Conquerors) V13:67

It was in and about the Martinmas time (Barbara Allan)
V7:10

It was many and many a year ago (Annabel Lee) V9:14

Its quick soft silver bell beating, beating (Auto Wreck)
V3:31

T

W

Y

Cumulative Index of First Lines

Cumulative Index of
Last Lines

A

A heart whose love is innocent! (She Walks in Beauty) V14:268

a man then suddenly stops running (Island of Three Marias) V11:80

a space in the lives of their friends (Beware: Do Not Read This Poem) V6:3

A sudden blow: the great wings beating still (Leda and the Swan) V13:181

A terrible beauty is born (Easter 1916) V5:91

About my big, new, automatically defrosting refrigerator with the built-in electric eye (Reactionary Essay on Applied Science) V9:199

Across the expedient and wicked stones (Auto Wreck) V3:31

Ah, dear father, graybeard, lonely old courage-teacher, what America did you have when Charon quit poling his ferry and you got out on a smoking bank and stood watching the boat disappear on the black waters of Lethe? (A Supermarket in California) V5:261

All losses are restored and sorrows end (Sonnet 30) V4:192

Amen. Amen (The Creation) V1:20

Anasazi (Anasazi) V9:3

and all beyond saving by children (Ethics) V8:88

And all we need of hell (My Life Closed Twice Before Its Close) V8:127

and changed, back to the class ("Trouble with Math in a One-Room Country School") V9:238

And Death shall be no more: Death, thou shalt die (Holy Sonnet 10) V2:103

And drunk the milk of Paradise (Kubla Khan) V5:172

And Finished knowing—then— (I Felt a Funeral in My Brain) V13:137

And gallop terribly against each other's bodies (Autumn Begins in Martins Ferry, Ohio) V8:17

and go back. (For the White poets who would be Indian) V13:112

And has not begun to grow a manly smile. (Deep Woods) V14:139

And his own Word (The Phoenix) V10:226

And I am Nicholas. (The Czar's Last Christmas Letter) V12:45

And in the suburbs Can't sat down and cried. (Kilroy) V14:213

And life for me ain't been no crystal stair (Mother to Son) V3:179

And like a thunderbolt he falls (The Eagle) V11:30

And makes me end where I begun (A Valediction: Forbidding Mourning) V11:202

And 'midst the stars inscribe Belinda's name. (The Rape of the Lock) V12:209

And miles to go before I sleep (Stopping by Woods on a Snowy Evening) V1:272

And not waving but drowning (Not Waving but Drowning) V3:216

And oh, 'tis true, 'tis true (When I Was One-and-Twenty) V4:268

And reach for your scalping knife. (For Jean Vincent D'abbadie, Baron St.-Castin) V12:78

and retreating, always retreating, behind it (Brazil, January 1, 1502) V6:16

And settled upon his eyes in a black soot ("More Light! More Light!") V6:120

And shuts his eyes. (Darwin in 1881) V13: 84

And so live ever—or else swoon to death (Bright Star! Would I Were Steadfast as Thou Art) V9:44

and strange and loud was the dingoes' cry (Drought Year) V8:78

and stride out. (Courage) V14:126

and sweat and fat and greed. (Anorexic) V12:3

And that has made all the difference (The Road Not Taken) V2:195

Cumulative Index of Last Lines

Y

Cumulative Index of Last Lines